JEREMIAH

THE OLD TESTAMENT LIBRARY

Editorial Advisory Board

WILLIAM P. BROWN
CAROL A. NEWSOM
DAVID L. PETERSEN

Leslie C. Allen

Jeremiah
A Commentary

Westminster John Knox Press
LOUISVILLE • LONDON

© 2008 Leslie C. Allen

All rights reserved. No part of this book may be reproduced or transmitted in any form or by any means, electronic or mechanical, including photocopying, recording, or by any information storage or retrieval system, without permission in writing from the publisher. For information, address Westminster John Knox Press, 100 Witherspoon Street, Louisville, Kentucky 40202-1396.

Scriptural quotations outside Jeremiah, unless otherwise indicated, are from New Revised Standard Version Bible. Copyright © 1989 National Council of the Churches of Christ in the United States of America. Used by permission. All rights reserved.

Book design by Jennifer K. Cox

First edition
Published by Westminster John Knox Press
Louisville, Kentucky

This book is printed on acid-free paper that meets the American National Standards Institute Z39.48 standard. ∞

PRINTED IN THE UNITED STATES OF AMERICA

08 09 10 11 12 13 14 15 16 17 — 10 9 8 7 6 5 4 3 2 1

Library of Congress Cataloging-in-Publication Data

Allen, Leslie C.
  Jeremiah : a commentary / Leslie C. Allen. — 1st ed.
    p. cm. — (The Old Testament library)
  Includes bibliographical references and index.
  ISBN 978-0-664-22223-9 (alk. paper)
  1. Bible. O.T. Jeremiah—Commentaries. I. Title.
  BS1525.53.A45   2008
  224'.2044—dc22   2008004989

*To Sylvia, the girl next door,
who under God started it all*

CONTENTS

Preface	xi
Abbreviations	xiii
Bibliography	xix
Introduction	1
1. Premises	1
2. Translation and Text	2
3. Genre	4
4. Style	6
5. Literary Development	7
6. Macrostructure	12
7. Purpose	14

COMMENTARY

1:1–2:3	Prologue: Introducing Jeremiah and His Message	21
1:1–3	Superscription	21
1:4–19	Jeremiah's Call and Commissions	23
2:1–3	The Honeymoon Is Over	33
2:4–10:25	Destruction and Eventual Reconstruction, Part One	
2:4–6:30	Coming Disaster and Its Causes	37
2:4–19	Judah's Apostasy	37
2:20–37	Judah's Apostasy Reaffirmed	44
3:1–18	Coming Back: A Distant Prospect	51
3:19–4:4	Coming Back: An Empty Claim	58
4:5–18	The Alarm Is Sounded	62
4:19–31	Three Visions of Doom	67

5:1–9	The Inevitability of Punishment	71
5:10–19	(Nonabsolute) Destruction of People and Land	74
5:20–31	Overstepping God's Limits	78
6:1–15	The Wages of Sin	82
6:16–21	Road Closed Ahead	87
6:22–30	Consequences of Failing the Test	89

7:1–10:25 The Self-Paved Road to Exile   **92**

7:1–20	The Exilic Outcome of Nominal and Pagan Worship	92
7:21–8:3	The Exilic Outcome of Nominal and Pagan Worship Reaffirmed	99
8:4–9:1 (8:23)	Paying the Price for Apostasy	105
9:2–16 (1–15)	What Happens When Solidarity Breaks Down	113
9:17–26 (16–25)	Exile: Prospect and Challenge	117
10:1–16	Exilic Faith in Yahweh	122
10:17–25	Coping with an Exilic Future	129

11:1–33:26 Destruction and Eventual Reconstruction, Part Two

11:1–13:27 A Broken Cycle of Rejection and Counterrejection   **133**

11:1–17	Pagan Worship as Breach of the Torah Covenant	133
11:18–12:6	An Exemplar of Rejection of Prophecy	142
12:7–17	Yahweh's Counterrejection and Eventual Wide Compassion	150
13:1–17	The Ruin of Exile and the Reason Why	155
13:18–27	The Peril of Ignoring Yahweh	161

14:1–17:27 Why God's Answer Was No   **165**

14:1–16	Unanswered Prayers	165
14:17–15:9	More Unanswered Prayers	171
15:10–21	The Messenger's Trauma over the Message	177
16:1–21	The Trouncing of Pagan Religion	186
17:1–13	Sins of the Heart	195
17:14–27	Reprisal for Scorning the Torah-Based Message	202

18:1–20:18 God and Prophet Ominously Rejected   **209**

18:1–23	The Spurned Message and Messenger of Disaster	209

Contents

19:1–20:18	The Spurned Message and Messenger Once More	220
21:1–24:10	**Doomed Kings and Discredited Prophets**	**234**
21:1–22:9	Doom for Court and Capital	234
22:10–30	Further Doom for Court and Capital	246
23:1–8	A Restored Court and Community	255
23:9–24	The Subversive Marks of Spurious Prophecy	260
23:25–40	Popular and Unpopular Types of Prophecy	268
24:1–10	Restoration and Judgment	274
25:1–38	**Doom for Judah and Other Nations**	**278**
26:1–29:32	**True and False Predictions**	**293**
26:1–24	Rejection of God's True Message and Messenger	293
27:1–22	Yoke Symbolism, Part One	302
28:1–17	Yoke Symbolism, Part Two	312
29:1–32	No Quick Return for the Deportees	319
30:1–31:40	**Covenant-Centered Hope**	**330**
30:1–31:1	Future Reversal of Past Reprisals	330
31:2–26	Promises of Homecoming and Blessing	340
31:27–40	Divine Guarantees for Israel's Future	351
32:1–33:26	**Covenant-Centered Joy**	**360**
32:1–44	Hope against Hope	360
33:1–26	Jerusalem's Role in the Reversal	372

34:1–51:64 Destruction and Eventual Reconstruction, Part Three

34:1–36:32	**The Dangers of Rejecting the Divine Word**	**381**
34:1–22	Capture of King and Capital: A Reason Why	381
35:1–39	An Object Lesson in Listening	388
36:1–32	Reaffirmation of the Rejected Word	393
37:1–39:18	**Retribution for Rejecting Message and Messenger**	**401**
37:1–21	Message and Messenger in Wartime	401
38:1–28a	Message and Messenger in Wartime Again	408
38:28b–39:18	Vindication of Message and Messenger	416
40:1–45:5	**Self-Imposed Exile**	**422**
40:1–43:13	A God-Given Opportunity Squandered	422

44:1–30	Fatal Consequences of a Besetting Sin	441
45:1–5	Promise of Survival to Baruch	449

46:1–51:64 Oracles against the Nations — **454**

46:1–47:7	Egypt and Philistia		454
	46:1–28	Egypt's Comeuppance and Israel's Security	454
	47:1–7	The Flooding of Philistia	469
48:1–47	Moab under Threat		473
	48:1–27	Moab's Coming Conquest and Destruction	473
	48:28–47	A Moabite Anthology	482
49:1–39	A Quintet of Foreign Oracles		488
50:1–51:64	Oracles against Babylon and Their Recitation		502
	50:1–46	Babylon's Fate and Israel's Fortune	502
	51:1–58	Babylon's Downfall and Israel's and Yahweh's Vindication	517
	51:59–64	Babylon's Fate Announced and Enacted	532

52:1–34 Epilogue: A Tale of Two Kings — **534**

Index of Modern Authors — **542**

PREFACE

Gedaliah's advice in Jer 40:10 to "commandeer wine, fruit, and olive oil, storing it in your own containers," may be taken to heart by contemporary Jeremiah commentators, since a plethora of academic study, especially that done in the last three decades, provides a rich store of insights. Warm thanks are due to Benjamin Galán and Micah L. Haney for bibliographical research that saved me a lot of time. The McAlister Library at Fuller Theological Seminary has been my second home for the past seven years. Its excellent collection of books and periodicals, interlibrary loan service, Internet facilities, and gracious staff have met my needs. Susan Wood in the faculty publications department has given painstaking technical aid that is much appreciated. Diana Parkhurst made an invaluable contribution by industriously acting as my typical informed reader for the first half of the commentary, as long as her health permitted. Dr. Genevieve Ramirez generously presented me with a laptop for use during a sabbatical term. During that term in 2004 I appreciated the quiet haven provided by Trinity College in Bristol, England, the city of my birth and upbringing. The dedication honors Mrs. Sylvia Bryant, whose role in that upbringing was to escort me Sunday by Sunday to Miss Palmer's class for infants.

ABBREVIATIONS

AB	Anchor Bible
ABC	A. Kirk Grayson, *Assyrian and Babylonian Chronicles*. Texts from Cuneiform Sources 5. 1975. Reprinted Winona Lake, Ind.: Eisenbrauns, 2006
ABD	*Anchor Bible Dictionary*. Edited by David N. Freedman. 6 vols. New York: Doubleday, 1992
ACEBT	*Amsterdamse Cahiers voor Exegese en bijbelse Theologie*
AGJU	Arbeiten zur Geschichte des antiken Judentums und des Urchristentums
AJBA	*Australian Journal of Biblical Archaeology*
AnBib	Analecta biblica
ANET	*Ancient Near Eastern Texts Relating to the Old Testament*. Edited by James B. Pritchard. 3d ed. Princeton: Princeton University Press, 1969
AOAT	Alter Orient und Altes Testament.
ASV	American Standard Version
ATANT	Abhandlungen zur Theologie des Alten und Neuen Testaments
ATSAT	Arbeiten zu Text und Sprache im Alten Testament
BA	*Biblical Archaeologist*
BBB	Bonner biblische Beiträge
BDB	Francis Brown, Samuel R. Driver, and Charles A. Briggs, *A Hebrew and English Lexicon of the Old Testament*. Oxford: Clarendon, 1907
BEATAJ	Beiträge zur Erforschung des Alten Testaments und des antiken Judentums
BETL	Bibliotheca ephemeridum theologicarum lovaniensium
BHK\SI3	*Biblia Hebraica*. Edited by Rudolf Kittel. 3d ed. Stuttgart: Württembergische Bibelanstalt, 1937
BHS	*Biblia Hebraica Stuttgartensia*. Edited by Karl Elliger and Wilhelm Rudolph. Stuttgart: Deutsche Bibelstiftung, 1983
BibB	Biblische Beiträge

BibInt	*Biblical Interpretation*
BibOr	Biblica et orientalia
BIOSCS	*Bulletin of the International Organization for Septuagint and Cognate Studies*
BN	*Biblische Notizen*
BT	*The Bible Translator*
BWANT	Beiträge zur Wissenschaft vom Alten und Neuen Testament
CAD	*Assyrian Dictionary.* Edited by Ignatius J. Gelb et al. Chicago: Oriental Institute of the University of Chicago, 1956
CBET	Contributions to Biblical Exegesis and Theology
CBQ	*Catholic Biblical Quarterly*
CC	Continental Commentaries
COS	*The Context of Scripture.* Edited by William W. Hallo. 3 vols. Leiden: Brill, 1996–2002
DCH	*Dictionary of Classical Hebrew.* Edited by David J. A. Clines. Sheffield: Sheffield Academic Press, 1993–
DDD	*Dictionary of Deities and Demons in the Bible.* Edited by Karel van der Toorn et al. Leiden: Brill, 1995
DJD	Discoveries in the Judean Desert
EBib	Études bibliques
ErIsr	*Eretz-Israel*
EstBib	*Estudios bíblicos*
ETL	*Ephemerides theologicae lovanienses*
EvQ	*Evangelical Quarterly*
EvT	*Evangelische Theologie*
EVV	English Versions
ExpTim	*Expository Times*
FAT	Forschungen zum Alten Testament
FB	Forschung zur Bibel
FRLANT	Forschungen zur Religion und Literatur des Alten und Neuen Testaments
GKC	*Gesenius' Hebrew Grammar.* Edited by Emil Kautzsch. Translated by Arthur E. Cowley. 2d ed. Oxford: Clarendon, 1910
GNB	Good News Bible
GTA	Göttinger theologischer Arbeiten
HALOT	Ludwig Koehler, et al. *The Hebrew and Aramaic Lexicon of the Old Testament.* Translated by Mervyn E. J. Richardson et al. 5 vols. Leiden: Brill, 1994–2000
HAR	*Hebrew Annual Review*
HDR	Harvard Dissertations in Religion

Abbreviations

HSM	Harvard Semitic Monographs
HTR	*Harvard Theological Review*
HUB	*The Hebrew University Bible: The Book of Jeremiah*. Edited by Chaim Rabin et al. Jerusalem: Magnes, 1997
HUCA	*Hebrew Union College Annual*
IB	*Interpreter's Bible*. Edited by George A. Buttrick et al. 12 vols. New York: Abingdon, 1951–1957
IBHS	Bruce K. Waltke and Michael O'Connor, *Introduction to Biblical Hebrew Syntax*. Winona Lake, Ind.: Eisenbrauns, 1990
ICC	International Critical Commentary
IDB	*The Interpreter's Dictionary of the Bible*. Edited by George A. Buttrick. 4 vols. Nashville: Abingdon, 1962
IDBSup	*Interpreter's Dictionary of the Bible: Supplementary Volume*. Edited by Keith Crim. Nashville: Abingdon, 1976
Int	*Interpretation*
Jastrow	Marcus Jastrow. *A Dictionary of the Targumim, the Talmud Babli and Yerushalmi, and the Midrashic Literature*. 2d ed. New York: Shalom, 1903
JBL	*Journal of Biblical Literature*
JNES	*Journal of Near Eastern Studies*
JNSL	*Journal of Northwest Semitic Languages*
Joüon	Paul Joüon. *A Grammar of Biblical Hebrew*. Translated and revised by Takamitsu Muraoka. 2 vols. Subsidia biblica 14/1–2. Rome: Pontifical Biblical Institute, 1991
JQR	*Jewish Quarterly Review*
JSNTSup	Journal for the Study of the New Testament: Supplement Series
JSOT	*Journal for the Study of the Old Testament*
JSOTSup	Journal for the Study of the Old Testament: Supplement Series
JTS	*Journal of Theological Studies*
K	Kethib
KJV	King James Version
LCL	Loeb Classical Library
LD	Lection divina
LXX	Septuagint
LXX^L	Lucianic recension of the LXX
LXX^O	Hexaplaric recension of the LXX
mg.	margin
MS(S)	manuscript(s)
MSU	Mitteilungen des Septuaginta-Unternehmens
MT	Masoretic Text

Mus	*Muséon: Revue d'études orientales*
NAB	New American Bible
NCB	New Century Bible
NEB	New English Bible
NIB	*The New Interpreter's Bible*. Edited by Leander Keck. 12 vols. Nashville: Abingdon, 1994–2002
NIDOTTE	*New International Dictionary of Old Testament Theology and Exegesis*. Edited by Willem A. VanGemeren. 5 vols. Grand Rapids: Zondervan, 1997
NIV	New International Version
NJB	New Jerusalem Bible
NJPS	New Jewish Publication Society Translation
NRSV	New Revised Standard Version
n.s.	new series
NT	New Testament
OBO	Orbis biblicus et orientalis
ÖBS	Österreichische biblische Studien
OBT	Overtures to Biblical Theology
OL	Old Latin
OPTAT	Occasional Papers in Translation and Textlinguistics
OT	Old Testament
OtSt	Oudtestamentische Studiën
OTWSA	Die Ou Testamentiese Werksgemeenskap in Suid-Afrika
PEQ	*Palestine Exploration Quarterly*
PIBA	*Proceedings of the Irish Biblical Association*
PTMS	Pittsburgh Theological Monograph Series
Q	Qere
RB	*Revue biblique*
RSV	Revised Standard Version
RV	English Revised Version
SBB	Stuttgarter biblische Beiträge
SBLAB	Society of Biblical Literature Academia Biblica
SBLDS	Society of Biblical Literature Dissertation Series
SBLMS	Society of Biblical Literature Monograph Series
SBLSCS	Society of Biblical Literature Septuagint and Cognate Studies
SBLSP	*Society of Biblical Literature Seminar Papers*
SBT	Studies in Biblical Theology
SEÅ	*Svensk exegetisk årsbok*
SJLA	Studies in Judaism in Late Antiquity
SJOT	*Scandinavian Journal of the OT*
SJT	*Scottish Journal of Theology*

SOTSMS	Society for Old Testament Studies Monograph Series
SSN	Studia semitica neerlandica
Syr.	Syriac version
TDOT	*Theological Dictionary of the Old Testament*. Edited by G. Johannes Botterweck et al. Translated by John T. Willis et al. Grand Rapids: Eerdmans, 1974–
Text	*Textus*
Tg.	Targum
TGUOS	*Transactions of the Glasgow University Oriental Society*
TLOT	*Theological Lexicon of the Old Testament*. Edited by Ernst Jenni and Claus Westermann. Translated by Mark E. Biddle. 3 vols. Peabody, Mass.: Hendrickson, 1997
TynBul	*Tyndale Bulletin*
USQR	*Union Seminary Quarterly Review*
Vg.	Vulgate
VT	*Vetus Testamentum*
VTSup	Vetus Testamentum Supplements
WBC	Word Biblical Commentary
WMANT	Wissenschaftliche Monographien zum Alten und Neuen Testament
WUNT	Wissenschaftliche Untersuchungen zum Neuen Testament
ZAW	*Zeitschrift für die alttestamentliche Wissenschaft*

BIBLIOGRAPHY

Commentaries

References to commentaries are indicated in this commentary by author and page.

Berrigan, Daniel. *Jeremiah: The World, the Wound of God.* Minneapolis: Fortress, 1999.
Boadt, Lawrence. *Jeremiah 1–25.* Old Testament Message 9. Wilmington, Del.: Michael Glazier, 1982.
———. *Jeremiah 25–52, Habakkuk, Zephaniah, Nahum.* Old Testament Message 10. Wilmington, Del.: Michael Glazier, 1982.
Bracke, John M. *Jeremiah 1–29.* Westminster Bible Companion. Louisville: Westminster John Knox, 2000.
———. *Jeremiah 30–52 and Lamentations.* Westminster Bible Companion. Louisville: Westminster John Knox, 2000.
Bright, John. *Jeremiah.* 2d ed. AB 21. Garden City, N.Y.: Doubleday, 1974.
Brueggemann, Walter. *A Commentary on Jeremiah: Exile and Homecoming.* Grand Rapids: Eerdmans, 1998.
Calvin, John. *Jeremiah and Lamentations.* 5 vols. Translated from the Latin and edited by John Owen. Repr. Grand Rapids: Eerdmans, 1950.
Carroll, Robert P. *Jeremiah, A Commentary.* OTL. Philadelphia: Westminster, 1986.
Clements, Ronald E. *Jeremiah.* Interpretation. Atlanta: John Knox, 1988.
Craigie, Peter C., Page H. Kelley, and Joel F. Drinkard Jr. *Jeremiah 1–25.* WBC 26. Dallas: Word, 1991.
Cunliffe-Jones, Hubert. *The Book of Jeremiah: Introduction and Commentary.* Torch Bible Commentaries. New York: Macmillan, 1961.
Davidson, Robert. *Jeremiah: Volume 1.* Daily Bible Study Series. Philadelphia: Westminster, 1983.
———. *Jeremiah: Volume 2, and Lamentations.* Daily Bible Study Series. Philadelphia: Westminster, 1985.
Duhm, Bernhard. *Der Prophet Jeremia.* Kurzgefasstes exegetisches Handbuch zum Alten Testament 11. Leipzig: Weidmannsche Buchhandlung, 1901.

Fretheim, Terence E. *Jeremiah*. Smyth & Helwys Bible Commentary. Macon, Ga.: Smyth & Helwys, 2002.
Harrison, Roland K. *Jeremiah and Lamentations*. Tyndale Old Testament Commentaries. Downers Grove, Ill.: InterVarsity Press, 1973.
Herrmann, Siegfried. *Jeremia*. Biblische Kommentar: Altes Testament 12/1–2. Neukirchen-Vluyn: Neukirchener Verlag, 1986–1990.
Hitzig, Ferdinand. *Der Prophet Jeremia*. Kurzgefasstes exegetisches Handbuch zum Alten Testament. Leipzig: Weidmannische Buchhandlung, 1841.
Holladay, William L. *Jeremiah 1*. Hermeneia. Philadelphia: Fortress, 1986.
———. *Jeremiah 2*. Hermeneia. Philadelphia: Fortress, 1989.
Hyatt, J. Philip, and Stanley R. Hopper. "The Book of Jeremiah." *NIB* 5:775–1142.
Jones, Douglas R. *Jeremiah*. NCB. Grand Rapids: Eerdmans, 1992.
Keil, Carl F. *Jeremiah, Lamentations*. Translated by David Patrick and James Kennedy. Commentaries on the Old Testament 8. Repr. Grand Rapids: Eerdmans, 1986.
Keown, Gerald L., Pamela J. Scalise, and Thomas G. Smothers. *Jeremiah 26–52*. WBC 27. Dallas: Word, 1995.
Kidner, Derek. *The Message of Jeremiah: Against Wind and Tide*. The Bible Speaks Today. Downers Grove, Ill: InterVarsity, 1987.
Lundbom, Jack R. *Jeremiah 1–20*. AB 21A. New York: Doubleday, 1999.
———. *Jeremiah 21–36*. AB 21B. New York: Doubleday, 2004.
———. *Jeremiah 37–52*. AB 21C. New York: Doubleday, 2004.
Martens, Elmer A. *Jeremiah*. Believers Church Bible Commentary. Scottdale, Pa.: Herald Press, 1986.
McKane, William. *Jeremiah i–xxv*. ICC. Edinburgh: T & T Clark, 1986.
———. *Jeremiah xxvi–lii*. ICC. Edinburgh: T & T Clark, 1996.
Miller, Patrick D., Jr. "The Book of Jeremiah." *NIB* 6:553–920.
Nicholson, Ernest W. *Jeremiah 1–25*. Cambridge Bible Commentary. Cambridge: Cambridge University Press, 1973.
———. *Jeremiah 26–52*. Cambridge Bible Commentary. Cambridge: Cambridge University Press, 1975.
Peake, Arthur S. *Jeremiah i–xxv*. Century Bible. London: Nelson, 1910.
———. *Jeremiah xxvi–lii and Lamentations*. Century Bible. London: Nelson, 1910.
Pixley, Jorge V. *Jeremiah*. Chalice Commentaries for Today. St. Louis: Chalice, 2004.
Rudolph, Wilhelm. *Jeremia*. Handbuch zum Alten Testament 1/12. 3d ed. Tübingen: Mohr (Siebeck), 1968.
Schreiner, Josef. *Jeremia 1–25,14*. Neue Echter Bibel 3. Würzburg: Echter Verlag, 1981.
———. *Jeremia 25,15–52,34*. Neue Echter Bibel 9. Würzburg: Echter Verlag, 1984.

Smith, George Adam, *Jeremiah*. 4th ed. New York: Harper, 1929.
Streane, Annesley W. *The Book of the Prophet Jeremiah together with the Lamentations*. 2d ed. Cambridge Bible for Schools and Colleges. Cambridge: Cambridge University Press, 1913.
Stulman, Louis. *Jeremiah*. Abingdon Old Testament Commentaries. Nashville: Abingdon, 2005.
Thompson, John A. *The Book of Jeremiah*. NICOT. Grand Rapids: Eerdmans, 1980.
Volz, Paul. *Der Prophet Jeremia*. 2d ed. Kommentar zum Alten Testament. Leipzig: A. Deichert, 1928.
Wanke, Gunther. *Jeremia*. 2 vols. Zürcher Bibelkommentare: AT 20. Zurich: Theologischer Verlag, 1995.
Weiser, Artur. *Das Buch der Propheten Jeremia, Kapitel 1–25,14*. 4th ed. Das Alte Testament Deutsch 20. Göttingen: Vandenhoeck & Ruprecht, 1960.
———. *Das Buch Jeremia, Kapitel 25,15–52,34*. 4th ed. Das Alte Testament Deutsch 21. Göttingen: Vandenhoeck & Ruprecht, 1966.

Monographs

Bach, Robert. *Die Aufforderungen zur Flucht und zum Kampf im alttestamentlichen Prophetenspruch*. WMANT 9. Neukirchen-Vluyn: Neukirchener Verlag, 1962.
Bak, Dong Hyun. *Klagender Gott—klagende Menschen: Studien zur Klage im Jeremiabuch*. BZAW 193. Berlin: de Gruyter, 1990.
Barthélemy, Dominique. *Critique textuelle de l'Ancien Testament*, vol. 2: *Isaïe, Jérémie, Lamentations*. OBO 50/2. Fribourg: Éditions Universitaires; Göttingen: Vandenhoeck & Ruprecht, 1986.
Baumgartner, Walter. *Jeremiah's Poems of Lament*. Translated by David E. Orton. Historic Texts and Interpreters in Biblical Scholarship 7. Sheffield: Almond Press, 1987.
Bellis, Alice O. *The Structure and Composition of Jeremiah 50:2–51:58*. Lewiston, N.Y.: Mellen Biblical Press, 1995.
Berridge, John M. *Prophet, People, and the Word of Yahweh: An Examination of Form and Content in the Proclamation of the Prophet Jeremiah*. Basel Studies of Theology 4. Zurich: EVZ, 1970.
Biddle, Mark E. *A Redactional History of Jeremiah 2:1–4:2*. ATANT 77. Zurich: Theologischer Verlag, 1990.
———. *Polyphony and Symphony in Prophetic Literature: Rereading Jeremiah 7–20*. Studies in Old Testament Interpretation 2. Macon, Ga.: Mercer University Press, 1996.
Böhmer, Siegfried. *Heimkehr und neuer Bund: Studien zu Jeremia 30–31*. GTA 5. Göttingen: Vandenhoeck & Ruprecht, 1976.

Bourguet, Daniel. *Des métaphores de Jérémie.* EBib n.s. 9; Paris: Gabalda, 1987.
Bozak, Barbara A. *Life "Anew": A Literary-Theological Study of Jer. 30–31.* AnBib 122. Rome: Pontifical Biblical Institute, 1991.
Broyles, Craig C. *The Conflict of Faith and Experience in the Psalms: A Form-Critical and Theological Study.* JSOTSup 52. Sheffield: JSOT Press, 1989.
Brueggemann, Walter. *The Theology of the Book of Jeremiah.* Old Testament Theology. Cambridge: Cambridge University Press, 2007.
Carroll, Robert P. *From Chaos to Covenant: Prophecy in the Book of Jeremiah.* New York: Crossroad, 1981.
Christensen, Duane L. *Transformations of the War Oracle in Old Testament Prophecy: Studies in the Oracles against the Nations.* HDR 3. Missoula, Mont.: Scholars Press, 1975.
Cloete, Walter T. W. *Versification and Syntax in Jeremiah 2–25: Syntactical Constraints in Hebrew Colometry.* SBLDS 117. Atlanta: Scholars Press, 1989.
Diamond, A. R. Pete. *The Confessions of Jeremiah in Context: Scenes of Prophetic Drama.* JSOTSup 45. Sheffield: JSOT Press, 1987.
Driver, Samuel R. *The Book of the Prophet Jeremiah: A Revised Translation with Introduction and Short Explanations.* London: Hodder & Stoughton, 1906.
Ehrlich, Arnold B. *Randglossen zur hebräischen Bibel: Textkritisches, sprachliches und sachliches*, vol. 4: *Jesaja, Jeremia.* Leipzig: Hinrichs, 1912.
Fischer, Georg. *Das Trostbüchlein: Text, Komposition und Theologie von Jer 30–31.* SBB 26. Stuttgart: Katholisches Bibelwerk, 1993.
Fishbane, Michael. *Biblical Interpretation in Ancient Israel.* Oxford: Clarendon, 1984.
Friebel, Kelvin G. *Jeremiah's and Ezekiel's Sign-Acts: Rhetorical Nonverbal Communication.* JSOTSup 283. Sheffield: Sheffield Academic Press, 1999.
Goldman, Yohanan. *Prophétie et royauté au retour de l'exil: Les origines littéraires de la forme massorétique du livre de Jérémie.* OBO 118. Freiburg: Universitätsverlag; Göttingen: Vandenhoeck & Ruprecht, 1992.
Graupner, Axel. *Auftrag und Geschick des Propheten Jeremia: Literarische Eigenart, Herkunft und Intention vordeuteronomisticher Prosa im Jeremiabuch.* Biblisch-Theologische Studien 15. Neukirchen-Vluyn: Neukirchener Verlag, 1991.
Herrmann, Siegfried. *Die prophetischen Heilserwartungen im Alten Testament: Ursprung und Gestaltwendel.* BWANT 5/5. Stuttgart: Kohlhammer, 1965.
———. *Jeremia: Das Prophet und das Buch.* Erträge der Forschung 271. Darmstadt: Wissenschaftliche Buchgesellschaft, 1990.
Hill, John. *Friend or Foe? The Figure of Babylon in the Book of Jeremiah.* Leiden: Brill, 1999.

Holladay, William H. *The Architecture of Jeremiah 1–20*. Lewisburg, Pa.: Bucknell University Press, 1976.

Hubmann, Franz D. *Untersuchungen zu den Konfessionen Jer 11,18–12,6 und Jer 15,10–21*. FB 30. Würzburg: Echter Verlag, 1978.

Huwyler, Beat. *Jeremia und die Völker: Untersuchungen zu den Völkersprüche in Jeremia 46–49*. FAT 20. Tübingen: Mohr Siebeck, 1997.

Ittmann, Norbert. *Die Konfessionen Jeremias: Ihre Bedeutung für die Verkündigung des Propheten*. WMANT 54. Neukirchen-Vluyn: Neukirchener Verlag, 1981.

Janzen, J. Gerald. *Studies in the Text of Jeremiah*. HSM 6. Cambridge: Harvard University Press, 1973.

Job, John B. *Jeremiah's Kings: A Study of the Monarchy in Jeremiah*. SOTSMS. Aldershot, Eng.: Ashgate, 2006.

Joo, Samantha. *Provocation and Punishment: The Anger of God in the Book of Jeremiah and Deuteronomistic Theology*. BZAW 361. Berlin: de Gruyter, 2006.

Kessler, Martin. *Battle of the Gods: The God of Israel versus Marduk of Babylon: A Literary/Theological Interpretation of Jeremiah 50–51*. SSN 42. Assen: Van Gorcum, 2003.

Kilpp, Nelson. *Niederreissen und aufbauen: Das Verhältnis von Heilsverheissung und Unheilsverkündigung bei Jeremia und in Jeremiabuch*. Biblisch-theologische Studien 13. Neukirchen-Vluyn: Neukirchener Verlag, 1990.

King, Philip J. *Jeremiah: An Archaeological Companion*. Louisville: Westminster/John Knox, 1993.

Kiss, Jenö. *Die Klage Gottes und des Propheten: Ihre Rolle in der Komposition und Redaktion von Jer 11–12, 14–15 und 18*. WMANT 99. Neukirchen-Vluyn: Neukirchener Verlag, 2003.

Lallelman-de Winkel, Hetty. *Jeremiah in Prophetic Tradition: An Examination of the Book of Jeremiah in the Light of Israel's Prophetic Traditions*. CBET 26. Leuven: Peeters, 2000.

Levin, Christof. *Die Verheissung des neuen Bundes in ihrem theologiegeschichtlichen Zusammenhang ausgelegt*. FRLANT 137. Göttingen: Vandenhoeck & Ruprecht, 1985.

Lundbom, Jack R. *Jeremiah: A Study in Ancient Hebrew Rhetoric*. 2d ed. Winona Lake, Ind.: Eisenbrauns, 1997.

McConville, J. Gordon. *Judgment and Promise: An Interpretation of the Book of Jeremiah*. Winona Lake, Ind.: Eisenbrauns, 1993.

Migsch, Herbert. *Gottes Wort über das Ende Jerusalems: Eine literar-, stil- und gattungskritische Untersuchung des Berichtes Jeremia 34,1–7; 32,2–5; 37,3–38,28*. ÖBS 2. Klosterneuberg: Österreichisches Katholisches Bibelwerk, 1981.

Miller, Patrick D., Jr. *Sin and Judgment in the Prophets: A Stylistic and Theological Analysis.* SBLMS 27. Chico, Calif.: Scholars Press, 1982.

Mowinckel, Sigmund. *Zur Komposition des Buches Jeremia.* Kristiania, Oslo: Jacob Dybwad, 1914.

Nicholson, Ernest W. *Preaching to the Exiles: A Study of the Prose Tradition in the Book of Jeremiah.* New York: Schocken, 1971.

O'Connor, Kathleen M. *The Confessions of Jeremiah: Their Interpretation and Role in Jeremiah 1–25.* SBLDS 94. Atlanta: Scholars Press, 1987.

Overholt, Thomas W. *The Threat of Falsehood: A Study in the Theology of the Book of Jeremiah.* SBT 2/16. Naperville, Ill.: Allenson, 1970.

Parke-Taylor, Geoffrey. *The Formation of the Book of Jeremiah: Doublets and Recurring Phrases.* SBLMS 51. Atlanta: Society of Biblical Literature, 2000.

Peels, Hendrik G. L. *The Vengeance of God: The Meaning of the Root NQM and the Function of the NQM-Texts in the Context of Divine Revelation in the Old Testament.* OtSt 31. Leiden: Brill, 1995.

Pohlmann, Karl-Friedrich. *Studien zum Jeremiabuch: Ein Beitrag zur Frage nach der Enstehung des Jeremiabuches.* FRLANT 118. Göttingen: Vandenhoeck & Ruprecht, 1978.

———. *Die Ferne Gottes—Studien zum Jeremiabuch: Beiträge zu den "Konfessionen" im Jeremiabuch und ein Versuch zur Frage nach den Anfängen der Jeremiatradition.* BZAW 179. Berlin: de Gruyter, 1989.

Polk, Timothy. *The Prophetic Persona: Jeremiah and the Language of the Self.* JSOTSup 32. Sheffield: JSOT Press, 1984.

Raitt, Thomas M. *A Theology of Exile: Judgment/Deliverance in Jeremiah and Ezekiel.* Philadelphia: Fortress, 1977.

Reimer, David J. *The Oracles against Babylon in Jeremiah 50–51: A Horror among the Nations.* San Francisco: Mellen Research University Press, 1993.

Reventlow, Henning Graf. *Liturgie und prophetisches Ich bei Jeremia.* Gütersloh: Gerd Mohn, 1963.

Rietzschel, Claus. *Das Problem der Urrolle: Ein Beitrag zur Redaktionsgeschichte des Jeremiabuches.* Gütersloh: Gerd Mohn, 1966.

Roncace, Mark. *Jeremiah, Zedekiah, and the Fall of Jerusalem.* Library of Hebrew Bible/Old Testament Studies 423. New York: T & T Clark, 2005.

Schmid, Konrad. *Buchgestalten des Jeremiabuches: Untersuchungen zur Redaktions- und Rezeptionsgeschichte von Jer 30–33 in Kontext des Buches.* WMANT 72. Neukirchen-Vluyn: Neukirchener Verlag, 1996.

Seidl, Theodor. *Texte und Einheiten in Jeremia 27–29.* ATSAT 2. St. Ottilien: EOS, 1977.

———. *Formen und Formeln in Jeremia 27–29.* ATSAT 5. St. Ottlien: EOS, 1978.

Seitz, Christopher R. *Theology in Conflict: Reactions to the Exile in the Book of Jeremiah.* BZAW 176. Berlin: de Gruyter, 1989.

Seybold, Klaus. *Der Prophet Jeremia: Leben und Werk.* Urban-Taschenbücher 416. Stuttgart: Kohlhammer, 1993.

Sharp, Carolyn J. *Prophecy and Ideology in Jeremiah: Struggles for Authority in the Deutero-Jeremianic Prose: Struggle for Authority in the Deutero-Jeremianic Prose.* London: T & T Clark, 2003.

Shead, Andrew G. *The Open Book and the Sealed Book: Jeremiah 32 in Its Hebrew and Greek Recensions.* JSOTSup 347. London: Sheffield Academic Press, 2002.

Skinner, John. *Prophecy and Religion: Studies in the Life of Jeremiah.* Cambridge: Cambridge University Press, 1922.

Smith, Mark S. *The Laments of Jeremiah and Their Contexts: A Literary and Redactional Study of Jeremiah 11–20.* SBLMS 42. Atlanta: Scholars Press, 1990.

Soderlund, Sven. *The Greek Text of Jeremiah: A Revised Hypothesis.* JSOTSup 47. Sheffield: JSOT Press, 1985.

Stipp, Hermann-Josef. *Jeremia im Parteienstreit: Studien zur Textentwicklung von Jer. 24, 36–43 und 45 als Beitrag zur Geschichte Jeremias, seines Buches und judäischer Parteien im 6. Jahrhundert.* Athenäums Monografien: Theologie 82. Frankfurt am Main: Hain, 1992.

———. *Das masoretische und alexandrinische Sondergut des Jeremiabuches: Textgeschichtlicher Rang, Eigenarten, Triebkräfte.* OBO 136. Freiburg: Universitätsverlag, 1994.

Stulman, Louis. *The Prose Sermons of the Book of Jeremiah: A Redescription of the Correspondences with Deuteronomistic Literature in the Light of Recent Text-Critical Research.* SBLDS 83. Atlanta: Scholars Press, 1986.

———. *Order amid Chaos: Jeremiah as Symbolic Tapestry.* Biblical Seminar 57. Sheffield: Sheffield Academic Press, 1998.

Thiel, Winfried. *Die deuteronomistische Redaktion von Jeremia 1–25.* WMANT 41. Neukirchen-Vluyn: Neukirchener Verlag, 1973.

———, *Die deuteronomistische Redaktion von Jeremia 26–45.* WMANT 52. Neukirchen-Vluyn: Neukirchener Verlag, 1981.

Tov, Emanuel. *The Septuagint Translation of Jeremiah and Baruch: A Discussion of an Early Revision of Jeremiah 29–32 and Baruch 1:1–3:8.* HSM 8. Missoula, Mont.: Scholars Press, 1976.

———. "Jeremiah." Pp. 145–207 in Eugene Ulrich et al., *Qumran Cave 4: X. The Prophets.* DJD 15. Oxford: Clarendon, 1997.

Unterman, Jeremiah. *From Repentance to Redemption: Jeremiah's Thought in Transition.* JSOTSup 54. Sheffield: JSOT Press, 1987.

Waard, Jan de. *A Handbook on Jeremiah.* Winona Lake, Ind.: Eisenbrauns, 2003.

Wanke, Gunther. *Untersuchungen zur sogenannten Baruchschrift.* BZAW 122. Berlin: de Gruyter, 1971.

Watson, Wilfred G. E. *Classical Hebrew Poetry: A Guide to Its Techniques.* JSOTSup 26. Sheffield: JSOT Press, 1984.

Weippert, Helga. *Die Prosareden des Jeremiabuches.* BZAW 135. Berlin: de Gruyter, 1973.

Westermann, Claus. *Basic Forms of Prophetic Speech.* Translated by Hugh C. White. Philadelphia: Westminster, 1967; reprinted with a new foreword by Gene M. Tucker. Louisville: Westminster/John Knox, 1991.

Ziegler, Joseph. *Beiträge zur Jeremias-Septuaginta.* Nachrichten der Akademie die Wissenschaften in Göttingen I. Phil.-Hist. Klasse 1958:2. Göttingen: Vandenhoeck & Ruprecht, 1958.

———. *Jeremias, Baruch, Threni, Epistula Jeremiae.* 2d ed. Septuaginta: Vetus Testamentum Graecum auctoritate Academiae Scientiarum Gottingensis editum 15. Göttingen: Vandenhoeck & Ruprecht, 1976.

Articles and Collections of Articles

Ackroyd, Peter R. "Historians and Prophets." *SEÅ* 33 (1968): 18–54.

Aejmelaeus, Anneli. "Jeremiah at the Turning-Point of History: The Function of Jer. xxv 1–14 in the Book of Jeremiah." *VT* 52 (2002): 459–82.

Aitken, Kenneth T. "The Oracles against Babylon in Jeremiah 50–51: Structure and Perspectives." *TynBul* 35 (1984): 25–63.

Albertz, Rainer. "Jer 2–6 und die Fruhverkündigung Jeremias." *ZAW* 98 (1982): 20–47.

Applegate, John. "Narrative Patterns for the Communication of Commissioned Speech in the Prophets: A Three-Scene Model." Pp. 69–88 in *Narrativity in Biblical and Related Texts.* Edited by George J. Brooke and Jean-Daniel Kaestli. BETL 149. Leuven: Leuven University Press, 2000.

Bach, Robert. "Bauen und Pflanzen." Pp. 7–32 in *Studien zur Theologie der alttestamentlichen Überlieferungen.* Edited by R. Rendtorff and K. Koch. Neukirchen-Vluyn: Neukirchener Verlag, 1961.

Becking, Bob. *Between Fear and Freedom: Essays on the Interpretation of Jeremiah 30–31.* OtSt 51. Leiden: Brill, 2004.

Bogaert, Pierre-Maurice. "Le livre de Jérémie en perspective: Les deux rédactions antiques selon les travaux en cours." *RB* 101 (1994): 363–406.

———, ed. *Le livre de Jérémie: Le prophète et son milieu, les oracles et leur transmission.* 2d ed. BETL 54. Leuven: Leuven University Press, 1997.

Brueggemann, Walter A. "Jeremiah's Use of Rhetorical Questions." *JBL* 92 (1973): 358–74.

———. "Israel's Sense of Place in Jeremiah." Pp. 149–65 in *Rhetorical Criticism: Essays in Honor of James Muilenburg.* Edited by Jared J. Jackson and Martin Kessler. PTMS 1. Pittsburgh: Pickwick, 1974.

Castellino, Giorgio R. "Some Observations on the Literary Structure of Some Passages in Jeremiah." *VT* 30 (1980): 398–408.

Clements, Ronald E. "Jeremiah 1–25 and the Deuteronomistic Tradition." Pp. 93–113 in *Understanding Poets and Prophets: Essays in Honour of George Wishart Anderson*. Edited by A. Graeme Auld. JSOTSup 57. Sheffield: JSOT Press, 1993.

Crenshaw, James L. "*YHWH Ṣ^{e}ba'ôt Š^{e}mô:* A Form-Critical Analysis," *ZAW* 81 (1969): 156–75.

Curtis, Adrian H. W., and Thomas Römer, eds. *The Book of Jeremiah and Its Reception: Le livre de Jérémie et sa reception*. BETL 128. Leuven: Leuven University Press, 1997.

Diamond, A. R. Pete. "Jeremiah's Confessions in the LXX and MT: A Witness to Developing Canonical Function?" *VT* 40 (1990): 33–50.

———, Kathleen M. O'Connor, and Louis Stulman, eds. *Troubling Jeremiah*. JSOTSup 260. Sheffield: Sheffield Academic Press, 1999.

Driver, Godfrey R. "Linguistic and Textual Problems: Jeremiah." *JQR* 28 (1937–38): 97–129.

Fischer, Georg, "Zum Text des Jeremiabuches," *Bib* 78 (1997): 305–28.

Fretheim, Terence E. "The Character of God in Jeremiah." Pp. 211–30 in *Character and Scripture: Moral Formation, Community, and Biblical Interpretation*. Edited by William P. Brown. Grand Rapids: Eerdmans, 2002.

Goldingay, John, ed. *Uprooting and Planting: Essays on Jeremiah for Leslie Allen*. Library of Hebrew Bible/Old Testament Studies 459. New York: T & T Clark, 2007.

Gosse, Bernard, "Trois étapes de la rédaction du livre de Jérémie." *ZAW* 111 (1999): 508–29.

Gross, Walter, ed. *Jeremia und die "deuteronomistische Bewegung."* BB 98. Weinheim: Beltz Athenäum, 1995.

Hermisson, Hans-Jürgen. "'Das Feind aus den Norden' (Jer 4–6): Zu einem Gedichtzyklus Jeremias." Pp. 233–51 in *Schriftprophetie: Festschrift für Jörg Jeremias zum 65. Geburtstag*. Edited by Friedhelm Hartenstein et al. Neukirchen-Vluyn: Neukirchener Verlag, 2004.

Hobbs, T. Raymond. "Some Remarks on the Composition and Structure of the Book of Jeremiah." *CBQ* 34 (1972): 257–75.

Holt, Else K. "The Meaning of an *Inclusio*: A Theological Interpretation of the Book of Jeremiah MT." *SJOT* 17 (2003): 183–205.

Janzen, J. Gerald. "A Critique of Sven Soderlund's *The Greek Text of Jeremiah*." *BIOSCS* 22 (1989): 16–47.

Kessler, Martin. "Jeremiah Chapters 26–45 Reconsidered." *JNES* 27 (1968): 81–88.

———. "The Judgment-Promise Dialectic in Jeremiah 26–36." *ACEBT* 16 (1977): 60–72.

———, ed. *Reading the Book of Jeremiah: A Search for Coherence.* Winona Lake, Ind.: Eisenbrauns, 2004.
Long, Burke O. "Two Question and Answer Schemata in the Prophets." *JBL* 90 (1971): 129–39.
Marx, Alfred. "A propos des doublets du livre de Jérémie: Réflexions sur la formation d'un livre prophétique." Pp. 106–20 in *Prophecy: Essays Presented to Georg Fohrer on His Sixty-Fifth Birthday, 6 September 1980.* Edited by John A. Emerton. BZAW 150. Berlin: de Gruyter, 1980.
McConville, Gordon. "Divine Speech and the Book of Jeremiah." Pp. 18–38 in *The Trustworthiness of God: Perspectives on the Nature of Scripture.* Edited by Paul Helm and Carl R. Trueman. Grand Rapids: Eerdmans, 2002.
McEvenue, Sean. "The Composition of Jeremiah 37:1 to 44:30." Pp. 59–67 in *Studies in Wisdom Literature.* Edited by Wouter C. van Wyk. OTWSA 15–16. 1976.
Murray, Donald F. "The Rhetoric of Disputation: Reexamination of a Prophetic Genre." *JSOT* 38 (1987): 95–121.
Neumann, Peter K. D. "Das Wort das geschehen ist. . . . Zum Problem der Wortempfangsterminologie in Jer. i–xxv." *VT* 23 (1973): 171–217.
O'Connor, Kathleen M. "'Do Not Trim a Word': The Contributions of Chapter 26 to the Book of Jeremiah." *CBQ* 51 (1989): 617–30.
Perdue, Leo G., and Brian W. Kovacs, eds. *A Prophet to the Nations: Essays in Jeremiah Studies.* Winona Lake, Ind.: Eisenbrauns, 1984.
Raitt, Thomas M. "The Prophetic Summons to Repentance." *ZAW* 83 (1971): 30–49.
Rofé, Alexander. "The Arrangement of the Book of Jeremiah." *ZAW* 101 (1991): 390–98.
Seitz, Christopher R. "The Crisis of Interpretation over the Meaning and Purpose of the Exile: A Redactional Study of Jeremiah xxi–xliii." *VT* 35 (1985): 78–97.
———. "The Prophet Moses and the Canonical Shape of Jeremiah." *ZAW* 101 (1989): 3–27.
Stipp, Herman-Josef. "The Prophetic Messenger Formulas in Jeremiah according to the Masoretic and Alexandrian Texts." *Text* 18 (1995): 63–85.
Stulman, Louis. "Insiders and Outsiders in the Book of Jeremiah: Shifts in Symbolic Arrangements." *JSOT* 66 (1995): 65–85.
Sweeney, Marvin A. "The Masoretic and Septuagint Versions of the Book of Jeremiah in Synchronic Perspective." Pp. 65–77 in *Form and Intertextuality in Prophetic and Apocalyptic Literature.* FAT 45. Tübingen: Mohr (Siebeck), 2005.
Tov, Emanuel. "Exegetical Notes on the Hebrew Vorlage of the LXX of Jeremiah 27 (34)." *ZAW* 91 (1979): 73–93.

Bibliography

———. "The Literary History of the Book of Jeremiah in the Light of Its Textual History." Pp. 211–37 in *Empirical Models for Biblical Criticism*. Edited by Jeffrey H. Tigay. Philadelphia: University of Pennsylvania Press, 1985.

Watts, James W. "Text and Redaction in Jeremiah's Oracles against the Nations." *CBQ* 54 (1992): 432–47.

Williams, Michael J. "An Investigation of the Legitimacy of Source Distinctions for the Prose Material in Jeremiah." *JBL* 112 (1993): 193–210.

Zimmerli, Walther. "Visionary Experience in Jeremiah." Pp. 95–118 in *Israel's Prophetic Tradition: Essays in Honour of Peter R. Ackroyd*. Edited by Richard Coggins et al. Cambridge: Cambridge University Press, 1982.

INTRODUCTION

Prophecy is a psychic gift that in many cultures has been harnessed to religion. Even now Protestant and Catholic charismatic groups practice it, in addition to Pentecostal denominations. According to the NT, the church was "built upon the foundation of the apostles and prophets" (Eph 2:20; cf. 3:5; 4:11). A major part of the OT canon is made up of the books of the classical prophets, while in the Hebrew Bible these "Latter Prophets" are traditionally associated with the "Former Prophets," the Deuteronomistic historical books that derive their theology from Deuteronomy and tell the story of Israel and Judah. The mission of the classical prophets clustered around political crisis. Their period, stretching from the eighth century to at least the fifth century B.C.E., embraced the dangerous eras of Assyrian and Babylonian dominance, eras that brought increasing loss of national independence and eventual deportation. The period extended to the Persian era, when a significant number of exiles returned and achieved an uneasy survival. The prophets refused to see national misfortune from a purely political perspective. They were religious idealists who insisted a higher agenda was being played out in the history of the two nations that shared a common theological tradition, Israel and Judah. They saw themselves as interpreters of crisis in terms of the ongoing will of Yahweh, the God of these twin nations. The lengthy book of Jeremiah stands at the epicenter of this prophetic witness, focusing on the crucial period around the final capture of Jerusalem in 587 that spelled the end of Judah. It also gathers up concerns of the wider prophetic canon, containing its own strong Deuteronomistic flavor and echoes of Deuteronomy and featuring Israel and Judah by exhibiting a keen interest in the future of them both.

1. Premises

Research for this commentary began with a parallel reading of three stimulating commentaries, those of Rudolph, McKane, and Holladay. It became evident that there were marked differences between them in commenting on the same passage. Each had his own agenda, a complex set of scholarly convictions that were rigorously applied throughout their books. Readers may find it helpful to have announced at the outset six main premises that govern this commentary.

1. The book of Jeremiah is religious literature and deserves to be approached from a religious perspective.
2. The focus of the commentary is on the final form of the book as the canonical version, theologically and literarily.
3. Nevertheless, I have listened to other ancient texts and versions with care and sometimes preferred them.
4. Nevertheless, too, I have made some effort to ascertain earlier stages of the literary process that led to the final form. The book is not less than the sum of its successive parts.
5. The commentary consists of context-driven exegesis that pursues the book's own interests. The necessary task of contemporary application is left to other commentaries, such as those of Miller and Bracke.
6. Nevertheless, in keeping with the spirit of the title of the series, the Old Testament Library, I have tried to observe echoes and parallels elsewhere in the OT and in the NT, in order to show the book's coherence with other parts of the biblical revelation and its abiding, even when disturbing, character.

2. Translation and Text

The translation incorporates interpretive conclusions reached in the notes and exegesis. Its style covers a spectrum from a free, natural-sounding rendering that expresses the sense of the original to ponderous literalness, polar ends represented respectively by two vintage scholarly renderings.[1] Earlier drafts were closer to the former end, but, since the commentary is based on the Hebrew text, accommodation increasingly had to be made to repeated terms that turned out to be exegetically crucial to a passage. Thus "burn down" became "burn with fire" in 21:10; 43:13; 51:38 because "fire" is a key word in the context. "Visited" had to be changed to "came to" in 40:8, 13; 41:1 under the constraint of a Hebrew catchphrase that also occurs in 40:6, 12. Another necessary constraint has been to retain the contours of Hebrew poetry.[2] An effort has been made to reflect the Hebrew word order and/or focus, for example, in 14:19, "Is Zion the object of your intense loathing?" and in 26:16, "Rather, what he has told us has been in the name of our God Yahweh." Bracketed material in the

---

1. Adam C. Welch, *The Book of Jeremiah Translated into Colloquial English* (2d ed.; London: National Adult School Union, 1928); Samuel R. Driver, *The Book of the Prophet Jeremiah: A Revised Translation with Introduction and Short Explanations* (London: Hodder & Stoughton, 1906).

2. Wilfred G. E. Watson, *Classical Hebrew Poetry: A Guide to Its Techniques* (JSOTSup 26; Sheffield: JSOT Press, 1984); Walter T. W. Cloete, *Versification and Syntax in Jeremiah 2–25: Syntactical Constraints in Hebrew Colometry* (SBLDS 117; Atlanta: Scholars Press, 1989).

Introduction

translation, like the italics in KJV, adds words necessary in English, such as "you [all]" in 28:27; 33:20; 37:18–19; 40:3; 49:6; 51:24 to indicate an otherwise undetectable plural pronoun. A question mark in parentheses warns of extreme uncertainty and a cautious attempt at translation. Italics are used to indicate what I judge to be expansions in the longer text of MT, over against the shorter LXX, so that readers can see at a glance such later stages of development in the literary tradition. The English numbering of verses and chapters is followed in the translation and elsewhere, with Hebrew variations in parentheses, unless otherwise noted.

The notes accompanying the translation justify it in matters of lexicography, syntax, poetic structure, and text criticism. A non-Hebraist finds such recondite issues daunting, and so they are often collated with standard English versions (EVV) in order that their impact may be appreciated. Seven versions were chosen for regular comparison, NRSV, NIV, REB, NAB, NJB, NJPS, and GNB, with occasional recourse to others, such as KJV, RSV, and NEB. The NRSV is also used in the commentary for biblical quotations outside Jeremiah, unless otherwise indicated, while the NRSV forms of Hebrew names have usually been followed. All seven versions except NJPS engage in text-critical changes to a greater or lesser degree. Textual criticism in Jeremiah mainly addresses the differences between MT and LXX.[3] Other ancient translations—Syriac (Syr.), Old Latin (OL), Vulgate (Vg.), Targum (Tg.), and the later Greek translations of Aquila, Symmachus, and Theodotion—play subsidiary roles.[4] LXX is about one-seventh shorter than MT. This difference in length involves both text-critical and redaction-critical issues. The majority of differences appear to fall into the latter category, but each case has to be separately judged either textual or redactional in nature.[5] In practice the distinction is often blurred, as when, for instance, explanatory glosses have been incorporated into the text. McKane (263) has used a pragmatic test of intelligibility in such cases, namely, that the redacted text is to be retained if it is intelligible, while textual error is to be gauged by unintelligibility. Thus the close of 51:64 in MT, "'Wearing themselves out' marks the conclusion of Jeremiah's messages," employs a cue word, citing v. 58, which is a characteristic of a textual gloss. All seven EVV wisely retain the clause. However, in 24:9 a misplaced gloss turns up awkwardly in MT; NAB, REB, as well as RSV, omit it.

---

3. For LXX, the critical edition of Joseph Ziegler, *Jeremias, Baruch, Threni, Epistula Jeremiae* (2d ed.; Septuaginta: Vetus Testamentum Graecum auctoritate Academiae Scientiarum Gottingensis editum 15; Göttingen: Vandenhoeck & Ruprecht, 1976), has mostly been used. Exceptions are in 29(LXX 36):11; 30(LXX 37):17; 37(LXX 44):21. McKane in his commentary exercises his text-critical skill on MT, but is sometimes too inclined to begrudge Ziegler's doing so in the case of LXX and to take LXX at face value.

4. For an overview see McKane 1:xv–xli.

5. The apparatus in *BHS* confusingly covers both textual and redactional issues.

Many scholars now recognize that the relationship between the MT and LXX is complex, involving both text-critical and redaction-critical problems.[6] Some scholars adopt more radical positions. Rudolph, who did most of his work in a pre-Qumran academic era, tended to explain LXX's shorter text as due to deliberate translational abridgment. Lundbom generally regards LXX's shorter text as the result of accidental oversight.[7] With the same result but a different premise, Barthélemy understands most variants in terms of a literary perspective and rarely corrects MT on the basis of LXX.[8] On the other hand, Janzen considers the differences between LXX and MT to be of a textual, rather than redactional, nature.[9] The issue of redaction will be further treated below under "Literary Development."

3. Genre

Knowledge of genre is an indispensable tool for exegesis. Recognition of this cultural feature brings readers into an initial engagement with the text, arousing their expectations as to its mood and function and prompting a search for formal guidelines throughout the passage. By this means a mass of strange material becomes more amenable. The proof of the pudding is in the eating—form-critical analysis of particular texts in the commentary itself.

A concatenation of oracles of disaster constitutes a backbone for the book, as it does in other prophetic books. Many oracles are composed of a reason for disaster and an announcement that the disaster is to come in the double form of a divine intervention into the human situation and the dire consequences of that intervention. The beginning of the oracle may be expanded in an attention-grabbing fashion, such as questions (e.g., 5:7; 15:5; 18:13–14) and imperatives (e.g., 5:10, 20–21; 7:21; 22:20). Oracles of disaster are sometimes combined

---

6. Cf. Andrew G. Shead, *The Open Book and the Sealed Book: Jeremiah 32 in Its Hebrew and Greek Recensions* (JSOTSup 347; London: Sheffield Academic Press, 2002), 263: "we must distinguish between the use of G [= LXX] to correct mistakes in M[T] and the use of G to undo revision in M." A good discussion is provided by James W. Watts, "Text and Redaction in Jeremiah's Oracles against the Nations," *CBQ* 54 (1992): 432–47; he rightly observes that textual error can occur at any stage of the history of the text (437–39).

7. Apart from his commentary see David N. Freedman and Jack R. Lundbom, "Haplography in Jeremiah 1–20," *ErIsr* 26 (1999): 28*–38*.

8. In A. E. Housman's words, he at times practices "the art of explaining errors instead of correcting them," according to Bertil Albrektson, "Translation and Emendation," in *Language, Theology, and the Bible: Essays in Honor of James Barr* (ed. S. E. Balentine and J. Barton; Oxford: Clarendon, 1994), 27–39, esp. 38. Readers without French can find summaries of Barthélemy's discussions in Jan de Waard, *A Handbook on Jeremiah* (Winona Lake, Ind.: Eisenbrauns, 2003).

9. J. Gerald Janzen, *Studies in the Text of Jeremiah* (HSM 6; Cambridge: Harvard University Press, 1973), 132. He regards only the position of the foreign oracles in chs. 46–51 and the material in 33:14–26, and 52:28–30 in redactional terms.

Introduction

with disputations, which have a basic form of thesis, dispute, and counterthesis.[10] There are a surprisingly large number of disputations in the book, and their recognition provides exegetical insight (see 2:23–25; 3:1–5; 8:8–9; 18:6; 28:2–4, 6–9, 14; 33:23–26; 37:9–10; 42:13–18; 44:1–30; 45:3–5a; 48:14–17).[11]

The oracle or its second part is frequently introduced by a quotation formula of the type "Here is what Yahweh said," to indicate the prophet's proclamation of the divine word.[12] Another kind of quotation formula, "declared Yahweh," can on occasion mark the opening of divine speech, though it follows the first phrase or clause.[13] It frequently signals the end of a unit or section. An oracle reception heading, generally in the form "A message that Jeremiah received from Yahweh," has an important structural function in the book (see "Literary Development" below). An oracle reception statement, "I/Jeremiah received Yahweh's message," often opens smaller sections. A recurring peculiarity of the book, seldom recognized, is that these and other introductory formulas can have an anticipatory role, alerting the reader to a divine oracle to be cited later on (see the commentary at 9:17 [16]; 14:1, 17; 17:5; 25:1; 30:5; 31:2, 10, 15; 32:1, 14; 40:1; 45:2; 48:40; 50:33).

Far fewer in the book than oracles of disaster, but fulfilling an important overall role, are proclamations of salvation, which announce God's positive intervention into a disastrous situation and the human consequences that were to flow from it (e.g., 30:18–22; 31:4–6, 8–9, 31–34).

The influence of the Psalms is evident in Jeremiah's confessions, which exhibit the genre of the individual lament. The divine answers to the first four

---

10. See Donald F. Murray, "The Rhetoric of Disputation: Reexamination of a Prophetic Genre," *JSOT* 38 (1987): 95–121, for this analysis and examples outside Jeremiah.

11. See Leslie C. Allen, "Disputations in the Book of Jeremiah."

12. It is often called a messenger formula, but, though in the OT messengers sometimes use it, it introduces a citation; a past tense for the verb, as in the second half of LXX and in NJPS, is necessary since another's words already spoken are being cited. See Samuel A. Meier, *Speaking of Speaking: Marking Direct Discourse in the Hebrew Bible* (VTSup 46; Leiden: Brill, 1992), 277–91. At times quotation formulas are used in what appear to be redactional contexts and so represent not Jeremiah's speaking to his own constituency but the redactor's literary elaborations for the reader, legitimating them as divinely inspired (3:16; 12:14; 24:5, 8; 26:2; 30:2; 32:36; 33:10, 12). Similarly, in material added in MT, quotation formulas feature at 33:14, 17, 20, 25. Unless this phenomenon is to be viewed as purely literary, readers are meant to regard the redactors in these cases as prophets in their own right. Henry Van Dyke Parunak, "Some Discourse Functions of Prophetic Formulas in Jeremiah," in *Biblical Hebrew and Discourse Linguistics* (ed. R. D. Bergen; Dallas: Summer Institute of Linguistics, 1994), 489–519, esp. 506, has observed that after *kî*, "for," and *lākēn*, "therefore," the quotation formula functions as an aside and the conjunctions introduce what follows it. His observation often applies (e.g., 6:21; 7:20; 14:15; 29:32), though on closer examination reasons emerge why it does not in some cases.

13. See Rolf Rendtorff, "Zum Gebrauch der Formel *ne'um jahwe* im Jeremiabuch," *ZAW* 66 (1954): 27–37; cf. Meier, *Speaking of Speaking*, 298–314.

confessions match the oracular response to a psalm of lament (11:21–23; 12:5–6; 15:11–12, 19–21; cf. Lam 3:55–57). A subgroup of the psalm of lament is the complaint.[14] This shriller form is represented in four of the confessions (12:1–4; 15:18; 20:7, 18; see too 45:3). A communal psalm of lament is echoed in the people's prayer (14:7–9), which receives a negative divine reply in v. 10. Communal laments also occur at 14:19–22 and earlier at 10:19–20, 23–25, in the final case taking the form of a complaint. In 8:19–20 the prophet cites the people's complaint, but sets it in the context of a type of funeral lamentation over Judah's future fate (8:18–9:1 [8:23]). Whereas the funeral lamentation engages in despairing grief over inexorable suffering, the psalm of lament characteristically turns to God in prayer and seeks help. Here the two different genres are strikingly juxtaposed, and doom rather than deliverance wins out. It was too late for the people to receive another chance. The same point is made by putting 10:19–20, 23–25 in a pall of punishment and by setting 14:19–22 after Jeremiah's heavyhearted lamentation (vv. 17–18). However, in 31:15–17 a despairing funeral-type lamentation unexpectedly—defying a form-critical norm—encounters a positive response from God. What made all the difference were prejudgment settings in chs. 8, 10, and 14, but a postjudgment one in ch. 31. After judgment redemption could come. In a similar vein chs. 50–51 are best understood as Yahweh's passionate response to laments uttered by exiled suppliants, promising to deal with their imperial oppressors.

4. Style

Genre can provide the skeleton of a passage, but rhetorical style is an aspect of its flesh and blood. If genre helps the informed reader by providing typicality, a stylistic analysis uncovers the passage's individuality that sets it apart from other examples of the same genre.[15] The purpose of this brief section is to alert readers to this exegetical dimension and so to justify the role it plays in the commentary. Focus and structural limits are often indicated by a frame that repeats a significant term or motif. For example, at the block level an interpretive prose frame in 21:1–10 and 24:1–10 has been editorially placed around the two collections of poetic oracles in 21:11–23:40, interacting with them in several ways. At the composition level 31:27–40 is framed by a verb of demolishing in vv. 28 and 40; MT augments the frame by adding uprooting in v. 28 to match v. 40. At the unit level the motif of marriage fittingly frames 16:2–9. At the verse level

---

14. See, in principle, Craig C. Broyles, *The Conflict of Faith and Experience in the Psalms: A Form-Critical and Theological Study* (JSOTSup 52; Sheffield: JSOT Press, 1989).

15. Pioneering work on rhetorical style in the book of Jeremiah has been done by William H. Holladay, *The Architecture of Jeremiah 1–20* (Lewisburg, Pa.: Bucknell University Press, 1976); and Jack R. Lundbom, *Jeremiah: A Study in Ancient Hebrew Rhetoric* (2d ed.; Winona Lake, Ind.: Eisenbrauns, 1997). In this commentary relatively narrow spans of text are generally in view.

Introduction 7

Yahweh's vigilant "eyes" hauntingly frame 16:17. Key words with different applications can pervade a passage, like the Hebrew root *ykl*, rendered "win," in 20:7–13. The same root is used as a powerful undercurrent in 38:1, 5, 22. In 40:7–41:18 key verbs pervade three subsections, "come" in 40:7–12, "kill" in 40:13–41:9, and "set off" in 41:10–18. The verbs divide the narrative development into a triptych of nullified hope.

5. Literary Development

Oral tradition credits H. L. Ellison with the statement that "no doctrine of inspiration is worth its salt that does not take the work of editors into account."[16] Readers of the NT Gospels can feel at home in the book of Jeremiah. Each Gospel possesses its own interpretive framework; its contents are nuanced differently, addressing the particular needs of the Christian community for which it was written. Each is a product of a later generation than the time of the scenes it narrates. Each Gospel shapes the Jesus tradition in its own way ("the Gospel according to . . ."), as it takes over and develops earlier oral and written records. Inspiration lies in the Gospels at book level, despite the red type used in some Bibles to highlight words attributed to Jesus.[17] In similar fashion the book of Jeremiah is best understood as a representation of the message and significance of the prophet substantially intended for the Jews in Babylonian exile. A complication arises because the book has been handed down in two canonical forms; one may compare the various endings of Mark's Gospel. For a long time scholars could write off the shorter text of LXX with different explanations, but most now accept that it bears witness to an older Hebrew text than that of MT. The issue is "not a *veritas graeca* over against a *veritas hebraica*, but two *veritates hebraicae*."[18] The sea change was caused by Hebrew manuscript fragments found at Qumran, 4Q71 (4QJer[b]) and 4Q71a (4QJer[d]), which remarkably, though in a tantalizingly scanty way, represent a short text closely related to that underlying LXX.[19] Because their brevity involves relatively dispensable types of

---

16. The third edition of Rudolph's commentary (1968) included in its revision careful consideration of Ellison's contributions to Jeremiah study in a series of articles entitled "The Prophecy of Jeremiah" in *EvQ* 31–40 (1959–1968).

17. Cf. the willingness of older commentators on Jeremiah to jettison material they considered non-Jeremianic. Smith (305 n. 1) said of 31:22b: "This couplet has been the despair of commentators. Its exilic terms 'created' and 'female' relieve us of it." For a discussion of the book of Jeremiah as word of God, see Gordon McConville, "Divine Speech and the Book of Jeremiah," in *The Trustworthiness of God: Perspectives on the Nature of Scripture* (ed. P. Helm and C. R. Trueman; Grand Rapids: Eerdmans, 2002), 18–38; and cf. John B. Job, *Jeremiah's Kings: A Study of the Monarchy in Jeremiah* (SOTSMS; Aldershot, Eng.: Ashgate, 2006), 171–201.

18. De Waard, *Handbook*, xxii.

19. See the survey in Emanuel Tov, *Textual Criticism of the Hebrew Bible* (2d ed.; Minneapolis: Fortress, 2001), 319–27.

material that are very often found throughout MT but tend to be absent from LXX, the reasonable conclusion is that MT has preserved a longer form of the Hebrew text than that attested by LXX. Indeed, examples of such a proto-masoretic form have also been discovered at Qumran, 2Q13 (2QJer), 4Q70 (4QJer^a), and 4Q72 (4QJer^c). The editors of the longer text apparently intended to develop the earlier one for their circle of readers and replace it. Because the Masoretes adopted the longer text, this replacement received in Judaism the official recognition that also prevailed eventually in most Christian circles. Only Greek Orthodox churches regard as canonical the translation of the shorter Hebrew canonical text, perpetuating its use in the Letter to the Hebrews (cf. Heb 8:8–12).

Emanuel Tov has defined the forms of text attested by LXX and MT as first and second editions of the book.[20] He analyzes the differences of the latter under six categories: text arrangement, addition of headings to prophecies, repetition of sections, additions of new verses and sections, additions of new details, and changes in content. He also defines its overall aim in terms of exegetical clarification.[21] A concern of this commentary will be to examine many of the additions and changes in the light of their contexts. The second stage, represented in MT, supplemented in various respects the first one, attested in LXX.[22] However, major redactional work had already been done at the earlier stage. Redactional shaping had taken place in terms of overall structure, superscriptions, assignment of historical settings, and arrangement of material. The short ch. 45 is a redactional showcase. A heading supplies a setting for the oracle, which reveals it to be historically earlier than the context in which it has been inserted. A prose sermonic statement occurs in v. 5b*a*. MT, in addition to a few minor extras, attests the incorporation of an interpretive gloss in v. 4b.

So-called prose sermons are already a feature of the book at the earlier stage attested by LXX.[23] They may be compared with the so-called Levitical sermons

---

20. "Some Aspects of the Textual and Literary History of the Book of Jeremiah," in *Le livre de Jérémie: Le prophète et son milieu, les oracles et leur transmission* (ed. P.-M. Bogaert; BETL 54; Leuven: Leuven University Press, 1997), 145–67. Another version written for non-Hebraists appeared under the title "The Literary History of the Book of Jeremiah in the Light of Its Textual History," in *Empirical Models for Biblical Criticism* (ed. J. H. Tigay; Philadelphia: University of Pennsylvania Press, 1985), 211–37, where Tov defines "editions" loosely as different stages in the development of the book (214 n. 17). The latter article was reprinted in idem, *The Greek and Hebrew Bible: Collected Essays on the Septuagint* (VTSup 72; Leiden: Brill, 1999), 363–84.

21. See also the overview of the MT material in Louis Stulman, *The Prose Sermons of the Book of Jeremiah: A Redescription of the Correspondences with Deuteronomistic Literature in the Light of Recent Text-Critical Research* (SBLDS 83; Atlanta: Scholars Press, 1986), 141–44.

22. In the commentary and notes, "MT" will often stand for the proto-masoretic form of text taken over in MT, and "LXX" for the earlier stage. Space constraints necessitate consideration of LXX mainly as it impacts MT and not in its own right. Thus readings judged inferior and those judged to be nonpreferable alternatives generally go unmentioned.

23. See esp. Stulman, *Prose Sermons*. To Stulman's credit he distinguishes between such material in LXX and in MT.

Introduction

in Chronicles and the long discourses in John's Gospel. The sermons stand out by the use of stereotyped formulations that are often, but by no means always, taken from Deuteronomy and the Deuteronomistic History and by quotations from these and other OT books. These solidly literary features are a mark of the prose sermons in 7:1–8:3; 11:1–14; 14:11–16; 18:7–12; 21:5–9; 22:1–5; 25:3–12; 26:3–6; 32:29–41; 34:8–22; 40:2–3; 44:2–10, 20–23. Prose sermonic language is also a sporadic editorial mark of other prose oracles and narratives and further prose passages (e.g., within 17:19–27; 32:17–25; 35:13–17).[24] The prose sermons and their echoes are best taken as a redactional feature of the book. In ch. 44 this material represents an adaptation of an earlier disputation, so that at the close of the book—the material in ch. 45 in MT and EVV comes just before ch. 52 in LXX and is numbered 51:31–35—the prose sermonic lesson that pagan worship was the divine reason for the tragedy of 587 might be given a last hearing. In some cases (e.g., 21:5–9; 25:3–12; 34:8–22) it is possible to see how prose sermons have been grafted onto earlier material. The prose sermons appear to be a version of Jeremiah's message written for a later generation. They are "not the firsthand voice of the prophet, but a voice filtered through memory and tradition."[25] Most of the prose sermons are organically linked to the book's structural framework, namely in chs. 7, 11, 14, 18, 21, 25, 26, 32, 34, and 40. A glance at the sectional headings listed in the table of contents shows that these chapters begin blocks of material. The prose sermons typically function as literary buttresses at the head of blocks, in some cases redefining and crystallizing their contexts in particular categories of thought and in other cases periodically providing essential summaries of lessons derived from Jeremiah's prophesying in general.[26] The relationship between the Deuteronomistic tradition and the prose sermons is difficult to identify because on both sides complex issues are at stake. Bright and Weippert made much of the fact that terminology in prose sermons is too broad to be simply identified with that tradition.[27] Although Stulman indicated that the text common to LXX and MT is closer to the tradition than MT's redactional material,[28] a significant area of disparity remains. Thus the prose sermons stand on the fringe of the tradition, though strongly influenced by its style and vocabulary.

24. Cf. in general Michael J. Williams, "An Investigation of the Legitimacy of Source Distinctions for the Prose Material in Jeremiah," *JBL* 112 (1993): 193–210.

25. Joel Rosenberg, "Jeremiah and Ezekiel," in *The Literary Guide to the Bible* (ed. R. Alter and F. Kermode; Cambridge, Mass.: Belknap, 1987), 184–206, esp. 188.

26. Cf. Stulman's contextual reading of the prose sermons in *Order amid Chaos: Jeremiah as Symbolic Tapestry* (Biblical Seminar 57; Sheffield: Sheffield Academic Press, 1998), 23–55.

27. John Bright, "The Date of the Prose Sermons of Jeremiah," *JBL* 70 (1951): 15–35; Helga Weippert, *Die Prosareden des Jeremiabuches* (BZAW 135; Berlin: de Gruyter, 1973).

28. *Prose Sermons*, 119–44; but see the critique of Stulman's conclusions by Raymond F. Person, *Second Zechariah and the Deuteronomic School* (JSOTSup 167; Sheffield: JSOT Press, 1993), 75 n. 48.

Major blocks in the book are nearly always introduced by an oracle reception heading, "A message that Jeremiah received from Yahweh" or "What Jeremiah received as Yahweh's message."[29] Jeremiah 37:1 and 52:1 lack them in both LXX and MT. MT sensitively adds them at 7:1 and 46:1. An oracle reception statement, "this message came from Yahweh," occurs at 26:1, and another type of introduction at 2:4. Oracle reception headings can also occur within blocks (34:8; 35:1; 44:1; 45:1; 46:13). Within the oracles against the nations in MT (chs. 46–51) the significance of oracle reception headings is difficult to gauge. While both MT and LXX have them at 46:13 and 50:1, MT adds them at 47:1, as well as at 46:1, but not at 48:1 or 49:1. In the book blocks are made up of compositions, which in turn are arrangements of units.[30] Especially in the case of the groupings of poetic material, the impression is given of a literary quilt. Small pieces of existing material have been joined together in sections, which have then been combined into a larger pattern.[31] Sometimes units and even compositions are sewn together with the redactional conjunction *kî*, usually rendered "For" in EVV (e.g., 2:20; 4:3; 15:5; 22:6; 26:15; 30:12), indicating elucidation. In chs. 2–6 units evidently reflecting Jeremiah's early prophetic activity have been grouped together with the addition of some post-Jeremianic prose. A similar impression of quilting is given by the originally independent collection of chs. 30–31, where some of Jeremiah's own oracles have been deliberately combined with later poetry and prose of a prophetic nature, and by the foreign oracles in chs. 46–51. In the second composition concerning Moab (48:28–47) an editor has assembled an anthology of Moabite poems from other books. In chs. 21–24 two preexisting collections of poems about kings and prophets have been set in compositions and inserted into a new frame to form a literary block. Overall the compositions vary in length; they often occur in pairs, as the headings in the table of contents show. Prose compositions can be narrative units centered on a single incident, which have then been skillfully assembled into blocks with a coherent message. Occasionally one can detect how a composition grew.

---

29. See Peter K. D. Neumann, "Das Wort das geschehen ist. . . . Zum Problem der Wortempfangsterminologie in Jer. i–xxv," *VT* 23 (1973): 171–217; Theodor Seidl, "Die Wortereignisformel in Jeremia: Beobachtungen zu den Formen der Redeöffnung in Jeremia, im Anschluss an Jer 27,1.2," *BZ* 23 (1979): 20–47, 184–99, esp. 23–27.

30. Space constraints prevent comparison with the delimitation systems found in MT and elsewhere. See Lundbom's commentary and Tov, "Sense Divisions in the Qumran Texts, the Masoretic Text, and Ancient Translations of the Bible," in *The Interpretation of the Bible: The International Symposium in Slovenia* (ed. J. Krašovec; JSOTSup 289; Sheffield: Sheffield Academic Press, 1998), 121–46.

31. The quilting analogy for redactional arrangement is taken from Gail P. C. Streete, "Redaction Criticism," in *To Each Its Own Meaning: An Introduction to Biblical Criticisms and Their Applications* (ed. S. L. McKenzie and S. R. Haynes; 2d ed.; Louisville: Westminster John Knox, 1999), 105–21, esp. 110. Jones (27) criticizes McKane's conception of a rolling corpus behind the book of Jeremiah on the ground that his view of uncontrolled, haphazard growth "overlooks the design in the putting together and assembly of originally independent oral units."

Introduction

Evidently the unit in 16:2–9 was once a companion piece to 15:15–21, but it has been made the nucleus of a separate composition decrying pagan religion, a theme that puts the basic piece to a new hermeneutical use.

The literary system of compositions and blocks has been retained in MT with additional units sometimes slotted into it. The fundamental arrangement in compositions reveals that the collection of foreign oracles placed in LXX in the middle of ch. 25 is a first attempt to integrate them in a foreign body, just as chs. 30–31 are on other grounds. MT restored an earlier redactional feature by moving the collection elsewhere, filling the gap with 25:14, which echoes one of the constituent oracles.[32] By placing them after ch. 45, MT gave a new overall shape to the book (see "Macrostructure" below). The editorial rearrangement has a loose parallel in the transfer of Jesus' cleansing of the temple to the beginning of his ministry in John's Gospel.

The book of Jeremiah is like an old English country house, originally built and then added to in the Regency period, augmented with Victorian wings, and generally refurbished throughout the Edwardian years. It grew over a long period of time. Jeremiah 36:32 refers to a book in the prophet's own time (604 B.C.E.), which received subsequent supplementation. In 25:13 there is a reference to the book at the stage of editing attested in LXX, when the foreign oracles immediately followed. In 30:2 the editorial incorporation of chs. 30–31 into the book seems to be in view. Of course, the dating of the LXX stage is not tied to that of the LXX itself (ca. 200 B.C.E.) or that of the Qumran finds that support it at the Hebrew level (the first half of the second century B.C.E.). This stage, attested in the LXX, may have been completed by the late exilic period. It steadfastly looks forward to the downfall of the Neo-Babylonian Empire and its later oracles align with those of Second Isaiah, while its perspective fits a Babylonian setting (see "Purpose" below). There are elements in MT that have a similar perspective—it has a special interest in Babylon and its king and in the Judean exiles[33]—and suggest a reshaping not long afterward, at least in its initial stages. The prose sermonic language of the earlier edition is freely echoed, though its lower frequency may indicate a time or locale in which Deuteronomistic literature was less influential.[34] The addition of patronymics in 29:21 and of Baruch's job description in 36:26, 32 indicates knowledge of early traditions. However, the unit added in 33:14–26 points to a setting in postexilic Judah.

---

32. Cf. the claim of Hermann-Josef Stipp, "The Prophetic Messenger Formulas in Jeremiah according to the Masoretic and Alexandrian Texts," *Text* 18 (1995): 63–85, that study of the quotation formulas expanded in MT, such as "Here is what Yahweh *Almighty, Israel's God,* has said," shows an incremental pattern from the beginning to the end of the book, yet one in which the oracles against the nations belong in the middle of the book, so that the expansions took place at a developmental stage underlying MT in which the LXX position of the oracles prevailed.

33. Stulman, *Prose Sermons*, 143–44, 146.

34. Ibid., 146.

6. Macrostructure

Bright (lvi) famously described the book of Jeremiah as giving the impression of "a hopeless hodgepodge thrown together without any discernible principle of arrangement at all." Does the MT redaction envision a structure? Here are two modern proposals for the way the book is structured.[35] Alexander Rofé sees four collections: visions, prophecies, and laments, mostly undated, in chs. 1–24; separate episodes, all dated, in chs. 25–36; continuous "biography" in chs. 37–45; and oracles against the nations in chs. 46–51.[36] Georg Fischer has divided the book into three sections, chs. 1–24, 26–45, and 46–51 + 52, with a pivotal ch. 25 concluding the first section and introducing the next two. Chapters 1–24 forecast the destruction of Judah and Jerusalem, while 25:1–14 introduces a double judgment of Judah and other nations, which 25:15–38 develops; then separately chs. 26–45 work out Judah's judgment and chs. 46–51 that of other nations.[37] Fischer regards as a subsequent development the different placement of chapters in LXX, where the foreign oracles were placed in the middle of ch. 25 and so chs. 26–45 + 52 dealt only with Judah's fate, reverting to chs. 1–24 in an ABA format. If a more common view is followed, however, the MT placement represents a significant rearrangement of that in LXX. Both scholars' analyses shed interesting light on the book's complex prehistory, but they leave out of account—Rofé explicitly—an elephant in the room, the two positive blocks of material in chs. 30–33, largely poetry in chs. 30–31 and prose in chs. 32–33, which, intrusive though they appear, were already in place at the LXX stage. What, one must ask, is the overall effect of the intrusion?

If the presence of these blocks is allowed structural significance, it recalls a literary pattern in the prophetic books in which a relatively short portion of positive material tends to conclude a mass of messages of doom.[38] At times the pattern can take a recurring form, such as in Hosea, which subdivides into three complexes, chs. 1–3, 4–11, and 12–14, each of which ends positively,[39] and in Micah, where the first and last of three complexes appear to do so (1:2–2:11/12–13; 6:1–7:7/8–20).[40] Is such a pattern present in MT? Childs has

---

35. For other proposals that take MT into account see Adri J. O. van der Wal, "Toward a Synchronic Analysis of the Masoretic Text of the Book of Jeremiah," in *Reading the Book of Jeremiah: A Search for Coherence* (ed. M. Kessler; Winona Lake, Ind.: Eisenbrauns, 2004), 13–24.

36. "The Arrangement of the Book of Jeremiah," *ZAW* 101 (1989): 390–98, esp. 395.

37. "Jer 25 und die Fremdvölkersprüche: Unterschiede zwischen hebräischem und grieschischem Text," *Bib* 72 (1991): 474–99, esp. 485, 488, 496–97.

38. See Ronald E. Clements, "Patterns in the Prophetic Canon," in *Canon and Authority: Essays in Old Testament Religion and Theology* (ed. G. W. Coats and B. O Long; Philadelphia: Fortress, 1977), 42–55.

39. See, e.g., Hans W. Wolff, *Hosea: A Commentary on the Book of the Prophet Hosea* (trans. G. Stansell; Hermeneia; Philadelphia: Fortress, 1974), xxix–xxxi.

40. John T. Willis, "The Structure of the Book of Micah," *SEÅ* 34 (1969): 5–42.

claimed that a movement from judgment to redemption is the agenda of the book in its present form.[41] Can this claim be substantiated in detail? The editorial movement was doubtless triggered to some extent by ch. 52—ironically so, since commentators hold the chapter in little esteem—where a lengthy narrative of destruction (vv. 1–30) is followed by a short one of tentative hope (vv. 31–34). Working backward, the foreign oracles in chs. 46–51, especially in their MT format, have been structured as a series of virtual pronouncements of salvation for Israel (see the introduction to chs. 46–51). Moreover, the happy endings for the Egypt, Moab, and Ammon oracles in MT, supplementing Elam's in the common text of LXX and MT, extend eventual hope to the nations. If the positive presence of chs. 30–33 signifies an interim conclusion, the negative material in chs. 34–45 forms a new beginning, to be concluded by chs. 46–51. This negative material constitutes a vast block made up of three smaller blocks: chs. 34–36, which relate the dangers of rejecting the divine word; chs. 37–39, which warn of retribution for rejecting the prophetic message and messenger; and chs. 40–45, which narrate the ill-fated rejection of a divine opportunity to stay in the land. In turn, chs. 30–33 follow a long run of negative material. Does a macrostructural scheme shed any light on that earlier material? Certainly the so-called confessions within chs. 11–20 seem to parallel the persecution narratives in chs. 37–39 as different cases of Judah's fateful rejection of God's prophetic revelation exemplified in Jeremiah's experience (see the introduction to 11:18–12:6). Within chs. 21–29 there is a series of minor but significant anticipations of the positive chs. 30–33. The block made up of chs. 21–24 concludes its first half with positive royal and national messages in 23:5–6, 7–8 at the close of a collection of royal oracles, and incorporates a positive note at the close of the block in 24:5–7. The limitation of the power of Judah's enemy in 25:12, which is amplified in MT at v. 14 (cf. MT's addition at v. 26b), has a hopeful ring. As for the block of chs. 26–29, MT adds positive notes that develop 25:12 at 27:7, 22; in turn 27:11 holds out a positive opportunity for the nations in both MT and LXX. Chapter 29 contains promises for Judean exiles in the common text at vv. 7 and 10–13, which MT develops at v. 14. Glancing back to chs. 11–20, one finds further anticipations. The composition of 12:7–17 closes in vv. 14–17 by holding out hope for the nations, while the composition of 16:1–21 ends by envisioning not only Israel's homecoming (vv. 14–15) but the nations' joining in Israel's praise of Yahweh (vv. 19–21).

One should conceive of a macrostructural span of chs. 11–29 + 30–33 because, already in ch. 10, there occurs upbeat material, the hymn of vv. 6–16,

---

41. Brevard S. Childs, *Introduction to the Old Testament as Scripture* (Philadelphia: Fortress, 1979), 351. Cf. Stulman's characterization of chs. 1–25 as "death and dismantling of Judah's sacred world" and of chs. 26–52 as "new beginnings emerging from a shattered world" in *Order amid Chaos*, chs. 1–3.

to which MT has contributed vv. 6–8, 9b*b*, 10; the hymn looks forward to the destruction of implicitly Babylonian idols in v. 15. Significantly 10:12–16 are also incorporated into ch. 51 (MT 51:15–19) in the common text. Within ch. 10, however, the positive material is not placed at the close, since the negative unit of 10:17–25 follows. In chs. 2–9, as in chs. 21–29, there are a few foretastes of a bright future, a substantial one in 3:14–18 and a series of hopeful qualifications within 4:27 and 5:10 and in 5:18. Moreover, a parallel to Jeremiah's confessions in chs. 11–20 and to the persecution narratives in chs. 37–39 occurs in this part of the book, in the form of a series of vehement reactions from the prophet in 4:10, 19–21; 5:4–5; 6:10–11a; 8:18–9:1 (8:23).

So there is evidence of an overall shape—a serial structure of closing hope with sporadic anticipations—that the MT redaction imposed on the older text, developing intimations it already found there. Toward this end it pushed the positive material into the limelight by making its own additions in ch. 10, as indicated above, and in chs. 30 (vv. 10–11) and 33 (vv. 14–26) and by rearrangement—both large-scale and local—and amplification in chs. 46–51. The reassuring promise that Israel's destruction would not be complete is sketched in 4:27; 5:10, 18, and elaborated not only in 46:27–28 but also in MT at 30:10–11. Finally, reference should be made to the book's prologue in 1:1–2:3 and epilogue in ch. 52. In the latter, MT recognized a scheme it could develop in the book, and within the former it recognized and augmented a long description of destruction and a short description of restoration for Judah and other nations, "to uproot and tear down and destroy *and demolish*, to build and plant" (1:10).

7. Purpose

A long and complex book like Jeremiah certainly leads the reader to hope for some guiding statements of purpose within its pages. They may be sought in passages that adopt a contemporary time frame that reflects a "now" in which the book addresses its intended readers over against a "then," whether the "then" of readers' history or the "then" of their future. This "now," if found, would be different from the "now" of Jeremiah's own oracles. Such passages might disclose a sense of purpose. A starting point is the series of prose "question-and-answer" passages that pervade a large part of the book. They envision a "then" that looked back to the fulfillment of Jeremiah's oracles of disaster. There are four such passages, at 5:19; 9:12–16 (11–15); 16:10–13; and 22:8–9. They have the same question-and-answer format, asking why it all happened and then explaining it as a response to preexilic pagan worship. They are more or less loosely tied into Jeremiah's preceding oracles of disaster. Worship of other gods is spiritually criminalized in 9:13 (12) and 16:11 as infringement of the torah and in 22:9 as abandoning the covenant relationship. All four passages are set at important structural junctures. Apart from the case in ch. 16, they occur at the end of compositions; in ch. 16 the answer introduces for the first time the theme of the composition of 16:1–21. To this group of passages should be added 32:21–23, 29b–35, verses that, as Fretheim (453–54) has recognized, are intended to answer Zedekiah's "why?" in 32:3. Here the issue of pagan worship is illustrated at some length. Jeremiah 32:29b–35 belongs to a prose sermon, while the prophet's earlier prayer in vv. 21–23 is itself suffused with prose sermonic language. In turn the four earlier question-and-answer passages are written in prose sermonic style, and it is significant that the same format also occurs in Deut 29:24–28 (23–27); 1 Kgs 9:8–9. The book's long prose sermons and the short question-and-answer units overlap and evidently belong to the same editorial stage. Units with this latter format look back at the destruction wrought by the disaster of 587 and, in the first three cases, also at the ensuing exile. They patiently explain repeatedly to the reader the theological necessity for the covenant God to inflict the catastrophe that Jeremiah continually predicted. They are editorial summaries of Jeremiah's oracles that frequently have their own indictments of pagan worship, and they provide a key for understanding much of the book as theodicy. Standing essentially in an editorial "now," the summaries look back to the "then" prophesied in terms of disaster. They derive their literary inspiration from one of the prophet's poetic oracles. In 13:22 the "why" of Jerusalem's coming disaster is answered in terms of Jerusalem's great "guilt," which is contextually defined in terms of Canaanite worship in v. 27.

A concentration on the book's "now" seems to mark some other examples of purposeful material. In 9:23–24 (22–23) there is a general exhortation evidently addressed to readers. Its call to "know" Yahweh follows in the wake of Jeremiah's accusation in 9:3 (2) that Yahweh's preexilic people did not know their covenant Lord, as their engaging in such vices as falsehood and untrustworthiness revealed. From such negative spirituality is extrapolated a contemporary call to a positive spirituality of knowing Yahweh and thereby engaging instead in the virtues of "loyalty, justice, and right dealing." There is not only dependence on 9:3 (2), but a gathering up of accusations of not knowing Yahweh earlier in the book (4:22; 5:4; 8:7) and also of forgotten virtues of loyalty (cf. 2:2), justice (4:2; 5:1, 4, 5; 7:5; 8:7), and right dealing (4:2). The editor surely had also in mind Jeremiah's expression, in God's name, of warm admiration for Josiah at 22:15–16: "he demonstrated justice and right. . . . That is what knowing me means, isn't it?" A similar hermeneutical application to that in ch. 9 is to be found at 2:31a*a*, if it is correct to understand it as a redactional aside. Readers are suddenly brought within the orbit of Jeremiah's addressees, the "you" of vv. 29–30. They are urged to take to heart the prophetic denunciation of repudiation of Yahweh's authority. The verb "consider" significantly echoes its challenging uses at vv. 10, 19, and 23, in contexts of preexilic unfaithfulness; it serves to reinforce the homiletical updating of Jeremiah's message.

The proverb-like generalities that mark most of 17:5–13 appear to point to hermeneutical application. Chapter 17 stands at the end of a block, chs. 14–17. The four units in 17:5–13 break away from the description of preexilic sin and its punishment in the first complex unit, vv. 1–4, and speak about sinning in more general terms. The options of curse and blessing in the unit of vv. 5–8 set out the importance of trust in Yahweh. The unit's reference to the "heart" echoes the preexilic "hearts" of v. 1, expounding their sin as a lack of trust that is liable to invade contemporary hearts. There is another such echo in the next saying in vv. 9–10, which warns not only of the wickedness of the human heart but of ensuing liability for divine judgment. Verse 11 gives ill-gotten gains as an example of human sinning. It appears to provide an illustration of the backsliding that was characteristic of exilic readers who were to be singled out for condemnation in vv. 12–13. This last unit of two verses has a literary air; it brings together in a grand finale a number of terms used previously in ch. 17. In particular, the phrase "the deviants in the country" (see the commentary) takes up "the country" of exile from v. 4 and combines with it the motif of deviating from Yahweh in v. 5. The exilic community had rebels within its ranks, and they needed to be purged by divine judgment, if the community was to prosper.

This community appears to be in view also within ch. 10, in continuation of the hermeneutical concerns expressed in ch. 9 and near the close of the block of chs. 7–10. The direct exhortations in 10:2 and 5b not to be intimidated by Babylonian religion and astrological divination are explained in the intervening verses by a satirical polemic in the Second Isaiah tradition. It is not surprising that the following hymn (vv. 12–16) was later cited in 51:15–19; the setting of Babylonian exile shared by these portions of ch. 10 and by ch. 51 must have encouraged the reuse. A place where Jeremiah's "now" remarkably overlaps with the book's "now" occurs in ch. 29, with respect to the letter the prophet sent to those exiled in 597. His unwelcome advice not to expect a quick return home was reinforced with positive exhortations on how to live as long-term exiles. At this juncture the letter's original readers and the readers for whom the book was intended have much in common. The latter group's customary overhearing of what the book says about preexilic Judeans must have given way to an avid hearing at this point. In the next composition, 30:1–31:1, if the interpretation proposed in the commentary is correct, there is a striking juxtaposition of a "then" referring to the exiles' past and another "then" relating to their future homecoming and renewal. Three reversals are set out; three times over, first one of Jeremiah's oracles of disaster is cited as having been fulfilled and then a reversing proclamation of future salvation is given (30:5–7 + 8–9, 12–15 + 16–17, 23–24 + 31:1). The exiles stood between the times, looking back to deserved judgment at God's hands and looking forward in hope to divine redemption. These two chapters, 29 and 30, sum up much of what the book as a whole seeks to accomplish in its retelling of Jeremiah's prophetic

Introduction 17

ministry, to give exilic readers an understanding of God's comprehensive will for Israel in the past and future and to encourage them to live faithfully as God's people in the present.

Scholars have suggested two false trails in their quest for purpose. The first relates to the prose sermons. One of their intentions has been described as presenting direct exhortations to the exiles to live in accordance with the torah and thus win divine blessing.[42] In particular, attention has been drawn to the setting out of spiritual alternatives in the course of sermon material at 7:1–15; 17:19–27; 22:1–5.[43] (These alternatives are grounded in the poetic oracle of 13:15–17.) While the prose sermon form has plausibly been derived from an exilic model,[44] its function in the book can only be deduced from the literary setting in which it is used. In each case a prejudgment setting determines that the alternatives have already been decided and that the road to disaster has been selected. The good options operate in each case as a lost opportunity, a road not taken, which serves to reinforce preexilic culpability. Some prose sermonic passages even go on to declare that the bad option was chosen (7:13; 18:12). The same reasoning applies to a second invalid claim of hermeneutical value. The calls to repentance in 3:22; 4:1–2, 3–4, 14 have often been hailed as transcending their preexilic time and place and as relevant to the book's exilic readers. However, these calls are set firmly in prejudgment contexts and draw implicit attention to the fact that repentance did not take place.[45] A range of other passages that move explicitly from such exhortations to relate failure to do so may be compared (18:11–12; 25:5–7; 27:12–15; 35:15; 36:3, 6–7, 31), as well as yet others that simply state a lack of repentance (5:3; 8:4–6; 9:5 [4]). Occasionally, however, a call to repentance occurs in a postjudgment setting (3:12, 14; cf. 30:9, 18; 31:21–22), and is meant to be taken at face value, with exilic readers in view.

Lastly, mention should be made of the purposeful trajectory of overriding grace that stretches over the book like a rainbow, already entrenched in the edition represented in LXX and enhanced in MT. Texts mentioned above in "Macrostructure" here feature again. Yahweh's bark was worse than the actual bite would turn out to be, in at least five respects. First, what becomes a programmatic statement for the book, announced at Jeremiah's call, the uprooting

---

42. Ernest W. Nicholson, *Preaching to the Exiles: A Study of the Prose Tradition in the Book of Jeremiah* (New York: Schocken, 1971), 71, 80–81.

43. Winfried Thiel, *Die deuteronomistische Redaktion von Jeremia 1–25* (WMANT 41; Neukirchen-Vluyn: Neukirchener Verlag, 1973), 118, 204–9, 290–95, 301. See too 18:5–11; 26:3, 13.

44. Nicholson, *Preaching*, 14–18, 134–35.

45. Cf. the role of positive exhortations in Amos as "a kind of backhanded way of affirming the certainty of judgment" according to Austin Vanlier Hunter, *Seek the Lord! A Study of the Meaning and Function of the Exhortations in Amos, Hosea, Micah, and Zephaniah* (Baltimore: St. Mary's Seminary and University, 1982), 122.

and replanting of Judah and other nations (1:10), is periodically reaffirmed, for Judah (24:6; cf. 31:40; 42:10), for Israel and Judah (31:28), and for Judah and other nations (12:14–17; cf. 18:7, 9). Second, in the middle of prejudgment oracles of unmitigated doom that belong to Jeremiah's early years in chs. 2–6 is set a blatant passage of promise (3:14–18), sparked by the prophet's own postjudgment message for the defunct northern kingdom (3:6a*a*, 11–14). Third, messages of utter doom in chs. 4–5 are flagrantly interrupted by postjudgment cries of "No, not complete doom!" (4:27; 5:10, 18), cries that are eventually confirmed by 46:27–28 and also in MT at 30:10–11.[46] Fourth, 16:14–15 flashes forward to return from exile after the prediction of exile in v. 13; in turn vv. 19–21 deal radically with Judah's problem of pagan worship by glancing ahead to Yahweh's dynamic self-revelation to the nations, the human source of such worship. Fifth, in the oracles against the nations, ultimate, postjudgment restoration is paradigmatically predicated of the first nation, Elam, according to LXX (25:19; also MT 49:39), while in MT it is perceptively extended to three more nations that have key structural positions in its own text (46:26; 48:47; 49:6). In conclusion it may be said in terms of Rom 5:20 (KJV) that, where sin (and judgment) abounded, grace was much more to abound. The overruling message of the book as a whole is that "weeping may linger for the night, but joy comes with the morning" (Ps 30:5 [6]), a morning yet to dawn.

---

46. Cf. Walter Brueggemann, "An Ending That Does Not End: The Book of Jeremiah," in *Postmodern Interpretations of the Bible—A Reader* (ed. A. K. M. Adam; St. Louis: Chalice, 2001), 117–28, esp. 120–25.

COMMENTARY

1:1–2:3
Prologue: Introducing Jeremiah and His Message

1:1–3 Superscription

1:1 The messages of Jeremiah ben Hilkiah, who was a member of a priestly family that lived at Anathoth in the Benjamin region, 2 what[a] he received as Yahweh's[b] message during the reign of King Josiah ben Amon of Judah in the thirteenth year of his reign 3 and [those which] he continued to receive during the reign of King Jehoiakim ben Josiah of Judah and down to *the end of*[c] the eleventh year of King Zedekiah ben Josiah of Judah, right down to the deportation of Jerusalem's population in the fifth month.

a. Verse 2 is not a subordinate relative clause (NRSV) but an independent one (cf. GKC §138e; *IBHS* 331). The objection that elsewhere (e.g., in 14:1) this version of the oracle reception heading names Jeremiah (Herrmann 4) ignores his mention in v. 1, which made naming unnecessary here.

b. LXX "God's" is a free rendering that occasionally occurs in only the first half of LXX for the divine name or an accompanying epithet (Hermann-Josef Stipp, *Das masoretische und alexandrinische Sondergut des Jeremiabuches: Textgeschichtlicher Rang, Eigenarten, Triebkräfte* [OBO 136; Freiburg: Universitätsverlag, 1994], 54).

c. Italics in the translation refer to redactional material present in MT and not in LXX (see "Translation and Text" and "Literary Development" in the introduction).

The composition of 1:1–2:3 introduces Jeremiah's prophetic ministry to readers. It is made up of three units: a superscription (1:1–3), a pair of accounts of Jeremiah's commissioning, the second a later one deliberately placed here (vv. 4–12 + 13–19), and a basic message that serves as a theological premise for all of Jeremiah's messages of disaster to Judah (2:1–3), somewhat like the motto in Amos 1:2. The clues to the literary grouping of this material are the oracle reception heading in 1:2 and the elaborating oracle reception statements in vv. 4, 11, 13, and added in MT at 2:1.[1]

[1:1–3] Like other prophetic books, Jeremiah's has a superscription editorially prefixed to introduce the written edition of messages associated with the prophet.[2] It marks for the ongoing religious community the importance of

1. Neumann, "Problem der Wortempfangsterminologie," 181–88.
2. For superscriptions to prophetic books see Gene W. Tucker, "Prophetic Superscriptions and the Growth of a Canon," in *Canon and Authority* (ed. G. W. Coats and B. O. Long; Philadelphia: Fortress, 1977), 56–70. The comments on vv. 1–3 are indebted to this article.

oracles that interpreted a cataclysmic period of Israel's history. It makes the claim that a written form of divine revelation is represented in this collection of prophetic addresses.

[1] A title in terms of the content and its human speaker is supplied in the first half of the verse, as in Amos 1:1. The speaker is identified by personal name and patronymic. The rest of the verse provides the first of two elaborations of the title. It gives information about the prophet's family and home. His priestly descent comes from a tradition outside the book. Anathoth was about three miles northeast of Jerusalem; it features in the book at 11:21–23; 29:27; 32:7–9. It was a priestly city according to Josh 21:18 and 1 Chr 6:60 (45). In Solomon's reign Abiathar, a priest descended from Eli who had officiated at the old northern sanctuary in Shiloh, was sent home to Anathoth by the king (1 Kgs 2:26–27). Did such a lineage prompt the historical precedent for the destruction of the Jerusalem temple in that of the Shiloh sanctuary (7:12–15; 26:6, 9)? Yet presumably a number of priestly families lived at Anathoth. There is no evidence that Jeremiah functioned as a priest; the reference to his youth in vv. 6–7 suggests that at his prophetic call he was not yet old enough to carry out priestly duties.

[2] The second elaboration of the title (vv. 2–3) relates to the divine source of Jeremiah's addresses and their overall dating in Judean history, calculated in terms of the regnal calendar with formal full titles for each king. There is awkwardness in the transition from v. 2 to v. 3; at least one expects a dating "from" rather than "in" Josiah's thirteenth year, as in 25:3. This suggests that one role of v. 2 is to give an overall introduction to the complex of oracles set out in 1:4–2:3. Verse 2, with its oracle reception heading, does double duty, as a composition heading as well as an element in the superscription to the book. The dating refers to 627/626 B.C.E., which creates some difficulty because there is scant evidence for Jeremiah's prophesying in Josiah's reign (cf. 3:6 and the summaries at 25:3; 36:2), and Josiah's cultic reforms hardly appear at all in the book (cf. 44:18).[3] But the date is embedded in the tradition and there is no textual warrant for a change.

[3] The duration of Jeremiah's prophetic activity is broadly presented in terms of Judah's last two major kings, passing over the three-month reigns of Jehoahaz and Jehoiachin. In MT the termination of Zedekiah's eleventh year refers not to the end of the royal calendar year but to the abrupt ending of his reign by conquest. The final phrase specifies the fate of Jerusalem's citizens in July/August 587, "the fifth month" (cf. 52:12, 15), and finds there climactic closure. Jeremiah continued prophesying after that date according to chs. 40–45. The main period of his prophesying, which culminated in an event that vindicated his repeated claims, is in historical view (vv. 2–3). Perhaps 1:1–3 func-

---

3. See Holladay 2:25–26; Thomas W. Overholt, "Some Reflections on the Date of Jeremiah's Call," *CBQ* 33 (1971): 105–84.

Prologue: Introducing Jeremiah and His Message 23

tioned at an earlier stage as a superscription to chs. 1–39 (Rudolph 3);[4] the reference to deportation would fit well as a reference to 39:9. However, the addition of ch. 52 to the book (non-Jeremianic as 51:64 admits) provides fresh coverage of the deportation of Jerusalem's citizens, since 39:9 is repeated at 52:15 and echoed in MT at 52:29.

The editors responsible for the superscription lived when the prophetic career of Jeremiah and the events he witnessed and interpreted were all past history. Nevertheless they recognized divine revelation in his prophesying, which could and must illumine God's ways with the later community of faith.

1:4–19 Jeremiah's Call and Commissions

4 I received Yahweh's message/communication *as follows*: 5 "Before I shaped you in the womb I had already taken note of you, and before you left the uterus I had marked you out for a sacred purpose: I made you a prophet for nations."[a] 6 "Oh no, Lord Yahweh," I said. "Look, I am not experienced in communicating. I am too young for that." 7 "Do not say 'I am too young,'" Yahweh said to me. "Rather, you are to go to all those I send you to and communicate all that I order you to. 8 Do not be afraid of their presence, because I will be there with you to rescue you," declared Yahweh. 9 Then Yahweh reached out his hand. Touching my mouth with it, Yahweh said to me, "Look, I have just put my communications in your mouth. 10 See, I hereby give[b] you today authority over nations and realms to uproot and tear down and destroy *and demolish*, to build and plant." 11 I received Yahweh's communication as follows: "What can you see, *Jeremiah*?" "An almond stick[c] *is what I can see*," I said. 12 "You have seen right," Yahweh said to me, "because I am going to watch[d] over my communication with the intent of making it happen."

13 I received Yahweh's communication a second time: "What can you see?" "A furiously heated caldron *is what I can see*," I said, "with its top[e] facing away from the north." 14 Yahweh said to me,

"From the north a bad fate will spill out
    over all who live in the country
15 because, look, I am going to summon
    all the realms[f] in the north,"
declared Yahweh,
"and they will come and each set up their tribunals
    in front of Jerusalem's gates

---

4. Chapters 46–51 would be included at an earlier redactional stage inasmuch as in LXX they appear after 25:13.

and they will surround all its walls
and all of Judah's cities,
16 and then I will present my case against them
for all their bad behavior in abandoning me,
by sacrificing to other gods
and worshiping what their own hands have made.
17 You, for your part, must hitch up your robe
and get going and communicate *to them*
all that I *personally* order you to.
Do not be scared of their presence
or else I will cause your discomfiture in their presence.
18 For my part, look, I hereby make you
today a fortified city,
an iron pillar, and bronze walls,
capable of resisting all *the country*,
for Judah's kings[g] and officials,
its priests, and the people of the country.
19 Fight you they will, but defeat you they will not
because I will be there with you,"
declared Yahweh,
"to rescue you."

a. REB and GNB take this verse as prose, the rest of EVV as poetry. EVV also vary for the divine statements in the rest of the chapter. I judge only vv. 14b–19 to be poetry.

b. The perfect is performative (*IBHS* 489). Another instance occurs in v. 18. Construing the last verb of v. 5 in this way (Herrmann 50) is unlikely in view of the flow of the sentence within past time.

c. Not "branch" (EVV); *maqqēl*, "stick," is not part of a living tree (see *DCH* 5:466b–67a).

d. Parallelism with v. 15 suggests future action rather than the present in EVV.

e. Literally the "surface" of its contents (Rudolph 8).

f. LXX lacks "clans" of MT. It probably originated as a marginal annotation, based on "all the northern clans" in 25:9 (*BHS*).

g. LXX has simply "for all Judah's kings." Then the first three cola in v. 18 constitute a tricolon. MT has borrowed from 15:10.

The rest of ch. 1 presents the call and twofold commissioning of Jeremiah as a prophet. His call/commissions and symbolic actions (e.g., 32:6–15) are presented in first person format, assuring the reader of bedrock experiences in the Jeremiah tradition. Here Jeremiah gives reports concerning Yahweh's announcement, including two visions he received and a closing message of encouragement that recapitulates part of the initial message. An obvious way to structure vv. 4–19 is to use as guides the introductory oracle reception statements in vv.

4, 11, and 13 and ensuing dialogues, and to discern three sections, vv. 4–10, 11–12, and 13–19.[5] Another approach that reflects diverse content as a clue to structural intent is to see a chiasm, ABB'A', in which "a second time" in v. 13 demarcates vv. 13–19 from vv. 4–12, rather than just the second vision from the first, assuming that the oracle reception statement in v. 11 has a lesser structural role. Then the two vision-oracle accounts in vv. 11–12 and 13–14 function as a double core for the passage and may be distinguished from the preceding and following messages in vv. 4–10 and 15–19 (Lundbom 1:227). There are two drawbacks to this particular scheme. First, parallel material in the flanking sections appears in vv. 7–10 and 17–19. Second, vv. 12 and 14–16 are formally parallel as interpretations of the visions, though of different lengths. So B' should be widened to vv. 13–16 and A' reduced to vv. 17–19.[6] In favor of linking the first vision with vv. 4–10 is the mixing of vocabulary from vv. 10 and 12 in 31:28. The two parts of the complex unit, united by "I hereby give/make you today" (vv. 10, 18), are surprisingly different despite their similarities.

[4–12] A report of Jeremiah's call (vv. 4–10) concludes with a vision-oracle report (vv. 11–12).

[4] After the heading embedded in the superscription (v. 2) comes a major oracle reception statement, the first in a series (cf. 24:4).[7] No interest is shown in the psychological means by which the divine message was apprehended by the human mind.

[5] Jeremiah's call is strikingly presented as the culmination of long-term divine planning that antedated his conception and birth. Elsewhere in the OT this sort of statement is at home in special birth narratives. On the human plane Hannah promised to dedicate her male child, should she be given one, to God's service as a Nazirite (1 Sam 1:11). Sometimes a divine purpose is announced. Samson was to be born to the life of a Nazirite and would "begin to deliver Israel from the hand of the Philistines," declared the angel of Yahweh (Judg 13:3–5). In Gen 17:19 Yahweh declared the unborn Isaac's destiny to be: "I will establish my covenant with him." There is nothing special about the language of fetal development; the attribution to a divine creative shaping is a glorious commonplace. Psalm 95:5 mentions "the dry land, which his hands have formed [or "shaped"]"; in the beginning "the LORD God formed man from the dust of the ground" (Gen 2:7). This kind of personal initiative is actualized by growth in the womb according to Job 10:11; Pss 119:73; 139:13. Long ago a divine decision had been made, to set Jeremiah aside to belong to God and to

---

5. Thus Bernard Renaud, "Jér 1: Structure et théologie de la rédaction," in *Livre de Jérémie* (ed. P.-M. Bogaert), 177–96, esp. 180–81.

6. Gunther Wanke, "Jeremias Berufung (Jer 1, 4–10)," in *Alttestamentliche Glaube und biblische Theologie* (ed. J. Hausmann and H.-J. Zobel; Stuttgart: Kohlhammer, 1992), 132–44, esp. 134.

7. Cf. Neumann, "Problem der Wortempfangsterminologie," 181–88.

be used by God, as if for priesthood (cf. Num 3:12–13; 8:14–18). The precise sacred purpose is stated in an abrupt and blatant climax. The divine plan was for Jeremiah to be "a prophet for nations," and he had already been designated for this task. The scope is left unelaborated until v. 10, so that a dynamic frame is provided for the call report; focus is achieved by the suspense. In its blatancy the statement matches the divine announcement to the pregnant Rebekah concerning Esau and Jacob: "Two nations are in your womb" (Gen 25:23).

[6] The term "nations" is tantalizingly shelved, and the focus in vv. 6–9 and 12 veers to "prophet," with special focus on communicating and communications (or speaking and messages), using variations of the Hebrew root *dbr*, "speak." That is why at v. 4 of the translation "message" was given an alternative, "communication," to prepare for the repetition that will be so important in vv. 6–12. The report now begins to conform to some elements of OT call traditions concerning national leaders and/or prophets. The protest of inadequacy is paralleled in Moses' adducing his stammer (Exod 4:10) and Gideon's and Saul's claiming to be nobodies (Judg 6:15; 1 Sam 9:21; cf. 18:18); it leaves traces in the NT, at Luke 1:18, 34. The effect after v. 5 is to stress that Jeremiah's prophetic career was not his own idea or achievement. The credit must go to the electing God, who chooses "what is low and despised in the world, things that are not, to reduce things that are, so that no one might boast in the presence of God" (1 Cor 1:28–29). Jeremiah's less than enthusiastic response is qualified: not yet, rather than no.[8] The vagueness of the Hebrew word translated "boy" in NRSV is captured by the LXX rendering "too young," echoed by NAB, REB, and GNB. Having waited so long, God can surely wait a little longer, until natural ability and social standing catch up. But that would miss the point. In Jeremiah's case supernatural equipping stands uncompromisingly over against nature and nurture, as v. 9 will confirm (cf. 1 Kgs 3:7, 9).[9]

[7–8] God's control, inexorably manifested in the past, is to mark Jeremiah's prophetic future. His obligation is to carry out the mission completely as to target—the mysterious "nations" is not yet repeated—and content. Natural fears are reassuringly transcended by the promise of the divine presence as a powerful factor to offset intimidating confrontation by human addressees. The one who sends Jeremiah will also be at his side. At this point negative features emerge momentarily; they will be explored further in vv. 17–19. The exhortation not to be frightened can have a background of warring hostility (cf. Num 21:34; Josh 1:9), which vv. 18–19 will express. Again, the promise of divine help typically follows protests in call narratives. Moses was similarly encour-

---

8. John Skinner, *Prophecy and Religion: Studies in the Life of Jeremiah* (Cambridge: Cambridge University Press, 1922), 34.

9. Cf. Brent A. Strawn, "Jeremiah's Ineffective Plea: Another Look at n^cr in Jeremiah i 6," *VT* 55 (2005): 366–77.

Prologue: Introducing Jeremiah and His Message 27

aged (Exod 3:12) as was Gideon (Judg 6:16). At an anxious time Paul received the same assurance (Acts 18:9).

[9] God's presence was not only promised for Jeremiah's future ministry but also manifested there and then in a striking experience, a commissioning act of sacramental symbolism. In Isa 6:7 the touching of Isaiah's mouth with a burning coal brought by a seraph had expiatory power. Here a divine touch transfers oracles to Jeremiah's mouth so that he can speak them. To put words in someone's mouth is to give that person a message to pass on (e.g., in Exod 4:15; Deut 18:18; 2 Sam 14:19).[10]

[10] The explanation of the dramatization continues, and with it the report comes full circle by reverting to v. 5: v. 9 alludes to "prophet," and the first part of v. 10 mentions "nations" again.[11] Verse 10 presents the prophetic commission earlier expressed in terms of divine purpose at v. 5. The main verb has a performative function, dynamically bestowing authority. The Hebrew verb elsewhere relates to political or military administration, as in 40:11 concerning Gedaliah, whom the Babylonian king "put in charge of" the people left in Judah as governor. The task that the prophet is delegated by the divine King to carry out is a double program, first negative and then positive; the positive element, though present in the book, will be redactionally developed there. Like Hosea, Jeremiah's message was to go beyond destruction to eventual restoration. The statement has a seminal role in the book in terms of both vocabulary and theme. Elsewhere in the book the range of the verbs, here the infinitive, has Yahweh as their subject (e.g., 12:14; 18:7). Describing this verbal activity as Jeremiah's work demonstrates his fully representative role as initiator of the outworking of the divine will (cf. 5:14; 6:9, 27; 23:29).[12] The book does not always conceive of prophecy in such absolute terms; in 18:5–11 an element of

---

10. The parallel in Deut 18:18 raises a question of literary dependence. The last clause in v. 7 is close to Deut 18:18, "... the prophet who shall speak to them everything that I command." Moreover, the Hebrew verbs for "put" (*ntn*) are the same in v. 9 and in Deut 18:18, but a different one occurs in similar passages (cf. Winfried Thiel, *Die deuteronomistische Redaktion von Jeremia 1–25* [WMANT 41; Neukirchen-Vluyn: Neukirchener Verlag, 1973], 67–68). If echoes of the post-Mosaic prophetic ministry envisioned in Deut 18:15–22 are present, an earlier account presumably was redactionally amplified. Rudolph (7 n. 3), McKane (13), and Jones (71) do not find literary dependence compelling. Verse 9 certainly lies at the pulsing heart of the section. Matthias Köcker, "Literargeschichtlicher Ort des Prophetengesetzes," in *Liebe und Gebot: Studien zum Deuteronomium. Festschrift zum 70. Geburtstag von Lothar Perlitt* (ed. R. G. Kratz and H. Spieckermann; FRLANT 190; Göttingen: Vandenhoeck & Ruprecht, 2000), 80–100, esp. 85–93, urges the dependence of Deut 18:18 on this text.

11. Gregorio del Olmo Lete, *La vocación del líder en el antiguo Israel: Morfología de los relatos bíblicos de vocación* (Bibliotheca Salamanticensis 3/2; Salamanca: Universidad Pontifica de Salamanca, 1973), 282.

12. Else K. Holt, "Word of Jeremiah—Word of God: Structures of Authority in the Book of Jeremiah," in *Uprooting and Planting: Essays on Jeremiah for Leslie Allen* (ed. J. Goldingay; Library of Hebrew Bible/Old Testament Studies 459; New York: T & T Clark, 2007), 172–89, esp. 178–79.

contingency is dominant in a context that echoes the negative and positive infinitives (cf. 42:10).

The "nations" of v. 5 are still not explained, just repeated with the addition of "realms." They are thus distinguishable from "the realms in the north" in v. 15, which are agencies of the divine will rather than its victims or beneficiaries. The book does not give the same weight to "nations" that this passage seems to. One expects here a reference to Judah as the target of Jeremiah's ministry, as later in vv. 14 and 18. Certainly Judah appears to be included; at least other passages in the book so assume. The application of the infinitives to God's people in 24:6; 31:28; and 42:10 reflects this implication. It also underlies the redactional inclusion of Judah in the list of nations at 25:18–26, in v. 18. Moreover, in 18:7, 9 the hypothetical reference to "this nation or that realm" along with the programmatic verbs, with Judah really in mind, presupposes the inclusion of Judah in such a wider scope. So does "any nation" in 27:8, 11, and 13 in a setting of Palestinian and Phoenician states. A plausible clue as to the identity of the other nations in this case may be derived from 12:14, in a passage that depends on 1:10. It mentions Yahweh's "neighbors" (v. 14), generally understood as the small kingdoms bordering on Judah, such as Edom, Philistia, Moab, and Ammon. Indeed, at 4:16 "the nations" seems to refer to local national allies of Judah (cf. 22:22; 25:9, 11). Palestine was to be caught up in a maelstrom of invasion. What Jeremiah had to say about Judah was to be momentous enough to produce repercussions among its immediate neighbors; "nations" is a premonition of its immense scope. The description of the enemy as "destroyer of nations" (4:7) in the context of Jeremiah's early prophesying strikes the same note. He became directly concerned with other nations late in his ministry (see chs. 25; 27; 46–49; 51:59–64).

At the earliest literary stage the programmatic verbs were four in number, in a chiastic order of building and agricultural metaphors, as the formulations in 24:6; 42:10; and 45:4 suggest. The positive pair is constant in the book, but the negative pair is variable. Here "destroy" has been supplied from the basic pair "uproot/destroy" in 18:7–9 (cf. 12:17), while "demolish" in MT is an addition derived from the pair "demolish/uproot" in 24:6; 42:10; 45:4.[13] The effect of the accumulation of verbs is to reflect the preponderance of negative oracles in the book and also to announce the book's overall structure (see "Macrostructure" in the introduction). This account of Jeremiah's commissioning marks him out as a proclaimer of Yahweh's comprehensive work that was to involve not only destruction but also reconstruction.

[11–12] The first person vision-oracle report supplements the call report in vv. 1–10, while "a second time" in v. 13 registers a fresh beginning for the rest of the chapter. The two vision-oracle reports may earlier have existed separately from their present context, paired by "a second time," corresponding to the pairs

---

13. Janzen, *Studies*, 35.

Prologue: Introducing Jeremiah and His Message 29

of vision-oracles in Amos 7:1–6 and 7:7–9 + 8:1–3. From the perspective of the call tradition, the vision takes on the value of a confirming sign or omen, like that to Gideon in Judg 6:17–21. The question-and-answer format in both reports is a standard one, found, for example, in Jer 24:1–3; Amos 7:7–9; 8:1–3. This report is based on wordplay; *šāqēd*, "almond," sounds like *šōqēd*, "watching," as *qayis*, "summer fruit," sounds like *qēs*, "end," in Amos 8:1–2. "Stick" has no significance except as the form the almond wood happened to take. (Almond sticks feature in Gen 30:37 and an almond staff in Num 17:8.) A commonplace sight is given revelatory value by Yahweh's drawing attention to it and interpreting it. The point of the question in this vision-oracle is to make Jeremiah pronounce the word and so provide a clue to the interpretation. Yahweh's "communication" sums up what God would order Jeremiah to communicate (v. 7) and what "my communications" (v. 9) were that God put in Jeremiah's mouth. Far from being Jeremiah's own feeble attempts to communicate (v. 6), the divine oracles would carry a guarantee of their eventual fulfillment in the form of God's providential alertness (cf. Dan 9:12, 14). As Second Isaiah stressed at beginning and end, "the word of our God will stand" and "my word . . . shall not return to me empty, but it shall accomplish that which I purpose, and succeed in the thing for which I sent it" (Isa 40:8; 55:11).

[13–19] The end of this new section (vv. 18–19) overlaps with material in 15:20 in the course of Yahweh's answer to one of Jeremiah's laments over communal opposition to his prophesying, while the initial "from the north" in vv. 13–15 recurs in 15:17. This similarity suggests not only the unity of vv. 13–19 but also that this section reflects the later situation of ch. 15 and, having a visionary introduction, was associated with the vision of vv. 11–12 and so placed here.[14] Its usefulness lies in its definition of Jeremiah's commission not in international but in national terms and in focusing on Jeremiah's negative ministry that dominates the book. Now, at a later date, the divine focus of v. 12 on waiting was to give way to action.[15]

[13] A second vision-oracle launches the next commissioning report; it is hinged with the former report by "realms" (vv. 10, 15). Another sign introduces a restatement of the prophet's task. The imagery operates not by wordplay but by featuring metaphor that uses a key word, somewhat as in Amos 7:7.[16] Jeremiah's

---

14. Cf. Claus Rietzschel, *Das Problem der Urrolle: Ein Beitrag zur Redaktionsgeschichte des Jeremiabuches* (Gütersloh: Gerd Mohn, 1966), 134; Hans-Winfried Jüngling, "Ich mache dich zu einer ehernen Mauer: Literarkritische Überlegungen zum Verhältnis von Jer 1,18–19 zu Jer 15,20–21," *Bib* 54 (1973): 1–24; Holladay 1:24–25; Jack R. Lundbom, "Jeremiah 15,15–21 and the Call of Jeremiah," *SJOT* 9 (1995): 143–55.

15. Gregory Y. Glazov, *The Bridling of the Tongue and the Opening of the Mouth in Biblical Prophecy* (JSOTSup 311; Sheffield: Sheffield Academic Press, 2001), 200.

16. Henning Graf Reventlow, *Liturgie und prophetisches Ich bei Jeremia* (Gütersloh: Gerd Mohn, 1963), 84.

reply describes a domestic mishap, a large cooking pot having slipped in a certain direction on the stones around the fire.

[**14–16**] The divine interpretation slides—like the caldron—from the danger that threatens in v. 13 to its feared sequel. The form of the interpretation closely parallels that in v. 12, but the symbolism demands two variations. First, an explanation of the impersonally expressed metaphor has to be given, displacing the approbation in v. 12. Second, the interpreting causal clause that sets out Yahweh's future activity needs to be longer. The activity is split into two parts, source-oriented in v. 15 and target-oriented in v. 16, in line with the north-south movement of the interpreted imagery in v. 14.

This commissioning report exhibits a narrower focus than the former one, in two respects. First, "the country" or "Judah" replaces the nations of vv. 5 and 10, and, second, Yahweh's message for Jeremiah to transmit is now only a negative one—a veritable avalanche of punishment. Both features are already evident in v. 14. Hebrew repetition in terms of effect and cause marks the boundaries of the interpretation in vv. 14 and 16: *rāʿâ* in the sense of a "bad fate" or "disaster" (NRSV) was to be the consequence of *rāʿâ* in the sense of "bad behavior" or "wickedness" (NRSV). This correlation also appears in prophetic oracles of communal disaster, for example, Mic 2:1–3.[17] Indeed, the interpretation in vv. 14–16 looks like an oracle of disaster; it summarizes the negative message Jeremiah was to prophesy. It combines elements of divine intervention, the results of that intervention, and the dire situation that warranted it. The orchestrated invasion of a mysterious northern coalition of nations is in view. The overwhelming nature of Jeremiah's prophecy is reaffirmed, but now presented in terms of its agents ("realms," v. 15), not its objects ("nations and realms," v. 10). From "realms" one has to infer that "they" in v. 15b refers to their kings. There is brusquely under stated allusion to both siege and conquest. The "tribunals" or thrones refer to the establishment of administrative control in the subject area, as in 39:3 and 43:10. Not only the capital would be involved, but "all of Judah's cities." The larger horizon resumes "all who live in the country" in v. 14 and serves as a transition to v. 16, where they are now the objects ("them," "their"). The royal tribunals represent thrones of judgment, as in Ps 9:4, 7 (5, 8), and Luke 22:30, and the human activity undertaken at Yahweh's behest becomes a window to a divine act of providential judgment. The grounds for such judgment are stated in religious terms, as outright apostasy along with rejection of the aniconic worship characteristically associated with Yahwism. The combination has a parallel in the traditions expressed in the first two of the Ten Commandments, to "have no other gods" and "not make for yourself an idol" (Exod 20:3–4; Deut 5:7–8).[18]

---

17. See Patrick D. Miller Jr., *Sin and Judgment in the Prophets: A Stylistic and Theological Analysis* (SBLMS 27; Chico, Calif.; Scholars Press, 1982), 29–31.

18. The language of the second bicolon in v. 16 was taken over into prose sermonic terminology (cf. Stulman, *Prose Sermons*, 34 no. 8, 38 no. 38).

Prologue: Introducing Jeremiah and His Message 31

[17–19] This passage turns to the prophetic role Jeremiah has to play. In the present context it harks back to the parallel section in vv. 7–10 and has a resumptive function in keeping with its tone of encouragement to shoulder the previously given responsibilities of being Yahweh's spokesperson. The task of communication presented in v. 7 is closely repeated in v. 17, though the content has been redefined in vv. 14–16. Verse 17 also echoes the urging not to fear given in v. 7. The performative utterance of v. 10 finds a partner in v. 18, while the assurance of Yahweh's rescuing presence is repeated in v. 19 from v. 8. The repetition has a rhetorical, persuasive role. The parallelism takes on a consecutive ABCDC′ shape in the supplemented text, with the factor of divine help being given climactic focus. This switch is in line with the passage's stressing how Jeremiah is to cope with the opposition he will have to face. The emphasis explains the element of divine threat in v. 17, which sounds like a warning against desertion by threatening a court martial or worse.[19] The positive focus on divine action in v. 18 suggests that the threat has a subsidiary role as a growled aside.

The rest of the motivational speech has a positive tone. The investiture of v. 18 grants armor-like resources of defensive power against comprehensive onslaught from Jeremiah's own countryfolk.[20] Repetition of "country" and "Judah" ties the passage to the divine message in vv. 14–16. "City" and "walls" echo terms used in v. 15. The motif of siege has supplied the imagery of v. 18, apart from the "pillar," which simply suggests a solid fixture.[21] The motif is given an ironic twist not only by its application to Jeremiah's coming persecution but also by its reversal of outcome. The victory northern kings were to achieve would in no way be matched by Judean kings and all their subjects in their own war against Jeremiah. Ultimate assurance of this surprising effect comes from the continuing support of Jeremiah's divine ally.

The negative and positive factors of v. 10 are manifested differently in this report; the latter is reserved for the prophet. If a communal oracle of disaster shaped vv. 14–16, an individual oracle of salvation has lent its form to vv. 17–19. Comparison with Isa 41:8–13 reveals a similar progression, from the "do not be afraid" formula to God's promise of intervention, then the results of that intervention and a closing divine explanation.[22] In the explanation the motif of divine rescue, repeated from v. 8, is rooted in the psalms of individual

---

19. The threat is sharpened by repetition of the same Hebrew verb *htt* in the two clauses in different senses; cf. NRSV and NJPS "break down/break."

20. "The people of the country" in v. 18 and elsewhere in the book is a comprehensive term for the rest of the population rather than a political class. See Ernest W. Nicholson, "The Meaning of the Expression ʿm hʾrṣ in the Old Testament," *JSS* 10 (1965): 59–66, esp. 65.

21. Shemaryahu Talmon's suggestion that it refers to the bar or bolt of a city gate ("An Apparently Redundant MT Reading—Jeremiah 1:18," *Text* 8 [1973]: 160–63) is appealing, but he was unable to provide linguistic corroboration.

22. Cf. John M. Berridge, *Prophet, People, and the Word of Yahweh: An Examination of Form and Content in the Proclamation of the Prophet Jeremiah* (Basel Studies of Theology 4; Zurich: Evangelischer Verlag, 1970), 198–99.

lament.[23] Laments derive their voice from a theological tradition that at times of crisis, in response to prayer, Yahweh rescues worshipers from premature death (Ps 91:14–16). So Jeremiah is not to be preserved from society's warring but brought through it by repeated saving acts, not unscathed but a survivor. The God "who rescued . . . will continue to rescue" (2 Cor 1:10).

The chapter serves as an introduction to the book; the superscription and the commissioning passage with its double premonition of disaster have the function of two prologues. I have already mentioned both continuity and discontinuity between vv. 4–12 and the book. The discontinuity suggests that this passage was not editorially made to measure for the book. It functions rather as a good rough fit. It claims the prophetic authenticity of the book's leading human character by giving evidence of his initial appointment by God, so that readers are predisposed to trust Jeremiah's interpretation of Judean history and to prefer him to prophets of a different stripe, who appear later in the book. The overall narrative introduces motifs and concepts that will appear throughout the book. Even admission of hardship and failure in the narratives of chs. 26–45 need raise no doubts in the light of 1:18–19, but rather provide corroboration, just as the call narrative in Isaiah 6, with its warning of hardened hearts, paves the way for the prophet's rejection in chs. 7–8. Jeremiah's panicky reaction in v. 6 will find poignant echoes in his prayers of lament scattered through chs. 11–20. The stark term "nations" in vv. 5 and 10 acquires applicability to the collection of oracles of disaster for foreign nations in chs. 46–51 and to their introduction in ch. 25. It has already been noticed that the double program of v. 10 bounces through the book; two separate redactional additions in the verse have reinforced the link.[24] Positive messages will be reserved mainly for God's own people, especially in chs. 30–33, but a promise of restoration occurs as an afterthought to a foreign oracle in 49:39, to which the MT adds others at 46:26; 48:47; 49:6, while unconditional promises occur in 3:17 and 16:19–21, and a conditional one in 12:14–17.

The commissioning accounts also prepare readers for chs. 2–6. While prediction of invasion from the mysterious north is widely featured in the book and eventually understood in terms of Babylon (25:9; cf. 20:4, 6; 36:29), references to it are clustered in 4:5–6:30. Other dominant motifs in chs. 2–6 are Israel's abandonment of Yahweh—the verb recurs in 2:13, 17, 19; 5:17, 19—and recourse to pagan deities, on which 2:4–4:4 focuses, along with specific reference to idols in 2:27; 3:9. Both of these motifs are introduced in 1:16. Chapter 1 broaches key motifs that the next five chapters will unfold.

A kaleidoscope of genres derived from Judah's cultural background adorns the passage. Special birth narratives, call traditions, vision-oracle reports,

---

23. See Broyles, *Conflict of Faith*, 222–23.
24. Similarly the addition of "priests" in MT at v. 18 feeds back the term from later listings in 2:26 and 32:32, where it accompanies "prophets" (Janzen, *Studies*, 35–36).

Prologue: Introducing Jeremiah and His Message 33

prophetic oracles of disaster and salvation, and a lament tradition have all made rich contributions and given vv. 4–19 its impressive shape. Such a bombardment of genres presents Jeremiah as an accredited prophet for the coming crisis, empowered to be Yahweh's plenipotentiary, despite the controversy he was to stir up among his contemporaries. The first account has left its literary mark on the Bible. The positive mission of Yahweh's servant in Isa 49:1, 5–6 is colored by Jer 1:5: "The LORD called me before I was born, while I was in my mother's womb he named me. . . . And now the LORD says, who formed me in the womb, . . . 'I will give you as a light to the nations.'" In the NT Paul found Jer 1:5 helpful for expressing his own sense of apostolic destiny: "God . . . set me apart before I was born and called me through his grace . . . so that I might proclaim [his Son] among the Gentiles [or nations]" (Gal 1:15–16).

2:1–3 The Honeymoon Is Over

2:1 *I received Yahweh's message as follows:*[a] 2 *"Go and proclaim in Jerusalem's hearing:* 'Here is what Yahweh said:

"What I remember about you is the commitment shown when you
    were young, the love at your wedding celebrations,
how you followed me through the wilderness,
    a nonarable region.
3   Israel was sacred to Yahweh,[b]
    the firstfruits of his harvest.
Any who ate such produce would be held guilty,
    experiencing a bad fate,"
declared Yahweh.'"

a. An introductory formula evidently fell out, as in 3:1. MT has supplied a first person oracle reception statement, aligning with 1:4, 11, 13 (cf. Janzen, *Studies*, 111–13).
b. For LXX in vv. 2b–3a*a* see McKane 1:27.

This oracle rounds off ch. 1 according to MT and introduces especially 2:4–6:30. What is to be proclaimed is a self-contained unit, with its own opening and closing quotation formulas. In genre the piece is related to the oracle of disaster, which generally falls into two parts, an announcement of disaster prefaced by the reason for it. The initial reason sometimes has its blameworthiness accentuated by a contrast motif.[25] The motif usually harks back to the basic

---

25. Claus Westermann, *Basic Forms of Prophetic Speech* (trans. H. C. White; Philadelphia: Westminster, 1967; repr. with a new foreword by G. M. Tucker; Louisville: Westminster/John Knox, 1991), 182–83.

work of God on Israel's behalf, as in Amos 2:9–11, but it can refer to Israel's early attractiveness to God, as in the first part of Hos 9:10. Here room is made for both, the latter in v. 2 and the former in v. 3. This motif fills the unit, implicitly providing positive antitheses for subsequent shocking changes in the relationship between Yahweh and Israel. Those changes will be explained in what follows as the negative ways Israel treated Yahweh and the negative ways Yahweh consequently had to treat Israel.

[**2:2**] The directive relating to Jerusalem in MT was added to provide an antecedent for the Hebrew feminine second person references in the divine statement that follows. "Jerusalem" as audience took its cue from 4:5, "make an announcement in Jerusalem" (cf. 4:3, 4). In the light of the reference to Israel in 2:3 it was presumably meant to refer to the Judean covenant community gathered in the capital at festival time. The two verbs of the directive recur in 3:12, "Go and proclaim." The second verb occurs with the prepositional phrase in Judg 7:3 with the sense "proclaim in the hearing of the troops."[26]

In another context Yahweh's recollection could have the flavor of a proclamation of salvation, with the sense "I remember and will act accordingly by blessing or saving you" (cf. Pss 105:42; 132:1). Against the somber backdrop that will emerge after v. 3, however, it refers to a nostalgic appreciation of a past memory. A happy wilderness experience is an echo of passages in Hosea (2:15–16 [16–17]; 9:10; 11:1, 4). In Hosea it always presupposes subsequent degeneration as soon as Israel reached the promised land, the very note to be sounded in vv. 6–7, and so it anticipates a relationship that turned sour.[27] This positive wilderness perspective stands at odds with the Pentateuch's tradition of a murmuring and disobedient Israel. It is unlikely, however, that the tradition represented here and in Hosea ever existed by itself; rather, it reflects simply a difference of perspective.[28] In terms of pentateuchal texts the faith and praise of Exod 14:31–15:21 (cf. Ps 106:12) and the people's affirmations in Exod 19:8; 24:3, 7 may be compared.

Much more commonly the great theological term *ḥesed*, here rendered "commitment," relates to Yahweh's covenant love and faithfulness, as at 31:3, along with "love." It does refer to Israel's response relatively frequently in Hosea (2:19 [21]; 4:1; 6:4; 12:6 [7]; cf. Rev 2:4), though it tends to focus on love of neighbor rather than of God. Clues to the divine interpretation here are

---

26. Mark E. Biddle, *A Redactional History of Jeremiah 2:1–4:2* (ATANT 77; Zurich: Theologischer Verlag, 1990), 160–61, has suggested that, since the combination has the sense "read out in (someone's) hearing" elsewhere in the book of Jeremiah (29:29 and six times in ch. 36), the sense of reading a written document applies here; the redactor was already working with a written text.

27. Christoph Barth, "Zur Bedeutung der Wüstentradition," in *Volum du Congrès: Genève 1965* (ed. P. A. H. de Boer; VTSup 15; Leiden: Brill, 1966), 14–23, esp. 19.

28. Brevard S. Childs, *The Book of Exodus, A Critical, Theological Commentary* (OTL; Philadelphia: Westminster, 1974), 263.

the adjacent reference to Israel's own activity of following Yahweh and the combination of that motif with Israel's love in 2:25.[29] The depiction of Israel as young depends on Hos 2:15 (17) (cf. 11:1), and the marriage portrayal of the covenant relationship depends on Hosea 1–3. The striking contemporization of past tradition ("you") aligns with Hos 13:4–5; other prophets also used this convention in relation to the exodus and wilderness (see Amos 2:10; Mic 6:4). The present generation was the current heir of such traditions and could spiritually identify with their forebears' encounter with God as a once-for-all experience. Time was bridged in a community whose religious heritage had been kept alive in worship down the centuries. The NT took up this concept of historical solidarity via a sacramental theology, for instance in Eph 2:5, "God made us alive together with Christ."

To "follow" or "go after" is an idiom of loyalty that is related to marriage in Gen 24:5 and 1 Sam 25:42. It refers to rival religious commitments in 1 Kgs 18:21 and to a wrong commitment to divine "lovers" in Hos 2:5 (7). The "wilderness" suggests a trusting dependence upon Yahweh for food to sustain life, as the parallel expression shows. Verse 2 lays a foundation for the large block of incriminating material in 2:5–4:4. The motif of the inhospitable wilderness will be resumed in 2:6, 31. Israel's following gods other than Yahweh will recur four times in ch. 2 (at vv. 5, 8, 23, and 25), while idols find specific mention at 2:27 and 3:9. Yahweh's remembering will find counterpoints in Israel's forgetting at 2:32 and 3:21—forgetting its wedding finery in 2:32.[30] Initial devotion to Yahweh as the ancestral God will have a shocking sequel in desertion and alien religious practices.

[3] There is a switch from the contemporizing "you" and "your" to a history-oriented presentation, as if to anticipate the shutter the covenant people put up between past and present. Third person references to Yahweh achieve similar distancing, unlike the intimate subjectivity of v. 2. While Israel's relationship to Yahweh was the focus of v. 2, now Yahweh's former protective relationship to Israel comes into view. The basis of the trust implicit at the close of v. 2 is presented as divine care. The underlying sense and the link between the verses are well expressed by Deut 32:10:

> He sustained him in a desert land,
>   in a howling wilderness waste;
> he shielded him, cared for him,
>   guarded him as the apple of his eye.

---

29. Michael DeRoche, "Jeremiah 2:2–3 and Israel's Love for God during the Wilderness Wanderings," *CBQ* 45 (1983): 364–76, esp. 366, 368–69. For a contrary view see Gordon R. Clark, *The Word Hesed in the Hebrew Bible* (JSOTSup 157; Sheffield: JSOT Press, 1993), 193–99, and literature there cited.

30. Cf. Holladay, *Architecture*, 32.

Cultic imagery is employed, perhaps sparked by reflection on the picture of Israel's attractiveness to Yahweh as "the first fruit [a different Hebrew term] on the fig tree" in Hos 9:10. The first picking of each fruit and cereal crop was traditionally sacrosanct, dedicated to the sanctuary and eaten by Yahweh's priestly representatives (Exod 23:19; Num 18:12–13; Prov 3:9). This exclusive right debarred secular use, and so infringement would carry a penalty; Lev 22:15–16 uses similar vocabulary. Here the envisioned offenders are Israel's national enemies, such as the Amalekites (Exod 17:8–13; cf. Jer 5:17). If the structural function of v. 2 was to introduce 2:5–4:4, that of v. 3 is to be the contrasting prelude for 4:5–6:30. Israel lost not only a close relationship to Yahweh but also the "hands off" privilege that went with it. Now, instead of a bad fate coming upon Israel's enemies, Israel was to be exposed to its own bad fate by way of punishment. In 5:12 an optimistic assertion, "We will not find a bad fate coming upon us," using the Hebrew verb of v. 3, is dismissed. In 4:6 and 6:19 Yahweh is to implement such a fate, and a causative form of the same verb is used.[31]

Verses 2–3, drawing heavily on traditions used by Hosea,[32] function as a keynote message and a frontispiece with 2:4–6:30 especially in view. It presents lost harmony as a measure of Israel's waywardness and as a hint of the danger to which Israel was thereby exposed.

---

31. Ibid., 57–58.
32. For these and further links between Hosea and Jeremiah see Holladay 2:45–47; Martin Schulz-Rauch, *Hosea und Jeremia: Zur Wirkungsgeschichte des Hoseabuches* (Calwer theologische Monographien 16; Stuttgart: Calwer, 1996).

2:4–10:25 Destruction and Eventual Reconstruction, Part One

2:4–6:30 Coming Disaster and Its Causes

2:4–19 Judah's Apostasy

4 Listen to Yahweh's message, Jacob's community, all you clans of Israel's community. 5 Here is what Yahweh said:

"What fault did your forebears find in me
    that they went so far from my side
    and followed a nonentity, becoming nonentities themselves?
6 They failed to ask, 'Where is Yahweh
    who brought us up from Egypt,
who guided us through the wilderness,
    a region of desert and ravines,
a region of drought and deep darkness,
    a region untraveled
    and unpopulated?'
7 I brought you into a fertile country
    so you could eat its fruit and other benefits,
but you came in only to defile my country,
    turning my property into something abominable.
8 The priests have failed to ask 'Where is Yahweh?'
    Those who handle torah have had no insight into my will.
The shepherd-kings have rebelled against me,
    while the prophets have prophesied in Baal's name.
So things that are useless are what they have followed.[a]
9 Therefore I will state my grievances against you also,"
    declared Yahweh,
    "and against your descendants I will state my grievances.
10 In fact cross to the coast of Cyprus and look,
    send messengers to Kedar and make careful observation,
    consider whether anything like this has ever occurred.
11 Has any other nation changed gods—
    though they are not really gods?

Yet my people have exchanged their glorious one
    for something useless.
12 Be shocked, you skies, at this,
    be horrified and utterly devastated,"
    declared Yahweh,
13 "because two bad choices have my people made:
    me they have abandoned,
        the spring of running water,
    to dig cisterns for themselves,
        cisterns that get cracked,
        which cannot hold water.

14 "Is Israel a slave?
    Is it some house-born slave?
    If not, why has it become plunder?
15 Over it the lions kept roaring,
        howling loudly.
    They turned its country into a shocking place.[b]
    Its towns were ruined, so nobody could live in them.
16 Indeed, the people of Noph and Tahpanhes
    will break[c] the crown of your head.
17 Is not the cause of this happening to you
    your abandoning[d] Yahweh as your God?[e]
18 So now what is the point of your journey to Egypt,
    to drink Nile water?
    And what is the point of your journey to Assyria,
    to drink Euphrates[f] water?
19 Your own bad behavior will get you punished,
        your backsliding ways convict you.
    So realize, consider how bitterly bad
        is your abandoning Yahweh your God
        and that you do not feel obliged to revere me,"[g]
    declared the sovereign Yahweh Almighty.[h]

   a. This is a climactic monocolon, for which cf. Watson, *Classical Hebrew Poetry*, 70–72. It is distinguished from the previous four cola by lack of an initial subject. The final colon sums up the waywardness of all the leaders (Daniel Grossberg, "Noun/Verb Parallelism: Syntactic or Asyntactic?" *JNES* 99 [1980]: 65–69, esp. 67–68; Holladay 1:88).
   b. For this meaning see *HALOT* 4:1553b.
   c. The vocalization of MT from *rʿh*, "graze," in the secondary sense of "devastate," produces an odd mixture of metaphors. The translation assumes a vocalization *yěrōʿûk* implied by Syr., from *rʿʿ*, "break," an Aramaism used in 15:12 and Ps 2:9. NRSV, REB,

Coming Disaster and Its Causes

and GNB have adopted this pointing, in the wake of KJV. The other EVV assume scribal metathesis of $yē^cārûk$ from ^crh, with the sense "lay bare, shave." This last suggestion has received much support from commentators and yields good meaning, but it is better in principle to retain the consonantal text when it gives adequate sense.

d. For the syntax see GKC §114a, which compares 1 Sam 18:23.

e. MT adds words not represented in LXX, $b^ct\ mwlykk\ bdrk$, "at the time when he guided you in the way," with an aramaizing use of a participle. This looks suspiciously like a garbled version—influenced by v. 6—of the next four words in v. 18, $w^cth\ mhlk\ ldrk$, "and now what to you with respect to the way." Probably correction has taken place in MT without removal of the corrupt text (cf. *BHS*). NAB deletes.

f. Literally "River" par excellence; see BDB 625b.

g. More lit. "and (that) reverence for me is not (an obligation resting) upon you," taking ^ʾel, "to," in the sense of ^cal, "upon." For this sense of ^cal see BDB 753; and for continuation of an infinitive with a separate clause cf. GKC §114r.

h. This is the rendering of NIV and GNB, derived from the standard translation in the LXX of Jeremiah in place of the traditional, enigmatic-sounding "of hosts." Whatever the precise meaning, the term carries a sense of divine omnipotence.

The literary block of 2:4–6:30 functions as a giant oracle of disaster, broadly stating first the grounds for it (2:4–4:4) and then its certainty (4:5–6:30). Two parallel compositions in 2:4–19 and 20–37 present religious and political accusations of unfaithfulness to Yahweh. The next pair in 3:1–18 and 3:19–4:4 continues with charges of religious infidelity and dismisses pious claims of Yahweh's commitment and Israel's contrition as insincere ploys. One day, however, all this would change for the better for God's people in north and south. As for 4:5–6:30, a pair of compositions in 4:5–18, 19–31 announces impending military doom, while the three compositions of 5:1–9, 10–19, and 20–31 affirm such coming disaster and ground it in both moral delinquency and religious infidelity. Yet in 4:27; 5:10, 18, the completeness of the destruction is qualified, with a positive sequel implicitly in view. The three compositions in 6:1–15, 16–21, and 22–30 proclaim utter military destruction in response to utter rejection of God's torah standards and prophetic overtures.

At first sight 2:4–37 gives the impression of being a random cluster of extracts from early oracles. There is a form-critical clue that a break occurs after v. 19. The various units all have the flavor of an oracle of disaster. Most units offer reasons for disaster, but v. 19 moves to the second stage, an announcement of disaster. This movement implies that vv. 5–19 represent an editorially produced version of a complete oracle, one that focuses on reasons. The first unit consists of vv. 5–9, demarcated by opening and closing quotation formulas; it has been turned into a complex unit by having vv. 10–11 and 12–13 appended to it, with the latter's quotation formula "declared Yahweh" used as a section opener. Verses 14–19, concluded by a closing formula, constitute a separate unit that ends the literary composition.

[4] A weighty, formal call to attention in prose announces a new beginning. It seems to be a redactional introduction. It is addressed to the covenant people as a whole and embraces all its parts. Later in the chapter (v. 28), "Judah" will be plainly invoked as the addressee, but here the theological term "Israel" of v. 3 is resumed, with "Jacob" as its parallel (cf. vv. 14, 26, 31). The Jerusalem festival setting of v. 2 in MT is envisioned.

[5–9] A history lesson turns into a confrontation with Jeremiah's contemporaries. The audience is drawn into an objective, relatively nonthreatening discussion, only to be trapped into finding themselves condemned. The procedure is reminiscent of the parable Nathan told David, ending with "You are the man!" (2 Sam 12:1–7). The trap is laid and activated by a chiasm, ABCB'A', which ties the two parts of this piece together by pitting past and present generations in vv. 5 and 9 and by asking old and new questions in vv. 6 and 8.[1]

[5–6] Verses 6–7 suggest that Israel's "forebears" are the generations who had the exodus and the wilderness wanderings behind them and had entered the promised land. The logical starting point occurs at v. 6, a recital of Yahweh's deeds that emphasizes a championing and protective role and thus recalls the final part of v. 2 and v. 3. God's protégés had been preserved from dire and ever-present dangers.[2] The unspoken question "Where?" belongs to the prayer of lament in which appeal is made to a once-saving God to save again (Judg 6:13; Ps 89:49 [50]; Isa 63:11, 15). The period of the judges is in view, when Israel's existence in the land was threatened by adjacent nations, but also a period marked by religious apostasy. This apostasy provides the background for the ironic protest of v. 5 in which the speculative and unlikely "fault" presupposes by contrast the parade of saving benefits in v. 6. There is allusion to worship of the Canaanite storm god Hadad, who was given the title "Baal," mentioned outright in v. 8, but here in terms of a dismissive pun, *hahebel*, "(the) nonentity," on *habbaʿal*, "the Baal, lord" (Bright 15). By appealing to what was powerless, the people only reinforced their own powerlessness.

[7] The exploits of v. 6 continue, now in a narrative form, to include provision of entry into the promised land, at which the phrase "brought up from Egypt" had already hinted. The forebears of v. 5 are still in view, with "you" logically functioning in an answer to the forebears, whose quoted question had employed "us." However, the sense of "you" also slides into a contemporizing usage matching that of v. 2, though now the Hebrew pronouns are plural, as later in v. 9. The exploit includes a focus on God's agricultural gifts that contrast with the "nonarable region" of the wilderness in v. 2. It accentuates the fol-

---

1. Lundbom, *Hebrew Rhetoric*, 94–98.
2. Othmar Keel, *The Symbolism of the Biblical World: Ancient Near Eastern Iconography and the Book of Psalms* (trans. T. J. Hallett; New York: Seabury, 1978), 76, has suggested that darkness in vv. 6 and 13 refers to the black basalt deserts of Transjordan. Darkness bears the metaphorical connotation of danger (cf. GNB "dangerous"), as in Ps 23:4.

lowing complaint of ungrateful abuse of the land. Once more Jeremiah depends on traditions in Hosea, traditions that associate occupation of the land with rot setting in. Israel seized the opportunity to adopt the Baal cult they found there (Hos 2:5, 8 [7, 10], 9:10; 11:2). The cultic language "defiled" and "abominable" expresses a change in religious affiliation, while the definition of the land as "my country" and "my property" upholds a claim of Yahweh's inalienable rights as landowner, which the Israelite tenants should have respected (cf. Lev 25:23).

[8] The unasked question of v. 6 is repeated, but now with a contemporary application that builds on the contemporizing usage of "you" in v. 7. Judah's present leaders, who set the tone for the community at large, had continued in the same bad attitude. In troublous times the priests who should have taken the lead in praying a communal lament to Yahweh—along the lines of Joel 2:17—had been silent. Those priests responsible for giving the inquiring people instruction based on torah traditions had misrepresented the divine will (cf. Hos 4:6). Judah's kings, here called "shepherds," as in Jer 3:15; 22:22; 23:1, also set a bad example, while some prophets had even turned openly to Baal for inspiration.[3] This failure of the leadership to propagate Yahwistic ideals was evidence of an underlying tendency to demote Yahweh in the interests of a rival faith. "The community . . . has lost its foundational point of reference" (Brueggemann 35). The derogative phrase "things that are useless" (*yôʿîlû*) represents a Hebrew play on "Baals" (cf. *habbĕʿālîm*, 2:23) by repeating two root components.

[9] "Therefore" is a conventional link between reasons for disaster and the announcement of disaster. Here it prefaces a warning of punishment, the pressing of charges against the covenant people.[4] Not only their forebears were guilty before God (v. 6); they had caught the old bug. And, since there was no sign of improvement, the next generation was likely to be embroiled.

[10–13] A pair of passages follows, parallel in their tone of outrage and pathos ("my people") and in their bridging of exclamatory command and content by "this." Linked editorially by the initial *kî*, "For" (NRSV), these passages look back to the reasons of apostasy given earlier and reinforce them. Oracles of disaster sometimes conclude with reasons after the announcement,[5] and that is the function of vv. 10–11 and 12–13.

---

3. Listing of leaders usually has the order of kings, priests, and prophets, as in v. 26, but presumably the rhetorical desire to echo the question of v. 6 distorts it here. Jacob Milgrom, "The Date of Jeremiah, Chapter 2," *JNES* 14 (1955): 65–69, esp. 67–68, observing that only here and in vv. 26–27 are Judean prophets rebuked for idolatry (cf. 23:13), has used this and other evidence in ch. 2 to date its oracles before Josiah's reform in 622 B.C.E.

4. The Hebrew verb and noun *rîb*, rendered "state grievances," are not to be understood form-critically in terms of a covenant lawsuit. See DeRoche, "Yahweh's *rîb* against Israel: A Reassessment of the So-Called 'Prophetic Lawsuit' in the Preexilic Prophets," *JBL* 102 (1983): 563–74; Dwight R. Daniels, "Is There a 'Prophetic Lawsuit' Genre?" *ZAW* 99 (1987): 339–60.

5. See Westermann, *Basic Forms*, 180–81.

[10–11] The charge that Judah had virtually exchanged Yahweh for Baal as the national god is hailed as outrageous. In v. 11 the derogatory wordplay used at the close of the main statement of the reasons for disaster (v. 8) is repeated. Enormity is expressed by an ethnological comparison. Searching from west to east, from Cyprus to the Arabian Kedar (cf. Isa 42:10–11), one could never find a parallel. A modification—"though they are not divine"—avoids seeming to bring other national gods up to Yahweh's unique level. Like Simple Simon, Judah had lost out by swapping substance for the insubstantial. Yahweh is described as *kābôd*, "weight, glory," as in the punning contrast between "weight of glory" and that which is slight in 2 Cor 4:17.[6]

[12–13] The comparison is broadened; no counterpart exists anywhere in the world. With impressive assonance the skies (*šāmayim*) above the wide world are invited to register their shock (*šōmmû*) at anything so unprecedented. The inequality already expressed in v. 11 is developed in terms of a choice of disproportionate alternatives. Saying no to Yahweh is folly; to fill the vacuum by saying yes to the Baals is madness. The pragmatic standard of uselessness (vv. 8, 11) is heightened to a metaphorical contrast between life and death. Yahweh is "a spring of running [lit. "living"] water," providing never-failing resources for coping with the real world. Yahweh's rivals are mere plaster-lined cisterns cut in the limestone rock and gradually leaking the stale water they hold from last winter's rains. They provide pseudospiritual sustenance by their rituals, but leave those who worship them with their thirst for effective living unquenched and so unable to survive. Only contact with the living God (10:10; 23:36; Ps 42:2 [3]; Hos 1:10 [2:1]) can bring true life, as Ps 36:9 (10); Prov 14:27; John 4:14; and Rev 21:6 reaffirm.

[14–19] This unit concludes the literary oracle of disaster that began in v. 5. It will culminate in the explicit reprisal of v. 19, but it derives the reason for it no longer from the religious sphere but from international politics. After the second masculine plural address in vv. 5–13, it uses second feminine singular language, at least in vv. 16–19, while "Israel" is discussed in third masculine singular terms in vv. 14–15. The unit is consistent with what precedes at three points: the water imagery (v. 18), the motif of abandoning Yahweh, and the description of Yahweh as "your God" (vv. 17 and 19). The last element echoes "my people" in vv. 11 and 13 as the other side of the double covenant formula (cf. 24:7; 31:33; 32:40).

[14–17] The main point of the unit will be reached at v. 18 with "And now" (NAB, REB), which in speeches and letters commonly marks a transition from preliminaries. These prior verses point out the failure of the political maneuvers of v. 18. It should have been a case of once bitten twice shy, yet Israel had not learned from its mistakes but blundered on from past failure to a worse one in the future.

---

6. A definition as "the object of their glorifying" (BDB 459b) loses this contrast.

[14–15] The three initial questions discuss that past failure, with the first two suggesting wrong answers to stimulate concern for the right answer to the third question.[7] Israel should have been a free agent under Yahweh, not subject to foreign powers. In the light of v. 3 it was an ominous sign that Israel had lost the divine protection it had once enjoyed. It had become "plunder" or prey, devoured by foreign nations as if by lions (cf. 30:16; Ezek 34:8). Such destruction may refer not to recent events in Judah but to its long history of subjection to Assyria, including its devastation at Sennacherib's hands in 701 B.C.E. (cf. Isa 1:7; 5:29; Rudolph 19).

[16] This reference to defeat at Egyptian hands, citing two cities in northern Egypt, is a historical enigma, if it is read in conjunction with vv. 14–15. The Hebrew imperfect verb can refer to the future, as REB takes it. If the verse belongs to one of Jeremiah's early oracles, it represents a premonition of Josiah's defeat at Pharaoh Neco's hands in 609 and Judah's subsequent spell of vassalage to Egypt.[8] Then not only do Assyrian and Egyptian defeats correlate with Judah's overtures to those powers in v. 18,[9] but the Egyptian defeat gives an objective definition of Judah's future punishment in v. 19.

[17] Both defeats are traced back to the outworking of divine providence in Judah's affairs, in reprisal for unfaithfulness to its covenant God. Here is the right answer in place of the wrong answers of v. 14 as to why Judah incurred its political failures in the past and would do so again in the future.

[18] Rivalry among pro-Assyrian and pro-Egyptian political parties in Judah may be in view. Since already by 616 Egypt and Assyria were allied against the Neo-Babylonians and Medes, a situation earlier in Josiah's reign may be envisioned.[10] Condemnation of Judah's vacillation between Assyria and Egypt echoes that of the northern kingdom in Hos 7:11. The depiction of the goal as a quest for a plentiful supply of water indicates a search for political and economic survival at a time when Judah's own resources were at a low ebb.

[19] In venturing out from Yahweh's protective reach, Judah would have to face the negative consequences. Its punishment, when it came, would be Judah's own fault. The right answer of v. 17 is reaffirmed with a call to take it remorsefully to heart as the inevitable aftermath of lack of spiritual commitment.

Verses 14–19 present a new message of political failure that at first sight strikes an alien note after the earlier religious charges, but in embracing both types of accusation Jeremiah showed himself to be Hosea's heir once more. This unit sketches the nature of the punishment Judah would suffer as a political one.

---

7. See Walter A. Brueggemann, "Jeremiah's Use of Rhetorical Questions," *JBL* 92 (1973): 358–74.
8. Milgrom, "Date of Jeremiah," 66 n. 8.
9. Holladay, *Architecture*, 37, notes the ABB′A′ order in the double reference to Assyria and Egypt.
10. Milgrom, "Date of Jeremiah."

In contrast to the happy scenario of v. 2, the nations who devoured Judah as their prey would be allowed to do so with impunity, now that Judah had abandoned its covenant God. Besides wrong religion, vv. 14–19 also identify a supplementary reason for that punishment, wrong politics, which is consistent with the charge of Judah's inordinate disloyalty to Yahweh.

2:20–37 Judah's Apostasy Reaffirmed

20 "In fact ages ago you broke[a] your yoke,
 you snapped[a] your harness,
 and said, 'I will not serve.'
Rather, on every high hill
 and beneath every leafy tree
 you have been sprawling as a prostitute.
21 Yet I it was who planted you as a red grape vine,
 wholly from true seed.
So how is it you changed into a rotten plant,[b]
 a foreign vine?
22 Even if you wash with soda
 and use a lot of lye on yourself,
 your wrongdoing leaves a stain I can see,"
declared *the Lord* Yahweh.
23 "How can you say, 'I have not defiled myself,
 the Baals I have not followed'?
Consider your conduct in the valley,
 realize what you have been doing,
you fast young camel, crisscrossing your[c] tracks,
24 you wild ass used to the wilderness—[d]
she sniffs the wind in her instinctive urge.
 It is her time to mate![e] She is out of control.
No males seeking her out need tire themselves;
 in her time of heat they will find her.
25 Stop running till your feet are left bare[f]
 and your throat is thirsty.
But you say, 'It is hopeless! No,
 I love the aliens
 and they are the ones I must follow.'

26 "As a thief is chagrined when he is caught,
 so Israel's community is chagrined.
They, their kings and officials,
 and their priests and prophets,[g]

Coming Disaster and Its Causes

27 have been saying to wood, 'You are my father,
  and to stone, 'You gave me birth.'
 In fact they have turned their backs on me
  instead of their faces toward me.
 Yet when times turned bad for them they kept saying,
  'Come and save us.'
28 Where are your gods then,
  those you made for yourself?
 Let them come, if they can save you,
  now that you are going through a bad time.
 In fact the number of your towns
  is matched by your gods, Judah.[h]

29 "How is it you state grievances against me?
  You have all rebelled against me,"
 declared Yahweh.
30 "In vain have I struck your children;
  they would not accept correction.
 Your own sword has devoured your prophets
  like a lion bent on destruction"—
31 You members of this generation should consider Yahweh's message—[i]
 "Have I been a wilderness to Israel?
  Or some shadow land?
 If not, why have my people said, 'We roam free,
  we will resort to you no more'?
32 Can a girl forget her jewelry,
  a bride her sash?
 Yet my people have forgotten me
  for a time too long to reckon.

33 "How well you direct your course
  in search of love!
 That is why, yes, in bad deeds[j]
  you have trained your ways.
34 Yes, on your skirts has been found
  the blood of innocent[k] persons,
   though you did not catch them in the act of burglary.
 But in spite of all this (?)[l]
35 you say, 'I am innocent.
  Surely his anger has veered away from me.'
 Look, I am going to pass judgment on you
  because of your saying 'I have not sinned.'

36 How very lightly you treat^m
   your change of course!
   Yes, in Egypt you will be disappointed,
   just as you were disappointed in Assyria.
37 Yes, you will only get out of this
   with your hands to your head,
   because Yahweh has rejected those you trust
   and you will have no success with them."

a. See *BHS* and cf. v. 33.
b. See *BHS* for this modest emendation of a corrupt text made by Duhm 25, and cf. *HALOT* 2:749a; *sôrîyâ* is to be taken as *Qal* feminine participle with retention of the original third radical (cf. GKC §75v), used nominally, "a stinking, rotten plant." In the contextual echo of Isa 5:2–4, the term corresponds to *bĕʾūšîm*, "stinking grapes." LXX *eis pikrian*, "to bitterness," implying *lĕmôrâ*, gives partial support to the change.
c. Literally "her." A third person suffix is sometimes found in an attributive clause after a vocative (cf. GKC §144p). The same usage probably explains the third person references in v. 24.
d. The Hebrew masculine forms must be epicene (GKC §122d).
e. For this exclamatory clause see GKC §147c.
f. Literally "Restrain your foot from (being) barefoot." For this compressed construction cf. GKC §119x with reference to 1 Sam 15:23, 26.
g. Against the MT punctuation, the translation takes these nouns with v. 27 as the subject of the verb. See the commentary.
h. The repetition of second singular suffixes suggests six cola, with the suffix at or near the end of each colon (Cloete, *Versification*, 144).
i. For LXX see Janzen, *Studies*, 85–86; cf. Yohanan A. P. Goldman, "Crispations théologiques et accidents textuels dans le TM de Jérémie 2," *Bib* 76 (1995): 25–52, esp. 42–47.
j. Similarly NAB and NJB; the other EVV interpret on the lines of teaching "wicked women." See McKane 1:53.
k. MT *ʾebyônîm*, "poor," is not represented in LXX and seems superfluous. Did it originate in a marginal exegetical note that compared 5:28 and found a similar forensic setting here? Then the trigger was *rāʿôt*, "bad deeds," in v. 33, which caused recollection of *dibrê raʿ* in the same sense at 5:28.
l. This is a feasible way of understanding the enigmatic phrase, taking it with v. 35; most EVV so interpret. Then the following *wāw* is one of apodosis (cf. Joüon §176). See the discussion of Dominique Barthélemy, *Critique textuelle de l'Ancien Testament*, vol. 2: *Isaïe, Jérémie, Lamentations* (OBO 50/2; Fribourg: Éditions Universitaires; Göttingen: Vandenhoeck & Ruprecht, 1986), 474–75.
m. See *BHS* and most EVV. NIV retains the pointing of MT, while NRSV "lightly you gad about" strangely combines both options.

The second composition which follows the pattern of vv. 5–19, is a literary oracle of disaster, one that offers a series of reasons for it. Verse 35b bluntly

Coming Disaster and Its Causes

announces divine punishment, with its results spelled out in vv. 36–37. Just as vv. 14–15 referred to the results of past punishment, so vv. 26, 30, and 36 refer to previous divine intervention and its results. Yet once more the structural focus is on reasons for coming disaster. There are a number of other reinforcing parallels between vv. 4–19 and 20–37, which will be noted as they occur. Nonetheless, vv. 23–25 possess their own form-critical status as a disputation, with the elements of a basic thesis that is queried in the quotation opening v. 23, a dispute of the thesis, and a final counterthesis in the new quotation that closes v. 25.[11] In its literary context the disputation has the subordinate role of contributing to a series of reasons for disaster. Three other units, vv. 26–28, 29–32, and 33–37, follow the disputation.

[20–25] Perhaps a pair of units should be envisioned, vv. 20–22 with their lively shifts from metaphor to metaphor and vv. 23–25 with their more consistent imagery. Both use second feminine singular pronouns and verbs, and the final quotation formula in v. 22 now functions only as a section divider. The first section addresses ancient religious apostasy, while the second deals with its contemporary manifestation, somewhat like vv. 5–9.

[20] The initial *kî* ("For," NJPS) unite vv. 20–37 with vv. 5–19, the latter verses elaborating the former ones. As in vv. 5–7, the new collection of prophetic pieces begins with ancient history. Its combination with the contemporizing "you," which traces a continuous line between past and present, indicates the seriousness of the charge leveled against the present generation. No first-time offenders here! Israel is depicted as a plow animal that refused to work for the plowman and defiantly broke its yoke and harness. The imagery of the farmer and the working farm animal functions as a covenant metaphor. Putting interpretive words into Israel's mouth is a mark of these combined sections, appearing also in vv. 23 and 25. It enables underlying attitudes to be made explicit, rather than purporting to give actual quotations.[12]

The second half of the verse moves from farm to family to illustrate a broken covenant (cf. Isa 1:2b–3). In tones reminiscent of v. 7 but now registering distaste in sexual rather than religious terms, rural shrines devoted to Canaanite worship are pictured as the rendezvous for illicit sex (cf. Deut 12:2; 1 Kgs 14:23; 2 Kgs 16:4). The metaphor is simply one of unfaithfulness to Yahweh,

---

11. For the elements of a disputation see Murray, "Rhetoric of Disputation," 95–121. Westermann, *Basic Forms*, 201, also cites vv. 29–30 and 34–35 as disputations, but the label is not so obvious in those cases. Werner H. Schmidt, "'Kann ich nicht mit euch verfahren wie dieser Töpfer?' Disputationsworte im Jeremiabuch," in *Nachdenken über Israel: Bibel und Theologie. Festschrift für Klaus-Dietrich Schunck zu seinem 65. Geburtstag* (ed. H. M. Niemann et al.; BEATAJ 37; Frankfurt am Main: Peter Lang, 1994), 149–61, defines the genre essentially in terms of provocative questions.

12. Cf. Thomas W. Overholt, "Jeremiah 2 and the Problem of 'Audience Reaction,'" *CBQ* 41 (1979): 262–73.

rather than reflecting Canaanite orgiastic rites of sexual prostitution, for which there is no evidence.[13] It is a flagrant metaphor Jeremiah borrowed once more from Hosea (cf. Hos 4:12–13), deliberately offensive in order to represent the passion of God's wounded love.

[21] Another reminder of v. 7 is provided by the reference to Israel's degeneration in the land. There is also a similar sense of outrage in the changing of gods at v. 11, though the Hebrew verbs are different. Appeal is made to Yahweh's initial work of planting Israel in the land (cf. Exod 15:17) in order to accentuate the contrast. Where was that high quality vine with its promise of luscious red grapes? In its place stood a grossly inferior product! Isaiah's indignant parable of the vineyard and its disappointing crop of wild grapes (Isa 5:1–4) may lie in the background.

[22] The new metaphor of trying to wash out an indelible stain offers another link with Isaiah, recalling Isa 1:15–16, 18. Here, however, the damned spot is left not by social apathy but by the adoption of Canaanite worship. The metaphor summarizes the ingrained and widespread nature of the community's failure (v. 20) and its radical change for the worse (v. 21).

[23–25] Commitment to a non-Yahwistic faith begins and ends this poem which repeats the motif of following the wrong gods.

[23] The denial put in the community's mouth is a rhetorical ploy that permits an indignant challenge. Self-defilement here has the nuance of sexual unfaithfulness, which picks up the second metaphor in v. 20.[14] The call for Judah to "consider" and "realize" the seriousness of its behavior reinforces the appeal in v. 19. The pluralization of Baal, already encountered through wordplay and metaphor in vv. 8 and 13, over against the references to Baal elsewhere, refers to local representations of the deity at different shrines. "Conduct in the valley" seems to refer generalizingly to non-Yahwistic practices in Ben Hinnom Valley, to which LXX alludes by rendering "cemetery" as in 19:6. The valley is associated with child sacrifice to the god Molech (7:31), but one may compare 19:5 and 32:35, which link Baal and Molech to this rite. The metaphor of the young camel reflects Judah's religious commitments as unstable.[15]

[24–25] The second animal metaphor bears a sexual import. It develops the camel's aimless chasing around into a fuller image of the sniffing of the female

---

13. See Wolfgang Herrmann, "Baal," *DDD* 249–63, esp. 254–55, 262; Judith M. Hadley, "Baal," *NIDOTTE*, 4:422, 426; Sabine van den Eynde, "Taking Broken Cisterns for the Fountain of Living Waters: On the Background of the Metaphor of the Whore in Jeremiah," *BN* 110 (2001): 86–96.

14. Arnold B. Ehrlich, *Randglossen zur hebräischen Bibel: Textkritisches, sprachliches und Sachliches*, vol. 4: *Jesaja, Jeremia* (Leipzig: Hinrichs, 1912), 239, citing Num 5:13, 14, 20; Hos 5:3; 6:10; BDB 379a.

15. See Kenneth E. Bailey and William L. Holladay, "The 'Young Camel' and 'Wild Ass' in Jer. ii 23–25," *VT* 18 (1968): 256–60.

Coming Disaster and Its Causes 49

ass in heat to pick up a male scent and track it down. The scathing application to a human search that is ready to wear out sandals and endure thirst uncovers a passionate obsession. In v. 21 Israel had been described as a foreign vine; now that reference is elucidated in terms of a fatal attraction to non-Yahwistic religion, putting faith in "aliens." That truth is admitted in v. 25b.

[26–28] A new unit combines charges of idolatrous worship with mention of bad times for which such worship provided no help. As in vv. 5, 8, and 11, the test of faith is a pragmatic one. Third plural references in vv. 26 and 27b give way to second masculine singular ones in the direct address of v. 28, for which the first singular pronouns in the quotation at v. 27a prepare. At beginning and end, the pervasiveness of the aberrant faith is presented, in terms of leaders (cf. v. 8) and towns.

[26–27a] The simile of the thief caught red-handed aptly sums up Judah's frustration in a reprehensible context. Its frustration in reaction to crisis will be made clear later in the piece, but the context is plainly and ironically described (vv. 26b–27) as rejection of Yahweh in favor of material objects that are credited with divine significance. Fatherhood and motherhood have covenantal associations (cf. Deut 32:6, 18). The wood and stone are not further defined; a context of blatant Canaanite worship seems to be implied. The comprehensive list, as in 44:17, shows that even community leaders had endorsed this aberration.

[27b–28] When life turned stormy, it was a different matter. The community was forced to switch back to praying for Yahweh's help (the Hebrew imperatives are singular). The question "Where?" no longer reflects the plea in communal laments, as it had in vv. 6 and 8. It reflects another part of the lament, citation of the scorn expressed by enemies when divine help was not forthcoming (cf. Pss 42:3 [4]; 79:10). "Gods" are satirically qualified by "those you made for yourself," in line with the negative qualification in v. 11. These fair-weather friends had no influence on the real world, with which only Yahweh could cope. The urban pervasiveness in v. 28 matches the rural range of v. 20.

[29–32] Further charges of apostasy are made against the community. Vehemence is expressed by total involvement ("all") at the outset, long duration at the end, and bewildered questions throughout. This piece is demarcated by its use of direct second masculine plural references in vv. 29–30 (and also in the aside in v. 31) and of indirect third plural ones with "my people" as subject in vv. 31–32.

[29–30] As in v. 5, hypothetical blame is laid at Yahweh's door, only to give way to countercharges that expose the truth. Rebellion, as in v. 8, is the challenge of divine authority over the community; it is shown in passive unwillingness to take seriously God's earlier providential action against its members ("children") and in active—though not further specified—persecution of the prophetic messengers God had sent them.

[31–32] The initial prose appeal is a redactional call to hearers of the text to search their own hearts for traces of this repudiation of divine authority.[16] The Hebrew imperative hints that the call is meant to relate to vv. 29–30 with their second person content. The verb "consider" is borrowed from earlier appeals in the text (vv. 10, 19, and 23), which suggests that for the redactor those appeals too should find listening ears whenever the text is read.

The possibility of blaming God, broached in v. 29, is explored further by means of the interrogative made present in v. 14. Blatantly wrong answers are suggested and implicitly dismissed as irrelevant. Readers can think back to the dangerous wilderness of v. 6, where Yahweh's care was its antithesis. There was no reason for Israel's attitude of striking out on its own and worshiping elsewhere. Its long history of forgetting Yahweh was as unnatural as a woman forgetting what she wore on her wedding day. The double "my people" conveys the same sense of poignant regret as in vv. 11 and 13, while the wedding comparison gains added insight from the introductory v. 2, which cited historical memories of the relationship with Yahweh that Israel had forgotten.

[33–37] This final unit is marked in Hebrew by second feminine singular references, unlike vv. 29–32. It makes political charges, like the closing piece in vv. 14–19. The political factor is explicit in v. 36; it is doubtless implied by the "love" of v. 33, as in 4:30, where Judah's allies are called lovers. The unit falls into two parallel sections, vv. 33–35 and 36–37, each introduced by a protesting "How!" in a charge relating to Israel's "course" and continuing with a double "Yes" (Lundbom 1:294).

[33–35] The sarcasm of "well" is shown by the ensuing "bad deeds," which are explained in terms of international alliance. Is the reference to the killing of Judean collaborators with Assyria, when the political tide had turned?[17] Judah is blamed for executions that did not fall within the guidelines for justifiable homicide. By way of definition, an ancient legal tradition that also appears in Exod 22:2 (1) is cited, about killing a nocturnal burglar with impunity. The politically motivated offense was compounded by a shoulder-shrugging lack of moral and spiritual concern. Providential judgment at Yahweh's hand was inevitable.

[36–37] The gist of vv. 33–35 is repeated with more political information. The complacency of v. 35 reappears in a switch of international treaty making, which earlier was the theme of v. 18. Already early in Josiah's reign, Assyria's weakness was evident, but Egypt was to bring no less disillusionment. The gesture of putting hands on or to one's head occurs elsewhere only in 2 Sam 13:19,

---

16. Barthélemy, *Critique textuelle*, 2:473–74; A. R. Pete Diamond and Kathleen M. O'Connor, "Unfaithful Passions: Coding Women Coding Men in Jeremiah 2–3 (4:2)," *BibInt* 4 (1996): 288–310, esp. 301.

17. Rainer Albertz, "Jer 2–6 und die Frühzeitverkündigung Jeremias," *ZAW* 94 (1982): 20–47, esp. 39 n. 64.

Coming Disaster and Its Causes 51

where it is associated with humiliation, as is the case here. Does it refer to putting one's hands over the face? Judah had not reckoned with Yahweh, its first and best ally, and with Yahweh's ultimate power of reprisal for Judah's misplaced trust in human allies (cf. Ps 118:8–9; Isa 31:1).

Verses 20–37 contain a second barrage of shocking charges against Judah, again mainly religious but also political, which made divine reprisal inevitable. This literary compilation reinforces that of vv. 4–19, passionately affirming how Judah had given up its exclusive commitment to Yahweh despite the grace it had received. Its accountability could not be evaded.

3:1–18 Coming Back: A Distant Prospect

3:1 . . . saying as follows:[a]

"If a man divorces his wife
    and she leaves his home
    and gets married to another man,
        can he resume relations with her[b] once more?
Gross pollution would befall
    that country, wouldn't it?
In your case, you have had love affairs with many paramours,
    so you cannot come back to me, can you?"
declared Yahweh.

2 "Look up to the bare places[c]
    and try to see where you have not been raped.[d]
At the roadsides you have sat waiting for them
    like a nomad in the wilderness.
You have polluted the country
    with your love affairs, your bad behavior.

3 So the heavy showers were held back,
    the spring rain did not come.
Yet you had the brazen face of a professional[e] prostitute,
    refusing to show remorse.

4 Indeed,[f] you have started to call to me, 'My father,
    the companion of my youth, is who you are,'

5 thinking, 'He will not retain his anger forever,
    keep it up perpetually, will he?'
Look, you have talked,
    but done as much bad as you could."

6 Yahweh said to me during King Josiah's reign: "Just look at what Backslider, Israel, did! She was going up every high mountain and beneath

every leafy tree and there she had love affairs. 7 I thought she would come back to me after she had done all this, but she did not. Faithless, *her sister* Judah, took note 8 and saw[g] that I divorced Backslider, Israel, on the grounds of adultery and gave her certificate of severed relations to her. However, Faithless, Judah *her sister*, was not afraid, but went off and had love affairs herself. 9 Because her love affairs came so easy to her, she polluted[h] the country and committed adultery with stone and wood. 10 Furthermore, in spite of all this, Faithless, *her sister* Judah, has not come back to me wholeheartedly, but only in pretense," *declared Yahweh*. 11 Yahweh said to me, "*Backslider*, Israel, has shown herself more in the right than Faithless, Judah. 12 Go and announce this message to the north, saying,

'Come back, Backslider,[i] Israel,'
declared Yahweh.
'I will not frown at you,
because I am loyal,'
declared Yahweh,
'and I will not retain my anger forever.
13 Just realize your guilt,
that against Yahweh your God have you rebelled—
you lavished your desires[j] on the aliens
under every leafy tree
and me you would not obey,'[k]
declared Yahweh."

14 "Come back, backsliding children,"
declared Yahweh,
"because I am your baal.
Then I will take you,
one from a city and two from a clan district,
and bring you to Zion.

15 "I will provide you with shepherd-kings who are likeminded with me, and they will shepherd you with knowledge and understanding. 16 When you multiply and are fruitful in the country, in those days," declared Yahweh, "people will mention no more the ark of Yahweh's covenant. It will not cross their minds, it will not be remembered. They will not miss it and it will not be remade. 17 At that time they will call Jerusalem Yahweh's throne and all the nations will gather to it in honor of Yahweh's name at Jerusalem.[l] People[m] will follow no more the stubborn inclination of their own bad attitude. 18 In those days Judah's community will accompany

Israel's community and together they will come from a north country to the country I let your forebears possess."

a. A relic of an introductory formula survives in MT, as in LXX at 2:1 (cf. NJPS, GNB). Its absence from LXX may indicate subsequent deletion.

b. The verbal phrase appears to be a development of *bô' 'el*, "come to," with the sense of engaging in sexual intercourse, and refers to its resumption.

c. The meaning of *šĕpayim* is not certain: see the discussions in *HALOT* 4:1628 and William McKane, "*špy(y)m* with Special Reference to the Book of Jeremiah," in *Mélanges bibliques et orientaux en l'honneur de M. Henry Cazelles* (ed. A. Caquot and M. Delcor; AOAT 212; Kevelaer: Butzon & Bercker; Neukirchen-Vluyn: Neukirchener Verlag, 1981), 319–35.

d. For the colon division and syntax, Cloete, *Versification*, 144–45, compares 2:10.

e. Cf. the vocational use of *'îš*, "man" (*HALOT* 1:43b).

f. For the exclamatory force see Joüon §161c; for that in v. 6 see §161b.

g. See *BHS*. The reading of MT and LXX suffered assimilation to the first verb in v. 7 (Holladay 1:58). EVV, except NIV and NJPS, emend MT.

h. See *BHS* for the repointing, which aligns with v. 2; EVV change. MT "she became polluted together with the country" seems to have v. 1 in view, but the text at this point is restating v. 2. Barthélemy, *Critique textuelle*, 2:481–82, takes the clause as a gloss, noting that LXX omits it, and so does Janzen, *Studies*, 37; however, the omission may simply be a case of parablepsis.

i. In Holladay's interpretation, "Turn a turning, Israel," *mĕšûbâ* functions as a cognate accusative with an emphatic force (1:59; cf. GKC §117p-q), a construction that has been misunderstood in vv. 6–11. But this ignores the fact that elsewhere in Jeremiah and in the OT the abstract noun is used in a negative sense. Somewhat strangely the abstract term is used in a concrete sense.

j. Literally "ways," here in the sense of sexual impulses. Ehrlich, *Randglossen*, 4:239, 245, compares Prov 30:19.

k. The plural verb in MT, a more blatant phenomenon than the Hebrew plural pronoun in the phrase "at you" in v. 12, is a redactional technique to integrate it with the next section. Cf. the third plural in a second plural context at Isa 1:29 and the opposite at Isa 61:7; and cf. GKC §144p. Similar phenomena will occur at Jer 5:14, 19; 13:20; 49:30 K.

l. "In . . . Jerusalem" is missing from LXX here, but turns up at 4:2 in the form "to God in Jerusalem" (*HUB*).

m. Since the following nominal phrase is used only of Israel in Jeremiah, the plural verb is presumably indefinite, like those in v. 16 and at the start of v. 17; "the nations" is not the subject. The repetition of "no more" from v. 16 favors this interpretation.

The next two compositions, 3:1–18 and 3:19–4:4, are governed at strategic points by the key word *šûb* meaning "come back" to Yahweh (3:1b, 7, 10, 12, 14, 22; 4:1a*b*; cf. 3:1a) and meaning "turn back" in repentance at 4:1a*a*. They tellingly couple that key word with hypocritical claims that rob it of reality (3:3b–5, 10, 22b–25). The need to come back is grounded in another use of *šûb* meaning "turn back" from Yahweh (3:19), which also appears in the forms *mĕšûbâ*, "Backslider" (3:6, 8, 12; also v. 11 in MT), *šôbābîm*, "backsliding" (3:1, 4, 22), and *mĕšûbōt*, "backsliding ways" (3:22). The double use of the root develops the negative tone of the two previous compositions.

The first composition falls into three units, vv. 1–5, 6–13, and 14–18.[18] It contrasts a polluted, barren country (vv. 1b–3a, 10) with one ultimately fertile with people (v. 16).

[3:1–5] The possibility of coming back to Yahweh is ruled out as a current option on grounds of past tradition and present insincerity. The unit takes the form of a disputation.[19] A provocative counterthesis in v. 1 is defended by a dispute in vv. 2–3; then a citation of Judah's own thesis in vv. 4–5a receives a disputatious coup de grace in v. 5b.

[1] A legal parallel is used to reinforce the argument. The ruling appears in Deut 24:1–4, forbidding remarriage of a divorced couple if the ex-wife had herself remarried and that marriage was terminated. The law is doubtless very old since it seems to be presupposed in Hos 2:7 (9).[20] The use of *hēn*, "if," is modeled on legal disputes (Exod 8:26 [22]; Lev 10:18, 19; 25:20).[21] In Num 35:33–34 the notion of a single offense polluting the whole land refers to a homicide (cf. Deut 24:4).[22] The vehemence of the second question presupposes the claim (v. 2) that Judah's apostasy had already polluted the land. A further step of resuming the earlier relationship would aggravate the problem, not solve it. Reference to this complication in the legal parallel rather than in the real case under discussion gives it the rhetorical force of objectivity. The religiously applied metaphor of sexual unfaithfulness already used in ch. 2 is now developed further. The worship of "Baals" (2:28) at local shrines throughout the country in both rural and urban settings (2:20, 28) represented promiscuity and so a worse case than the legal parallel. The parallel is a loose one in that prior divorce had not been arranged by Judah's divine partner. One could improve the parallelism by regarding sexual intercourse as itself creating a marriage-like bonding, as Paul argued in 1 Cor 6:16. The verb *znh* and its noun, rendered "(have) love affairs," had been used by Hosea (e.g., Hos 1:2; 6:10). Their use clears the way for *zōnâ*, "prostitute"—already used in Jer 2:20—in v. 3 to heighten the symbolism.

---

18. Mary E. Shields, *Circumscribing the Prostitute: The Rhetorics of Intertextuality, Metaphor and Gender in Jeremiah 3.1–4.4* (JSOTSup 387; London: T & T Clark International, 2004), 18, also divides 3:1–4:4 into 3:1–18 and 3:19–4:4 and subdivides the first half as here.

19. Cf. Burke O. Long, "The Stylistic Components of Jeremiah 3:1–5," *ZAW* 88 (1976): 386–90, esp. 387–88. Westermann, *Basic Forms*, 201, so labels it.

20. Holladay 1:112, citing Hans W. Wolff, *Hosea* (trans. G. Stansell; Hermeneia; Philadelphia: Fortress, 1974), 36. Schulz-Rauch, *Hosea und Jeremia*, 177–78, claims the ruling underlies Hos 3:1. It is often urged that *šûb*, "come back," with the husband as subject, reflects the same verb in Deut 24:4, but there it has an auxiliary force, "again."

21. Long, "Stylistic Components," 388–89.

22. James D. Martin, "The Forensic Background to Jeremiah iii 1," *VT* 19 (1969): 82–92, esp. 84.

Coming Disaster and Its Causes

[2–3a] The seventh colon in v. 1 is developed with reference to worship at shrines in the open country. The crudity of "raped" labels the new relationship(s) as devoid of true gratification and not worth comparing with the covenant relationship between Yahweh and Israel. The simile of the nomad selling his wares to travelers presupposes a prostitute touting for trade and anticipates the reference to prostitution in v. 3b (cf. Gen 38:14; Prov 7:12). The charge of land pollution is defended by evidence of a ruinous drought in the late winter, when copious rain normally permitted the early summer crops to grow.

[3b–5] The notion of prostitution is given a twist by referring to its related attitude of defying convention (cf. Prov 7:13). Describing Judah's optimistic statement in this way discredits it, as does its being termed a recent phenomenon, presumably a response to the drought. The thesis makes an appeal to the covenant bond in terms of long-lasting father-daughter/husband-wife relationships. That bonding, belatedly recognized, and Yahweh's predisposition to forgiveness are not enough. The reason given in v. 5b for dismissing the thesis as insincere picks up from v. 2 the charges of bad behavior and of the pervasiveness of the wrong worship, which was the form the bad behavior took.[23] The argument has shown the covenant community to be locked into inescapable charges of religious unfaithfulness. It must squarely take the blame and cannot talk its way out of it by misapplied theology.

[6–13] This complex unit reinforces the impossibility of Judah's restoration to a covenant relationship by contrasting it with the northern kingdom and providing a measure of its deterioration. It is important to recognize in vv. 6 and 11 the technique of repetitive resumption, which marks the insertion of a self-contained unit into another literary context.[24] The introduction to v. 6 originally stood in place of the briefer, resumptive one at v. 11; it prefaces a small group of oracles, vv. 12–13 and 14, addressed to nondeported members of the former northern kingdom. The oracles align with early material in chs. 30–31, in which a positive appeal is made to this constituency. The collection is prefaced with a brief comparative statement in prose at v. 11, which fits with the sentiments—though they are politically and not religiously applied—expressed in Ezek 16:43b–58, a postexilic text. Ezekiel often took up material from earlier prophets, including Jeremiah, and developed them in his own way and at greater length. The narrative introduction to the northern oracles, now in v. 6 and resumed in v. 11, has a format also employed in the commissioning narratives (1:7, 9, 12, and 14).

---

23. The equivalence is facilitated by wordplay between *rēʿîm*, "paramours" (v. 1), and *rāʿâ*, "bad (behavior)" (vv. 2, 5) (Walter Brueggemann, "Israel's Sense of Place in Jeremiah," in *Rhetorical Criticism: Essays in Honor of James Muilenburg* [ed. J. J. Jackson and M. Kessler; PTMS 1; Pittsburgh: Pickwick, 1974], 149–65, esp. 155).

24. Cf. Shemaryahu Talmon, "Ezra and Nehemiah," *IDBSup* 317–28, esp. 322, with reference to those books; Moshé Anbar, "La 'reprise,'" *VT* 38 (1988): 385–98.

[6–10] A prose redactional expansion elaborates the negative comparison of v. 11.[25] "Her sister" in vv. 7, 8, and 10, lacking in LXX, is a still later redactional addition not from Ezekiel 16 or 23:32–34, where the sisters are Jerusalem and Samaria, but from associating 23:2–27, where the sisters signify Judah and Israel,[26] with 16:15–22, where Jerusalem's turning to Canaanite religion is condemned. In v. 8 "and saw" probably derives from Ezek 23:11. Language from Deut 24:1–4 is also present. Most of the explanatory expansion leans heavily not only on the basic v. 11 below but also on preceding material about Judah, which in part it applies to the northern kingdom. Israel is personified as a woman, like Judah in vv. 1–5. What she did matched what Judah had done (v. 5). Specifically Judah's "love affairs" were replicated at Israel's own rural shrines (cf. 2:20; 3:2). The downfall and mass deportation of Israel was evidence of divorce, God's final break in the covenant relationship. The ground for the divorce was adultery, a formal term new to the context; it is used as religious metaphor, as in 13:27.

The reaction of Judah, the second of two wives, was not to appreciate Yahweh's disappointment at Israel's failure to return to an exclusive relationship, but to deliberately and defiantly engage in love affairs (vv. 1–2), land-polluting activity (v. 2), and idolatry (2:27). Her own religious aberration is now branded with the stronger term "adultery." Such aberration takes on a more reprehensible character when set against the background of the fall of the northern kingdom, which is understood in terms of moral providence. Nor was this Judah's only fault. The shallow claim of v. 4 plus persistence in her bad old ways meant that she aggravated her guilt by insincerity, only pretending to come back, even after theological history had taught the consequences of religious infidelity. By comparison Israel's behavior, so black when viewed by itself, looked merely gray.

[11–13] A brief explanatory statement of the situation precedes the command to prophesy. For the adverse comparison 23:13–14 may be compared; it is echoed in Ezek 16:51. The label "Backslider" anticipates v. 12, while Judah's nickname "Faithless" matches a verb used later (v. 20). The incorporation of this northern material was presumably encouraged by this match, as well as by the identity of the opening appeals (vv. 14 and 22). The invitation to return, earlier denied to Judah, here serves as a snub that reinforces Judah's guilt. Underlying the invitation may have been Hos 14:1 (2), "Return, O Israel," addressed to the northern kingdom. The oracle is a summons to repentance, with a double structure of first exhortation and promise, then exhortation and accusation.[27]

---

25. Stulman, *Prose Sermons*, 132, found in the wording of 3:6–13 common to MT and LXX 12 percent of the range of stereotyped vocabulary used in the prose sermons, compared with 33 percent in both 7:1–8:3 and 11:1–14.

26. The reference in Ezek 23:4 is widely recognized as a gloss. See Leslie C. Allen, *Ezekiel 20–48* (WBC 29; Dallas: Word, 1990), 43.

27. Thomas M. Raitt, "The Prophetic Summons to Repentance," *ZAW* 83 (1971): 30–49, esp. 35.

Framed by opening and closing quotation formulas, it ironically promises what Judah had presumed in v. 5: Yahweh's basic commitment to the covenant relationship. What makes all the difference is the accompanying call to true repentance (cf. 2:8, 29). Rebellion against the covenantal ("your") God by engaging in non-Yahwistic rites amounted to rank disobedience (for "aliens" see 2:25).

[14–18] Whereas vv. 6–13 have an overall negative function, this mainly prose unit flashes forward to a positive future. The initial call to repentance in v. 14 originally belonged with the basic material in vv. 6 and 11–13 as a second oracle addressed to the northern kingdom. It has been dovetailed into a proclamation of salvation in vv. 15–18. Representatives of the northern kingdom are still ostensibly in view in vv. 15–16, as v. 18 confirms with its explicit change of subject to "Judah's community." However, a broadening of perspective emerges in the course of v. 16 and in v. 17, and the restoration of Judah from exile is presupposed; v. 18 belatedly recognizes this development. The parallel synchronisms "in those days" at vv. 16 and 18 are pointers to redaction,[28] but the general theme of postexilic restoration set out in vv. 16–18 already appears in v. 15. So vv. 15–18 give the impression of being redactional, not least because of their violent jump to a new kind of topic. The expansion carries its own prophetic authority, conveyed by the quotation formula in v. 16. It impatiently embraces the larger agenda of the book, to uproot *and* to plant (1:10), and reminds readers of the essential blessings that would accrue to God's people. What triggered this jump is the allusion to northern exile in v. 8. It created a hermeneutical desire to engage with both that and Judean exile and with the hope for return and for a better future that might reverse Judah's accursed past. However, it also implies that such a hope does not bypass deserved punishment. Jeremiah's postjudgment message of hope for the northern kingdom is extended to a similar message for Judah.

[14] The northerners' worship in Zion is reminiscent of 31:6, 12, while their paucity reflects postdeportation conditions in the north. The motivation echoes the problem of religious aberration adduced earlier in oracles to Judah, but innovatively clarifies who the true *baʿal* is. In a double entendre, the rival Baal is discredited and Yahweh's covenant role as "husband" (NIV) is reaffirmed.

[15] The horizon of thought now widens considerably, with a postexilic renewal of monarchy that uses the promise of shepherd-kings and efficient government in 23:4–5 as an assurance, thus reversing Judah's wretched preexilic experience. It reflects a desire to counter 2:8.

[16–17] Attention flickers back to the northern attenuation (v. 14b), which is remedied in the prolific growth of God's postexilic flock in 23:3. A new topic,

---

28. Simon J. De Vries, *From Old Revelation to New: A Tradition-Historical and Redaction-Critical Study of Temporal Traditions in Prophetic Prediction* (Grand Rapids: Eerdmans, 1995), 68, 141–42.

the restoration of postexilic worship, is now generated by "Zion." A religious loss is adroitly turned into a theological gain. The ark that in preexilic times resided inside the holy of holies as a sign of Yahweh's presence disappeared, presumably in connection with the defeat of Jerusalem in 597 or 587. The "ark of the covenant of the LORD of hosts, who is enthroned on the cherubim" (1 Sam 4:4; cf. 2 Sam 6:2), represented the throne on which Yahweh invisibly sat, and in earlier times its loss had to be made good by David before Solomon's temple could be built to house it. Its loss must have caused great grief during the exile. However, the eschatological tradition of a new and glorious Jerusalem, a positive magnet for the nations (cf. Isa 2:2–4; Mic 4:1–4), would mean that Yahweh's ark-linked presence was released to pervade the city. In Rev 21:22–25, in a development of this motif, the new Jerusalem to which the nations come has no need of a material temple. The final negative statement, which lacks any positive development, is also triggered by prior material, the end of v. 13, "and me you would not obey." The stubborn attitude of v. 17b is closely associated with disobedience elsewhere in the book (7:24; 9:12–13 [13–14]; 11:8; 13:10; 16:12). Reversal of such disobedience-related willfulness fittingly marks the new era.

[18] Judah's return from exile has been implicitly presupposed in vv. 15b–17 as a parallel to Israel's, but now it is explicitly declared, thus preparing for the resumption of an address to Judah (v. 19). The "north country" anticipates the threat of the foe from the north that will pervade 4:5–6:30 and will lead to exile there (23:8). Threat is transcended by a prospect of repossessing the land, something in line with Yahweh's desire that will be expressed in v. 19. The motif of return from exile suggests that already in v. 14 the call "Come back" in its present setting has been reinterpreted with a territorial as well as a spiritual force, so that the oracle of vv. 14–18 is framed by return from exile. The oracle is a literary celebration, looking beyond the gathering clouds of disaster and assuring exiled Judeans that their banishment was the prelude to glorious restoration. The recourse to contextually based reversals is reminiscent of Amos 9:11–15, which gives negative motifs used earlier in the book a positive reversal.

3:19–4:4 Coming Back: An Empty Claim

19 "For my part, how much I wanted
    to treat you as family
and to give you a desirable country,
    a possession more glorious than any other nation has!
I thought you would call me 'my father'
    and would never turn back from following me.
20 However,[a] just as[b] a woman can be faithless for her paramour's sake,[c]
    so you have faithlessly let me down, Israel's community"
declared Yahweh.

Coming Disaster and Its Causes

21 Hark! On the bare places can be heard
    the pleading sobs of Israel's children,
  because they have gone off course,
    forgetting Yahweh their God.
22 "Come back, backsliding children.
    I will cure you of your backsliding ways."
  "Here we are, coming to you,
    because you, Yahweh, are our God.[d]
23 In fact the hills have proved to be a delusion,
    the mountains a rabble.[e]
  In fact in Yahweh our God
    lies Israel's salvation,
24 whereas that shameful god has eaten
    the fruit of our forebears' labors since our youth—
  their flocks and herds,
    their sons and daughters.
25 Let us lie down in our shame,
    let our disgrace cover us,
  because against Yahweh our God have we sinned,
    both we and our forebears,
  from our youth up to the present day,
  and we have not obeyed
    Yahweh our God."

4:1 "If you turn back, Israel,"
  declared Yahweh,
    "to me you may come back.[f]
  And if you remove your detestable gods from my presence
    and never wander away,
2 but swear 'By Yahweh's life'[g]
    honestly, justly, and fairly,
  then nations will win blessing from him[h]
    and proudly give him their praise."
3 In fact here is what Yahweh said to the Judeans and to Jerusalem:
  "Plow up your fallow ground
    instead of sowing among thorns.
4 Circumcise yourselves in commitment to Yahweh,
    removing the foreskins over your hearts,
    you Judeans and you residents of Jerusalem—
  or else my fury will flare up like fire
    and burn out of control
    in reaction to your bad activities."

a. For the idiomatic usage see BDB 38b.

b. For the Hebrew juxtaposition see GKC §161b.

c. As in v. 1, *rēaʿ* refers to a paramour, rather than "husband" (NRSV, NIV).

d. NJPS so renders against the accentuation of MT, which regards the divine name as predicative.

e. The earlier *lāmed* does double duty to indicate result. The first colon is problematic. Godfrey R. Driver, "Linguistic and Textual Problems: Jeremiah," *JQR* 28 (1937–38): 97–129, esp. 99, suggested that the noun *migbāʿâ* has a primary sense of "peaked height" as well as a secondary one of "peaked cap."

f. The syntax of the eight cola of vv. 1–2 is not clear; see the table of six options in Holladay 1:126–27. The translation substantially aligns with NIV.

g. Thus REB. For the nominal function of *hay* see *HALOT* 1:307b–8a; Moshe Greenberg, "The Hebrew Oath Particle *Hay/Hē*," *JBL* 76 (1957): 34–39.

h. The antecedent appears to be Yahweh, as EVV except REB and NJPS take it. In this verbal phrase Israel is usually the means or agent, but Isa 65:16 provides an exception. In the parallel clause the prepositional phrase with the verb *hithallēl* elsewhere refers only to Yahweh, and so the same is probably true in the first colon (Barthélemy, *Critique textuelle*, 2:485–86). The third person is occasioned by the oath formula. For the indirect reflexive sense of the verb *hitbārēk*, cf. NRSV "gain blessing for themselves" in Gen 22:18 and 26:4, and GKC §54f; *IBHS* 430; Josef Schreiner, "Segen für die Völker in der Verheissung an die Väter," *BZ* 6 (1962): 1–31.

This composition develops the pretense of 3:10 that summed up vv. 3b–5. Preexilic Judah is once more in view, after the digression concerning the northern kingdom and postexilic blessings. A negative attitude toward Judah's coming back to Yahweh is resumed from vv. 1–5. In 3:19–4:2 a dialogue between Yahweh and Israel highlights the difference of their perspectives. It embraces four formal elements: a reason for disaster (vv. 19–20), a summons to repentance (v. 22a), a communal lament (vv. 22b–25), and a further call to repentance (4:1–2), which functions as a conditional oracle of response to a lament. Another call to repentance has been appended in 4:3–4. It refers to Judah and Jerusalem, that is, the people gathered for worship (cf. 2 Chr 20:15), providing an interpretive key for "Israel" earlier. There are three units, 3:19–20, 21–25, and 4:1–4.[29]

[19–20] The charge of infidelity in v. 20 is accentuated by a contrasting motif that serves to express Yahweh's disappointment in the light of earlier plans for Israel. The last two cola of v. 19 allude to fatherhood and marriage, both of which illustrate the covenant relationship (so 2:2; 3:4, 14). The latter metaphor continues in v. 20, while the former image governs the first four cola of v. 19. Family and inheritance belonged together; in turning its back on the relationship Israel was losing the territorial rights that went with it. The promised land was "a land flowing with milk and honey, the most glorious of all lands,"

---

29. Shields, *Circumscribing the Prostitute*, 18, so divides.

Coming Disaster and Its Causes

according to Ezek 20:6, 15 (cf. Deut 8:7–10). It is the first of a number of missed opportunities presented in the passage. There is a contrast with the polluted, accursed land (vv. 2b–3a), while in the light of 12:10 the bleakness of destruction caused by invasion lurks below the surface.

[21–25] After a prophetic introduction that sets the human scene, Yahweh's invitation and Israel's fervent response make up this section. Readers are meant to move on to 4:1–4 and judge the response accordingly. It turns out to be a replay of 3:4–5, talk without the walk to back it up. Judah's professions of repentance could not be taken at their face value.

[21–22a] The recognition of "forgetting Yahweh their God" introduces Israel's own confession set out in vv. 22b–25 and draws attention to the covenant formula that will be echoed four times in Israel's speech. But first a call to repentance is combined with a promise of forgiveness that would heal the breach caused by their apostasy (cf. Hos 14:4 [5]) and give them a fresh start.

[22b–25] The response is word perfect. Long-standing worship of Baal at the rural shrines is renounced in favor of Yahweh. It had provided no benefits; the pragmatic test of 2:27–28 is now applied by Israel. Baal was unable to deliver the people when times turned bad. In fact Baal—or *bōšet*, "shame," a derogatory term the OT often uses and v. 25 echoes—had proved a liability over generations, with demands for agricultural products as offerings and even for child sacrifice. At this point Baal and Molech are loosely equated, as at 2:23. Mourning rites of prostration are advocated, and the garb of humiliation. A confession of sin and disobedience comes readily to their lips.

[4:1–2] A good start, but was it enough? Yahweh's renewed call to repentance in response both spells out the essence of repentance and motivates it with an incentive. The first conditional sentence plays on different senses of the verb *šûb*, "come back," meaning first to turn from wrongdoing to Yahweh and so repent and then to restore the covenant relationship. The next sentence defines what repentance means, in two ways. First, the Baal cult, identified by the negative cultic term "detestable ones (= gods)" (cf. 13:27; Hos 9:10), was Judah's cardinal sin. It was incompatible with God's presence among the covenant people (cf. Exod 33:14–16), which must be matched by constant exclusiveness on their part. Second, Yahweh ups the ante with a radical demand. Exclusive faith had to be worked out in integrated living. By way of illustration, the common oath formula that invoked Yahweh to confirm the truth of an assertion must be accompanied by sincerity, instead of being used nominally (cf. Zech 8:16–17). The example echoes the empty talking of 3:4–5 and the pretense of 3:10. An external incentive is offered, after the internal incentive of Yahweh's accepting the community back. The ancient tradition of Israel's role as a mediator of divine blessing to the nations (cf. Gen 22:18; 26:4) could then find fulfillment.

[3–4] Another oracle has been appended to 4:1–2 by way of explanation, as the redactional *kî* ("For," NRSV) indicates. It includes its own quotation formula, which identifies the hearers from the information in v. 4. The piece lacks the key word of the foregoing material, *šûb*, "come back," but develops the changes of heart and life advocated in v. 2 and balances the earlier combination of exhortation and promise with one of exhortation and threat.

The agricultural metaphor of using the plow to remove weeds and so ensure a good harvest recalls Hos 10:12. It expresses the need for a fresh start. In the metaphor of circumcision, which also occurs in Deut 10:16, foreskins correspond to the thorns in the earlier image, as a barrier that stands in the way of once more belonging exclusively to Yahweh. Repetition of the verb "remove" suggests that pagan worship constitutes the barrier. The positive implications of the circumcision metaphor are openness to Yahweh's influence and obedience to the divine will.[30] The metaphor harks back to the wholeheartedness lacking in 3:10 and to the shepherd-kings' like-mindedness to Yahweh ("after my own heart," NRSV) in 3:15. Paul would develop the metaphor in Rom 2:29. After the carrots of vv. 1–2 comes a stick to urge compliance. The people's "bad activities"—plain speaking for the thorns and foreskins—would otherwise take their toll, provoking an inevitable backlash of God's vehement intervention, instead of the diminution of anger and displays of loyalty and forgiveness that repentance could have achieved (cf. vv. 5, 12, 22).

There is no positive response; the dialogue peters out. The negativity pervading the sections that toy with Judah's coming back, from 3:1 onward, has already pointed in that direction; 3:14–18 speaks from a postcatastrophe perspective. So this composition presents a series of missed opportunities—a land that enjoys divine blessing, restoration to covenant favor, and the spread of faith in Yahweh to other nations. Instead Judah faced divine reprisal, for which 2:4–4:4 has provided ample reason. The threat of punishment in v. 4b provides an anticipatory summary of the next series of messages in 4:5–6:30.

4:5–18 The Alarm Is Sounded

5 "Make a proclamation in Judah
and in Jerusalem an announcement,[a]
blowing the horn throughout the country.
Shout loudly and say,
'Mobilize yourselves and let us go
into the fortified towns.
6 Set up a marker pointing to Zion,
make for shelter, do not stay behind.'

---

30. Roger Le Déaut, "Le thème de la circoncision du coeur (Dt. xxx 6; Jér. iv 4) dans les versions anciennes (LXX et Targum) et à Qumrân," *Congress Volume: Vienna 1980* (ed. J. A. Emerton; VTSup 32; Leiden: Brill, 1981), 178–205, esp. 183.

The reason is that I am bringing from the north a bad fate,
   an immense calamity.
7 A veritable lion has advanced from its bushes,
   a destroyer of nations has set out,
      leaving his base,
   to make your country a shocking place—
      your towns will be ruined, left uninhabited.
8 For this reason wrap sackcloth around your waists,
      lament and wail,
   'Unaverted is
      Yahweh's *burning* anger from us.'"[b]

9 "What will happen on that day," declared Yahweh, "is that
   the king will lose heart
      and so will the royal officials;
   the priests will be shocked
      and the prophets dumbfounded."

10 "Oh no, Lord Yahweh," I said, "you have undoubtedly deceived this people and Jerusalem with the promise 'Peace will be yours,' while the sword presses against the throat."
   11 At that time it will be said concerning this people and Jerusalem:

"A searing wind from the bare places [is blowing]
   through the wilderness toward my dear people,
      not to winnow or cleanse.
12 A wind too strong for that
      is coming at my behest.
   Now I myself am passing
      judgment on them."
13 Look, like a cloud mass he will advance,
      and like a whirlwind his chariots.
   Faster than eagles will be his horses—
      poor us, we are done for!
14 Wash your heart clean of bad behavior, Jerusalem,
      so you may be saved.
   How much longer will you harbor[c] in your mind
      your evil schemes?

15 "In fact, hark, news is coming from Dan,
      announcement of an evil fate is heard from Ephraim's ridge.

16 Proclaim it to the nations,
    come on,[d] announce it concerning Jerusalem:
    'Besiegers[e] are coming from a distant country,
    raising shouts against Judah's towns.
17 Like guards around an estate
    they surround it.'
    The reason is that it has defied me,"
    declared Yahweh.
18 "Your own conduct, your own practices
    have brought this on you.
    Such is your bad fate—it is bitter indeed,
    reaching your very heart."

a. MT includes *wěʾimĕrû*, "and say," introducing a quotation, which seems to be an inappropriate anticipation of the phrase later in the verse (*BHS*). NAB and REB delete it.

b. The direct speech is introduced by *kî* (cf. BDB 471b–72a; *HALOT* 2:471a). This usage has been denied in principle in a number of studies; contrast the affirmation of Anneli Aejmelaeus, "The Function and Interpretation of *kî* in Biblical Hebrew," *JBL* 105 (1986): 193–209, esp. 208. The switch to a third person reference to Yahweh and to a first person reference to the lamenters corroborates the presence of direct speech. NAB and NRSV take it thus, along with Rudolph 32 and Holladay 1:154. There is another instance in 9:21 (20), as NRSV, REB, and NJB acknowledge.

c. The rendering is dictated by the word order and does not parse *tālîn*, lit. "will lodge," as *Hiphil*, which *HALOT* 2:529 considers an option; a feminine form would then be expected. For the singular verb see GKC §145k.

d. Barthélemy, *Critique textuelle*, 2:480, so takes *hinnēh*, following the MT accentuation and citing Ps 134:1. Cf. the same use of *hēn* before an imperative in Isa 64:9 (8).

e. Thus NAB, NRSV, and similarly NIV. The root *nṣr*, "keep," can evidently have the developed sense "besiege," like the synonym *šmr* in 2 Sam 11:16 (Barthélemy, *Critique textuelle*, 2:486–87).

Jeremiah 4:5–6:30 announces disaster rather than the reasons for it, which dominated 2:4–4:4. When reasons are given, they tend to feature moral issues rather than religious apostasy, a trend anticipated in 4:2a. This group of passages will explore the exposure of an unfaithful Israel to a "bad fate," after 2:3 affirmed, by contrast, the liability of the enemies of a faithful Israel to such a fate. The reader initially finds in 4:5–31 the same jumble of separate units as in ch. 2. The series of vision reports throughout vv. 19–31 suggests a literary composition. As for vv. 5–18, first person divine explanations in vv. 6b (or 6b–7), 11–12, and 17b–18 and human responses advocated in vv. 8 and 14 recur. Such parallelism provides evidence of separate units: vv. 5–8, 9–14, and 15–18. They are bonded by the repetition of *rāʿâ* in the senses of "a bad fate" at vv. 6 and 18 and of "bad behavior" at v. 14, a combination of cause and effect that appeared earlier in 1:14, 16; also *ʾāwen*, "evil/evil fate," hinges units in 4:14–15.

Coming Disaster and Its Causes

[5–8] Repetition of "country" and "towns" in v. 7 ties together the first two sections, vv. 5–6a and 6b–7, and expresses the national import of the coming invasion, while "For this reason" identifies the call for a response in the third section, v. 8, as a necessary consequence.

[5–6a] A dramatic description of the approach of a national enemy runs through vv. 5–31. In form-critical terms it represents an expansion of the announcement of disaster.[31] Here the description takes the form of a summons to flight, ordering the strategic withdrawal of the rural population behind town walls.

[6b–7] There is movement to a metaphysical level with an announcement of divinely backed disaster on a momentous scale. The geographical source of the enemy, "from the north," picks up the divine summons to "all the realms in the north" at 1:15. The tantalizing ambiguity will recur in 6:1, 22, and then in 10:22; 13:20. There is no mention of Babylon until the Pashhur episode of ch. 20. The impression is of a mysterious premonition that can only become specific as history unfolds.[32] Lions signified the Assyrians in 2:15. Here too the term (a different Hebrew word) refers to a national enemy, just as wild animals do in communal laments in the Psalms (e.g., Ps 80:13 [14]). "Jeremiah's description of this foe has been primarily governed by traditional terminology inherited from his prophetic predecessors, and not by the characteristics of a particular historical enemy."[33] Jerusalem ("your" is feminine singular) is bluntly warned that the devastation the enemy is to cause will embrace not only the countryside but even the towns thronged with refugees. Judah's defensive measures will be nullified!

[8] The prophet seeks to anticipate the dire crisis with the garb and speech of ritual lamenting of the dead. The admission that Yahweh's inevitable anger is the force behind the invasion functions as a providential confirmation of v. 6b, while in the larger literary context it counters the optimism of 3:5.

[9] This first section of the complex second unit, vv. 9–14, is a short oracle that defines the consequences as a total inability of Judah's leadership, secular

---

31. Westermann, *Basic Forms*, 186.

32. Hans-Jürgen Hermisson, " 'Der Feind aus den Norden' (Jer 4–6): Zu einem Gedichtzyklus Jeremias," in *Schriftprophetie: Festschrift für Jörg Jeremias zum 65. Geburtstag* (ed. F. Hartenstein et al.; Neukirchen-Vluyn: Neukirchener Verlag, 2004), 233–51, esp. 247. The old explanation of Scythian long-term control of Syria and Palestine with appeal to Herodotus (*Hist.* 1.103–7) is no longer regarded as historically credible or intended by Herodotus; see Richard P. Vaggione, "Over All Asia? The Extent of the Scythian Domination in Herodotus," *JBL* 92 (1973): 523–40; idem, "Scythians," *IDBSup* 797–98. Herodotus does mention a Scythian raid through Syria and Palestine in Psammetichus I's reign, i.e., sometime before 610 B.C.E. Edwin M. Yamauchi, *Foes from the Northern Frontier: Invading Hordes from the Russian Steppe* (Grand Rapids: Baker, 1982), 98–99, has suggested that the raiding Scythians functioned as a mercenary vanguard for the Babylonians. Be that as it may, a raid hardly satisfies the drastic language of the text.

33. Berridge, *Prophet, People*, 81.

and religious, to cope. The oracle is introduced by a connecting temporal formula and a quotation formula.

[10] The explanation of the crisis as divinely caused (vv. 11–12) is prefaced with a prose interjection from the prophet. The introduction to the oracle in v. 11 picks up from v. 10 "this people and Jerusalem" as the addressees. Jeremiah's protest also follows on from the dumbfounding of the prophets at the close of v. 9 since the message of *šālôm*, "peace," was implicitly theirs (cf. 6:14; 14:13). The tension between such a life-threatening crisis and such a prophetic message permitted by—though not derived from—Yahweh (McKane 1:94–95) was too acute to tolerate. Yahweh had failed to correct the claim. The protest anticipates Jeremiah's series of laments, which will begin in ch. 11.

[11–12] Yahweh does not give a direct answer to the protest. Instead a later oracle is placed here, one that like vv. 6b–7 verifies the divine origin of the invasion that was by now taking place. The metaphor of the hot, dry sirocco from the desert replaces that of the lion. The wind's vehemence is brought out by contrasting the breezes used in the winnowing process to separate chaff from grain. Divine anguish is evident in the phrase "my dear people" (lit. "my daughter people"), that the well-deserved punishment of war had to take the place of peace.

[13–14] The call for a response, now directed to Jerusalem, is prefaced by the prophet's description of the enemy that continues the analogy and envisions wind-driven dust clouds (cf. Isa 17:13; Nah 1:3). Use of simile allows the military juggernaut behind the analogy to be exposed. On behalf of his fellow citizens, Jeremiah groans at the prospect. He employs the dire threat as a last-minute motivation for repentance and for commitment to a new lifestyle far different from the "bad behavior" that had triggered the "bad fate" (v. 6). Jeremiah "clings to that thin possibility, but nothing comes of it" (Brueggemann 56). Is the chance of deliverance intended as the prophet's own riposte to his protest, that peace might after all lie within the community's grasp and that, if not, the blame was theirs rather than Yahweh's?[34]

[15–18] The third unit starts like the first with a military announcement, but now one that menacingly concentrates on the enemy and so relates to invasion and siege rather than defense. The initial *kî* (NRSV "For") defines this unit as an elaboration of the foregoing description of invasion. The geographical progression echoes "from the north" in v. 6, but now "a distant country" is the enemy's origin, as later in 5:15 and like Isa 5:26. Local national allies are to be alerted. Specification of "Jerusalem" in v. 16 indicates that a siege of the capital is in view at v. 17a. The divine explanation, introduced by a quotation formula, grounds Jerusalem's fate in behavior that revealed its treatment of Yahweh; wordplay, *mār*, "bitter," echoing *mārātâ*, "defied," clinches the connection (Schreiner 1:36). As by a sword (cf. v. 10), fatality would ensue. There

---

34. Cf. the association of "peace" and "salvation" in Ps 85:8–9 (9–10); Isa 52:7.

Coming Disaster and Its Causes 67

is a switch to direct address in v. 18, as in vv. 7b and 14 and later in v. 30. In this case there is no call for a response, either lamentation or repentance, and the absence of such a call is ominous.

Verses 5–18 have defined divine providence in terms of a devastating invasion that will negate defensive measures and leave Judah's political and religious leadership at a loss. The root of the problem lies in the ethical sphere; bad behavior can only culminate in a bad fate.

4:19–31 Three Visions of Doom

19 My guts! My guts! I writhe in pain.
    My heart is constricted (?),[a]
  my heart is palpitating.
    I cannot keep silent
  since hearing[b] the blast of the horn,
    the battle shout.
20 Calamity after calamity is announced,
    in fact the whole country is destroyed.
  Suddenly my tents are destroyed,
    in a moment my tent sheets.
21 How much longer will I see the standards,
    will I hear[c] the blast of the horn?
22 "The reason is that my people are fools,
    of me they know nothing.
  They are stupid children,
    they are devoid of sense.
  They are only clever at behaving badly
    and about good behavior they know nothing."

23 I looked at the earth and found it a *chaotic* wasteland,[d]
    at the sky and it had no light.
24 I looked at the mountains and found them quaking;
    all the hills were moving to and fro.
25 I looked and found no people
    and all the birds in the sky had flown away.
26 I looked and found the fertile country a wilderness
    and all its towns were ruined
  due to Yahweh,
    due to his burning anger.
  27 In fact here is what Yahweh said:
    "A devastated area is what the whole country will become—
    though I will not do away with it completely.

28 The reason why the earth will mourn
and the sky above turn drab
is that I have spoken and will not change my mind,
I have made my plans and will not alter them."ᵉ

29 At the noise of horsemen and archers
every townᶠ is taking flight;
they enter caves, hide in thickets,ᵍ
and into rocks they climb.
Every town is abandoned
and nobody lives in them.

30 As for you, you who are to be destroyed,ʰ what are you doing,
dressing up in scarlet,
putting on gold ornaments,
widening your eyes with kohl?
To no avail you are making yourself beautiful.
The sex partners have rejected you,
they have designs on your life.

31 In fact I can hear crying like that of a woman in labor,ⁱ
anguish like that of a primipara,
the crying of Lady Zion, gasping for breath,
as she holds out her hands:
"Wretched me!
I am losing consciousness before my killers."

a. Literally an exclamation, "The walls of my heart!"
b. For the mixed construction see Joüon §151c.
c. For the pseudo-cohortative form see *IBHS* 576–77.
d. LXX lacks *wābōhû*, "and emptiness." MT *tōhû wābōhû* echoes the phrase in Gen 1:2, "a formless void." "Chaotic" is an attempt to give the sense of the addition. LXX *outhen*, "nothing," renders *tōhû* in 1 Sam 12:21; Job 26:7; Isa 40:23, and so the note in *BHS* is mistaken (Cloete, *Versification*, 149–50; cf. Katherine M. Hayes, *"The Earth Mourns": Prophetic Metaphor and Oral Aesthetic* [SBLAB 8; Atlanta: Society of Biblical Literature, 2002], 66–67).

e. The word order in LXX is to be followed on stylistic grounds; see Holladay 1:144. NAB, NIV, and GNB render similarly.

f. Cf. Joüon §139g and v. 29b.

g. MT "They enter thickets" is to be corrected according to the longer text of LXX, as NEB recognized; see *BHS*, though a verbal form, *neḥbĕʾû* (Barthélemy, *Critique textuelle*, 2:490), is better.

h. Uncertainty attaches to *šādûd*. LXX lacks it and it does not agree with the feminine context. In the absence of a convincing text-critical or redactional argument to explain its presence, it may be taken in a future sense, as in NAB and NJPS. Cf. *haššĕdûdâ* in Ps 137:8, if the interpretation "doomed to destruction" (NIV, NJB; cf. GNB) is correct. The verb also occurs in vv. 13, 20.

i. See *BHS*; cf. GKC §72p.

This composition is a parallel piece to the former one in vv. 5–18, as suggested by the repetition of vocabulary from vv. 5–6: "horn" that frames vv. 19–21, *nēs*, "standards" (rendered "marker" in v. 6), and "calamity." It too falls into three units, vv. 19–22, 23–28, and 29–31. Each unit reports a prophetic vision of a doom-laden event.[35] The first two are capped with divine explanations.

[19–22] The initial vision is prefaced by Jeremiah's strong emotional reactions to it as the people's representative. He describes its psychosomatic effect upon him when he received it, his severe pain in stomach and chest, and his need to verbalize the mind-blowing experience (cf. Isa 21:3–4). The actual vision has both auditory and visual aspects. It was a battle scene, as big as Judah and as close as his own home, destroyed as he watched. The military sights and sounds overwhelmed him and he longed for it all to stop. An unannounced divine explanation for the invasion abruptly follows the prophet's vision report. The invasion's necessity and vehemence were dictated by the covenant people's attitude to Yahweh. It was providential reprisal for their refusal to comply with the divine will. The reason for punishment piles up negative wisdom vocabulary that carries a connotation of moral willfulness and satirically uses *ḥăkāmîm*, "wise," with the meaning "clever," all to reinforce their failure to fulfill a covenant responsibility. Knowing Yahweh involved ethical commitment (cf. 22:16). "Behaving badly" (*hāraʿ*) echoes the bad behavior (*rāʿâ*) of v. 14.

[23–26] The second vision vividly depicts a scene of desolation, again for "the whole country" (vv. 20, 27). It adopts a typical pattern—a verb of seeing followed by *hinnēh*, here rendered "found"—to introduce the description of a scene, but goes its own way by investing each detail with the same pattern in an overwhelming series of disasters (cf. v. 20a*a*). The "wasteland" (*tōhû*) in v. 23 is resumed by "wilderness" in v. 26 (cf. their pairing in Deut 32:10 [NRSV "desert . . . wilderness waste"]); both refer to the degradation of a cultivated or urban landscape, with "towns" echoing 4:5, 7, 16. The scene is dramatically highlighted by references to darkness, which was an uncanny feature of the wilderness in 2:6, 31; to earthquake as a symbol of the sudden upset of the established order by invasion; and to the total absence of living beings, even birds. The Hebrew addition (see textual note d) takes the metaphorical hyperbole further by finding creation virtually undone in a reversion to cosmic chaos.[36] The closing interpretation in terms of divine anger reinforces the lamentation of v. 8, as MT accentuates by adding "burning" there.

35. See Walther Zimmerli, "Visionary Experience in Jeremiah," in *Israel's Prophetic Tradition: Essays in Honour of Peter R. Ackroyd* (ed. R. Coggins et al.; Cambridge: Cambridge University Press, 1982), 95–118, esp. 97–104.

36. Michael Fishbane, "Jeremiah iv 23–26 and Job iii 3–13: A Recovered Use of the Creation Pattern," *VT* 21 (1971): 151–67, esp. 151–53, though he credits Jeremiah with this redactional interpretation, has explored its affinities with the Priestly creation account in Gen 1:1–2:4a.

[27–28] A formal divine explanation closes the unit. It reiterates the meaning of the vision in terms of the devastation of Judah and grounds it in the single-mindedness of a God for whom no options were left. The effect on earth and sky is now refigured as a response of mourning for the devastation. Darkness can refer to drab mourning garb, as in 14:2, which uses the same verb; Keil (1:117) paraphrases as "shrouds itself in darkness." The second colon in v. 27 surprisingly qualifies the totality affirmed in the vision and confirmed in the first colon. An intrusive negative also occurs at 5:10, while a longer qualification will occur at 5:18. These all appear to be redactional afterthoughts that aim to moderate the rhetoric with the long-term reality of an eventual aftermath of Judah's fall, when Yahweh's positive purpose would be implemented. The intention is to reaffirm the ultimate truth of 46:28, which MT repeats in 30:11: "I will not do away with you completely." Beyond destruction lies reconstruction; as in 3:15–18, it was judged fitting to bear witness to this larger theme of the book.

[29–31] The third unit reserves its vision report until the last section. For the first two sections it has its own agenda, reverting to issues found at the beginning of the former composition, defensive measures in vv. 5–7 and an appropriate response in v. 8. In this way an inclusive frame is provided for vv. 5–31, one that underlines their overall negativity.

[29] The issue of what defensive measures to take was left unresolved earlier. The command to retreat to urban areas proved inadequate because they would eventually be captured. The question is now reopened; townspeople would be reduced to taking refuge in rural hiding places. The overthrow of towns, mentioned in v. 26, is also developed here.

[30] In v. 8 the people were urged to dress in sackcloth in response to the coming crisis. Here a contrary response is deprecated. Personified Jerusalem, the last of the towns to fall, is warned that attempts to court the favor of her enemies, evidently former allies (cf. 2:33), would be a waste of time. It would be too late for manipulative overtures of conciliation, illustrated by attractive dress, jewelry, and eye makeup.

[31] The final vision, which like the first one (vv. 19b–22) is both auditory and visual, powerfully reinforces Jerusalem's coming destruction announced at the end of v. 30. In perpetuation of the imagery, shrieks, gasps, and hands craving mercy that would never come all preface Jerusalem's dying moan.

The vision reports in vv. 15–31 present with the aid of psychic imagination the results of Yahweh's future intervention in terms first of Judah's being engulfed in battle and desolation and then of Jerusalem's death throes. As in the earlier composition, moral issues left Yahweh no alternative. Into the dire darkness of such a future, however, a ray of hope is permitted for readers; such destruction, real and terrible though it was, was not to be God's last word.

Coming Disaster and Its Causes

5:1–9 The Inevitability of Punishment

5:1 "Roam the streets of Jerusalem,
  looking and inquiring,
  and search its squares
    to see if you can find anybody—
  if there is anyone practicing justice,
    aiming at trustworthiness,
      so I can forgive it;
2 or if rather they say 'By Yahweh's life,'
  but in fact[a] swear deceitfully."

3 Yahweh, your eyes are looking for trustworthiness, aren't they?
    You struck them, but they felt no pain;
    you destroyed them—they refused correction.
  They made their faces harder than rock,
    refusing to come back.
4 I for my part had thought,
    "The poor, only they prove stupid,
  because they do not acknowledge Yahweh's way of life,
    the justice required by their God.
5 I must go to the important people
    and talk with them.
  They are surely the ones who acknowledge Yahweh's way of life,
    the justice required by their God."
  However, like the others they had broken the yoke,
    snapped the harness.
6 That is why a lion from the forest must strike them,
    a desert wolf ravage them,
  with a leopard lying in wait around their towns,
    mangling any who venture out.
  The reason why is that their acts of rebellion are so many,
    their backsliding ways so numerous.

7 "On what grounds[b] can I forgive you?
  Your children have abandoned me,
    swearing by nongods.
  Though I satisfied them, they committed adultery
    and frequented[c] brothels.
8 They have been horses in heat,[d] replete with testicles,[e]
    each individual whinnying after his neighbor's wife!
9 With these folk[f]
    must I not deal?"

declared Yahweh.
"And should not such a nation
incur my vengeance?"

a. The usual sense "therefore" for *lākēn* hardly applies here, though BDB 487a suggests an implicit consequence presupposed from v. 1, i.e., "because there is no trustworthiness, accordingly. . . ." An adversative term is expected. G. R. Driver, "Textual Problems," 100–101, compared Arabic *lākin, lākinna,* "but," and suggested the same sense here. There is a little textual support (see *BHS*) for *ʾākēn* with this sense, but it looks suspiciously like a secondary reading.
b. See Joüon §143g. The first colon is a monocolon (Holladay 1:175).
c. See *BHS* and Barthélemy, *Critique textuelle,* 2:495–97, for the emendation, which EVV follow, correcting a common *r/d* error. MT *yitgôdādû,* "gashed themselves," imports a confusing note of reality into the metaphorical context.
d. See *HALOT* 2:401b; *DCH* 4:194a.
e. See *HALOT* 4:1488b. LXX represented both terms with a paraphrase, "mad after women."
f. For the construction see Holladay 1:181–82.

Conspicuous landmarks that provide bearings for analyzing the varied pieces in ch. 5 are three sets of plural imperatives (vv. 1, 10, 20) and a refrain (vv. 9, 29). This evidence points to a group of three literary compositions: vv. 1–9, 10–19, and 20–31. The first composition, like the other two, reflects the genre of an oracle of disaster. Its two parts of reasons and announcement duly appear. The accent is on the former element, with the latter only emerging in vv. 6a and 9. Two voices are heard, Yahweh's in vv. 1–2 and 7–9 and Jeremiah's in vv. 3–6, adducing arguments for the inevitability of Yahweh's punitive intervention against Judah. Verses 1–8 are marked by a chiasm, noted (slightly differently) by Lundbom (1:373), that moves inward from shared motifs of individual failings, wrong oaths, and divine forgiveness (A, A', vv. 1–2, 7–8) to punitive strikes in the past and future, respectively (B, B', vv. 3, 6), and then to a core of failure to live up to Yahweh's covenant expectations (C, C', vv. 4–5). This tight structuring suggests that at least vv. 1–8 function as a single unit with sections in vv. 1–2, 3–6, and 7–8, but within the chapter vv. 1–9 have a compositional role. The forecast of invasion and destruction in v. 6a echoes the dominant theme of 4:5–31.

[5:1–2] The reasons for disaster are introduced by an expansion that highlights the comprehensiveness of the charges that will be leveled against the community.[37] A rhetorical call goes out for a team of inspectors to conduct a thorough investigation in Jerusalem. The quest assigned to God's moral police is the broad social virtues of "justice" and "trustworthiness." Yahweh's goal is to find enough proof of the presence of such virtues to counteract contrary

---

37. Westermann, *Basic Forms,* 185.

tokens of vice and so permit exoneration. Yahweh is accommodatingly prepared to take any evidence as enough (cf. Gen 18:23–32). But, it is implied, such a quest would be unsuccessful. The negative example of lying oaths involving the name of Yahweh recalls 4:2 and the clustered ideal of acting "honestly, justly, and fairly" presented there.

[3–6] The prophet breaks in, reinforcing the difficulty of finding "trustworthiness" (v. 3) and "justice" (vv. 4–5) and affirming a consequent need for punishment (v. 6). A frame of "come back" and "backsliding ways" echoes 3:1–4:4.

[3] The covenant community's failure to satisfy the divine quest is exemplified by its refusal to take any warning from Yahweh's earlier acts of providential reprisal. It confronted its past failures stony-faced, with no regrets (cf. 2:30). Such intransigence amounted to an aggravation of initial wrongdoing, a significant rise in the level of spiritual accountability (cf. 3:3). To spurn God's further window of opportunity was a dangerous proof of incorrigibility.

[4–5] Jeremiah records from experience his own disappointment at the result. He had already passed a conventional verdict on the economically struggling class of society, dismissively expecting a higher crime rate and less spirituality. Does not poverty bring with it a tendency to "steal and profane the name" of God (Prov 30:9)? But he had volunteered to respond to Yahweh's call, with the upper class in view, expecting better results, compliance with the moral standards Yahweh had set for the covenant people. His hopes were dashed. If the lower class was "stupid," a wisdom term that carries overtones of moral reprehensibility (cf. 4:22), the upper class was equally ready to break off the yoke of the covenant (cf. 2:20).

[6] Jeremiah draws the obvious conclusion. With animal imagery (cf. 4:7) he spells out necessary consequences: enemy invasion and urban blockades that will be the human results of Yahweh's intervention, building on earlier intervention ("struck"/"strike," vv. 3, 6). The prophet justifies such consequences with a general statement about the widespread breach of covenant standards, recapitulating vv. 1–2.

[7–8] Yahweh resumes addressing the inappropriateness of divine forgiveness with a rhetorical question, turning to address Jerusalem directly, and then gives examples of religious and moral delinquency in the lives of individual members of the community, headed by the metropolis. First, oaths made in the names of other deities, "nongods" though they were (cf. 2:11), lead into a general charge of religious infidelity, portrayed in sexual terms—a shocking return for Yahweh's own input into the relationship! The contrast motif accentuates the charge. Second, by an association of ideas religious metaphor gives way to literal sexual immorality in a deliberately disgusting charge of animal passion demonstrated in chasing after other men's wives within the community.

[9] Further rhetorical questions cap the initial one in v. 7, in a closing announcement of disaster that is also used in v. 29 and 9:9 (8); it falls outside

the compact structure of vv. 1–8 and sounds redactional, expressing the implication of lack of forgiveness. Yahweh had no alternative but to "deal with" them punitively and so provide a fitting return for such provocation. The announcement fittingly concludes this passage, which has argued for the necessity of military invasion in reprisal. Even Jeremiah, who had reacted vehemently to such a prospect in 4:19, now agreed. The reprisal is couched in terms of vengeance, which expresses Yahweh's commitment to retributive justice. "[God's] vengeance is in no way illegitimate, but is precisely intended to bring the punishing judgment of the kingly Judge, who comes into action to avenge the transgression of his justice and to save the oppressed."[38] The concept survives in the NT, notably in eschatological passages (2 Thess 1:8; Rev 19:2) and in ethical contexts (Rom 12:19; 1 Thess 4:6).

5:10–19 (Nonabsolute) Destruction of People and Land

10 "Go up through its vine terraces and cause destruction—
but do not do away with it completely—
remove its tendrils,
because they are not Yahweh's.
11 The reason why is utter faithlessness to me
on the part of Israel's community
and Judah's community," *declared Yahweh.*

12 They have denied Yahweh,
claiming, "He is not a factor.
We will not find a bad fate coming upon us;
sword and famine we will never see."
13 As for the prophets, they will prove to be mere wind,
not having the message[a] in them.
That is what they themselves will suffer.

14 Therefore here is what Yahweh, *God* Almighty, said:

"Because they[b] have made this claim,
look, I am going to turn my messages
in your mouth into fire

---

38. H. G. L. Peels, *The Vengeance of God: The Meaning of the Root NQM and the Function of the NQM-Texts in the Context of Divine Revelation in the Old Testament* (OtSt 31; Leiden: Brill, 1995), 280; cf. Wayne T. Pitard, "Amarna *ekēmu* and Hebrew *nāqam*," *Maarav* 3 (1982): 5–25; idem, "Vengeance," *ABD* 6:786–87. Both scholars counter the widely adopted views of George E. Mendenhall, "The 'Vengeance' of Yahweh," in *The Tenth Generation: The Origins of the Biblical Tradition* (Baltimore: Johns Hopkins University Press, 1973), 69–104.

Coming Disaster and Its Causes 75

and this people will be sticks,
which it will consume."

15 "Look, I am going to bring upon you
a nation from far away, Israel's community,"
declared Yahweh.
"It is a long-established nation,
it is an age-old nation,
a nation whose language you will not recognize,
so you will be unable to understand what it says.
16 Its quiver is like an open tomb;
all of them are warriors.
17 It will consume your harvest and bread;
they will consume your sons and daughters.[c]
It will consume your flocks and herds;
it will consume your vines and fig trees.
It will batter your fortified towns,
in which you have put your trust, with the sword."

18 "However, in those days," declared Yahweh, "I will not do away with you completely. 19 When they[d] ask, 'Why has Yahweh our God done all this to us?' you should tell them, 'Just as you have *abandoned me and served foreign gods* in your own country, so you must serve aliens in a country not your own.'"

a. For the noun *dibbēr* in the sense of "divine word, revelation" (cf. LXX "word of the Lord" [*BHS*]), see Holladay 1:187; Richard C. Steiner, "A Colloquialism in Jer. 5:13 from the Ancestor of Mishnaic Hebrew," *JSS* 37 (1992): 11–26. The latter regards it as a colloquialism.

b. MT "you" (plural) represents a secondary alignment with "upon you" in v. 15; see note k on 3:13. The colon is best taken as a monocolon. For the determination of colon length in v. 14 see Cloete, *Versification*, 150–51.

c. KJV "which thy sons and thy daughters should eat," endorsed by Samuel R. Driver, *The Book of the Prophet Jeremiah: A Revised Translation with Introductions and Short Explanations* (London: Hodder & Stoughton, 1906), 30, who assumes that the switch to a plural verb suggests a relative clause. The plural does have a parallel in v. 16b.

d. The textual tradition has "you" (plural). See note b above. In this case the text has been aligned with "you" in v. 18.

Destruction, yet not absolute destruction, was to overwhelm people and land. This next composition develops the motifs of invasion and destruction broached in v. 6. Verses 10–17 repeat the pattern of vv. 1–9, punctuating divine declarations with a statement from the prophet.[39] These verses are marked by an ABB'A' structure, in that the destruction of vv. 10–11 (A) is developed in vv. 15–17 (A') and the issue of false and true prophecy pervades vv. 12–13 (B) and 14 (B'). But there are also links between the B and A' parts and between the B' and A' parts. First, vv. 12 and 15 juxtapose the people's skepticism about a bad fate "coming upon us" with Yahweh's confirmation, "I am going to bring upon you" an invading nation, with the latter verb turning into a causative form the Hebrew verb used earlier (*tābôʾ, mēbîʾ*). As for the second case, vv. 14 and 15 repeat a divine initiative, "Look, I am going to . . ." and the verb "consume" in v. 14 recurs in v. 17. This network of associations brings to vv. 10–17 a complex unity that looks like a literary arrangement rather than an oral presentation. The appended vv. 18–19 are a prose elaboration of elements found at the beginning of the composition, in v. 10, held over until its close.

[10–11] This self-contained oracle of disaster inverts the announcement and the grounds for it because the former takes the shape of military orders for destruction of the country, as vv. 15–17 will explain. Initially Jerusalem still seems to be in view ("its," "it," feminine pronouns), as in v. 1. The orders are dressed in a metaphor of reprisal for breach of covenant. A vineyard earlier planted and tended by the divine vinedresser is to be systematically destroyed (Isa 5:1–7; cf. Ps 80:8–15 [9–16]). The disowning of the tendrils as no longer belonging to Yahweh, which finds a somber parallel in the NT at John 15:6, is justified by "faithlessness." It was a charge leveled at "Israel's community" in Jer 3:20 and made the basis of Judah's nickname "Faithless" in 3:6–11. Mention of both "Israel's community" and "Judah's community," obviously with reference to the northern and southern kingdoms, strikes a discordant note in the context, since the former phrase is used of Judah in v. 15, while "Jacob's community" is so used in v. 20. "Judah's community" appears to be a differentiating addition motivated by the comparison of both communities' sinfulness in 3:6–11. There is further evidence of redaction in the surprising negative that appears in the second colon of v. 10. It is the continuation of a larger agenda met recently at 4:27, one that v. 18 will underline, though it is lacking in ch. 6.

[12–14] These verses belong together; in v. 14 Yahweh validates the charges against the people brought by Jeremiah in v. 12. Verse 12 is to be ascribed to the prophet, as the addition of the closing quotation formula in MT at v. 11 clarifies. As for v. 13, elsewhere in the book the plural term "prophets" with reference to Jeremiah's contemporaries regularly signifies his rivals who prophesied "peace" (*šālôm*).[40] So it is unlikely that v. 13 is a continuation of the

---

39. Holladay, *Architecture*, 87–88.

40. Cf., e.g., 2:8; 5:31. Georg Schmuttermayr, "Beobachtungen zu Jer 5, 13," *BZ* 9 (1965): 215–32, esp. 220, has distinguished this regular usage from positive cases where the reference is to prophetic activity in past history, in most of which, apart from 2:30 and 28:8, "prophets" is qualified by "(Yahweh's) servants" in apposition (e.g., 7:25).

Coming Disaster and Its Causes

people's claim in v. 12, as EVV apart from NRSV interpret; it represents Jeremiah's perspective.

[12] The citation of the people's attitude functions as a damning illustration of the general faithlessness predicated in v. 11. Jeremiah asserts that they are denying Yahweh's coming intervention when they reject oracles that threaten military disaster. His assertion assumes that he is a true prophet and that, in rejecting his oracles, they are rejecting Yahweh.

[13] The denial that military attack and consequent privation lie in Judah's future is part of the reassuring message of the šālôm prophets in 14:13, 15; 23:17.[41] Accordingly in v. 13 the initial focus on "the prophets" exposes the source of the people's attitude. Jeremiah is warning that their assurances would be shown to lack substance, and is denying that they represent true oracles from God. Instead, such prophets would find themselves victims of the very disaster they were encouraging the people to deny. "Sword and famine will be the very means by which these prophets will perish" (14:15).[42]

[14] Yahweh's announcement of disaster reassuringly addresses Jeremiah. It begins by resuming his assertion (v. 12) about the people's claim that was based on the other prophets' assurances. Divine intervention would validate Jeremiah's prophetic oracles. The vivid imagery of fire and firewood clinches Yahweh's powerful involvement as "Almighty," Jeremiah's role as Yahweh's authentic spokesperson (cf. 1:9), and Judah's disastrous end.

[15-17] A further announcement of disaster speaks of Yahweh's intervention and the results of that intervention. Its most obvious purpose is to expand the figurative reference to consuming at the end of v. 14 by spelling out in v. 17 the range of Judah's ongoing vitality that would suffer from such consumption. In v. 14 Yahweh's initiative had in primary view Jeremiah's prophetic role; now it confronts the faith community, both developing the invasive destruction of Yahweh's vineyard in v. 10 and defining the coming of a "bad fate" in v. 12 in terms of the hostile incursion of a powerful nation. A series of statements is made about that nation, and another series about Judah's suffering at its hands. In wider terms the message of the invasion in 4:6b-7, 13, 16b-17a continues.

[15-16] Remoteness, antiquity, longevity, and unintelligibility convey an overwhelming sense of inexorable and intimidating purpose. That purpose is defined in military terms—it is a nation of warriors. No question of a little tribal raid that could be repulsed with ease! The simile in v. 16a, like a black hole, evokes both fatality and insatiability (cf. Hab 2:5; Ps 5:9 [10]; Prov 27:20).

[17] In Psalm 127 towns, bread, and sons all stand potentially under the sustaining care of Yahweh in the ongoing life of the blessed people of God. Here, along with flocks and fruit, they are targets for divinely instigated disaster. All

---

41. Schmuttermayr, "Beobachtungen," 224.
42. Schmuttermayr, "Beobachtungen," 231, has observed the parallelism of 5:13 and 14:13-15, though there the prophets' punishment features in a divine oracle.

these symbols of building, sowing, and nurturing figure in Israel's future in terms of futility. Trust in fortified towns could be no enduring substitute for trust in God. The consuming of the vines echoes the destruction of the spiritual vineyard in v. 10. Likewise, "with the sword" not only provides forceful closure for vv. 15–17, but also articulates a final yes to the people's no in v. 12.

[18] This first of two separate prose supplements is loosely connected to the foregoing by a redactional and temporal link (cf. 3:16, 18). It calls the reader's attention to the reservation added in v. 10, lest it be overlooked. It is a testimony given in God's name to future survival, which should not be confused with the cloudless message of the šālôm prophets.

[19] The second supplement resumes Yahweh's address to Jeremiah in v. 14, but reinforces the announcement of disaster with another one that includes its own reason. The disaster looks beyond the contextual destruction of land and people toward exile, and so presents a different aspect of survival than v. 18. Jeremiah, at last vindicated by the turn of events, was to be acknowledged as a true prophet. The question-and-answer format has parallels elsewhere in the book, most closely in 16:10–13 and 22:8–9.[43] The supplement explains the claim of breach of covenant in v. 10. A shocked protest referring to Yahweh as (still) "our God" is silenced by a logical correspondence drawn between cultic service of foreign gods in their own land (cf. v. 7) and political service of aliens elsewhere. This choice carries with it no less a corollary. In MT the extra charge of abandoning Yahweh provides its own anchor for the supplement from v. 7.[44] The charge of pagan worship recalls not only v. 7 but also the emphasis in 2:4–4:4.

The composition in vv. 10–19 is made up of uncompromising announcements of disaster, which triggered qualifications at beginning and end (vv. 10 and 18). The community's refusal to listen to Jeremiah as Yahweh's mouthpiece is labeled as conclusive warrant for punishment; such action is consistent with the refusal to come back to Yahweh (v. 3). Yahweh adjudicates in Jeremiah's favor the communal clash over prophetic authority by announcing afresh Judah's bleak future. Before that materialized, however, the public debate was to go on, as later chapters will attest.

5:20–31 Overstepping God's Limits

20 "Give this report among Jacob's community,
    announce it in Judah:
21 Listen to this,
    you silly, senseless people,

---

43. See Burke O. Long, "Two Question and Answer Schemata in the Prophets," *JBL* 90 (1971): 129–39.
44. Janzen's derivation of the addition from 16:11; 19:4; and 22:9 (*Studies*, 36) adduces a contributing factor without addressing the contextual motivation.

      who have eyes but do not see,
         who have ears but do not listen.[a]
22 Should not I be the object of your reverence?"
    declared Yahweh.
      "Should not I be the object of your trembling awe,
    I who have set the sand as a boundary for the sea,
        a permanent barrier it cannot cross?
    Tossing about without succeeding,
        roaring in turmoil are its waves, but failing to cross it.
23 Yet this people possesses
      an uppity, rebellious attitude;
      they have upped and gone,
24 never thinking to themselves,
      'We should show reverence to Yahweh our God,
    who gives the rain,
      early and late, in its season,
    who the statutory weeks for harvest
      maintains for us.'
25 It is your wrongdoings that have diverted such occurrences,
      your sins that have deprived you of the bounty.

26 "In fact wicked folk have been found among my people.
      Each lies in wait as in a birdcatcher's hide.[b]
    They have set traps
      to catch human beings.
27 Like cages full of birds,
      their houses are filled with proceeds of fraud.
    That is how they have grown powerful and rich,
28   so fat and sleek.
    Yes, they overlook[c] bad verdicts,
      they fail to uphold justice
    by winning the just cases of orphans,
      and the rights of the poor they do not defend.
29 With these folk
      must I not deal?"
    declared Yahweh.
    "And should not such a nation
      incur my vengeance?

30 "A shocking, horrifying phenomenon has occurred in the country:
31   prophets have prophesied false oracles,
      while priests have been exercising control at their direction,[d]

and my people love this situation—
but how will you cope at its final outcome?"

    a. The Hebrew third person references at v. 21b, taken by Lundbom 1:402–3 as a reference to idols, are another case of the principle noted at 2:23 (note c).
    b. MT *kĕšak*, "as (birdcatchers) crouch (?)," is problematic since elsewhere the verb is not so used. An ingenious and simple repointing to *kĕšʾōk*, "as (in) a hide" (cf. Lam 2:6), was proposed by John A. Emerton, "Notes on Some Problems in Jeremiah v 26," in *Mélanges bibliques et orientaux en l'honneur de M. Henri Cazelles* (ed. A. Caquot and M. Delcor; AOAT 212; Kevelaer: Butzon & Bercker; Neukirchen-Vluyn: Neukirchener Verlag, 1981), 125–33, esp. 131–32.
    c. Thus Bright 40 and McKane 1:134; cf. REB. Vg. lends support.
    d. The meaning of the verbal phrase is uncertain. This option was adopted by Aubrey R. Johnson, *The Cultic Prophet in Ancient Israel* (2d ed.; Cardiff: University of Wales Press, 1962), 63–64, and has been followed by NRSV and GNB. Probably LXX originally interpreted the verb thus (Ziegler, *Jeremias*, 176).

This composition combines three oracles of disaster. First, a general charge justifies disaster already inflicted by God (vv. 20–25). Then specific charges preface an announcement of future disaster (vv. 26–29). Finally, in a self-contained brief oracle, another type of specific charge culminates in an oblique announcement of disaster (vv. 30–31). Accordingly development from general grounds to particular ones marks the composition. To this end the second unit is introduced by a redactional *kî* (NRSV "For"), so that what follows is presented as an elaboration of the preceding.

[20] Like the two earlier compositions in ch. 5, this one begins with a set of plural imperatives, here in a generic call for the following oracle to be disseminated throughout the Judean community.

[21] The focus on listening at beginning and end expresses both exasperation and forbearance (cf. v. 1). It presupposes that this was by no means the first time that such a lesson needed to be taught, but represents another try. Contextually the reminder matches the refusal of the community to listen to Yahweh's messages of disaster through Jeremiah (v. 12). As in 4:22, negative wisdom vocabulary is used to reprimand the community, here for failure to learn an obvious lesson.

[22–23] Now the message proper starts. Yahweh's role as creator and sustainer of the world is often used in the OT as warrant for adherence to the covenant, just as in the NT believers are exhorted to "entrust themselves to a faithful Creator" (1 Pet 4:19). Here the limitation put upon the sea, preventing the irruption of chaos on the earth, is used to set up a model of compliance. Yet while in the natural order God's "Thus far and no farther" (Job 38:11) met with conformity, the covenant community had gone out of control, showing no parallel respect for Yahweh. The wordplay of *sôrēr* and *sārû* is captured in the

Coming Disaster and Its Causes

translation by "uppity" and "they have upped" (lit. "stubborn" and "they have turned aside," NRSV); this alliteration underlines the community's contrariness. The switch from direct address to "this people," itself a phrase implying distaste (cf. Isa 6:10; 8:6), expresses pointedly the distance they have put between themselves and Yahweh.

[24] Obligation, rather than self-interest, is at stake. The covenant norm ("our God") was a cycle of divine giving and human gratitude, but Israel had blithely accepted the boons of the agricultural calendar with no demonstration of corresponding reverence.

[25] Such a break in the cycle had caused a break on Yahweh's side. Lack of reverence, now put in blunt terms of "wrongdoings" and "sins," led to the withholding of the autumn and spring rains and so of the harvest's "bounty" (cf. 3:3).

[26–28] The general charge of lack of reverence and the undefined sins of v. 25 are now spelled out in a catalog of particular issues relating to social justice. The metaphor of hunting is taken over from individual laments in the Psalms (e.g., Ps 140:4–5 [5–6]). Human beings had been caught and their property illegally commandeered for personal profit. The sins were ones of judicial omission as well as of economic commission. Despite the social positions of power the perpetrators enjoyed, they failed to stand up for justice; they condoned wrong decisions and made no efforts to secure the legal rights of underprivileged members of the community.

[29] The refrain used in v. 9 now reappears, characterizing Yahweh's intervention in punishment as inevitable.

[30–31] A new charge, a religious one, rounds off the composition. The approval given by "my people" bridges a conceptual gap between vv. 26–28, which place the wicked "among my people" (v. 26), and v. 29, where the "nation" is liable for punishment. A device of delayed explication builds up suspense and emotionally preconditions the hearer.[45] The context of vv. 12–13 encourages readers to think about the *šālôm* prophets whose message represented a perversion of true faith in Yahweh. The priests' basing their leadership role on the prophets' social prognosis meant that they neither instigated services of lamentation and repentance (cf. Joel 1:14; 2:15–17) nor emphasized social justice in their traditional task of teaching the torah. The switch to direct address in the closing question augments the effect of startling challenge.

Verses 20–31 place more emphasis on reasons for disaster than did earlier compositions from 4:5 onward (apart from 5:1–9). The analogy of the sea held in check highlights the anomaly of Judah's untrammeled loss of reverence for its covenant God. The virtual definition of such reverence in terms of social justice, in addition to faithful religious leadership, paves the way for James's interpretation of religion as "to care for orphans and widows in their distress" (Jas 1:27).

---

45. Watson, *Classical Hebrew Poetry*, 336–37.

6:1–15 The Wages of Sin

1 "Make for shelter, Benjaminites,
  and get outside Jerusalem,
 in Tekoa blow the horn,
  and on Beth-hakkerem light a beacon,[a]
 because a bad fate is looming from the north,
  an immense calamity.
2 That beautiful, refined woman
  I will destroy—Lady Zion.[b]
3 She will find shepherds coming with their flocks,
  who will pitch tents all round her,
  each grazing his patch.[c]
4 'Prepare for battle against it.
  Come on, let us mount a noon attack.'
 'What a pity! The daylight is fading,
  evening shadows are lengthening.
5 Come on, let us mount a night attack
  and destroy its fortified buildings.'"

6 In explanation here is what Yahweh *Almighty* said:

"Cut down its trees[d]
  and pile against Jerusalem a ramp of earth.
 This is the city that must be handed over.[e]
  There is nothing except exploitation inside it.
7 Like a well keeping its water fresh,[f]
  it has kept fresh its bad behavior.
 The cry 'Violence! Assault!' is heard in it.
  I am confronted continually by pain and injuries.
8 Accept correction, Jerusalem,
  or else I will turn away from you in disgust,
  or else I will make you a waste,
  an area where nobody lives."

9 Here is what Yahweh *Almighty* said:

"Glean, glean out[g]
  like a vine what is left of Israel.
 Pass your hand again
  like a grape picker over the branches"—
10 Who can I speak to
  and give a warning they will listen to?

Look, their ears are uncircumcised
and they cannot pay any attention.
Look, Yahweh's message
they regard with contempt
rather than welcoming it.
11 So I am full of Yahweh's fury,
I am tired of holding it in—
"Overwhelm with it children in the streets
and groups of young men as well.
Indeed, men and women will be captured,
and gatherings of old, aged men.
12 Their houses will be turned over to others,
fields and wives as well.
That is because I will brandish my fist
to strike the country's population,"
declared Yahweh.
13 "The reason why is that, ranging from lowest to elite,
every single one of them is greedy for profit,
and prophet and priest alike
are all acting falsely.
14 They try to heal my people's wounds superficially,
saying, "You are well, quite well,"
when they are not well at all.
15 They have been humiliated for acting abominably,
but they do not feel in the least humiliated,
they do not even know how to feel guilty.
Therefore they will fall where others have fallen,
they will tumble at the time when I deal with them,"
Yahweh said.

a. The noun $mś^{c}t$ is so used in the Lachish ostraca (4.10; see *COS* 3:80).
b. This bicolon is of uncertain meaning because its first and last words are ambiguous. The first word, $nāwâ$, may be regarded as a noun meaning "pasture" (NRSV) in line with the imagery of vv. 2b–3 or taken as short for $nā^{ʾ}wâ$, an adjective meaning "beautiful" (other EVV). The final verb may be (1) derived from roots meaning "be like" (NRSV) or "destroy" (other EVV), (2) regarded as first person (most EVV) or second (NAB), in which case "Lady Zion" is vocative, and (3) taken as past or future. My translation aligns with NIV, NJB, and NJPS.
c. For colon lengths in vv. 3, 9, 10, 20, 22, 24, and 25 see Cloete, *Versification*, 153–57.
d. See *BHS*.
e. The basic meaning "hand over" for the Hiphil of *pqd* (*HALOT* 3:957b) suggests such a passive sense here, apparently in an impersonal construction in an asyndetic relative clause.

f. LXX and Vg. so render, deriving from *qrr*. NRSV, REB, NJB, and GNB follow suit.

g. MT, upon which LXX is secondarily dependent, has a plural verb after an infinitive absolute, ʿôlēl yĕʿôlēlû, "Let them glean thoroughly," with reference to the invaders. This sense stands in tension with the third colon, which is evidently addressed to Jeremiah as Yahweh's agent. External parallelism is expected. Accordingly, a slight emendation to a singular imperative ʿôlēl is commonly made, with construal of the first verb as also an imperative. NAB, NRSV, and REB render along these lines, while NJPS mentions the emendation. The divine command to the invaders in v. 6 caused a copyist to think of the plural verbs used in the vine metaphor at 5:10.

Chapter 6 defines Judah's "final outcome," broached in 5:31. In broader terms, though ch. 6 does not lack reasons for disaster, it functions as a massive announcement of disaster after the concentration on the reasons for destruction identified in ch. 5, inasmuch as it devotes more space to announcements of disaster and tends to set them before the reasons. The numerous occurrences of the formula "Here is what Yahweh said," five in all, are important for determining the chapter's structure. Their subordination to the preceding context in vv. 6 and 21 shows that they do not have a single function. Two of the remaining cases, in vv. 16 and 22, appear to introduce compositions, while the one at v. 9 begins a unit. A number of repeated elements indicate that there are three compositions, vv. 1–15, 16–21, and 22–30, of which the middle one appears to be a single, if complex, unit, while the other two are literary amalgamations made up of basic units. First, "the north" is the invaders' place of origin in vv. 1 and 22. Second, personified "Lady Zion" stands for Jerusalem in vv. 2 and 23. Third, the verb "tumble" (*kšl*) occurs in vv. 15 and 21. Fourth, terms found in the course of vv. 1–15 recur in a cluster at vv. 18–19, "a bad fate" from v. 1 and terms of warning and listening and Yahweh's "message(s)" from v. 10. Indeed, the first composition supplies key elements that are selectively resumed in the other two. The first and third compositions are closely matched, in two respects. The switch from Jerusalem as the focus in vv. 1–8 to the people at large in vv. 9–15 finds a parallel in vv. 22–26 and 27–30 respectively; in particular not only is "Lady Zion" present in vv. 2 and 23, but "my people" appears in vv. 14 and 27. Moreover, a motif in the first composition that is repeated in the third is the comprehensiveness of the people's wrongdoing in vv. 13 and 28. Verses 1–15, then, have a fundamental role in the chapter. This composition grounds the completeness of military destruction in the comprehensive way both the capital and the wider community had gone awry.

[6:1–8] Jerusalem is the target of disaster in a self-contained oracle that moves from announcement in vv. 1–6a to reasons in vv. 6b–7 and back to announcement in the course of v. 8 ("or else . . ."). The unit is shot through with wordplay, *bitqôaʿ tiqʿû*, "in Tekoa blow," in v. 1, *tāqʿû*, "they will pitch," in v. 3, and *tēqaʿ*, "turn away in disgust," in v. 8 (Rudolph 44, following Albert Condamin). It bonds the human outworking of disaster with divine involve-

Coming Disaster and Its Causes 85

ment; nothing less than a grim encounter between Jerusalem and Yahweh underlies the coming invasion. Coherence is also provided for the passage by the loose chiastic shape reflected in the repetition of *qereb* ("outside, inside") in v. 6 from v. 1 and the repetition found within the military orders of vv. 4–5.[46]

[1] As in 4:5–6a, the announcement of disaster is expanded by a summons to flight, defensive orders given by Yahweh.[47] The location of Beth-hakkerem is uncertain, but since Tekoa lies twelve miles south of Jerusalem, the prospect for the capital's future is that it would be engulfed. People from the region of Benjamin who had already taken shelter in Jerusalem to the south are ordered to retreat still farther south, even as the danger spreads in that direction. The northern origin of the invaders reflects 4:6, and indeed v.1b echoes 4:6b. The difference is that there Jerusalem was hailed as a refuge, but now no longer.

[2–3] The focus on Jerusalem continues with a personification that reflects urban splendor and sophistication—qualities soon to be lost. A blatantly rural analogy ironically ensues, illustrating Yahweh's military means of destruction. The shepherds are kings, as in 2:18, and their flocks are the regional companies under their command. A siege is envisioned, as in 4:17.

[4–5] The military setting comes plainly to the fore in this summons to fight, an imaginative overhearing of snatches of deliberation in the enemy camp, with which Judg 7:10–14 may be compared. The ominous issue is a surprise attack, perchance at midday, siesta time (Peake 1:137). Even night would afford no respite for the besieged city, since an attack under cover of darkness was possible (cf. Judg 7:9, 19; Neh 4:9, 22 [3, 16]).

[6–7] Yahweh briefly endorses the siege preparations—acquiring lumber and moving soil—before justifying such a disaster as reprisal for the social disorder rampant in the capital. Jerusalem had an uglier side than the beauty and refinement of v. 1. The well analogy is a cynical indictment of a perversion of values that preserved only the bad. As in 1:14, 16, and 6:14, 18, $rā^câ$, "bad behavior," would find its own nemesis: the term echoes v. 1, where it was rendered "a bad fate." The danger that was to engulf it already stalked its streets in another form. A high level of street crime is an illustration of "exploitation." Its victims' calls for help (cf. 20:8) went unanswered. Only Yahweh heard the screams and was shocked by the resultant injuries.

[8] Jerusalem is directly addressed, as the grounds for disaster are expanded into a final warning.[48] The prospect of vv. 1–6a was almost inevitable, given the capital's bad record. The alternative to taking the warning seriously was

---

46. So Lundbom, *Hebrew Rhetoric*, 104–5, who, however, takes vv. 1–7 as a unit.
47. The three cases of assonance in v. 1, *běnê binyāmīn*, lit. "sons of Benjamin," *bitqôa^c tiq^cû*, "in Tekoa blow," and *śĕ'û maś'ēt*, "light a beacon," reinforce the exhortations.
48. See Westermann, *Basic Forms*, 184.

twofold: the withdrawal of a God whose presence was offended by intolerable sights (v. 7) and catastrophe that spelled the city's destruction. The appeal reveals Yahweh's reluctance to punish. Rather than expressing a realistic hope, it seals Jerusalem's fate, once refused. Earlier chapters have mentioned the refusal of correction (2:30; 5:3), and the next unit will refer frankly to lack of remorse (vv. 10, 15).

[9–15] Instead of Jerusalem this unit has a larger target, the people as a whole. It follows the same basic structure as vv. 1–8; it is an oracle of disaster that begins with an announcement and concludes with reasons for the disaster. Here the intervening speech is Jeremiah's (vv. 10–11a).

[9] Jeremiah is given a decisive role in the realization of the disaster (as in 1:10 and 5:14). His oracles were to unleash the final destruction.[49] The metaphor for punishing a breach of the covenant used of the enemy in 5:10 is now applied to the prophet's performative speech. Nothing was to be left.

[10–11a] Jeremiah loyally takes Yahweh's side, expressing his own passionate intuition of divine anger (cf. 15:17; 20:9), like Jesus fulminating against the unrepentant towns of Galilee (Matt 11:20–24). The sin that provokes it is not basic wrongdoing but a secondary development, a blatant refusal to take correction seriously. Uncircumcised ears are those willfully closed to prophetic indictment, as if by foreskins. The phrase is echoed at the close of Stephen's speech to the Sanhedrin in Acts 7:51–53.

[11b–12] In line with v. 9, Jeremiah is given permission to launch pent-up messages of military destruction that was to engulf the various sectors of the Judean community, as they and their homesteads felt the brunt of Yahweh's intervention.

[13–15] A divine analysis of the reasons for such a comprehensive disaster follows. It reverts to a primary stage of sinfulness, a breakdown in the community's ethical solidarity. Materialistic greed is cited, a different example from that in v. 6. The Hebrew term *šālôm*, which is generally used in the book for peace and security, is applied three times in v. 14 to the health of the social body diagnosed by Jeremiah's prophetic rivals ("well"). Implicitly the country's refusal to hear Jeremiah's messages from Yahweh (v. 10) was grounded in the popularity of the other prophets' wrong diagnosis, endorsed as it was by the priests, as 5:31 had stated. This was why previous divine intervention, intended to correct Judah's intolerable attitude, had bounced off ineffectively, so that now further intervention was necessary, causing much worse disaster. "Acting abominably" summarizes in strong language what was morally wrong with Judean society by metaphorically extending a religious concept used in its basic sense at 2:7.

---

49. Rudolph 44 and Berridge, *Prophet, People*, 79, understand the gleaning metaphor in a positive sense of trying to save a few, but Holladay, *Architecture*, 92, has observed the destructive force of the verb ʿôlēl, "glean," in Judg 20:45, where NAB, NJPS, and REB render "picked off."

Coming Disaster and Its Causes

Verses 1–15 trace a close link, both for Jerusalem and for Judah, between an extreme antipathy to Yahweh's covenant ideals and the extreme measures Yahweh must take in reprisal. Jeremiah was caught up in the process as God's prophetic agent, reporting the people's damning deafness and responsible for releasing Yahweh's vehement intervention.

6:16–21 Road Closed Ahead

16 Here is what Yahweh said:

"Stand at the crossroads and look,
    and ask about the age-old paths,
inquiring which is the road to what is good,
    and go that way.
Then you will find rest for yourselves."
    But they said, "We will not go that way."
17 "I have been appointing lookouts for you,
    who told you to pay attention to the sound of the horn."
But they said, "We will not pay any attention."
18 "Therefore hear, you nations, what is to befall them,[a]
19   hear, earth, and become aware of the warning:[b]
Look, I am bringing a bad fate
    to this people,
    the consequence of their own schemes,
because they have not paid any attention to my messages
    and my torah—they have rejected it.
20 What do I want
    with frankincense imported from Sheba
    or with aromatic grasses from a country far away?
Your burnt offerings are not acceptable
    and your sacrifices give me no pleasure.
21 Therefore"—here is what Yahweh said—
"look, I am going to place in this people's way
    obstacles for them to tumble over.
Fathers and sons alike,
    neighbors and friends, will perish."

a. Thus Ehrlich, *Randglossen*, 4:258, comparing Exod 8:17 (13) for the hostile sense of the preposition.

b. The latter clause appears in MT in the middle of v. 18. Its feminine imperative *děʿî*, "become aware of," suggests that, before it was misplaced, it belonged here with the feminine noun *hāʾāreṣ*, "earth," where it is metrically appropriate, and then the accompanying noun functions as the object of the verb (Holladay 1:218). The noun ʿēdâ is to be understood as "testimony," as Aquila rendered it (*martyrian*), more precisely as "warning" in light of that sense for the related verb used at v. 10 (wĕʾāʿîdâ, "and I give a warning") amid a number of other terms that are echoed in v. 19.

Now that the people had rejected Yahweh's directions for life's journey, death confronted them. This is the message of the grounds and announcement of disaster, which are reinforced by the initial quotation formulas in vv. 16 and 21. In between them another announcement is already made in v. 19a, so that there is an overall ABA′B′ structure, with reasons given in the course of vv. 16–17 and resumed in vv. 19b–20, and announcements introduced by "Therefore" and "Look" issued in vv. 18–19a and in v. 21.

[16] The quotation formula does not just introduce what follows as oracular, but opens a report of previous dialogue, as the subsequent narrative statements in vv. 16b–17 show (Peake 1:141). The people had refused the basic revelation given by Yahweh, which was a prescription for living. Life is pictured as a journey for which moral choices had to be made at every juncture. Only thus could one stay on the path that led to blessing and travel restfully or without mishap, unimpeded by self-generated crisis (cf. 45:3; Ps 16:8, 11). "Age-old paths" refer to torah traditions in light of the resumptive reference to the torah in v. 19. Each generation faced a divine challenge to govern their lives by its teachings for their own good.

Jesus included the last colon of the divine command in his own invitation at Matt 11:28–30, which should be connected with the next two pericopes about resting on the Sabbath (Matt 12:1–14). The issue in both cases was the torah, for Jeremiah whether it was honored, for Jesus how it was interpreted (cf. Matt 5:17–20), with or without the oral torah of the Pharisees.

[17] Yahweh had supplied a second channel of revelation, a series of prophets who warned of impending crisis when the people's behavior warranted it. They are pictured as lookouts, blowing their horns when danger loomed (cf. Hos 8:1; 9:8; Ezek 33:1–7). This back-up provision was also ignored.

[18–19] A rhetorical call is issued to the world, to mark Yahweh's words, to formally witness an unerring threat, that "this people"—a phrase as distasteful as it was in 5:23—who had disdained those two channels of revelation was indeed heading for danger. It was a self-incurred danger of "a bad fate," after abandoning the right path that led to "good" (v. 16). The two revelatory channels are repeated inversely as Yahweh's prophetic "messages" and "torah."[50] In the context of vv. 13–14 there is an implicit critique of Jeremiah's prophetic rivals as not bearers of such messages, and of the priests as poor teachers of the torah (cf. 2:8). The refusal to pay attention is consistent with v. 10 and so con-

---

50. See J. Philip Hyatt, "Torah in the Book of Jeremiah," *JBL* 60 (1941): 381–96, esp. 389–90.

Coming Disaster and Its Causes 89

nects with Yahweh's "message" through Jeremiah. Accordingly he stands in noble succession to earlier prophets of judgment.

[20] An objection from the people is forestalled and a regular component of earlier prophecy is cited (cf. Isa 1:10–17; Hos 6:6; 8:13; Amos 5:21–24). Did not their sacrificial gifts to Yahweh show sincere commitment on their part? And did not exotic imports from abroad—frankincense from the Sabeans in South Arabia to make into incense (cf. Exod 30:34–38) and aromatic grasses as an ingredient for the anointing oil (Exod 30:23)—prove their generous devotion? No, as Jer 7:21–24 will later explain, such worship only worked when it meshed with a more broadly based journey through life. "Surely to obey is better than sacrifice" (1 Sam 15:22). Cultic frills could not compensate for this basic lack, nor even sacrifices of worship. A traditional priestly formula regarding their acceptability is echoed in Yahweh's name (cf. Lev 22:20; 23:11).

[21] A formal announcement of disaster at Yahweh's hand rounds off the oracle. It glances back over the piece, emotively repeating "this people" from v. 19 and resuming the motif of a journey from v. 16. It would not be a quiet and comfortable journey for them, but one that was impeded by roadblocks and ended in death. All the groups in the community would be involved; their capture in v. 11 is now taken further. They would "tumble," as v. 15 had said. The oracle in vv. 16–21 explains what this meant in terms of the larger picture of life's journey with God as guide.

6:22–30 Consequences of Failing the Test

22 Here is what Yahweh said:

"Look out, a people is coming
    from the north country,
a powerful nation is being roused
    from the remotest parts of the earth.
23 Bows and javelins[a] they grip;
    a cruel entity, they are merciless.
The noise they make is like the roaring sea,
    as they ride upon horses.
Each of them[b] is deployed for battle
    against you, Lady Zion."
24 We have heard news of them,
    we have lost our nerve.
We are gripped with anguish,
    with pain such as a woman in labor feels.
25 Do not go out into the countryside,
    do not use the roads,

>   because the enemy's sword is there,
>   terror is everywhere.
> 26 My poor people, wrap sackcloth around your waists
>   and roll about in the dust.
>   Engage in mourning as you would for an only son,
>   in bitter lamentation,
>   because suddenness will mark the coming
>   of the destroyer against us.
> 27 "An assayer I have made you among my people,[c]
>   so you may learn and assay their behavior."
> 28 They are all stubborn rebels,
>   going about badmouthing others.
>   Copper and iron are they all,[d]
>   acting corruptly.
> 29 The bellows were scorched by the fire,
>   the lead was used up.
>   Futile has been the smelter's refining work;
>   the bad elements are not separated out.
> 30 Reject silver is what they are called,
>   because Yahweh has rejected them.

a. For *kîdôn*, "javelin," and its later meaning "scimitar," for which REB wrongly opts, see Holladay 1:224.

b. MT *kĕʾîš*, "like a man," for which LXX secondarily presupposes *kāʾēš*, "like fire," is generally understood either as "as one man" (NJB) or as "like a warrior" (NRSV), but neither alternative is viable. John A. Emerton, "A Problem in the Hebrew Text of Jeremiah vi. 23 and l. 42," *JTS* 23 (1972): 106–13, has plausibly proposed early dittography of *kap*, so that *ʾîš* in the sense of "each, every one," is the subject. NAB concurs.

c. The textual tradition adds *mibṣār*, "fortification," probably the result of incorporating a marginal gloss that related *bāḥôn*, "assayer," to *bāḥûn*, "watchtower," an allusion to Yahweh's defensive equipping of the prophet in 1:18 (*BHS*). Thus NAB, NJB, and GNB omit the term. An alternative is to repoint to *mĕbaṣṣēr*, "refiner" (NRSV, NJPS; cf. REB).

d. A change in the phrasing of MT integrates the metals with the context and provides external parallelism (Holladay 1:230). The mixture of metaphorical and moral terms has prompted the deletion of these metals as a further gloss, either from 1:18 or from Ezek 22:18, 20 (*BHS*, NAB). Perhaps, however, the presence of "copper [or bronze] and iron" was a factor that encouraged the gloss relating to 1:18 in v. 27.

Eventual invasion was inevitable because Yahweh's people failed Jeremiah's test. This composition follows a pattern laid down in vv. 1–15, featuring first "Lady Zion" and then "my people" in two units (vv. 22–26 and 27–30). Moreover, it too moves from a description of the northern invaders in an announcement of disaster to a role for Jeremiah that discloses reasons for the disaster. Here also appears a mixture of divine and human speech, as in the units in vv. 1–8 and 9–15. In this case the human speech is Jeremiah's in vv. 24–26, 28–30, like vv. 10–11a.

[22–23] The divine intervention announced in v. 21a finds virtual continuation in these human consequences, which parallel those set out in vv. 1–6a. The present passage is similar to 4:5–8, 15–17, and especially 5:15–17, with its description of the invaders and the threat they would pose. "The farther the land is from which the enemy comes, the more strange and terrible he appears to the imagination" (Keil 1:146). This military juggernaut is delineated with a mass of such frightening details. Here its target is finally disclosed as Jerusalem, which is suddenly addressed in a disturbing climax.

[24–26] Jeremiah empathically projects himself into the coming disaster as one of the victims inside Jerusalem. The "gripping" of v. 23 is echoed in the reaction of v. 24; the climactic "against you" finds a counterpart in "against us" (v. 26). The prophet uses the cultural convention of reaction to bad news.[51] The news causes demoralization and agonizing distress. The prophet urges the citizens not to go outside the city for work or travel and risk death from a ubiquitous enemy. He appeals to them to engage in mourning rites with the terrifying awareness that the invasion spelled a futureless end for a number of families in Jerusalem. Jeremiah is summoning the people to an anticipatory funeral dirge (cf. 2 Sam 3:31).[52]

[27] The prophet is given a metaphorical role as an analyst testing for metallic purity, a role similar in meaning to that of the inspectors in 5:1–2. The role assigns to him part of the responsibility for determining judgment. Elsewhere in the book it is Yahweh's task to do the assaying (e.g., in 9:7 [6]).

[28–30] This passage is Jeremiah's report, first translating the analogy of silver analysis into moral language and then highlighting metaphorical terms taken from the production of pure silver, a complex and difficult task that here proves a waste of time. The imagery is a sophisticated version of giving reasons for disaster; as in v. 13, it finds the people's wrongdoing to be all-inclusive. The Hebrew phrase rendered "stubborn rebels," *sārê sôrĕrîm*, uses the same assonance of homonyms to reinforce the meaning as in 5:23. There were two stages in obtaining silver: smelting the crude ore and then refining it into pure silver. Both stages had been used metaphorically by Isaiah (Isa 1:21–26). Jeremiah developed the second stage, while Ezekiel was later to develop the first (Ezek 22:18–22). In the refining process bellows raised the temperature of the furnace, but here they were damaged by the heat, so long did the work take.

---

51. See Delbert R. Hillers, "A Convention in Hebrew Literature: The Reaction to Bad News," *ZAW* 77 (1965): 86–90.

52. See Karl-Friedrich Pohlmann, *Die Ferne Gottes—Studien zum Jeremiabuch: Beiträge zu den "Konfessionen" im Jeremiabuch und ein Versuch zur Frage nach den Anfängen der Jeremiatradition* (BZAW 179; Berlin: de Gruyter, 1989), 155–57.

Lead was added as a flux to carry off the other metals and leave the silver, but a sufficient quantity was required for it to be effective. In this case it was used up before the refining was complete.[53] The prophet is reporting that the experiment to extract pure silver proved a failure. He has evidently pronounced his decision so that now it is generally acknowledged that here was no "choice silver" (Prov 10:20) but reject silver. In plain terms, since he was functioning as God's agent, it meant divine rejection of the covenant people—who had rejected Yahweh's torah traditions (v. 19). As in 5:1–2, no redeeming core could be found, and so the judgment of vv. 22–26 was inevitable.

An intriguing feature of this composition is the contrasting roles played by Jeremiah. In vv. 24–26 he functions as representative of the city's population, siding with them emotionally (cf. 4:19–21). In vv. 28–30, however, his role is to represent Yahweh over against the people at large, as earlier in v. 9. It is not difficult to appreciate the tension resulting from having a foot in each camp, which would find expression in the laments that begin in ch. 11.

7:1–10:25 The Self-Paved Road to Exile

7:1–20 The Exilic Outcome of Nominal and Pagan Worship

> **7:1** *A message that Jeremiah received from Yahweh, which said:* **2** "Stand by the gate of Yahweh's temple and there proclaim this message, saying, 'Listen to the message from Yahweh, all you Judeans *who are coming through these gates to worship Yahweh.* **3** Here is what Yahweh *Almighty*, Israel's God, said: "Let your conduct, your practices, be good so I can let you go on living[a] in this place. **4** Stop putting your trust in the false slogan, 'The complex is[b] Yahweh's temple, Yahweh's temple, Yahweh's temple!' **5** Instead, if you let your conduct, your practices, be good, if you act with justice in individual relationships, **6** not exploiting resident aliens, orphans, or widows and never[c] spilling innocent blood in this place, and if you do not follow other gods, which will prove bad for you, **7** then I will let you go on living in this place, in the country that ages ago was my gift to your forebears forever. **8** Look, you are putting your trust in a false slogan that will prove useless. **9** What![d] You steal, murder, commit adultery, swear false oaths, and sacrifice to Baal and follow other gods you did not know before, **10** and then you come and stand in my presence in *this* temple[e] that goes by my name and claim, 'We are saved'—only to go on committing all these abominable sins! **11** Is a cave occupied by

---

53. For the explanation I am indebted to Holladay 1:230–32. See also Robert J. Forbes, "Extracting, Smelting, and Alloying," in *A History of Technology*, vol. 1: *From Early Times to Fall of Ancient Empires* (ed. C. Singer et al.; Oxford: Clarendon, 1954), 572–99, esp. 581–85.

The Self-Paved Road to Exile 93

thugs the way you regard in your mind's eye *this* temple that goes by my name? Look out, I can see too!" declared Yahweh.

12 "Go, for example, to my place at Shiloh, where I formerly localized my name, and see how I treated it because of the bad behavior of my people Israel. 13 So now, because you have committed all these sins," *declared Yahweh,* "and when I spoke to you[f] you did not listen and when I called you you did not respond, 14 I will treat the temple that goes by my name, in which you have put your trust, and the place I gave you and your forebears just as I treated Shiloh. 15 I will also throw you out of my presence, just as I threw out *all* your kinsfolk, all of Ephraim's descendants."

16 "As for you, do not pray on behalf of this people, do not raise a shrill plea or any petition, and do not implore me, because I am not going to listen to you. 17 Can you not see how they are behaving in Judah's towns and on Jerusalem's streets? 18 Sons are collecting sticks, fathers are getting the fire to burn, and the womenfolk are kneading dough to make cakes for the Queen[g] of Heaven. They are also offering libations to other gods, making me upset as a result. 19 Am I the one they are upsetting?" declared Yahweh. "Is it not themselves, with the prospect of being so shamefaced? 20 Therefore"—here is what *the Lord* Yahweh said—"look out, my furious anger is about to descend in a deluge on this place, on humans and animals, on trees in the countryside and crops in the ground, and it will burn out of control."

a. NAB and NRSV, following Ehrlich, *Randglossen*, 4:259–60, and Rudolph 50, repoint and translate, "I will live with you," here and in v. 7, with minimal textual support; cf. *BHS*. See the critique of McKane 1:160–61.

b. Literally "They are," with reference to the complex of rooms and buildings in the temple area (cf. 2 Chr 8:11).

c. See Joüon §160f, for this negative expression.

d. See Joüon §§161b, 123w, for the exclamatory nuance of the interrogative particle.

e. LXX has "the temple" and in v. 11 "my temple."

f. LXX lacks *haškēm wĕdabbēr*, "over and over again," which was imported into MT by assimilation to a similar, shorter formula in 35:14, with which 35:17b may be contrasted. Reminiscence of the two juxtaposed formulas in a section of ch. 35, where v. 15 is very similar to vv. 3, 6–7 here, probably encouraged the addition. See Janzen, *Studies*, 37. EVV retain MT.

g. See *BHS*. MT points as "work (of heaven)," with "the host of heaven" (8:2, NRSV) in view, via Gen 2:1–2 (Duhm 79).

Jeremiah 7:1–8:3 consists of a collection of prose passages with cultic overtones. It falls into five oracles of disaster, with the first two functioning as a literary composition (7:2–20) and the last three as another (7:21–8:3). The collection marks the first appearance in the book of a series of what are called prose sermons, since these prose oracles are all marked by recurring solemn, sermonic phraseology.[54] So it stands apart from the poetic oracles that precede and follow. MT places in v. 1 an oracle reception heading (cf. 11:1) similar to the one in 1:2, and so explicitly invests 7:1–8:3 with a macrostructural role parallel to that of 1:2–2:3.[55] The two passages buttress the intervening poetic oracles, and both find the root of Judah's problems in its religious attitude (cf. 1:16). The function of the collection will be further assessed after the commentary on 7:1–8:3, but for now it can be noted that its most distinctive content is not new. Its dominant theme of the divine revelation of torah and prophets (7:5–6, 9, 13, 23, 25–26, 28) has been anticipated in 6:16–19 and its derogatory references to burnt offerings and sacrifices (7:21–22) in 6:20.

Within the collection the double literary shaping is outlined by the initial quotation formulas that occur at vv. 3 and 21. The identity of divine titles achieved by MT in these formulas has accentuated the structuring as a pair of compositions. The formula at v. 20 has a subsidiary role in view of the prefixed "Therefore"; it provides the final part of an overall framework for vv. 3–20. Similarly the closing quotation formula in MT at 8:3 makes a structural statement in that it rounds off 7:21–8:3. The embellished divine titles in MT at 7:3, 20, 21, and 8:3 draw attention to these formulas and enhance their role as structural signposts, while other quotation formulas are left unadorned.

The two pieces of the first composition, vv. 1–15 and vv. 16–20, are closely related, as their common words and phrases show: "place," vv. 3, 6, 7, 12, 14/20; "listen," vv. 2, 13/16; "see," vv. 11, 12/17; and "other gods," vv. 6/18. In each case a single occurrence in the second piece caps the earlier instance(s).

[7:2–15] The first oracle of disaster has an elaborate structure. Basically it consists of reasons (vv. 8–11a) and an announcement (vv. 13–15). MT signals the formal announcement with its own quotation formula (v. 13). Both parts have preparatory exhortations (vv. 3–7 and 12). Verse 11b initiates the process of disaster emanating from Yahweh, as the quotation formula indicates; it refers to the registering of incriminating evidence. The reasons and the enlarged announcement are demarcated by *hinnēh*, "Look," "look out," in vv. 8 and 11b.

[2] The earlier text has simply a call for attention like 2:4; it identifies the addressees of the following oracle as "Judeans." MT provides greater specificity, creating links between vv. 3–15 and the temple sermon in 26:1–6 by giving this oracle a temple setting and identifying the hearers as worshipers. It is similar to 26:2, "Stand in the court of Yahweh's temple . . . coming to worship." However, the different location, "by the gate of Yahweh's temple," suggests that the redactor was taking pains not to identify the two oracles as different versions

---

54. See "Literary Development" in the introduction.
55. Neumann,"Problem der Wortempfangsterminologie," 210.

of the same oracle but simply to associate them.⁵⁶ Reference to the temple as the scene for the oracle is continued in MT by the specification "this" when the temple is mentioned in vv. 10 and 11, which copy 26:6, 9. At an earlier stage there was no interest in providing a particular setting.

[3–7] The long hortatory passage has an ABA′ structure. Two exhortations are given in vv. 3b and 4, and then the first is repeated in an expanded conditional form in vv. 5–7. In light of the offenses listed in vv. 8–11a, the exhortations have a hypothetical role, setting up positive possibilities that the oracle recognizes were not realized and broaching negative possibilities that must eventually be realized instead because of the people's wrong choice (vv. 14–15). "Conduct . . . practices" echoes 4:18.

[3] A "place" refers to "storied" space.⁵⁷ The term brings with it a host of associations that invite reflection. Here it connotes "a permanent haven of security."⁵⁸ In this first, positive exhortation "this place" refers to the land, as it often does in Deuteronomy (e.g., Deut 9:7; 11:5; 26:9). It is appositionally defined thus in v. 7, in the condensed version of v. 7 at v. 14, and also in v. 20. Yet a twofold organic relationship between temple and land is presupposed in vv. 3–15. First, in v. 12 "my place" refers to the old sanctuary at Shiloh, presumably as a place given over to Yahweh's use in differentiation from an implicit "your place," or more exactly "the place I gave you" (v. 14). The repetition of "place" in a different sense, as God's space over against Israel's space, seems significant. Second, throughout the passage there is oscillation between the two entities. While in v. 3 occupation of the land is tied to a good lifestyle, this conditional exhortation is immediately followed in v. 4 by a second exhortation related to the temple. Later, v. 10 will complain of temple worship that was disconnected from a lifestyle befitting the people. Land, temple, and people function as a vital triangle, and the sort of people the Judeans should be is the focus with which the oracle begins. The basic connection between temple and land for the people in the OT was that their privilege of worshiping in the temple carried with it the further privilege of living in Yahweh's land.⁵⁹ One element of this tradition was the lifestyle of the worshiping people, expressed in the entrance liturgies of Psalms 15 and 24:3–6.⁶⁰ This element receives focus at the

---

56. Janzen, *Studies*, 36–37, observes that the phrase "come through these gates" has been borrowed from 17:20 and 22:2, where it refers rather to the gates of the city and palace, respectively; it was attracted by the call for attention in both verses.

57. Walter Brueggemann, *The Land: Place as Gift, Promise, and Challenge in Biblical Faith* (OBT; Philadelphia: Fortress, 1977), 187.

58. Donald F. Murray, "*mqwm* and the Future of Israel in 2 Samuel vii 10," *VT* 40 (1990): 298–320, esp. 319, with reference to 2 Sam 7:10.

59. Ronald E. Clements, "Temple and Land: A Significant Aspect of Israel's Worship," *TGUOS* 19 (1961/62): 16–28. He refers to vv. 3, 5–7 on p. 23 n. 1.

60. Cf. ibid., 26–27.

outset and in the fuller repetition of vv. 5–7, expressed in terms of the land. The people's lifestyle functions here as the condition of living in the land and in v. 10 as the criterion for worshiping in the temple. So large does this element loom that, if it is negated, it is capable of nullifying in turn both the temple privilege and the land privilege; once this element goes missing, the rest of the triangle collapses.

[4] The second exhortation, now a negative one about the temple complex, involves a "false slogan," which will be explained further in the accusations of vv. 8–11. For now it is provocatively dismissed as an empty claim, ironically enhanced by fulsome repetition, as if saying something often enough makes it true. In another context such a statement could have been meaningful, as when Jacob exclaimed, "This is none other than the house of God, and this is the gate of heaven" (Gen 28:17; cf. 1 Chr 22:1). Here, however, it has a hollow, unspiritual ring because the temple, rather than Yahweh, was the skewed object of the people's trust, as the oracle will reiterate in the accusation of v. 8 and in the announcement of punishment at v. 14.

[5–7] The first of the two exhortations is repeated in an explicit conditional statement that defines the "good" behavior of v. 3 in terms of a sketch of sins to be avoided. Failure to avoid such sins would lead to "bad" consequences, it is ominously added. "Justice" is used as a comprehensive ethical principle, as in 5:1, 4–5. The sketch is intended as a rough summary of torah traditions like those in Hos 4:2 and in the entrance liturgies, except that here pagan worship is included. The corollary of continued life in the land is not only related to God's ancient gift (cf. 2:7), but counterpoised with the disappointed intention that the gift should be permanent (cf. 1 Sam 2:30).

[8–11a] The oracle moves to direct accusation, which builds in an inverse order on the exhortations of vv. 3–4. Now the slogan is judged by the test of pragmatism. It is "useless," like pagan worship in 2:8, 11, and can bring no real blessing. The continuation of the accusation in vv. 9–10 explains the false slogan as a replacement of sincere acknowledgment of a moral God with nominal worship. Now the lifestyle criterion no longer mentions the land, but is linked with temple worship, in keeping with the basic theological principle that linked all three. The sketch of offenses is here slightly different, placing climactic emphasis on religious sins as befits the temple link. It is reminiscent of the formal summary found in the Ten Commandments (Exod 20:1–17; Deut 5:1–21). The novelty of pagan worship invokes Deut 11:28; 13:2, 13 (3, 14). The claim to be "saved" seems to echo Zion theology. Israel was protected by Yahweh's presence in the temple, which spread "a security blanket" (Miller 635) over Jerusalem and the land (cf. NIV "to save all the afflicted of the land," Ps 76:9 [10], using a different Hebrew verb; Isa 31:5). The accusatory section of the oracle is capped in v. 11a by the comparison of a criminals' hideout (cf. 1 Sam 22:1–2; 24:3; 27:8–9). Jesus reapplied the striking comparison when he cleansed the temple, protesting commercial transactions in the outer court (so Mark 11:17).

[11b] The transition to an announcement of disaster is marked by a play on the people's presumed mental perception of the temple and Yahweh's visual perception of their impropriety (cf. Holladay 1:247). As in Gen 6:12–13; 11:5, 7–8, divine observation is the prelude to punishment.

[12] An exhortation, parallel to those in vv. 3–4, introduces the announcement of disaster at Yahweh's hand. The verb "see" is repeated, but now in a call to the people to inspect the ruins of Shiloh some twenty miles to the north, the location of Yahweh's former sanctuary (cf. Ps 78:60; 1 Sam 4:11).[61] The historical precedent is explained in terms of "bad behavior," an ill-boding echo of the present generation's implied repudiation of "good" behavior in vv. 3 and 5, and the prospect of "bad" treatment in v. 6. So why should the Jerusalem temple be spared? The phrase "localized my name" (*šikkēn šĕmî*) is Deuteronomic (cf., e.g., Deut 12:11). However, it does not carry any specialized theological meaning here, but functions simply as a stylistic variant of the naming phrase used in vv. 10 and 11, which itself underscores "Yahweh's temple" in v. 4. It looks like a "deuteronomizing" adaptation of (*ʾōhel*) *šikkēn*, "(the tent) He had set" (NJPS), used of the Shiloh sanctuary in Ps 78:60.

[13] A summary of the accusation adds a new element, the rejection of Yahweh's prophetic revelation as well as of the torah, a motif that echoes 6:17 and that vv. 25–26 will repeat more fully. In light of this failure to listen to earlier warnings, the initial "Listen" (v. 2) is an ironic introduction to an oracle that initially sounds like another warning, but becomes an outright message of disaster.

[14–15] The disaster first picks up the cultic precedent of v. 12, but then affects the land. It fits the oracle as a whole in that it concerns the people's loss of both temple and land privileges. Their interconnectedness is underscored by repetition of the motif of the divine presence (cf. 4:1), which was used of the Jerusalem temple in v. 10 and now relates to the people's loss of the land, here by exile. The structure of v. 14 is repeated in v. 15, first a future intervention and then a historical comparison. The latter in the second case cites the end of the northern kingdom, and "Ephraim" refers to what it was reduced to, the rump state that existed between 733 and 722 B.C.E. There is probably literary dependence on Ps 78:67 ("He rejected . . . the tribe of Ephraim"), after the Shiloh reference in Ps 78:60. Exile has not been mentioned in the poetic oracles of Jeremiah 2–6; the reference to exile echoes the redactional prose of 5:19.

---

61. Whether the text envisions the destruction of the sanctuary at the hands of the Philistines (cf. Ps 78:60) or of the Assyrians at the fall of the northern kingdom (cf. Jer 7:14–15; Judg 18:30–31)—or fuses the two—is uncertain. For discussion of the archaeological evidence see Israel Finkelstein, "Seilun, Khirbet," *ABD* 5:1069–72.

[16–20] The second oracle of disaster addresses the unfinished business of the "other gods" mentioned in vv. 6 and 9. So it reads like a sequel to the first, as its shared vocabulary and lack of an introduction suggest. The oracle is addressed to Jeremiah and features at beginning and end two of the three linked entities of the previous piece, "this people" (v. 16) and "this place" (v. 20) in the sense of the land again. The third entity, Yahweh's temple, is replaced by worship of "the Queen of Heaven" and "other gods'" (v. 18). Both the reason for disaster (vv. 17–18) and the announcement (v. 20) are prefaced with intensifying remarks (vv. 16 and 19).

[16] The reason for the coming disaster will conclude with Yahweh's reaction of anger (v. 18). It is this anger that underlies the initial warning that intercession would prove ineffective, as comparison with 18:20 shows, where Jeremiah's intercession has the explicit purpose of averting Yahweh's anger from its intended victims. Intercession on behalf of the people was a regular part of a prophet's ministry since a prophet was not only Yahweh's representative in addressing the people but the people's representative in addressing Yahweh (cf. 18:20; 27:18; 1 Sam 12:23; Amos 7:2–3, 5–6). Paul would later integrate this element into his apostolic mission (e.g., Col 1:9–12; 2 Thess 1:11–12). In this case the people's religious offenses are judged to be so flagrant that the normal prophetic service had to be suspended, letting Yahweh's anger take its destructive course, as v. 20 will affirm—in striking contrast to Moses' successful pleading after the golden calf incident (Exod 32:11–14). If the people did not listen in v. 13, now Yahweh would not listen to their advocate.

[17–18] The call for Jeremiah to "see" echoes Yahweh's seeing in v. 11 and justifies divine implacability. The offenses are presented as prevalent throughout Judah's urban communities. There is a disconcerting perversion of family values in the contributions to the worship of the Queen of Heaven (Akkadian *šarrat šāmē*). This imported Mesopotamian cult featured worship of the goddess Ishtar, to whom were offered special cakes (Hebrew *kawwānîm*, a loanword from Akkadian *kamānu*); she was syncretistically identified with the Canaanite goddesses Astarte and Asherah.[62] The cult was especially practiced by women (cf. 44:19), who here co-opt other family members for the preparations.[63] This cult is selected for mention as the most provocative instance of a number of pagan cults.

[19] Divine anger, which dominates this short oracle of disaster, here provides a preface for the announcement, as the short quotation formula implies.

---

62. See Renate Jost, *Frauen, Männer und die Himmelskönigin: Exegetische Studien* (Gütersloh: Kaiser, 1995), 39–61; John Day, *Yahweh and the Gods and Goddesses of Canaan* (JSOTSup 265; Sheffield: Sheffield Academic Press, 2000), 144–50.

63. Cf. Susan Ackerman, "'And the Women Knead Dough': The Worship of the Queen of Heaven in Sixth-Century Judah," in *Gender and Difference in Ancient Israel* (ed. Peggy L. Day; Philadelphia: Fortress, 1989), 109–24.

The Self-Paved Road to Exile

The people's provocation of Yahweh would boomerang and bring about their humiliating loss of face.[64]

[20] MT has amplified the announcement proper with the epithet "the Lord," which aptly affirms the royal status of Yahweh over against the Queen of Heaven (cf. 34:5; Isa 6:1 ["the Lord"]). The spread of pagan cults throughout the community's towns and families (vv. 17–18) was to find a corresponding but much wider effusion of punishment throughout the land. The verb "burn" is repeated from v. 18 to show that the boomerang of v. 19 would take the form of the fire of divine fury.[65]

The composition of 7:1–20 has paired nominal worship of Yahweh and pagan worship as inevitable causes of the future disaster. A combination of blind faith in the temple with rejection of Yahweh's claim on everyday life was incriminating enough, but to such sins Judah had infuriatingly added blatant worship of other gods.

7:21–8:3 *The Exilic Outcome of Nominal and Pagan Worship Reaffirmed*

7:21 Here is what Yahweh *Almighty, Israel's God,* said: "Use your burnt offerings to supplement your sacrifices—and eat the meat! **22** But I gave your forebears no such instructions. I gave them no orders at the time I brought them out of Egypt concerning burnt offering or sacrifice. **23** No, the substance of my orders to them was as follows: 'Obey me, and I will be your God and you will be my people. Go only along the road I order you to, to ensure a good future for yourselves.' **24** But they would not listen, turning a deaf ear. They went by the stubborn inclination[a] of their own bad attitude. They went backward, not forward. **25** From the time your forebears got out of Egypt, right up to the present, I have been sending you all my prophetic servants[b] over and over again. **26** But they have not listened to me, turning a deaf ear. Instead, they have dug in their heels, *behaving worse* than[c] *their forebears.* **27** *You are to speak all this to them, but they will not listen to you. Proclaim it to them, but they will not respond to you.* **28** So you are to say to them, 'This is the nation that has not obeyed Yahweh *its God* and would not accept correction. Trustworthiness is dead, banished from their lips.

29 Cut off your hair and throw it away,
    and raise a funeral lament in the bare places,

---

64. For the verb of provocation used in vv. 18–19 and elsewhere in the book as the pivot between sin and punishment, see Samantha Joo, *Provocation and Punishment: The Anger of God in the Book of Jeremiah and Deuteronomistic Theology* (BZAW 361; Berlin: de Gruyter, 2006).

65. Cf. Charles D. Isbell and Michael Jackson, "Rhetorical Criticism and Jeremiah vii 1–viii 3," *VT* 30 (1980): 20–26, esp. 22.

because Yahweh has rejected
and renounced the generation that deserves his wrath.'

30 "In fact the Judeans have behaved in a way I regard in my mind's eye as bad," declared Yahweh. "They have put their detestable gods in the temple that goes by my name, defiling it. 31 They have also constructed the Topheth shrines that are in Ben Hinnom Valley, at which to set fire to their sons and daughters—something I never ordered, something that never crossed my mind. 32 Therefore, look out, the time is coming," declared Yahweh, "when Topheth and Ben Hinnom Valley will no longer be so called, but [the latter will be called] Slaughter Valley, while Topheth will be a cemetery, as long as it has any room left. 33 Then the corpses of this people will become food for birds in the sky and for beasts on the ground, with nobody to scare them off. 34 I will also eliminate from Judah's towns and Jerusalem's streets sounds of joy and gladness, such as the shouts of bridegroom and bride, because the country will be turned into a devastated area.

8:1 "At that time," declared Yahweh, "the bones of Judah's kings and its officials, of priests and prophets, and of Jerusalem's populace will be taken out of their graves 2 and exposed to the sun, moon, and all the other heavenly bodies that they loved and served and followed, which they turned to and worshiped. Instead of being collected and buried again, the bones will be left lying on the ground like dung. 3 Death will be preferable to life for all the survivors, the surviving members of these *bad* folk living in all the[d] places I will have driven them away to," *declared Yahweh Almighty.*

a. LXX lacks *bĕmōʿēṣôt*, "by plans," which is intrusive in this formula. It probably originated as a marginal gloss that had the parallelism of Ps 81:12 (13) in view and was offered as an alternative construct noun (Janzen, *Studies*, 11). NAB, NIV, and GNB omit.

b. The textual tradition adds *yôm*, "day," which was understood in the context as *yôm yôm*, "day by day." It probably represents an inappropriately incorporated marginal anarthrous alternative to *hayyôm*, "the day" (translated "the present"), for which cf. 1 Sam 29:8 and Neh 5:14. Dittography (*BHS*) is less likely. NAB, REB, and GNB omit.

c. LXX "more than."

d. LXX and Syr. lack *hannišʾārîm*, "remaining," the product of vertical dittography in MT. The term (in a feminine form) is written above the line as a correction in 4Q72 (cf. *BHS*). Janzen, *Studies*, 38, observes its intrusive position in a set formula. EVV except NJPS omit.

[7:21–8:3] These next three oracles of disaster (vv. 21–29, 30–34, and 8:1–3) make up a companion set to the first two oracles. Like the first set, it

The Self-Paved Road to Exile 101

moves in theme from Yahweh-related temple worship (v. 21) to pagan worship (v. 31; 8:2), via the bridging 7:30, and first addresses the people (vv. 21–25) and then speaks of them in the third person (7:26–8:3). As in vv. 12 and 16, it moves away from "my people" to "this people" (vv. 23, 33). It shares a number of motifs and terms with the previous composition, such as polarity between "good" and "bad" (vv. 3, 5, 6, 12/23, 24, 30, accentuated in MT at v. 26 and 8:3), the motifs of rejection (vv. 15/29) and of anger (vv. 18, 20/29), the term "forebears" (vv. 7/22, 25, 26), the novelty of paganism (vv. 9/31), Israel's failure to "listen" to Yahweh (vv. 13/26, amplified by v. 27 in MT), "the temple that goes by my name" (vv. 10, 11, 14/30), "Judah's towns" and "Jerusalem's streets" (vv. 17/34; cf. "Judah" and "Jerusalem," 8:1). An overarching frame for the pair of compositions is provided by "this place" of present domicile (7:3) and the "places" of subsequent exile (8:3), while another appears in MT, a contrast between worship of Yahweh and worship of celestial bodies (7:2; 8:2).

[21–29] This oracle explains why disaster has to come. It begins with an exhortation like those of vv. 3–4, 16. Just as the exhortation of vv. 3–4 was amplified in vv. 5–7, so this one is explained in vv. 22–23 in a divine report. The report continues in vv. 24–28, giving reasons for disaster, while v. 29 briefly alludes to the disaster itself.

[21] The sarcasm of the exhortation is obvious from its conclusion. "Sacrifices" were a type of animal offering that was only sacrificed partially on the altar, while the rest was handed back for a sacred meal. Here they are supplemented by burnt offerings, another type of animal offering that was wholly sacrificed. The priority of "sacrifices" and the option of two types of offering suggest that the cultic situation in view is the private temple ritual associated with an individual's payment of a vow, voluntary offering, or thanksgiving offering. In such cases either a (partial) sacrifice or a burnt offering was permissible according to Lev 22:18–21; Num 15:3, 8, with the latter option being an extravagant sign of greater personal devotion (cf. 2 Chr 29:31; Ps 66:13–15). Individuals are exhorted to go the extra mile in their ritual worship—but then told they might as well eat the burnt offerings. The implication is that it was all a matter of indifference to Yahweh.

[22–23] The explanation is closely akin to 6:16–20, where "burnt offerings" and "sacrifices" are rejected as a one-sided response to Yahweh. They ignored the way of life urged in the ancient torah traditions and reaffirmed by the prophets. Here, however, the same point is made much more strongly in terms of an apparent denial that the whole cultic system summed up in terms of "burnt offering" and "sacrifice" belonged to the older tradition of the covenant. The switch from suffixed plural nouns in v. 21 to generic singulars, "burnt offering or sacrifice," in v. 22 seems to widen the cultic reference to public services of worship at which burnt offerings were regularly followed by a host of voluntary offerings before a communal meal (cf. 2 Chr 29:27–31; Ezek 43:27).⁶⁶ The older covenant tradition is given a broader, moral definition as a way of life, which is regarded as the indispensable condition for the covenant relationship between Yahweh and Israel. Exodus 19:5 is comparable, though here a two-sided formulation characteristic of the book of Jeremiah is used; it matches "Israel's God" and "my people Israel" in the first composition (vv. 3, 12; cf. MT in v. 28). This critique of sacrificial ritual is akin to Amos 5:25, but goes farther in denying not early practice but even instructions for it. Did it emanate from a circle that did not know of the Priestly claim that Israel's sacrificial system was as old as the Mount Sinai revelation (e.g., Lev 7:37–38)—or even of the literary propinquity of the Ten Commandments in Exod 20:1–17 to divine instructions for an altar for "burnt offerings" and "offerings of well-being" (a synonym of "sacrifices") in Exod 20:22–26? Or does the oracle reflect a deliberate choice to ignore such contrary evidence as was available? It is difficult to imagine a rarified form of Israelite religion that was devoid of sacrifice, and so a degree of hyperbole should be assumed, whereby the priority of Yahweh's moral demands is put in the form of a provocative overstatement.⁶⁷

[24–25] The report of Yahweh's dealings with Judah's forebears continues, but now initiates recriminations that will continue to v. 28. A mirror to present behavior in Judah is found in their forebears' repudiation of Yahweh's lifestyle mandate. Instead of making moral progress (v. 23), they regressed. The grim story continues up to the present, with the torah tradition of v. 23 being supplemented by a long prophetic tradition, which seems to be presented as inaugurated by Moses (Deut 18:15).

[26] In anticipation of the direct address of v. 28 (or vv. 27–28), the oracle turns implicitly to address Jeremiah, as if in distaste, and characterizes his contemporaries as surpassing their forebears' example.

[27] This verse, missing from LXX,⁶⁸ echoes the language of v. 13b and applies the rejection of Yahweh's prophetic revelation to Jeremiah's ministry. "Proclaim" here corresponds to "call" there, with a new sense for the same Hebrew verb *qārāʾ*. The sentence provides a bridge between vv. 26 and 28 by

---

66. Jacob Milgrom's explanation that v. 22 has in view not mandated public services but purely voluntary private sacrifices, so that Israel was providing Yahweh with optional religious extras without honoring the fundamental moral mandate ("Concerning Jeremiah's Repudiation of Sacrifice," *ZAW* 89 [1977]: 273–75), ignores the difference between vv. 21 and 22.

67. Thus McKane 1:173 finds here "not a denial that sacrifices have been a feature of empirical or institutional Yahwism . . . but . . . a denial that they are of the essence of Yahwism." However, he rightly rejects the simplistic reduction of the passage to an idiom such as Hos 6:6 employs, whereby "not . . . but" means "not only . . . but also" (e.g., Heinz Kruse, "'Dialektische Negation' als semitisches Idiom," *VT* 4 [1954]: 385–200, esp. 393–95; Harold H. Rowley, *The Unity of the Bible* [Philadelphia: Westminster, 1957], 30–41). The idiom characteristically appears in compact two-part sentences.

68. Cf. Janzen, *Studies*, 37–38.

The Self-Paved Road to Exile

explicitly including Jeremiah in the chain of prophetic witness and making his work a clinching proof of Judah's repudiation of Yahweh, on the lines of Jeremiah's complaint in 6:10.

[28] The message Jeremiah was to give begins with the form of a summary-appraisal, typically introduced by "This."[69] The lack of obedience picks up the negative reaction of vv. 24–26 (27) to the call "Obey me" in v. 23. The matching refusal of correction echoes the charges in 2:30 and 5:3 (cf. 6:8). Just as in v. 5 "justice" in the sense of an ethical principle was borrowed from 5:1, 4–5, now "trustworthiness" with the same function draws on 5:1, 3. Its oral dimension corresponds to the false oaths of 7:9.

[29] This snatch of poetry announces disaster and a crowning reason for it, in order to round off the oracle (cf. 6:30). It sounds a death knell, making an oblique reference to disaster with a call to engage in mourning rites of lamentation. The addressee of the Hebrew feminine singular imperatives, whether Jerusalem or Judah, is unclear.

[30–34] This oracle adds to vv. 24 and 27 further examples of bad behavior that must be punished. So the initial *kî* (NRSV "For"), as often, presents the oracle as an elaboration of the former one. More space is devoted to the announcement of disaster than in the previous oracle; it begins with a formal "Therefore, look out," like the second oracle in the first composition (v. 20).

[30–31] The bad behavior is religious in nature and is presented in two brief but shocking reports that feature first the installation of pagan images in the temple, with consequent defilement of its holiness, and second the building of "Topheth shrines" in the valley south of Jerusalem for child sacrifice (cf. 2 Kgs 23:10, but here the distinctive language of Deut 12:31 is used, as in Jer 19:5); "Topheth" means "the [cultic] burning place." The victims were ritually slaughtered, then burned (Ezek 16:21). The second offense is immediately denounced as utterly alien to Yahwistic tradition.

[32–33] The reprisal takes the form first of a name change that implies heavy war casualties among Jerusalem's citizens, and then of a new role for the illicit sanctuary as a burial place. This would implicitly cause defilement, thereby matching the earlier defilement of the temple. Yet so numerous would be the casualties that others would be left unburied, suffering the indignity of a standard but shocking curse (cf. 1 Sam 17:44), which is here cited in the precise terms of the covenant curse of Deut 28:26. Shocking offenses deserved a shocking fate.

[34] This extra punishment is unrelated to what immediately precedes and seems to hark back to v. 18, as the echo of "Judah's towns . . . Jerusalem's streets" (v. 17) suggests. It supplements the destruction of v. 20 as a further fitting punishment for pagan festivities. Deathly silence would replace such

---

69. Holladay 1:259, with reference to Brevard S. Childs, *Isaiah and the Assyrian Crisis* (SBT 2/3; Naperville: Allenson, 1967), 128–36.

family celebrations; in particular, wedding revelry, with its promise of the continuance of family life, would disappear (cf. 16:9).

[**8:1–3**] This final oracle, like 7:34, has a resumptive function. The reason for disaster, which is here woven into the announcement at v. 2, features worship of heavenly bodies, an Assyrian cult like the worship of the Queen of Heaven in 7:18 (cf. Deut 4:19; 17:3). Moreover, a second announcement of disaster in v. 3 amplifies the reference to Judah's exile in 7:15. So 7:34–8:3 represents three supplements to the former of the pair of literary compositions that at an earlier stage consisted of 7:1–33. In the present ordering of the text, 8:1–3 functions as a conclusion for the second composition that is parallel to that of the first and presents a horrifying and unrelieved climax.

[**1–2**] A supplementary formula, "At that time," introduces an oracle that announces a further shocking event, the widespread desecration of graves. As v. 2 explains, it is meant as a gruesome reprisal for astral worship, evidently popular among the upper classes and throughout Jerusalem (cf. 2 Kgs 21:5; Zeph 1:5).

[**3**] The exiles of 7:15 would escape such indignities. However, instead they would suffer a living death in exclusion from their proper "place," choosing death in a bitter parody of Deut 30:19.

The double block of prose oracles in 7:1–8:3 has spelled out the people's accountability for worship-related offenses, both nominal worship of Yahweh that ignored its corresponding lifestyle and various types of non-Yahwistic worship. Two features predominate. First, 7:1–8:3 is marked throughout by recapitulation. It looks back over earlier chapters and picks up their terms and themes, mainly from chs. 5 and 6. Robert R. Wilson has summed up its overall purpose thus: It "summarizes and simplifies the preceding poetic material, underscoring some of it but eliminating much content in the process. The various themes of the earlier oracles are now reduced to a simple, unambiguous message having to do with the inevitability of judgment."[70] And, it may be added, moral and religious issues are again presented as grounds for the coming disaster, which was to result in exile from the land.

A second feature that distinguishes these oracles from preceding ones is a literary one. They depend heavily on earlier texts, especially Deuteronomy and Psalm 78. These two features, along with the pervasive sermonic phraseology, suggest that these oracles in their present form are the product of redaction.[71] They represent an exilic tradition whereby Jeremiah's essential message was

---

70. Robert R. Wilson, "Poetry and Prose in the Book of Jeremiah," in *Ki Baruch Hu: Ancient Near Eastern, Biblical, and Judaic Studies in Honor of Baruch A. Levine* (ed. R. Chazan et al.; Winona Lake, Ind.: Eisenbrauns, 1999), 413–27, esp. 423.

71. Stulman, *Prose Sermons*, 132, has found 33 percent of the wording common to LXX and MT in 7:1–8:3 to consist of stereotyped terms, with the densest grouping in 7:1–6, 22–26, and 33–34.

The Self-Paved Road to Exile

relayed to a later generation. Their oracle quotation formulas lay unambiguous claim to their own prophetic authority.

A further factor must be mentioned. The repetition of "And say to them," from 7:28 in MT at 8:4, asserts a bonding between 7:1–8:3 and what follows. Is this link justified? If so, in what respects? To answer, a consideration of the relationship between the prose buttress and 8:4–10:25 is required. That literary block continues to mention many of the themes already met in chs. 2–6, while 7:1–8:3 highlights a number of the themes common to both blocks. The fate of exile that occurs in 7:15 and 8:3 glances back at the redactional prose of 5:19 and forward to 9:16 (15), which is set in another prose supplement, and to the following exile-oriented collection of texts in 9:17–10:25. The double revelation of the torah and prophecy, broached in 6:16–19, not only becomes a dominant theme of ch. 7 but reappears in 8:8–9 and the redactional 9:13 (12). The pervasive accent on pagan religion in 7:1–8:3 recalls 1:16 and runs through chs. 2–6 and also looks forward to 8:19, the redactional 9:14 (13), and the hermeneutical application to exilic conditions in 10:1–16. Key ethical vocabulary continues to be a hallmark of the text. "Trustworthiness" (7:28), itself an echo of 5:1, 3, is repeated at 9:3 (2), while "justice" (7:5), picked up from 5:1, 4–5, returns at 8:7 and 9:24 (23). Thus 7:1–8:3 functions as a focal point to call attention to certain themes that appear in the blocks that precede and follow it.

8:4–9:1(8:23) Paying the Price for Apostasy

8:4 "*And say to them*, 'Here is what Yahweh said:

"When anybody falls, they get up, don't they?
 If anybody goes away, they come back, don't they?
5 Why then has this people's[a] backsliding
 been a chronic backsliding?
[Why] have they clung to deception,
 refusing to come back?
6 I have paid close attention:
 they speak dishonestly,
while nobody shows remorse for wrong committed,
 exclaiming, 'What have I done!'
They have one and all gone away on their own course,
 like horses rushing into battle.
7 Even a stork flying in the sky
 knows its seasons,
and a dove, swift, or thrush
 observes its time for migrating here,

	but my people do not know
	Yahweh's justice.
8	How can you say, 'We are wise
	because we have in our possession Yahweh's torah'?
	In fact, look, it has been transformed[b] into falsehood
	by the false pens of scribes.
9	The 'wise' will be humiliated,
	defeated, and captured.
	Look, Yahweh's message they have rejected:
	so what kind of wisdom can they have?
10	Therefore I will give their wives to other men,
	their fields to new owners.
	The reason why is that, ranging from lowest to elite,
	every single one is greedy for profit,
	and prophet and priest alike
	are all acting falsely.
11	*They try to heal my poor people's wounds superficially,*
	saying 'You are well, quite well,'
	when they are not well at all.
12	*They will be humiliated for acting abominably,*
	though they do not feel in the least humiliated,
	they do not even know how to feel guilty.
	Therefore they will fall where others have fallen,
	they will tumble at the time when they are dealt with,"
	Yahweh said.
13	"I will gather them and destroy them,"[c]
	declared Yahweh.
	"There will be no grapes on the vine
	nor figs on the fig tree.
	The foliage will drop off,
	and what I have given to them will leave them.""(?)[d]
14	Why are we staying here? Mobilize yourselves
	and let us go into the fortified towns
	and perish there,
	because our God Yahweh means us to perish
	and has given us poison to drink
	because of our sinning against Yahweh.
15	We hoped for peace, but a good outcome has never come,
	for a time of healing, but have found terror.
16	From Dan can be heard the snorting of their horses.
	At the noise of their neighing steeds

The Self-Paved Road to Exile 107

          the entire country shakes.
          They come and devour the country and everything in it,
              each town and its populace—
17   "In fact, look out, I am releasing among you
              snakes, vipers,
          that cannot be charmed away,
              and they will bite you,"
          declared Yahweh.

18   My grimace^e is because of the sorrow,
              I feel my heart is sick.
19   Hark, listen to my poor people's cry for help
              from the distant parts of the country,
          "Isn't Yahweh present in Zion?
              Isn't its King there?"—
          "Why have they upset me with their images,
              with foreign nonentities?"—
20   "Harvest is past,
              summer is over,
          but we have not been saved!"
21   The wounding of my poor people has wounded me.
          I am in mourning, gripped by shock.
22   Is there no balm in Gilead?
          Are there no doctors there?
          Why else has there not grown
              new skin over my poor people's injury?
9:1 (8:23) I wish my head were water
              and my eyes a wellspring of tears,
          so I could weep day and night
              for the casualties of my poor people!

    a. MT represents a conflated text into which *hāʿām hazzeh*, "this people," has intruded between *šōbĕbâ yĕrûšālayim*, "Jerusalem has apostasized," as an alternative subject. LXX represents an earlier stage of the text, lacking "Jerusalem" and implying a masculine verb (cf. *BHS*; EVV except NJB, NIV, and NJPS so judge). A marginal reference to Jerusalem, which came to dominate MT, probably arose because the fourth colon of v. 5 is predicated of the residents of Jerusalem in 5:3. Verses 4–7 have a number of affinities with 5:1–9, as I observe in the commentary.
    b. See *BHS* for the repointing, which EVV apart from NJPS assume.
    c. The combination of roots in MT is acceptable; see Barthélemy, *Critique textuelle*, 2:526–27; McKane 1:189; Lundbom 1:523.
    d. The interpretation above has been retained from KJV by NRSV, NIV, and NJPS. Barthélemy, *Critique textuelle*, 2:527–29, defends it; cf. Joüon §125n. As Barthélemy

observes, the text is too difficult to have originated as a gloss. Hence the lack in LXX may simply reflect the translator's frustration.

e. Barthélemy, *Critique textuelle*, 2:529–32, has suggested that *mablîgîtî*, from a root *blg*, "smile," in this context means "my rictus," a meaning Jerome proposed in Amos 5:9 and one that here Vg. *dolor meus*, "my pain," may represent. "Incurable" and the like in some EVV assume a word division reflected in LXX (cf. *BHS*).

The literary block of 8:4–10:25, for which 7:1–8:3 functions as a prefatory block, explains why Israel could not remain in the land (7:3, 7, 15; 8:3) but had to endure exile. A pair of compositions in 8:4–9:16 (15) traces the destructive consequences of the people's apostasy from torah standards and their lack of social cohesion. Then three compositions in 9:17 (16)–10:25 are dominated by exile, both as a future threat and as a present opportunity to live up to and stand firm in their traditional faith.

Amid what at first seems a confusing mass of units, the initial quotation formulas in 8:4 and 9:17 (16) function as an organizing device that demarcates material extending from 8:4 to 9:16 (15). These formulas are to be distinguished from the subsidiary ones preceded by "Therefore" in 9:7, 15 (6, 14). The material subdivides into a pair of compositions, 8:4–9:1 (8:23) and 9:2–16 (1–15). The main evidence for this subdivision is the fourfold parallelism of the two opening units, 8:4–13 and 9:2–9 (1–8). They are both oracles of disaster that introduce the announcement phase with "Therefore" (8:10; 9:7 [6]). They both accuse the people of lack of knowledge ("know," 8:7, and "acknowledge," 9:3, 6 [2, 5], rendering the same verb, *yādaʿ*). Another of their common reasons for disaster is a related pair of terms, "deception" (*tarmît*, 8:5, and *mirmâ*, 9:6, 8 [5, 7]) and also "falsehood" (*šeqer*, 8:8, 10; 9:3, 5 [2, 4]). Furthermore they deplore the lack of two ethical principles that were paired at 5:1–5 and appeared separately at 7:5 and 28, *mišpāṭ*, "justice," in 8:7 and *ʾĕmûnâ*, "trustworthiness," in 9:3 (2). The opening units are supplemented with two more that reinforce the disaster intimated in the initial ones. They appear in 8:14–17, 18–9:1 (8:23), and 9:10–11 (9–10), 12–16 (11–15), respectively.

[4–13] This oracle of disaster, which speaks of the community in the third person (apart from v. 8), is basically made up of reasons in vv. 4–7 and announcements in vv. 9a, 10a, and 13. The third person reference to Yahweh in v. 7 appears in a stereotyped phrase and so permits a divine speaker (McKane 1:183). The oracle has been expanded in MT by the redactional insertion of vv. 10b–12 from 6:13–15, a passage that in genre is also a two-part oracle of disaster. Apart from that insertion, the piece has its own intricacy in that vv. 8–9 represent a disputation used to corroborate the foregoing reasons for disaster. In v. 4 MT bonds what follows to ch. 7 by echoing Yahweh's introductory directive to Jeremiah in 7:28.

[4–7] A syllogistic argument is used to establish the abnormality of the covenant people's persistent apostasy. "Backsliding," *mĕšûbâ*, and its associated verb, *šûb*, stand at the logical heart of the section. The root verb *šûb*, "turn," means "go away" at vv. 4 and 6 and "come back" at vv. 4 and 5, while the analogy of seasonal migration in v. 7 echoes the verb's movement to and fro. The factor of abnormality is accentuated by the exasperation detectable in the phrase "this people" in v. 5a and by the question in which it is set. The general accusation of apostasy appeared earlier at 5:6. It is explained in 8:5b in terms of "deception," which is itself amplified in v. 6. Yahweh's "close attention" is another link with the oracle of 5:1–9; it parallels the call for inspectors to thoroughly search Jerusalem in 5:1. The charge of deception is grounded in what was spoken and what was left unspoken; truth was denied both by explicit statements and by reluctance to admit failure. The key word *šûb* can connote repentance and this sense is present here; the fourth colon of v. 5 has already occurred in 5:3. The simile of warhorses caught up in the frenzy of attack captures the reckless impetuosity of the community, somewhat like the simile of the wild ass in 2:24. The avian illustration in v. 7, however, works by contrasting the unnatural with what is natural, like the sea analogy in 5:22–23. "My people" suggests the constraint of covenant standards that should have motivated the community, while the ethical principle of divine "justice" stands for those covenant standards, which, as in 5:4–5, are described as unacknowledged and ignored.

[8–9] The grounds for future disaster are underscored by a disputation, a genre used earlier (2:23–25; 3:1–5).[72] The change to a confrontational genre encourages a momentary switch to direct address, which is dropped in v. 9. The disputation rebuts a claim to wisdom, the opposite of a lack of knowledge, which was linked with folly at 4:22 (cf. 5:21). An objection the community might or did make represents the thesis.[73] There follow a dispute and, in the concluding colon, a counterthesis that inveighs against the wise. The proud claim to wisdom is backed by possession of the torah traditions that enshrined covenant standards (cf. 6:19). The rebuttal is two-pronged and in each case opens with *hinnēh*, "look." Evidently the traditions were available in a written form since the basic charge of deception in v. 5 is now developed into an accusation of scribal adaptations that misrepresented the truth. It is tempting to try to find some reference to Deuteronomy here, as older scholars did, but there seem to be in view amendments and codicils that evaded the spirit of the torah in general, such as Jesus claimed to find in the oral traditions of the Pharisees

---

72. Cf. Westermann, *Basic Forms*, 201; Adrian Graffy, *A Prophet Confronts His People: The Disputation Speech in the Prophets* (AnBib 104; Rome: Biblical Institute Press, 1984), 31–35.

73. For the community as the addressees see Roger N. Whybray, *The Intellectual Tradition in the Old Testament* (BZAW 135; Berlin: de Gruyter, 1974), 22–24.

(Mark 7:9–13). In the sphere of civil law Isa 10:1–2 may be compared. In Jer 8:9 the self-professed wise are in view, the community that spoke in v. 8 (cf. Deut 4:6). Their prospect can only be humiliation, which is spelled out in terms of military defeat. Is the root *bôš*, "be humiliated," used as a deliberate play on the root *šûb* that dominated vv. 4–6? If so, it nicely reflects the abnormality of those verses in terms of a reprisal that is a back-to-front reversal. The second prong of the rebuttal takes the community's rejection of the other channel of divine revelation, prophecy, as further proof of lack of wisdom. Thus the dispute echoes the concerns of 6:16–19 and a dominant theme of ch. 7.

[**10a**] This announcement of disaster develops the motif of military defeat already used in v. 9a. It envisions the breakdown of normal social conditions as appropriate punishment for the community's spiritual abnormality.

[**10b–12**] The redactional insertion from 6:13–15 restates the grounds for disaster within the announcement, but the inclusion of its own announcement (8:12b) before the oracle's earlier one in 8:13 betrays its secondary nature.[74] The insertion was doubtless triggered by the occurrence of the verb "captured" and of lost wives and fields in 6:11–12a. It corroborates the original oracle with five echoes. (1) The entire community was to blame, as in v. 6. (2) The reference to "prophet and priest" reinforces the critique of the double revelation of torah and prophecy in vv. 8–9. (3) "Acting falsely" echoes the falsehood of v. 8. (4) "They will be humiliated" (*hōbîšû*) repeats the verb of v. 9; in the new context the Hebrew perfect tense takes on a sense of future certainty it did not have in 6:15. (5) The reference to falling draws an arc back to the opening of the oracle—but now the falling was to be permanent. So the insertion forms an excellent redactional fit. For good measure it also anticipates terms used in the next unit at v. 15, "peace" (*šālôm*, rendered "well" in v. 11) and "healing," while "my poor people's wounds" paves the way for v. 21.

[**13**] This verse is a continuation of v. 10a, perhaps due to an editorial hand in view of the fresh quotation formula. Significantly it repeats *ʾettēn*, "I will give," in the form *wāʾettēn*, "and (what) I have given." God's own gifts to the community would be given to others. The harvest and drought metaphors symbolize the utter loss of Yahweh's usual blessings in a final endorsement of the mad world the covenant people had created for itself.

[**14–17**] This announcement of disaster is unusual in that Jeremiah mainly speaks it and includes himself with the people as he delivers it. Only at the end does Yahweh speak in confirmation, addressing "we" as "you." The announcement reinforces the preceding oracle of disaster, which focused on the rationale, and provides balance by emphasizing the shocking reality of the coming disaster; accusation is limited to the last colon of v. 14. There are no lexical links

---

74. There are differences between 6:13–15 and 8:10b–12 that are not simply orthographical in nature (Janzen, *Studies*, 95–96) but recensional (McKane 1:187–88).

with the preceding (pre-MT) piece except for "our God," which matches "my people" that was used in v. 7 in the context of an equally negative attitude to the covenant relationship. Indeed, the addition of vv. 10b–12 may have been intended to supply a parallel for v. 15 in v. 11.

[14–16] Though similar to 4:5–18, these verses tend to reflect a grimmer stage. Verse 14a echoes the initial call to take shelter in the towns (4:5), but sardonically reissues it in the light of the realization (4:7, 16) that the towns would be threatened by and eventually fall to the invading enemy. The truth of the wages of sin eventually dawns, too late. The hope of "peace" in v. 15 picks up Jeremiah's complaint in 4:10, but now as a failed hope. Verse 16a recalls the advance of the foe from the north in 4:15, including *qôl*, rendered "noise" here and "hark" there. The combination of "country" and "each town" as scenes of destruction in v. 16b is close to 4:7b. The oracle is uttered in a mood of resigned despair, in anticipation of inevitable disaster at Yahweh's hands. It also contains imaginative touches that add to the anguish, the metaphor of drinking poison and the frightening detail of earth tremors caused by countless hooves—4:13b mentioned only the horses' speed (cf. 4:24).

[17] Another new element is the snakebites in the divine punch line, which MT clarifies by adding a closing quotation formula. In 4:15–18 the metaphors for the enemy were a lion (4:7) and an east wind (4:11–12). Is an echo of Amos 5:19 intended, where by way of climax an evidently fatal snakebite is the unexpected sequel to anticipated security? In that case Yahweh's announcement develops the reversal of v. 15.

[8:18–9:1 (8:23)] This unit presents Jeremiah's own reaction to the coming disaster. Affinity with the previous piece, at least in the redactional arrangement of units, is indicated by deriving the source of the people's cry for help "from the distant parts of the country" (v. 19). The phrase recalls the news "from Dan" of an invasion that was to make "the entire country" shake (v. 16). Jeremiah's response mirrors the enormity of the disaster.[75] It recalls his passionate vision report of 4:19–21, but here with an extra element of poignancy, the fourfold "my poor people" that punctuates the piece (cf. 6:26). Jeremiah, as a Judean, could not remain unmoved by Judah's future fate. Yet there is no note of appeal, except that of the people cited in the course of vv. 19–20 as doomed to go unheard. Comparison with psalms of lament that culminate in cries to God to stop or mitigate a disaster would be misleading. The mood is not that of Lam 3:49–50:

> My eyes will flow without ceasing . . .
> until the LORD from heaven
> looks down and sees.

---

75. The text hardly supports the popular understanding in terms of divine sympathy; cf. the critique of Joseph M. Henderson, "Who Weeps in Jeremiah viii 23 (ix 1)? Identifying Dramatic Speakers in the Poetry of Jeremiah," *VT* 52 (2002): 191–206.

A more helpful parallel is the weeping of Jesus over the coming, inexorable destruction of Jerusalem (Luke 19:41–44). Form-critically it is an adaptation of the funeral lament that mourns irrevocable disaster.[76] Jeremiah speaks as an insider, yet one who has been won over to the rival cause of his divine patron. The prophet's outburst registers a heartfelt regret in face of the inevitable. The moral explicability of a tragedy does not preclude grieving its terrible consequences, especially when he has close ties with the victims. Here grief is a measure of the extent of the disaster.

The unit receives its stylistic structure from the three expressions of personal grief at the beginning, middle, and end. Inset are two barrages of triple interrogation in vv. 19 and 22; the first case is amplified by a despairing statement in v. 20.

[19] The people's questions represent a complaint based on their belief in Yahweh's royal presence in the city (cf. Pss 48:2–3 [3–4]; 99:1–2) and cited to express the extremity of the disaster. Typically in Jeremiah's oracles the third of a group of three questions asks "Why?" and leads to the resolution of a problem posed by the first two questions or to their essential point (cf. 2:14; 8:4–5). Such is the function of this third question, but here it is spoken by a different person—by Yahweh, who intervenes with an implicit answer to the first two questions. One may compare 4:19–22, where Jeremiah's response of grief to a vision of disaster was followed by a short divine explanation of the disaster. The explanation went unannounced and only its content indicated that Yahweh was the speaker. Here the shift to divine speech is more blatant in taking the form of a quotation that counters a quotation. Certainly the instant retort to the pointed, personal accusation is effective here; it exploits the convention of the third, crucial question.[77] The retort not only accuses the people of pagan worship in a dismissive, derogatory fashion ("nonentities"; cf. 2:5), but mentions its foreign origin as a damning denial of the community's right to appeal to the indigenous tradition of Zion theology.

[20] There is a proverbial ring to this statement of despair. It portrays the precarious lateness of the hour in terms of the gradual passing of the agricultural year. Here is another element of complaint—now shown to be without merit by the "why" question—that the window of opportunity was practically closed, but still God had not intervened, thus failing to maintain a long-standing tradition of delivering the covenant people.[78]

[22] This second set of questions bitterly regrets the anticipated "wounding" of Judah (v. 21). In 4:20 and elsewhere the same term, *šeber*, may be rendered

---

76. Pohlmann, *Ferne Gottes*, 166–69; cf. Westermann, *Basic Forms*, 202–3, who, however, does not cite this passage.

77. Cf. Holladay's defense in "The So-Called 'Deuteronomic Gloss' in Jer. viii 19b," *VT* 12 (1962): 494–98.

78. Cf. the commentary on 1:17–19. For the accusation of culpable delay in the complaint type of psalm lament, see Broyles, *Conflict of Faith*, 122–27.

The Self-Paved Road to Exile

"calamity," but here its pathological connotation is evident not only from the empathic, stigmata-like wounding it produced in Jeremiah's psyche, but from the medical analogies that dominate the questions. This was a fatal wound, one that medication could not cure (cf. 46:11; Gen 37:25). The third question points instead to an unspoken malignancy that left no hope of survival but only grief that time could scarcely heal.

The blend of units in this composition does the work of an extended oracle of disaster. It matches grim outcome against ghastly input, not only by the plain announcement of disaster but also by viewing it obliquely through Jeremiah's tearful eyes.

9:2–16 (1–15) What Happens When Solidarity Breaks Down

2 (1) "I wish I had available in the wilderness
    a travelers' shelter,
so I could leave my people
    and get right away from their company!
As to why, they are all adulterers,
    a pack of traitors.

3 (2) They use their tongues as they string^a their bows,
    while falsehood and untrustworthiness^b are prevalent in the country.
In fact they go from one bad act to another
    and fail to acknowledge me,"
    declared Yahweh.

4 (3) "Let everybody beware of a community member
    and put in a^c family member no trust,
because every family member launches an insidious attack
    and every community member goes around bad-mouthing.

5 (4) They all cheat on other members of the community,
    never telling the truth.
They have trained their tongues to utter falsehood,
    they do wrong and have lost their will to come back.

6 (5) Oppression after oppression, deception after deception!^{d}
    They refuse to acknowledge me,"
    declared Yahweh.

7 (6) "Therefore"—here is what Yahweh *Almighty* said—
"look out, I am going to refine them, test them—
    how else can I act since my very own people are involved?

8 (7) Deadly arrows are what their tongues are,
    deception is their talk,
With their mouths they talk peaceably to other community members,
    but in their minds they are setting traps for them.

9 (8) From these folk
         must I not exact punishment for such offenses?"ᵉ
       declared Yahweh.
       "And should not such a nation
         incur my vengeance?

10 (9) "For the mountains' sake breakᶠ into weeping and lamentation,
         for the wilderness pastures' sake into a dirge.
       The reason why is that they are laid waste and emptied of humans,ᵍ
         and the noise of cattle is unheard.
       Birds flying about, beasts—
         they have all fled, they are gone.
11 (10) Also I will turn Jerusalem into heaps of rubble,
         a haunt for jackals,
       and Judah's towns I will turn into desolate areas
         where nobody lives."

12 (11) Who is the wise person that can understand the reason, or who is qualified as someone to whom Yahweh's mouth has spoken to explain why the country was destroyed, becoming as waste and untraveled as a wilderness? 13 (12) Yahweh replied: "The reason is that they abandoned my torah that I put in front of them and did not obey me *by walking in its track*, 14 (13) following instead the stubborn inclination of their own thinking and the Baals, as their forebears had taught them." 15 (14) "Therefore"—here is what Yahweh Almighty, Israel's God, said "look out, I am going to give them—*this people*—wormwood to eat and poison to drink. 16 (15) Then I will disperse them among nations unknown to them and their forebears alike and get the sword to chase them until I have annihilated them."

   a. Literally "tread," in order to string. See John A. Emerton, "Treading the Bow," *VT* 53 (2003): 465–86. REB so renders in 46:9; 50:14, 29; 51:3, and NIV in 51:3.
   b. The former noun is to be taken with the following clause; so LXX. The negative functions as the first element of a compound noun (cf. BDB 519b). The *lāmed* before the second noun is to be deleted (cf. *BHS*). A marginal gloss comparing 5:3, *lōʾ leʾĕmûnâ*, "not to trustworthiness," seems to have eventually displaced *lōʾ ʾĕmûnâ*, "untrustworthiness," unless simple dittography was the cause.
   c. MT *kol-*, "every," missing from LXX, anticipates the parallelism of the next colon (Janzen, *Studies*, 65).
   d. This slight reconstruction of the last colon of v. 5 (4) and the first colon of v. 6 (5) depends on LXX; see *BHS*. NRSV, NAB, REB, and GNB change thus. MT has wrongly divided the consonants. In support of the change Barthélemy, *Critique textuelle*, 2:535, joins

The Self-Paved Road to Exile 115

other scholars in appealing to the association of *tōk*, "oppression," and *mirmâ*, "deception," in Pss 10:7; 55:11 (12).

e. See Holladay 1:181–82 for the value of the prepositions.

f. MT *ʾeśśāʾ*, "I break into," has assimilated the verb to the first person imperfect verbs in vv. 9 (8) and 11 (10); reminiscence of 9:1 (8:23) may have been a contributing factor. LXX, OL, and Syr. attest a plural imperative (see *BHS*); thus NRSV and NAB.

g. MT has "human travelers," adding from v. 11 *ʿōbēr*, which LXX lacks. For the resultant triple sequence of human absence in vv. 10–12 (9–11), Janzen, *Studies*, 38, has compared Zeph 3:6.

A cosmetic hinge is provided between the pair of compositions by the wishes of 9:1–2 (8:23–9:1). Their mood and focus are quite different, sympathy over the coming disaster in the former case and disgust at its underlying causes here. This composition is made up of three units, vv. 2–9 (1–8), 10–11 (9–10), and 12–16 (11–15). The first and third are complete oracles of disaster, including both reasons and reprisals, while the second is an announcement of disaster that elaborates the disaster of the prior unit. The first unit is similar to 8:4–13, while the second begins on the same mourning note as 8:18–9:1 (8:23) and concludes with the rural and urban destruction mentioned in 8:14–17. The third unit has a larger agenda, resuming material found in both compositions and elaborating it by way of summary; likewise MT adds "this people" to 9:15 (14) from 8:5.

[9:2–9 (1–8)] This oracle of disaster falls into three sections, two dealing with reasons and one with the consequent disaster. MT draws attention to the tripartite structure by adding closing quotation formulas in vv. 3 (2) and 6 (5) to match loosely the short intermediate formula in v. 9 (8). A distinctive feature of the oracle is the expansion of the reason with a wish (v. 2 [1]), to signal the heinousness of the charges.

[2–3 (1–2)] The divine wish to give a wide berth to "my people" is intended to evoke questioning surprise and so highlight the explanation. Similar imagery of Yahweh as the insider who insists on acting as an outsider occurs in a communal complaint at 14:8 in tones of astonishment. Here it is explained as a response to the people's alienation from Yahweh's standards for them. Trustworthiness, negated in v. 3 (2), was earlier used as a summarizing ethical key word for those covenant standards, in 5:1, 3; 7:28. The alignment with 5:1, 3 is striking, because there are other echoes of ch. 5 here: adultery (cf. 5:7–8), treachery ("traitors," like "faithlessness" in 5:11, renders the root *bgd*), while "deception" in 9:6, 8 (5, 7) occurred in 5:27. Adultery and treachery could be either spiritual metaphors with Yahweh as victim or literal offenses within the community. The lack of communal solidarity that dominates the oracle suggests the latter, so that "untrustworthiness" involves the breakdown of human commitments. Ultimately, however, they all function as evidence of a lack of commitment to Yahweh, since at stake were covenant standards and an unwillingness to acknowledge their upholder. The hunting metaphor for sins of speech derives from lament psalms (cf. Pss 57:4 [5]; 64:3–4 [4–5]).

[4–6 (3–5)] The second section continues the reasons for disaster. It elaborates the sins of speech from the middle colon of v. 3 (2) and develops the next phrase "from one bad act to another" into a damning description of habitual sins that had a willful, hardening effect. Not acknowledging Yahweh is heightened into a refusal to do so. "Come back" (*šûb*) in the sense of repentance briefly resumes the key word of 8:4–6.

[7–9 (6–8)] The announcement of disaster at Yahweh's hands uses the metaphor of a metal refiner, which in 6:27–30 was used of Jeremiah's ministry but here refers to Judah's ordeal as it undergoes divine punishment (cf. Isa 48:10). The covenant relationship establishes its own accountability, the cold logic of Amos 3:2. The middle portion of the section recapitulates sins of speech as the most glaring example of Judah's moral failure. Another announcement of disaster, one used already (5:9, 29), adds reinforcement.

[10–11 (9–10)] The gravity of the anticipated disaster is underscored by a plural imperative that calls for mourning as an appropriate response (cf. 4:8; 6:26; 7:29; 9:17 [16]). Focus is laid on the countryside, eerily drained not only of farmers and herds but also of birds and wild animals. Destruction suffered by urban communities, including the capital, is reserved for the climax of this portrayal of total ruin.

The message of vv. 2–11 (1–10) is that the breakdown of social cohesiveness can only issue in the dissolution of the land, including its urban structures, which had been the setting for so much misconduct. People and land were inextricably linked, and Yahweh was to preside over a collapse that would drag down people and land in a common fate.

[12–16 (11–15)] This redactional supplement (in prose apart from the bicolon of v. 12b [11b]) provides a summarizing elaboration of 8:4–9:11 (10). It is like the prose supplement of 5:19, which elaborated 5:10. As that passage did, this one gives an answer to the key question "Why?" that must have reverberated through the minds of Judean victims of invasion and exile. Verse 12 (11) looks back at an accomplished fact from the vantage point of exile, though vv. 15–16 (14–15) present what had by now happened as future events because they are intended as a representation of Jeremiah's future-oriented message. The unit is furnished with full prophetic authority in vv. 13 (12) and 15 (14). This unit takes phraseology from other parts of the book and reapplies it in an elaboration of Judah's fate.

[12 (11)] The desolation of the whole land is echoed from vv. 10–11 (9–10). The question "Why?" that is so often the bewildered, rhetorical cry of the lament psalms is fittingly attached to this terrible event. If the question is taken seriously and an answer is sought capable of satisfying mind and heart, the task is difficult enough to tax both the expert trained in wisdom traditions and the prophet—two of the three representatives of the usual channels of divine revelation that will be mentioned in 18:18. Reference to the wise alludes to the wisdom theme attested in 8:8–9a.

[13–14 (12–13)] A claim is here made, however, to have a definitive answer that has divine endorsement. The reference to torah alludes to the motif of 8:8 and puts it in general terms also present in 26:4, which MT insightfully uses in amplifying the verse. The abandoning of the torah is defined as religious (cf. 11:8 and commentary), and the deviation is seen as the culmination of a long history (cf. 2:5, 20).

[15–16 (14–15)] There was therefore no alternative to dire punishment. The metaphor of poison is an echo of 8:14 with its context of invasion and defeat; it is elaborated with the language of 23:15, which is there the punishment of the people of Jerusalem. Earlier prose supplements ended on the specific note of exile (5:19; 7:15; 8:3), and that pattern is followed here. The trigger in this case is the failure to acknowledge or know Yahweh and Yahweh's justice (8:7; 9:3, 6 [2, 5]). After mention of the empty land in vv. 10–11 (9–10), it provokes a corresponding reprisal in terms of the unknown—dispersal to unknown nations (cf. Deut 28:36). The experience of exile was to be the fate of Judeans in the land (so 24:10; 29:17–18).

Jeremiah 9:2–16 (1–15) paints a grim picture of the collapse of social solidarity and presents the desolation of the land and the dispersal of its people as inevitable consequences. The covenant triangle with Yahweh, Israel, and the land as its fixed points could continue no longer.

9:17–26 (16–25) Exile: Prospect and Challenge

17 (16) Here is what Yahweh *Almighty* said.

    Put your minds to it, call for the mourning women to come,
        send for the wise women
    to come[a] quickly
18 (17)   and utter a lamentation over us,
        so our eyes run with tears,
            our eyelids[b] are awash with water.
19 (18) Hark, here is why: a lament
        can be heard coming from Zion,
    "How terrible! We are done for,
        utter humiliation is ours,
    now that we must leave[c] the country,
        now that our homes have been demolished!"[d]
20 (19) In fact, listen, you women, to Yahweh's message,
        let your ears take in the message from his mouth,

and teach your daughters a lamentation,
    one another a dirge:
21 (20) "Death has climbed through our windows,
    has gained entry to our fortified houses,
emptying the streets of infants
    and the squares of young men,
22 (21) while[e] human corpses lie fallen[f]
    like dung spread over a field
or like swathes behind a reaper,
    left ungathered."

23 (22) Here is what Yahweh said:

"The wise should not boast about their wisdom
    nor the powerful about their power;
the wealthy should not boast about their wealth.
24 (23) Instead, this is what one should boast about:
    applying acumen to knowing me
to be[g] Yahweh who acts out of loyalty,
    justice, and right dealing in the earth,
because these are virtues I appreciate,"[h]
    declared Yahweh.

25 (24) "Look out, the time is coming," declared Yahweh, "when I will deal with all those who, though circumcised, have foreskins, 26 (25) the Egyptians, Judeans, Edomites, Ammonites, Moabites and all those denizens of the wilderness who have their temples shaved, because all the nations have foreskins—in the case of Israel's community they all have foreskins on their hearts."

    a. The repetition of the verb "(and) come" is suspicious, especially since the different vocalized forms, an unusual *ûtĕbô'ênâ* and a usual *wĕtābô'nâ*, look like alternatives. However, LXX already reflects both words, in the second case with a degenerate variant (cf. Holladay 1:309; for the omission of the next verb in LXX see Janzen, *Studies*, 119). The repetition appears to reflect urgency. The verse division in MT, after the second "(and) come," is clumsy.
    b. Or "pupils" (NJPS). See Holladay 1:313.
    c. The Hebrew perfect indicates certainty (Streane 67; Rudolph 68).
    d. Literally "they have demolished," with an indefinite plural referring to the enemy and, evidently, a developed sense of the verb (cf. Dan 8:11), which basically means "throw." LXX has a first person plural verb, a distortion under the influence of the preceding verb.
    e. MT, but not LXX, prefaces with "Speak: 'Here is what Yahweh declared,'" which NAB and REB properly do not attempt to translate. The first term, *dabbēr*, which Syr. too

The Self-Paved Road to Exile

does not represent, is reflected in later Greek translations as *deber*, "pestilence" (see *BHS*). In this sense it probably originated as a marginal interpretive comment on "death" (thus, e.g., McKane 1:209). The following quotation formula is odd and intrusive here. It seems to be a secondary textual development that presupposes the mispointing of the previous term in MT.

f. The inverted perfect corresponds to an imperfect of durative action (cf. Joüon §119u-v).

g. Literally "that I am." As in 24:7, the preceding *ʾôtî*, "me" (omitted in LXX, probably secondarily), has an anticipatory role (Rudolph 68; Holladay 1:318).

h. A monocolon closes the poetic unit (cf. Watson, *Classical Hebrew Poetry*, 169–72).

Jeremiah 9:12–16 (11–15) gave so strong an impression of literary closure to 8:4–9:11 (10) that a reader aware that the next prose buttress appears in ch. 11 is left wondering what the role of the rest of ch. 9 and ch. 10 can be. This material all flows from the motif of exile introduced in 9:16 (15) and elaborates that crisis. Thus 9:17–22 (16–21) have been included for their grief-stricken statement "we must leave the country" (v. 19 [18]), vv. 23–24 (22–23) for the worldwide role they assign to Yahweh (v. 24 [23], "in the earth"), and vv. 25–26 (24–25) for their key word "nations" that echoes the term in v. 16 (15). This key word reappears in 10:2 (and vv. 6–7, 10) as the justification for the presence of 10:1–16. Expulsion from the country (10:17–18) is the clue for explaining 10:17–25, which accordingly echoes the initial passage, 9:17–22 (16–21), rounding off the whole group. The redactional passage 9:12–16 (11–15) has set the tone for a collection of passages with similar content, 9:17 (16)–10:25, which falls into three compositions, 9:17–26 (16–25); 10:1–16; and 10:17–25. One may compare the collections of royal passages in 21:11–23:8 and of oracles about prophecy in 23:9–40, though both those collections have distinct headings.

The first composition is made up of three heterogeneous units, vv. 17–22 (16–21), 23–24 (22–23), and 25–26 (24–25), loosely tied by the overarching theme of exile and its implications. A quotation formula marks the opening of the composition, though the poem that follows does not appear to be a divine oracle.[79] It has an anticipatory role, preparing for the next quotation formula in v. 23 (22) and the other type in v. 25 (24), both of which introduce oracles.

[17–22 (16–21)] The first unit falls into two sections, vv. 17–19 (16–18) and 20–22 (19–21). Each opens with references to women mourners and moves to

---

79. Lundbom 1:557, 559, takes the rest of v. 17 (16) as spoken by Yahweh and vv. 18–22 (17–21) by Jeremiah and the people. Plural imperatives do appear in divine oracles at 5:1 and 9:10 (9), but the continuity between v. 17 (16) and the next verse (in Lundbom's terms "and let them hurry") makes a change of voice unlikely at this point.

quotations that define the anticipated disaster in first person plural language. The unit, an anticipatory summons to a funeral lament, is spoken by Jeremiah, as the third person reference to Yahweh in v. 20 (19) suggests. It echoes the divine summons in v. 10 (9) and has the same role of reinforcing the gravity of the coming disaster. So it functions as an indirect announcement of disaster, but one spoken by the prophet, as in 8:14–16. Exile, mentioned in v. 19 (18) is the warrant for the unit's inclusion here.

[17–19 (16–18)] The prophet issues a call for professionals ("wise women") to be summoned. These specialists gave expression to grief after a death or comparable crisis and so helped the survivors' transition from stunned silence to open sorrow.[80] Jeremiah looks for support in verbalizing his own grief of 8:18, 21; and 9:1 (8:23) in anticipation of the coming crisis. In justification he cites his premonitory audition of a cry of distress emanating from Jerusalem (cf. "in Zion," 8:19) in reaction to the city's fall. The cry opens with the typical *ʾêk*, "How (terrible it is that)" (cf. 2 Sam 1:19, 25, 27). Exile is spelled out as a foregone conclusion.

[20–22 (19–21)] Now the professional mourners, a family guild, are themselves addressed and urged to act as the prophet's allies in communicating the coming disaster and to let his divinely given announcements of it strike the note for their own keening. The reader has a sense of the unspecified oracles from the preceding context. An appropriate dirge is offered. Death from war and pestilence gain easy access to homes, even well-secured homes, rob the capital of two generations, and leave in its wake masses of unburied corpses.[81] Closure is achieved by hyperbolic similes that heighten the horror, similes drawn from different points in the agricultural year (the first echoes 8:2).

[23–24 (22–23)] This short piece has the most tenuous role of all those in the collection, but that it has been placed here intentionally is shown by the parallel beginnings of "the wise women" in v. 17 (16) and "The wise (man/men)" here. The unit strikingly lacks any reference to disaster, but has the form of a positive exhortation that challenges social regard for wisdom, power, and wealth and commends a different triad of priorities, the covenant virtues of loyalty (cf. 2:2), justice, and right dealing (cf. 4:2; 22:3, 15–16 [juxtaposed with "know me"]). The standard ethical principle of justice (cf. 5:1, 4, 5; 7:5; 8:7) is here expanded with two others. Those who shared Yahweh's appreciation of such virtues should show them in their community. The phrase "in the earth" is important since it anticipates the series of references to the earth (10:10–13) that refer to Yahweh's universal work as creator, maintainer of the created

---

80. Cf. Saul M. Olyan, *Biblical Mourning: Ritual and Social Dimensions* (Oxford: Oxford University Press, 2004), 49–51.

81. For a possible Ugaritic background see the discussion of Day, *Yahweh and the Gods*, 188–90.

world, and instigator of disaster. Here God's positive providential control of the world is in view. This striking piece encourages the exiles to identify themselves in faith and lifestyle with this universal God who was on their side. It is a counterchallenge to earlier accusations of not knowing Yahweh (9:3, 6 [2, 5]; cf. 4:22; 5:4; 8:7). The ironic exhortation to "boast in the Lord" reappears twice in Paul's letters to Corinth as an echo of this text, at 1 Cor 1:31 in a contrast with human wisdom and power and at 2 Cor 10:17 in an attack on unjustified self-commendation on the part of rival missionaries who were boasting "according to human standards" (2 Cor 11:18).

[25–26 (24–25)] Like the previous piece, this prose one is attached to its context by a linguistic thread, in this case "the nations." It echoes the term in 9:16 (15), one that will also appear in 10:2, 7, 10, and 25. The tantalizingly brief passage is an oracle of disaster that moves back from announcement to reason. It reinforces Jeremiah's constant message of merited disaster. It may represent a retort to an anti-Babylonian alliance made between Egypt and Judah, the Transjordan states, and Arab tribes, whose rallying cry was the shared practice of circumcision, in opposition to the uncircumcised Babylonians (Rudolph 70–71).[82] The validity of such a rallying cry is then questioned in v. 26b (25b). Both Judah and the other nations have their circumcision denied, in different ways. They both retain their foreskins, spiritually so in Judah's case. The reference in the case of the other nations is evidently to partial circumcision, whereby the foreskin was cut through and left hanging, not amputated.[83] This was not so for Judah; instead, the presence of a foreskin is metaphorical, which is underlined by a switch from a political label, "Judah," to a theological one, "Israel's community." Its circumcision, though physically complete, was "a sacrament skin-deep" (Kidner 56); there had been a failure to live up to it with a committed spiritual attitude. One may compare the charges of uncircumcised hearts in 4:4 and uncircumcised ears in 6:10. There is a contextual correlation with 9:16 (15). Judah was no better than other nations, notably those that practiced circumcision, and to be grouped with them was ironically fitting. So, it is implied, Judah could not cavil at an exilic fate among the nations.

Verses 17–26 (16–25) affirm Judah's fate of exile and its own absorption into the world of "the nations" that made such a fate inevitable. However, these verses also contain a positive message, that in exile Judah was still confronted by the God of the world and had an obligation to model itself upon virtues displayed in Yahweh's universal work.

---

82. For the widespread practice of circumcision outside Israel see Jack M. Sasson, "Circumcision in the Ancient Near East," *JBL* 85 (1966): 473–76; and Holladay 1:319. For the Arab reference see the commentary at 25:23.

83. See Richard C. Steiner, "Incomplete Circumcision in Egypt and Edom: Jeremiah (9:24–25) in the Light of Josephus and Jonckheere," *JBL* 118 (1999): 497–505.

10:1–16 Exilic Faith in Yahweh

10:1 Listen to the message Yahweh spoke to you, Israel's community. 2 Here is what Yahweh said:

"The [other] nations' ways should not be what you learn,
    and signs in the sky must not scare you
    just because the nations are scared of them.
3 As to why, the peoples' customs are inane.
    For example, a tree cut from the forest
    is made [into an idol] with a chisel by a craftsman*'s hands.*
4 Silver and gold he uses to beautify it,
    then nails and hammers;
    they fasten them[a] to stop it wobbling.
5 A scarecrow in a cucumber patch is what such things are like,
    unable to talk.
They actually have to be carried[b] around
    because they cannot walk.
Have no fear of them because they cannot do any harm—
    nor is anything beneficial within their scope!"

6 *There is nobody[c] like you, Yahweh.*
    You are so great
    and your name is powerfully great.
7 *Who should not fear you,*
    King of the nations?
    Such is your due,
because among all the wise experts of the nations,
    through all their realm,
    there is nobody like you.
8 *One and all they are stupid, moronic.*
    The nonentities they teach about are wood.[d]
9 *Hammered silver is brought from Tarshish*
    and gold from Uphaz;[e]
they are made by a craftsman, handmade by a metalsmith.
    Violet and purple fabrics are used to clothe them;
    they are all made by wise experts.
10 *But Yahweh is truly God,*[f]
    the living God and everlasting King.
    His wrath causes the earth to quake
    and the nations cannot endure his rage.

The Self-Paved Road to Exile 123

11 (Here is what you are to say to them:^g "May^h the gods who the sky and earth did not make perish from the earth and from under this sky.")

12 He is the one who made the earth by his might,
    fixed the world in place by his wisdom,
    and by his insight spread out the sky.
13 At the sound of his shoutingⁱ there is a massing of water in the sky,
    as he brings clouds up from the end of the earth.
  Lightning flashes he makes for the rain
    and he brings wind out from his warehouses.
14 Everybody is shown to be stupid, devoid of knowledge,
    every metalsmith is discredited by the idols,
  because those metal figures of his are a lie,
    lacking any breath.
15 They are nonentities, ludicrous, made objects;
    at the time when they are dealt with they will perish.
16 Not like them is Jacob's portion;
    rather, his possession is the one who shaped the universe—^j
  Yahweh *Almighty* is his name.

    a. The plural subject and object of the Hebrew verb refer to the hammers and nails, respectively, in which case the nouns qualify the earlier verb, "beautify" (Cloete, *Versification*, 161). The reverse order, "hammers and nails," in 4Q71 and LXX appears to presuppose this interpretation and may be original.

    b. See *BHS* for the Hebrew slip in the Leningrad Codex.

    c. Here and at the end of v. 7 REB prefers a pointing *mēʾayin*, "from where," presupposed by the later Greek translator Theodotion (*pothen*). This pointing is also adopted by BDB 35a, McKane 1:223–24, and Holladay 1:323. However, a negative statement or a question using "who?" is the form-critical norm with "is like" (see Casper T. Labuschagne, *The Incomparability of Yahweh in the Old Testament* [Pretoria Oriental Series 5; Leiden: Brill, 1966], 8–28). The question appears to be an easier and so secondary reading, prompted by the rhetorical question in v. 7a and by the admitted difficulty of MT *mēʾên* in place of *ʾên*, "nothing," which was perhaps corrupted by dittography of *mêm* (cf. 30:7).

    d. More lit., "(The subject of) their instruction, relating to nonentities, is wood." Cf. NAB "these idols they talk about are wooden."

    e. The location of Uphaz is unknown. It recurs in Dan 10:15, probably based on this text, which at least verifies its presence. NAB, NJB, and REB opt for the easier reading of Syr. and Tg., "Ophir."

    f. Contrary to MT, the colon ends with *hûʾ* in a resumptive sense, as in vv. 3, 8, 16 (Holladay 1:333; Cloete, *Versification*, 162–63).

    g. NAB and REB render "of them," with reference to the pagan gods or idols. But see the commentary.

h. The verb is jussive (Franz Rosenthal, *A Grammar of Biblical Aramaic* [6th ed.; Porta Linguarum Orientalium n.s. 5; Wiesbaden: Harrassowitz, 1995], §108).

i. The accentuation in MT takes *tittô*, "his giving," as an ellipsis for *tittô qôlô*, "his producing his voice, shouting." LXX has no equivalent here, but presupposes MT at the parallel 51:16. The ellipsis is feasible after the initial *lĕqôl*, "at the sound of."

j. LXX lacks *wĕyiśrāʾēl šēbeṭ*, "and Israel is the tribe (of)," while in the parallel 51:19 MT lacks *yiśrāʾēl*, "Israel," and LXX lacks both terms. This textual evidence suggests that originally Yahweh was the focus of the second colon, as of the first, and that expansion creating a third colon with a reciprocal focus on Israel took place in two stages (cf. Duhm 103; Streane 73). Initially *naḥălātô*, "his possession," was glossed with *šēbeṭ*, "the tribe of (his possession)," with reference to Jacob, in reminiscence of Ps 74:2, *šēbeṭ naḥălātekā*, "the tribe of your heritage" (NRSV). Then an explanatory "Israel" was added to 10:16 for clarity. The existence of parallel passages has made it possible to trace the textual growth developing partially in the more remote context of ch. 51, but fully here. The force of *kî* was changed from an adversative sense after a negative ("rather") to a causal one, "because he is the one who shaped the universe and Israel is the tribe that is his possession." Cf. Janzen, *Studies*, 39, 61. A two-stage textual development also occurred at 9:22 (21). The creation of an extra colon may have been motivated in part by a desire to match the pattern of two bicola in the parallel v. 10. It is tempting to take this case as a redactional issue rather than a textual one, but 51:19 hardly fits this category.

Jeremiah 10:1–16 is composed of units that are linked by their opposition to pagan religion that used images in its worship. It was later used as the basis of the apocryphal Letter of Jeremiah. The composition consists basically of two units, a divine oracle of warning exhortation, vv. 2–5, and a hymn, vv. 12–16. The intervening vv. 6–10 contain a further unit, which is structurally patterned on the hymn that follows. The structure of vv. 12–16 is threefold, an ABA′ format in which praise of Yahweh (three lines [a tricolon and two bicola], vv. 12–13, and one line [a tricolon], v. 16) is punctuated by disparaging denunciation of idol worship (three lines [bicola], vv. 14–15). This structure has been copied in vv. 6–10; hymnic material in vv. 6–7 (three lines [tricola]) and v. 10 (two lines [bicola]) is interwoven with idol material in vv. 8–9 (three lines [two bicola and a tricolon]). Verses 6–8 and 10 are absent from LXX and represent a later stage of redaction in MT. Though the Hebrew fragment 4Q71 contains no whole lines, its extant text has no room for these verses in its column arrangement, so that it corroborates the LXX evidence and shows that the latter's distinctiveness goes back to a Hebrew source. Verse 9 as far as v. 9bα is present in LXX, but appears in v. 5, after the first bicolon, and the letter spacing in 4Q71 seems to indicate that it stood there in the text of the Qumran fragment.[84] Rudolph (72) and Bright (80) wanted to put v. 9 with v. 4, but in the original order of vv. 3–5a that included v. 9, within the framework of exhortations in

---

84. See Tov's reconstruction of the text of 4Q71 in DJD 15:176.

vv. 2 and 5b, an ABA'B' structure was intended, alternating the manufacture of religious images with negative statements. Verse 9 resumed vv. 3–4 with an overlap of vocabulary, "silver," "gold," "work," and "craftsman."

[10:1–5] The piece opens with an introductory, prophetic call to attention that identifies the otherwise unidentified target of the oracle as "Israel's community." The phrase provides a neat overlap with the end of the preceding composition (9:26 [25]). The oracle takes the form of a warning exhortation and has an ABB'A' structure, a simplification of the overall ABCB'A' pattern it had when v. 9 was included in it. Exhortations frame the unit, while two reasons are inserted, the process by which divine images were made and the lack of animate features that are the marks of personhood.

The unit fits well into the collection of exile-oriented passages. In terms of vocabulary "the nations" (twice in v. 2) is its passport to membership. The question of provenance is often raised. Preuss, for example, has argued that some of its language is comparable with 1:16 and with earlier prophetic texts, Isa 2:8; Hos 8:4–6; 13:2.[85] Holladay (1:329–30) has listed lexical links with other places in the book of Jeremiah, links that do not occur in Second Isaiah. The content does fit a setting of Babylonian exile, which is consistent with the redactional intent of the collection to which it belongs. The unit seems to reflect the defiant stance of a religious minority living in the midst of a pagan environment in which astrology played a key role ("signs in the sky," v. 2), as it did in Mesopotamian religion. It is possible to compare Jeremiah's letter to the exiles in ch. 29, and interestingly the Targum claims for v. 11 the setting of a letter to the exiles. However, McKane (219) has pertinently distinguished between material decrying idolatry elsewhere in the book, such as in 1:16; 2:28; and 16:20, and a separate type of elaborately developed polemic that describes the manufacture and nature of divine images in tones of satire and ridicule, the sort of literature that appears in the tradition of Second Isaiah (Isa 40:18–20; 41:6–7; 44:9–20). So a purely exilic setting seems to be implied, with a conscious development of the prophet's teaching that used some of Jeremiah's phraseology and was intended as a continuation of his prophetic witness, as the oracle's introduction and quotation formula indicate. Along with the hymnic material that follows, the unit updates the book's denunciation of pagan religion for an exilic audience.

Here, as in other treatments of idolatry in the OT, there is a dogged refusal to admit that divine images were representational. Instead, they are identified with the gods they depicted in a humanistic and rationalizing manner that rigorously denied they shared in any supernatural reality.[86] Such a satirical tirade was

---

85. Horst D. Preuss, *Verspottung fremder Religionen im Alten Testament* (BWANT 5/12; Stuttgart: Kohlhammer, 1971), 167.

86. Gerhard von Rad, *Old Testament Theology*, vol. 1: *The Theology of Israel's Historical Traditions* (trans. D. M. G. Stalker; New York: Harper & Row, 1962), 216–17.

intended not as serious debate but as propaganda for the exiles, to enable their survival in a cultural environment that would otherwise have overwhelmed them as a religious minority. The humor of in-jokes was judged the best weapon for waging this ideological warfare. Underlying this stance was the theological claim that Yahweh is the only true God,[87] as v. 10 will later declare. The only exception to this nonrepresentational view of religious images appears in Gen 1:26–27. Humanity was God's only earthly representation.

[2] The exiles were to avoid the religious norms of the Babylonian society in which they had to live. They are warned against both intellectual indoctrination and emotional intimidation in face of the claims of astrology to find life-determining omens in the sky (cf. Isa 44:15; 47:13).

[3–4] The curtain is whisked away from the Wizard of Oz, exposing the mystique as a facade. The reality behind Babylon's religious pomp is seen to be a series of mundane technicalities that attest merely human artistry capable of transforming a tree into a metal-plated icon.

[5a] The negative clause at the end of v. 4 introduces two negative statements that poke fun at the image's inanimateness. The first is accentuated by a homey, demeaning comparison that strips the image of its awesome glamour. It lacks basic functions of personhood, talking and walking. The latter defect was ironically evident in the very processions in which they were displayed to foster their worshipers' faith (cf. Isa 46:1).

[5b] After such deconstruction, the opening exhortation is repeated with clinching arguments; both images and astrology were manifestations of the Babylonian religion encountered by the exiles. First, an assurance is given that such idols were incapable of retaliating against the lese majesty that was being advocated. Second, any exile who might be tempted to convert (cf. vv. 2, 8; Deut 29:17–18) is warned to think again; the idols had no power to bestow blessing.

[6–10] The text turns from the empty flashiness of pagan religion to positive praise of the true God, just as in Rom 1:25 Paul broke out of the foul atmosphere of idolatry into the fresh air of a doxology. This passage has been creatively composed from preceding and following elements to form a hymn parallel to the one in vv. 12–16. The hymn begins and ends with the key word "nations," now used in a new, inferior sense, and with praise of Yahweh's kingship, first in spatial and then in temporal terms.

[6–7] Statements of incomparability frame a rhetorical question in the hymnic prayer. The "nations" within the Babylonian Empire are subjects of Yahweh, whom their religious experts who make idols (cf. the last colon of v. 9) cannot emulate by their divine reproductions. The verb "fear" is taken from v. 5, but now in the positive sense of reverence, as in 5:22, 24. The sarcastic term

---

87. Marilyn J. Lundberg, "The *Mis-Pi* Rituals and Incantations and Jeremiah 10:1–16," in *Uprooting and Planting* (ed. John Goldingay), 210–27, esp. 224.

"wise experts" has been inspired by contrast with Yahweh's wisdom in v. 12, while the negative expression of incomparability derives from v. 16.

[8–9] Verse 9 is now woven into the hymn as an enhancing contrast and "wise experts" is reused. The new introduction in v. 8 leans forward to vv. 14–15 to borrow "stupid" and "nonentities" and back to vv. 2–3 to borrow ʿēs, "wood" (rendered "tree" in v. 3), and the idea of learning.

[10] A hymnic confession crowns the passage. It finds in the person of Yahweh divine reality and the quintessence of life and power. The positive motifs of truth and life have been generated by contrast with the idols' characterization as a lie and lacking breath (v. 14b). As evidence of divine power, appeal is made to Yahweh's providential control whose dynamic effects in the world made "the nations" shudder, though they did not know that Yahweh caused them.

[11] Strikingly, this verse is written in Aramaic. What is it doing in a Hebrew book? Also striking is its often noted intricate chiastic structure (ABCDD′C′B′A′), which my translation has tried to capture by its order, though it cannot convey the assonance of ʾĕlāhayyāʾ, "gods," and ʾēlleh, "this," or of ʿăbadû, "did make," and yēʾbadû, "may they perish." The vocabulary is taken from v. 12 ("made the earth," "sky"); from v. 13, where the order of nouns is reversed ("sky . . . earth"); and from v. 15 ("will perish" [yōʾbēdû]). The Targum interprets the citation as a response the exiles were to give to Babylonians who urged them to worship local gods. In that case "to them" refers to "the nations," harking back to v. 2, which was nearer in the older text, though now the term recurs in v. 10, perhaps as an intended antecedent. The language used would be Aramaic, as a common tongue, and not unnaturally the introductory words were written in Aramaic.[88] The following unit gave rise to a cursing formula, expressed in a memorable word pattern, that would boldly express the exiles' faith, and this formula was inserted here. It was a way to "make your defense" to inquirers, to use the terms of 1 Pet 3:15, though it lacks the "gentleness" counseled in that text, apart from the concession "gods"—if such it is, since they are firmly relegated to an earthly habitat, "under this sky." The formula implies an idea new to the context, that divine making is restricted to Yahweh. The Aramaic interestingly uses different words for "earth" in stylistic dissimilation, first an older term, ʾarqāʾ, and then a later term that eventually replaced it, ʾarʿāʾ. The two terms were used together in Egyptian Aramaic in the fifth century B.C.E.,[89] which may be the historical context of v. 11.

[12–16] This unit, verified as such by its reappearance in 51:15–19, functions as a hymnic development of vv. 1–5, one that became the literary inspiration for vv. 6–10 and was already a firm part of the written tradition before

---

88. Meshulam Margaliot, "Jeremiah x 1–16: A Re-Examination," *VT* 30 (1980): 295–308, esp. 302.

89. See Arthur E. Cowley, *Aramaic Papyri of the Fifth Century B.C.* (Oxford: Clarendon, 1923), 277, and the particular instances listed there.

ch. 51 was added. The unit is a type of participial hymn that concludes with the refrain "Yahweh (Almighty) is his name."[90] A Hebrew participle begins the hymn (v. 12, ʿōśēh, "the one who made"), which continues in v. 13 with finite verbal forms; then separate sentences intervene before the refrain. The use of the refrain is facilitated by a fresh participle, yōṣēr, "the one who shaped." This type of hymn occurs only in the prophetic literature, not in the Psalms; it celebrates Yahweh's work in nature and among humanity at large, rather than covenant theology. It regularly includes motifs of idolatry and judgment.[91] In this case idolatry is prominent in the intervening sentences of vv. 14–15 and judgment in v. 15b.

[12] Israel's courageous faith in the universal power of Yahweh is expressed so that believers' minds and hearts were filled with positive traditional formulations instead of being mesmerized and demoralized by grand spectacles of Babylonian religious processions. The first word, ʿōśēh, "the one who made," blatantly challenges the pagan image as something "made" (maʿăśēh) by the human craftsman (vv. 3, 9). The fixing of the world in place contrasts with the use of hammer and nails to stop the image wobbling. Here is a superior deity that must leave the discriminating consumer dissatisfied with other brands on offer; there is no comparison.

[13] Yahweh can put on a spectacle too, which true faith appreciates and applauds. The storm phenomena of thunder, lightning, and wind, rightly interpreted, are the dynamic outworking of Yahweh's will in maintaining the natural world. The last three cola are appreciatively repeated in the late, anthological Psalm 135 (v. 7).

[14–15] It is time to make the contrast crystal clear. Images reflect stupidity rather than divine wisdom. They are a sham, big dolls, mere jokes. Icons that reflect the power of the totalitarian state are ruthlessly demystified. They are repackaged as "nonentities"—puffs of air that could never match the solid grandeur of Yahweh—and in light of v. 12 paltry objects made by humans. The coup de grace is inevitable; eventually they could only be destroyed at Yahweh's time of judgment (cf. 6:15; 8:12). No wonder this unit will be quoted in ch. 51. Its corollary was the fall of Babylon itself.

[16] The last step in the process of ideological deconstruction was to affirm the bond between the creator Yahweh and the exiles. The traditional term ḥēleq, "portion," is a spiritual metaphor derived from the tribe of Levi's dependence on Yahweh instead of being allotted tribal land (Num 18:20). The metaphor was used as an individual avowal of faith in the Psalms (Pss 16:5;

---

90. See Frank Crüsemann, *Studien zur Formgeschichte von Hymnus und Danklied in Israel* (WMANT 32; Neukirchen-Vluyn: Neukirchener Verlag, 1969), 111–12.
91. James L. Crenshaw, "YHWH Ṣᵉbaʾôt Šᵉmô: A Form-Critical Analysis," *ZAW* 81 (1969): 156–75, esp. 164–65.

The Self-Paved Road to Exile

73:26; 119:57; 142:5 [6]). Here, however, it is used collectively of the community's dependence on Yahweh. The term is backed by another land-based one, *naḥălâ*, "property," "possession," which was also used of Yahweh with reference to Levi in Num 18:20 (and Deut 10:9). Yahweh was Israel's ultimate means of living, the very ground of its being.

Jeremiah 10:1–16 breaks out of the preexilic setting that has hitherto dominated the book and addresses the Babylonian exiles, in pursuance of the exile-related agenda set by 9:16 (15). Its defiant call to faith in Yahweh turns into a hymnic celebration of Yahweh's superiority to Babylon's icons. This passionate composition was regarded as still so relevant for Israel's faith that it generated not only a formula of witness attached in v. 11, but also a further hymn in the Hebrew text (vv. 12–16). The entire composition offers a spirited testimony to aniconic monotheism in an alien, threatening culture.

10:17–25 Coping with an Exilic Future

17 Gather up your baggage [and get] out of the country,
    you group living under siege.
18 As to why, here is what Yahweh said:
    "Look out, I am going to sling away
       those who live in the country
       right now,
    loading them
       so they hit the target."ᵃ
19 "I feel so bad about my wounds,
       my injuries are so severe,
    though I thought
       this would be just an affliction I could bear!ᵇ
20 My tent is torn down,
       all my ropes are snapped.
    My children are gone from me and are no longer here,
       leaving nobody to pitch my tent again,
       to put up its sheets."

21 In fact the shepherd kings were stupid
       in not consulting Yahweh.
    Consequently they had no success
       and their entire flock is scattered.
22 Hey, here comes news
       about a great commotion originating in the north country
    that will turn Judah's towns into devastated areas,
       the haunts of jackals.

23 "I know, Yahweh,
   that human beings do not control their own courses,
   that individuals walk life's path,
   but cannot determine their steps.[c]
24 Chastise me, Yahweh, but only with justice,
   not in your anger, or you will reduce me to a few.
25 Overwhelm with your fury
   the nations who do not acknowledge you,
   the clans who do not worship you,[d]
   because they have devoured Jacob and finished him off,[e]
   devastating his pasture."

a. Barthélemy, *Critique textuelle*, 2:547, following J. D. Michaelis and F. Böttcher, has plausibly taken the two verbs as technical terms relating to the military practice of slinging, the first verb, *ṣrr* Hiphil, to loading the ammunition (cf. the *Qal* used of binding a stone in a sling at Prov 26:8) and the second verb, *mṣʾ*, "find," to hitting a target (cf. 1 Sam 31:3, of archers; Deut 19:5, of an ax).

b. Cf. Bright 70, NJB, and GNB. This nuance is part of the range of meaning of the modal imperfect, for which see Joüon §113l-n.

c. For the continuation of a participle with an infinitive absolute (cf. Ezek 7:14), see Joüon §123s with reference to Esth 9:4.

d. For the colon divisions see the discussion of Cloete, *Versification*, 165–66.

e. For the last verbal phrase MT has a conflated text, *waʾăkāluhû wayĕkallūhû*, "and devoured him and finished him off"; LXX represents only the second verb. In MT two variants stand side by side, an error caused by confusion with the previous verb and its correction.

This composition closes the collection of exile-related passages. It not only echoes the earlier key word "the nations" (v. 25), but also speaks plainly of exile (vv. 17–18). The accusation of stupidity in v. 21 forges an artistic link with the previous passage (vv. 8, 14). Like vv. 1–16, this composition concludes with a reference to "Jacob" as the covenant community. The composition brings closure to the collection by presenting exile as a sure prospect, like the initial unit at 9:17–22 (16–21). The two units, vv. 17–20 and 21–25, form a literary pair in that their second halves are quotations of the people's reaction to the disaster that share a collective first person speaking voice and a lament genre (vv. 19–20, 23–25). The second unit explains the first one ("For," NRSV, v. 21).

[17–20] The coherence of the unit lies in the identity of the group addressed in the vocative at v. 17 and the speaking voice in vv. 19–20. Since the vocative is a collective singular, the response uses first person singular forms.

[17] An announcement of exile takes the form of a command for victims of siege to prepare for deportation. The command is issued by the prophet; it anticipates a military invasion of Judah that will lead first to a successful siege of

The Self-Paved Road to Exile

Jerusalem and then to deportation of Judah's population. The reference to "Judah's towns" (v. 22) suggests that the siege was to mark the downfall of the state, as the phrase "those who live in the country" (v. 18) implies.

[18] The command is backed by a specific oracle that uses the military metaphor of slinging to convey the idea of deportation to an exilic destination (cf. 1 Sam 25:29). The Hebrew wordplay between *māṣôr*, "siege" (v. 17), and *wahăṣērôtî*, "loading," may suggest that the enemy siege is itself regarded as Yahweh's preliminary loading of the weapon before the shot is discharged.

[19–20] This quotation bears the stamp of a description of personal crisis in an individual psalm of lament.[92] It represents the voice of the collective group addressed in v. 17. Like earlier quotations put in the people's mouths, such as in 9:19 (18), it registers the bitter extremity of the coming disaster. It would bring material destruction compounded by exile of the population, which would make rebuilding impossible. There is some tension in the image of the speaker as Jerusalem rather than its people; the image represents a slight shift of perspective from vv. 17–18. Similarly, in vv. 23–25, there will be a degree of dissonance within the quotation—between the suffering of the collective speaker and that of "Jacob" as an objective entity in v. 25.

[21–25] The unit is framed by negative metaphors involving sheep.[93] Moreover, the two sections into which the unit falls end on the same note of devastation (vv. 22 and 25).

[21–22] The first section follows the contours of an oracle of disaster, but is spoken by the prophet rather than Yahweh. Verse 21 provides the reason, and v. 22 the announcement, couched as the report of an audition (cf. 9:19 [18]). Blame is laid squarely on the royal administration (cf. 2:8). However, whereas earlier blame has been grounded in not listening to Jeremiah's prophecy, here the leaders are indicted for not seeking such prophecy (cf. 21:2). Jeremiah anticipates the failure of this shortsighted policy and dispersal of their national flock, as in 23:1–2. He announces a military attack from the north and predicts the disintegration of Judah's urban centers (cf. 8:16). Now the past perspective of v. 21 has given way to a premonition of disaster ahead. The scattering of the flock (v. 21) symbolizes exile.

[23–25] The reference to reducing "me" to a few (v. 24) shows that this quotation is spoken by a personified, collective voice, which LXX recognizes by an exegetical rendering "us." The genre is a psalm of lament, as in the previous quotation; now elements of affirmation of faith and petition are reflected in vv. 23 and 24–25, each using the vocative "Yahweh." Jeremiah's choice in reaction

---

92. For *ʾôy lî*, "Woe is me" (NRSV; "I feel so bad" in my translation) cf. 15:10; 45:3; and *ʾôyâ lî*, "woe is me," Ps 120:5.

93. In v. 25 EVV have not recognized the link, rendering "home" or the like. For the primary meaning "pasture" for *nāweh* see BDB 627b, and cf. 23:2. Holladay 1:339 and Lundbom 1:611, 613 recognize the sense but not the symmetry.

to the national crisis was not for a psalm of lament in hope that prayer would change things, but for a dirge that accepted the inevitable. It was too late for a petitionary lament.

[23] The force of the affirmation of faith can be ascertained from the parallel and clearer Ps 119:75: "I know, O LORD, that your judgments are right, and that in faithfulness you have humbled me." It is an admission of Yahweh's moral, providential control over human affairs, specifically in being responsible for the speaker's trials.

[24] Nevertheless, as in Ps 119:76–77, the speaker goes on to plead for favorable treatment, that punishment should be seasoned with equity, wrath with reasonableness. The plea that by this means not too many should be killed reminds the reader of Abraham's bold argument against Yahweh's wholesale destruction of Sodom, "Should not the judge of all the earth do what is just?" (Gen 18:25 REB).

[25] The last verse is remarkably similar to Ps 79:6–7, though with a few recensional differences. Since the psalm appears to have an exilic origin and is written in an anthological style,[94] it is reasonable either to postulate a cultic source that both texts have used (Kelley in Craigie et al. 164; Jones 181) or to regard this text as the source. Certainly the material fits this context well, both the immediate one and the larger one due to its use of "the nations." There is a parallel between v. 24b and Psalm 79 in that the motif of excessive anger recurs at Ps 79:5; both include complaining questions urging that Yahweh's punishment be modified. Instead of continuing to punish Israel, divine anger should be redirected to Judah's enemies, who carry their own guilt (cf. Ps 79:1–3, 11–12) and cannot claim Yahweh's covenant favor.

The quotation of vv. 23–25 functions as a complaint, a blunter development of the lament, like Psalm 79 itself.[95] Jeremiah has cited the people's complaints before, in the course of 8:19–20; but despite his intense sympathy with their plight, it was there made very clear that he distanced himself from their complaining and the quotation was included as an ironic part of a mirror for the community's merited disaster. Likewise here the punch line of utter devastation in v. 25b is the real point, and the people's anguished reaction is cited as evidence of their extreme suffering. From a broader perspective, there is tension between two spiritual models of suffering. The complaint is presented as an authentic reaction in Psalm 79, but implicitly as an overreaction here, and yet both texts appear to refer ultimately to the disaster of 587 B.C.E. Both texts are given to the faith community, believers at different stages of processing their grief.

Jeremiah 10:17–25 reiterates Yahweh's punishment of exile, portraying it in military and pastoral terms, and pairs it with the people's reactions to the disaster, which expose the depth of suffering into which Judah is plunged.

---

94. See Marvin E. Tate, *Psalms 51–100* (WBC 20; Dallas: Word, 1990), 299–300.
95. For the role of Psalm 79 as a complaint see Broyles, *Conflict of Faith*, 157–60.

11:1–33:26 Destruction and Eventual Reconstruction, Part Two

11:1–13:27 A Broken Cycle of Rejection and Counterrejection

11:1–17 Pagan Worship as Breach of the Torah Covenant

1 A message that Jeremiah received from Yahweh, which said: 2 "'Listen to the terms of this covenant'—you are to declare them[a] to the Judeans and Jerusalem's residents 3 and tell them, 'Here is what Yahweh, Israel's God, said: "A curse is laid on anyone who does not listen to the terms of this covenant, 4 which I mandated for your forebears at the time I got them out of that iron-smelting furnace, Egypt, with the promise, 'Obey me and act[b] in accord with all my orders to you, and then you will be my people and I in turn will be your God,' 5 so I could fulfill the oath I swore to your forebears, promising to give them a country awash with milk and honey, an experience duly enjoyed at the present time." "Amen, Yahweh," was my reply. 6 Yahweh said to me, "Make this *entire* proclamation among Judah's towns and on Jerusalem's streets: 'Listen to the terms of this covenant and put them into practice. 7 The reason why is that I solemnly warned your forebears at the time I brought them up from Egypt and through the present, warning them over and over again to obey me. 8 But they would not listen, they turned a deaf ear. One and all they followed the stubborn inclination of their own bad attitude, and so I inflicted on them the threats of this covenant, whose terms I had ordered to be put into practice,[c] but they had failed to do so.'" 9 Yahweh said to me, "A conspiracy has been discovered, perpetrated by the Judeans and Jerusalem's residents. 10 They have gone back to the errors of their forebears, the previous generations who refused to listen to my terms. They too have followed other gods and served them. The communities of Israel and Judah have broken my covenant, the one I made with their forebears. 11 Therefore"—here is what Yahweh said—"look, I am going to inflict on them a bad fate impossible to get out of. When they cry out to me, I will not listen to them. 12 Judah's towns and Jerusalem's residents will then go off and cry out to the gods they have been sacrificing to, but no way will they save them when their bad fate comes. 13 (In fact, the number of your towns is matched by your gods, Judah, and the number of Jerusalem's streets is matched by the altars

you [all] have set up in honor of the shameful one,^d altars for sacrificing to Baal.) 14 And as for you, do not pray for this people, do not raise a shrill plea or any petition on their behalf, because I am not going to listen when they call on me about^e their bad fate.

15 "What does my loved one in my temple
 mean by carrying out wicked scheming?^f
Can pieces of fat^g or sacred meat
 avert^h your bad fate from you?^i
In that case you could celebrate with joy!"
16 A leafy olive tree with a beautiful shape^j
 was Yahweh's designation for you.
With a loud, roaring sound
 he will set fire to it^k
 and its branches will suffer damage.^l

17 So Yahweh *Almighty*, who planted you, is the one who has threatened you with a bad fate, on account of the bad behavior of the communities of Israel and Judah—"a bad fate they will have brought on themselves by upsetting me over sacrificing to Baal."

a. The Leningrad Codex that is the basis of *BHS* reads *wĕdibbartām*, "and you [singular] are to declare them," whereas the standard MT reading has a pointing *wĕdibbartem*, "and you [plural] are to declare." Barthélemy, *Critique textuelle*, 2:551–55, has plausibly argued that the codex contains the original reading and that the standard text represents an easier and so inferior one that simply continues the initial plural imperative *šimʿû* (KJV "Hear ye"). LXX implies *wĕdibbartā*, "and you [singular] are to declare," which looks like an adaptation of the codex reading. In the light of Jeremiah's reply in v. 5b, vv. 2–5a function as an oracle addressed to the prophet. In v. 2, however, the singular command is put second and an element of the prophet's public message is pushed forward into first place. The deliberate nature of this reversal is indicated by the resumption of "the terms of this covenant" with the suffix "them." It is impossible to streamline the text into a purely personal oracle by regarding v. 2 and the initial command of v. 3 as an addition (*BHS*; McKane 1:237). As McKane observes, in place of the plural suffix of *ʾăbôtêkem*, "your forebears," in vv. 4–5 a singular form would then be expected.

b. The addition of *ʾôtām*, "(do) them," in MT copies v. 6 (*BHS*). LXX and Vg. lack the addition. Two separate formulations have been confused in MT, "do" (with direct object) and "act in accord with."

c. LXX lacks vv. 7–8 except for the last clause. The similarity of v. 6b and the material in v. 8 at the end of the lacuna could have caused the omission, especially if the LXX or underlying Hebrew text at v. 8 represented an extra *ʾôtām*, "(to do) them," like Theodotion and thence LXX^O and LXX^L (Janzen, *Studies*, 39, 119). Janzen, *Studies*, 39–40, leaves open the possibility of redactional expansion in MT, based on 7:24–26. In that case the last clause in v. 8 with its third person verb originally acted as the prophet's narrative report of the nonfulfillment of the divine exhortation in v. 6 and went closely with the introduction to a new, explanatory oracle at the start of v. 9. However, Rudolph 77 observed the stylistic homogeneity of vv. 6–8 with their context and other prose sermons, while Thiel, *Redaktion von Jeremia 1–25*, 148–50, has noted that the parallels between vv. 7–8 and 7:24–26 are of a piece with those between vv. 4–5 and 7:22–23. As a result, no separate redactional process should be postulated in MT. Verse 10 appears to presuppose the presence of vv. 7–8.

d. LXX lacks "altars in honor of the shameful one," so it is often deleted as a gloss that conventionally substitutes *bōšet*, "shame," for "Baal"; NAB and REB omit. But parablepsis is more probably to blame in view of the presence of the replacement term in 3:24 and the verbose style of this passage.

e. EVV uniformly prefer *bĕʿēt*, "at the time of," presupposed by LXX and the other ancient translations, in place of MT *bĕʿad*, "about." Either works in the context. Did assimilation occur to the earlier double *bĕʿad* (rendered "for" and "on their behalf") or to *bĕʿēt rāʿātām* (rendered "when their bad fate comes") in v. 12? Barthélemy, *Critique textuelle*, 2:556–58, has argued for MT as the more difficult reading, noticing that the unusual construction with an impersonal object recurs in Exod 32:30.

f. MT presents a number of textual challenges in vv. 15–16. However, the masculine form *lîdîdî*, "for my loved one," can stand as epicene before the following feminine references. The infinitive *ʿăśôtāh*, "her carrying out," is also feasible; it seems to function as subject, a variant for the standard *kî*, "that," with finite verb (cf. Judg 9:2).

g. MT *hārabbîm*, "the many," is problematic, though NIV and NJPS struggle to keep it. OL *adipes*, "pieces of fat," can hardly stand for *ḥălābîm* with the same meaning (cf. BHS); it is unlikely to have been corrupted to the present form. It more probably stands for *habĕrîyîm* with an interrogative *hē*; than metathesis has occurred in MT (G. R. Driver, "Textual Problems," 109; cf. BHS; thus REB). Driver compared Ezek 34:20 for the defective spelling without *ʾālep*. His rendering "fatlings" is less likely than "pieces of fat" in view of the pairing with sacred meat; cf. 1 Sam 2:13–16; Hab 1:16. LXX *mē euchai* is helpful in its clause division and in taking the initial *hē* as interrogative, but "vows" does not fit the context; the consonants of a postulated *nĕdārîm*, "vows" (NAB, NRSV, NJB), are too far from MT.

h. Cf. GKC §53n for vocalic weakening in a *Hiphil*, as in 9:2 MT. LXX and other versions imply a transitive form.

i. MT *kî*, "that," probably arose by dittography from a longer form *mēʿālayĕkî*, "from you," as LXX and Vg. seem to imply, with the same archaic suffix as on the next word.

j. In MT *pĕrî*, "fruit," and *tōʾar*, "shape," are alternatives. LXX and Tg. represent the latter, though they both add a reference to shade, which Barthélemy, *Critique textuelle*, 2:565, has explained as a separate exegetical reference to Ezek 31:3. Did "fruit" originate as a gloss comparing Jer 12:2?

k. Since the antecedent *zayit*, "olive tree," is masculine, the Hebrew feminine form is unexpected. McKane 1:251 has adopted from Kimchi the explanation that the feminine referent has influenced the symbol. Elsewhere the verbal phrase is continued with the preposition *bêt*, but *ʿal* seems a permissible variant (Driver, "Textual Problems," 110).

l. The root of *rāʿû* is disputed, as in 2:16. HALOT 3:1269b derives from the root *rʿʿ*, "be bad," which LXX presupposes. It then clinches the "bad fate" (*rāʿâ*) of v. 15. BDB 949b derives from the homonym meaning "break" (cf. 15:2; Ps 2:9), and so evidently did Paul in his allegory at Rom 11:19–20. Most EVV follow the latter course, but it does not fit the imagery of combustion so well. NRSV and REB "will be/are consumed" seems to relate to *rʿh*, "graze, feed on," an even less likely expedient.

The literary block of 11:1–13:27 consists of five compositions, 11:1–17; 11:18–12:6; 12:7–17; 13:1–17; and 13:18–27. The first composition repeats the book's earlier contention of rejection of Yahweh's torah, while the so-called confessions in the second represent the rejection of Yahweh's prophetic revelation. The rejection in the first takes the form of pagan worship, a charge that the closing compositions in ch. 13 repeat, envisioning exile as the consequence. The central composition affirms that exile would be the outworking of Yahweh's rejection of the covenant people—and yet beyond it lay hope of return and blessing that would overflow to Judah's neighbors.

The first composition is made up of three units, a complex prose one (vv. 1–14) that represents an oracle of disaster, and two supplementary units (vv. 15–16 and 17). Verses 15–16 are a brief poetic oracle of disaster, linked to the previous one by the catchword *rāʿâ*, "bad fate." The same catchword appears in v. 17, a short oracle of disaster, but now in prose, which functions as a comprehensive summary for the composition. In part the composition is intended to underline the references to pagan religion in 8:4–10:25 and to find there a prime cause of Judah's downfall and an outworking of a covenant curse laid down in the torah. Two other factors anchor 11:1–17 to its context. In the collection of sayings found in 11:1–13:27, the "bad fate" of 11:1–17 will be increasingly defined in terms of exile, which was the focus of 9:17 (16)–10:25. And, like 7:1–8:3, the composition carries forward the book's theme of the rejection of the double revelation of torah and prophecy. The rejection of the prophetic messenger (11:18–12:6) constitutes an ominous sign for the nation's rejection of the message that will prompt Yahweh's counterrejection of Israel in 12:7–17.[1] Moreover, the failure to listen to the torah (here "covenant"; 11:1–17) will be matched by a failure to listen to prophetic messages (13:1–17).

The best way to understand this composition is to compare it with 7:1–8:3 and to observe five basic similarities. First, the oracle reception heading, which is similar to the one in 1:2, occurred in MT at 7:1 as a structural marker. Second, accordingly this composition functions as another (largely) prose buttress that interrupts Jeremiah's poetic oracles and draws attention to their purport. Jeremiah 7:1–8:3 contained two lines of poetry in 7:29, while this one has four in 11:15–16. Third, apart from the poem, the composition bears the marks of a prose sermon characterized by stereotyped phraseology (e.g., 7:1–8:3).[2] This

1. Franz D. Hubmann, *Untersuchungen zu den Konfessionen Jer 11,18–12,6 und Jer 15, 10–21* (FB 30; Würzburg: Echter Verlag, 1978), 168, 172–73; Diamond, *Confessions*, 153–54.
2. See Stulman, *Prose Sermons*, 64–67. He took into account only vv. 1–14, but there is evidence of the same style in v. 17. He computed the amount of stereotyped language in vv. 1–14 as

feature indicates that it too is redactional in nature. Such a conclusion at first sight conflicts with the explicit derivation of the material from Jeremiah, in the formula of v. 1 and in the first person language at vv. 5, 6, and 9. These statements indicate that the redactional material faithfully interprets Jeremiah's message. Jeremiah did refer to torah traditions (2:8; 6:16, 19; 8:8). The third section (vv. 9–14), with its unique metaphor of conspiracy and its echo of 2:27b–28a, probably develops one of his poetic oracles, which was prefaced with 11:2–8 as a literary backdrop (cf. Schreiner 1:79). Fourth, like 7:1–8:3, this composition has an allusive character, depending on texts in Deuteronomy: Deut 27:15–26, especially 27:26, in vv. 3 and 5; Deut 4:20 in v. 4; Deut 7:8 in v. 5; and Deut 4:13 in v. 8;[3] also Deut 29:9 (8) for the recurring phrase "terms/threats of this covenant." Fifth, there are close parallels between 7:22–26 and 11:1–8 in that vv. 4–5 align with 7:22–23, and vv. 7–8 with 7:24–26. Also v. 14 is a close parallel of 7:16. Verses 4–5 have dropped the specific comment about sacrifice (7:22) and now speak generally of obedience to Yahweh. Verses 7–8 repeat the general language of 7:24–26, but play down the prophetic element, in keeping with the emphasis on torah in the composition. The same material appears in both passages so that this composition underscores the message of the former one, concerning Judah's failure to honor the covenant obligations of the torah by its adoption of pagan religion.

[11:2–14] The passage falls into three sections (vv. 2–5, 6–8, and 9–14), as is clear due to separate introductions and gradual development. The oracular introductions that appear in vv. 6 and 9, "(And) Yahweh said to me," introduced divine statements in ongoing narrative in ch. 1;[4] they have a similar role here, especially in light of Jeremiah's response to Yahweh in v. 5b. The first two sections (vv. 2–8) jointly present exhortation and warning that build up a case for the reason for disaster (vv. 9–10), before the announcement of disaster is pronounced (v. 11a). The explicit exhortations (7:3–4) and the implicit ones (7:5–6) had the same function. The overall coherence of vv. 3–10 is demonstrated by their frame of a "covenant" made with "forebears" in vv. 3–4 and v. 10.[5] Verses 2–14 provide the thread for the discourse: Yahweh's commands to the people, "Listen to the terms of this covenant" (vv. 2–3, 6), are met by a

---

33 percent in the material common to MT and LXX and 34 percent in MT, the same percentages he gave for 7:1–8:3 (*Prose Sermons*, 132).

3. Ibid., 66.

4. In 3:6, 11 the second case is a resumptive repetition of the first. Curt Kuhl, "Die 'Wiederaufnahme'—ein literarkritisches Princip?" *ZAW* 64 (1952): 1–11, esp. 4–5, found the same phenomenon here, judging vv. 2b–6 to be an addition, but Thiel, *Redaktion von Jeremia 1–25*, 139 n. 4, rightly dismissed his claim.

5. Thomas Römer, *Israels Väter: Untersuchungen zur Väterthematik im Deuteronomium und in der deuteronomistischen Tradition* (OBO 99; Freiburg: Universitätsverlag; Göttingen: Vandenhoeck & Ruprecht, 1990), 423.

refusal to "listen" (vv. 8, 10) and so by Yahweh's own disinclination to "listen" to the people's prayers (vv. 11, 14). Similar counterpointing of the verb "listen" occurred in the course of 7:2–20, though on a lesser scale. The first two sections have their own frame, "the terms/threats (*dibrê*) of this covenant" (vv. 2–3 and 8).[6] The resumption of the phrase in v. 6 creates the same frame for the second section.

[2–5] The first section is basically a personal message to Jeremiah, requiring him to publicly transmit an oracle of exhortation backed by a warning and a promise. The prophet's response in v. 5b makes clear the individual nature of the oracle.

[2] Accordingly the initial public exhortation is out of place. It has been pushed forward from v. 6 to place the focus on the exhortation, which uses language that is structurally important.[7] Surprisingly, no setting is provided for "this covenant," and so here and in v. 3 the demonstrative has the role of pointing forward to the definition of the covenant in v. 4, whereas in vv. 6 and 8 it looks back (Rudolph 78). In the third section, at v. 10, the style changes to "my terms" and "my covenant." The prophet is to "declare" the undefined terms by drawing attention to them and stating their significance for the covenant people. The phrase "Judeans and Jerusalem's residents," who appeared in 4:4 as addressees of an oracle, sets the tone for vv. 2–14, reappearing precisely at v. 9 and in versions with "towns" and/or "streets" at vv. 6 and 12 (cf. v. 13), each time marking developments in the sermon. The version in v. 6 appeared in 7:17, 34. In light of v. 12, "towns" in v. 6 seems to refer to townspeople gathered in Jerusalem at festival time.

[3] It is easy to overlook "Israel's God" in the quotation formula. Along with "your God" in v. 4, it is a positive preparation for the negative theme of the sermon. The theme will ultimately be clarified in the third section, the worship of other gods, which is what unleashes the curse of v. 3. The indeterminate exhortation, "Listen to the terms of this covenant," is thereby eventually unpacked as a summons to exclusive allegiance to Yahweh in keeping with the covenant bond. The curse is regarded as a closing constituent of the covenant. The singular application of the curse (*'ārûr*, "cursed") and Jeremiah's response with "Amen" in v. 5 presuppose the formulations in Deut 27:15–26, especially the final, comprehensive curse relating to "the words [NJPS "terms"] of this law" in Deut 27:26. The curse is adduced by way of warning, but in the present context both the exhortation and the warning function without any expectation of their being heeded but rather as justification for the oracle of disaster in the third unit, like the exhortations in 7:3–6. While there is a direct allusion to Deut 27:26, the

---

6. Cf. Holladay, *Architecture*, 161.
7. Lothar Perlitt, *Bundestheologie im Alten Testament* (WMANT 36; Neukirchen-Vluyn: Neukirchener Verlag, 1969), 16 n. 2; cf. Hubmann, *Untersuchungen*, 119.

A Broken Cycle of Rejection and Counterrejection 139

text is applied in a general way to contemporary Judah's obligation to maintain the covenant relationship. No use is made of the fact that the text referred to a ceremony carried out in Moab by the second wilderness generation. (Nor is there any hint of a covenant renewal ceremony in Josiah's reign.) The text is used simply to illustrate the general liability of the people in the wilderness and to draw an arc of spiritual solidarity between them and later generations—in particular the last preexilic generation.

[4–5] The covenant is defined in general terms as that made after the exodus and so at Sinai—or Horeb, as Deuteronomy would say (Deut 5:2–3), though the cursing awaited arrival in the land of Moab (Deut 29:1 [28:69]). The promise defines the people's corresponding commitment to an exclusive relationship with Yahweh. Appeal is made to prior and consequent demonstrations of divine grace that should have deepened the people's sense of obligation and liability into an unbreakable constraint, namely, to the rescue from the oppressive ordeal of Egypt and to the gift of the land in fulfillment of an earlier promise to the patriarchs. The image of the iron-smelting furnace refers to Deut 4:20 (cf. 1 Kgs 8:51), while the winsome description of the land reflects a widespread tradition. The representation of the land promise as an oath harks back to Deut 7:8. It is invested with a conditional quality of dependence on the people's obedience. As Calvin (2:78) commented, "they, if ungrateful to God, might justly be deprived of the promised inheritance." The added factor of historical fulfillment means that Yahweh's side of the covenant had been kept. On the other hand, the shift to Jeremiah as the respondent, rather than the people, is a first hint that the people have failed to honor the covenant relationship, which is expressed in terms of a double covenant formula, as at 7:23. Here, however, the order is reversed and the divine aspect is placed second, as a climax that highlights the divine exclusiveness created by the covenant.[8]

[6–8] The second section accentuates the first. Again warning follows exhortation, but now the warning has a historical basis rather than the hermeneutical, torah-based one (v. 3). The warning is presented as a negative reason why the present generation should have obeyed Yahweh.

[7] The switch from bringing the people "up from" Egypt, rather than "out of" Egypt as in v. 4, presupposes possession of the promised land (v. 5).[9] There is reference to the divine initiative of prophecy whereby more recent generations received a warning (cf. 7:25). The point is the concurrence of the warning with divine grace in vv. 4–5, from the exodus down to the present.[10]

---

8. Christof Levin, *Die Verheissung des neuen Bundes in theologiegeschichtlichen Zusammenhang ausgelegt* (FRLANT 137; Göttingen: Vandenhoeck & Ruprecht, 1985), 78.

9. Joanne Wijngaards, "*Hwṣyʾ* and *hʿlh*, a Twofold Approach to the Exodus," *VT* 15 (1965): 91–102, esp. 98–101.

10. Hubmann, *Untersuchungen*, 114.

[8] Disobedience was the people's response, which meant that the curse of v. 3 was incurred, no longer as an individual threat but in a communal punishment. In light of the imminent context, stubbornness does not have a general moral reference, as in 7:24, but alludes to pagan worship, as in 9:14 (13) and 13:10. The description of the punishment as having already occurred, in contrast to future punishment (v. 11), refers to the downfall and deportation of the northern kingdom, as older scholars such as Keil (1:212–13) held.[11] Mention of the "communities of Israel and Judah" as having "broken my covenant" in the third section (v. 10), is the clue to this interpretation. It presupposes a reference to the disaster of more than a century before. Verses 8 and 10 are thus parallel to 3:6, 8, and to the redactional shape of 5:11.

[9–14] The third section ties up loose ends left by the two earlier ones and brings the unit to a coherent conclusion. The exhortations and warnings of vv. 2–8 now turn out to have been a backdrop to Judah's own liability, which age-old obligation accentuated and which was the climax of age-old disobedience that had met with recent reprisal. The section follows the regular outline of an oracle of disaster, first the reason and then the announcement of disaster. The latter, vv. 11–14, has a chiastic frame, ABCC′B′A′, in vv. 11 and 14b: Judah's bad fate, Judah's crying out or calling to Yahweh, and Yahweh's turning a deaf ear. In this section Yahweh ominously speaks to Jeremiah alone, with Judah appearing in the third person.

[9–10] The reason for coming disaster is framed by political metaphors. The image of conspiracy is only used here of spiritual infidelity; it occurs with the verb $mṣ^{ʾ}$, "discover," in a political setting at 2 Kgs 17:4. The political nature of covenant breaking is not so obvious until one compares the same Hebrew phrase used of breaking off an alliance in 1 Kgs 15:19. In between the political metaphors lie two explanatory clauses. The first resumes the historical sweep of vv. 7–8a, sums it up structurally as marked by failure to listen to Yahweh's covenant terms, and includes Judah in its scope. The second clause specifies the nature of the disobedience, defiance of the exclusive relationship of v. 4b. So not only Israel (v. 8) but also the contemporary generation of Judah were guilty.

[11a] Accordingly Judah must suffer the same curse (v. 3) as the northern kingdom. The verb "inflict" (*Hiphil* of $bô^{ʾ}$) repeats its use as a past tense in v. 8b. Verses 4–5 dropped a hint that the curse would involve loss of the land, but it is not developed here. Instead Judah's fate is contrasted with the ordeal of Egypt in v. 4 by repetition of the verb used there, "get out." There would be no divine rescue this time.

[11b–12, 14] The conclusion of the section provides three reasons why Judah's fate would be inescapable. First, this time Yahweh would not listen to their lament, as had implicitly happened at the exodus (cf. Exod 2:23–25; 3:9).

---

11. Hubmann, ibid., 114, agrees.

A Broken Cycle of Rejection and Counterrejection 141

The punishment is a fitting response to the covenant people's own refusal to listen (vv. 8, 10). Second, Judah would find its substitute gods unable to live up to the pragmatic, lament-related tradition of Yahweh's role as deliverer (2:27b–28a finds an echo here). Third, another loophole, prophetic intercession, considered earlier at 7:16, is regarded as already ruled out by Yahweh's initial, categorical refusal.

[13] The secondary nature of this sentence is evident from the second person references to Judah (singular in v. 13a and plural in v. 13b) in an oracle addressed to the prophet (v. 9). It is a longer version of 2:28b, added because of the link between v. 12 and 2:27b–28a. Originally a marginal gloss, it has become part of the text attested in LXX and is indeed presupposed by v. 17. It serves as a comment on "Judah's towns" and "the gods they have been sacrificing to" in v. 12.

[15–16] A fourth option, the winning over of Yahweh by sacrifice, is adduced and dismissed. This first of two supplementary units both illustrates Judah's "bad fate" and further defines its inescapability. As in 7:29, the composition incorporates one of Jeremiah's poetic oracles. It is a short oracle of disaster in which Yahweh gives the reason and the prophet proclaims the disaster, as in the following unit.

[15] As in 6:20 and 7:21–22, the validity of temple sacrifices is challenged, here with sarcastic questions, as in 6:20a. Loving ties of covenant no longer counted. "Wicked scheming" acquires from the context an association with pagan worship, referring to hypocritical sacrifices to Yahweh to win favor while being committed to alternative worship (cf. 7:9–10, 30). In these circumstances portions of fat (cf. Lev 3:3–4) and other acceptable offerings of meat must lose their acceptability and yield no anticipated joyful celebration.

[16] Judah's fate is represented with a standard metaphor of fire, but tragic poignancy is achieved by its combination with an image of beauty and vitality, the olive tree. The train of thought between vv. 15 and 16 may have been suggested by the presence of olive trees in the temple courts (Ps 52:8 [10]; cf. Ps 92:12–14 [11–13]). The olive tree symbolizes Israel as the covenant partner, as does the vine elsewhere (cf. Jer 2:21; Ps 80:8–12 [9–13]; Isa 5:2). In Hos 14:6 (7) Yahweh's renewing love would make Israel as beautiful as an olive tree. Here, however, Judah was to find God's protective love forfeited.

In Rom 11:16–26 Paul was so impressed by the imagery of Israel as the olive tree and its broken branches[12] that he used it as an allegorical model for the ongoing community of faith, some of whose Jewish branches had been broken off "because of their unbelief." In Paul's telling of the story the imagery acquired two glorious new chapters of grace and hope. First, the eschatological theme of the incorporation of Gentiles into God's kingdom (cf. Jer 4:2;

---

12. See note 1 on v. 16.

12:14–17; 16:19–21) was interpreted in terms of branches from a wild olive being grafted into the tree's stock. Second, the old branches were to be grafted back, so that finally the faith community could stand complete and better than ever before, an amalgamation of Israel and Gentiles.

[17] A concluding reflection refers back to the first and second units. It picks up the bad fate from both units, the twin communities and the sacrificing to Baal from v. 13 (cf. v. 10), which already seems to be presupposed, and the tree image from v. 16 by means of the clause "who planted you." This oracle of disaster moves from announcement to reason because it answers an implicit question: How can one explain Yahweh's change of attitude from planting the covenant people in the land (v. 5) to announcing a bad fate (*rāʿâ*) to the northern and southern kingdoms (v. 10)? It was triggered by their own *rāʿâ*, "bad behavior," as 1:14 and 16 had stated at the outset. As there, it is elucidated in terms of pagan worship, in this case Baal worship, as in 7:9.

11:18–12:6 An Exemplar of Rejection of Prophecy

18 Furthermore it was Yahweh who let me know, and then I knew—that was when you let me see their sinister activities, 19 whereas I for my part had been like a docile lamb led off to be slaughtered, not knowing I was the victim of the plot they had hatched.

"Let us destroy the tree, sap and all,ᵃ
   and sever him from the world of the living,
   so his name is remembered no more."
20   But Yahweh *Almighty* judges aright,
   probing conscience and will—
may I see your vengeance on them,ᵇ
   because you are the one I discloseᶜ my cause to.

21 Therefore here is what Yahweh said: "About the men from Anathoth who have designs on your life, with the threat, 'You must not prophesy in Yahweh's name or else you will die at our hands': 22 Look,ᵈ I am going to deal with them.

The[ir] young men will die by the sword,
   their sons and daughters will die of famine,
23   and they will have no survivors,

because I am going to inflict a bad fate on the men of Anathoth, in the year when they are dealt with."

12:1 You are in the right, Yahweh,
      when I take issue with you.
   Nevertheless, I am going to plead my case with you.
   Why is the track record of the wicked so successful
      and comfort the lot of all those who let people down?
2 You planted them—yes, they took root.
      They went on growing—yes, they have produced fruit.
   You are present on their lips,
      but far from their consciences.
3 But you, Yahweh, know me, *you can see me*,
      and you probe my will in relation to you.
   Drag them off like sheep for slaughter,
      set them apart for when they are to be killed!
4 How long is mourning[e] to grip the country
      and the vegetation throughout the countryside to be withered?
   The bad behavior of those who live in it is the reason why
      beasts and birds have disappeared.
   It is because they say, "He cannot see how we will end up!"[f]
5 "If running in a footrace has tired you out,
      how will you compete with horses?
   And [if] easy terrain is where you fall down,[g]
      how will you get on in Jordan's jungle?
6 Yes, your brothers, indeed, your own family,
      yes, they are the ones who have let you down,
      yes, they have chased you in full cry.
   Do not trust them
      when the way they talk to you is good."[h]

a. MT *bĕlaḥmô*, "with its bread," and thence, hardly permissibly, "fruit" (NRSV, NIV, NJPS), is better pointed *bĕlēḥāmô*, "with its sap" (thus REB "while the sap is in it"; cf. Leonard H. Brockington, *The Hebrew Text of the Old Testament: The Readings Adopted by the Translators of the New English Bible* [Oxford: Oxford University Press, 1973], 203); cf. GKC 302 n. 3; Bright 84; McKane 1:253, 257.

b. There is the same pattern of third person reference to Yahweh before direct address as in v. 18 (Hubmann, *Untersuchungen*, 78–79, 95). The first clause corresponds to the use of *wāw* adversative and a statement about Yahweh in the lament psalm (cf. Claus Westermann, *Praise and Lament in the Psalms* [trans. K. R. Crim and R. N. Soulen; Atlanta, John Knox, 1981], 70–71). LXX took the divine name as a vocative (and did the same in v. 18) and has been followed by EVV.

c. A repointing of MT *gillîtî* to *gallôtî*, "I have committed" (BHS; NRSV, NIV, REB; cf. NAB), is unnecessary. See the discussions of Barthélemy, *Critique textuelle*, 2:570–71; and McKane 1:259.

d. MT, but not LXX, prefixes a repetition of the introduction to v. 21, but qualifies the divine name with "Almighty." It represents a wrongly incorporated marginal reading supplying the variant and cue words. NJB reflects the shorter text.

e. Or "dryness"; cf. REB and NIV, and *HALOT* 1:7a. See the discussion of Hayes, *Prophetic Metaphor*, 12–18.

f. In place of MT *ʾet-ʾaḥărîtēnû*, "our future," LXX implies by metathesis *ʾorḥōtēnû*, "our ways," which *BHS* and NAB, NRSV, REB, and GNB prefer. The line is a closing monocolon (cf. Watson, *Classical Hebrew Poetry*, 170–71).

g. A second root *bṭḥ* appears here; see *HALOT* 1:120b. NJPS ("are secure only") and NJB ("feel secure") relate to the first root, which means "trust." Correspondence with the parallel metaphor suggests an expression of physical failure. See the discussions of McKane 1:263–64 and Mark S. Smith, *The Laments of Jeremiah and Their Contexts: A Literary and Redactional Study of Jeremiah 11–20* (SBLMS 42; Atlanta: Scholars Press, 1990), 10.

h. For the poetic character of v. 6 see A. R. Pete Diamond, *The Confessions of Jeremiah in Context: Scenes of Prophetic Drama* (JSOTSup 45; Sheffield: JSOT Press, 1987), 41–42; Cloete, *Versification*, 166–67; cf. Watson, *Classical Hebrew Poetry*, 47–48.

Jeremiah 11:18–12:6 is a composition made up of two separate units, dialogues between Jeremiah and Yahweh (11:18–23; 12:1–6). The initial sections of these units present the first two of the eight so-called confessions of Jeremiah, which appear between chs. 11 and 20 and reflect the tradition of individual lament prayers in the Psalms.[13] The latter sections feature divine responses. In addition to the units' form-critical similarities, the composition is unified by an overarching frame, the motif of naive, misplaced trust, admitted metaphorically by Jeremiah (11:19) and deprecated in plain terms by Yahweh (12:6). The final polarizing of a bad fate in 11:23 and deceptively good talk in 12:6 is also significant. Both passages appeal to Yahweh's attitude as a just judge who is able to probe human motives (11:20; 12:1, 3). The divine answers are linked in that they specifically identify the adversaries left suspensefully undefined in Jeremiah's prayers, in the first case "the men of Anathoth," the prophet's home village (1:1; 29:27; 32:7–9), and in the second case his own family. In other respects, however, the two units differ in form and content. MT has artistically linked the units by importing two new parallels in 12:3, the reference to seeing to match the "know/see" pair in 11:18 and the sheep simile to match the one in 11:19 (cf. Ps 44:11, 22 [12, 23]).

The confessions of Jeremiah are scattered through chs. 11–20. They are neither confessions of sin nor basically confessions of praise. The traditional label,

---

13. For a classic treatment of the relationship between Jeremiah's confessions and psalms of lament see Walter Baumgartner, *Jeremiah's Poems of Lament* (trans. David E. Orton; Historic Texts and Interpreters in Biblical Scholarhip; Sheffield: Almond Press, 1987). See too Robert C. Culley, "The Confessions of Jeremiah and Traditional Discourse," in *A Wise and Discerning Mind: Essays in Honor of Burke O. Long* (ed. S. M. Olyan and R. C. Culley; Brown Judaic Studies 325; Providence: Brown Judaic Studies, 2000), 69–81.

influenced by Augustine's *Confessions*, is a misnomer for a series of prayers and outbursts in the style of psalms of lament, spoken out of situations of distress and adapted to a prophetic setting: "there is no compelling reason not to place them within the prophet's ministry."[14] However, they do not have a biographical role in the book, fascinating though that suffering-laden perspective is to modern readers. The confessions lack explicit settings apart from references to village and family discord appended to the first two (11:21–23; 12:6). An incident of persecution is present in 20:1–2, typifying the punishable persecution mentioned or implied in the closing pair of confessions in 20:7–18. The confessions illustrate, from Jeremiah's experience, the book's contention that the faith community had rejected the whole of God's prophetic revelation in addition to the revelation grounded in torah traditions. Jeremiah functions as "the paradigmatic illustration of the degree of total national rejection of the message of the prophets."[15] The community had thus incurred a double measure of culpability. There could be no third chance; they had committed the equivalent of the NT's mortal sin or blasphemy against the Holy Spirit (Mark 3:28–29; 1 John 5:16–17; cf. Heb 6:4–6). Jeremiah 7:25–26 laid down this theological axiom in respect of the prophets, after a torah reference in 7:24, and it is recapitulated in 25:4. The last of the three compositional blocks of chs. 11–13, 14–17, and 18–20 carefully repeats it at 19:15 in explanation of the confession of 18:19–23. The first block mentions the rejection of the torah at 11:8, like 7:24, so that the first pair of confessions within 11:18–12:6 provides its prophetic counterpart, which MT reinforces at 13:10. The second block incorporates torah rejection in 17:23, complementing the prophetic force of the confession in 17:14–18. Jeremiah's reactions of pain and utter unease reflect the way the people were treating Yahweh. The confessions are variously keyed into their individual contexts to show that corporate rejection of Jeremiah as Yahweh's prophetic messenger meant nothing less than spurning the divine message and will for the covenant people.

[**11:18–23**] Jeremiah appeals to Yahweh to vindicate his prophetic ministry. Verses 1–17 had reached back into a torah tradition to find an incriminating basis for Judah's disaster. There had been a side glance at the subsequent role of prophetic ministry, at v. 7, and indeed Jeremiah's own task as a prophet was defined in vv. 2–10 in terms of reaffirming the torah's covenant accountability, while in v. 5 Jeremiah had sided with Yahweh. Now the prophetic aspect is explored further ("Furthermore," v. 18). The first part of the unit can be regarded as a development of 6:10–11a, where the prophet identified himself with Yahweh's message of destruction and found in his own soul a reflection of

---

14. Smith, *Laments of Jeremiah*, xviii.
15. Ronald E. Clements, "Jeremiah 1–25 and the Deuteronomistic History," in *Understanding Poets and Prophets: Essays in Honour of George Wishart Anderson* (ed. A. G. Auld; JSOTSup 152; Sheffield: JSOT Press, 1993), 93–113, esp. 102.

the divine anger at the people's refusal to take the prophetic message seriously. Here, however, that refusal flares up much closer to home, in fact in his home village, and takes a sinister turn as a death threat.

The most obvious characteristic of this complex unit is its focus on prophecy. Notably vv. 21–23 present an oracular announcement of disaster addressed to Jeremiah, and so vv. 18–20 look like a version of the reason for disaster, proffered in this case by Jeremiah. A second significant factor is that the unit has the skeletal structure of an autobiographical report that states Yahweh's revelatory intervention (v. 18) and the background of the prophet's experience (v. 19a), and furnishes (v. 21) the divine response to a request made by the prophet (cf. 6:16). Poetic elements (vv. 19b–20 and 22b–23a) provide the core of the exchange.

[18–20] Surprisingly vv. 18–19 follow the general style of a psalm of thanksgiving, recording Yahweh's earlier intervention and describing a past crisis that had nearly overwhelmed him. The description of the crisis borrows from laments the subjective reference to personal suffering and the objective reference to the work of enemies. The vague references to "their," "they," and "them" are consistent with the broad language that can appear in the lament (cf. Ps 142:3 [4]; Jer 17:15). The primary focus is thereby put on Yahweh and the prophet.[16] Oscillation between third and second persons in referring to God (v. 18) is a feature of the thanksgiving psalm, which mingles testimony to the congregation and thanksgiving prayer. In this case the mood of thanksgiving is an interim one, and it shifts to pure lament in v. 20. It is clear that the crisis had not yet been resolved and required Yahweh's further intervention. Accordingly v. 20 presents in lament style an affirmation of faith and a petitionary wish.

[18] The report starts in medias res, with a minimum of background information necessary to introduce Jeremiah's prayer. Yahweh's revelatory intervention is a prophetic trademark (cf. 32:8; 1 Sam 9:15–17); so too is an experience of second sight (cf. 2 Kgs 5:26; John 1:48–50). The prophetic shaping of the unit and Yahweh's eventual disclosure (v. 21) that the hostility shown to Jeremiah was based on the discharge of his prophetic commission indicate that Jeremiah's prophetic role was at stake (vv. 18–20).

[19] Jeremiah alludes to walking into mortal danger, which conveys his relief and gratitude to God. His naive trust is uniquely captured by the lamb simile.[17] It is elucidated in terms of malign plotting, like that of Pss 56:5 (6) and 140:2 (3); the quotation has a parallel in a communal lament (Ps 83:4 [5]). The striking metaphor of the tree full of sap refers to human life, as the next colon

---

16. Dong Hyun Bak, *Klagender Gott—klagende Menschen: Studien zur Klage im Jeremiabuch* (BZAW 193; Berlin: de Gruyter, 1990), 108.

17. In Isa 53:7, which may have been inspired by this text, it refers rather to unresisting compliance. A comparable simile in Prov 7:22 refers to deception, as here.

explains. The vehemence of the death wish is expressed in terms of the obliteration of Jeremiah's very name from human memory.

[20] The affirmation of trust appeals to Yahweh's attributes of providential justice and ability to penetrate human motives by deduction, here with reference to Jeremiah's enemies (cf. Pss 7:9 [10]; 26:2).[18] The kidneys (*kĕlāyôt* here and in 12:2; KJV "reins") were regarded in Hebrew psychology as the seat of the conscience, while the heart functioned as the seat of the will.[19] The lament reaches its appropriate climax with a petition for justice, which represents a direct turning to ask God for help. "Your vengeance" seems to imply vengeance not merely to be carried out by Yahweh but for an offense committed against Yahweh insofar as it was committed against Yahweh's representative (cf. 15:15). The reader is invited to hear an echo of Yahweh's national commitment to vengeance in the refrains of 5:9, 29; 9:9 (8).

[21–23] This passage functions as an oracular response to prayer (cf. Lam 3:55–57; for a communal setting see Ps 85:8 [9]), but it has the form of an announcement of disaster. It possesses a double frame, with references first to "the men of Anathoth" in vv. 21 and 23 and then to Yahweh's dealing with them in vv. 22 and 23.

[21] The prophetic character of the unit is now brought into the open both by the nature of Yahweh's response and by the disclosure that Jeremiah's role as prophet lay behind the plotting (v. 19). The identification of the enemies elaborates Yahweh's letting the prophet in on the secret of the plot (v. 18). What the prophet then learned is resumed in an introduction to the announcement of disaster that recapitulates its reason. The change from a secret plot (v. 19) to an open threat marks the escalation that evidently occasioned Jeremiah's lament. Prophesying in Yahweh's name has a sinister parallel in 26:20–23, with reference to Uriah ben Shemaiah, a prophet of Jeremiah's ilk who met an untimely death.

[22–23] Yahweh's dealings by direct intervention frame a tricolon that sets out the results of that intervention. The tricolon is a deliberate match of the one in v. 19b, so that the punishment fits the intended crime, the first two lines again speaking positively of death and the third negatively of absolute extinction.[20] Moreover, the threat of death in v. 21 becomes a boomerang. By way of reprisal

---

18. This verse recurs substantially in Jeremiah's final confession, at 20:12; it does fit well here. The redactional significance of the repetition is difficult to assess. For example, it has been regarded as an addition either here, as a poetic island in a sea of prose, by McKane 1:154–55, who does not regard v. 19b as poetry (cf. REB, NJB); or at 20:12, to provide a stylistic frame for the confessions as a whole, by Geoffrey Parke-Taylor, *The Formation of the Book of Jeremiah: Doublets and Recurring Phrases* (SBLMS 51; Atlanta: Society of Biblical Literature, 2000), 13–14.

19. See Hans W. Wolff, *Anthropology of the Old Testament* (trans. M. Kohl; Philadelphia: Fortress, 1974), 51–54, 65.

20. Hubmann, *Untersuchungen*, 79–81; Holladay 1:367.

the local community would lose its best and youngest members. The references to "sword" and "famine" (cf. 5:12), to inflicting "a bad fate" (cf. 6:19), and to a coming "year" of retribution (cf. 23:12 in a national context) allude to a postponed punishment—when Anathoth would be caught up in the destruction that was to befall the community at large.

Verses 18–23 focus on Judah's rejection of Yahweh, in terms of a village's reaction to Yahweh's prophetic messenger. That place warrants the same message of doom hitherto announced to the nation.

[12:1–6] The second unit in the composition loosely follows the format of the first, the prophet's appeal (vv. 1–4) and Yahweh's response (vv. 5–6). The same generality obtains in the earlier part and specificity in the latter about Jeremiah's opponents, who are eventually identified as his own family. The unit is marked by a frame (vv. 1 and 6), the charge of letting down those who should be loyally supported. The unit offers the reason for coming disaster. It presents a microcosm of a national failing. The root *bgd*, here rendered "let down" and used in a social context, was so employed in 9:2 (1), rendered "traitors" with reference to a wider constituency, God's "people."

[1–4] Jeremiah's prayer, compared with the lament of 11:18–20, represents an intensification of a psalm of lament, now become a complaint.[21] It is signaled as such by the telltale questions in vv. 1 and 4, "Why?" and "How long?"[22] Whereas the lament persuasively pleads with God, the complaint accusingly argues against God. It is marked by a shrillness that is absent from the typical lament. The closest parallel is Psalm 35, a complaint that is a cry for justice, which asserts the psalmist's innocence (vv. 7, 19), asks "How long?" (v. 17), and appeals to Yahweh's righteousness (v. 24).[23] Here the prophet's two questions dominate the prayer. The pairing is accentuated by their shared chiastic structure, which I have tried to reproduce in the translation. They are the backbone of the prayer, which falls into two parallel halves: an address to Yahweh in which the prophet engages with Yahweh as judge (vv. 1a, 3), a chiastic question (vv. 1b, 4a), an elucidation of the question (vv. 2a, 4b*a*), and the pertinent others' relation to Yahweh (vv. 2b, 4b*b*).[24]

[1] A belligerent note is evident from the outset in that the ironically polite admission of Yahweh's justice is followed by a determination to challenge it (cf. Gen 18:25). The question is an indirect petition. "The question is challenge,

---

21. See Broyles, *Conflict of Faith*, passim, for this development of the lament genre in the Psalms and its characteristics.

22. See ibid., 80–82. A difference is that the Psalms use *lāmmâ* for "why," while the customary term in the book of Jeremiah, *maddûaʿ*, is employed here, as a "prophetizing" element. For the virtual equivalence of the terms, at least in these cases, see Berridge, *Prophet, People*, 162 n. 257; James Barr, "Why? in Biblical Hebrew," *JTS* 36 (1985): 1–33, esp. 33.

23. Cf. Broyles, *Conflict of Faith*, 48, 193–96.

24. Hubmann, *Untersuchungen*, 82–86.

accusation, and demand in one. The only acceptable answer would be action, not words."[25] It is not surprising, then, that a direct petition will appear in v. 3b. Though the question is posed in a speculative form, its general language conceals an intensely personal interest that will gradually be revealed. In Hab 1:13 the juxtaposition of "Why," "the wicked," and "the treacherous" (*bôgĕdîm*, the same verb as here) is set in a protest against Yahweh's using the Babylonians to punish Judah's breach of covenant. There Yahweh's moral tolerance is explicitly criticized, as it is implicitly here.

[2] Yahweh's alleged complicity now surfaces. If there is a divine source for human life and blessing, the prosperity of these undeserving folk raises suspicions. Such fertility and fruitfulness suggest Yahweh's ongoing support: "God gave the growth" (1 Cor 3:6). If so, it is not reciprocated. Their relation to Yahweh is a nominal one, in Isaiah's terms:

> These people draw near with their mouths
> and honor me with their lips,
> while their hearts are far from me.
> (Isa 29:13)

Or they are those who swear loudly "By Yahweh's life," but whose lives contravene God's will (Jer 4:2; 5:2; cf. 7:9; 12:16).

[3] Jeremiah begins again by appealing to Yahweh's judicial insight into his own life. The polarization between vv. 2b and 3a is not merely a stylistic hinge between sections but points to Jeremiah's conflict with personal opponents. He asks Yahweh to take his side as the innocent party and pass upon them the death sentence they deserve.

[4] The second complaining question has been widely judged to be secondary, but its structural fit justifies its presence.[26] A period of intense drought is interpreted as nature's symbiotic reaction to human wickedness, as in 23:10 and Hos 4:1–3. Yahweh needed to restore the disturbed equilibrium by sentencing the guilty parties.[27] They are further defined by their refusal to believe in the prospect of Yahweh's providential judgment upon their lives (cf. Deut 32:20; Lam 1:9).[28]

[5–6] The divine answer is surprising, compared with the parallel in Jer 11:21–23. First, it lacks an introduction, as in 4:22; 5:7–9; 6:11b–12. Second, it does not overtly take Jeremiah's side, not even with an assurance of postponed

---

25. Sheldon H. Blank, "The Confessions of Jeremiah and the Meaning of Prayer," *HUCA* 21 (1948): 331–54, esp. 342.

26. Hubmann, *Untersuchungen*, 139.

27. Ibid., 140–43.

28. LXX provides "God" as subject of the verb, while in the fragmentary 4Q70 the first two letters of the divine name are preserved (DJD 15:160). That these additions exegete correctly is shown by the structural correspondence with v. 2b (Hubmann, *Untersuchungen*, 144).

punishment, as in 11:22 or 12:3b.[29] The divine judge refuses to take the case, but issues an advisory brief. It commences with a chiastically shaped pair of questions that correspond to the prophet's questions,[30] continues with an elucidation that exposes the reality behind Jeremiah's complaint, and closes with a kindly warning.

[5] There are times of dire extremity when shrill complaint is the only form of prayer left to a distraught believer, as the presence of over a score of complaints in the Psalms implies. Jeremiah's predicament is judged not to be such a time, just as the people's complaints in 8:19–20 and 10:23–25 were not taken at face value. The counterquestions do not address theological conundrums and pointed challenges, but rather challenge Jeremiah. They make a pastoral comment on his prophetic relationship to Yahweh, envisioning it in terms of an arduous struggle. Jeremiah was not to overreact to his experience, but must learn to take such problems in his stride, as preparation for more daunting ones ahead. Eventually he would have to cross tougher terrain, terrain as challenging as the tangled growth of trees, bushes, and reeds alongside the Jordan, where lions lurked (49:19; Zech 12:3).[31]

[6] The problem turned out to be serious familial discord, distressing indeed (cf. Mic 7:6), but an issue he had to address. (One day he would have to resist the whole country [1:18; cf. 15:10]—and Yahweh's hard-line answer is not unlike the growled aside in 1:17b.) His family would show the same duplicity to Jeremiah as they did to Yahweh according to v. 2b. They were liable not to live up to fine words (cf. 9:8 [7]).

Jeremiah 12:1–6 presents his experience of prophetic hostility as a reflection of the hostility shown by Judah to the God he served. Such hostility was to grow in intensity. In 11:18–12:6 Jeremiah discovers, like Jesus, that "prophets are not without honor, except in their hometown, and among their own kin, and in their own house," and encounters a response of "unbelief" (Mark 6:4, 6).

12:7–17 Yahweh's Counterrejection and Eventual Wide Compassion

7 "I have left my family,
    abandoned my home.
I have surrendered the love of my life
    to their enemies' clutches.
8 My home's attitude to me became
    like that of a forest lion.

---

29. Diamond, *Confessions of Jeremiah*, 201 n. 24, has compared the rejection of prayer in Hos 6:4–6.
30. Hubmann, *Untersuchungen*, 87.
31. See Menashe Har-El, "The Pride of the Jordan, the Jungle of the Jordan," *BA* 41 (1978): 65–75.

>   They roared at me
>   and so I have come to hate them.
> 9   Did my home treat me as a denful of hyenas[a] would?
>   Well, birds of prey are hovering around it.
>   Come on, gather all the wild animals,
>   bring them here to devour.
> 10 Shepherd-kings aplenty ruin my vineyard,
>   trampling down my field.
>   They have remade my desirable field
>   into a wilderness that is desolate.
> 11 They make[b] it desolate;
>   it mourns on my account, desolate.[c]
>   Desolate is laid the whole country,
>   because nobody shows any concern."

12 The reason why all the bare tracts in the wilderness are invaded by raiders is that Yahweh's sword devours the country from one end to the other, and so everybody lacks security.

> 13 They sowed wheat, but thorns are what they reap.
>   They exhausted themselves, without achieving anything—
>   feel disappointment, then, over your harvest,
>   which is due to Yahweh's burning anger.

14 Here is what Yahweh said: "About all my bad neighbors who have encroached on the home I gave my people Israel the right to occupy: Look, I am going to uproot them from their native soil—and *the community of* Judah I will uproot from among them. 15 But, after uprooting them, I will turn to show them compassion and bring back each group to its own territorial home. 16 Then if they are prepared to learn my people's spiritual traditions, swearing in my name the oath 'By Yahweh's life,' as once they taught my people to swear by Baal, they will be rebuilt among my people. 17 But if they do not listen, I will uproot that nation with the intention of destroying it," *declared Yahweh.*

    a. LXX "a hyena's cave" seems to be a correct interpretation of ʿayiṭ ṣābûaʿ (REB "a hyena's lair"). See *HALOT* 2:816b; 3:997b; John A. Emerton, "Notes on Jeremiah 12:9 and on Some Suggestions of J. D. Michaelis about the Hebrew Words *nahā, ʿaebrā,* and *jadăʿ*," *ZAW* 81 (1969): 182–91, esp. 182–88; and Barthélemy, *Critique textuelle,* 2:572–73. There is wordplay with the next colon, where ʿayiṭ, though again rendered "cave" in LXX, is a homonym meaning "birds of prey"; a pointing with the definite article

(BHS) is preferable to the interrogative particle of MT. Just as *naḥălâ*, "home," is used in the sense of a social unit, so evidently is "den."

b. The Hebrew indefinite singular verb is more naturally pointed as plural; see BHS.

c. For the division into cola see Cloete, *Versification*, 167–68. For the rendering of *ʿālay* as "on my account," see Holladay 1:388, though there is no need to change the punctuation of MT.

Jeremiah 12:7–17 covers a lot of ground, moving from invasion to exile and back to possession of the land. It is made up of three units (vv. 7–11, 12–13, and 14–17), the first of which is an oracle of disaster spoken in Yahweh's name. The second unit, which plays a supplementary role, is a brief announcement of disaster that presents Yahweh's work of judgment in the third person. The third unit also depends on the first one, but it looks forward to a positive future in a conditional proclamation, which includes elements of disaster for Judah's enemies. To mark its different message and its role as a conclusion, the oracle is introduced by its own quotation formula.

[12:7–11] The previous composition dealt with Jeremiah's rejection as a prophet and understood it as a picture of the people's rejection of the God in whose name he prophesied (11:21). Such an understanding is presupposed by these verses, which declare Yahweh's counterrejection of the hostile covenant community. Jeremiah's "tragedy is a miniature of mine," Yahweh virtually declares (Kidner 61). The unit picks up from v. 6 "your family" (*bêt ʾābîkā*, KJV "the house of thy father") with reference to Jeremiah and reuses it in a shorter version, "my family" (v. 7, *bêtî*, NRSV "my house"), with reference to Yahweh's covenant people.[32] The unit falls into two sections. The first (vv. 7–9) speaks of a broken relationship between Yahweh and the people, describing the latter three times as "my home," while the second (vv. 10–11) describes the destruction of the land.

[7] The reason for the disaster will be given in v. 8. It is prefaced with Yahweh's stark announcement of a drastic personal decision: to abandon the covenant people and to withdraw the protective presence entailed in the covenant relationship, so that national enemies could attack with impunity (cf. 2:3). The relationship is described in intimate terms: the people are "my family," "my home," and "the love of my life." "Home" renders *naḥălâ*, which was used of the land in 2:7 and 3:19, and translated "property" and "possession," respectively. Here it refers to the people, as it did in the secondary text of 10:16, and as often in the OT (e.g., Deut 32:8–9).

[8–9] Leaving home was a last resort. It was Yahweh's response to provocation, in the form of hostility so extreme that it managed to turn divine love to hatred or implacable opposition (cf. Pss 5:5 [6]; 11:5; Hos 9:15). So the punishment was to fit the crime. Hostility described in terms of wild creatures on

---

32. Hubmann, *Untersuchungen*, 172–73; Diamond, *Confessions of Jeremiah*, 153.

the attack would be the trigger for their reappearance as a standard metaphor for invaders (cf. Jer 4:7; 5:6), and the latter feature in a rhetorical call for them to do their destructive work.

[10–11] The disaster is not the destruction of the people but that of the land. So its executors are kings leading their military detachments on the rampage through the vineyard or field that represents Yahweh's beautiful land (cf. 3:19; 6:3). The provocation that transformed family love into hatred in the first section now meets its match in the destruction that transforms God's vineyard into a wilderness. Bell-like, the term "desolate" tolls at the end of three successive cola and at the start of a fourth. Behind the human agents lies a divine cause ("on my account"). These agents of destruction would carry out their work dispassionately. Whereas once Yahweh had cared for the land (cf. Deut 11:12), there would be nobody to care for the land anymore.

[12–13] This unit picks up "wilderness" and "devour" from vv. 9–10 and echoes "the whole country" in v. 11b, but it primarily elucidates "on my account" in v. 11a. The announcement of disaster has at its core the parallel phrases "Yahweh's sword" and "Yahweh's burning anger." The previous unit envisioned the withdrawal of Yahweh's protective presence, an absence that left a vacuum into which destruction and desolation would flood, but this unit, with greater intensity, speaks of a negative divine presence actively directing the destruction.

[12] This prose sentence finds in "Yahweh's sword" the fundamental agency behind the coming invasion and the cause of comprehensive woes.

[13] The first of two poetic bicola concentrates on the disruption of the crop routine the war would cause, and the sheer waste of effort it would represent. Then, with a sudden turn, hearers are directly challenged and told to interpret such destruction all in terms of the irruption of a providential factor, "Yahweh's burning anger" (cf. 4:26).

[14–17] This prose unit impatiently leaps ahead—to Judah's being exiled and to its return from exile. It follows the separate agenda of the redactional unit 5:18–19, which looked beyond the destruction of the land (5:15–17) to exile and hinted at a positive future for Judah. However, this unit consciously builds on the preceding two units by echoing "home," the key term of vv. 7–9, though in vv. 14 and 15 with the more common sense of land, and by elucidating the enemies of vv. 7–12 in terms of neighboring nations. Moreover, in MT the added "community" (NRSV "house") in v. 14 provides a further stylistic link by echoing "my family" (NRSV "my house") in v. 7. "My home" in the communal sense of vv. 7–9 is now explained by the standard covenant phrase "my people," which dominates the unit, occurring four times. The unit also qualifies the denial of divine compassion in 13:14 by affirming its eventual reappearance at v. 15. In God's long-range purposes "there is a time to break down and a time to build up" (Eccl 3:3).

The unit begins as an oracle of disaster for Israel's neighbors, a disaster that would catch up Judah in its sweep. But since disaster was to give way to a restoration that would include Judah, the oracle becomes an explicit proclamation of salvation. Although God's people stand in the background for most of the oracle—it is the target of divine action only in the closing clause of v. 14—they function as the key to the oracle, as motive and model for the nations' experiences. The unit alludes to a range of material in the book and so has a redactional air; it is probably exilic in origin.

[14] This verse is a self-contained oracle of disaster, presenting the reason in the heading and then the divine intervention. The invaders mentioned in vv. 7–12 were not specified; anyone who has read thus far in the book would think of foes from afar. Here, however, local nations are singled out. There appears to be a reference to Nebuchadnezzar's use of vassal troops from Moab and Ammon to punish Jehoiakim's rebellion about 600 B.C.E. (2 Kgs 24:2; cf. v. 10 above), though there may be a more general reference to their earlier threats of encroachment (Zeph 2:8).

Yahweh's sovereign control over Israel's land is invoked ("my neighbors"). Those who took over any Israelite land were answerable to Yahweh (cf. Ps 79:1). If the privilege of Jer 2:3 was forfeited in v. 7, it is now gloriously reaffirmed. Encroachment on the land would entail the perpetrators' loss of their own land. Judah's similar fate is mentioned in passing to pave the way for their return and subsequent role as a spiritual magnet for the nations. The verb "uproot," used three times in vv. 14–15 and again in v. 17, is one of the key terms of the unit. It echoes not so much 1:10 as the application of 1:10 in 18:7–11. There, not only is the uprooting of nations (including Judah) a logical prelude to their being (planted and) built again, as 12:16 states, but there are two specific links between 18:7–11 and this unit. First, the conditions of 12:16–17 seem to be based on those of 18:7–10, especially v. 10.[33] Second, "that nation" in 12:17 echoes that phrase in 18:8.

[15] Yahweh's gracious renewal would extend not only to Judah, which appears to be included here in view of its role in v. 16, but also to Judah's exiled neighbors. Divine compassion, reserved for Israel's return in 30:18; Zech 1:16; 10:6, reaches out more widely here.

[16–17] Physical return was to be the setting for spiritual transformation. Whereas the conditionality derives from ch. 18, learning Israel's "ways" (NRSV) reverses Israel's learning "the way of the nations" (10:2, NRSV).[34] The change of oath formulas depends not only on the "swearing by nongods" in 5:7 but also on swearing "by Yahweh's life" at 4:2, in a conditional statement that refers to the nations' winning blessing from Yahweh (cf. 3:17). Appeal is being made to

---

33. Cf. Thiel, *Redaktion von Jeremia 1–25*, 163, 166.
34. LXX "way" in 12:16 (cf. *BHS*) probably sharpens an allusion to 10:2 by assimilation.

the OT tradition of the nations' turning to worship Israel's God. However, the tradition is clothed in terms dear to Jeremiah and with the same two expectations Jeremiah's God had for Israel: swearing by Yahweh, here used as a badge of Yahwism, and the need to "listen," a term for conformity to the torah tradition, as 11:2–10 had recently affirmed. With that qualification, uprooting would give way to (re)building in close association with Judah. The preposition of disintegration, "from among" (v. 14), is replaced by one of magnetic integration, "among." Nevertheless, an irreversible uprooting could follow. The condition of 18:10, with its reference to "not listening to my voice" (NRSV), is taken with absolute seriousness at this point.

The implicit goal of the unit is the vindication of Yahweh and of Yahweh's people. This unit purposefully breaks into the series of oracles of disaster directed at Judah. It strains forward in hope for a time when Yahweh would remake the spiritual geography of Judah's world and put its pernicious influence into reverse. So 12:14–17 encompasses not only the alienation of exile but reconciliation, which would spill beyond Judah's borders to the glory of God. The oracle offers just a sketch of future spirituality, but its open-ended human accountability presents a disturbing conclusion (cf. Zech 14:18–19). Yet there is a remarkable rapport with the contextual theme of the consequences of not listening to Yahweh, broached in Jer 11:1–17. Was this piece also intended as an oblique warning to a later generation, as Calvin (2:159) suggested? "God is not mocked . . ." (Gal 6:7).

13:1–17 The Ruin of Exile and the Reason Why

13:1 Here is what Yahweh said to me: "Go and buy yourself a linen sash[a] and put it round your waist, but do not put it in water." 2 So I bought a sash, as per Yahweh's message, and put it around my waist. 3 Then I received another message from Yahweh: 4 "Take the sash you bought, the one you are wearing, and go off to Parah[b] and hide it there, in the crevice of a rock." 5 So I went off and hid it at Parah, as Yahweh had ordered me. 6 Much later Yahweh said to me, "Go off to Parah and retrieve the sash I ordered you to hide there." 7 So I went off to Parah and after a search retrieved the sash from the place I had hidden it—only to find it ruined, no use for anything! 8 Then I received a message from Yahweh: 9 "Here is what Yahweh said: 'This is like the way I will ruin Judah's prestige[c] and Jerusalem's enormous prestige. 10 This bad people, who refuse to listen to my messages, who *go off after the stubborn inclination of their own thinking and* go off after other gods, serving and worshiping them, will become[d] like the sash that is no use for anything. 11 In fact the close cling of a sash to a man's waist is like the way I made Israel's entire community and Judah's entire community[e] cling to me,' *declared Yahweh*, 'so they would become my people, a source of my renown, praise, and glory—and yet they have not listened.'

12 "Now tell this people:ᶠ 'Every jar is supposed to be filled with wine.' When they tell you, 'Don't we know for a fact that every jar should be filled with wine?' 13 tell them, 'Here is what Yahweh said: "Look out, I am going to get *all* who live in this land full to the point of inebriation, and in particular the kings of David's line who sit on his throne, the priests, prophets, and all others who live in Jerusalem. 14 Then I will smash them against each other, even parents in a clash with children," declared Yahweh, "without pity or mercy or any compassion that stops me ruining them."'"

15   Listen, pay attention—do not be arrogant—
     because it is Yahweh who has spoken.
16   Give honor to Yahweh your God
     before he brings darkness
     and before your feet stumble
        on twilit mountains
     and you look for light,
     but he makes it deep darkness,
        turning it into black clouds.
17   But if you will not listen to this,
     in secret I must weep
     in face of such pride.ᵍ
  My eyes will run with tears
     and shed tears aplenty
     because Yahweh's flock will be carried off captive.

    a. Usually *ʾēzôr* is rendered "loincloth," an undergarment, but the reference in v. 11 to "renown, praise, and glory" reflects the ornamental quality that a girdle or "waist-sash" can have (Kelvin G. Friebel, *Jeremiah's and Ezekiel's Sign-Acts: Rhetorical Nonverbal Communication* [JSOTSup 283; Sheffield: Sheffield Academic Press, 1999], 102), for which *ḥăgôr* or *ḥăgôrâ* is the common term. "Prestige" in v. 9 points in the same direction. Cf. LXX *perizōma*, "girdle, apron," KJV and NEB "girdle," and NIV "belt."

    b. MT *pĕrātâ* refers to the Euphrates (NRSV, NJB, GNB), and LXX so rendered, even adding "river" in v. 7. However, Aquila translated "Phara" (see *BHS*; cf. NAB "Parath," and REB and NJPS "Perath"). If this is correct (see the commentary), a repointing to *pārātâ* is necessary, here and in vv. 5–7. At v. 5 4Q70 has *bprth* (cf. GKC §90e), which may have been revised in MT to *biprāt*, as an unambiguous reference to the Euphrates.

    c. EVV render *gĕʾôn* "pride," but for a positive sense here see BDB 144b–45a; Friebel, *Sign-Acts*, 110 n. 81. Calvin 2:164 rendered "excellency."

    d. The odd verbal form is apparently a weak *wāw* with a meaningless jussive; cf. GKC §109k; Joüon §114l.

e. The latter phrase may have originated as an explanatory gloss on the former one, recalling the mention of Judah in v. 9. It is less likely that the former phrase is an amplification (cf. *BHS*); cf. 5:11. See the commentary.

f. MT adds a quotation formula, "Here is what Yahweh, Israel's God, said." It is absent from LXX and hardly fits at this juncture; the divine oracle appears in v. 13. It doubtless originated as a longer variant of the formula there, incorporated from the margin, as in 11:22. Just before, MT has "Now tell them this message," a reading that probably developed secondarily to accommodate the insertion and was influenced by 14:17. The reference to "this people" in LXX (see *BHS*) nicely harks back to v. 10. Holladay 1:394–95, 399–400, prefers the form of the directive in MT and takes it with v. 11 as a concluding directive to report the symbolic action. This would fit well, but leaves the oracle of vv. 12–14 without any introduction. Have MT and LXX preserved two halves of a longer text?

g. For the cola division see Cloete, *Versification*, 168–69.

Ruin and failure to listen are the twin foci of this composition. It falls into three units, a main one (vv. 1–11) and two supplementary ones (vv. 12–14 and 15–17) that pick up terms from the first as catchwords. The second unit is linked to the first by the final verb "ruin" (*šḥt*, *Hiphil*) with Yahweh as subject and Judah and Jerusalem as object, echoing v. 9. The third repeats from the close of the first unit the motif of "not listening" at v. 17.

[13:1–11] The first unit is a first person report of a symbolic action. It has the three standard parts of the genre, divine command and prophetic performance (vv. 1–7), and divine interpretations of the action (vv. 8–11). Symbolic actions were carried out by prophets as a powerful means of communicating in a dramatic manner. In this case the communication does not include a public enactment but lies simply in the report that is presented here. The interpretive element is similar to an oracle of disaster. The report as a whole is carefully structured in a chiastic format. A series of divine orders is given and each time carried out exactly (vv. 1–2, A; vv. 3–5, B; vv. 6–7a, C). A shocking discovery follows (v. 7b, D). In the interpretation, first the discovery is explained (v. 9, D′), then the second executed order (v. 10, B′), and finally the initial executed order (v. 11, A′).[35] The reference at the end of v. 10 to language used in v. 7b is intended for the purpose of identification rather than of explanation. The third executed order (vv. 6–7a, C) does not reappear in the course of the interpretation because it is merely an incidental preparation for the discovery.[36]

[1–2] Jeremiah was to purchase and wear a linen sash. Its material is not mentioned again and serves only to indicate that it could be ruined.

[3–7a] Where was Jeremiah to first hide it and then retrieve it from? MT "Euphrates" raises the logistical problem of a journey that took Ezra and his

---

35. This chiastic scheme is a refinement of two others, proposed by Brueggemann 128 and Friebel, *Sign-Acts*, 100–101.

36. Friebel, *Sign-Acts*, 108, 112.

party three and a half months (Ezra 7:9; 8:31), and the narrative would surely have referred to the arduousness of two such round trips. Calvin 2:161–63, among others, believed that a vision is reported here rather than a real experience, but it is not presented as such and the lapse of time in v. 6 suggests otherwise. Alternatively it has been regarded as a fictional, allegorical account (for example, by McKane 1:286, 291–92), but the tone of the report does not support this view. Accordingly a widely held solution, first made in the eleventh century and revived by Conrad Schick in 1867 (see McKane 1:286), is that the reference is to Wadi Fara, five miles northeast of Jerusalem and not far from Anathoth, a place that may be compared to the town "Parah" in Benjamin listed in Josh 18:23. There would then be an implicit metaphorical association with the Euphrates by wordplay, *pārātâ*, "to Parah," sounding much like *pĕrātâ*, "to the Euphrates." Some modern versions postulate "Perath" as the place name, so that the words would sound the same.

The appeal, homonymous or literal, to the Euphrates would evoke the idea of exile. True, the place name occurs only in the report of the symbolic action and not in its interpretation, but this aspect of the symbolism was evidently regarded as too obvious to articulate. Reference to exile accords with its recurrence at the end of the supporting unit (v. 17), while in the companion composition explicit mention of exile occurs in vv. 19 and 24. Presumably the unit 12:14–17, with its exilic associations, was partly prefixed to ch. 13 because the latter contained a series of exilic references, not least the initial allusions to the Euphrates in vv. 4–7. This is the first crack in the anonymity of the foreign, northern foe, which will be abandoned in the mention of Babylon at 20:4–6.

[7b] The statement of Jeremiah's shocking discovery stands outside the formal structure of divine command and prophetic compliance.[37] The discovery is an isolated climax, important enough to be repeated at the beginning of the interpretation (v. 9). The cause of the damage is not given, nor is it necessary because Yahweh's own agency will come to the fore in v. 9, cutting across any intermediate cause. If, however, the sash had been hidden near a wadi in summer, Jeremiah's long absence would have included a winter when floodwaters reached it, soaking it and rotting it. In Isa 7:19 rock crevices are associated with wadis (NRSV "ravines"). The addition of "river" in LXX at v. 7 interprets in terms of water damage, while the allusion to water in v. 1 may already anticipate such a catastrophe.[38]

[9] The first of three interpretive statements focuses on the fate of Judah and Jerusalem, finding in it the humiliating end of their prestigious history. The interpretation moves from the result, "ruined" in v. 7, to divine intervention, "I will ruin" (cf. 12:10). The overall interpretation of the symbolic action is

---

37. Daniel Bourguet, *Des métaphores de Jérémie* (EBib n.s. 9; Paris: Gabalda, 1987), 242.
38. Ibid., 248–49.

expressed as an oracle of disaster, and here a future disaster initiated by Yahweh is announced.

[10] The second interpretive statement, like the third in v. 11, also functions as the underlying reason in an oracle of disaster. The two statements are linked by a frame, the reference to not listening that begins v. 10 and ends v. 11. Now it is the turn of the second stage of the symbolic action (vv. 4–5) to be interpreted. The element of going off (*hālak*) to Parah/Euphrates is picked up and associated not with going into exile but with its fundamental religious cause, the following (*hālak*) of other gods, which must result in alienation not only from Yahweh but from Yahweh's land (cf. 5:19). MT reinforces the reason for disaster by repeating the same verb in the formulation that was used in 9:13 and 11:8 with reference to pagan worship.[39] Yahweh's "messages" (*dĕbāray*) are meant to be understood primarily as prophetic, especially in view of the use of the singular noun in vv. 2, 3, and 8 (cf. 6:17; 7:13; 11:21), rather than referring to the "terms" of the covenant, as in 11:3, 8, though the later amplification probably understood it thus.

[11] The failure to listen is highlighted by a contrast motif that alludes to a pristine period of fellowship with God. It draws a stark comparison between that period and the present. The verse returns to Jeremiah's initial wearing of the sash in vv. 1–2, and, in so doing, gives closure to the report. Its snug fit is interpreted in terms of the prior harmonious relationship between Yahweh and the covenant people (cf. 2:2–3a). This verse reflects editorial amplification. First, "clinging" has Deuteronomic associations of spiritual allegiance (e.g., Deut 11:22, rendered "holding fast"). Second, the trio of nouns recalls Deut 26:19, which differs only in word order (NRSV "in praise and in fame and in honor"). The trio serves as a parallel to the "prestige" of v. 9 (*gā'ôn*, "prestige, pride," and *tip'eret*, "glory," are associated in Isa 4:2; 13:19). It again alludes to the ornamental quality of the sash. Third, "to be my people" (NIV) is a reprise of "to be his . . . people" (Deut 26:18). Moreover, the reference to the two communities creates a long-range link with Jer 11:10, 17, underscoring the refusal to listen (13:10 and 11:10). The observation of Holladay (1:397) that the resumption of *tip'eret*, "glory," as a catchword in vv. 18 and 20 already presupposes its presence here is not necessarily an argument against redactional activity.

[12–14] This originally independent unit has been attached to the previous one to reinforce it. It too concerns Judah and Jerusalem. Its closing verb "ruin" with Yahweh as agent now echoes v. 9. As an announcement of disaster it amplifies the one reported in v. 9. The unit is a variant of the question-and-answer format

---

39. "Bad" (*hāra'*) earlier in v. 10 is in a strange position in the Hebrew and may represent the wrongly placed insertion of a marginal gloss that assimilated the later phrase to the longer form it had in 11:8. Cf. the text-critical evidence for the addition of the adjective to the formulation in *BHS* at 9:14(13).

used earlier (5:19; 9:12–16 [11–15]). In this case, as in 15:1–4 and 23:33, it is an example of one pattern of Jeremiah's preaching.[40] The prophet is directed to make a statement to the people, a seemingly commonplace remark that is disparaged, only to be justified by being interpreted in a metaphorical way.

[12–13] The negative response suggests that the initial statement was not a proverb but an inconsequential-sounding statement that "triggers the process of communication."[41] The metaphorical interpretation launched by the announcement of divinely initiated disaster is related to the more common cup of wrath motif used by the prophets (cf. 25:15, 27; Ezek 23:32–33). It spells the collapse of the country's population, a collapse that operates from the top down, with the failure of the capital's establishment, both the royal family and religious leaders.

[14] The metaphor is developed further with the smashing of the storage jars.[42] Now the choice of jars rather than a cup becomes evident; the fragility of jars is exploited. Whereas in v. 13 the disintegration was to occur from the top down, here it develops from the inside out, with the family unit at the heart of society that is falling apart. In both vv. 13 and 14 the disintegration comes not from an outside human agency as in 51:7, but from inside, with an internal collapse caused by divine providence. The categorical, implacable nature of such providence is spelled out at the end as a terrible singleness of purpose that blocks Yahweh's traditional grace. Such stark closure has occurred before, in 4:8, 28, and in the refrain of 5:9, 29; 9:9 (8). In this case it has been toned down earlier, in 12:15, as God's short-term policy.

[15–17] The final unit of the composition, like the second, reinforces the first. It refers in v. 17 to the failure to listen (vv. 10–11) and to the prognosis of exile. Moreover, in v. 16 it gives the obverse of "my people" (v. 11) in calling Yahweh "your God." This covenantal language is resumed at the end with the metaphor of "Yahweh's flock." The piece, spoken by Jeremiah, is an exhortation that presents with pathos a two-sided prospect, either humbly listening to Yahweh and avoiding coming disaster (vv. 15–16) or arrogantly refusing to listen and experiencing the disaster of exile (v. 17). If the first half is given full weight, the unit hardly accords with the no-option finality of v. 14. Its editorial placement at this point implies that the focus is on the second half and that the first part is used to portray a wasted opportunity and the direness of the disaster.

---

40. Long, "Question and Answer Schemata," 134–35, 138.

41. McKane, "Jeremiah 13:12–14: A Problematic Proverb," in *Israelite Wisdom: Theological Essays in Honor of Samuel Terrien* (ed. J. G. Gammie et al.; Missoula: Scholars Press, 1978), 107–20, esp. 114.

42. Bourguet, *Métaphores de Jérémie*, 267 and n. 62, has observed that, apart from the citation of false prophecy in 27:16, the announcements of disaster that begin with *hinnēh*, "look," and a participle are always followed by another verb in the book of Jeremiah and that this practice renders unlikely McKane's view that v. 14 is secondary ("Problematic Proverb," 117–18; idem, 11:297).

[15–16] The prophet brought a warning that the people were walking into danger. The danger is illustrated by travel continued too late into the evening. If the people claimed the covenant tradition of divine deliverance and looked for its light on their path (cf. Ps 27:1), they were liable to find themselves plunged into utter darkness.

[17] One expects the people's refusal to lead straight on to Yahweh's punishment, as in 12:17 (Holladay 1:406). However, an announcement of the prophet's private grief comes first. Rejection of Jeremiah's message would mean withdrawal from public ministry, as in Isaiah's case (Isa 8:16–17). There was nothing else to say. As in 4:19; 8:18; 9:1 (8:23), his emotional reaction is a premonitory measure of the overwhelming nature of the disaster, which is spelled out metaphorically by referring to the covenant people's loss of the land.

Jeremiah 13:1–17 comprises an oracle of disaster. It accuses the people of forfeiting its covenant birthright by pagan worship and failing to listen to prophetic warnings. It forecasts exile, which would accomplish Yahweh's twofold reprisal, the extinction of national prestige and the collapse of political and social solidarity.

13:18–27 The Peril of Ignoring Yahweh

18 "Tell the king and queen mother:
    'Take lower seats,
because falling off are your insignia of headship,[a]
    each of your glorious crowns.
19 The Negeb towns are closed off
    and relief is impossible.
Judah is to be deported in its entirety,
    totally deported.'[b]

20 "Raise your eyes[c]
    and see the invaders from the north![d]
Where is the flock that was committed to you,
    the sheep that have been your glory?
21 What will you say
    when they punish you,[e]
after you have gotten them used
    to being leaders[f] over your head?
Spasms of pain will seize you, won't they,
    as they seize a woman in labor.
22 And if you ask yourself,
    'Why have such things happened to me?'

> it is because your guilt is so great that your skirts will be lifted up,
> your limbs exposed[g]—
> 23 Can Nubians[h] alter their skin color
> or leopards their spots?
> Well, you are no more capable of doing good,
> so used are you to doing bad!
> 24 (So I dispersed them, like so much chaff
> carried off by[i] the desert wind.)
> 25 This is to be your lot,
> the deal doled out to you[j] by me,"
> declared Yahweh,
> "because you have forgotten me
> and put your trust in lies.
> 26 So I for my part will pull up
> your skirts right over your face,
> and your nudity will be brought into shameful view.
> 27 Your adulteries and mare-like cries!
> Your lascivious affairs!
> On the hills, in the countryside,
> I have seen your detestable acts.
> How deplorable, Jerusalem, that you are not cleansed!
> How much longer can this go on?"[k]

a. Most EVV adapt to *mērā'ăšêkem* or *mērā'šôtêkem*, "from your heads," following LXX, Vg., and Syr. (*BHS*), but MT *mar'ăšôtêkem* can probably stand with the sense "your signs of headship," as Kimchi suggested (Barthélemy, *Critique textuelle*, 2:580–81); cf. ASV "headtires" and NJPS "diadems."

b. MT may be retained; see Rudolph 92; McKane 1:302, 305.

c. In view of the feminine singular suffixes in vv. 20b–22, the masculine plural suffix must reflect a secondary literary device that relates to the previous unit, specifically with v. 18. See note k on 3:13.

d. For the cola division see Cloete, *Versification*, 169–70.

e. LXX so understands the verb, unlike EVV. A plural verb with LXX (*BHS*) seems required by the plurals before and after. MT takes Yahweh as subject, which suits neither context nor genre.

f. "Friends" (NJB, GNB; similarly most other EVV) is a possible meaning for *'allūpîm*, but the poetic structure does not favor it. Cf. KJV "captains," NEB "leaders," NAB "rulers," and the discussion of McKane 1:308–9.

g. NJPS; cf. REB "uncovered." LXX, Syr., and Tg. so render. See John A. Emerton, "The Meaning of the Verb *ḥāmas* in Jeremiah 13,22," in *Prophet und Prophetenbuch: Festschrift für Otto Kaiser zum 65. Geburtstag* (ed. V. Fritz et al.; BZAW 185; Berlin: de Gruyter, 1989), 19–28, who compares Akkadian *ḫamāṣu*, to "strip."

h. See Donald B. Redford, "Kush," *ABD* 4:109–11.

i. For the verb cf. Isa 29:5; the *lāmed* indicates the agent (Holladay 1:416). LXX, Vg., and Tg. so rendered.

j. Literally "the portion of your measures." For LXX, adopted by *BHS*, see the discussion of McKane 1:311–12.

k. Literally "After when still?" It is hardly an implicit call to repentance, as EVV take it with undue reliance on v. 16.

Jeremiah 13:18–27 is a companion piece to vv. 1–17, underlining and elucidating its key contents. Its two units (vv. 18–19 and 20–27) share in the theme of the loss of political power. The first amplifies v. 13 with its forecast of royal and national collapse. The second unit also elucidates the first composition. The pagan worship of v. 10 is revisited (vv. 26–27) in greater detail, while the description of the people as "bad" is amplified (v. 23). The key term "glory" (*ʿăṭeret*), as in v. 18, echoes v. 11, now with reference to the nation, as there. The "flock" in v. 20 looks back to v. 17, with its presentiment of exile, while exile comes into plainer view in v. 24.

[18–19] Jeremiah is commanded to deliver a brief message to the royal family, an announcement of disaster that predicts the royals' loss of power and the mass deportation of Judah. The oracle reflects events in 597 B.C.E. and the misfortunes of Jehoiachin and his mother Nehushta (see 2 Kgs 24:8), whose deportation to Babylon is recorded in 2 Kgs 24:12, 15 after a reign of only three months (cf. Jer 22:24–27). The eminent position of the queen mother reflects not only its political importance but the special role as counselor she would have had in the transition of royal power to a young king.[43]

The loss of Judean control over territory in the Negeb, evidently at the hands of Edomite forces working in league with Babylon, substantiates both the impending royal downfall and Judean exile. (An ostracon found at Arad and written in Hebrew warns of an imminent Edomite attack, though the ostracon may belong to Zedekiah's reign rather than Jehoiachin's.[44]) The communal deportation turned out to be a selective one (2 Kgs 24:14–16), and Judah staggered on for another ten years.

[20–27] This unit is dominated by second feminine singular references, which are ultimately explained by the vocative "Jerusalem" (a feminine noun) at the close; for clarity LXX added it in v. 20. This oracle of disaster announces disaster (vv. 20–22) and gives the reason for it (vv. 25–27). The two sections are separated by vv. 23–24, where there is a switch to second masculine plural references at v. 23 and to third plural ones at v. 24. Verse 23 gives

43. See Niels-Erik A. Andreason, "The Role of the Queen Mother in Israelite Society," *CBQ* 45 (1983): 179–94.

44. See John Lindsay, "The Babylonian Kings and Edom, 605–550 B.C.," *PEQ* 108 (1976): 23–39, esp. 24–25; Yohanan Aharoni and Michael Avi-Yonah, *The Macmillan Bible Atlas* (3d ed.; New York: Macmillan, 1993), 124–25 and maps 161 and 162.

its own reason for the coming disaster, while v. 24 confirms that disaster did happen.

[20–22] If v. 19 spoke of trouble in the south, v. 20a finds trouble coming from the north, reverting to that description of the national enemy in earlier chapters. A series of four questions follows in vv. 20b–22. The first three are rhetorical and related to the disaster; the last one searches for a reason and provides one. The first question gives a warning to check on the "flock," for which disaster looms. In Mic 4:8 Zion is called "watchtower of the flock" (NIV), but here the capital is its shepherd, as steward and beneficiary of an important state under God. The second and third questions envision the capital of a vassal country allied to an imperial power and enjoying the benefits of that alliance—but liable to suffer severely at its hands when the relationship went awry. The fourth question discloses a spiritual factor, that the disaster would be reprisal for "great guilt," which relates not to political offenses but to theological ones. Jerusalem's conquest is described now not in terms of a woman in labor (v. 21), but brutally and shockingly as a rape inflicted by the military enemy, supplementing suffering with humiliation. "Limbs" (REB, NJPS), literally "heels" (KJV), are a euphemism for genitalia.

[23–24] These verses do not cohere with their immediate context, but function as separate sayings that comment on the coming crisis and its cause.

[23] A fresh pair of rhetorical questions appears, now in definition of "great guilt." The metaphors are explained in terms of bad habits to which Judah has become addicted (cf. 2:22).

[24] This comment looks beyond invasion and the conquest of Jerusalem to Judah's exile as an act of God, whether the exile of 597 or that of 587 B.C.E. The winnowing image, used earlier at 4:11–12, points both to Yahweh's destructive power and to the insignificance to which Judah had shrunk—mere chaff, gone with the wind.

[25–27] This section has more to say about the reason for Jerusalem's coming downfall, but mingles it with an insistence that not only would disaster come, but it would do so by Yahweh's direct intervention.

[25] Verse 25a summarizes the disaster, then v. 25b supplies the reason. It is now a religious reason, the abandonment of traditional faith in Yahweh and a novel "trust" in gods that had no basis in reality. The triangle of characters, Jerusalem, Yahweh, and the "lies," will develop in vv. 26–27 into an exploration of Yahweh's future involvement with Jerusalem by way of reprisal and of Jerusalem's past and present involvement with the "lies."

[26] The metaphor of ultimate degradation used earlier of a wartime eventuality is strikingly echoed in a divine mandate. It now takes the form of public pillorying that would expose the capital's wrongdoing (cf. Ezek 16:37–38; Hos 2:10 [12]; Nah 3:5).

[27] That the punishment would fit the crime is now explained. Pagan worship, carried out at Canaanite-type rural shrines, represented acts of marital infi-

delity to Yahweh (cf. 2:20 and commentary there). It all boded ill for Jerusalem, as unchecked provocation that could not for long go unpunished. The oracle ends as it began, with a rhetorical question. Perhaps the comment at v. 24 was originally generated by "the hills," wryly noting that they came to serve a new purpose as winnowing places and that expulsion from the misused land was the price that was duly paid.

Jeremiah 13:18–27 envisions the loss of political power, as invasion and exile loom, and explains it in terms of a providential response for adopting pagan religion and ignoring Yahweh.

14:1–17:27 Why God's Answer Was No

14:1–16 Unanswered Prayers

1 What Jeremiah received as Yahweh's message[a] About the drought:

2   Judah is lamenting
        and its towns flop down,
    in mourning garb lying on the ground,
        while Jerusalem's crying is directed upward.
3   Their grandees sent their minions to the water;
        they came to the cisterns,
    found no water,
        and returned with their pots empty.[b]
4   Because of the ground that is cracked
        for lack of rain *throughout the country*,
    farmworkers are humiliated and dismayed,
        and they cover their heads.[c]
5   *Yes*, the very doe in the countryside
        abandons the young she bears
    for lack of vegetation,
6   while wild asses, standing in the open spaces,
        pant for air like jackals,
    bleary-eyed
        for want of grass.
7   "Although our wrongdoings give evidence against us,
        Yahweh, act for your name's sake,
    though[d] our backsliding ways are so many,
        [though] against you we have sinned.
8   You hope of Israel, its savior in times of trouble,
        why are you like a visitor to the country
        or like some traveler who stops off for a night's rest?

9   Why are you like somebody caught off guard,ᵉ
       like a warrior who has lost his power to save?
    Yet you are here among us, Yahweh,
       and your name is the one we are called by—
    do not leave us!"ᶠ

10 Here is what Yahweh said about this people:

   "That is the way they love to wander,
      they do not keep their own feet under control."
   So Yahweh has not given them his approval;
      right now he will remember their wrongdoing
   and deal with their sins.

11 Moreover, Yahweh said to me: "Do not pray on this people's behalf for a good outcome. 12 Even though they fast, I will not listen to their shrill crying. Though they sacrifice burnt offerings and grain offerings, I will not give them my approval. Instead, I will use sword, famine, and pestilence to put an end to them." 13 Then I said: "Oh no, Lord Yahweh! Here are the prophets telling them, 'You will not see a sword, and famine you will not experience, but stable peace is what I will give you in this place.'" 14 But Yahweh said to me: "It is false, what the prophets are prophesying in my name. I never sent them nor gave them any orders, I never spoke to them. False visions, worthless divinations, and delusions generated by their own minds are what they are prophesyingᵍ to you.ʰ 15 Therefore," here is what Yahweh said, "about the prophets who are prophesying in my name—though I never sent them—and saying that neither sword nor famine will materialize in this country: Sword and famine will be the very means by which *those* prophets will perish. 16 Moreover, the people they are prophesying to will be thrown out onto Jerusalem's streets and left there,ⁱ victims of the famine and sword. There will be nobody to bury them or their wives or their sons and daughters either. That is how I will overwhelm them with the consequences of their own bad behavior."

   a. The oracle reception statement found in LXX (*BHS*) has a minimal role in the book.
   b. MT adds "They are humiliated and dismayed and they cover their heads," which LXX lacks. The addition is best understood as a longer variant of v. 4b that was wrongly incorporated from the margin (*BHS*; NEB).
   c. See the previous note.
   d. As in v. 12, *kî* means "though" (NAB, NJPS).
   e. For the root *dhm*, which only occurs here in Biblical Hebrew, see *HALOT* 1:214b.
   f. This colon is a closing monocolon (Watson, *Classical Hebrew Poetry*, 171), as its climactic content suggests.

g. The *Hithpael* of *nbʾ* is used as a synonym of the earlier *Niphal* (Ivo Meyer, *Jeremia und die falsche Propheten* [OBO 13; Göttingen: Vandenhoeck & Ruprecht, 1977], 60–62; Robert R. Wilson, "Prophesy as Ecstasy: A Reexamination," *JBL* 98 [1979]: 321–37, esp. 335–36).

h. "To them" (cf. *BHS*; NEB) is logically expected after Jeremiah's report in v. 13 referring to the people as "them," but the report's quotation using second plurals for the people has exerted an understandable influence; there is no need to depart from MT.

i. See Holladay 1:436; Joüon §121e.

Judah's fate was sealed whatever Jeremiah's prophetic rivals might imagine, and no prayer could avert it, according to this composition. It begins with an oracle reception heading, that is used editorially as a block heading in the book, using the less common type found earlier in 1:2. Hitherto such formulas have introduced long prose passages that have framed the surrounding poetry, highlighting certain themes. In this case the poem in vv. 1–10 paves the way for a prose passage in vv. 11–16 that in content corresponds on a smaller scale to the buttresses of 7:1–8:3 and 11:1–17.[45] Not only does it, like them, summarily declare the inevitability of divine punishment, but it does so by repeating aspects of earlier passages: the prohibition of Jeremiah's intercession to avert doom (7:16; 11:14; 14:11), the failure of sacrifice to do so (7:21–22; 11:15; 14:12), and the horror of coming disaster that would leave its victims unburied (7:33; 8:2; 14:16). It bears the terminological trademark of 7:1–8:3, "this place" in the sense of the land (v. 13), and that of 11:1–17, "a bad fate" (*rāʿâ*, v. 16, rendered "consequences of bad behavior"). In the earlier passages religious deviation involved nominal worship of Yahweh or outright pagan worship; here it is the misleading contribution of false prophets.

This next block of material (chs. 14–17) consists of six compositions. It bears further witness to the inevitability of coming disaster construed as divine punishment, and in this loose sense the unit (14:11–16) forms a fitting summary. The block includes interrelated themes. The ban on prophetic intercession in 14:11 suits the motif of the people's unanswered prayers featured in the twin compositions of 14:1–16 and 14:17–15:9. The repeated word pair epitomizing disaster, "sword" and "famine" (14:12, 13, 15, 16), surfaces again in 14:18; 15:2; 16:4, and so does "sword" by itself in 15:2, 3, 9. "Peace," vainly promised in 14:13, reappears in negative contexts in 14:19; 15:5 (rendered "welfare"); 16:5. The terrible fate of lack of burial (14:16) emerges again in 16:4. Mainly, however, this block continues the emphases of the previous one, chs. 11–13. A "bad fate" or "bad times" occurs in 15:11; 16:10; 17:16, 18. It takes

---

45. Stulman, *Prose Sermons*, does not include this passage. However, Thiel, *Redaktion von Jeremia 1–25*, 182–88, regards vv. 11–16 as a Deuteronomistic product because of literary borrowings and Deuteronomistic terminology; cf. McKane 1:326–28. The overlap of motifs with the sermons in chs. 7 and 11 is a significant factor.

the form of exile in 15:2, 14; 16:13; 17:4. The practice of pagan religion is the major accusation in 16:1–21 and it continues into 17:2–3. In the compositions of 17:1–13 and 14–27, the definition of reprehensible sin gradually widens beyond pagan religion to charges of ignoring the Divine, of general immorality, and of Sabbath breaking. This final charge illustrates a failure to honor the revelation of the torah, which in general terms also appears in 16:11. A passage characteristic of blocks earlier in the book is the redactional summary (16:10–13), which corresponds to 5:19; 9:12–16 (11–15). As one would expect from its preceding parallels, the passage highlights pagan religion, not keeping the torah, and the fate of exile and so bears witness to the context in its selection of motifs. Three more of Jeremiah's confessions are woven into the block, a pair in the composition of 15:10–21, which presents him as Yahweh's agent whose rejection spells that of Yahweh, and a third in 17:14–18, which calls for punishment for the community that rejects his (torah-based) message.

The block interweaves Jeremiah's oracles with redactional material. Two striking examples of the latter, in which the exilic community raises its own voice in reverent harmony with the earlier message, occur in 16:19–21 and 17:12–13. The former unit echoes and develops Israel's confession of wholehearted praise in 10:11–16, now incorporating the hope for Gentile praise to be added, after a divine promise of return from exile in 16:14–15 (cf. 12:14–17). The unit in 17:12–13 pleads with Yahweh to deal with contemporary deviants in the land of exile, just as earlier deviants in Judah had been punished. These redactional innovations reveal how closely the exilic constituency had been listening to the divine message and endeavored to appropriate it.

The first composition consists of two units, vv. 1–10 and 11–16, which establish a pattern of human prayer and its divine rejection that will be continued in 14:17–15:9.

[14:1–10] This poetic unit presents a communal lament (vv. 2–9), followed by a divine answer (v. 10). The focus of the heading is on the latter part, to which the earlier verses are a necessary preliminary. The heading takes the topic of drought from vv. 3–6 and anticipates the divine answer in v. 10. The climatic hazard of drought has been prominent in Jeremiah's earlier oracles, as a minor motif of providential punishment at 3:3 and 5:24–25, and also as evidence of human disarray at 12:4. Here it is a crisis for which Yahweh's help was sought.

[2–9] The elements of a communal lament are used as the basis for a report setting the scene for Yahweh's answer. Jeremiah apparently speaks in vv. 1–6, presenting "suggestive pictures of atmosphere."[46] A lament, accompanied by appropriate dress and prostration and uttered by Judah and Jerusalem, is

---

46. Wim A. M. Beuken and Harm W. M. van Grol, "Jeremiah 14,1–15,9: A Situation of Distress and Its Hermeneutics, Unity and Diversity of Form—Dramatic Development," in *Livre de Jérémie* (ed. P.-M. Bogaert), 297–342, esp. 311, 314.

announced in v. 2. A description of the drought is given in vv. 3–6, first from Jerusalem's perspective in v. 3 and then from Judah's in vv. 4–6. The lament announced in v. 2—Jerusalem's cry is directed to God (cf. Exod 2:23)—is at last cited in vv. 7–9.[47]

[2–6] Just as three cola are devoted to Judah and one to Jerusalem in v. 2, the same proportion of vignettes is inversely devoted to Jerusalem (v. 3) and to Judah (vv. 4–6).

[3] Jerusalem's cause for lament is empty cisterns, as a brief narrative explains. "Their" refers to its citizens who were crying out. An ironic contrast is drawn between the capital's powerful elite, who have lesser mortals at their beck and call, and their failure to get a basic need supplied.

[4–6] Three other vignettes, now in a rural setting, are presented as warrant for the lament. The addition "throughout the country" underlines the change of scene; it also provides a stylistic match for the parallels "in the countryside" and "in the open spaces" in vv. 5–6 and so reinforces the existing triple parallelism of "for lack of rain," "for lack of vegetation," and "for want of grass." Farmworkers, unable to produce crops, cover their heads in a mourning rite (cf. 2 Sam 15:30; Esth 6:12), while the stark suffering of wild creatures is sensitively sketched to portray the extent of the crisis (cf. Hos 4:3; Joel 1:18, 20). The wild asses pant openmouthed in canine fashion, a sorry sight.

[7–9] This is a vocal response to the crisis of drought. Whether Jeremiah cites a contemporary lament or composes an appropriate one remains unclear. The vocative "Yahweh" and the appeal to Yahweh's "name" or reputation provide a frame that is a focal point for the lament, insofar as the genre took its rationale from the tradition of Yahweh as deliverer of the covenant people from crisis (cf. Pss 79:9; 106:8).

[7] Unfortunately the tradition was only held to work if the covenant relationship was healthy (Pss 34:15, 17, 19 [16, 18, 20]; 91:14–15; 145:18–19). Yet Yahweh usually forgave sins that stood in the way, accepting confession in lieu of conduct. Accordingly, the effusive admission of sins is designed to remove any barrier to divine help.

[8–9] A new and fitting frame, "savior/save," is supplied for the divine vocatives and the pair of double rhetorical questions. The "why" questions are an element of complaint, as in 12:1.[48] Accusing questions are not uncommon, but the similes are novel. Yahweh is accused of lack of commitment to the covenant people and of failing to intervene with power (cf. Zeph 3:17 NJB). But there is a chance for rectification. Appeal is made to the tradition of the helping presence of God and to the covenant relationship, in order to support the climactic

---

47. Cf. Baumgartner, *Poems of Lament*, 88, who identifies parallels from the Psalms. He misses the point of v. 2.

48. But here and in 15:18 the psalm term *lāmmâ* is used, unlike 12:1; 14:19.

negative petition. "Do not leave us" gains emotional weight as a synonymous echo of the doe's abandoning her young in v. 5.

[10] The process of lament, though punctiliously followed, does not work. In direct speech Yahweh denies the people's plea. It is a caustic reply to the first pair of complaining questions in v. 8 (Holladay 1:434). On the issue of absenteeism the fault lay on the people's side. They had distanced themselves by their lavish sinning, which remained a rigid barrier to divine deliverance. The punishment of v. 16 is anticipated. MT adds a parallel colon derived from Hos 8:13;[49] it echoes the parallelism of v. 7, embellishing a frame for vv. 7–10.

[11–16] The accompanying prose unit reinforces the message of v. 10. It too relates to unanswered prayer, but it is now concerned with a military disaster, not an ecological one; its "famine" reflects siege conditions (cf. v. 18). The unit is neatly hinged to the prior one by disparaging repetition of "this people" and by Yahweh's lack of approval. The unit is a three-statement dialogue between Yahweh and Jeremiah, in which the prophet's protest (v. 13) to Yahweh's blunt rejection of the people (vv. 11–12) is answered by an oracle of disaster (vv. 14–16). The pitting of "their own bad behavior" (v. 16) against the people's desire for "a good outcome" (v. 11) provides a frame for the unit.[50] From the standpoint of vv. 1–10, this prose unit supplements the longer poem, but from an editorial perspective it provides the heart of the composition, dealing with the radical crisis of national defeat and as a counterpart to the literary landmarks in chs. 7 and 11. The drought was a dress rehearsal for coming total disaster.

[11–12] Yahweh's deafness to the people's prayers (v. 10) is reinforced by a ban on the prophet's intercessory praying because it would consequently be doomed to failure. Recourse to fasting, a traditional accompaniment of urgent prayer to show that those who prayed meant business, or to sacrificing would prove equally unsuccessful (contrast 1 Sam 7:5–9). Divine "acceptance" or "approval" (*rṣh*) of a sacrifice or of a person bringing a sacrifice is a cultic term (cf. Lev 7:18), which in v. 10 was extended to bringers of prayer. Nothing could avert the coming military catastrophe as Yahweh's final punishment. The concessive clauses confront those in v. 7. The triad "sword, famine, and pestilence" is a redactional feature in the book; MT often adds the third item to an earlier pair of terms.[51] The triad has a poetic basis in 15:2, and 18:21, with "plague" (*māwet*) in place of "pestilence" (*deber*). Elsewhere in this unit "sword and famine" occur three times, and here the third term looks like a redactional flourish.

[13] In the style of 1:6 and 4:10, Jeremiah pleads an excuse for the people. Prophetic peddlers of *šālôm*, "peace," were to blame. In Yahweh's name they had explicitly and misleadingly denied the threats of "sword and famine" voiced by

---

49. Janzen, *Studies*, 40.
50. Gregorio del Olmo Lete, "La unidad literaria de Jer 14–17," *EstBib* 30 (1971): 3–46, esp. 13.
51. See Janzen, *Studies*, 43–44; McKane 1:505–6.

Jeremiah (5:12; cf. 23:17). "In this place" refers to Judah, as its echo "in this country" in v. 15 (and ch. 7) verifies. LXX explains this identification in an addition.

[14] An oracle of disaster begins here, offering a vehement accusation. Despite the divine "I" of v. 13, Jeremiah's prophetic rivals lacked authenticity and were preaching a message that mistakenly confused revelation with their own expectations of what Yahweh should do. The initial statement about falsehood (cf. 5:31) is amplified in a triple denial of their validity and a triple reaffirmation of the falsehood of their message.

[15] A quotation formula introduces what Yahweh had to say, an announcement of disaster, first for the fake seers. The prophetic stratagem of a punishment that fits the crime emerges here in the boomerang effect of the "sword and famine" denial.[52] They would be among the victims when the military catastrophe eventually struck (cf. 11:22–23).

[16] Now Jeremiah's protest that there was reason to excuse the people receives a response. The disaster would not exclude the credulous people; there was warrant enough irrespective of the prophets' incitement. Their "bad behavior" would wreak its own nemesis (cf. 2:19). It would take the form of the ultimate curse of lack of burial, which would engulf them all in a terrible solidarity.

Jeremiah 14:1–16 sounds an emphatic no in response to the people's prayers of hope, whether in the face of drought or military defeat. Nothing could avert their rightful fate, neither the cultic tradition of Yahweh's promise of deliverance, which they had forfeited, nor a prophet's intercession nor fasting nor sacrifice. And false prophets who could not excuse communal culpability are denounced as make-believe.

14:17–15:9 More Unanswered Prayers

17 "You are to tell them this message."
  Let my eyes run with tears
    night and day without stopping,
  over the *great* injury suffered by my poor *virgin* people,[a]
    wounding most severe.
18 If I go out to the countryside,
    I find casualties of the sword;
  if I come into the city,
    I find cases of suffering from famine.
  Yes, both prophet and priest
    wander around[b] the country, clueless.[c]
19 "Have you rejected Judah outright?
    Is Zion the object of your intense loathing?

---

52. Miller, *Sin and Judgment*, 67–68.

Why else have you inflicted on us wounds
   that will not heal for us?
We hoped for peace, but a good outcome has never come,
   for a time of healing, but have found terror.[d]
20 We acknowledge, Yahweh, our wickedness
   and our forebears' wrongdoing,
   our own sinning against you.
21 Do not show scorn, for your name's sake,
   do not discredit your glorious throne!
   Remember—do not break—your covenant with us!
22 Can any of the nonentities the nations worship bring rain?
   Can the sky of itself produce heavy showers?
   Aren't you the one who can, *Yahweh our God*?
   So we put our hope in you
      because you are the one who brings all this about."

15:1 Yahweh said to me: "Even if Moses or Samuel were to stand in my presence, I would not be inclined toward this people. Send them out of my presence, so they go away! 2 If they ask you where they are to go, tell them, 'Here is what Yahweh said:

"Those designated for plague,[e] to plague,
   those for sword, to sword,
those for famine, to famine,
   and those for captivity, to captivity.

3 "I will subject them to four classes of fate," declared Yahweh, "the sword to kill, dogs to drag off, and birds in the sky and beasts on the ground to devour and destroy. 4 I will make them people the rest of the kingdoms in the world shudder at, on account of King Manasseh ben Hezekiah of Judah, because of what he did in Jerusalem."'"

5 *Here is the explanation.*

"Who will show you any pity, Jerusalem?
   Who will give you a sympathetic nod
or stop to ask
   after your welfare?
6 You are the one who has abandoned me,"
   declared Yahweh,
   "continually moving away.
So I deal *you* a blow with my fist and destroy you,
   having grown tired of relenting.

Why God's Answer Was No 173

7   Moreover, I winnow them with a winnowing fork
       in the towns throughout the country.
    Bereaved by destruction, I leave my people—
       they have not turned back from their ways.
8   Their widows *at my behest* become more in number
       than the sand by the sea.
    I bring upon *their* mothers of young men
       a raider at noon;
    I suddenly cause to fall on such
       shock and terror.
9   A woman who has given birth to seven flops down
       and faints away.
    Her sun sets while it is still day
       in humiliation and consternation—
    the last of them I will surrender to the sword,
       as they face their enemies,"
    declared Yahweh.

   a. For the sympathetic assimilating additions in MT that LXX lacks, see Janzen, *Studies*, 40.
   b. The preposition ʾel is used in the sense of ʿal.
   c. Cf. NJB "at their wits' end."
   d. For the delimitation of the cola in v. 19 see the discussion of Cloete, *Versification*, 176.
   e. For this sense of *māwet*, usually "death," see *HALOT* 2:563b.

   This companion piece to 14:1–16 is a more vehement rerun. It falls into three units, 14:17–22, 15:1–4, and 15:5–9. That it is to be read in conjunction with the former piece is indicated by the ties between 14:17–22 and vv. 11–16, namely, the references to "sword" and "famine" in v. 18 and the lack of "peace" and "a good outcome" in v. 19. The first unit also has links with vv. 1–10, including the need for rain in v. 22. The communal lament of vv. 19–22 recalls vv. 7–9 in the confession of wrongdoing and sinning, in the clinging to "hope," and in the appeal "for your name's sake." As for the second unit, "sword" and "famine" still dominate. The third unit harks back to the first unit of the former composition so that a frame is constructed for the double literary block. "Towns" (15:7) echoes 14:2, and so does the flopping down of 15:9, while "humiliation" in 15:9 echoes that in 14:4.[53] The directive in v. 17, rather like the heading in 14:1, looks ahead to the divine oracles in the second and third units, regarding the first unit as a prelude to the main performance.

   53. Holladay, *Architecture*, 146.

[17–22] As in vv. 2–10, the communal lament (vv. 19–22) is prefaced by description (vv. 17–18). The alignment of its subject matter with the future military disaster of vv. 11–16 suggests that the descriptive element functions as a premonition and so that the lament is put on the people's lips as a hypothetical response to that coming crisis. The triple questioning (v. 19) is characteristic of Jeremiah (cf. 2:14; 8:19, 22). There is striking affinity between vv. 17–22 and the two units in 8:14–9:1 (8:23). Verse 17a and b are similar to the intense grief expressed by the prophet in 9:1 (8:23) and 8:21, respectively; v. 18 repeats the "casualties" of 9:1 (8:23); the final bicolon of v. 19 matches 8:15 exactly, and v. 22 echoes a term used in 8:19, "nonentities."

[17–18a] These verses, similar in tone to 8:21 and 9:1 (8:23), convey personal emotion lacking in their counterpart (vv. 2–6). The unit in 8:18–9:1 (8:23) registered the prophet's heartfelt reaction to the coming disaster in the mood of a funeral dirge. These verses (17–18) have a radically different tone from the ensuing psalm-like lament in which the people still believe that deliverance is a possibility. The description anticipates with a heavy heart the divine no of the next unit.

[18b] This bicolon is a bridge to the people's lament. Physical suffering is matched by religious leaders' disorientation and bewilderment (cf. 4:9). "The religious establishment is bankrupt."[54] The people are left to bring their own lament to God, unlike the lead taken by prophet and priest in Joel 1:13–20 and 2:15–17.

[19–22] The communal lament moves through various stages: accusing questions, a description of unexpected crisis, a confession of long-standing sins, imploring petitions, and an affirmation of faith expressed by means of questions and a closing statement.[55] In this context the lament is a tragic exercise in futility, but it bears eloquent witness to the people's suffering.

[19] The bewilderment of v. 18b spills over into the opening of the lament. The first two questions broach the unthinkable possibility of Yahweh's utter rejection to explain the fact of unmitigated disaster disclosed in the third question. "Judah" and "Zion" are the equivalents of "countryside" and "city" in v. 18a; "Zion" anticipates a cultic allusion in v. 21. "Wounds" resumes the metaphor of v. 17, and the motif of healing unites the second and third bicola.

[20–21] As in v. 7, acknowledgment of sins is the conventional way of removing an obstacle to divine deliverance. A battery of arguments is used in the petitions: the tradition of Yahweh as deliverer, as in vv. 7–8; the powerful, protective presence of Yahweh enthroned in the Jerusalem temple (cf. 8:19; Ps 99:1–2; Ezek 43:7); and the onus upon Yahweh to maintain the covenant rela-

---

54. Martin Kessler, "From Drought to Exile: A Morphological Study of Jer 14:1–15:4," in *SBLSP 1972* (ed. L. C. McGaughy; 2 vols.; n.p.: Society of Biblical Literature, 1972), 2:505–25, esp. 511.
55. See Baumgartner, *Poems of Lament*, 88, for Psalms parallels.

tionship. There is "no awareness of Jeremiah's own conviction that the very disasters of which they complained were evident signs that God was taking his covenant obligations very seriously indeed" (Cunliffe-Jones 120).

[22] At first sight the crisis of vv. 1–6 is again in view, but in this military context the need for rain refers to its healing effect on ground desolated by war (McKane 1:332–33). Yahweh is persuasively acclaimed as the providential source of rain (cf. 5:24), rather than the gods of other nations or even the sky by inherent capacity. MT adds a covenantal reference, "Yahweh our God," that reinforces v. 21. The people want Yahweh's power to be used in their own interests.

[15:1–4] Apart from the pair of bicola in v. 2, this unit is in prose. It is a counterpart to the divine refusal in 14:11–16. After the explicit rejection in v. 1, vv. 2–4 present three different announcements of disaster that rhetorically reinforce it. The first case concentrates on human consequences, while the other two focus on divine agency.

[1] The people stood no chance of having their prayers answered. As in 14:11, Yahweh's reply is inauspiciously addressed not to the lamenting people but to the prophet, and again there is a disdainful reference to "this people." Whereas Jeremiah was forbidden to intercede in the former case, here Yahweh's negative response is presented hypothetically in terms of a historical tradition of covenant mediators' intercession for Israel. Successful as Moses and Samuel had been, even they would have no chance of succeeding now. The tradition also appears in Ps 99:6, with the addition of Aaron. In OT narratives the tradition of intercession is present in Exod 32:11–13; Num 14:13–19; 1 Sam 7:5, 8–9; 12:19, 23. Here, however, the people had no mediator to present their prayers and they presented them on their own behalf. Jeremiah himself is not compared with Moses and Samuel; there is no mention of his interceding. The mediatory role he is now assigned is ironically the opposite of intercession, to communicate the rejection of their appeal.

[2] A question-and-answer format explains an anticipated question, as in 13:12.[56] The answer is a chilling one. It describes the disaster in comprehensive and inescapable terms of four alternatives. The fatality of the first three raises doubt about the fit of the fourth until one recalls that exile is portrayed as a fate worse than death in 8:3 (cf. Amos 9:1–4).

[3] The four fates in this announcement of disaster do not correspond to the four in v. 2. They function instead as a development of the second fate, the sword, into a ghastly series of consecutive tragedies in which death at enemy hands is capped by lack of burial and dismemberment by wild creatures (cf. 7:33). Ezekiel 14:13–20 appears to show an awareness of vv. 2–3, but condenses the two foursomes into a new configuration: famine, wild animals, sword, and pestilence.

---

56. Long, "Question and Answer Schemata," 134–36.

[4] The final statement differs from the previous two in that it is an oracle of disaster that combines announcement and reason with "king(doms)." It appears to be a redactional climax added to vv. 1–3, on two scores. First, the assignment of blame to a particular Judean king, Manasseh, is an accusation present in the Deuteronomistic History (2 Kgs 24:3–4). Second, the punishment is couched in a formulation characteristic of redactional prose sermons in the book (Jer 29:18; 34:17), which itself depends on the curse in Deut 28:25.

[5–9] MT has supplied the third unit of the composition with a redactional link as an elucidation of what precedes (KJV "For"; Rudolph 102; McKane 1:337). The unit is an oracle of disaster heavily weighted on the side of announcement. So the primary function of the unit is to give further details of the disaster deprecated in the first unit and endorsed in the second. The disaster's military nature is confirmed; the closing reference to "the sword" brings to a climax its presence in 14:18; 15:2, 3. The refusal to relent anymore (v. 6b) amplifies the absolute rejection of v. 1. The reference to Jerusalem in v. 5 provides a hinge with the end of the former unit. The placing of vv. 5–9 justifies the presence of v. 4. The unit provides a premonition of coming disaster, with explicit future verbs at beginning and end, and in between Hebrew perfect verbs that speak as if future disaster were already present (McKane 1:342–43). The emphasis on divine agency (vv. 3–4) is a prominent feature in this unit; Yahweh is to be responsible for military defeat. MT accentuates this feature in v. 8 by borrowing "at my behest" from 4:12.

The unit falls into two unequal sections, vv. 5–6 addressed to Jerusalem and vv. 7–9 that speak of victims in the third person and identify an inexplicit "them" in v. 7a with "my people" in v. 7b.

[5–6] Verse 6 constitutes a little oracle of disaster in its own right, with v. 5 functioning as a preliminary expansion that supports the accusation by hailing the punishment as well deserved. The oracle proper is signaled by its own quotation formula. Verse 6a and the last colon in v. 7 frame Yahweh's intervention with reasons, which function contextually as an answer to the people's pleas in 14:21. The people, here represented by Jerusalem, had broken off the covenant relationship with Yahweh and so earned reprisal. Yahweh's relenting was no longer a possibility (cf. Amos 7:3, 6, 8; 8:2).

[7–9] Winnowing is a metaphor for divine judgment; victims are pictured as so much chaff tossed into the wind. The metaphor has exile in view in 13:24, but not here or in 4:11–12. As in 51:1–2, it is a striking image that is subsequently explained in terms of military destruction. "Bereaved" at the head of v. 7b announces the theme of the rest of the section. Before its threefold development, such a tragic fate is briefly explained in terms of the covenant people's failure to reform. The bereavement would leave behind widows beyond number (cf. Job 6:3 and Ps 78:27 for the hyperbole). And noon raiders would surprise not only Judah's soldiers (cf. Jer 6:4, 26), but by a domino effect their mothers at home when they heard the news of their sons' deaths. The motif of motherhood is developed in v. 9, with a return to the number of casualties mentioned in v. 8. A mother of seven—a picture of totally fulfilled womanhood (Ruth 4:15; 1 Sam 2:5)—would swoon at the news of every one of her sons dying on the battlefield. She would live out the rest of her days a shadow of her former self, never recovering from the shock (cf. Mic 3:6). In this section women civilians are portrayed as the ultimate victims of war, caught up in the solidarity of national suffering.

Jeremiah 14:17–15:9 reissues the message of the former composition, but now wholly in terms of the final military disaster. Jeremiah knew that only a funereal lamentation was in order, but the people persisted in a psalm-like lament to persuade Yahweh otherwise. Its rejection is backed by announcements of utter disaster for the people and the capital, not least stunning bereavement after Judah's army was wiped out in battle.

15:10–21 The Messenger's Trauma over the Message

10 What a tragedy for me, my mother, that you ever gave birth to me,
    a man all the country opposes and is at odds with!
  I have not lent money nor has anybody lent to me—
    they all curse me.[a]

11 Yahweh said,[b]

"I promise you a good outcome by setting you free.[c]
    I promise to cause you to be entreated[d]
in bad, distressing times
    by the enemy.
12 Can he break iron,[e]
    iron from the north, and bronze?
13 'Your wealth and your treasures
    I will hand over for plunder,
as the price[f] to pay for all your sins
    committed inside all your borders.[g]
14 I will also make you work[h] for your enemies
    in a country you have never known,
because a fire has been ignited by my anger,
    which will flare up against you.'"[i]

15 *You know*, Yahweh!
    Remember me and pay attention to me,
    and take revenge for me on my persecutors.
Do not be so patient[j] *you do away with me*!
    Take into account I am suffering insults for your sake.

16   Your messages appeared[k] and I devoured them.
   Your messages became my joy,
      my heart's delight,
   because I was called by your name,
      Yahweh, *God* Almighty.
17   Instead of sitting in a group of merrymakers, having fun,
      your hand has caused me to sit alone,
   because you have filled me with indignation.
18   Why has my pain been so chronic
      and my wound incurable,
         reluctant to heal?
   You have in my experience become like an unreliable watercourse,
      where water cannot be counted on.
19   "Therefore"—here is what Yahweh said—
   "if you turn back so I can take you back,
      you will stand in my very presence.[l]
   If you utter[m] what is valuable rather than trivialities,
      you will become like my very mouth.
   It must be a case of others turning to you,
      not you turning to them.
20   Then I will make your relation to this people
      that of a fortified bronze wall.
   Fight you they will,
      but defeat you they will not,
   because I will be there with you,
      ready to save you and rescue you,"
         declared Yahweh.
21   "I will rescue you from the clutches of bad folk
      and *retrieve you* from the hands of the ruthless."

   a. MT reflects textual imprecision. EVV are divided between "everyone . . ." (Joüon §146j) and changing to "they all . . ." (*BHS*; GKC §61h).
   b. LXX implies *ʾāmēn*, "surely," for MT *ʾāmar*, "said," changing the perspective; the divine name is then a vocative and the whole is a continuation of Jeremiah's speech. This understanding has received considerable scholarly support, including Shemaryahu Talmon, "*Amen* as an Introductory Oath Formula," *Text* 7 (1969): 124–29; it is reflected in NAB, NJB, and GNB. However, *ʾāmēn* is never used elsewhere to introduce an oath of the type used here (see Barthélemy, *Critique textuelle*, 2:591). Moreover, the pattern of prophetic confession and divine answer in the adjoining unit (vv. 15–18 + 19–21) and the same double structuring in 11:18–12:6 support MT, in which v. 11 functions as Yahweh's answer. For the introductory clause cf. 46:25; Ps 68:22 (23).
   c. For a review of options for this interpretive crux see *HALOT* 4:1652b–53a. A decision whether Jeremiah or Yahweh speaks limits the options. Here I follow Q (cf. *HALOT*

4:1658a). The Hebrew verb, here in the Piel, is evidently an Aramaism; cf. the Peal in Dan 5:12, 16, and the Qal in Job 37:3. In later Aramaic both the Peal and the Pael are used in this sense (Jastrow 1630). Cf. NIV "deliver."

d. The Hiphil verb appears to be a causative of the Qal, which is used in the sense "plead with (*b*) someone" in 7:16; 27:18; and 36:25, though the Hiphil conjugation is not used elsewhere in this sense. Thus NIV "make your enemies plead with you," KJV, and probably NEB. For a "prophetic" perfect in an oath cf. Isa 14:24.

e. "The enemy" of v. 12 is the subject of the verb. This is more obvious than assuming an indefinite subject with a passive sense, "Can . . . be broken" (cf. NIV and GNB). The metals in the second colon appear to be amplifications of "iron" in the first, rather than objects after "iron" as subject of the verb, as NJB construes (cf. NRSV, NJPS, and REB). Hubmann, *Untersuchungen*, 264, has drawn attention to the parallelism that runs through vv. 10–12, "a man of strife and a man of contention" (KJV, v. 10), "in a time of trouble and in a time of distress" (NRSV, v. 11), and now the appositional repetition of "iron." For the division of cola see Cloete, *Versification*, 179.

f. LXX rightly lacks the preceding *lōʾ*, "not," which is also absent from MT at 17:3 (*BHS*; thus GNB). As the punctuation of MT infers, it was inserted due to false alignment with the previous clause ("for plunder, not for a price") under the influence of Ps 44:12 (13); Isa 52:3 (Barthélemy, *Critique textuelle*, 2:594). The colon distribution suggests otherwise (see Cloete, *Versification*, 183). The error led to the addition of *wāw*, "and," before the next phrase in MT here (*BHS*; contrast 17:3) and a failure to appreciate the *bêt* of price.

g. Again *wāw*, "and," is to be omitted as in MT at 17:3 (*BHS*), though LXX already reflects MT here. It is an addition that thoughtlessly linked this phrase with the superficially similar previous one.

h. Most EVV render with LXX here and with MT at 17:3, taking the root as *ʿbd*, "work," and not *ʿbr*, "pass." Barthélemy, *Critique textuelle*, 2:598–600, agreeing that an error has occurred in this passage, has taken up earlier suggestions that MT here took "wealth and treasure" as the object of the verb, "I will make (them) pass with your enemies" (cf. 20:5). MT in 17:4 and LXX here supply a suffix "you," but the suffixless verb may be taken as a recensional variant with the literal sense "cause (your enemies) to be served" (cf. *IBHS* 442–43). The verb *ʿbd* is needed for its hermeneutical role; see the commentary.

i. After a series of collective second singular suffixes, MT, supported by LXX, has a second plural, *ʿălêkem*, "against you," evidently with no change in the reference to Judah. MT at the parallel 17:4 has *ʿad-ʿôlām*, "forever," which is sometimes adopted here (*BHS*; NRSV, GNB). However, MT at 17:4 has its own second plural reference in the form of *qĕdahtem*, "you have ignited," in place of *qādĕḥâ*, "has been ignited." Barthélemy, *Critique textuelle*, 2:613, has suggested that the shifts to a plural echo Deut 32:22, which employs third plural references.

j. See *BHS* for the repointing as a noun, as LXX implies. For the clause cf. 5:3; 15:1. The second clause is a consecutive one (GNB).

k. Or "were given"; lit. "were found" (*mṣʾ*); cf. Lam 2:9.

l. For a discussion of the syntactical alternatives of the bicolon see Holladay 1:462–63.

m. See Holladay 1:461–62.

The composition in 15:10–21 is remarkably like 11:18–12:6; both consist of two units in which Jeremiah brings his own lament to Yahweh and then Yahweh gives a reply. In each composition the first reply is positive and the second less so. This pair of confessions and responses appears in vv. 10 + 11–14 and 15–18 + 19–21. The second unit is distinct from the first and may have been placed beside it because of its greater clarity; it sheds light on the more obscure one. This composition has links with the immediately preceding one—in the resumption of motherhood and giving birth from vv. 7–9 in v. 10. This link highlights the difference between the pair of unanswered prayers of the people in the compositions (14:1–16 and 14:17–15:9), on the one hand, and the new pair of answered prayers of the prophet, on the other. Rudolph (105–6) observes that, while "a good outcome" (*lĕṭôbâ*, 14:11) was denied to the people, it is offered to the prophet (*lĕṭôb*, 15:11). One may add that the denial of a good outcome for the people was grounded in "the consequences of their own bad behavior" (14:16), while the prophet's opportunity of a good outcome is now associated with "bad times" for the people (15:11). They or their representatives are characterized as "bad folk" from whom the prophet would be delivered if he was faithful to his ministry (15:21). Prophet and people basically stood on either side of a great divide, for or against Yahweh and headed for deliverance or doom. The prophet had to anticipate the wounding and lack of healing that was to be the people's fate (14:17, 19), both by proclaiming them and reflecting their severity in his own grief (15:18).

[15:10–14] The first unit consists of a brief lament (two bicola) and a similarly brief reply (three bicola), but the divine answer has been redactionally extended with a quotation of four bicola from 17:3–4 that is a little shorter than the original and has a few recensional differences.

[10] The lament begins with a speech addressed to Jeremiah's mother, expressing regret that she ever brought him into the world. The cry of exasperation is grounded in a sense of utter alienation from the rest of the community; "all the country" (cf. 1:18) had turned against him. Yet Jeremiah was conscious of having done nothing wrong. For example, it was not as if he had been involved in inappropriate financial transactions, a typical reason for friction with one's fellows. Although Jeremiah's outburst does not take the form of a prayer, it is similar to individual lament psalms, which include a claim of innocence and a twofold description of crisis grounded in the activity of one's enemies and in one's own feelings of hurt. In its sense of isolation, this verse is comparable to Ps 102:7, "I am like a lonely bird on the housetop." The initial exclamation, *ʾôy lî* ("Woe is me," NRSV), is not characteristic of lament psalms, but apart from 10:19 it does have counterparts in 45:3 and Ps 120:5, *ʾôyâ lî*, "Woe is me." The extreme wishing away of one's birth is not found in lament psalms, but it does appear in Job 3:2–12. What is more significant about the frantic outburst is its eloquent silence as to the source of the problem. Jeremiah's intolerable role as a prophet whose message of doom ran counter to the expectations of the community is undoubtedly the implicit reason for his vehemence, which is expressed in a virtual lament prayer that warrants the divine reply (vv. 11–12).

[11] This verse is notorious for the range of its interpretation, as the widely divergent translations in EVV testify. The translation above corresponds to that of NIV. It takes the verse as a double assurance. The first is a general promise of eventual deliverance from the present crisis. The second assurance spells out a particular consequence. The vindication of the prophet's dire message is illustrated in terms of the entreaties of those who now opposed him, for him to intercede in prayer on their behalf (cf. 21:1–2; 37:3; 42:2–4). An ironic contrast is drawn between such "a good outcome" for Jeremiah and the fulfillment of his oracles of disaster in "bad times" for the hostile community, which is collectively called "the enemy" (cf. the adversarial language of v. 20).

[12] A further assurance is given. Again this verse has taxed the ingenuity of interpreters and even evoked despair. One may construe it with both v. 10 and v. 11 by taking the collective "enemy" as the subject of the rhetorical question and finding a reference to Jeremiah's prophesying of disaster as possessing the unbreakable quality of metal. "Bronze" occurs in the parallel divine reply at v. 20 with reference to Yahweh's strengthening of the prophet, while "iron" appears alongside "bronze" at 1:18 in a similar sense. However, here the precise reference seems to be the infallible content of Jeremiah's negative oracles, which the Judean community can do nothing to annul (cf. 28:14). "From the north" can hardly be taken as anything other than a pointer to this meaning. It echoes the persistent premonition earlier in the book about the direction from which a ruthless invader would come (1:14–15; 4:5; 6:1; 13:20; cf. 6:22; 10:22). There seems to be a subtle double entendre in that "iron from the north" refers also to the hardened iron or "steel" (REB) manufactured in the region south of the Black Sea (cf. Holladay 1:454).

[13–14] The divine reply continues, but now "the enemy" of vv. 11–12 is addressed. The presence of this material at 17:3–4, where it is more at home, and the sudden shift of address suggest that these verses function as a redactional insertion to illustrate and reaffirm Jeremiah's oracles of disaster.[57] It is not immediately clear why this example should have been chosen as typical; an oracle that specified the northern foe would be more natural. A possible reason for selecting this passage is the affinity between v. 12 and the oracle of 28:13–14, where an unbreakable iron yoke is metaphorically promised for the

---

57. There is hardly need to explain away vv. 13–14 by the supposition that it originated as a marginal variant of 17:3–4 that became wrongly inserted into the adjoining column (Janzen, *Studies*, 133). These verses appear to be a redactional addition and must be retained. "The true scepticism is the critical scepticism whether it is possible to dissolve the unity created by the redactor" (Jones 219).

nations, compelling them to serve (ʿbd) Nebuchadnezzar, with whom the narratives later in the book identify the northern foe. That oracle is connected to the topic of the Judean deportation of 597 B.C.E. (28:3–4). However, it was not suitable for citation because the victims are described too broadly as "the nations." The oracle in 17:3–4 was chosen instead. It does include the other oracle's key word ʿābad (here rendered "work"). It also addresses Judah as collective victim of invasion and deportation at the implicit hands of the Babylonians, and so is related to the collective "enemy" (vv. 11–12).[58] The extract constitutes an oracle of disaster that is mostly an announcement of double intervention on Yahweh's part, but a reason, "all your sins," is cited within the announcement. It was this reason that aroused divine anger, which in turn was to set ablaze a firestorm of reprisal. The oracle presents a reversal of the normal tradition of life in the land under God's blessing, whereby work resulted in wealth. Judah's sins were to set into motion a contrary pattern at Yahweh's hands. Wealth would be plundered and work no longer done for one's own benefit but for masters in another land.

[15–21] This second unit goes through the same sequence of prophetic protest and divine response as the first one. However, this one is longer; the protest has more specificity, while the reply is pointedly qualified. The unit has a frame of a granted request in that the appeals for help in v. 15 lead eventually to a promise of deliverance in v. 21.

[15–18] Jeremiah's lament begins with direct appeal and moves (vv. 16–17) to a description of crisis that incorporates a claim of faithfulness to God.[59] It closes (v. 18) with a description of personal lament set in the form of first a complaining question and then a plain statement of protest that echoes the negative perception of Yahweh's attitude found in complaint psalms.[60] KJV, RSV, NIV, and GNB tone it down into a more respectful question of fact. By carrying over the force of "Why," one may regard it as a question of circumstance that does not lose any of its bluntness. The lament has been suffused with a prophetic perspective.[61] Structurally v. 18 functions as a forceful pair of indirect petitions that correspond to the explicit series in v. 15. The whole is a challenge that operates on an "I-you" axis. To this end the phrase "for your sake" that closes v. 15 functions as a headline for two linked examples in vv. 16 and 17, each ending with a causal clause that focuses on the polarity. The bipolar axis develops into

---

58. "Enemies" in v. 14 functions not as an elucidation of "the enemy," but simply as an ironic catchword (Hubmann, *Untersuchungen*, 257, 271).

59. Baumgartner, *Poems of Lament*, 51.

60. See Broyles, *Conflict of Faith*, 37–40, 55–82. Broyles finds this God-related element the most characteristic evidence of a complaint. He cites Pss 44:9a (10a); 60:1 (3); 89:38 (39); and 90:8 as examples of negative statements relating to God's disposition toward the speaker(s).

61. Baumgartner, *Poems of Lament*, 51.

a triangular nexus at two places by incorporating "my persecutors" in v. 15 and "merrymakers" in v. 17, but mainly in order to enhance the basic axis.

[15] The barrage of direct petitions to which a lament psalm usually builds up slowly is here set abruptly at the beginning. "Persecutors" will eventually be picked up in the divine reply as "this people" (v. 20) and "bad folk" and "the ruthless" (v. 21). The communal opposition to Jeremiah's prophesying in the previous unit recurs, though vv. 15 and 21 seem to refer to particular spokespersons.[62] Jeremiah's appeals reflect his sense of being threatened. MT spells out that threat in terms of fatality ("you do away with me"); it also anticipates the closing appeal to "take into account" (NAB "know") Jeremiah's situation by using the same Hebrew verb in a definite statement, "You know," in the style of Ps 69:19 (20); Jer 17:16; 18:23. Jeremiah yearned for Yahweh's just retribution. A number of psalms appeal to God's loss of honor from the suffering of the covenant community or member. Psalms 44:22 (23) and 69:7 (8) are the closest parallels, and the latter example may help to explain the earlier addition in MT from the same psalm. In this case, however, the prophet's mission is particularly in view (cf. Jer 20:8).

[16] The first elaboration of "for your sake" establishes Jeremiah's commitment to the mission. He had accepted each oracle as it was revealed to him and willingly identified himself with its tenor, proud to function as Yahweh's designated representative. Like Jesus, "his food" was "to do the will of him who sent me" (John 4:34). Jeremiah's metaphor of eating divine oracles was to become the basis of Ezekiel's visionary experience of eating God's scroll of judgment in a rite of ordination as prophet (Ezek 2:8–3:3).

[17] Commitment had come with a heavy cost. The second elaboration describes a sinister side of the mission. Ironically, rejoicing in the divine messages had caused joy to disappear from the rest of his life. The normal enjoyment of social relaxation and the lighter moments of fun that leaven the human lot (cf. 30:19; 31:4) had been taken from him. He had not indulged—"but he certainly would have liked to."[63] Bitter resentment was his response. The impediment was Yahweh's "hand," which blends the prophetic sense of divine manipulation by inspiration or empowerment (e.g., 2 Kgs 3:15 NIV; Isa 8:11) with the lament psalm's sense of a hostile providence (Pss 32:4; 38:2 [3]; 39:10 [11]). Jeremiah's identification with prophetic messages whereby he shared divine anger (cf. Jer 6:11) left him ostracized.

[18] The prophet's resentment surfaces fully. The lament takes on the form of a complaint with the question "Why" (cf. 14:8–9). Terms used elsewhere of the disaster to befall the community, "wound" (*makkâ*, 6:7; 14:17) and lack of

---

62. These have been identified as false prophets by Hubmann, *Untersuchungen*, 279–80; and Holladay 1:459; and as Jehoiakim and his counselors by Duhm 138 and Nicholson 141, but there is no evidence for these identifications. The divine deception in connection with false prophecy at 4:10 is a different issue.

63. James Muilenburg, "A Confession of Jeremiah," *USQR* 4 (1949): 15–18, esp. 17.

healing (*rpʾ*, 8:15, 22; 14:19), are transferred to his own experience in order to convey his mental suffering and stress. It is significant that elsewhere he had used this and similar language to describe his own grief over the people's coming disaster, already feeling its brunt (4:19; 8:18, 21; 10:19). Indignation and grief had been twin forces taking their toll on his soul. He finally accuses Yahweh of letting him down. The metaphor of the dried-up wadi that disappoints travelers is developed in Job 6:15–20 with reference to Job's friends, but here, spat out in briefer form, it provides strong closure for the lament. In the light of the opening appeals, the deep disappointment reflects a lack of support from Yahweh and nonfulfillment of the oracles of disaster (cf. "patient," v. 15), as well as discontent with the social restrictions demanded by his prophetic ministry. In 2:13 Jeremiah had transmitted Yahweh's self-description as "the spring of running water," but now he was reflecting the subversive mood of the complaint version of the lament psalm. "God behaves in the Psalms in ways he is not allowed to behave in systematic theology."[64] The prophet felt he had been left in the lurch, not only a social outcast but lacking his patron's backing. It was all too much.

[19–21] Yes, Yahweh would help, but first Jeremiah had to help himself, came the reply. The initial lament receives an affirmative answer (vv. 20–21), a proclamation of salvation, but only via a summons to repentance (v. 19) that confronts Jeremiah's complaint and lays down necessary conditions for deliverance. There is thus an overall ABB′A′ pattern.[65]

[19] Jeremiah's perception of his problems had started with human persecutors and ended with Yahweh. At a deeper level of truth he himself was the problem and his own enemy. The response to his blunt complaint is an equally blunt call to repentance presented with standard elements of a quotation formula, admonitions, promises, and accusation.[66] The divine reply in 11:21 was also introduced by "Therefore" and a quotation formula as a preliminary to an announcement of disaster for Jeremiah's foes. Perhaps with this parallel in mind, the conjunction has been called "threatening,"[67] but its combination with a quotation formula can introduce a proclamation of salvation (Isa 29:22; 37:33; Zech 1:16). Jeremiah's complaint about Yahweh is dismissed as a dangerous misconception—so dangerous that it jeopardized his role as a prophet. This danger is treated first, in two parallel conditions, before the misconception in the final bicolon. The danger and misconception are interlinked by pairings of the verb *šûb*, "turn back/take back," and the double "turning." A term used of

---

64. Kathleen Norris, *The Cloister Walk* (New York: Riverhead Books, 1996), 91, quoting a Benedictine monk.
65. Diamond, *Confessions of Jeremiah*, 68–69.
66. Raitt, "Prophetic Summons," 35.
67. Hubmann, *Untersuchungen*, 251; similarly Blank, "Confessions of Jeremiah," 334.

Israel throughout 3:1-4:2 is now shockingly applied to the prophet himself. If Jeremiah was disappointed with Yahweh, the latter was even more disappointed with Jeremiah. The distance between them was of the prophet's making and the onus was upon him to bridge it. Only then could he resume his prophetic role in terms of regular audiences with Yahweh (cf. 1 Kgs 17:1; 2 Kgs 3:14 KJV; Jer 23:18) and subsequently heralding Yahweh's messages. Jeremiah's becoming like Yahweh's mouth is a trenchant counterpart to Yahweh's becoming like an unreliable watercourse in the complaint.[68] In the second condition "what is valuable" refers to the divine messages of v. 16, while "trivialities" is a dismissive reference to Jeremiah's wrong perception voiced in v. 17. That is clear from the closing sentence. Hitherto the focus in the reply has been on the "I-you" axis of relationship between Jeremiah and Yahweh, which is presented afresh by way of correction, but now the focus shifts to the third party that in Jeremiah's lament had been described in terms of both hostility and envy. It is the latter element that comes to the fore in the final sentence of v. 19, while the former one will dominate vv. 20-21. If Jeremiah was to be on Yahweh's side, as a prophet he must unreservedly represent that side instead of theirs.

The juxtaposition of 16:2-9 and this passage, with its austere call to sacrifice normal marital happiness and social fraternizing, furnishes readers with insight into the meaning of this verse and its relation to v. 17. In Matt 24:38-39 and Luke 17:27, Jesus compared the end time with Noah's day, when people "were eating and drinking, marrying and giving in marriage," unmindful of the flood that would sweep them all away. Again, in Matt 16:1-4 he contrasted a skill in weather forecasting with an inability to "interpret the signs of the times." Here Jeremiah was siding with those who lacked such discernment and went on living normal lives. There is "a time to weep, and a time to laugh; a time to mourn, and a time to dance" (Eccl 3:4). Jeremiah was called to announce an emergency, warning of a hurricane of disaster bearing down on Judah. Did not v. 11 warn of "bad, distressing times" that would ironically spell Jeremiah's vindication? So he had to throw in his lot with Yahweh, instead of hankering after social normality—a normality that the redactor in vv. 13-14 had already characterized as doomed to end. Only such integrated commitment would permit Jeremiah to continue as a prophet.

[20-21] Then, and only then, Jeremiah's prayer for deliverance in v. 15 would be answered. The proclamation of salvation overlaps with the oracle of salvation given to Jeremiah in his prophetic commissioning at 1:18-19. The proclamation functions for readers as an opportunity for the renewal of support earlier promised. But, as there, it is an assurance not of the absence of crisis but of crisis finding resolution. "The Lord will rescue me from every evil attack," affirmed Paul (2 Tim 4:18; cf. 2 Cor 1:10), and Jeremiah was offered no less

---

68. Lundbom, "Jeremiah 15, 15-21," *SJOT* 9 (1995): 147.

and no more. Neither the prophet nor the apostle had an inalienable right to the pursuit of happiness in his distinctive mission.

Jeremiah 15:10–21 has presented two more dialogues of prophetic lament and divine reply, repeating the pattern of 11:18–12:6. As there, both encouragement and reprimand are conveyed in Yahweh's answers. Jeremiah is directed to accept wholeheartedly his alienation from the people, in acknowledgment of the spiritual gulf that divided Yahweh and people, a gulf that was to be exposed by coming disaster. His solitary role and even the promise of survival accentuated the communal fate (cf. 39:16–18; 45:4–5). As God's agent ("for your sake," v. 15) Jeremiah's experience intrinsically illustrated the community's rejection of Yahweh.

16:1–21 The Trouncing of Pagan Religion

16:1 *I received the following message from Yahweh:*[a] **2** "You must not marry and have sons and daughters in this place." **3** The reason why is that here is what Yahweh said about any sons and daughters born in this place and about their mothers who give birth to them and their fathers who procreate them in this country: **4** "Deadly diseases will cause their deaths; getting no mourning or burial, they will lie like dung on the surface of the ground. Sword and famine will be causes for others to perish, and their corpses will get eaten by birds in the sky and beasts on the ground." **5** Here[b] is what Yahweh said: "Do not enter a house where a funeral feast is being held, do not go there to mourn, and do not offer them any sympathy. The reason why is that I have taken away from this people my peace," declared Yahweh, "loyal love, and compassion.[c] **6** So elite and lowly alike will die in this country; they will get no burial and nobody will engage in mourning for them or in self-mutilation and head shaving for them. **7** People will not break bread[d] for the mourners[e] to comfort them for the deceased nor will they give them[f] a drink that comforts for the loss of their fathers or mothers. **8** Moreover, a house where people are having a party you must not enter, intending to sit with them, eating and drinking. **9** The reason why is that"— here is what Yahweh *Almighty*, Israel's God, said—"look out, before your very eyes and in your own lifetimes I am going to eliminate from this place noise expressing joy and delight, such as shouts of bridegroom and bride."

10 "When you tell this people all such matters and they ask you, 'Why has Yahweh issued against us all these threats of a*n extremely* bad fate? What is our wrongdoing? What is our sin that we have committed against Yahweh our God?' **11** you are to tell them: 'It is because your forebears abandoned me,' declared Yahweh. 'They followed other gods, serving and worshiping them, while I was abandoned by them and my torah was not kept. 12 As for you, you have behaved worse than your forebears. Here you are, every one of you, following the stubborn inclination of your own bad attitude, instead of obeying me. 13 So I will hurl you away from this country, over to a country neither you nor your forebears have ever known, and there you will serve other gods *day and night*, because I will show you no favor.'

14 "Therefore, look, the time is coming," declared Yahweh, "when people will no longer swear the oath, 'By the life of Yahweh who brought the Israelites up from the country of Egypt.' 15 Instead they will say, 'By the life of Yahweh who brought the Israelites up from the north country or any of the other countries he had driven them away to.' I will bring them back to their own soil, my gift to their forebears.

16 "Look out, I am going to send for fishers aplenty," declared Yahweh, "and they will catch them. Next I will send for hunters aplenty, who will hunt them down, retrieving them from every mountain and every hill, even from crevices in the rocks. 17 This will happen because my eyes detect all their behavior. It cannot be hidden from my presence nor can their wrongdoing be concealed from my eyes. 18 *First of all* I will pay them back twice over for their wrongdoing and sin, evidenced in their desecrating my country with their detestable 'corpses' and with their abominations filling my property."[g]

19 Yahweh, my strength and my stronghold,
   my refuge in times of trouble,
  to you nations will come
   from the ends of the earth and say,
  "Utterly false gods were the heritage of our forebears,
   nonentities and none of them any use.
20 Can human beings make gods,
   though they are not really gods?"
21 "Therefore, look, I am going to give them knowledge,
   right now I will give them the knowledge
   of my power and my might.
  Then they will acknowledge that my name is Yahweh."[h]

a. LXX has instead a quotation formula, "says the Lord, Israel's God," after v. 2a (see *BHS*). The variation indicates independent secondary activity in both traditions in order to signal a separate piece. See the commentary.

b. MT, unlike LXX, prefaces with *kî*, "For" (NRSV), which is inappropriate, since v. 5 opens a new section. Verses 5–7 are structurally parallel to vv. 2–4 and 8–9. Assimilation to vv. 3 and 9 has occurred (cf. Holladay 1:468). NAB rightly omits.

c. The suffix on the first noun does triple duty (William L. Holladay, "The Recovery of Poetic Passages of Jeremiah," *JBL* 85 [1966]: 401–35, esp. 418; Thompson 400 n. 5).

d. As NJPS recognizes, MT *lāhem*, "for them," is an error for *lehem*, "bread," caused by assimilation to *lāhem* twice in v. 6. MT assumes an elliptical use of the verb, which occurs in Lam 4:4, but here the plural reference does not fit the following *lĕnaḥmô*, lit. "to comfort him." LXX, followed by Vg., has both terms in a conflate text.

e. MT (ʿal) *ʾēbel*, "(in accordance with/on the occasion of) mourning," is more naturally pointed *ʾābēl*, "(for) the mourner," with Vg. (*BHS*), as EVV acknowledge.

f. The translation loosely uses plurals for the bereaved throughout this verse, but a mixture of collective singulars and plural forms continues in MT, with *ʾôtām*, "them," in place of an expected "him," which is how LXX renders. It is arguable that despite the following Hebrew singular suffixes the grammatical lapse is tolerable here because of the greater distance between the different pronouns in v. 7b than in v. 7a (cf. Barthélemy, *Critique textuelle*, 2:604–5).

g. EVV except REB have repunctuated MT.

h. For the climactic monocolon see Watson, *Classical Hebrew Poetry*, 170–72.

Jeremiah 16:1–21 is a long composition of five separate units, all in prose except for the last, climactic unit. The clue to its coherence as a redactional collection is the steady repetition of *ʾereṣ*. It occurs in the phrase "this country" in the first unit (vv. 3, 6). There is conscious widening from "this country" to the "country" of exile in the second (v. 13), then to the "country" and "countries" of exile in the third (vv. 14–15). The fourth unit reverts to the earlier sense, with the variation "my country" (v. 18). In the fifth the term occurs with the collective meaning "earth" (v. 19), developing in a new direction the non-Israelite usage in the second and third units.

[16:1] It is not difficult to discern that 16:2–9 was originally appended to 15:15–21 because of the links between 15:17 and 16:8–9, namely, a verbal link "sit" and a thematic link of social alienation. There is also a contrasting link between Jeremiah's "joy" and "delight" in Yahweh's messages (15:16) and the future absence of such communal expressions (16:9). MT has provided an oracle reception statement to introduce the composition that was subsequently developed from this unit.

[2–9] Jeremiah is to disengage from social activities and so be a witness to coming disaster. The unit, written in "rhythmic prose" (Holladay 1:467–68), reports a series of related symbolic actions to be performed by Jeremiah, like 13:1–11; in this case the actions represent a refraining from normal activities. The second plural references in v. 9 (cf. v. 10) suggest that the report is made to the people. The unit falls into three sections, vv. 2–4, 5–7, and 8–9, which present divine commands (vv. 2, 5a, and 8) and divine interpretations of the commands (vv. 3–4, 5b–7, and 9). The expected element of prophetic performance is missing; in the present context 15:17 presumably fits that role. The divine interpretations take the form of announcements of disaster. The initial reference to marriage (v. 2) and the closing mention of "bridegroom and bride" (v. 9) provide a frame for the unit. Indeed, a chiasm may be detected, with "mothers" and "fathers" (v. 3) echoed in reverse (v. 7) and the motifs of death, mourning, and burial (v. 4) resumed (v. 6).[69] The second and third sections are run together, with no introductory formula (v. 8), because of the complementary nature of the commands (vv. 5 and 8). The reverse order of the command to enter a house in v. 8 compared with v. 5 has the same bracketing effect. The reason for both the chiastic scheme and the running together of the sections is the intent of these sections to pick up separate aspects of the first one. Death and lack of burial (v. 4) are pursued in the second section, while marriage (v. 2) is developed in the third. Throughout the unit the phrase "this place/country" underlines the national dimension of the disaster (vv. 2, 3, 6, 9). The passage has received some editorial amplification with later prose styling in vv. 4, 6, and 9.[70]

[2–4] The first command and its interpretation are the fundamental set, which will be supplemented in the other two sections. So this prohibition of marriage is more radical than the other two commands to disengage from normal social activities. To abstain from marriage would be strikingly abnormal. Here not simply marriage but parenthood is in view, and it is with this prospect that the interpretation is concerned. The disasters of v. 4 depend upon the families in v. 3. The phrase "mothers who give birth" recalls 15:8–9, but now the perspective is no longer one of battle casualties but of a more comprehensive disaster bringing death to entire families. The disaster was to cause the suspension of family life throughout the nation, and Jeremiah had to be an anticipatory witness to that suspension by refusing to start a family. The disaster would gruesomely chase its victims beyond their deaths, whether caused by disease or by the effects of battle and siege. The dishonor of lack of burial and mutilation of corpses accentuates the horror of these deaths.

[5–7] The basic command that made the shadow of the country's future fall upon the prophet's present life generates two supplementary commands. The first is a corollary of the mortality broached in the interpretation of the first command. Jeremiah was to live out that interpretation by disengaging from contemporary funeral observances. Verses 5a and 6–7 explore how extensive they were. Apart from burial, there was the "funeral feast," a sort of wake at which family and friends could share in the mourning of the bereaved and be a consoling presence (v. 5a).[71] The mourning involved rites of self-mutilation and

---

69. Friebel, *Sign-Acts*, 83; cf. the more complex scheme in Holladay, "Poetic Passages," 419–20.

70. See Stulman, *Prose Sermons*, 69. Following Rudolph, Stulman has unfairly characterized the whole of vv. 2–15 as a late prose sermon. In LXX the disorder in v. 4 and the omission in vv. 5–6 (see *BHS*) are text-critical errors (Janzen, *Studies*, 98).

71. The *marzēaḥ*, here rendered "funeral feast," in extrabiblical texts, notably those from Ugarit, refers to religious associations concerned with funeral rites and to the social meals they

head shaving, frowned on as pagan in Israel's law codes (Lev 19:28; 21:5; Deut 14:1) but evidently widely practiced. Verse 7 develops the motif of sympathy in v. 5a in terms of a ritualized provision of food and drink. The death of aged parents is envisioned since it was the most common occasion of funerals. Jeremiah was not to engage in these rituals, established though they were in Judean society, as a sign that the disaster would create such chaos that these cherished conventions could no longer be maintained. The divine action of v. 5b does not deal with Yahweh's coming intervention, unlike v. 9. Rather, it reflects a divine decision already implemented, which would trigger the communal disintegration portrayed in vv. 6–7. Yahweh's blessing of peace, motivated by covenant love and compassion, which kept the community afloat, no longer exerted a protective role, and the culture of death would not survive the disaster. Jeremiah's present abstention symbolizes the situation when the stunning reality of communal catastrophe was to overtake death's tidy rituals. Ezekiel was similarly called to suspend the norms of disorientation (Ezek 24:15–24).

[**8–9**] The second supplementary command reverts in closing to the motif of marriage (v. 2). Again the focus of the first section is generalized, now from a prohibition of marriage to a wider ban on engaging in social celebrations. Jeremiah's abstinence from such camaraderie and fun was to reflect a time—not too distant—when not only funerals but happy festivities, including weddings, would cease to be held because of the breakdown of the social order. Jesus' teaching about his eschatological coming in Matt 24:38–39 and Luke 17:26–30 echoes such a catastrophic breakdown (cf. 1 Cor 7:25–31). Here the interpretation stands out from the two earlier ones as a climax. It predicates not merely the experience of disaster or the withdrawal of divine protection but Yahweh's own hostile intervention—direct confrontation between the divine "I" and the communal "you." Jeremiah was to testify to the people's fate by his disengagement. The oral proclamation of his behavior at Yahweh's behest and of Yahweh's ominous purpose would reinforce the lessons of his social withdrawal. "In all three prohibitions Jeremiah functioned in the role of the people, representing to them what their future life would be like when the judgment came."[72] He had to representatively and predictively take up the cross on which the community soon would die.

[**10–13**] The second unit and also the third one are redactional supplements replete with later prose stylization.[73] The first unit cries out for a reason for the disaster announced there. This editorial supplement spells it out, using the ques-

---

held. See the surveys of the term in Hans M. Barstad, *The Religious Polemics of Amos* (VTSup 34; Leiden: Brill, 1984), 127–42; Susan Ackerman, "A *marzēaḥ* in Ezekiel 8:7–13?" *HTR* 82 (1989): 267–81, esp. 275–79.

72. Friebel, *Sign-Acts*, 96.

73. See the list in Stulman, *Prose Sermons*, 69.

Why God's Answer Was No

tion-and-answer format employed earlier at 5:19 and 9:12–16 (11–15), and merging motifs from both passages.[74] Here, however, the reaction is not to the experience of disaster but to its announcement. The climactic absence of divine favor (v. 13) reinforces the withdrawal of compassion (v. 5), while "from this country" reorients "from this place" (v. 9) in an alarmingly worse direction. Taken by itself, the unit is a variation of an oracle of disaster with its own announcement held back until the very end. The emphasis on pagan worship in this unit is one that will engage the rest of the composition. This overall focus raises a question whether it was not seen to be present in the first unit. The obvious place to look is v. 6, with its reference to self-mutilation and head shaving. Commentators (such as McKane 1:367) tend to say that proscription of such practices in the legal codes is not exegetically relevant. In terms of the basic meaning of the unit, one may agree. However, redactionally the pagan nature generally ascribed to such practices seems to leap into prominence. The explanation in the second unit wants to say so, while ensuing units elaborate the theme. The redactional interpretation supplied to the first unit means that rites associated with pagan worship must receive their comeuppance, with an exilic punishment that fits the crime.

[10] A national disaster so extreme as that presented in the preceding unit demanded a convincing cause. The barrage of outraged questions paves the way for the chilling divine replies in vv. 11–12, while the closing covenant claim "our God" is met head-on with a rebuttal, as in 5:19. The embellishment "extremely" has been borrowed from 32:42.[75] That passage moves on to gracious renewal on Yahweh's part, so the addition indirectly signals the turnaround in vv. 14–15.

[11–12] The reason for the disaster is the pagan worship of earlier generations, which represented rejection of Yahweh and of the explicit prohibition in Yahweh's torah tradition. The present generation is accused of perpetuating and even escalating such apostasy (cf. 7:26). Such a "bad attitude," here used specifically of idolatrous religion as in 9:14 (13), deserved the "bad fate" of v. 10.

[13] An even worse fate than the social chaos of the previous unit is threatened, the practice of pagan worship outside Yahweh's and Israel's own land, in the land of exile "where they can worship other gods to their hearts' content" (Davidson 1:134). The violent expulsion ("hurl") generalizes the royal fate in 22:26, 28, and varies the slinging of 10:18 and also the throwing of 7:15. The enhancement "day and night" in MT is a loose reminiscence of exilic anguish in Deut 28:66.[76] The unit follows the pattern of earlier prose supplements by sounding the shrill note of exile as the ultimate punishment, as at 5:19; 7:15; 8:3; 9:16 (15).

---

74. Long, "Question and Answer Schemata," 134–35.
75. Janzen, *Studies*, 40.
76. Ibid.

[14–15] Promise would eventually transcend punishment. This second supplementary unit ventures to build on the previous one with a positive message, as in 3:14–18. The redactional nature of this unit is evident from its exilic setting, while its redactional placement is evident from its recurrence with recensional differences in 23:7–8, where it is a more natural fit. As in ch. 3, the deliberate intent of the unit inserted here is reassuringly to jump ahead to a hopeful, post-catastrophe future. In this new context "Therefore," introducing a proclamation of salvation as in 15:19, blatantly expresses divine logic that defies human possibility, like the new life rising from the grave of exile in Ezek 37:1–14. The oracle announces a radical innovation that launches a fresh era of revelation, as in Jer 3:16–17. A new oath that celebrated an exodus from exile would transcend an old one that voiced faith by invoking Yahweh's reality and power as manifesting the exodus. This theme of a new exodus recurs in Ezekiel (Ezek 20:33–34) and functions typologically in Second Isaiah, notably at Isa 43:14–21; 51:9–11.[77] The extra reference to the Diaspora, which in Jer 23:8 is promised as a bonus, is here folded into the oath formula. Yahweh's continuing dealings with Israel are expressed by the added reference to the ancient role of the land as divine gift (cf. 3:18), implicitly a permanent gift (cf. 7:7). The sense of the unit in its new context derives from the observation that oaths are linked with pagan worship in a variety of OT passages.[78] Here taking an oath in Yahweh's name functions positively. Moreover, a transition from home to exile is capped with a new homecoming.

[16–18] The insertion of vv. 14–15 interrupted the negative rhetoric in vv. 10–13 and in this unit (note "wrongdoing" and "sin" in vv. 10 and 18).[79] To accommodate the insertion MT adds "First of all" in v. 18 (Streane 105). The unit is an oracle of disaster that sets the announcement of v. 16 before the reason of v. 17, and then resumes both in v. 18, identifying the reason explicitly as pagan worship. There are no grounds for denying the unit to Jeremiah. It has been placed here to develop the accusation of pagan worship and its punishment in vv. 10–13, no matter that the people are addressed in vv. 10–13 but mentioned in the third person here.

[16] The announcement functions as a restatement of Yahweh's hurling away the people (v. 13). Now the focus is on the military attack that will inexorably achieve this end. The attack is depicted using the metaphors of fishing and hunting. In the lament psalms hunting is a figure for persecution (e.g., Pss 10:9; 57:6 [7]; 64:4–5 [5–6]); here the figure is imaginatively developed and applied to the military disaster that would overtake the whole land. Fishing is also used in Hab 1:14–17 for the imperial advance of the Babylonians, while

---

77. Cf. Fishbane, *Biblical Interpretation*, 362.
78. Crenshaw, "Form-Critical Analysis," 170–71.
79. Del Olmo Lete, "Unidad," 30.

being hunted down is more specifically applied to the Babylonian pursuit of refugees from Jerusalem in Lam 4:18-19.

[17] The tracking down of each and every quarry depends on Yahweh's meticulous observation; "my eyes" frame the verse (Lundbom 1:767). What Yahweh sees is Israel's "behavior," which is also generically described as "wrongdoing."

[18] The announcement and reason are replayed. The two images of fishing and hunting that were presented consecutively in v. 16 to convey the utter military disaster are summarized as a double punishment. There is no need to see in either verse a reference to the separate invasions of 597 and 587 (cf. Holladay 1:478) nor a parallel to the language of Isa 40:2 (e.g., McKane 1:377-78). Resumption of the metaphorical double trouble of v. 16 is explanation enough. The reason is now presented in the specific terms of pagan worship, in God's own country a travesty of faith. The term *šiqqûṣîm*, rendered "detestable," is a scathing resumption of the "detestable gods" of 4:1 and 7:30 (cf. 13:27). The striking term "corpses" alludes to them as "lifeless forms" (NIV). This term creates a ghastly sequence of effect and cause with "their [human] corpses" in v. 4. The parallel term "abominations" is used similarly of pagan gods, rather like 2:7; in 6:15 (= 8:12) and 7:10 it had an ethical connotation. The accusation of vv. 11-12 is rigorously reinforced.

[19-21] The last unit goes to the root of the problem of pagan worship, presenting a climax stylistically enhanced by using the divine name as a frame. It falls into two parts, a two-part affirmation of faith addressed to Yahweh (vv. 19-20) and a proclamation of salvation in response (v. 21). The poem seems to be exilic in origin, on three counts. First, it expects Yahweh's imminent intervention, presumably by bringing Israel back from exile, which would conclusively prove the power of Yahweh. The insertion in vv. 14-15 admirably prepares for such a demonstration. Second, it alludes to the exilic passage 10:1-16 or at least an important portion thereof. It does so by the use of *šeqer*, rendered "false gods" here and "a lie" in 10:14, and of collective *hebel*, "nonentities," here and in 10:15 (and thence in 10:8), while the refrain "Yahweh (Almighty) is his name" in 10:16 receives a divine amen in the closing "my name is Yahweh." Jeremiah 16:19-21 develops exilic Israel's own confession of faith in Yahweh, which appears in 10:1-16, by claiming that the nations would join in the chorus of praise. Third, the author apparently modeled vv. 19b-20 on 2:5-11. The combination of "nonentities" collective (*hebel*) with "forebears" is echoed from 2:5 and the motif of uselessness (*wĕʾên-bām môʿîl*, "with none of them any use") from 2:8, 11 (*lōʾ-yâʿîlû/lôʾ yôʿîl*, "useless"), while the qualification "though they are not really gods" is also borrowed from 2:11. Israel's own experience is transposed to a different key by using it of Gentiles. One of the criteria for identifying non-Jeremianic material is the reapplication of the prophet's own language to new settings (McKane 1:382), which

[19a] The vocatives represent an affirmation of faith that is typical of lament psalms (e.g., Pss 9:9 [10]; 59:9 [10]; 70:5 [6]). The speaker is to be understood as a collective entity, Israel (so Isa 12:1–2). At last—after generations of pagan worship—the religious community avows its faith in Yahweh, acknowledging the divine help consistently received in the past. A new Israel has learned its lesson and abandoned its preexilic penchant for pagan religion. The affirmation of faith performs a function similar to the oath, celebrating future return from exile. An exilic setting seems to be presupposed here, since the affirmation of faith is grounded in the lament.

[19b–20] Not only would Israel confess its newly restored faith in Yahweh, it looks forward to the tradition that the other nations would "come" for worship to express their own faith in Israel's God. The hopes voiced in 3:17; 4:2; and 12:14–17 move toward fulfillment ("right now"). The second affirmation is put on Gentile lips, as in Isa 2:3 and 45:14. It achieves its purpose by means of a repudiation of old-style pagan religion that only new devotees of Yahweh can utter. Ironically Gentiles here profess the faith that Judah failed to profess (ch. 2) and hopefully would learn to profess in exile (ch. 10).

[21] In this proclamation of salvation, introduced by "Therefore," as in v. 14 and 15:19, Yahweh caps the lament-laden confidence of a reformed Israel with the promise of a dynamic intervention. The restoration of Israel to its own land appears to be in view (cf. Ps 126:1–2). Divine self-revelation is the focus of the oracle, as the triple use of the same verb yd^c indicates ("give knowledge/ acknowledge"). Yahweh's "power," literally "hand," was to trigger profound knowledge (cf. Ps 98:1–3). The "nations who do not acknowledge" Yahweh (Jer 10:25) would at last do so. The recognition formula "know that I am Yahweh" is used elsewhere in the OT to express the purpose of revelatory action. It occurs in exilic texts concerning the nations or a similar non-Israelite subject concerning a momentous divine act, often in Ezekiel (e.g., 25:7, 11, 17) and in Isa 45:6; 49:26. In the formula here, "my name" replaces "I," somewhat like Ps 83:18 (19), but here as a closing part of an arc that stretches back to ch. 10 (v. 16).

Jeremiah 16:1–21 celebrates Yahweh's stand against pagan religion in Israel and the world at large. The bubbling spring of the composition is vv. 10–13, which plainly present Israel's problem and Yahweh's drastic solution of exile. This key unit co-opts the symbolic activity of vv. 2–9 into the service of its theme. Then vv. 14–16 look forward to Israel's restoration from exile and even from the Diaspora, which would trigger a new spiritual allegiance. However, first Judah's pagan religion must be punished, vv. 16–18 maintain. That done, in vv. 19–21 Israel in exile turns back to Yahweh with fresh faith and with morale high enough to assert that the other nations who practiced the non-Yahwistic worship (v. 13) would put their own faith in the true God. Israel looks forward to the realization of Yahweh's own oracle of promise, one that matches the great claim of Isa 45:22–23.

17:1–13 Sins of the Heart

17:1[a] "Judah's sin is written
   with an iron stylus.
With a diamond[b] point it is engraved[c]
   on the tablets of their hearts
   and on[d] the horns of their[e] altars,
2 while their children remember
   their altars and their Asherim
beside leafy trees on the high hills,
3 the mountains[f] in the countryside.
Your wealth, all your treasures
   I will hand over for plunder
as the price[g] to pay for the sin
   committed inside all your borders,
4 and you will lose your hold[h] on your ancestral property,
   my gift to you.
I will also make you work for your enemies
   in the country you have never known,
because you have kindled the fire of my anger,
   which will burn forever."

5 Here is what Yahweh said.

A curse rests on the man
   who puts his trust in humanity,
who makes mortals his support,
   and whose heart deviates from Yahweh.
6 So he will be like a juniper[i] in the wilderness,
   which never sees any good coming its way,
but lives in a parched place[j] in the wilderness,
   in an uninhabited salt region.
7 A blessing rests on the man
   who puts his trust in Yahweh,
   for whom Yahweh is the one to trust.
8 So he will be like a tree planted by water,
   which by a stream stretches out its roots,
and so it has no fear[k] when heat comes,
   but its foliage stays luxuriant,

while in the year of drought it has no anxiety,
but never stops producing fruit.

9 "The heart is more insidious than anything else,
it is incurably sick—
who can understand it?
10 I, Yahweh, can, searching the heart,
probing the conscience,
and I repay[l] one and all what their behavior warrants,
in accord with the fruit their conduct represents."[m]

11 A partridge that hatches eggs it did not lay
is what anybody is like who makes money by unjust means.
By middle age it will abandon him,
and by his final years he will be proved a fool.

12 You glorious throne, exalted from the beginning,
our place of sanctuary,[n]
13 you hope of Israel, Yahweh,
let[o] all who abandon you suffer humiliation,
and let the deviants[p] in the country be written down [as such],[q]
because they have abandoned the spring of running water
(namely, Yahweh).[r]

a. LXX does not represent vv. 1–5a*a*, jumping in error from the divine name in 16:21 to the one in 17:5 (Janzen, *Studies*, 117). Bernard Gosse, "Jérémie 17, 1–5a*a* dans la rédaction massorétique du livre de Jérémie," *EstBib* 53 (1995): 165–80, discerns a redactional problem here; so does Pierre-Maurice Bogaert, "Jérémie 17,1–4 TM, oracle contre ou sur Juda propre au texte long, annoncé en 11,17–18 TM et en 15,12–14 TM," in *La double transmission du texte biblique: Études d'histoire du texte offertes en hommage à Adrian Schenker* (ed. Yohanan Goldman and Christoph Uehlinger; OBO 179; Fribourg: Editions Universitaires; Göttingen: Vandenhoeck & Ruprecht, 2001), 59–74, esp. 70–74.

b. Cf. *HALOT* 4:1562b–63a.

c. The punctuation in MT is generally disregarded on metrical grounds; see *BHS* and Cloete, *Versification*, 183.

d. The preposition *lāmed* can be used to continue another preposition (Joüon §133d).

e. MT *mizbĕḥôtêkem*, "your [plural] altars," is an anomaly in the midst of third plural suffixes, much more so than the second plural verb *qĕdaḥtem*, "you have kindled," after singular references in v. 4, for which see the textual note on 15:14. There is considerable evidence for a third person suffix (see *BHS*; even NJPS so renders) in line with the form in v. 3. The corruption has not received adequate explanation. Division into two words, *mizbēaḥ tōkām* (or *tôkām*), "(on the horns of) the altar is their oppression"

(Hubmann, "Textgraphik und Textkritik am Beispiel von Jer 17, 1–2," *BN* 14 [1981]: 30–36, esp. 33; Holladay 1:483–84, 486), labors under the difficulty of the ethical content of *tōk*, "oppression" (cf. 9:6 [5]), which hardly fits a solidly religious context.

f. Generally MT *hărārî*, "my mountain," is repointed *harărê*, "mountains," and the whole phrase is linked with v. 2, with some textual support in both cases (*BHS*). Wrong alignment with v. 3, which has a first person verb, presumably caused the pointing error, which envisions the capture of Jerusalem. NIV and NJPS endeavor to retain MT.

g. The correct text is preserved in 15:13, *bimḥir*, "as the price" (*BHS*). MT *bāmōtêkā*, "your high places," doubtless originated as a contextually appropriate annotation to explain "sin," but it was wrongly taken as a correction of the adjacent, similar-looking word; cf. Mic 1:5, where the specification "high places" actually displaced "sin" (Leslie C. Allen, "More Cuckoos in the Textual Nest: At 2 Kings xxiii.5; Jeremiah xvii.3, 4; Micah iii.3; vi.16 (LXX); 2 Chronicles xx.25 (LXX)," *JTS* n.s. 24 [1973]: 69–73, esp. 70–71).

h. In place of the strange *ûbĕkā*, "and in/with you," a conjectural emendation *yādĕkā*, "your hand," is frequently read (see *BHS*; NRSV, NIV, and NJPS dissent); cf. Deut 15:3, though the construction is different. A direct object seems to be required. Again, an erroneous textual displacement is to blame. The MT consonantal reading *wbk* was meant to be a scribal abbreviated form of *wbkl*, "and for all." This was a marginal comment, noting an alternative in the preceding colon for *bkl*, "for all" in the parallel passage at 15:13. It came to displace *ydk*, which looked sufficiently similar to cause confusion (Allen, "More Cuckoos," 71). The textual evidence for *lĕbaddĕkā*, "by yourself" (see *BHS*), may reflect jumbled conflation of the correct reading *ydk* and a fuller form of the annotation, *bkl*.

i. See *HALOT* 2:887b for identification with the juniper via Arabic. Michael Zohary, *Plants of the Bible* (Cambridge: Cambridge University Press, 1982), 117, identifies the shrub with the Phoenician juniper, whose branches bear tiny, scale-like leathery leaflets.

j. Thus BDB 359b and McKane 1:388, 390. *HALOT* 1:357a and Holladay 1:492 interpret as a lava field or stony area.

k. K is to be followed with some ancient support (*BHS*). See the commentary.

l. An infinitive with *lāmed* can continue another verbal form and have the same sense (Joüon §124p).

m. The genitive is epexegetical or appositional; cf. GKC §128k-q.

n. Taking these phrases as vocative with NRSV and NJPS provides a desired connection with v. 13. LXX and Vg. so construe; the shorter text of LXX is accidental (Janzen, *Studies*, 117).

o. This verb and the next are to be taken as jussive in a lament, as LXX took them and as the setting of the vocative in 14:8 suggests (Holladay 1:502).

p. Q is to be followed but pointed *wĕsûrê*, with the use of a construct before a preposition, as at the beginning of v. 3 (Duhm 147; NEB); cf. GKC §130a for the construction and GKC §72p for the form. LXX, Syr., Vg. (cf. Barthélemy, *Critique textuelle*, 2:470, rather than McKane 1:407 and Lundbom 1:798; *a te* is secondary in Vg.), and Symmachus so presuppose; 4Q70 has the letters *wswry*. The compositional factor of word repetition adduced in the commentary below militates against the root attested by K.

q. The text has been queried (see *BHS*), but see the commentary.

r. The gloss, indicated as such by its third person reference but already attested by LXX and, less usefully, 4Q70, is to be regarded as part of the literary tradition; it falls outside the poetry.

The next composition must end with 17:13, since the confession of Jeremiah in vv. 14–18 certainly looks like the beginning of a new one. The translation has demarcated five separate units. The redactional coherence of the first three is indicated by repetition of *lēb*, "heart," at vv. 1 (rendered plural), 5, 9, and 10.[80] "Fruit" (*pĕrî*, vv. 8, 10) creates a further link between the second and third units, rounding off each unit. In fact, whereas the third unit picked up the second term in the phrase "producing fruit," the fourth reuses the first term, ʿ*śh*, here rendered "makes" (v. 11). Moreover, "money" echoes the parallel terms "wealth" and "treasures" in the first unit (v. 3). The first four units provide a range of sins that merit divine reprisal. By way of closure the fifth unit reaches back to the second one, repeating in v. 13 the verb *swr*, "deviate" (v. 5), and "water" (v. 8); also "abandon" in the fourth unit (v. 11) gets double repetition in v. 13. For good measure a frame for the composition as a whole is supplied by the writing of vv. 1 and 13. This complex network of repeated terms demands an interpretation not merely of the individual units but also their interrelationships. The composition provides a panorama of "Judah's sin" (v. 1), while the generalities of vv. 5–13 apply its message by way of hermeneutical warning to later readers.

[17:1–4] The first unit is a poetic oracle of disaster that duly moves from reason (the practice of Canaanite religion) to announcement of Yahweh's punitive intervention (by means of invasion and exile). The two halves are bonded by resumption of "sin" (v. 1) in v. 3, a term that echoes 16:10, while the unit's charge of pagan religion echoes ch. 16 as a whole. However, the unit includes some tensions: a switch from a third person description of Judah in the reason to direct address in the announcement, and the explanatory expansion of the metaphor in v. 1 with a list of religious terms.[81] The unit looks like a literary patchwork in which pieces have been sewn into a redactional whole. The recurrence of the bulk of vv. 3–4 in 15:13–14 reinforces this impression, though at least the material seems more at home here. The unit is also plagued with textual issues that complicate the interpreter's task.

[1a–b*a*] Judah's sinning was no superficial or temporary phenomenon. Rather, it was deeply ingrained in the communal psyche. The same point was made in 2:22 in terms of an indelible stain and in 13:23 in terms of ineradicable skin coloring and fur markings. Now it resurfaces with a metaphor of chiseling on a stone tablet with sharp instruments that bite deep. In Job 19:24 inscription on rock is used as an illustration of the future preservation of Job's words. Here v. 2 refers to a long period of apostasy. The text emphasizes the impossibility of removing sinful habits, hence the implication that divine reprisal is inevitable.

---

80. Holladay, *Architecture*, 151.

81. Verses 2–3a*a* are sometimes taken as prose and so as a redactional insertion (thus NAB), though NEB and NRSV regard vv. 1–4 in their entirety as prose.

[1b*b*–3a*a*] The extension of the metaphor to a religious sphere, the four projections on the top corners of stone altars, specifies the nature of Judah's sinning. Verses 2–3a*a* amplify this religious interpretation as Baal worship at rural shrines, including the wooden poles that probably represented the Canaanite goddess Asherah (cf. 2:20, 23, 27). Such worship has lasted for a long time (so 2:20). A new generation was willfully perpetuating the religious deviations of former generations (cf. Ps 78:3–4).

[3a*b*–4] A normative triangle of land, work, and wealth is deconstructed. The divine punishment is spelled out as a revoking of the land-gifted covenant whereby working as one's own master resulted in wealth as Yahweh's blessing. Instead, military invasion would make such wealth evaporate and subsequent deportation would lead to life in a different country and loss of economic and political independence. The oracle achieves closure by mentioning divine anger as the motivation for such sweeping deconstruction and by the vehement characterization of the punishment as permanent. So radical a reprisal is a measure of the radical nature of Judah's religious sin.

[5–8] This piece looks forward and backward as the middle of three "heart"-based units. Its anticipatory perspective is clear from the quotation formula, which properly introduces the divine oracle of the third unit. The formula implies that the intervening statement, which has third person references to the divine name, operates as an explanatory preface to the oracle, just as 14:1, 17 looked ahead to vv. 10 and 15:1–9, respectively. Curses and blessings were used in a variety of social settings, though formal antitheses like this one occur in OT texts only at Gen 9:25–26; 27:29; Num 24:9; and Deut 27–28.[82] Here the characterizations of two men as cursed in one case and blessed in the other identify the consequences of trust in Yahweh and lack of trust. At first glance the focus seems evenly distributed between the curse and blessing sections, each with its statement and supporting expanded simile, the latter marked by a contrasting Hebrew wordplay, not seeing (*rʾh*) good (v. 6) and not fearing (*yrʾ*) harm (v. 8). Indeed, greater emphasis seems to be given to the blessing section, three bicola in v. 8 over against two in v. 6. However, relating the piece to its literary context tells a different story. The compositional key word "heart" appears in the curse section; and hence suggests that it is the intended focus.

[5–6] The curse section functions as an oracle of disaster, even though it does not feature Yahweh as speaker (cf. 6:28–30; 10:21–22). Whereas the previous unit specified Canaanite religion as the implicit alternative for allegiance to Yahweh, this one draws a contrast between such allegiance and trust in human self-sufficiency. "Mortals" is literally "flesh," and the same parallelism of "humanity" and "flesh" occurs in Isa 31:3, with Egyptian allies and military resources in view. Here the self-sufficiency is simply contrasted with faith in

---

82. See William J. Urbrock, "Blessings and Curses," *ABD* 1:755–61, esp. 756–58.

Yahweh. A grim prognosis is supplied by the imagery of a shrub eking out a miserable existence in the desert. There is leakage between subject and symbol in the anthropomorphic description of the shrub never seeing good, just as in the counterpart at v. 8 lack of fear or anxiety is an anthropopathism. These are allegorical elements of realism in the similes.

[7–8] The antithesis has the force of a missed opportunity, like those presented in 3:19–4:4. The road not taken is tantalizingly elaborated in lavish, positive terms. It would have provided a vital source of sustenance beyond the limitations of the human ecosystem, a source that would have stayed available in worst-case scenarios. The simile of the riverside tree recurs in Ps 1:3, symbolizing those who meditate on the book of Psalms as God's written revelation, for an ethical purpose. Here the simile portrays commitment to Yahweh as the only means of living a blessed life.

[9–10] This third unit is bonded to the former two by a double repetition of "heart" and by repetition of "fruit." It functions as a divine oracle of disaster and so at last justifies the quotation formula in v. 5. A reason for the disaster is given (v. 9) and a reprisal is assured (v. 10). (For a divinely spoken rhetorical question, one may compare 18:14 and 30:21.) The generalities of vv. 9–10 are carefully integrated into the context, redactionally reusing Jeremiah's language. Insidiousness (ʿqb) was featured in 9:4 (3), incurability (ʾānūš) in 15:18, the motif of divine insight in a participial formulation in 11:20, and a similar use of "fruit" in 6:19 (there rendered "consequence").

[9] The radicality of human sin was portrayed in terms of deep etching on the heart in v. 1. Now that same extremity is presented in a triple crescendo: a heart morally insidious beyond compare, sick beyond hope of recovery, and therefore located far beyond the limits of human comprehension.

[10] The motif of mystery broached at the end of v. 9 continues here, but its accompanying negative factors also implicitly carry over, namely, a moral crisis and a terminal disease. The rhetorical question in v. 9 is now taken seriously and receives an answer. Penetrating a facade to detect underlying purpose and finding sufficient clues in overt behavioral patterns are divine means for bringing a resolution that satisfies justice; and so, in light of vv. 1–4, Judah's fate is sealed (cf. too 16:17). Ironically "fruit" is no longer the healthy phenomenon hypothetically envisioned in v. 8 but a real and ugly perversion.

[11] The first three units have been supplemented with two others. This little unit continues to speak in the general terms of the previous one, but defines its sinning in moral terms, with a precise example. Just as the hypothetical fruit (v. 8) was belied by grim reality (v. 10), its production (ʿśh) is now given a negative sense as the unjust making (ʿśh again) of money. The proverbial form of the unit acts as a sophisticated vehicle for a pronouncement of disaster, though there is no evidence that Yahweh speaks it. Reason and ensuing disaster are communicated by the two sentences, while the certainty of the disaster is set out in two

stages (cf. 16:16), in terms of human consequences rather than by the divine intervention of v. 10. The "wealth" and "treasures" in the first unit (v. 3) have influenced the incorporation of this unit: "the image in v. 3 of Judah's sudden loss of wealth is mirrored in v. 11."[83] Overall, Judah's lack of allegiance to Yahweh in the initial unit was amplified in the second by trust in human entities. In the third unit, culpability has widened to an ethical charge of inward insidiousness, and this ethical charge now finds a precise counterpart in this fourth one.

The partridge simile is generally explained in terms of a popular belief that this bird took eggs from the nests of other birds, which when hatched and reared flew back to their own kind. In favor of this interpretation is the parallelism of eggs not laid and money acquired by unjust means, a closer parallelism in the Hebrew, with repetition of *wĕlōʾ*, "and not," introducing the clause or phrase at the ends of the first two cola (KJV "and hatcheth them not... and not by right").[84] The proverbial quality of the unit reflects the world of wisdom literature.

[12–13] The last unit includes a grand medley of terms culled from the previous four units. It is a literary creation that passionately amasses earlier vocabulary in a closing prayer of communal lament for Yahweh's announcements of disaster to offer fresh hope to the Judean exiles. This lyrical shout of amen selects "abandon" from v. 11, deviating from v. 5, "in the country" from v. 4, writing from v. 1, and "water" from v. 8. It also plucks "suffer humiliation" from the next composition (v. 18). It ranges further afield by recalling a charge of abandoning "the spring of running water" in 2:13. It borrows "hope of Israel," a divine vocative in 14:8, and also co-opts "glorious throne" from 14:21 and *mārôm*, "height" (here rendered "exalted"), from 31:12 (cf. 25:30), both in new vocative senses. Yet the unit, for all its heterogeneous elements, has been crafted into a whole by Hebrew alliteration. Yahweh's roles as Israel's *miqwēh*, "hope," and *mĕqôr*, "spring," are anticipated in that of *mĕqôm miqdāšēnû*, "our place of sanctuary."[85]

---

83. Timothy Polk, *The Prophetic Persona: Jeremiah and the Language of the Self* (JSOTSup 32; Sheffield: JSOT Press, 1984), 144.

84. KJV "As the partridge sitteth on eggs and hatcheth them not" adopts a different interpretation, that the bird's large clutch of eggs was whittled down to a few by wastage. It is theoretically possible to take *yld*, "give birth," when applied to birds, to mean either laying eggs or hatching them out; the Greek equivalent *tiktō* has the same range of meaning. However, the parallel endings of the first two cola suggest otherwise. John F. A. Sawyer, "A Note on the Brooding Partridge in Jeremiah xvii 11," *VT* 28 (1978): 324–29, has argued in favor of KJV's interpretation. Carroll 356–57 and Holladay 1:498–99 have followed his lead, but see the critique of McKane 1:400–401. The grammatical objection that in the first colon the conjunction *wāw*, "and," indicates an event later in time, namely, hatching, and that a relative clause would be needed for an earlier event, laying eggs, is not cogent; cf. *IBHS*, 490 (with reference to 1 Sam 28:3), 551–53.

85. Martin Metzger, "'Thron der Herrlichkeit': Ein Beitrag zur Interpretation von Jeremia 17, 12f," in *Prophetie und geschichtliche Wirklichkeit im alten Israel: Festschrift für Siegfried Herrmann* (ed. Rüdiger Liwak and Siegfried Wagner; Stuttgart: Kohlhammer, 1991), 237–62, esp. 238–39.

[12] This initial bicolon addresses a series of vocatives to Yahweh. Terms used elsewhere in the book concerning the temple ("glorious throne," 14:21) or Zion ("height," 31:12) are applied to God now that the preexilic counterparts are things of the past. The latter term is probably used of Yahweh in Ps 92:8 (9) and also in Ps 56:2(3) as a vocative, while *miqdāš*, "sanctuary," is similarly used of Yahweh in Ezek 11:16 and perhaps in Isa 8:14, if the text is correctly preserved. This amassing of cultic terms provides a counterpart to the pagan terminology (vv. 1–3) in a final affirmation of allegiance to Yahweh, Israel's age-old God.

[13] The issue of allegiance is pursued, but now with an awareness that among God's exilic people there were still those who pledged allegiance elsewhere, as in the first two units, deviants who rejected the spiritual "water" (v. 8). The resumption of "in the country" (of exile) from v. 4 implies the fulfillment of the threat of deportation, but there is an appeal for Yahweh's intervention even there. The terse reference to writing is at first sight surprising, but its presence reflects the allusive style of the unit. The incriminating sense of the verb in v. 1 is balanced by a punitive one here. There is a reference to divine record keeping of past human deeds for a future settling of accounts (cf. Neh 13:14; Pss 56:8 [9]; 149:9; Isa 65:6; Dan 7:10). The author asks God to record the names of deviants so that justice would eventually be done.

This closing unit is a spirited application of units earlier in the composition. From the standpoint of exile, it appeals to Yahweh to vindicate such threats anew, as the community faces a resurgence of deviation in its ranks. The generalities of vv. 5–11 point to a contemporary crisis, which the composition as a whole has presented as a range of sins.

17:14–27 *Reprisal for Scorning the Torah-Based Message*

14 Heal me, Yahweh, so I can get healed.
    Save me, so I can get saved,
      because you are the God I praise.
15 Hey, they have been saying to me:
    "Where is Yahweh's message? Let it come true!"
16 As for me, I have not pestered you for a bad fate[a] to happen
    and times of despair are not what I have wanted.
    You know full well what has left my lips,[b]
      it has been open to your scrutiny.
17 Do not be the cause of my discomfiture—
    you have been my shelter in bad times.
18 Let my persecutors suffer humiliation—
    do not let me suffer humiliation!
    Let them be the ones who are discomfited—
      do not let me be discomfited!

Why God's Answer Was No

Inflict bad times on them,
wound them twice over.

19 Here is what Yahweh said *to me*: "Go and stand at the public gate[c] through which the Judean royals enter and leave, and then at each of the other gates of Jerusalem. **20** Tell those who are there: 'Listen to Yahweh's message, you royals of Judah and all you of Judah and *residents of Jerusalem who enter by these gates.* **21** Here is what Yahweh said: "At the risk of your lives[d] mind you do not carry loads on the Sabbath day and bring them through the gates of Jerusalem. **22** You are not to carry loads out of your houses on the Sabbath day either, or do any other work. You are to keep the Sabbath day holy, as I commanded your forebears, **23** though they would not listen, they turned a deaf ear, digging in their heels and refusing to listen or accept warnings. **24** If you do listen to me," declared Yahweh, "so you do not carry in loads through the gates of this city on the Sabbath day, but keep the Sabbath day holy by not doing any work *on it,* **25** then there will come[e] through the gates of this city kings, with officials,[f] who occupy David's throne, riding in horse-drawn chariots. They [will come accompanied by their officials and so will Judeans and residents of Jerusalem, and this city will be populated forever. **26** People will come in from Judah's towns and the vicinity of Jerusalem, from the territory of Benjamin, from the foothills, mountain region, and Negeb, bringing burnt offerings and sacrifices, grain offerings and incense, and also bringing thank offerings to Yahweh's temple. **27** But if you do not listen to me in the matter of keeping the Sabbath day holy and not carrying loads when you come[g] through the gates of Jerusalem on the Sabbath day, I will set fire to its gates, and the fire will get out of control and burn down Jerusalem's fortified mansions."'"

a. MT *mērōʿeh* seems to mean "not to be a shepherd," with a privative use of the preposition (GKC §119x), a singular way of referring to the prophetic role. Parallelism with the next colon suggests a repointing to *mērāʿâ* with Aquila, Symmachus, and partially Syr., and a loose causal use of the preposition, "because of a (future) bad fate." NAB, REB, and NJB render on these lines.

b. The punctuation in MT is to be ignored. Metrically the second bicolon in v. 16, like the first, is to be taken as 4 + 3 (*BHS*). NAB, NRSV, and NJPS construe thus.

c. "Benjamin" (RSV, NAB, REB) represents an unattested emendation in line with 37:13 and 38:7. MT "(gate of) the sons/members of the people" should be kept as contextually fitting (see the commentary). It refers to a public gate, one generally used by commoners. Cf. 26:23, "the burial ground of the common people" or "the public burial ground" (GNB); 2 Kgs 23:6.

d. For the sinister connotation, recognized by EVV, though not NIV and NJPS, cf. BDB 90a.

e. The sense is "will continue to come" (NAB; cf. NJB). The same applies to v. 26. Alex Varughese, "The Royal Family in the Jeremiah Tradition," in *Inspired Speech: Prophecy in the Ancient Near East: Essays in Honor of Herbert B. Huffmon* (ed. J. Kaltner and L. Stulman; JSOTSup 378; London: T & T Clark International, 2004), 319–28, esp. 322 n. 10, finds in this promise of continuation evidence of a preexilic setting.

f. The textual tradition attests "and officials," which intrudes between "kings" and "who sit on David's throne" (cf. 13:13; 22:4) and anticipates the later reference to officials. However, it may be kept as a legitimate instance of poor style (Barthélemy, *Critique textuelle*, 2:618–69; McKane 1:415).

g. Literally "and coming" (rather than "nor coming," as if a separate prohibition, as LXX renders under the influence of its rendering in v. 21), which closely qualifies the previous verbal phrase as in v. 21. LXX seems to have in view the postbiblical tradition of a ban on travel on the Sabbath (Fishbane, *Biblical Interpretation*, 133 n. 74).

Jeremiah 17:14–27 is the composition that rounds off chs. 14–17. It is made up of two disparate units (vv. 14–18 and 19–27). The bond between them is "Yahweh's message" (vv. 15, 20), so that the second unit functions as a redactional illustration of Jeremiah's prophesying that is belittled in the first. Another link is that the threefold occurrence of *yôm*, "day," rendered "times" in negative contexts (vv. 16–18), corresponds to a sevenfold usage in the second unit with reference to the Sabbath. The penalty for infringement of the Sabbath command (v. 27) is thereby adumbrated.

This composition is loosely related to the previous one. The first unit is related to vv. 5–8 in the absence of "good" (v. 6) and the prospect of "bad (times)" (vv. 16–18). "Bad times," more literally "the day of a bad fate," appears to be an interpretation of the metaphorical "year of drought" (v. 8). Calling Yahweh "my shelter" (*maḥăsî*, v. 17) parallels the characterization of Yahweh as "his one to trust" (*mibṭāḥô*, v. 7); indeed, the two devotional terms appear in close proximity in Ps 71:5, 7. Alternative scenarios are presented in both vv. 5–8 and 24–27. The Hebrew diction is the same in this unit and the one in vv. 9–10—*ʾānûš*, "incurably sick" (v. 9), is echoed by the same term rendered "despair" at v. 16. It has already been noted that "suffer humiliation" (v. 18) was deliberately anticipated in v. 13. As for the second unit, a further item is added to the catalog of sins.[86] The quotation formulas in vv. 19 and 21 echo the one in v. 5. Moreover, the "fire" of divine anger (v. 4) materializes in the divine fire that would burn down Jerusalem (v. 27). Hence an overall frame has been provided for what seem to be intentionally juxtaposed compositions.

[17:14–18] This poem is the fifth of Jeremiah's so-called confessions, following those in 11:18–20; 12:1–4; 15:10, 15–18. The poem is neatly ringed by the pairing of opposites, healing for Jeremiah (v. 14) and wounding for his per-

86. Cf. Thiel, *Redaktion von Jeremia 1–25*, 209.

secutors (v. 18), terms that occur together in 6:14; 8:11; and in a confession at 15:18. The opposites are both set in double petitions, at beginning and end. Elements drawn from the genre of the individual lament psalm appear here, though the genre has been adapted to reflect the prophetic role of the lamenter, as in earlier cases.[87] Explicit Hebrew pronouns portray the prophet's relationship to Yahweh as disrupted by human adversaries: "you" three times in vv. 14, 16, and 17, "they" twice in vv. 15 and 18, and "I" three times in vv. 16 and 18.

[14] The prophetic lament opens with a pair of petitions. Healing is not a reference to literal sickness but a metaphorical indication of the need for resolution of a personal crisis, in fact a reaction of disbelief and persecution to his prophetic ministry. Divine intervention was judged the only means of obtaining such resolution, and so the prophet turned to Yahweh for help. The petitions are supported with an affirmation of faith, personal commitment to Yahweh expressed in terms of regular praise and worship (cf. Ps 71:6).

[15] A description of the crisis follows, formulated as a quotation of Jeremiah's enemies, who are vaguely referred to as "they," as in 11:18. Yahweh needed no further clarification; they will be defined as "my persecutors" in v. 18 (cf. 15:15). In psalmic laments a standard taunt is "Where is your God?" (Ps 42:3, 10 [4, 11]; cf. 79:10; Joel 2:17). Here it is adapted to the prophetic context, the delayed fulfillment of oracles proclaimed in Yahweh's name (cf. Isa 5:19).

[16] This is a kind of protestation of innocence, again with a prophetic orientation, as in 15:17. Jeremiah did not deserve the brunt of hostility he had to bear from other members of the community. He had only been the messenger, not the initiator of the message of doom. Is there an oblique reference to his intercession on the doomed people's behalf (cf. 18:20)? The protestation is defended by an appeal for Yahweh's corroboration. The final colon indicates that Jeremiah's statements were not made to Yahweh, but were overheard by God and monitored, and so they refer to a lack of personal hostility in his communications to the people, whether in his prophetic capacity or otherwise.

[17] The negative petition (v. 17a) guards against another aspect of the crisis. Whereas in v. 14 a positive petition was presented for divine intervention on the prophet's side, now there is a fear of a negative intervention that would take the side of his detractors and providentially endorse it by letting their malevolence triumph, to his own loss. In v. 17b an affirmation of faith is offered again, reminding Yahweh of previous intervention on Jeremiah's behalf in deliverance from crisis and implicitly urging that Yahweh should do so again, rather than intervening as an enemy.

[18] A double expression of a two-sided wish now follows. This element is more common toward the end of a communal lament, but does occur in

---

87. Cf. Baumgartner, *Poems of Lament*, 54–55.

individual laments (Pss 31:17 [18]; 35:26–27; 109:28–29).[88] Jeremiah's vindication could be made evident only by the downfall of his persecutors. Dire provocation has transformed the goodwill of v. 16 into a demand for tough justice.[89] The closing double petition has the stridency of a sobbing scream. It corresponds to the opening pair in v. 14, but now reflects the dark perspective the prophet has maintained since v. 17. A direct appeal is made for Yahweh's punitive intervention. The coming true of "bad times" refers back to the negative content of Jeremiah's oracles, whose coming true was described as "a bad fate" and in terms of "times of despair" in v. 16 (cf. 28:9). Jeremiah was praying that his persecutors might be included in the calamity that was to befall the people at large (cf. 11:22–23; 14:15; 20:6), but that their punishment should be deservedly greater—"twice over," which means, as Streane (111) says, "the one part for their apostasy as a nation, the other for their treatment of Jeremiah." Such turning of the tables would spell the prophet's eventual vindication.

The lament gives vent to Jeremiah's frustration and resentment as he was caught up in a prophetic situation he could not handle. The biblically minded and compilers of a postmodern lectionary may note that it has a (more assertive) counterpart in 2 Tim 4:14–15. The lament is close to a complaint in that just beneath the surface of the prayer is an unspoken "for your sake" (15:15), a sentiment found in psalms of complaint, for instance at Ps 44:22 (23) ("Because of you"). What distinguishes this prayer from such psalms is the special relationship between the prophet and his God. "If Yahweh got Jeremiah into his present predicament, he should rescue him from it" (Holladay 1:506). Contextually this lament paves the way for the sequel; Jeremiah is presented as a messenger whose torah-promoting message was scorned, and so his plea for just retribution would be honored.

[19–27] This prose unit sends out a number of mixed signals, both internally and contextually. First, it gives a stern warning, with the hope that the warning will be effective (vv. 24–26). Yet in light of vv. 14–18 the unit functions as "Yahweh's message" of doom (vv. 15, 20), a message that Jeremiah's contemporaries were failing to take seriously. The arrangement suggests that the onus is meant to be on the possibility of disaster for Jerusalem (v. 27), and that the unit is intended to be an oracle of disaster in which the initial warning constitutes the reason for it. The framing parallelism of the inextinguishable fire of divine fury (v. 4) and that of Jerusalem's destruction at Yahweh's hands (v. 27) supports this impression. On the heels of Jeremiah's confession the unit functions as a virtual divine reply (Fretheim 261), promising punishment.

---

88. See Claus Westermann, *Praise and Lament in the Psalms* (trans. K. R. Crim and R. N. Soulen; Atlanta: John Knox, 1981), 52, 64.

89. Polk, *Prophetic Persona*, 211 n. 49, has noted a similar shift in other confessions, 11:19–20; 18:19–23; 20:7–12, while Baumgartner, *Poems of Lament*, 55, compared Ps 35:12–14, 22–26.

Second, the unit purports to be the report of a preexilic oracle, though "to me" (v. 19) is a redactional addition in MT, intended to bond the unit more closely to Jeremiah's own words in the preceding one. However, serious objections have been raised. Does the specificity of Sabbath breaking fit Jeremiah's attitude to the torah elsewhere? Would it not better fit an exilic or postexilic setting, in which defense of Sabbath observance became increasingly necessary (cf. Ezek 20:12–13, 20–21, 24; Isa 56:2, 4, 6; 58:13–14; Neh 13:15–22)? Moreover, this oracle places a high premium on this single issue as capable of triggering the very downfall of Jerusalem. Furthermore, the general address to Judean "kings" (EVV) in v. 20 has an unhistorical ring, suggesting a rhetorical projection from a later period when the monarchy no longer existed. The dating of the oracle in the postexilic period, with which McKane (1:417–19), for instance, has sided, suits its affinities to the Sabbath problem of Neh 13:15–22, in that both passages mention bringing in goods to Jerusalem for sale and "loads" (*maśśāʾ*, Jer 17:21, 22, 24, 27; Neh 13:15, 19 [NRSV "burdens"]). It also respects the oracle as confronting a real-life issue in the Judean, Jerusalem-based community. For all the similarities, however, the Nehemiah passage is concerned with the complication of Judeans purchasing goods at a market staffed by foreign vendors (cf. Neh 10:31 [32]), whereas the present issue relates to Judeans and residents of Jerusalem offering goods for sale. Besides, although this oracle is not cited, Neh 13:18 seems to be aware of it, using the fulfillment of Jer 17:27 in the downfall of the capital as a historical precedent.[90] The parallels between the texts are cases of intertextuality designed to bolster Nehemiah's case.

The oracle is often ascribed to exilic, Deuteronomistic circles responsible for editing the book. However, Herrmann has warned that the issue of keeping the Sabbath was never a special concern of either Deuteronomy or the Deuteronomistic History nor was it linked to the fate of the Judean community, as it is in vv. 21 and 27.[91] Certainly the oracle reflects in places the phraseology of the exilic prose sermons found in the book (e.g., in 7:1–8:3). Yet a reservation must be made. Stulman has observed that such diction is "distributed sparsely."[92] He finds it mainly confined to vv. 21 ("At the risk ... mind"), 23, and 25.[93] In addition, at vv. 22 and 24 there appears to be literary dependence on an earlier text, Deut 5:12–14, in the references to keeping the Sabbath day holy and not doing any work.[94] This evidence of redaction suggests the existence of an earlier

90. Cf. Fishbane, *Biblical Interpretation*, 131–32.
91. Siegfried Herrmann, *Die prophetischen Heilserwartungen im Alten Testament: Ursprung und Gestaltwendel* (BWANT 5/5; Stuttgart: Kohlhammer, 1965), 172–73. In the priestly passages Exod 31:14–15; 35:2; and Num 15:32–36 Sabbath breaking is a capital offense.
92. *Prose Sermons*, 72.
93. Ibid., 71.
94. Fishbane, *Biblical Interpretation*, 132. The amplification "on it" in MT at v. 24 continues the literary trend; cf. Exod 31:14; 35:2; and the textual tradition in Deut 5:14 supplied in *BHS*.

prophetic core that linked a triangle of factors: Sabbath observance, the gates of Jerusalem, and the monarchy (cf. Weiser 1:155–56; Rudolph 119–21; Jones 249). Sabbath observance that prohibits selling merchandise appears in a preexilic prophetic oracle (Amos 8:5). Jeremiah's own oracles were aware of the Yahwistic torah tradition and its crucial potential for good or ill for the Judean community (e.g., 6:16–21), and concentration on what must have been a part of it is not an implausible corollary. Nor is it surprising that it underwent redactional amplification to drive home to a later constituency the serious import of the oracle.

The unit commences with a personal introduction to the oracle from Yahweh to the prophet (v. 19) and a public introduction from the prophet to his audience (v. 20). The oracle itself falls into three parts: warning exhortations backed by a negative precedent (vv. 21–23), an incentive (vv. 24–26), and a deterrent (v. 27). Most of these sections are highlighted by fourfold use of the verb "listen," used positively and negatively (vv. 20, 23, 24, 27). Other key terms in the unit are "the Sabbath day" (seven times) and "the gates of Jerusalem" (vv. 19, 21, 27a), which are also mentioned with inversion of the terms ("Jerusalem . . . gates," vv. 20, 27b) and in the form "the gates of this city" in the incentive (vv. 24, 25), again a total of seven times. These heptads are surely not coincidental.

[19–20] The introductions to the oracle prepare for it by specifying first a particular gate and then other gates as places where the oracle was to be delivered. An open square suitable for a market generally stood inside a city gate, and the cases of Sabbath breaking focused on such markets. A further preparation for the oracle is provided by the initial reference to a gate convenient for access to the palace, on the northern stretch of the eastern wall of the city, perhaps the Horse Gate (cf. 31:40). It was also a public gate, so that it was used both by commoners and the royal family, the joint recipients of the oracle. The Hebrew term usually rendered "kings" presumably means the royal family or its leading members, at least in the vocative of v. 20 (Hitzig 141, citing Syriac and Latin parallels; cf. 2 Sam 15:1; Jer 13:13). The mention of such "royals" and their access to the city anticipates v. 25.

[21–23] The portion of the exhortation has been fleshed out with a sinister introduction that already anticipates v. 27 and a conclusion that warns of earlier willful deviations, and also with scriptural elucidation. The conveying of goods to the gate markets implies commerce, whether by Judean vendors into the city (v. 21) or by residents who had shorter journeys from their city homes (v. 22). The double reference corresponds to the Judean and Jerusalemite addressees in v. 20.

[24–26] Yahweh offers an incentive to support the exhortation. The greater space given to it than to the deterrent (v. 27) matches the pattern of alternatives in the parallel composition at vv. 5–8. Here too the focus in the present literary setting is on the shorter, negative alternative, and this one functions as another missed opportunity, a mirage of what might have been. The condition recapitulates the essence of vv. 21 and 23. The sketches of royal cavalcades and more ordinary traffic depict maintenance—rather than restoration—of regular life in this bustling metropolis, a seat of government and commerce (cf. 22:24). The closing characterization refers to another aspect of Jerusalem, which was the religious center of Judah where pilgrims were glad to exclaim, "Our feet are standing within your gates, O Jerusalem" (Ps 122:2). At festal times they came to worship from six areas of the state, including the tribal areas of Judah and Benjamin, and the Negeb in the far south, which was lost to encroaching Edomites in the exilic period and thereafter. The continuity of such worship hung in the balance.

[27] The briefer alternative again consists of a condition, formally constructed like v. 24, but now paired with an announcement of disaster. The burning was presumably to occur in the context of military invasion, but the agency is firmly expressed as divine. It would mean the destruction of Jerusalem's gates—and so its markets—and of the grand buildings that reflected its God-given glory (cf. Pss 48:12–13 [13–14], where "citadels" renders the term translated "mansions" here; 122:3).

Jeremiah 17:14–27 exposes the reprehensibility of the faith community in refusing to heed from the prophet "Yahweh's message," here illustrated with a torah-based message relating to the Sabbath. This refusal must usher in the collapse of Jerusalem and its valued traditions.

18:1–20:18 God and Prophet Ominously Rejected

18:1–23 The Spurned Message and Messenger of Disaster

18:1 A message Jeremiah received from Yahweh that said: 2 "Get going, down to a potter's workshop, where I will let you hear my message." 3 So I went down to a potter's workshop, and there he was busy making things at the wheel. 4 If the pot he was making *with the clay*^{a} got spoiled in the potter's^b hand, he would remake it into another pot of whatever kind the potter deemed appropriate to make. 5 Then I received this message from Yahweh: 6 "What this potter did cannot I do likewise in your case, Israel's community?" *declared Yahweh*. "Look, clay in the potter's hand is what you are like in mine, *Israel's community*. 7 On one occasion I may announce threats relating to any nation, any realm, to uproot it, *demolish it*,^{c} and destroy it, 8 but if that nation veers from its bad behavior, *which caused*^{d} me to threaten it, I change my mind about the bad fate I was planning to put into effect in its case. 9 On another occasion I may announce promises relating to any nation, any realm, to build it and plant it. 10 But if it puts into effect what I deem bad behavior, refusing to obey me, I change my mind about the good I promised it. 11 The upshot is that you are to tell the Judeans and Jerusalem's residents *as follows*: 'Here is what Yahweh *said:* "Look out, I am shaping a bad fate in your case and planning a scheme against you. So veer one and all from your bad courses and let *your courses*,[e] your conduct, be good."'" 12 But they kept saying,[f] "It is hopeless, because we have our own schemes we are going to follow, and one and all we will put into effect the stubborn inclination of our bad attitude."

13 Therefore here is what Yahweh said:

"Ask among the nations
   if anybody has ever heard of such a thing!
Something extremely horrible has been put into effect
   by virgin Israel.
14 Is the rocky terrain[g] ever left[h]
   by the snow of Lebanon?
Or is there a running dry[i] of water from afar,
   of cool streams?
15 Yet my people have forgotten me,
   sacrificing to worthless gods,
which[j] have made them flounder in their courses,
   the age-old paths,
so they follow other roads,
   unmade courses,
16 with the prospect of turning their country into a shocking place,
   a place people will ever whistle at,
at which all who pass by will be shocked,
   shaking their heads in scorn.
17 Force like that of the east wind I will use to scatter them
   in front of the enemy.
A back view, not a front view, I will have of them[k]
   on their day of calamity."[l]

18 "Come on," they said, "let us plan schemes against Jeremiah, because the priests must never stop giving torah, or the wise their advice, or the prophets their messages. Come on, let us denounce him, so we will not have to pay attention[m] to any of his messages."[n]

19 Pay attention to me, Yahweh,
   and listen to my opponents' talk.
20 Should good be repaid with bad?
   In fact they have dug a pit for me.

God and Prophet Ominously Rejected

Remember how I stood in your presence
pleading to their good advantage,
to avert your fury from them.
21 Therefore turn over their children to famine
and consign them to the power of the sword!
Let their womenfolk become childless and widowed,
their menfolk be killed by plague,°
their young men struck down by the sword in battle.
22 Let cries be heard from their homes,
when you instigate a sudden attack on them by invaders,
because they have dug a pit to catch me
and laid hidden snares for my feet.
23 But you yourself know, Yahweh,
all their plotting for my death.
Do not forgive their wrongdoing
and their sinning do not blot out^p from your sight.
But let them be overthrown at your direction.^{q}
At your time of anger deal with them!

a. MT has been influenced by v. 6 (Janzen, *Studies*, 74), relating symbol and subject more closely, and may also intend "clay" to function as the antecedent for "(remake) it," instead of the first pot.

b. LXX uses pronouns, probably free renderings, for both occurrences of "the potter"; in the first case correspondence with v. 6 appears significant.

c. MT adds a precise contrast to "build" in v. 9; cf. 1:10.

d. The loose use of *ʾăšer* with the sense, "in connection with which," was observed by Ehrlich, *Randglossen*, 4:289. EVV construe differently and less plausibly than this interpretation, taking "that nation" as the antecedent. The relative clause is a linking exegetical comment.

e. MT's insertion assimilates to 7:3, 5; 26:13; contrast 35:15 (Janzen, *Studies*, 40–41).

f. EVV render as future, apart from the present of NRSV. The sense is a frequentative past (Holladay 1:517; Lundbom 1:816), to which the past renderings of the ancient versions approximate.

g. The genitive appears to be appositional (cf. *IBHS* 153); cf. NIV and REB "rocky slopes," and similarly NAB and NJB.

h. For the anomalous preposition after the transitive verb (Gen 24:27 and Lev 26:43 are hardly parallel) cf. its use after *škḥ*, "forget," in Ps 102:4 (5).

i. See *BHS* for this old conjectural emendation, which assumes metathesis under the influence of the root *ntš*, "uproot," in v. 7. Apart from NJPS, EVV so read.

j. In the previous colon *šāwʾ* has a collective sense, "worthless gods," and so can be the antecedent of the plural verb (Barthélemy, *Critique textuelle*, 2:624–25, comparing 2 Chr 28:23; McKane 1:428, 432–33; Holladay 1:520; cf. NIV and REB).

k. Cf. NJPS. All other EVV repoint to a Hiphil, like *BHS*, following the ancient translations. The nouns function as accusatives of limitation (Barthélemy, *Critique textuelle*, 2:625–26; cf. Joüon §126g).

l. For the cola division in v. 17 see Cloete, *Versification*, 188.

m. For the consecutive sense see NJPS and Ehrlich, *Randglossen*, 4:291; cf. GKC §109g; Joüon §116j.

n. For a defense of MT in this sentence see McKane 1:435–37.

o. Rather than "death" (NIV); cf. 15:2, where NIV also opts for "death."

p. For the verbal form see *BHS* and GKC §75hh, but also Lundbom 1:833.

q. Cf. the sense "under one's eye or oversight" for *lipnê* in Deut 25:2; 1 Sam 3:1 (BDB 817a).

The first unit begins with an oracle reception heading, which typically opens a new block of material. Another will appear in ch. 21, so that this next block consists of chs. 18–20. The redactional nature of the formula is evident from its third person format, whereas first person references appear in vv. 3 and 5. The block is made up of two compositions, 18:1–23 and 19:1–20:18, which form a pair marked by numerous parallels. They both open with pottery narratives and related oracles, the first with a visit to a potter's workshop and the message of Yahweh's shaping "a bad fate" for Judah and Jerusalem (18:11), and the second with the breaking of a jug at the Potsherd Gate and the message of Yahweh's inflicting "a bad fate" on Topheth, Jerusalem, and the other cities of Judah (19:3, 15). The pair of compositions is enveloped by the Hebrew verb *niḥam*, the changing of the divine mind about Judah's "bad fate" (18:8), which the context denies, and its explicit denial in the case of Judean cities being "relentlessly" overthrown by Yahweh (20:16). Both compositions envision the coming disaster to involve "enemy/ies" (18:17; 19:9), "the sword" (18:21; 19:7; 20:4), and shocking devastation for Judah (18:16) or Jerusalem (19:8). Both include accusations of pagan worship ("worthless gods," 18:5; "Baal," 19:5; "other gods," 19:4, 13) and also suggest nominal worship of Yahweh (18:18; 20:1–2) by claiming that the religious establishment was following a course diametrically opposed to the divine will. Whereas the first composition portrays the stance of the entire religious establishment as contrary to that of Jeremiah (18:18), in the second a high-ranking priest has that role (20:1–2). Both also accuse Israel of rejecting the divine "message(s)" (18:2, 18b; 19:15) and the prophetic messenger (18:18a; 20:7b–10), to the point of death threats (18:23; 20:18). Both compositions conclude with Jeremianic confessions (18:19–23; 20:7–13, 14–18) that reflect the community's rejection of Yahweh in the prophet's own rejection.

Divine power justifiably wielded against Israel is a prominent motif in the first composition, whether illustrated by the way a potter reshapes botched clay before starting over (v. 4) or in terms of the east wind that symbolizes military invasion (v. 17), or elaborated in the literal language of famine, sword, and plague as God's means of punishment (v. 21). The key words of vv. 11–12 also dominate the composition. These climactic verses of the first unit (vv. 1–12) provide a nucleus whose vocabulary is echoed in the other two units (vv. 13–17, 18–23). As for the second unit, "put into effect" (ʿśh) in v. 13 reflects the verb used in vv. 10 and 12, while in v. 15 "courses" repeats v. 11 and "follow" repeats v. 12. In the third unit "they said" (v. 18) resumes "they kept saying" in v. 12, and another sinister echo is "schemes" as the content of what they said, while the polarized "bad" and "good" in vv. 19–20 link especially with v. 11 (cf. vv. 8–10, 12). The three units have been deliberately juxtaposed and their overall significance is meant to overshadow their individual features.[95]

[18:1–12] This prose unit resembles the report of a symbolic action, like 13:1–11; it has the same three standard parts of divine command, prophetic performance (vv. 1–4), and divine interpretation (vv. 5–11). However, symbolic action reports relate to actions carried out by the prophet, whereas here he observes someone else's activity. The unit is a hybrid between such a report and a vision-oracle report, such as those in 1:11–14, in which Yahweh draws Jeremiah's attention to everyday phenomena and then explains their significance. There appears to be disparity between vv. 2–6 and 7–12 regarding both message and style. As to the latter, vv. 7–12 exhibit characteristics of the prose sermon, examples of which have occurred earlier in chs. 7, 11, and 14.[96] These verses are best understood as a redactional continuation of the oracle. They comprise theological reflection (vv. 7–10) and its application to the community in the form of a call to repentance (v. 11), while there is a concluding report of a negative response to the divine invitation (v. 12). Verses 7–12 can be defined as a prose buttress, like 7:1–8:3; 11:1–17; and 14:11–16. In general it shares with them mention of "a bad fate" (rāʿâ) and the inevitability of divine punishment. Although many of the specific features in the earlier buttresses are not present here, vv. 10–12 offer a conglomeration of five parallels to the first and/or second buttresses: addressing "Judeans and Jerusalem's residents," as in 11:2, 9; Yahweh's standard of bad behavior, as in 7:30; the motif of obedience, as in 7:23, 28; 11:4, 7; the repudiated alternative of good conduct, implicitly in 7:3, 5; and the sin of a stubborn attitude, as in 7:24 and 11:8. Some of these elements are resumed from the previous block. "A bad fate" has been prominent in 16:10 and 17:16. The stubborn attitude or heart has occurred in 16:12, while the negativity of the human heart has been a recurring theme in 17:1–10. Refusal to listen—the same verb šmʿ rendered "obey" elsewhere—has come to the fore in 17:23, 27.

---

95. The coherence of vv. 1–23 has been maintained by Terence E. Fretheim, "The Repentance of God: A Study of Jeremiah 18:7–10," *HAR* 11 (1987): 82–92, esp. 83–84, 89. It is fairly common for scholars to see redactional affinity between vv. 1–12 and 13–17.

96. See Stulman, *Prose Sermons*, 73–76.

[2–5] The initial personal command is a prelude to the public oracle given to the prophet in v. 5. The workshop was situated in a lower area of Jerusalem, with easy access to a water supply. Jeremiah briefly describes the potter at work. He evidently stayed quite a while, waiting for the oracle and meantime admiring the dexterity with which the potter handled the clay, the adroit way he could cope with any mishap by reshaping as necessary. The "wheel" is literally a pair of stone disks, which would revolve, one pivoted by a vertical shaft above the other, with a heavier lower disk that, periodically kick-started or shoved by the left hand, gave steady, freewheeling momentum.[97] The prophet clarifies the divine interpretation in v. 6, supplying eyewitness information that fills out the demonstrative interjection rendered "Look."

[6] The public perspective will be reinforced by v. 11 as it closes the complex oracle. This succinct explanation focuses on the potter's control of his medium. "Did" and "do" render the verb ʿśh translated in terms of (re)making (vv. 3–4), and so there is greater continuity than the English translation suggests. The potter's adept control becomes an analogy for Yahweh's control over the covenant community. The oracle in vv. 7–11 continues on a different tack, and v. 6 looks like an independent saying.[98] The issue of God's power suggests that this saying reflects an incomplete disputation, a dispute and counterthesis that assumes a thesis that about Yahweh's providential control of the community's present and imminent history, in the categorical spirit of 5:12: "He is not a factor."[99]

[7–10] The theological reflection that follows and prepares for the application in v. 11 makes a different, more elaborate point, moving away from the generality of parable to the detail of allegory and arguing for an ultimate control that takes human contingencies into account. The rapid whirl of the manufacturing process described in v. 4 now slows down. Each of the constituent

---

97. See further Philip J. King, *Jeremiah: An Archaeological Companion* (Louisville: Westminster/John Knox, 1993), 166–67.

98. Cf. Gunther Wanke, "Jeremias Besuch beim Töpfer: Eine motivkritische Untersuchung zu Jer 18," in *Prophecy: Essays Presented to Georg Fohrer on His Sixty-Fifth Birthday, 6 September 1980* (ed. J. A. Emerton; BZAW 150; Berlin: de Gruyter, 1980), 151–62, esp. 152.

99. As to theme, see Christian Brekelmans, "Jeremiah 18,1–12 and Its Redaction," in *Livre de Jérémie* (ed. P.-M. Bogaert), 345–50, esp. 346. As to genre see Jenö Kiss, *Die Klage Gottes und des Propheten: Ihre Rolle in der Komposition und Redaktion von Jer 11–12, 14–15 und 18* (WMANT 99; Neukirchen-Vluyn: Neukirchener Verlag, 2003), 172, 174–75, though he defines a disputation and the meaning here differently. Cf. the disputations in Ezek 12:21–25, 26–28, rendering at vv. 25 and 28: "Whatever word I speak is fulfilled" (Leslie C. Allen, *Ezekiel 1–19* [WBC 28; Dallas: Word, 1994], 185, 188, 199). "Is fulfilled" is more literally "is done," reflecting the same verb ʿśh rendered "make" and "do" here in vv. 4 and 6. For the incomplete genre see the analysis of Nah 1:2–3:19 as counterthesis (1:2–10) and two-pronged dispute (1:11–15 [2:1; 2:1[2]–3:19), with an implicit thesis of Yahweh's impotence, made by Marvin A. Sweeney, "Concerning the Structure and Generic Character of the Book of Nahum," *ZAW* 104 (1992): 364–77, esp. 374–75.

elements is treated in detail: an initial course of action, an interruption or disruption of that course, and a new course. Divine providence is still in view, but a human response can trigger a response from Yahweh. This human element is surprising and marks a novel interpretation of the metaphor. Elsewhere the potter metaphor is used to rule out human interference (Isa 29:16; 45:9; 64:8; and also in Rom 9:20–21). This reflection depends on at least three presuppositions. First, a knowledge of Jer 1:10 is implied, where Yahweh's negative work of uprooting and demolishing parallels the positive work of planting and building, affecting not only the covenant nation but other "nations" and "realms," though there the divine working is consecutive and here it is alternative. Second, the imagery of the potter (*yôṣēr*) implicitly embraces the theological tradition of creation. The associated root is used in Gen 2:7, 19, according to which Yahweh "formed" or shaped the human being and the other animate creatures, while in Jer 10:16 Yahweh is "the one who shaped (*yôṣēr*) the universe." Creation is not a static notion, but involves Yahweh's lordship over the nations of the world, as the movement from Isa 45:12 to vv. 13–14 illustrates, after the potter metaphor of 45:9. Third, in Jer 27:1–11 by right of creation Yahweh assigns providential power to "anybody I deem appropriate" to have it (27:5; cf. 18:4), in this case Nebuchadnezzar. Through Jeremiah Yahweh offers choices to "any nation, any realm" (27:8). The options are destruction or survival on its native soil, depending on whether it accepts or rejects the Babylonian yoke. That oracle (27:1–11) is presupposed in the alternatives of 18:7–10 and helps to explain the novel focus on human activity.

The general statement of v. 6 is amplified in two hypothetical scenarios. They incorporate a conditional proclamation of salvation and a conditional announcement of disaster. Both paraphrase the potter's new intent, the deeming of what was appropriate (v. 4), in terms of changing the mind, a motif expressed in 15:6 and 20:16, where the same Hebrew verb, *niḥam*, rendered "relenting" and "relentlessly," has the same meaning as in the first scenario (vv. 7–8).[100] This is the more crucial scenario. It lays a foundation for the application (v. 11) by predicating the canceling of an oracle of disaster by means of repentance. The second scenario (vv. 9–10) is logically closer to the potmaking imagery than to the application, introducing not only a new, contrary factor that causes revision of the original intent, but also a bad factor that corresponds to the spoiling (v. 4). The Hebrew verb *nišḥat*, "got spoiled," used there occurs in the symbolic action of 13:1–11 at v. 7, where it refers to the "ruined" waistcloth. In another respect the first scenario is closer, in the way Yahweh's planning to "put into effect" (*ʿśh*) the intent of "a bad fate" parallels the potter's (re)making (*ʿśh*) a different pot. The new pot is interpreted as the

---

100. See in general Terence E. Fretheim, "The Repentance of God: A Key to Evaluating Old Testament God-Talk," *HBT* 10 (1988): 47–70.

new situation Yahweh creates in the history of a claylike nation. In the second scenario, on the other hand, the putting into effect is credited to the human agent and its object is "bad behavior" (v. 10). The subject strains the symbol as it focuses on human choice. Moreover, the divine "deeming" (v. 10) refers not to the potter's eventual "deeming" (v. 4) but to the interim stage of spoiling. Metaphorical terms function in diverse ways such that the level of coherence between symbol and subject becomes complex. The second scenario, which envisions an initial proclamation of salvation, is hardly relevant to Judah's situation expressed in v. 11. Its purpose as a theoretical possibility reinforces the moral dimension of God's effective providence, which complements human tendencies fairly, as the contrasting of "good" and "bad" indicates. Its negative vocabulary, "bad behavior, refusing to obey me," bolsters the reference to "bad behavior" in v. 8.

[11] A deduction from the theorizing of vv. 7–10 now appears. The initial wĕʿattâ, literally "And now" (NJPS), typically introduces a conclusion at the end of a speech. The deduction applies the "any nation, any realm" scenario (vv. 7–8) to Judah and Jerusalem. The "planning" of "a bad fate" (v. 8) now reappears, and so does the "veering from" a "bad" tendency. Continuity with the potter imagery is maintained by repetition of *yôṣēr*, "potter," from vv. 2–3/4, now a participle with a divine subject, "shaping," which is a variation of the putting into effect or making of v. 8. The conclusion takes the form of a summons to repent, made up of a threat, a double admonition, and an inset accusation ("your bad courses").[101]

[12] But, of course, they did not repent. The fatal attraction of 2:25, "It is hopeless," reappears here. The report of the outcome caps the conclusion of v. 11 and transforms the whole argument leading up to a call to repentance into a virtual oracle of disaster. "The certitude of judgment is unexpressed but also unmistakable."[102] The warning about "a bad fate" issuing from "bad behavior" hereby becomes a certainty, now that the previously open window of gracious opportunity has been closed from the human side. The contingent message of disaster cannot be canceled after all; though originally not cast in concrete, it has become so. The quotation format is a rhetorical device for summing up a popular attitude, as in 2:20, 23, 25. There are echoes of v. 10 in the terms "putting into effect" and "bad." Moreover, a stubborn attitude is closely associated with the disobedience of v. 10 elsewhere in the book (7:24; 9:12–13 [13–14]; 11:8; 13:10; 16:12). The scenario of vv. 9–10, minimally useful for v. 11, is presupposed and emphasized in v. 12. The unit has ended up affirming

---

101. Raitt, "Prophetic Summons," 35. The quotation formula added in MT supplies a frequent element of the formulation (cf. 7:3).

102. Walter Brueggemann, *The Theology of the Book of Jeremiah* (Old Testament Theology; Cambridge: Cambridge University Press, 2007), 100.

the rejection of the prophet's message of disaster, rejection that was reported earlier at 6:17, 19; 7:13, 26, 28; 8:9; 13:10 (cf. 17). No wonder a frequentative tense, "they kept saying," opens v. 12. Regularly in the book, calls for repentance are cited as lost opportunities. Israel's last chance had come and gone. The book of Jonah was able to exploit knowledge of 18:7–11 and weave the passage with its explicitly international setting (*gôy*, "nation") into its narrative at Jonah 3:8–10. The passage became ammunition for the book's antichauvinistic campaign on behalf of the nations' reprieve from the prophetic proclamation of divine punishment if an opportunity for repentance was given and taken. Not only did the focus shift to the international reference, but a reverse argument was drawn from the passage. An olive branch of positive potentiality was held out, that a pagan nation might be treated in the same gracious way as Yahweh traditionally treated Israel (cf. Jonah 4:2). "Is God the God of Jews only? Is he not the God of Gentiles also?" (Rom 3:29).

[13–17] The second unit reinforces the first. It is an oracle of disaster whose poetry moves from reason (vv. 13–15) to announcement (v. 17) via an anticipation of disaster (v. 16). The redactional word, "Therefore," integrates it with the preceding unit. It builds on the closing declaration in v. 12 as a decisive reason for disaster and focuses on v. 17 as the expected announcement. The intervening verses now function as a recapitulation of the reason in v. 12, explaining the community's vague "schemes" and "bad attitude" as pagan worship. A clue to such interpretation is the recurrence of the verb "put into effect" (*ʿśh*, v. 12) in v. 13, looking ahead to the accusation of pagan worship in v. 15. It is also significant that the admission "It is hopeless" in v. 12 is related to such worship in 2:25. The present oracle has a number of links with ch. 2, and the shared admission in v. 12 presumably triggered its placement at this point.

[13] Emotional abhorrence frames vv. 13–16, first by way of a passionate reaction to Israel's wrongdoing and finally in the shocking v. 16. Verses 13–14 expand the reason for disaster, a rhetorical outburst that sets the tone for the precise accusation of v. 15 by exposing its heinousness. Verse 13 reads like a combination of 2:10 and 12, with its vehement vocabulary and claim that no other nation would commit Israel's religious crime. That crime is expressed in 2:11 in an indignant question about any nation ever changing its gods. The "nations," models of providential normality in vv. 7–10, are now presented as properly distant from Israel's religious abnormality. The epithet "virgin" refers to the community's ideal and honorable status under the patronage of Yahweh, a status that had been compromised by the unfaithfulness that v. 15 will openly broach.[103]

[14] "Does not nature itself teach" otherwise (1 Cor 11:14)? Here is another proof of Israel's horrendous innovation. The persistent snows that cap the Lebanon range and the permanent waters of the Jordan, itself fed from

---

103. John H. Walton, "*bĕtûlâ*," *NIDOTTE* 1:781–84, esp. 783.

Anti-Lebanon springs (cf. Ps 42:6 [7]), are object lessons of consistency; similar appeal was made to natural phenomena in 5:22 and 8:7.

[15] Israel, however, had become a law unto itself, defying traditional norms of exclusive religious loyalty. The charge of forgetting Yahweh recalls 2:32, which was echoed in 3:21 and 13:25. The imagery of abandoning the traditional journey of religious faith for inferior roads (cf. 6:16) reinforces and interprets "bad courses" (v. 11) and self-centered behavior (v. 12).

[16–17] Logic points to only one consequence. The emotional shrinking from the unheard-of crime in v. 13 culminates in a no less shocking reaction to Israel's fate. As often in the OT, the land is the barometer that registers Israel's spiritual relationship to Yahweh; its inevitable destruction marks a terrible nadir. Such logic is confirmed with an announcement of Yahweh's overwhelming intervention by military means, causing defeat and headlong retreat. As in 13:24–25, Yahweh's destructive power is compared with the east wind, scattering those who forget Yahweh. If the charge of v. 15 was meant to define the "bad behavior" and "attitude" of vv. 8, 10–12, the doom of vv. 16–17 spells out the "bad fate" of vv. 8, 11.

[18–23] This final unit is a poetic prayer of lament from Jeremiah, introduced by a redactional prose citation that explains his "opponents' talk" (v. 19). Both the introduction and the poem are important, yielding illustrations of, first, Judah's rejection of Yahweh (v. 12: "they kept saying," "schemes" against Yahweh; v. 18: "they said," "schemes" against Jeremiah) and, second, their "bad" response to Yahweh's "good" intent (vv. 10–12, 19–20). Verse 18 contains a separate allusive clue to this interpretation in that failure to pay attention to messages had Yahweh as its object and the people as subject in 6:19. The poem constitutes the next in the group of intermittent confessions. It is a psalm-like individual lament in which an initial general petition (v. 19) leads into a description of the enemies' misconduct in the form of a rhetorical question (v. 20a) and a profession of innocence introduced by a petition (v. 20b). A barrage of petitions for divine intervention (vv. 21, 22a, 23b) is interspersed with a pair of supporting statements, a motivation that reverts to the enemies' misconduct (v. 22b) and an affirmation of faith (v. 23a). The lament psalm tradition obviously provided a form of prayer that individuals could use to address God. In this case prophetic elements emerge in vv. 20b–22a, and the compositional meaning of the unit will take its cue from such elements. The poem breaks into two unequal sections, vv. 19–20 and 21–23, punctuated by "Therefore" in v. 21. The parallelism of "they have dug a pit" (vv. 20a, 22b), followed by divine "fury" or "anger" (vv. 20b, 23b), confirms this structuring.[104]

---

104. Cf. the fuller listing of parallels in Kathleen M. O'Connor, *The Confessions of Jeremiah: Their Interpretation and Role in Jeremiah 1–25* (SBLDS 94; Atlanta: Scholars Press, 1987), 55–56.

God and Prophet Ominously Rejected

[18] Jeremiah faces persecution due to his prophetic message. His prophesying of national doom made him an enemy of the religious establishment. Its three pillars—the priesthood, the wisdom movement, and the prophetic movement—now ironically stood as a solid bulwark in opposition to his stance (cf. Ezek 7:26). Elsewhere in the book Jeremiah's oracles pit him against a religious coalition committed in its ministries to upholding Judean society in its present form (e.g., 4:9; 5:31; 8:8–9). Here the coalition's supporters have turned on Jeremiah. His subversive prophesying is categorically denied, as by the community in 6:10, 17, 19; it is made the ground of a plot to silence him (Rudolph 124–25; cf. 11:19). The planned judicial indictment evidently constituted a threat to Jeremiah's life, as v. 23 states (cf. 26:10–11). McKane (437) observes that the introduction presupposes the poem and so did not intend to contradict it.

[19–20] The introduction moves with ironic smoothness into Jeremiah's prayer via the repetition of "pay attention." The repetition counters vigorous rejection of his prophesying with an appeal for divine vindication. To that end he pleads the injustice of the persecution, using a hunting metaphor, which is prominent in the Psalms (cf. Pss 35:7; 57:6 [7]; 142:3 [4]). The persecution was poor return for his own prophetic intercession on the people's behalf. Lament psalms often include the charge of receiving something bad after having acted in a good way (Pss 35:12; 38:20 [21]; 109:5); here it is given a prophetic twist, though interestingly at Pss 35:13 and 109:5 prayer is also cited as an example of earlier "good." A shift from goodwill to hostility marks the rest of the prayer, as elsewhere in the confessions.[105] Here virtual refusal of intercession leaves only judgment as an option.

[21–22a] Jeremiah's oracles of disaster concern his opponents. "What might seem to be a very personal vendetta is, in fact, a conformation of the prophet's words to the message of the wrath of God."[106] They and their families will find themselves caught up in the disaster that was to engulf Judah (cf. 17:18 and the commentary there).[107] Both civilians and soldiers related to them would suffer. They, in particular, had proved their liability for such prophetic judgment by their rejection of Jeremiah's oracles. "Therefore" is not characteristic of the lament psalm; it typically introduces an announcement of disaster in a divine oracle, and that sense is echoed here. At a more basic level death was to be their fate for plotting death (v. 23).

---

105. See n. 88 above on 17:18.
106. Terence Fretheim, *The Suffering God: An Old Testament Perspective* (OBT 14; Philadelphia: Fortress, 1984), 158.
107. Hans-Jürgen Hermisson, "Jahwes und Jeremias Rechtsstreit: Zum Thema der Konfessionen Jeremias," in *Altes Testament und christliche Verkündigung: Festschrift für A. H. J. Gunneweg* (ed. M. Oeming and A. Graupner; Stuttgart: Kohlhammer, 1987), 309–43, esp. 333. Kiss, *Klage Gottes*, 191–92, traces particular links with 11:21–23.

[22b–23] His opponents' entrapment tactics to this end were no news to Yahweh, who is implicitly urged to act upon that knowledge (cf. 15:15; 17:16). Such blatant opposition to a true prophet deserved punitive intervention. Yahweh's "time of anger" refers back to the coming disaster (vv. 21–22a) and compositionally to "their day of calamity" (v. 17). Prophetic intercession against such "fury" (v. 20b) had by now been forfeited. The time for it was definitely over, as for the community in general (cf. 7:16; 11:14). The vehemence of all these petitions is overwhelming. Peake (1:229) hoped that vv. 21–23 were redactional: "it would be a relief to think Jeremiah did not utter them." Baumgartner showed more empathy in claiming, "We have no right to turn the angry prophet into a gentle Christian theologian."[108] There is in fact another type of Christian theologian, represented in the NT itself, for example, at 2 Thess 1:6–10; Rev 6:9–10. Baumgartner's term "prophet" is significant, inasmuch as Jeremiah was daring to echo and apply the dire language and tone of God-given oracles of disaster out of sensitivity to his own representative role.

The punchline "deal with them" uses the Hebrew verb ʿśh, which ran as a refrain through the first unit, variously rendered "make, do, put into effect." The "bad fate" spoken by Yahweh (v. 8) is now in view. There was no option; the scheming against the prophet typifies the scheming against Yahweh in v. 12. In vv. 20 and 22 (Q) šûḥâ, "pit," provides a wordplay with nišḥat, "got spoiled," in v. 4.[109] The wordplay illustrates Israel's general deterioration, explained as "bad behavior" in v. 8. The rejection of Yahweh's spokesperson illustrates their rejection of Yahweh. The "bad" way Jeremiah was treated in v. 20 reinforces the community's own bad behavior in the first unit, which the second unit analyzed in terms of pagan worship. Moreover, the second unit defined divine reprisal as military invasion (v. 17), and in the third unit such invasion is spelled out in gruesome detail (vv. 21–22a). "Therefore" appropriately introduces such elucidation, as an echo of v. 13. Jeremiah's prayer of lament endorses the verdict of a bad fate, egging Yahweh on to implement it (cf. 6:11a). The introductory v. 18 adds the only new element. The community's scheming and bad behavior lay in the area of pagan worship, claimed the second unit. Now it is also claimed to lie in a nominal form of Yahwism, as the misguided attempt to support the religious establishment by opposing Yahweh's true witness reveals.

19:1–20:18 The Spurned Message and Messenger Once More

1 Here is what[a] Yahweh said: "Go and buy a potter's earthenware jug, along with[b] some of the elders of the people and the[c] priests. 2 Then go

---

108. Baumgartner, Poems of Lament, 58.
109. Philip R. Davies, "Potter, Prophet and People: Jeremiah 18 as Parable," HAR 11 (1987): 23–33, esp. 30–31.

God and Prophet Ominously Rejected

out to Ben Hinnom Valley just outside the Potsherd Gate and there make the announcement I am going to tell you. 3 You are to say: 'Listen to Yahweh's message, you kings of Judah and you residents of Jerusalem. Here is what Yahweh *Almighty*, Israel's God, said: "Look out, I am going to inflict on this site a bad fate that will set the ears of everybody who hears about it ringing. 4 The charges are that people have deserted me and treated this site as foreign by sacrificing to other gods in it, gods unknown both to them and to their forebears and also to Judah's kings, and they have filled this site with the blood of the innocent 5 and constructed shrines in honor of Baal for setting fire to their children *as burnt offerings to Baal*—something I never ordered *or mentioned*, something that never crossed my mind. 6 Therefore, look out, the time is coming," declared Yahweh, "when this site will no longer be called Topheth or Ben Hinnom Valley, but Slaughter Valley. 7 I will wreck[d] the planning of Judah and Jerusalem because of this site; at my direction they will fall by a sword in the presence of their enemies, at the hands of people who have designs on their lives. I will let birds in the sky and animals on the ground have their corpses for food. 8 I will make this city a shocking scene, a scene that makes people whistle. Every passerby will be shocked and react with whistling to all the damage it has suffered. 9 At my direction they will eat the flesh of their sons and daughters. People will eat one another's flesh because of the restrictions caused by the siege imposed by their enemies, *people with designs on their lives.*"' 10 Then you are to break the jug, witnessed by the men accompanying you, 11 and say *to them*: 'Here is what Yahweh *Almighty* said: "That is how I will break this people and this city. Just as when a pot made by a potter gets broken so much it can never be mended,[e] 12 that is the way I will treat this place," declared Yahweh, "and its residents too. I will make[f] this city like Topheth, 13 so Jerusalem's houses, including those of Judah's kings, become like the Topheth site—those that are defiled, namely, all the houses on whose roofs sacrifices have been made to all the heavenly bodies and libations have been poured out to other gods."'"

14 Jeremiah came back from Topheth, where Yahweh had sent him to prophesy, and stood in the court of Yahweh's temple and addressed all the people: 15 "Here is what Yahweh *Almighty, Israel's God,* said: 'Look out, I am going to inflict on this city and *all* its cities the sum total of the bad fate I threatened it with, because they have dug in their heels, refusing to listen to my messages.'" 20:1 Now Pashhur ben Immer, a priest who was chief administrator in Yahweh's temple, heard Jeremiah giving this prophecy. 2 *Pashhur* had *the prophet Jeremiah* beaten and put in the stocks[g] that were at the Upper Benjamin Gate at the temple. 3 *The next day* Pashhur released Jeremiah from the stocks and Jeremiah said

to him, "Not Pashhur but Terror-*everywhere* is the name Yahweh now gives[h] you, 4 because here is what Yahweh said: 'Look out, I am going to make you a terror to yourself and to all your friends. They will fall by their enemies' swords and you will be an eyewitness. Moreover, all Judah I will hand over to Babylon's king, who will deport them *to Babylon* and strike them down with a sword. 5 I will hand over all of this city's wealth, all its profits and valuables; even all the treasures of Judah's kings *I will hand over* to their enemies. They will *plunder them and carry them off, and* take them to Babylon. 6 As for you, *Pashhur,* you and all those who live in your house will go off as prisoners. Babylon is where *you will come. That is where* you will die and that is where you will be buried, along with all your friends to whom you have given false prophecy.""

7 You have shown me up as a fool,[i] Yahweh—and I let myself be fooled![j]
    You have overpowered me[k] and won.
  I have come to be a laughingstock all the time,
    derided by all.
8 Indeed, whenever I speak, I have to cry out;
    "Violence! Assault!" is what I shout,
  because Yahweh's message has brought me insults
    and scorn all the time.[l]
9 But if I decide, "I will not recall it[m]
    or speak anymore in his name,"
  it becomes *in my mind* a sort of blazing fire,
    it is trapped[n] in my very bones.
  I am tired of suppressing it,
    I cannot win.
10 The basis for this is that I have heard a lot of people talking,
    "'Terror everywhere'!
  Denounce him, let us denounce him!"
  All the folk I am on friendly terms with
    are the ones watching for me to slip up:
  "Perhaps he can be shown up as a fool, then we will win where
    he is concerned and have our revenge on him."
11 But Yahweh is with me, like a formidable champion—
    that is why my persecutors must falter
    and cannot win.
  They will be bitterly humiliated over their lack of success,
    permanently and unforgettably discredited.
12 And so, Yahweh *Almighty*, you who probe the innocent,
    you who can see conscience and will,

> let me see your vengeance on them,
> because you are the one I have disclosed my cause to.
13 Sing to Yahweh,
> praise Yahweh
> for rescuing the life of the poor person
> from the hands of people who behave badly!

14 A curse rests° on the day
> I was born.
> Let the day my mother gave birth to me
> not be celebrated as a blessed one!
15 A curse rests on the man
> who brought my father the news,
> "You have a son, a baby boy,"
> offering him warm congratulations.P
16 That man's fate will be like that of the cities
> Yahweh relentlessly overthrows.q
> He will hear shrieks in the morning,
> battle shouts at noontime
17 for not declaring me deadr alreadys in the womb,
> so my mother would have been my grave
> and her womb always pregnant.
18 Why ever did I exit the womb,
> only to see trouble and sorrow
> and have my days brought to a humiliating end?

a. LXX has "then" and adds "to me" (see *BHS*), interpreting the unit as Yahweh's response to Jeremiah's previous confession by associating "plotting/planning" (both $^{c}\bar{e}ṣ\hat{a}$) in 18:23 and 19:7 (Bourguet, *Métaphores de Jérémie*, 441–42).

b. Literally "and," coordinating loosely and tersely with what precedes. The ancient translations expanded for stylistic improvement (cf. *BHS*). Bourguet, *Métaphores de Jérémie*, 442, notes the difficulty of explaining how MT, if secondary, could have arisen.

c. Unlike LXX, MT inserts "elders of" by assimilation to the preceding phrase (*BHS*; Janzen, *Studies*, 41). For the phrase in MT cf. 2 Kgs 19:2.

d. See *HALOT* 1:150b.

e. LXX lacks MT's addition, "and in Topheth burials will take place as long as it has any room left for burying," which disturbs the train of thought. The marginal gloss is a slightly adapted version of 7:32b meant to qualify v. 6 (= 7:32a). It was realigned (and subsequently inserted) here because $^{c}ôd$, "(no) longer, (n)ever," occurs just before "Topheth" in both vv. 6 and 11. Cf. Janzen, *Studies*, 43. The insertion interrupts the second comparison, which continues into v. 12 (cf. 13:11).

f. For the construction cf. Joüon §124p.

g. Here and in 29:26 this is an approximate rendering for some such apparatus of punishment.

h. The perfect has a performative function (see Joüon §112f).

i. A factitive sense (see Joüon §52d), "show to be a fool," for the Piel of *pth* in v. 10 and correspondingly for the Pual here in v. 10 has plausibly been suggested by Rudolf Mosis, "Ez 14,1–11—ein Ruf zur Umkehr," *BZ* 19 (1975): 161–94, esp. 164; idem, "*pth*," *TDOT* 12:162–72, esp. 169–71.

j. The use of a Niphal, as distinct from the Pual as a passive in v. 10, suggests a reflexive sense (Holladay 1:552; cf. *HALOT* 3:984b–85a).

k. For the datival suffix see 1 Kgs 16:22; Holladay 1:552–53; Joüon §125ba.

l. See Cloete, *Versification*, 89–91, for the division of cola here and in vv. 14–15.

m. Thus REB; or "him," as the other EVV render.

n. The gender shows that the message, not the fire, remains the subject (McKane 1:473).

o. For the declaration of a fact here and in v. 15, as in 17:5, see Leo Prijs, "Jeremia xx 14ff.: Versuch einer neuen Deutung," *VT* 14 (1964): 104–8, esp. 105–6; Holladay 1:561. The wish in v. 14b expresses a consequence of the curse of v. 14a.

p. For the sense of the verb see Ehrlich, *Randglossen*, 4:294–95; McKane 1:486–87.

q. The Hebrew perfect either reflects a general experience or is prophetic. See the commentary.

r. Ehrlich, *Randglossen*, 4:295, suggested a declarative force for the Polel such as a Piel verb can have. Declaration of death then balances the declaration of birth in v. 15.

s. Literally "from" but in a temporal sense, "from the time when I was in" (Drinkard in Craigie et al. 277, 279). Cf. NJPS "before birth."

Yahweh's message of disaster was rejected and with it the prophetic messenger, declares the composition of 19:1–20:18. Jeremiah 19:15 plays a central role in the composition. That verse belongs in 19:14–20:6, and provides a fourfold nucleus for the three adjacent units, the preceding 19:1–13 and the following pair, 20:7–13 and 14–18. First, its divine announcement of disaster, "a bad fate" to be inflicted "on this city," reinforces 19:3, the inflicting of "a bad fate" on Topheth, a fate to be shared by Jerusalem, "this city" (19:8, 11, 12), because of pagan worship. Second, the new reason that is given for the community's downfall in 19:15, the refusal "to listen to" divine "messages" of prophecy, is related to "Yahweh's message" as the source of the prophet Jeremiah's persecution in 20:8. Third, "the bad fate" (*rāʿâ*) of 19:15 (and 19:3) is capped by the description of Jeremiah's persecutors as those "who behave badly" (*měrēʿîm*) in 20:13, a term that matches effect with cause. Fourth, the "cities" of Judah that were to be victims of the disaster in 19:15 are revisited in 20:16, "the cities Yahweh ruthlessly overthrows." So 19:15 acts as a hub for a compositional wheel. From it radiate stylistic spokes to all the other units, to 19:1–13 at the point of v. 3, to 20:7–13 at the two points of vv. 8 and 13, and to 20:14–18 at the point of v. 16. A coherent message emerges from the composition: Yahweh's announcement of disaster for Judah for its religious defection had a further ominous reason, the community's rejection of Yahweh's prophetic messages, a rejection that found tragic illustration in the confessions of the

God and Prophet Ominously Rejected

rejected prophet. The second, central unit, 19:14–20:6, illustrates a different kind of punishment meted out to Jeremiah by a temple official because he prophesied doom. Jeremiah's oracle in response spells out in concrete terms the nature of the disaster that would befall Judah. That disaster would consist of not only the siege and destruction of Jerusalem (19:7–9, 13), but of Jerusalem's sacking and Judah's exile to Babylon (20:4–6).

[19:1–13] The first unit depicts disaster for Jerusalem by means of symbolic action and metaphor and gives pagan worship as the reason. Yahweh issued a series of orders that may be literally presented as follows: "Go and buy . . . and go out . . . and make an announcement . . . and say . . . and break . . . and say." Divine speeches occur in vv. 3–9 and 11–13 after the twin orders "and say." Taken together, the speeches make up a complex oracle of disaster. It has a summary announcement of disaster in v. 3b, reasons in vv. 4–5, and two sets of announcements, one in vv. 6–9 introduced by "Therefore" and a supporting one in vv. 11–13a that concludes with a recapitulating reason in v. 13b. The unit also includes elements of a symbolic action report. The command to carry it out comes in vv. 1 and 10, and the interpretation in vv. 11–13, the second divine speech. Its execution is not reported, though v. 14 assumes it. The first divine speech (vv. 7–9) plays yet another role in the unit, to interpret the Hebrew term *baqbūq*, "jug," used in v. 1 as a metaphorical omen in its own right—apart from the symbolic action—by linking it by wordplay with the verb *bqq*, "lay waste, wreck," in v. 7. From these separate perspectives each divine speech describes the fate of the people and capital, the first in vv. 7–9 and the second in vv. 11–13. The first puts the blame on the practice of pagan worship in Topheth (v. 4) and the second on such worship in Jerusalem itself (v. 13); they have in common the key phrase "other gods." The destruction of Topheth (vv. 3, 6) twice becomes a model for the destruction of Jerusalem in vv. 12b–13. This means that in vv. 11–13 two comparisons of a different type are made, an interpretive comparison with the breaking of the jug in the symbolic action and an associative comparison with the destruction of Topheth predicted in v. 6.

The unit covers a lot of ground. Verses 3–9 reflect the language of the prose sermons that have punctuated the oracles in the book of Jeremiah thus far, and so they reveal themselves as a redactional supplement to the preexisting symbolic action report.[110] The supplement pushes Topheth to the fore. The core of the oracle is vv. 5–7, which incorporate material concerning Topheth from 7:31–33, part of an earlier prose sermon. Verse 8 has adapted the land-related material of 18:16 to Jerusalem. There is further evidence of intertextuality whereby other works are quoted: In v. 3b material from 2 Kgs 21:12 that originally related to Jerusalem and Judah, and in v. 4b material from 2 Kgs 21:16 and 24:4 that related to Jerusalem, are both reapplied to Topheth. In v. 7a Isa

---

110. See Stulman, *Prose Sermons*, 76–79.

19:3, "Egypt shall be drained (*wĕnābqâ*) of spirit, and I will confound its plans (*ʿăṣātô*)" (NJPS), appears to be compressed as the literary basis of the wordplay "I will wreck (*ûbaqqōtî*) the planning (*ʿăṣat*)." In v. 9 a covenant curse from Deut 28:53 is cited as due for fulfillment. After the redactional insertion of vv. 3–9, vv. 12b–13 with their two Topheth references were added to cement the oracle more firmly into place.[111] The overall intention of the redaction was twofold, to provide examples of pagan worship inside and outside the city and to detect in the distinctive word *baqbuq*, "jug" (v. 1), an omen that pointed to divine reprisal against Jerusalem. Thus the announcement of disaster in vv. 11–12a has been vigorously reinforced.

[**1–2**] The scene is set for the symbolic action of v. 10, the breaking of the jug. Its fragile nature is indicated by its specification as "earthenware." The jug, *baqbūq*, had a large spherical body and a narrow neck that caused a gurgling noise (glug-glug) as its contents were poured out, accounting for its onomatopoeic name. Verse 10 indicates that the invited group of significant people were to function as witnesses of the symbolic action and so auditors of its sinister interpretation (cf. the added "to them" in v. 11). The Potsherd Gate is mentioned only here; it must have been on the south side of the city. Its very name made it an appropriate place to create yet more potsherds. The reference to the adjacent Ben Hinnom Valley may be a redactional tie-in to v. 6, unless it simply encouraged the Topheth emphasis of the appended oracle. Originally the announcement referred to the interpretive oracle of vv. 11–12a that was to follow the symbolic action (cf. 18:2, 5), but it now introduces vv. 3–9.

[**3**] The vocatives are surprising after v. 1. They highlight the victims of the ensuing oracle. "Residents of Jerusalem" are the focus of v. 9 (and also v. 12) and "the city" is cited in v. 8. From the mention of "Judah and Jerusalem" in v. 7a and the national focus in vv. 4–5, 7b, one might have expected "Judeans" in place of "kings of Judah," and indeed LXX inserts "and men of Judah" between the vocatives of MT, but "kings of Judah" does anticipate the reference in v. 4 (also v. 13). It may also allude to the intertextual use of material in vv. 3b and 4b that originally referred to Manasseh's impious innovations. The epithet "Israel's God" in the quotation formula has particular relevance in view of the charge of worshiping "other gods" in v. 4. The element of shock in the summary announcement of disaster at Yahweh's hands corresponds to that near the end, at v. 8, so that an emotional frame is provided for the oracle.

[**4–5**] The religious practice of child sacrifice at Topheth is disowned. It is interpreted in theological terms as doubly wrong, involving desertion of Israel's traditional God and espousal of "other," non-Israelite "gods" (cf. 2:11, 13), and in moral terms as unconscionable (cf. Ps 106:38). The reference to "Judah's

---

111. Cf. the discussions of redactional growth in Gunther Wanke, *Untersuchungen zur sogenannten Baruchschrift* (BZAW 122; Berlin: de Gruyter, 1971), 8–13; McKane 1:451–56.

God and Prophet Ominously Rejected

kings" hints at the special relationship between Yahweh and the Davidic monarchy and at the impropriety of permitting such worship in the realm. "Other gods" are narrowed down to the archrival "Baal"; MT underscores this focus, which will be echoed in 32:35 (cf. 7:9; 11:13, 17 and the commentary on 2:23).

[6–7] Topheth's fate as a scene of military destruction and the horrendous scale of that destruction are sketched from 7:32a–33 and bridged by explicit reference to military casualties. It functions as an interpretation of the distinctive term *baqbūq*, "jug" (v. 1), a wordplay with *bqq*, "lay waste, wreck." The jug in Jeremiah's hands is regarded as an omen of Yahweh's nullifying the community's political policies by military means, in reprisal for the religious betrayal represented by Topheth.

[8–9] The phrase "Judah and Jerusalem" in v. 7 functioned as a headline. The fate of Judeans was the focus of the rest of v. 7, while vv. 8–9 turn to Jerusalem's fate. By reuse of 18:16 the disaster of the capital is portrayed, as if in a mirror, from the perspective of later spectators of its ruin. Then the harrowing conditions of Jerusalem under siege are depicted as a grimly ironic requital for the sacrificing of children (vv. 4–5; cf. Lam 2:20; 4:10).

[10–13] The symbolic action and its interpretation continue. The verb "break" (v. 11) connects with the noun *šeber* often used in the book, rendered "calamity" or "injury" or "wounds" (e.g., 6:14; 14:17). The interpretation develops the shared fate of "this people and this city" that vv. 7–9 have already broached to supply details lacking in vv. 11–12a. "This city" (v. 11) was given an anticipatory echo in v. 8. "This place," though the same Hebrew that was rendered "this [religious] site" in vv. 3–4, 6–7, now refers to the capital. In a nightmarish way Topheth and Jerusalem merge in a commonality of doom. The merging is justified by repeating the charge of worshiping "other gods" in v. 4 (cf. 7:18), the Topheth-related charge in v. 4, amplifying it with specific reference to defiling astral worship prevalent in Jerusalem (cf. 8:2 and commentary).

The unit in 19:1–13 has a basic role in the composition, to present in a vivid way Yahweh's announcement of disaster and to ground it in pagan worship.

[19:14–20:6] The second unit gives the rejection of Yahweh's prophetic messages as a confirming reason for coming disaster and portrays that rejection in terms of an official punishment of the messenger, a rejection that only seals Judah's fate. The unit consists of two oracles of disaster, one communal and the other individual, each prefaced with interconnected passages of narrative. But this ABA′B′ structure does not tell the whole story, because the A′B′ elements present an individual affirmation of the B element, the first oracle; the two parts of B are repeated in a reverse order of human rejection and divine reprisal. The introductory narrative in v. 14 presupposes the fuller, redactional form of vv. 1–13, with its mention of "Topheth." This structure strengthens the parallelism of the threat of "a bad fate" for Jerusalem, "this city," in v. 15 with the preceding oracle, where "a bad fate" (v. 3) for Topheth was extended to Jerusalem, "this city like Topheth" (v. 12). In turn MT has boosted the similarity of vv. 3 and 15 by its addition of the epithets "Almighty, Israel's God," to v. 15, after adding "Almighty" to v. 3.

[19:14-15] This oracle concerning the temple is a prelude to the detailed sequel of 20:1-6. The oracle consists of an announcement of disaster and an appended reason; both use language found in prose sermons. The reason is not the same as the one in vv. 3-13; it represents a typical second stage in the book of Jeremiah, the rejection of prophetic oracles of disaster, whereas acceptance could have averted or at least postponed the disaster. So the oracles in 19:1-15, taken together, refer to the two stages of divine revelation: torah and prophets. The unusual combination, "this city and all its cities," recurs in 34:1 in the form "Jerusalem and *all* its cities." There LXX gives an exegetical rendering for the second phrase, "the cities of Judah." "All" here in MT is borrowed from 34:1.

[20:1-2] The narrative illustrates the refusal to listen to Yahweh's messages by the punishment of Jeremiah as messenger. The addition of "the prophet Jeremiah" in MT after "Jeremiah giving this prophecy" (cf. 19:14) heightens the connection between message and messenger. Pashhur, head of temple security, expressed this refusal by a flogging and a stay—for a night according to MT—in the stocks (cf. 29:26). The Upper Benjamin Gate was evidently a temple gate on the north side, differentiated from the Benjamin Gate in the city wall (37:13; 38:7) because it stood at a higher elevation. "For the first time in the prose narrative, the persecution of the prophet appears outside the confessions."[112]

[3-6] Like Amos responding to the priest Amaziah (Amos 7:16-17), Jeremiah announces Yahweh's doom-laden name for Pashhur in acknowledgment of his new role as catalyst of terror. The oracle is a sustained announcement of disaster; the reason was by now self-evident, though a fresh reason is introduced at the end. Pashhur, by his active refusal to listen to Jeremiah's messages, had caused an onslaught of disaster to be unleashed. At Yahweh's behest a sinister solidarity was to spread throughout his environment, affecting "all" of Pashhur's "friends," "all Judah," "all" of Jerusalem's "wealth," "all his household," and, sealing the circle, "all" his "friends" again. His friendship was to be a kiss of death, his social importance a blight on Jerusalem's material prestige, and his home at the top of a list for rounding up Judean deportees. Eventually he himself would die, like his friends, in a distant land. Behind the exuberance of "all" with double reference to the friends seems to lie a sense of some suffering one fate and some another (Peake 1:241). For the first time in the book the anonymity of Judah's military foe is discarded and free mention is made of Babylon and its king. The threat of invasion and exile is brought disturbingly closer by the disclosure of a concrete power and person. From now on in the book Babylon would be explicitly used by God. Surprisingly in closing the

---

112. O'Connor, *Confessions*, 144.

priest Pashhur is charged with a new accusation, of being an agent of false prophecy. His implicit message of peace was to be rudely contradicted by bloody invasion, capture, and permanent exile. Rejection of Yahweh's message and true messenger could not be perpetrated with impunity.

[7–13] The third unit is the first of the final pair of Jeremiah's confessions. The pair illustrates in graphic and emotional terms the community's rejection of the messenger, while the former unit in broaching Jeremiah's vindication alludes to the inevitable disaster that rejection incurs. From start to finish the first unit takes the shape of an individual lament psalm.[113] In a direct address, "Yahweh" introduces a description of divinely caused distress in which Yahweh is primarily the subject (v. 7a). Personal distress is described at greater length in vv. 7b–9, where first person verbs predominate.[114] The role of enemies in the distress comes to the fore in v. 10. A cluster of affirmations of faith is interspersed with a related assurance of vindication and a petition (vv. 11–12). The lament closes with an anticipatory thanksgiving (v. 13). As in earlier confessions, the lament psalm has been adapted by the incorporation of prophetic references, notably in vv. 8–9. The resulting poem is marked by a threefold structure. The pivot of the poem is v. 10, whose initial $kî$ ("For," NRSV) signals a basis for vv. 7–9, which redefines the negative human situation of v. 10 in divine terms. If v. 10 is presupposed in vv. 7–9, it is countered in vv. 11–13 by the grouping of positive elements. Again the human situation of v. 10 is redefined, but now positively. The $wāw$ adversative ("But") that begins vv. 11–13 typically marks a transition in lament psalms.[115] The key word of the unit, ykl, rendered "win," tracks the unit's development of thought in a fourfold usage. The enemies' hope of winning in the pivotal v. 10 is echoed in the frame of vv. 7–9 by the admission of Yahweh's winning through taking the enemies' side (v. 7) and by Jeremiah's frustrated conclusion, "I cannot win" (v. 9).[116] However, vv. 11–13 open with the counterassertion that Jeremiah's enemies "cannot win," since Yahweh was really on his side.

One reason why the unit has been placed alongside the previous one is because of the shared term "terror" in vv. 3–4, 10, which operates as a catchword. Indeed, MT has underscored the match by adding "everywhere" to v. 3, in line with v. 10. The parallel does not so much identify the unit's situation with the Pashhur incident as see in that incident an illustration of the sort of crisis reflected in the poem, so that the poem invests the narrative with typicality.[117]

---

113. Cf. David J. Clines and David M. Gunn, "Form, Occasion and Redaction in Jeremiah 20," *ZAW* 88 (1976): 390–409, esp. 391–92.

114. Westermann, *Praise and Lament*, 182; Bak, *Klagender Gott*, 189–90.

115. Cf. Westermann, *Praise and Lament*, 70–74.

116. Norbert Ittmann, *Die Konfessionen Jeremias: Ihre Bedeutung für die Verkündigung des Propheten* (WMANT 54; Neukirchen-Vluyn: Neukirchener Verlag, 1981), 173 and n. 605.

117. Polk, *Prophetic Persona*, 157–58.

Another reason is the echo of "my messages" (19:15) to be heard in "Yahweh's message" (20:8). Jeremiah is an example of the ominously rejected prophetic revelation.

[7a] Blame is laid at Yahweh's door for the human opposition Jeremiah was encountering. Yahweh is accused of taking his persecutors' side and being behind their attacks. Complaining psalms of lament typically interpret God as actively involved against the lamenter.[118] A close parallel to v. 7 as a whole occurs in Ps 44:13–14 (14–15), "You have made us the taunt of our neighbors...." No less than a cruel providence was at work, collaborating with Jeremiah's adversaries. This "most unkindest cut of all" expresses the worst of his distress. Sometimes a sexual connotation is assigned to the verbs rendered "shown up as a fool" and "overpowered," with the senses of "seduced" (NJB) and rape. The verbs can be so used, but "to suppose that such a contextually determined usage carries overtones into other passages is to commit the error of 'illegitimate totality transfer.'"[119] Moreover, since v. 7a is intended as an extrapolation of v. 10, the first Hebrew verb, *pth*, there in the passive and rendered "be shown up as a fool," must be used here in a sense compatible with that usage. What is envisioned in terms of a malicious scheme that may or may not happen (v. 10) is here vehemently portrayed as having already materialized in the experience of being discredited, which Jeremiah proceeds to describe. He has even now been brought into an intolerable and belittling situation, and ultimately it must be Yahweh's work of victimization.

[7b–9] The report of distress changes its focus to the personal hurt Jeremiah was suffering while functioning as a prophet. The personal element was already anticipated in "and I let myself be fooled." The vehement tone of v. 7a continues in (the repeated) "all the time," "all," "whenever," and in the extreme metaphor of "burning fire." The topic of prophesying comes to the fore, implicit in "speak" (*ʾădabbēr*) and explicit in Yahweh's "message" (*dĕbar*) and the phrase "speak in his name." Oscillation between second person divine references (vv. 7a, 12) and third (vv. 8–9, 11, 13) occurs often in lament psalms (e.g., in Psalms 42–43). Here the special bond between Yahweh and Jeremiah as prophet brings a new dimension to the lament form.[120] The universal and unremitting ridicule of v. 7b is explained as the reaction to Jeremiah's prophesying (cf. 6:10). There is external parallelism in v. 8; "Violence! Assault!" is Jeremiah's response to intimidating public abuse that always followed his prophesying.[121] "Violence" (*ḥāmās*) is a Hebrew exclamation of distress (Hab

---

118. See Broyles, *Conflict of Faith and Experience*, 76–78.
119. D. J. A. Clines and D. M. Gunn, "'You Tried to Persuade Me,' and 'Violence, Outrage!' in Jeremiah xx 7–8," *VT* 28 (1978): 20–27, esp. 21, citing James Barr. Cf. O'Connor, *Confessions*, 70–71.
120. Cf. Baumgartner, *Poems of Lament*, 75.
121. Cf. Clines and Gunn, "You Tried to Persuade Me," 25–26.

1:2; Job 19:7) like "Fire!" or "Help!" in English; here and in 6:7 it is reinforced with "assault." The cry reflects the intensity of his adversaries' attacks. Is it intended as an appeal to God, which it is explicitly in Hab 1:2? If so, it anticipates the positive turning to Yahweh in vv. 11–12 and highlights the tension of an appeal to God against God. Receipt of a divine oracle evidently brought with it a compulsion to declare it, and so silence was not an option (cf. 6:11). Fire in one's bones signifies a fever in an individual lament psalm (Ps 102:3 [4]; cf. Job 30:30), but in this prophetically charged lament the reference is to intolerable mental pressure, as the addition of "in his mind" in MT helpfully clarifies (cf. Luke 24:32). "The Lord GOD has spoken; who can but prophesy?" (Amos 3:8; cf. Acts 4:20; 1 Cor 9:16). So Jeremiah is "damned if he does" prophesy "and damned if he doesn't" (Holladay 1:558).

[10] The core of the problem, which was extrapolated in divine terms in v. 7a and in personal terms in vv. 7b–9, is now presented in this description of social opposition to Jeremiah. The motif of ridicule develops into plotting; the two are juxtaposed in lament psalms, for instance Ps 31:11, 13 (12, 14). Indeed, the first two cola of v. 10 recur in Ps 31:11 (12). Which influenced the other is difficult to say, though "terror everywhere" is characteristic of the book of Jeremiah (6:25; 46:5; 49:29). The phrase functions as a dismissive quotation, referring to Jeremiah's oracles of disaster—"Yahweh's message" in v. 8—and in particular to the invading foe that was often prominent in them, as in 6:25. In the present editorial context, however, the phrase is meant to hark back to the related new name for Pashhur in v. 3 and its explanation in v. 4. The addition of "everywhere" in MT (v. 3) makes the connection clear. The vehemence expressed earlier recurs in the size of the opposition ranged against Jeremiah and its inclusion of "all" of his friends. Further poignancy comes from the involvement of the latter (cf. 12:6). They watch him like a hawk, planning to use his oracles or ordinary speech against him in an incriminating way by denouncing him to the authorities. Jeremiah has emerged as a loser, under attack from his human constituency that feels threatened by him and, as he argued earlier, from his supposed divine patron.

[11] Jeremiah rebounds with surprising resiliency. The surprise is minimized when one realizes that the lament psalm genre by its very nature presupposes the tradition of divine rescue from crisis. Nevertheless the mixture of the complaint feature (v. 7a) and the barrage of affirmations of faith (vv. 11–12) is unusual (cf. Ps 10:14, 16 in a complaint psalm).[122] There is probably an echo of the divine answer to an earlier confession in the fresh beginning and the ending of this one; this echoing helps to explain the shift to optimism. In 15:20–21 (cf. 1:19) Yahweh gave the qualified promise, "Defeat you [or "win where you are concerned," Hebrew *ykl* again] they will not because I will be there with

122. Cf. Broyles, *Conflict of Faith and Experience*, 41–42.

you. . . . I will rescue you from the hands of bad folk and . . . the ruthless (ʿărîṣîm)." Here rendered "formidable," ʿārîṣ is now provocatively used of Yahweh, who is more than a match for all their hostility. So the tables would eventually be turned. They would "falter" instead of Jeremiah's slipping up (v. 10) and be humiliated after deriding Jeremiah; the two motifs belong to the same semantic field. Like a psalmist, he speaks of his "persecutors," as in 15:15; 17:18.

[12] This verse occurred in an earlier confession (11:20) in a somewhat different form. Here there is a sharper focus on Yahweh's mind-reading ability.[123] The material does fit snugly here, with "vengeance" completing the contextual reversal by picking up the close of v. 10. And the petition for Yahweh's intervention supplies requisite underpinning for Jeremiah's assurance of vindication in v. 11. Yahweh is now portrayed not as military champion but as omniscient judge who can see beyond a facade to motivation. The praise has an edge, as repetition of the verb "see" indicates. There is an appeal for Yahweh to live up to a reputation for justice in Jeremiah's particular case. Divine "vengeance" is not to be taken in a vindictive sense. As in the Psalms, it connotes a welcome restoration of the rule of justice (cf. Ps 94:1–3).[124]

[13] This call for others to offer praise would be more obviously at home at the end of a thanksgiving psalm that celebrated the resolution of a crisis (cf. Ps 32:11). It could have an anticipatory role after a lament prayer had been assured of an answer, as in Ps 22:23 (24). Here it expresses Jeremiah's conviction of eventual vindication in line with his earlier affirmations of faith. There is a close parallel in the lament of Psalm 64, if the interpretation of admittedly difficult Hebrew in NRSV and NIV (cf. NJPS) is correct. There confident claims of Yahweh's future intervention (64:7–9 [8–10]) are followed by an exhortation to others to share the psalmist's thanksgiving (64:10 [11]). The double reference to "Yahweh" matches that in vv. 7–8 and so brings closure to the unit (Drinkard in Craigie et al. 271). "Poor" is a spiritual metaphor for a lack of resources to cope with a crisis apart from divine help, as often in the Psalms (e.g., Ps 37:14). It reverts to the distress of vv. 7b–10 at the hands of human enemies and so provides further closure for the piece. It is possible that the Hebrew plural imperatives imply public proclamation of the confession, and the third person references to Yahweh earlier may point in the same direction.[125]

[14–18] This separate unit is the last of Jeremiah's confessions. At first sight it is disconcertingly pessimistic, but the theme of the composition is rejection. The two curse formulations of vv. 14–17 provide a preparatory expansion for the punchline of the unit (v. 18). The unequal parts are hinged by "womb"

---

123. See Michael Carasik, "The Limits of Omniscience," *JBL* 119 (2000): 221–32, esp. 225–26.
124. See Erich Zenger, *A God of Vengeance? Understanding the Psalms of Divine Wrath* (trans. Linda M. Maloney; Louisville: Westminster John Knox, 1996).
125. Cf. Clines and Gunn, "Form, Occasion and Redaction," 400–402.

(*mērehem*, lit. "from the womb"). Although v. 18 does not directly address Yahweh, it laments Jeremiah's personal crisis, like vv. 7b–9, here prefaced with a "why" reminiscent of psalm complaints.[126] In the Psalms the question is generally used in a description of divinely caused distress, but one may compare Ps 43:2, "Why must I walk about mournfully because of the oppression of the enemy?" McKane (1:482–84) has outlined the four elements the unit shares with Job 3, ascribing them to a common literary convention: an opening curse relating to the day of birth (v. 14; Job 3:3–10), the announcement of birth (v. 15; Job 3:3), fatality in connection with the birth (v. 17; Job 3:11, 16), and a protesting "why" at being born for a wretched life (v. 18; Job 3:20–26). A frame for the unit is supplied by "day(s)." Jeremiah's "days" of misery may all be traced back to the "day" of his birth as their prerequisite. "My mother" fittingly frames vv. 14–17.

[14] In an earlier confession, 15:10, which functions as a lament prayer inasmuch as it elicits a divine reply in 15:11–12, Jeremiah regretted he had ever been born. He went on to ground his lament in the communal rejection he was facing. Here, in a chiastically constructed pair of bicola, there is the same negative focus on his birth as in 15:10a. The anniversary of his birth date was by no means to be celebrated each year as a happy birthday. As v. 18 will indicate, however, "the real issue . . . is not Jeremiah's birth but his life" as a prophet.[127]

[15–17] The chiastic structure of v. 14 is echoed in the second curse of v. 15;[128] the content of and reason for this curse are added in vv. 16–17. The focus shifts to a close-up, a particular incident associated with the birth event. The congratulatory messenger of new life ironically created for himself a sword of Damocles that would eventually cause his own death. Unwittingly he was setting himself up for such a fate, quite unaware that the baby would grow up to announce the disaster of the whole community.[129] Verse 16b echoes the martial language in Jeremiah's oracles of disaster (4:19; 6:4; 15:8) and so specifies in terms of military invasion the general, divinely instigated destruction mentioned in v. 16a. The hapless messenger was to find himself caught up in urban destruction. He would be involved in the collapse of Judah's cities (cf. 4:16), after the daily bombardment of enemy attack. "Like" is used of an experience in common, as in 19:12b. "He is representative of all those who later encountered [Jeremiah's] message and are the objects of the judgment" (Jones 276). There is hardly room for the allusion to Sodom and Gomorrah that is generally seen in v. 16a; it spoils the contextual flow of both the unit and the composition (cf. Fretheim 296–97). The irony of vv. 15–16 is maintained in v. 17. The bad

---

126. As in the Psalms, *lāmmâ* underlies "why"; see n. 22 above on 12:1–4.
127. O'Connor, *Confessions*, 76.
128. Diamond, *Confessions*, 116.
129. Prijs, "Versuch," 106–7.

news of a dead fetus would have prevented Jeremiah's ministry of doom and saved the news bearer's life.

[18] As in 15:10b, Jeremiah's despair is evidently grounded in the community's rejection of his messages of disaster. It reflects "the full extent of this rejection."[130] He was stuck in the middle, between Yahweh's oracles of ruthless destruction and a community that resented them, refusing to accept them as true. "The whiplash of the poem falls . . . upon the people and their stubborn will" (Hopper in Hyatt and Hopper 976). Jeremiah's protest sounds at first like that of Habakkuk, "Why do you make me see wrongdoing and look on trouble [ʿāmāl, as here]?" (Hab 1:3). Habakkuk was complaining about Yahweh's nonintervention to deal with a corrupt society. Yet the trouble in Jeremiah's case was not an objective breakdown of society but the subjective factor of his unbearable persecution that was threatening his own life.[131] So his expostulation is like that in Psalm 31, in a context of social ridicule: "My life is spent [the same root *klh*, rendered here "brought to an end"] in sorrow [*yāgôn*, as here] and my years in sighing" (Ps 31:10 [11]).

The juxtaposition of the last two units (vv. 7–13 and 14–18) throws into relief the negative perspectives of vv. 7–10 and the final unit. Room is left for the positive material of vv. 11–13, but it recedes to a secondary role. Passionate focus is laid on Jeremiah's role as a rejected prophet, even while his prophetic vindication and Yahweh's own eventual vindication in support of the prophet by wreaking disaster are affirmed. The rejection of the messenger of Yahweh's destruction is reflected through the mirror of Jeremiah's cry of despairing pain. These two units have a function similar to that of an oracle of disaster, one that first moves from reason to announcement and then returns to the reason in order to spell out beyond all doubt the justification for the disaster.

21:1–24:10 Doomed Kings and Discredited Prophets

21:1–22:9 Doom for Court and Capital

21:1 A message Jeremiah received from Yahweh when King Zedekiah sent to him Pashhur ben Malkiah and the priest Zephaniah ben Maaseiah with the request, 2 "Consult Yahweh for us about the attack on us by King *Nebuchadnezzar* of Babylon. There is a chance Yahweh will do *in our case* something on the lines of all his wonders, making him retreat and leave us alone." 3 But Jeremiah told them: "Here is what you are to tell Zedekiah: 4 'Here is what Yahweh, *Israel's God,* said: "Look out, I am going to divert the weapons in your hands, which you are using to combat *Babylon's king and* the Chaldeans who are besieging you outside the

---

130. Clements, "Jeremiah 1–25," 101.
131. O'Connor, *Confessions*, 76–79.

wall, *and I will move them* to the interior of this city. 5 I will attack you myself with outstretched hand and strong arm, in anger, fury, and extreme rage!^a 6 I will strike down the residents of this city, animals along with people, by means of a severe pestilence, which will be fatal.^b 7 Next," declared Yahweh, "I will hand King Zedekiah, together with his officials and the people—any^c in this city who survive pestilence, sword, and famine—over *to King Nebuchadnezzar of Babylon and* to their enemies *and to* people who have designs on their lives. He will strike them down with the edge^d of the sword, without showing them any clemency, mercy, or compassion. 8 As for this people, you should tell them: 'Here is what Yahweh said: "Look, I am presenting you with a way to live and a way to die. 9 Any who stay in this city will die from sword, or famine, *or pestilence*, while any who leave and desert to the Chaldeans who are besieging you will survive, getting away with just their lives. 10 The explanation is the attitude toward this city I have adopted, a bad one instead of a good one," *declared Yahweh*. "Babylon's king will have it handed over to him, and he will burn it with fire." ' "

11 On the theme of:^e Judah's royal house

Listen to Yahweh's message, David's house. 12 Here is what Yahweh said:

"Pass verdicts with justice in the morning
   and rescue robbery victims from oppressors' hands,
or else my fury will flare up like fire
   and burn out of control."^f

13 "Look out, I am your opponent, you who are enthroned over the valley,
    you rock in the plain,"
declared Yahweh,
"you folk who claim, 'Who can come down against us?
    Or who can get into our homes?'
14 *But I will deal with you as your behavior warrants,"* declared Yahweh.^g
"I will light a fire in her forest
    that will consume the entire area around her."

22:1 Here is what Yahweh said: "Go down to the palace of Judah's king and there give this message. 2 You are to say: 'Listen to Yahweh's message, Judah's king, occupant of David's throne—you, your ministers, and other staff members^h who are coming through these gates. 3 Here is what Yahweh said: "Carry out just and right policies. Rescue robbery victims from oppressors' hands. As for resident aliens, orphans, and widows, you are not to exploit or physically abuse them. The blood of the innocent you are not to spill in this place. 4 The reason why is that if you do carry out these policies, then kings of David's line occupying his throne will continue to come through the gates of this palace on horse-drawn chariots—each king, his ministers, and other staff. 5 But if you do not listen to these instructions, I swear by my very self," declared Yahweh, "devastation will be the fate of this palace."' 6 The explanation is that here is what Yahweh said about the palace of Judah's king:

"As Gilead I appreciate you,
    as Lebanon's summit.
I swear I will turn you into a desert,
    an area of ghost towns.
7 I will assign[i] agents of your destruction,
    each equipped with his tools,
who will cut down the best of your cedars
    and throw them on the fire.

8 "So people from *many* other nations, passing by this city, will ask one another, 'Why did Yahweh do such a thing to this great city?' 9 'It was because they abandoned the covenant with Yahweh, their own God,' they will say, 'and worshiped other gods and committed themselves to them.'"

    a. The longer text of MT is to be preferred to the two nouns of LXX; cf. the discussion of Janzen, *Studies*, 43.
    b. The coherence of the sentence requires fresh punctuation and reading with LXX *wāmētû*, "and they will die" (Ehrlich, *Randglossen*, 4:296; cf. *BHS*).
    c. It is necessary to delete *wĕʾet*, "and," with LXX and other textual witnesses (see *BHS*); it was added by assimilation to the previous phrases. EVV, apart from NIV and NJB, concur. The phrase develops the reference in v. 6 to residents dying of the plague by adding other ills.
    d. This is the traditional interpretation; cf. *HALOT* 3:914b and references; Lundbom 2:104–5.
    e. Unlike LXX, MT prefaces with "and," wrongly construing v. 11 as a continuation of v. 8, with the sense "and to Judah's royal house (say)," and understanding Zedekiah and his court to be the addressees, like v. 3. As in 23:9, a superscription for 21:11–23:8 is intended, as NAB, REB, NJB, and NJPS interpret. However, the sense of *lāmed* is not "to," as they translate, but "concerning." The parallel heading in 23:9, which has the same preposition, is rightly rendered "concerning" (NAB, NJPS), "on" (NJB), or "of" (REB).
    f. MT adds "in reaction to their bad activities," a marginal comment, as the third person suffix indicates, which was subsequently taken into the text. It was derived from the similar 4:4. Q has changed to a second person suffix to match the context.
    g. MT has borrowed from 23:2, thus encouraging the expansion in v. 12 above (cf. Janzen, *Studies*, 44). The verb *pqd*, rendered "deal with" here, is translated "take care of" there.

h. See McKane 1:516.
i. REB renders lit. "consecrate" and NJB "dedicate," but a faded expression is generally seen here and also earlier in 6:4, following the lead of LXX.

The first unit opens with an oracle reception heading that regularly begins a new block of material. The next will appear in ch. 25, and so chs. 21–24 are demarcated as a block. The block consists of two collections of oracles, one royal (21:11–23:8) and the other attacking Jeremiah's prophetic rivals (23:9–40). The collections have been set in an editorial prose frame, 21:1–10 and 24:1–10.[132] Both parts of the frame are explicitly related to Zedekiah's reign and provide a terrible description of the results of the Babylonian invasion in 588–587 B.C.E. His reign would end with Yahweh's handing over Jerusalem to be destroyed by "pestilence, sword, and famine" (21:7) and by the dying off of Judah's populace by divinely sent "sword, famine, and pestilence" (24:10). There is deliberate polarization between the two parts of the frame, in that Yahweh's "bad," rather than "good," attitude to the city (21:10, "I have set my face against this city for evil and not for good," NRSV) is matched with Yahweh's looking out for the good of the earlier exiles (24:6, "I will set my eyes upon them for good," NRSV).

The outer frame of the block is linked with the intervening pair of collections in four ways. First, the collection of royal oracles reinforces the initial announcement of the fall of Jerusalem and its court with two damning reasons, a disregard for the Davidic tradition of social justice and a refusal to heed either torah traditions or prophetic warnings. These reasons are supplemented with a third, in a redactional oracle (22:8–9), the worship of pagan gods in Jerusalem. Second, within the other collection the message of the rival prophets is summed up as promising "peace" and denying the "bad fate" predicted by Jeremiah (23:17), a fate that was to be the consequence of Yahweh's "bad attitude" announced in 21:10. So in reaction the divine "fury" and "anger" of 23:19–20 reinforce 21:5. The prophets' own claims are discredited by their immoral lifestyle and amoral messages, while their general claim to truth is vigorously countered with an insistence that truth rests in Jeremiah's representation of Yahweh. Third, both 21:1–10 and 24:1–10 show signs of editing as prose sermons, but the same is true of 22:1–5. In each case sermon language has been inserted into earlier material. In 21:5–9 destruction at Yahweh's hands is vehemently intensified, while in 24:6–7, 9–10 both divine judgment and grace are accentuated. In 22:2–4 there is a focus on Yahweh's demand for social justice as an underlying reason for divine judgment. Fourth, the divine grace to those taken into exile (24:6–7) develops throughout the block. The motif of exile is mentioned alongside that of destruction of the homeland. It is the fate of all of

132. Thiel, *Redaktion von Jeremia 1–25*, 230, 260.

Judah's kings in 22:22 and specifically of Jehoahaz in 22:10–12 and of Jehoiachin ("Coniah") in 22:26, 28. The exile of the people is broached in 23:1–2; vv. 3–4 continue this motif with the promise of return, prosperity, and good government. Jeremiah's forecast of restoration of good monarchy in vv. 5–6 has been integrated with this promise. The prospect of the people's return from exile and diaspora is celebrated in vv. 7–8. It is upon this foundation that the positive summary of 24:6–7 builds. It follows renewed mention of exile in 24:5, for which the exile-related addition "right away from my presence" in MT at 23:39 has paved the way. The generalized tone with which the block treats the topics of exile and return has the effect of blurring the specificity of the reference to the exiles of 597 in 24:5 and loosely regarding them as covering the exiles after 587, despite the insistence of v. 10. Moreover, the doom-laden reference to the Diaspora (24:9) is not meant to be taken as God's last word in view of 23:8. Radical and final judgment was eventually to be trumped by postjudgment grace, as in 13:14b (cf. 12:15).

The literary core of the next three compositions in 21:1–23:8 is a collection of poetic royal oracles, which has its own heading at 21:11; a fresh collection, relating to prophecy, will be introduced in 23:9. There are three indications that the first collection has been supplemented with other material. First, it has been prefaced with a different sort of oracle, a prose and only partially royal one, in 21:1–10; second, a nonroyal oracle in prose has been inserted in the middle (22:8–9; the royal prose oracle in 22:1–5 is a further addition); third, another nonroyal one has been added at the end (23:7–8). These additions provide clues to the compositional structuring. The first composition consists of 21:1–22:9. An older group of royal oracles has been supplied with a new beginning and ending. A third composition, evidently 23:1–8, has been capped with a new conclusion. That leaves 22:10–30 as the second composition, with attention to three consecutively reigning kings. Two cases of stylistic repetition are important. First, all three compositions place a premium on the royal attributes of "justice" and "right" (22:3 [in a supplementary unit; cf. "justice" by itself in 21:12], 13, 15; 23:5). Second, the first two compositions have similar references to kings occupying David's throne (22:5 [in a supplementary unit], 30) and the first a reference to "David's house" (21:12), while the third mentions a king of David's line (23:5). The three compositions are interrelated further by various patterns of alignment. The first one is set apart from the next two by its own key word "fire," while the third is distinguished from the first two by its mainly positive perspective after the complete negativity of the others. The first two both have metaphorical references to "Lebanon" (22:6, 23 [and a literal one in v. 20]) and "cedar(s)" (22:7, 14–15, 23), and the last two contain oracles introduced by "Woe betide" (22:13; 23:1). Enough of the stylistic material falls into a sectional format in the core collection of oracles to suggest that the redactor recognized three existing sections, one in 21:11–14 and 22:6–7, a longer one in 22:10–30, and a short one in 23:1–6, and developed them further.[133]

The first composition is made up of six units, 21:1–10 (actually two interrelated oracles), 11–12, 13–14, a pair of oracles consisting of 22:1–5 plus vv. 6–7, and vv. 8–9. The key word of the composition is "fire." It sounds a recurring and strident note, occurring in 21:10, 12, and 14 and once in the pair of oracles, at 22:7, in each case in a climactic position. The closing unit does not have it, but instead provides a frame for the composition by echoing "this city" (22:8, twice) from the opening unit, where it is found no less than five times (21:4, 6, 7, 9, 10), with reference to Jerusalem. The oracle in 21:13–14 also has Jerusalem wholly in view. The combination of royal court, capital, and fire creates a lurid impressionistic picture for the composition. Further discussion of its structure awaits the exegesis of 22:1–5.

[21:1–10] This unit was inserted as a preamble to the collection of royal oracles and to the block of chs. 21–24, in particular to the first composition. The oracle conveniently contains the composition's key word "fire," though it refers to the king only in v. 7. In advance it provides the reader with the assumption of a negative response to the exhortations (v. 12 and 22:3) and it paves the way for the later messages of destruction (22:5, 6–7); in these ways it creates coherence for the composition. Moreover, its focus on Jerusalem ("this city") spells out the dire implications of royal policy for the capital and elucidates the presence of the unit concerning Jerusalem (21:12–13), as well as finding an echo in the closing unit (22:8–9). The unit of 21:1–10 includes two interrelated oracles, vv. 4–7 and 8–10, each introduced with a quotation formula. The first is set in a narrative report of a response to a royal inquiry, like 37:3–10, a passage that relates to a later stage of the siege, while the second is a message to the people in Jerusalem ascribed to the same setting. The setting is given by the repeated phrase "the Chaldeans who are besieging you" (vv. 4 and 9). At the LXX stage of the text the unit was framed by "Babylon's king" in vv. 2 and 10. However, a more intricate pair of frames has been created in MT, using "King Nebuchadnezzar of Babylon" in vv. 2 and 7 to wrap the request and reply together and "Babylon's king" in vv. 4 and 10 to encompass the two oracles. The open identification of the enemy as the king of Babylon in 20:4–6 continues here, with

---

133. Mention should also be made of the pervasive use of the Hebrew verb *yšb*, basically "sit." Two cases occur in the supplementary first unit of the first composition, rendered "residents" and "stay" (21:6, 9). The first two compositions are also marked by double use of the verb at 21:13 (rendered "enthroned") and 22:4 ("occupying," in a supplementary unit) in the first composition and at 22:23 ("perched") and 30 ("occupying") in the other; the second of the first two instances (22:4) appears to copy the final case (22:30). The presence of *yšb*, "reside," in a supplementary unit of the third composition at 23:8 in MT is accordingly fitting, over against the recensional variant at 16:15 and in LXX at 23:8.

added reference to the Chaldeans; the former is now further identified as Nebuchadnezzar in MT. Of course, from a historical perspective, one expects such openness. The use of an oracle from Zedekiah's reign, despite oracles relating to earlier kings later in the royal collection, provides a fitting introduction to the theme of the downfall of the court and capital that terminated his reign.

The beginning of a literary block tends to be marked by a prose sermon, and this block is no exception. In this case characteristic vocabulary is concentrated in vv. 5–9.[134] Some have argued that older material can be detected within vv. 4 and 9,[135] and v. 7 must have been uttered before the fact. The passage may be regarded as a makeover of Jeremiah's own prophesying. One feature of the makeover is the incorporation of texts from Deuteronomy. Verse 5 echoes the triple phrasing of Deut 29:21, while v. 8 contains a virtual parody of Deut 30:15, 19, offering an option not of a richly blessed life but of mere survival.

[1–2] A chronological setting for the unit in the reign of the last Judean king, Zedekiah, will be made more precise by the reference to the Babylonian siege of Jerusalem (588–587 B.C.E.; vv. 4 and 9). Such a setting highlights the crisis for the Judean monarchy and capital. Jeremiah, as Yahweh's mediatory channel, is asked by Zedekiah via an official delegation that represents royal and religious interests to request a divine oracle, which is duly given and passed on in the prophet's response in vv. 3–7. History was here repeating itself, doubtless by royal design; over a century before, Hezekiah had sent a similar delegation to the prophet Isaiah at the time of an Assyrian blockade of the capital (2 Kgs 19:1–4; Isa 37:1–7). A proclamation of salvation is politely requested. Some hope is entertained of Yahweh's miraculous intervention on Judah's side, in line with a tradition of saving events, doubtless including the sparing of Jerusalem recorded in 2 Kings 19 and Isaiah 37. The name "Pashhur" provides a loose link with the previous block of material (18:1–20:18), though referring to a person different from the priest of 20:1–6. The priestly delegate, Zephaniah, has the same role in 37:3 and is also mentioned in 29:25, 29, and evidently 52:24, while his partner reappears in 38:1 (in MT at least).

[3–6] Jeremiah offers no comfort. Instead he passes on an oracle that announces disaster. The military "attack" (v. 3) is brusquely endorsed by news of Yahweh's own "attack," to which it was the prelude (v. 5). There is also a bitterly ironic echo of the tradition of divine salvation, in the use of the double phrase "with outstretched hand and strong arm," which has associations of Yahweh's positive intervention in the Deuteronomistic exodus tradition (e. g., Deut 4:34; 1 Kgs 8:42). There, however, the adjectives are reversed, "with strong hand and outstretched arm." The present order appears to be influenced by the phrase "outstretched hand" used in a refrain in Isaiah (Isa 5:25; 9:12, 17, 21 [11,

---

134. See Stulman, *Prose Sermons*, 79–81.
135. Thiel, *Redaktion von Jeremia 1–25*, 233, 236.

Doomed Kings and Discredited Prophets 241

16, 20]).[136] Now Yahweh would side with the enemy. While the Babylonians ("Chaldeans") were conducting the siege from outside, Yahweh would be at work inside, bringing about death-dealing "pestilence" in the besieged city. The oracle lacks any reason for the disaster; other units later in the composition will fill this gap. For now the composition concentrates on the disaster. Zedekiah spoke as representative of the Jerusalem community in saying "us" (v. 2), and the Hebrew plurals for "you" and "your" in the response at vv. 4–5 have the same role. The oracle starts in v. 4 with a dramatic omen of defeat. Weapons now aimed at the enemy would end up in useless piles inside the fallen city, having been surrendered by defending troops.[137] Yahweh's achievement of this about-face is perhaps meant as an ironic use of the motif of disarmament in the Zion tradition (cf. Pss 46:9 [10]; 76:3 [4]). So v. 5, with its bad news of Yahweh's fighting on the enemy side, looks backward and forward, backward to the divine agency of military defeat in v. 4 and forward to that of the complementary outbreak of pestilence among the civilian population in v. 6.

[7] The note of Yahweh's surrendering the people is now sounded more plainly, as the penultimate blow for the survivors after pestilential siege—to be followed by postvictory massacre. While Zedekiah's wistful hope of a miracle in v. 2b was countered in vv. 4–6, now his wish that the Babylonian king would withdraw is challenged.[138] In MT "He" is elucidated with a precise antecedent. The royal surrender and death are an important reason why this unit has been placed at this point, as a preface to royal oracles. A much longer story is told about Zedekiah's eventual end (39:4–7; 52:7–11), a story that makes room for a promise of royal survival (34:1–5), but this prediction, which, as Jones (279–80) observes, can hardly have originated after the fact, functions as a rhetorical flash of premonition concerning the king's fate in enemy hands, one from which he was literally spared, doubtless to his own regret. The triple reference to Nebuchadnezzar's ruthlessness matches that to Yahweh's anger (v. 5) as its human outworking in a powerful closure.

[8–10] This supplementary oracle, which originally was probably independent of the first, offers a means for bare survival, but says nothing about escaping deportation. Yahweh addresses it to Jeremiah, rather than through him to the delegation, as a message to be transmitted to the besieged commoners. It focuses on the fate of the capital. Desertion offered the only chance of survival, so dire was Jerusalem's doom. In MT the addition of "pestilence" ties this oracle more closely to the previous one (vv. 6–7), in particular to the triple means

---

136. Helga Weippert, "Jahwekrieg und Bundesfluch in Jer 21:1–7," *ZAW* 82 (1970): 396–409, esp. 399 n. 20.

137. The apparent ambiguity in MT—as to whether "them" refers to the Chaldeans or the weapons—does not arise in the shorter text of LXX, which MT clarifies.

138. Karl-Friedrich Pohlmann, *Studien sum Jeremiabuch* (FRLANT 118; Göttingen: Vandenhoeck & Ruprecht, 1978), 35 n. 95.

of death in v. 7. "Fire," the catchword of the composition, is the unit's last, ill-omened word.

[11–12] The second unit is the first of an older collection of royal oracles, whose heading has been preserved. The prophet transmits a brief but categorical call for justice to mark the verdicts delivered by the palace. The call is backed by a severe warning of divine reprisal. However, in the collection's new context the oracle is transformed into a virtual oracle of disaster, made up of reason and announcement. "Fury" now harks back to the certain retribution of v. 5, while "fire" has become the second case of a compositional catchword and gives a theological basis for the literal "fire" of destruction grimly promised in v. 10. So this second unit reinforces the first. The exhortation supplies a reason for its announcement of disaster, while the warning echoes that announcement.

The vocative phrase "David's house" deliberately recalls not only the dynasty represented by the present king, who is left unidentified, but also its traditional obligation to uphold justice among the community. Holladay (1:575) has compared Isaiah's ironic use of the same vocative in addressing faithless Ahaz in Isa 7:13. The plural imperatives in the Hebrew (vv. 11–12) refer to the king and the members of his administration assigned to judicial duties (cf. 22:2), who are regarded in the present context as typical of a series of reigns (Jones 284; cf. 22:22; 23:2). Earlier in the book "justice" was widely used as a general virtue of social ethics, but now it is traced back to the Davidic king's prime responsibility in his judicial role. That responsibility was a feature of ancient Near Eastern royal ideology, which Israel shared (cf. 2 Sam 8:15; 15:1–6; 1 Kgs 3:28; Ps 72:1–4, 12–14). Evidently there were or should have been regular morning sessions in which cases were heard by the king or his representative (cf. Jer 22:2–3), to which 2 Sam 15:2 and Ps 101:8 refer (cf. Zeph 3:15). After a general exhortation a particular crime is mentioned by way of example, as in Isa 61:8, the crime of robbery (*gzl*), that is, misappropriation of another's property by open force.[139] "Oppression" (ʿ*šq*) is a wider term referring to exploitation. The failure of the Davidic judge to remedy such social wrongdoing must ignite an inferno of divine reprisal.

[13–14] At first sight this odd oracle has no claim to be included in a royal collection, apart from the catchword "fire" it shares with its fellows. Its right to belong is derived from the feminine singular participle *yōšebet*, which means not "inhabitant" (NRSV), like the plural in v. 6, but "enthroned one" (Weiser 1:182, followed by a number of later commentators; GNB mg.). It refers to Jerusalem as the royal city. The unit takes the form of an announcement of disaster for the city at Yahweh's hands. It reinforces the message of the downfall of Jerusalem in the first unit and functions as a firm announce-

---

139. Cf. the discussion of Jacob Milgrom, *Cult and Conscience* (SJLA 18; Leiden: Brill, 1976), 89–102.

ment of disaster after the quasi-reason in v. 12a, thus backing up the quasi-announcement in v. 12b.

[13] The oracle is introduced by a formula of hostile orientation, "Look out, I am your opponent," whose note of challenge is maintained in the vocative phrases and clauses that express a false sense of security. Defensibly surrounded by valleys on three sides (cf. 31:40; Isa 22:7), Jerusalem felt safe from all attack. Its seemingly impregnable position is verbalized by the rhetorical questions of its citizens in further vocative expressions. Does the unusual verb "come down" have the sense of coming down from the north?[140]

[14] MT has regarded the fresh set of vocatives, now plural, as incomplete and rounded them out with a prose statement of punishment with plural pronouns, inspired by 23:2. The closing references to Jerusalem are expressed in the third person after the intervening address to its citizens. "Forest" is best taken literally, as a reference to the wooded area that once surrounded Jerusalem (cf. Neh 8:15), as the parallelism suggests (McKane 1:513). As in v. 10, "fire" was to be the instrument of aggression, now wielded not just by Nebuchadnezzar but by the divine enemy who stood behind him.

[22:1–5] This prose unit presents a demand for royal justice (v. 3) backed by an incentive (v. 4) and a deterrent (v. 5). Verse 3 contains a repetition of the example given earlier at 21:12, while the venue of the oracle, the palace (*bayit*), looks like a reinterpretation of the "house" (*bayit*) in 21:11–12, where it had the sense of dynastic representative. The unit also constitutes a prose sermon that shares language with 7:2 in v. 2, 7:6 in v. 3, and 17:25 in v. 4.[141] This evidence suggests that the unit predominantly represents a literary revamping of 21:12 that maintains the perspective of exhortation, widens the call for social justice, and undergirds it with alternatives that spell out the serious consequences (in general agreement with 17:24–25). Exhortation now functions as a literary device to indicate that a wrong choice had already been made and spells out the terrible consequences that such a choice entailed. This was the redactional role of 21:12, but in this case such exhortation constitutes the basic meaning of the secondary unit. The question arises why the unit was not set immediately beside its source. Stylistic structuring supplies the answer. There appears to be a chiastic ordering, ABABA, in which the central Jerusalem-focused unit of 21:13–14 matches 21:1–10 and 22:8–9, both of which deal with "this city," while the royal units of 21:11–12 and 22:1–5 + 6–7 are interposed. This means that, though the heading of a collection of royal oracles has been preserved in 21:11, the backbone of the composition has as its main theme the fall of Jerusalem, while the issue of monarchy plays a supporting role.

---

140. Cf. *DCH* 4:284b; Godfrey R. Driver, "On ʿlh, 'Went Up Country,' and yrd, 'Went Down Country,'" *ZAW* 69 (1957): 74–77.

141. See Stulman, *Prose Sermons*, 81–82.

[1] The order to "go down" to the palace presupposes reception of the oracle in the temple area (cf. 26:10; 36:12; Rudolph 137). Did this detail preface the oracle of 21:11–12 at an earlier literary stage or is it a redactional embellishment? Mention of the palace introduces a keynote for this unit. "This palace" will occur in vv. 4–5, and "these gates" in v. 2 refer to palace gates. The keynote will carry over as the topic of the accompanying unit, vv. 6–7, as "the palace of Judah's king" (v. 6) announces, reprising the phrase here in v. 1. However, "this place" in v. 3 must refer to Jerusalem, anticipating "this city" in v. 8 and recalling "this city" in the first unit, 21:1–7.

[2] This is a longer version of "Listen to Yahweh's message, David's house," in 21:11–12. Now not simply the palace is in view, but the organizational network of the royal administration that controlled the affairs of the community. The catalog explains the plural imperatives of 21:11–12.

[3] Whereas in 21:12 the judicial wing of royal government was in view, here a much broader perspective is presented, rule according to the ethical virtues of justice and right.[142] These social virtues were binding on any member of the covenant nation and as such have appeared before in the book (4:2; 9:24 [23]). They are a cardinal feature of the composition and will recur in v. 13 and 23:5. The particular positive detail of checking robbery is maintained, but accompanied by negative demands borrowed from 7:6a—neither to take advantage of underprivileged members of society nor to use execution as an immoral political or economic tool. These demands are similar to the royal duties outlined in Ps 72:12–14 and Ezek 45:9. In the context they represent a lost opportunity.

[4–5] The options of 17:24–27 recur here, now more precisely related to the continuance of the monarchy and the fate of the palace that was its material symbol. They function in the context as yesterday's alternatives, already decided and leaving a foregone conclusion. "The time for a positive choice has passed" (Brueggemann 196).

[6–7] This poetic oracle explains and develops the foregoing prose unit, specifically the climactic devastation of the palace in v. 5, as the prose introduction to the poetry infers with its opening Hebrew conjunction ("For," NRSV) and its resumption of the language of v. 1. The introduction defines the palace as the rhetorical addressee. The oracle is an announcement of divinely instigated disaster with a short form-critical expansion in the first bicolon, "As . . . summit," which presents a contrast with the palace's existing splendor. No reason is given in the oracle, but the reader is meant to extrapolate one from the previous unit. Here is the fate of royal injustice.

---

142. Cf. Moshe Weinfeld, "'Justice and Righteousness'—*mšpṭ wṣdqh*—The Expression and Its Meaning," in *Justice and Righteousness: Biblical Themes and Their Influence* (ed. H. Graf Reventlow and Y. Hoffmann; JSOTSup 137; Sheffield: JSOT Press, 1992), 228–46. Cf. Lundbom 2:119: "the covenant at issue is the Sinai covenant."

[6a] The divine compliment invites comparison with the description of the significant other in Song 5:15: "His appearance is like Lebanon, choice as the cedars." In the case of the palace the overlap between subject and symbol includes a material factor, the lavish use of cedar in its construction (cf. v. 14; 2 Sam 7:2; 1 Kgs 7:11–12), wood felled in the forest of Lebanon (1 Kgs 5:6 [20]). Moreover, there may be an allusion to the name of one of the buildings in the palace complex, "the House of the Forest of Lebanon" (1 Kgs 7:2). Gilead too was known for its dense forests in ancient times (cf. 2 Sam 18:6, 8). All such magnificence would be lost.

[6b–7] In a terrible reversal the devastation would strip the grand buildings, city landmarks, from the extensive palace area, leaving an empty space where each had stood. The woodcutters, who, in the composition, hark back to the Chaldeans of the first unit, were to wield their axes at Yahweh's command and chop down the fine wooden structures like so many trees. As in the first, second, and third units, "fire" is the terrible climax.

[8–9] The final unit provides another reason for the fall of Jerusalem. Failure to maintain the standards of the Davidic dynasty had previously been to blame (21:12; 22:3), but now the practice of pagan religion is added to the indictment, an accusation often leveled earlier in the book. A question-and-answer format is used (as in 5:19; 9:12–16 [11–15]; 16:10–13), and it closes the composition with a definitive flourish, as in the first two cases. However, whereas in the other examples future prophetic answers were given to Judeans' questions, here aliens are envisioned as posing and answering the question.[143] The setting of the destruction of Jerusalem in 21:10, 14 is presupposed in the question, while the destruction of the palace in 22:5, 7 is assumed to entail that of the capital. It is hardly fair to claim that here "an image of ravaged Jerusalem sits uneasily in its royal company."[144] The composition has deliberately set royal material into a wider message of doom for the capital.

Like the earlier cases, this prose supplement appears to be of exilic origin. It has parallels with Deuteronomistic literature: Deut 29:24–26 (23–25) and 1 Kgs 9:8–9; the reference is extended to foreigners in Deut 29:22, 24 (21, 23). Not content with ethical and royal accusations, the unit pairs them with the religious sin of pagan worship committed by the community at large, a sin that amounted to the breaking of Yahweh's covenant. It is worth asking whether the epithet "Israel's God" appended in MT at the start of the composition (21:4) was meant to be a framing device that anticipated and lent extra weight to this closing charge of extreme gravity. The unit is similar to an oracle of disaster, mentioning first the disaster and then the reason for it, though Yahweh is mentioned in the third person. The intent of the order of first disaster and then reason is to

---

143. See Long, "Question and Answer Schemata," 129–32.
144. Ibid., 129.

make a claim of theodicy for Jerusalem's fall, insisting that it amounts to fair punishment for a sin of equal seriousness.[145]

The composition in 21:1–22:9 has used royal oracles as the basis for a proclamation of the fall of Jerusalem. Both the capital and the court were doomed. The reason was twofold: first, the royal disregard of social ethics, whether binding on the king as the upholder of justice (21:12) or equally applicable to the community at large (22:3); and, second, the communal practice of pagan religion (22:9).

22:10–30 Further Doom for Court and Capital

10 Do not shed any tears over the one who is dead,[a]
    do not grieve over him.
  Shed tears instead[b] over the one who has gone away,
    because he will never come back again
    or see his native country.[c]

11 Here is the warrant, what Yahweh said about *King* Shallum ben Josiah *of Judah*, successor to his father Josiah, who left this place: "He will not come back to it[d] again, 12 but the place he has been deported to is where he will die and this country he will never see again.

13 "Woe betide you,[e] whose palace building is marked by lack of right,
    whose building of penthouses is marked by injustice,
  in getting your countrymen to work for nothing,
    in failing to pay them their wages,
14 you who assert, 'I want to build myself an extensive palace
    with spacious penthouses,
  which has wide windows[f] cut out for it
    and cedar paneling
    and vermilion paint'![g]
15 Does it make you a king, your competing in cedar?
    Your father ate and drank, didn't he?
  But he demonstrated justice and right;
    then it went well for him.
16 He defended the cases of the poor and needy;
    then it went well.
  That is what knowing me means, isn't it?"
    declared Yahweh.[h]

---

145. Thomas M. Raitt, *Theology of Exile: Judgment/Deliverance in Jeremiah and Ezekiel* (Philadelphia: Fortress, 1977), 90–94.

17 "But the only things your eyes
  and mind focus on are your selfish gain,
 spilling the blood of the innocent,
  and engaging in oppression and in crushing people."

18 Therefore here is what Yahweh said about King Jehoiakim ben Josiah of Judah:

"Nobody will lament him,
 'So sorry about my brother,
 so sorry about my[i] sister.'
Nobody will lament him,
 'So sorry about my[i] sovereign,
 so sorry about his royal majesty.'
19 A donkey's burial is what he will be given—
  dragged away and dumped
  well outside Jerusalem's gates.
20 "Climb Lebanon and shout,
  then in Bashan call at the top of your voice,
 and shout from Abarim,
  over the shattering of all your lovers.
21 I warned you in your time of prosperous ease—
  you said, 'I will not listen.'
 That has been your attitude from your youth,
  never to listen to what I say.
22 All your shepherd-kings will be shepherded away by the wind,
  while your lovers will go off as prisoners.
 Then you will certainly experience shameful humiliation
  in return for all your bad behavior.
23 Perched in Lebanon,
  nesting among the cedars,
 how loudly you will groan[j] when you encounter anguish,
  pain like that of a woman in labor!

24 "By my very life," declared Yahweh, "I swear[k] that King Coniah ben Jehoiakim of Judah will not be the signet ring on my right hand—I will wrench you off. 25 I will put you in the hands of people who have designs on your life, *in the hands of* people you are afraid of, *in the hand of King Nebuchadnezzar of Babylon,* in the hands of the Chaldeans, 26 and hurl you and your mother, the woman who bore you, into the country[l] where neither of you was born and both of you will die. 27 But the country they long to come back to will never witness their return."

28 Is he a despicable, broken pot,
    this man Coniah?ᵐ
    Is he an unwanted jar?
    Why else has heⁿ been hurled out and flung
    to the country he never knew?
29 Country, country, country,
    listen to Yahweh's message!

30 *Here is what Yahweh said:*

"Record this man as childless,
    a male who will have an unsuccessful life.°
The reason is that none of his children will be successful
    in occupying David's throne
    and ruling Judah anymore."

a. External parallelism suggests repointing with the article, with some ancient support; see *BHS*. EVV so presuppose.

b. The infinitive absolute reinforces the contrast, as EVV (apart from GNB) recognize; cf. *IBHS* 586–87.

c. For the ellipsis whereby "never again" carries over, see Francis I. Andersen and David N. Freedman, *Hosea* (AB 24; Garden City, N.Y.: Doubleday, 1980), 189–90; Lundbom 2:130; cf. GKC §152z. For the cola division rather than that of *BHS* in this verse and vv. 17a, 18b, see Cloete, *Versification*, 191.

d. Literally "there," reflecting the perspective of the exiled king.

e. For the vocative understanding of the participles here and in v. 14, see Waldemar Janzen, *Mourning Cry and Woe Oracle* (BZAW 125; Berlin: de Gruyter, 1972), 21–23, 72; Delbert R. Hillers, "*Hôy* and *Hôy*-Oracles: A Neglected Syntactic Aspect," in *The Word of the Lord Shall Go Forth: Essays in Honor of David Noel Freedman in Celebration of His Sixtieth Birthday* (ed. C. L. Meyers and M. O'Connor; Winona Lake, Ind.: Eisenbrauns, 1983), 185–88; GKC §144p.

f. The suggestion of Barthélemy, *Critique textuelle*, 2:637, is noteworthy, that *ḥallônāy* here and in 1 Kgs 6:4 means a row of windows, with a noun ending -*ay* (cf. GKC §86i).

g. REB and NJPS extend the quotation thus far, taking *qāraʿ*, here rendered "has cut out," as indefinite and referring *lô* not to the king but to the palace ("for it") (thus McKane 1:528).

h. For a discussion of LXX variants in vv. 15–16, 18, see McKane 1:529–30, 532. For the closing monocolon in v. 16 cf. Watson, *Classical Hebrew Poetry*, 171–72.

i. The earlier suffix does double and triple duty (so David N. Freedman, referred to by Janzen, *Mourning Cry*, 72 n. 109).

j. See *BHS*. EVV so understand the verb, apart from NJPS and GNB; see the discussion of Barthélemy, *Critique textuelle*, 2:640–41.

k. For the construction see NEB; McKane 1:540–41; Holladay 1:605. The initial oath formula suggests that an oath follows.

Doomed Kings and Discredited Prophets 249

l. MT ungrammatically adds "another," which LXX lacks. It originated as a marginal annotation, reflecting Deut 29:28 (27) (McKane 1:545; cf. Thiel, *Redaktion von Jeremia 1–25*, 243).

m. The shorter text of LXX in the latter part of v. 28a*a* (cf. *BHS*) appears to be accidental (Janzen, *Studies*, 119); the earlier term ʿeṣeb, "pot," may have been omitted because the translator did not know what it meant. For the poetic nature of the unit cf. Cloete, *Versification*, 138, who finds many textual problems in v. 28 and restricts the poetry to vv. 29 and (apart from the quotation formula) 30; Holladay 1:608–9. NAB, NRSV, NJB, and NJPS all regard it as poetry.

n. MT supplements the shorter text of LXX with "he [explicit pronoun] and his children" and then makes the verbs plural. The phrase probably originated as a marginal comment that took its cue from v. 30b, explaining that the king's children could not occupy the Judean throne because they too were exiled.

o. Omission of the relative clause in LXX was probably due to parablepsis (*HUB*; Holladay 1:609).

This composition reaffirms that court and capital must fall and again offers the reasons. Made up of five units, the composition has retained the collection's exclusive focus on Judean royalty, unlike the former one. It presents in order oracles associated with three consecutive kings, Jehoahaz, Jehoiakim, and Jehoiachin. The composition has evidently taken over a distinct section in the collection, with the topic of exile constituting a sinister frame in the first unit, vv. 10–12, and in the final three units in vv. 20–30. There is a close stylistic parallelism between the first unit and the last pair, the repeated use of ʾereṣ, "country," with overtones of exile (vv. 10, 12, 26–29). This peripheral focus on the form disaster will take is counterbalanced by a central accent on the reasons for it, in the course of the units in vv. 13–19 and 20–23. An overlap in this ABA structuring occurs not only in the notes of disaster present in the middle units but also in the precise repetition of the Hebrew verb hšlk, rendered "dumped" in v. 19, at v. 28, where it is translated "flung." First Jerusalem, then Judah would have no room for their royalty. MT has made a compositional feature of royal names and titles. "King Jehoiakim ben Josiah of Judah," a prose element in the second unit (v. 18), and "King Coniah ben Jehoiakim of Judah" in the prose fourth unit (v. 24) have been supplemented with "*King* Shallum ben Josiah *of Judah*" in the first (v. 11) and capped with grim eloquence by "*King Nebuchadnezzar of Babylon*" in the fourth (v. 25). There was no place for such kingly formality in the third unit, which is concerned with Jerusalem and owes its presence to royal allusions. Its presence does make the composition a good match for the former one, with a similar concern for the doom of capital as well as court.

[10–12] The first unit begins with an admonition from the prophet, one that introduces a prose divine oracle. "Shallum" is another name for Jehoahaz; it appears in the Davidic genealogy at 1 Chr 3:15 and the latter was evidently his throne name, which was little used since his reign lasted only three months (2 Kgs 23:30–31). Public mourning over the shocking death of his popular father, Josiah, must have been intense, as a tradition preserved in 2 Chr 35:24b–25 attests. Yet even greater grief is counseled on behalf of Josiah's exiled son, his youngest, to whom the focus of communal popularity had shifted, only to be disappointed. The historical setting is clear, the period when Jehoahaz, Judah's choice to succeed Josiah, was forcibly detained in Riblah in north Syria (609 B.C.E.) and then exiled to Egypt at the hands of Judah's new and temporary overlord, Pharaoh Neco. "He took Jehoahaz away; he came to Egypt, and died there" (2 Kgs 23:34; cf. Ezek 19:4).

[13–19] This oracle of disaster concentrates on a double presentation of the reason for it in vv. 13–17 and adds a briefer announcement of coming disaster in vv. 18–19. The oracle takes the form of a woe saying. The exclamation, "Woe" (NRSV), here rendered "Woe betide" with REB, introduces the reason with a sharp note of protest and, perhaps, one of foreboding that anticipates the disaster explicitly stated in the latter part. Both sections of accusation (vv. 13–14 and vv. 15–17) refer to justice and right. In vv. 15–16 there is an expansion that heaps on blame by means of an unfavorable comparison with Josiah; it is demarcated by a closing quotation formula. The announcement is formally introduced in v. 18 by a redactional prose sentence. Like v. 11, it helps the reader by identifying the royal addressee of the oracle as Jehoiakim, who was the successor of Jehoahaz, and his father (v. 15) as Josiah.

[13–14] The king is addressed in vv. 13–17, though vv. 18–19 use the third person, which may suggest that they were originally separate. He is taken to task for conduct unbefitting a member of the covenant nation. The virtue of justice (cf. v. 3 and commentary) had not been a feature of his rule, and his fellow countrymen or "neighbors" (NRSV) had been the victims of this failure. "In Israel the king and his carpenter were 'neighbours'" (Nicholson 1:186). The great example of this lack of solidarity with his own people is the building and remodeling program he undertook for the royal quarters. First, it was achieved by forced labor that was uncompensated and claimed as a fiscal right. Second—and here the prophet offers a quotation as an ironic comment—it was marked by ostentation and self-aggrandizement, as Jehoiakim built for himself a lavish palace. Frescoes seem to be in view in the last colon (Carroll 427; Lundbom 2:137–38 with reference to Ezek 23:14).

[15–17] This section addresses the issue of proper royal rule. As a counterblast to Jehoiakim's extravagance, another model is affirmed, that of his father, Josiah. The figure of Josiah haunts the first two units; dead and alive he was a difficult king to follow. Certainly he was not abstemious; he enjoyed a good standard of living. But, unlike his son, he displayed neighborly qualities. For a king, as head of the judicial system, that meant ensuring fair trials and in particular seeing that the case of the underdog did not go unheard (cf. Isa 1:23)

Doomed Kings and Discredited Prophets 251

nor was mishandled (cf. Prov 31:8-9 in a royal context). The bare bones of this section consist of a repeated verb and a contrasting pair of nouns in inverse order, AB+B'/C+C'A, *wĕʿāśâ mišpāṭ ûṣĕdāqâ*, "and he demonstrated justice and right," in v. 15, and *wĕʿalhāʿōšeq wĕʿal-hamměrûṣâ la ʿăśôt*, "and on oppression and on victimization to demonstrate (them)," in v. 17. The latter case is prefaced with claims of single-minded obsessiveness and of "selfish gain" and manslaughter; the final charge evidently involves injustice beyond the building projects. By contrast, Josiah is held up as an example of proper rule. The way he served the community as king illustrates what it means in practice to "know" the moral will of God (cf. 9:24 [23]; 1 John 2:3-4; 4:8).

[18-19] The aftermath of Jehoiakim's death was to be marked by a double reversal of the ostentation he had indulged during his life. First, his corpse would be accorded no proper burial with its ritual cries of *hôy*, "woe, alas" (here rendered "So sorry"; cf. 34:5). The absence of any *hôy* in a funerary sense balances in an ironical play the *hôy* of the prophetic woe saying in v. 13 that anticipated coming disaster. "Jehoiakim's situation calls for a *hôy* now . . . because there will be no *hôy* later."[146] The reference to "my sister" is not clear. Is the funeral of the queen mother envisioned as taking place at the same time? Or are condolences offered to her at her son's funeral? The mourning is presented at two levels, grieving for a fellow member of the community (cf. 1 Kgs 13:30) and for a person of royal rank, as in Jer 34:5. Jehoiakim lived up to neither role. Second, instead of a decent burial the king is promised dishonorable exposure of his corpse. A "donkey's burial" is an oxymoron, for a donkey would not be buried.[147] It was an epitaph the king deserved. Jeremiah predicts a similar end in 36:30, which at least shows that "he meant what he said" (Jones 291). The record in 2 Kgs 24:6 is silent on this point and gives no hint of anything untoward, though the account given of his reign is very brief.[148]

[20-23] The Hebrew feminine singular references throughout this unit are addressed to personified Jerusalem. Three elements earned it a place in the collection of royal sayings, the reference to "shepherds" in the sense of kings (v. 22), the palace associations of "Lebanon" and "cedars" (v. 23, as in vv. 6-7), and the near-repetition of *yōšebet*, "enthroned," of 21:13 in *yōšabtî* (Q *yōšebet*)

---

146. Janzen, *Mourning Cry*, 72.
147. Watson, *Classical Hebrew Poetry*, 313.
148. The expression "sleep with one's ancestors" refers to a natural death, not burial; see Nicholas J. Tromp, *Primitive Conceptions of Death and the Nether World in the Old Testament* (BibOr 21; Rome: Pontifical Biblical Institute, 1969), 169-71; Thomas H. McAlpine, *Sleep, Divine and Human* (JSOTSup 38; Sheffield: JSOT Press, 1989), 145-46. The LXX of Chronicles, in a supplement apprently derived from a Hebrew text of Kings, intriguingly adds to 2 Kgs 24:6a, "and he was buried in the garden of Uzza with his ancestors" (2 Par 36:8), on the general lines of 2 Kgs 21:18, 26. Cf. Oded Lipschits, "Jehoiakim Slept with His Fathers . . . (II Kings 24:6)—Or Did He?" *Journal of Hebrew Scriptures* 4 (2002): 1-33.

(v. 23), though it now means "perched," reflecting an avian metaphor. So Jerusalem functions as the royal capital. The oracle fits well with compositions celebrating the doom of royal court and capital. Verses 21–22 follow the pattern of an oracle of disaster, giving first the reason and then the announcement. The expansions at beginning and end (vv. 20, 23) frame the oracle with reactions of lamentation to be expressed by Jerusalem. "Lebanon" provides a reinforcing lexical frame, though used in different senses. The divine "I" in v. 21 brands the saying as an oracle.

[20] "Climb every mountain" is the invitation, the mountain ranges of Lebanon in the north, of Bashan in the northeast, and of Abarim in the southeast, in Moabite territory (cf. Num 33:47–48). It is a call to dirge-like lamentation in response to a communal catastrophe. Holladay (1:602) has compared Jephthah's daughter going to mourn her fate in the mountains in Judg 11:37–38, which may reflect a custom of leaving one's home to engage in lament over the inevitable. Had disaster already begun to strike, in which case the Hebrew verb *nišběrû* has the literal sense "have been shattered," or is it a prophetic perfect referring to future defeat? The former is the more likely occasion for the oracle. The reference is to a defeat suffered by Jerusalem's political and military allies (cf. 2:33; 4:30) in the buffer zone, as the prelude to her own defeat in v. 22. The placing of this oracle in a chronologically ordered series, after one about Jehoiakim (vv. 13–19) and before two that refer to his successor Jehoiachin (vv. 24–30), suggests that the oracle relates historically to the Babylonian capture of Jerusalem in the latter's reign (597 B.C.E.; cf. 2 Kgs 24:10–11).

[21] The initial defeat is invested with theological dimensions. Prophetic warnings that, taken seriously, could have prevented national tragedy had been disregarded. Economic prosperity and Babylonian noninterference muffled them. This skepticism is traced back to the preprophetic period, to a history of disregarding Yahweh's earlier revelation, presumably the torah traditions. As earlier in the book, notably in 6:16–19, disregarding the double revelation is the prescription for sure disaster.

[22] Jeremiah promises deportation for the defeated allies and for Jerusalem's royal administration (cf. 17:20 and commentary; 29:2; 2 Kgs 24:12). The violent wind from the east that stands for Yahweh's intervention by military force (as in 18:17) was to be the shepherds' shepherd for migration to new and unpleasant pastures! "Bad behavior," a general charge that sums up Jerusalem's failure to mend its ways in v. 21 and cleverly plays on the noun and verb for "shepherd" with the same Hebrew letters *rʿ*, would receive its humiliating deserts.

[23] The oracle reverts to its opening note of grief, no longer in an exhortation but in an exclamation that evokes the coming humiliation in emotional terms. Like a plaintively crying bird, Jerusalem would squawk as its nest was

attacked, a nest exquisitely constructed with twigs that represented palace woodwork (cf. vv. 6–7). A different image, that of a woman shrieking with labor pangs terrifyingly unimaginable to listening males, provides firm closure.[149]

[24–30] These last two announcements of disaster refer to "Coniah" and highlight a hurling into exile, a term of violent expulsion earlier used of the people in 16:13. Not surprisingly, the term "country" comes to the fore again, whether relating to Judah (vv. 27, 29) or to Babylonia (vv. 26, 28). "Coniah," which is also used in 37:1, is a name similar to "Jeconiah" in 24:1; 27:20; 28:4; 29:2; and 1 Chr 3:16–17. The names reverse the Hebrew elements of "Jehoiachin," the name that in Jer 52:31; 2 Kgs 24:6, 8–17 refers to Judah's penultimate king—who, like Jehoahaz, reigned merely three months. This pair of units and the initial unit create compositional bookends. They become the motif of royal exile, which poignantly features a land of no return. These final units represent parodies of positive royal oracles. Coniah is spurned as Yahweh's plenipotentiary ("signet ring"), permitted no secure roots in the homeland, and promised no one to sit on his throne after him.[150]

[24–27] There is no reason to doubt that this unit, though in prose, in essence belonged to the royal collection taken over by the redactor who created these compositions. The change to third person references in v. 27 may imply that the sentence is a supplementary comment, one that is echoed in 44:14, and is meant to reinforce the framing link with the first unit in the composition (vv. 10–12). The unit is a divine announcement of disaster marked by flat denial and finality. First, Coniah's prestigious role as Yahweh's "signet ring" of authority in the dynastic succession (cf. Hag 2:23) is annulled in a peremptory oath, which is made harsher by the switch to direct address. The realization of his worst fears, being captured by the Babylonians as a prelude to exile, would take place by divine mandate. MT cannot resist capping in a literary flourish the formal Judean title with its superior enemy counterpart. Second, he and the queen mother are doomed to permanent exile and aching nostalgia for their lost homeland (cf. 13:18 and commentary; 29:2; 2 Kgs 24:15). Popular expectations of his return (Jer 28:4) would come to nothing. Verse 26 has an overarching focus on birth, birthplace, and death that expresses a sharp separation from one's roots culminating in fatality. Whereas fear would materialize, hope would crumble.

[28–30] The final poetic unit is an announcement of disaster concerning Jehoiachin (v. 30), introduced by a reinforcement proffered by Jeremiah (v. 28) and his call for national attention (v. 29). It presupposes the king's exile, forecast in the previous unit, as a threat now fulfilled.

---

149. Watson, *Classical Hebrew Poetry*, 261.
150. Wilhelm J. Wessels, "Jeremiah 22,24–30: A Proposed Ideological Reading," *ZAW* 101 (1989): 232–49, esp. 235–36.

[28] Before the divine announcement the prophet bewails the king's deportation. The passive verbs in v. 28b work with Yahweh as implicit agent, as the active use of the same verb in v. 26 with a divine subject suggests. The deportation spelled outright rejection on Yahweh's part. There is a derogatory sense to the label "this man," a phrase quoted from the oracle in v. 30. The ex-king is judged no better than trash to be thrown out; he no longer had any right to the Judean throne. Jehoiachin's rejected status is set in the context of his deportation, which was nothing less than forcible ejection at Yahweh's hands. The format of the threefold series of questions common in Jeremiah's poetry reappears here. It culminates in a "why" question that explains the essential point of the two striking previous ones. The format is used in three genres in the book, in divine oracles (2:14, 31; 8:4–5; 49:1; cf. 30:6), in petitionary communal laments (8:19; 14:19), and in Jeremiah's own dirge-like lamentation of hopelessness (8:22). The present case is parallel to the last-mentioned usage. The prophet engages in an anticipatory, despairing dirge before the negative oracle of v. 30, rather like his role in 14:17–18 before 15:1–4.

[29–30] The entire national community is urged to pay serious heed in a solemn threefold call, since Judah's governance was at stake, as the close of the oracle will affirm. Jehoiachin could be written off as a failure in terms of his manhood, in that he lacked any children who would inherit his throne. No matter that doubtless he already had sons, since he had a harem who went into exile with him according to 2 Kgs 24:15. Eventually he had seven sons according to the genealogy in 1 Chr 3:17–18 and five sons to feed in exile according to a Babylonian ration docket.[151] From the divine perspective it was as if he had none. He could be placed on record for the benefit of future generations (cf. Ps 102:18 [19]) as virtually childless—childless "in the only way meaningful for a king" (Holladay 1:611). This unit underscores the prediction of Coniah's deportation (v. 26). However, in its broader literary setting, it has another role. The reference to David (v. 30) echoes a two-part warning about the continuance of the monarchy in a parallel composition (22:4–5). The monarchy was staggering on in the person of Zedekiah, but the beginning of the earlier composition had branded his reign too as doomed (21:7). Now a dark shadow is cast over the long-term survival of the institution of monarchy, at least through Jehoiachin. Whether the unit was intended to discourage national support for the young ex-king is unclear and beyond the interest of the book. It may be noted that later genealogical representations of the royal family did trace it via Jehoiachin (1 Chr 3:16–17; Matt 1:12).

Jeremiah 22:10–30 has announced once more the downfall of the royal court and with it the capital, and grounded it in unethical behavior that had flouted both torah traditions and prophetic warnings.

---

151. *ANET*, 308.

23:1–8 A Restored Court and Community

23:1 "Woe betide you shepherd-kings who have lost the flock I shepherd and got it scattered!" *declared Yahweh.* 2 "Therefore"—here is what Yahweh, *Israel's God,* said—"concerning the shepherds who should be[a] shepherding my people: You it is who have scattered my flock and driven it away, failing to take care of it. Look out, I am going to take care of the problem of your bad activities!" *declared Yahweh.* 3 "And I, for my part, will collect what is left of my flock from all the countries I have driven it away to, bringing them back to their own pasture, where they will be fruitful and multiply. 4 And I will put them in the charge of shepherds who will shepherd them properly, so they will never be afraid and scared again *and none of them will go missing,"* declared Yahweh.

5   "Look, a time is coming," declared Yahweh,
    "when I will put in charge a rightful scion of David,
      who will rule as king effectively,
      bringing about justice and right in the country.
6   In his reign Judah will enjoy salvation,
      while Israel will live securely,
    and this will be his name, what he will be called:
      'Yahweh-Is-Our-Righteousness.'"

7 "Therefore look, a time is coming," declared Yahweh, "when people will no longer swear the oath, 'By the life of Yahweh who brought the Israelites up from the country of Egypt,' 8 but say instead, 'By the life of Yahweh who brought in[b] the descendants[c] of Israel from the north country'—or from any of the other countries I have driven them away to. They will reside on their own soil."[d]

    a. Thus NJPS.

    b. MT has a doublet, "who brought up and who brought in." The former clause, lacking in LXX, came about by assimilation to 16:15. The error was corrected but not expunged.

    c. MT adds *bêt,* "house," to the shorter text of LXX. The addition seems to be related to LXX's recensional alternative for *běnê,* "sons (of Israel)," in v. 7 (see *BHS*). The alternative was evidently preserved as a marginal annotation in an earlier literary stage of MT and strayed into the text as a qualification of the comparable phrase in v. 8.

    d. For the presence of vv. 7–8 after v. 40 in LXX cf. Janzen, *Studies,* 92–93; and the critiques of Johan Lust in "'Gathering and Return' in Jeremiah and Ezekiel," in *Livre de Jérémie* (ed. P.-M. Bogaert), 119–42, esp. 135 n. 70, and of Yohanan Goldman, *Prophétie et royauté au retour de l'exil: Les origines littéraires de la forme massorétique du Livre de Jérémie* (OBD 118; Freiburg: Universitätsverlag; Göttingen: Vandenhoeck & Ruprecht, 1992), 48–51. The placement in MT appears to be correct.

Apart from vv. 7–8, this composition follows the contours of the short, last section of the collection of royal oracles. It now falls into three units, vv. 1–4, 5–6, and 7–8. The first two units manifest a triangle of characters, Yahweh, the royal representatives of Yahweh, and the community of Israel to and for whom the kings represented Yahweh. The addition of vv. 7–8 changes the overall focus in the composition from the first two factors to the first and last. Already vv. 1–6 had a concluding role in the collection, with "Woe betide" (v. 1) harking back to 22:13, "shepherds" (vv. 1–2, 4) and related wordplay (v. 2) to 22:22, "bring back" (v. 3) to "come back" in 22:10, 27, and "justice and right" (v. 5) to 22:3, 13, 15 (cf. 21:12). This concluding role is taken over and amplified in the composition, in that its nonroyal final unit has a double echo of the divine oath formula that appeared in 22:24. There is an organic relationship between the three units that reveals vv. 3–4 to be the center of the composition. Verses 3–4 are a positive development of vv. 1–2, while vv. 5–6 and 7–8, marked by parallel temporal introductions, separately develop vv. 3–4, with vv. 5–6 illustrating v. 4 and vv. 7–8 taking further the communal emphasis of v. 3. Another, complementary way to look at the structure is in terms of the triple *hinnēh*, "look (out)," in vv. 2, 5, 7, which draws attention to divine interventions in the first two cases and to a reaction to a divine intervention in the third. In the first case the reader, led on by the two conjunctions "And" in vv. 3 and 4, is meant to see an initial series of interventions in vv. 2–4 that start negatively but develop to a positive pair that matches the two following cases.

[1–4] MT cuts across the second scheme by its insertion of the closing quotation formula, "declared Yahweh," at the conclusions of vv. 1 and 2. The formula construes vv. 1–4 as an overall unit divided into three sections, vv. 1, 2, and 3–4, thus downplaying the two constituent parts of an oracle of disaster and highlighting their positive resolution.

[1–2] This prose oracle of disaster is a continuation of what has preceded in the royal collection. Both this fact and the echoes of ch. 22 in vv. 1–2 point to their literary role as a provisional summary. Indictments of individual kings are now replaced by a generalizing accusation. The essence of the accusation is that the kings have been responsible by their malfeasance for the deportation of their subjects during the Babylonian invasions of 597 and 587 B.C.E. The verses offer a comprehensive comment about the exile of specific Judean kings (22:10–12, though this was at Egyptian hands). The national exile pertaining to the end of Zedekiah's reign seems to be presupposed as a historical fact, whereas previous royal exile was put in future terms (22:22). Only the Egyptian exile of Jehoahaz and the Babylonian one of Jehoiachin lay in the past for the text. The literary dependence of the oracle of vv. 1–2 on foregoing oracles and its being in prose imply the redactional nature of this oracle. Its relatively early provenance is suggested by the fact that it was already pre-

Doomed Kings and Discredited Prophets

supposed at the basis of the multilayered extravaganza using the sheep-shepherd motif in Ezekiel 34.[152]

[1] The sinister *hôy*, "Woe betide," in this oracle of disaster anticipates the specific announcement in v. 2. It typically goes on to threaten an upper class of society with irresponsible maltreatment of lower classes, who are defined as "my people" (v. 2), here pictured as "my flock."[153] The addition of the epithet "Israel's God" in MT at v. 2 will further clarify the covenant relationship that prompts Yahweh's punitive reaction. The phrase *ṣōʾn marʿît*, "flock of shepherding," with a divine pronoun is standard cultic language (Pss 74:1; 79:13; 100:3). Here the assumption is that Yahweh is the shepherd to whom under-shepherds report (cf. Heb 13:20; 1 Pet 5:2–4). The notion is a development of the metaphorical covenant formula that builds into it the common ancient Near Eastern concept of the human king as shepherd of his people. Another development in this verse, one that pushes the metaphorical envelope, is the description of the kings' irresponsibility in terms of losing sheep under their care and causing them to stray outside the land into exile.

[2] After the formal quotation formula prefaced by "Therefore" that links the two parts of the oracle, the announcement is preceded by a forceful repetition of the accusation of irresponsibility, a not unparalleled form-critical device.[154] The development of *pqd*, "take care," leads into the announcement of divinely instigated disaster by means of a play on a different sense of the same verb, "deal with" in the sense of "punish." The translation has attempted to catch the insistent logic of the divine judgment by repeating "take care." A final accusation follows, a general one that uses the emotional tool of wordplay again, this time capping the metaphor of shepherding (*rʿh*) with "bad" (*rōaʿ*), as in 22:22.[155]

[3–4] The unit continues with a prose proclamation of salvation, one that moves from the punishment of the oppressing group to the vindication of the oppressed one, like Ezek 34:11–16 after vv. 2–10. The form-critical development of an oracle of disaster into a positive reversal does occur elsewhere, for example at the close of Isa 1:21–26, but in this case it seems to be a redactional amplification, especially in its switch from the kings' driving the people into exile to Yahweh's doing it, concepts that belong to "two separate worlds of ideas" (McKane 1:557). The new oracle presupposes vv. 1–2 and was designed to follow them smoothly, with the pronouns *ʾattem*, "You it is who," and *ʾănî*, "I, for my part," expressing antithesis. Now the good shepherd would take over

---

152. See Leslie C. Allen, *Ezekiel 20–48* (WBC 29; Dallas: Word, 1990), 160–61; also Jeremiah Unterman, *From Repentance to Redemption: Jeremiah's Thought in Transition* (JSOTSup 54; Sheffield: JSOT Press, 1987), 167.
153. Janzen, *Mourning Cry*, 73; cf. Isa 3:11–12; 10:1–2.
154. Westermann, *Basic Forms*, 180–81.
155. Miller, *Sin and Judgment*, 68.

from the bad underlings, first restoring the flock and then appointing good undershepherds.

[3] Two new ideas appear here. The first has already been mentioned, the concept of exile as providential punishment for the entire nation rather than simply the kings' fault. This brings the treatment into line with the more prevalent message of the book, that a comprehensive mass of wrongdoing throughout society had warranted Yahweh's radical intervention (cf., e.g., 5:4–5; 8:3 which use the same prose sermonic vocabulary as here). The covenant people were as much sinners as sinned against and deserved their exile. But there is a theological corollary. "With Yahweh involved, the stakes are raised; a solution can come only if his commitment to banish his people is reversed."[156] Second, the background of Babylonian exile has been widened to the Diaspora ("all the countries"). This change was motivated by a desire to take into account the deportation of Jehoahaz to Egypt, to which 22:10–12 implicitly refers. Otherwise, the sheep-shepherd analogy is developed in positive terms of restoration that use the language of covenant blessing in Lev 26:9, terms that were echoed in Jer 3:16.

[4] The issue of governance after the exile rounds off the unit. It harks back to the phrase in v. 2, "the shepherds who should be shepherding my people," with "shepherds who will shepherd them properly." The threat of external invasion that had been a menacing undercurrent of the earlier royal material is finally removed. MT provides rhetorical closure for the unit by further wordplay on the verb *pqd*, now in the sense of sheep going missing. The addition also creates a poignant frame for the proclamation of salvation by resolving the ravages implied in "what is left of my flock" (v. 3).

[5–6] This royal proclamation of salvation expands on the good governance of v. 4. The Hebrew verb *wahăqīmōtî*, "when I will put in charge," repeats exactly the beginning of v. 4, rendered "And I will put . . . in the charge." The Davidic kings (21:12; 22:2, 4, 30) who typified monarchy gone wrong earlier in the collection are finally balanced by one who will typify what is right. The Hebrew root *ṣdq* appears in the poem at three points: *ṣaddîq*, "rightful" or "legitimate," *ṣĕdāqâ*, "right," and *ṣidqēnû*, "our righteousness." The compositional function of this poem as an elucidation of v. 4 does not demand that its origin be judged chronologically later, any more than the poem in 22:6–7 is required to be later than the secondary 22:1–5, to which it is now subordinated. The symbolic name of the king who typifies a new regime seems to be a defiant play on that of the last king of the bad old regime, Zedekiah, and the oracle may well reflect Jeremiah's prophesying during his reign, as a corollary of the hope for new life in the land then given to him (32:6–15).[157] Tension

---

156. Ralph W. Klein, "Jeremiah 23:1–8," *Int* 34 (1980): 167–72, esp. 168.
157. Cf. Marvin A. Sweeney, "Jeremiah's Reflection on the Isaian Royal Promise: Jeremiah 23:1–8 in Context," in *Uprooting and Planting* (ed. J. Goldingay), 308–21.

with the apparent finality of the prophet's denunciation of preexilic monarchs is only intolerable when the surprising grace of God is left out of account. The old structures had to be cleared away before the new could be set in place. The poem promises a future Davidic monarchy, but it is not "eschatological" in the sense that it contains anything that deviates from the course of ongoing human history under Yahweh's providential control.[158] The phrase "scion (*ṣemaḥ*) of David" was echoed in postexilic promises concerning Zerubbabel (Zech 3:8; 6:12).

[5] Although the text speaks in individual terms, the reader should not imagine a single messianic figure. The king stands for the new regime or as the inaugurator of a fresh branch of the royal line (cf. the way this text is interpreted in 33:17; note also Ezek 46:16–18). Accordingly the echo of v. 5 that is sounded in 3:15 has the "shepherds" of v. 4 still in view. Of course, the oracle did become part of the general messianic expectation that developed by NT times. In the present context, membership of the Davidic dynasty remains a sine qua non, but it is the only thing the new regime would have in common with the old. What were to be the marks of proper shepherding on the part of the kings installed by God, according to the headline in v. 4a? This tricolon provides the answer in terms of ruling "effectively" (McKane 1:559, 562)[159] and reestablishing in the community the ancient moral values of "justice and right" on which, apart from long-gone Josiah, the old regime had set no value (22:3, 13, 15).

[6] And what could be said about the fearlessness of v. 4b? Verse 6a provides an elaboration of such security from external attack (cf. Ezek 39:25–26). It is arguable that "Judah" and "Israel" refer to the southern and northern kingdoms (cf. 3:11, 18; 31:31; and especially 33:14 as an introduction to 33:15–16, which reuses 23:5–6). However, in the present context the terms should be understood as synonymous parallels, in the light of "Israelites" and "descendants of Israel" in vv. 7–8, while MT's "Israel's God" in v. 2 points in the same interpretive direction. The symbolic name that is the climactic focus of the royal oracle is enigmatic. Since the previous parts of the oracle have proved to have an interpretive function, however, the meaning of *ṣedeq*, "righteousness," should be defined in the light of the context, which in narrower terms is the communal benefit of v. 5b and in wider terms the social demand in 22:3, 13, 15. Also significant for the divine subject in the name is the positive initiative taken by Yahweh at the start of vv. 3, 4, and 5. "Righteousness" has a divine source. The name thus reflects a communal confession of praise that righteousness at last prevails in the land and that the glory must go to Yahweh for setting up the new regime (cf. "Immanuel,"

---

158. For such a definition of eschatology see Yair Hoffman, "Eschatology in the Book of Jeremiah," in *Eschatology in the Bible and in Jewish and Christian Tradition* (ed. H. Graf Reventlow; JSOTSup 243; Sheffield: Sheffield Academic Press, 1997), 75–97, esp. 77–79, 88–89.

159. The term *whśkyl* is echoed in 3:15, but in another sense, "and with understanding."

"God is with us," Isa 7:14; 8:8, 10).[160] That regime was to be a celebration of divine grace in action throughout the community.

[7–8] Verse 6 marked the end of the royal collection, but the composition adds as a final unit a nonroyal supplementary oracle in prose. If vv. 5–6 function as an elucidation of v. 4, vv. 7–8 do the same for v. 3. One might have expected a different order, but the climactic focus is placed on God's people, whom the king was only to serve under God. As in the first composition, monarchy is assigned a supporting role. Indeed, this oracle is able to continue the communal references within vv. 5–6, "in the country" and "Our-Righteousness," while the people's oath in Yahweh's honor fits well the worshipful name of the king by which the community was to glorify Yahweh. This oracle has been used before in the book, at 16:14–15, with recensional differences.[161] That version was taken from this one. The language of 23:3, "from all the countries I have driven it away to," was incorporated as a quotation and put to new use in 16:15. Even here the oracle is a redactional supplement. In its interpretive role "their own pasture" in v. 3 becomes "their own soil," while the exilic reference of the oath formula is adapted to the extra Diaspora emphasis there (cf. NAB, NJPS). The oracle offers hope by celebrating a new revelation of Yahweh in a second redemptive act that would eclipse the exodus and bring about a wonderful reversal of Israel's punishment by the regaining of the land.

The brief composition in 23:1–8 rounds off the previous two by summarizing their negative series of oracles in terms of bad kings who caused Judah's exile and by adding promises of a capable monarchy in the future and the restoration of the banished community.

23:9–24 The Subversive Marks of Spurious Prophecy

9 On the theme of the prophets
Inwardly my mind is shattered,
   my whole body is shaking.
I have become like a drunk,
   somebody overwhelmed by wine,
in reaction to Yahweh,
   in reaction to his holy message:
10 "Indeed, adulterers fill the country—[a]
   indeed, as the result of a curse the country is in mourning,[b]
the wilderness pastures are parched—

---

160. LXX *Iōsedek*, "Josedek," lacks the communal reference. As a reversed form of "Zedekiah" (cf. the introductory comment on 22:24–30), it may be intended as a differentiating allusion to him.

161. See the comparative analysis of McKane 1:374–75.

the course the population[c] follows is a bad one,
   and the power they exercise is immoral.
11 Indeed, both prophet and priest are godless;
   in my very temple I have discovered their badness,"
declared Yahweh.
12 "Therefore their path will turn for them
   like slippery places in the dark;
   they will fall headlong and lie prostrate in it,[d]
because I will inflict a bad fate on them
   in the year when they are dealt with,"
declared Yahweh.

13 "On the one hand[e] among Samaria's prophets I saw a stupid sight:
   they prophesied in Baal's name,
   leading my people Israel astray.
14 On the other hand among Jerusalem's prophets I see some
horrifying sights:
   adultery, practicing deceit,
and encouraging people who behave badly in what they do,
   so nobody's bad behavior is renounced.[f]
I deem them all like Sodom,
   and its residents like Gomorrah.
15 Therefore"—here is what Yahweh *Almighty* said *about the prophets*—
"look, I am going to give them wormwood to eat
   and poison to drink,
because Jerusalem's prophets are the source
   from which godlessness has spread throughout the country.

16 "Do not[g] listen to the messages of the prophets
who are prophesying to you.[h]
   They are giving *you* empty talk,
expressing just the visions of their own minds,
   and nothing from Yahweh's mouth.
17 They say[i] to those who despise Yahweh's message,[j]
   'You will have peace.'
And as for[k] all those who follow the stubborn inclination of their own minds,
   they say [to them], 'No bad fate will befall you.'"

18 Indeed, who [of them] has had a place in Yahweh's council, with the opportunity of perceiving his message?[l] Who has listened *to his message* and heard?

19 Look, Yahweh's storm wind,
       the onset of fury!
    The wind is whirling around.
       Around the heads of the wicked it will whirl.
20 Yahweh's anger will not subside till he has worked through it
       and till he has accomplished the purposes he has in mind.ᵐ
    When time has elapsed,
       you will understand this *clearly*.

21 "I never sent the prophets,
       but off they ran.
    I never spoke to them,
       but they gave prophecies anyway.
22 Yet if they had had a place in my council,
       they would have let my people hear my messages
    and gotten them to renounce their bad conduct,
       the bad things they have done.
23 Am I just a God who is nearby,"
       declared Yahweh,
    "and not a God who is far off?
24 Can a person hide anywhere secret
       and keep out of my sight?"
    declared Yahweh.
    "Are not sky and earth
       filled by me?"
    declared Yahweh.

a. LXX omitted by parablepsis (Rudolph 148; McKane 1:570; *HUB*). McKane observes that the next clause in LXX presupposes this material.

b. Or "is dry"; cf. NIV and REB and note e on the translation of 12:4.

c. Literally "they," which loosely refers back to "the country" in terms of its inhabitants.

d. For the delimitation of cola see the discussion of Cloete, *Versification*, 194. "In it" refers to the "path" (*derek*), now treated as feminine.

e. The Hebrew conjunctions at the beginning of vv. 13 and 14 evidently correspond (Duhm 184; Rudolph 150).

f. See *BHS* for standard improvements of ungrammatical MT.

g. MT prefaces with a quotation formula that is a development of the erroneous single first person reference in MT (v. 17) and K *děbārî*, "my word" (v. 18b), for which see *BHS*. The rendering in the Greek tradition represents a prehexaplaric revision that points to the redactional nature of the formula (Janzen, *Studies*, 85). It could be judged an anticipatory introduction to the oracle of vv. 21–24 (cf. 14:1, 17), and this may be its redactional function.

Doomed Kings and Discredited Prophets 263

h. MT fills out along the lines of 27:15 in a similar context.

i. See BHS. Perhaps ʾāmôr, attested only in MT, represents an alternative form; cf. the infinitives absolute in v. 14. The colon is overloaded.

j. MT is to be repointed along the lines of LXX: see BHS, NAB, NRSV, and REB. The first person reference to Yahweh in MT hardly fits this unit so full of third person references. Holladay 1:633 notes the better poetic balance thus achieved for the pair of bicola. Part of the problem was that MT fell under the influence of *dibber yhwh*, "Yahweh spoke," in vv. 35, 37.

k. For the hanging construction cf. GKC §116w. Lundbom 2:192 suggests double duty of the *lāmed* before the earlier participle.

l. MT supplements the earlier text represented in LXX with "and in order that he may hear," which probably originated in a marginal explanation of the preceding unusual verb *wĕyereʾ*, "in order that he may perceive," lit. "see," as in 2:31, where it was rendered "consider" (McKane 1:581).

m. See Cloete, *Versification*, 197, for the bicolon.

Jeremiah 23:9–40 is a collection of originally separate sayings concerning prophets, with its own topical heading, the collection of oracles concerning kings (21:11–23:8). This collection divides into two sections, one primarily poetry (vv. 9–24) and another entirely prose (vv. 25–40). These sections were taken over as twin compositions. There are four important elements in the compositions: the charge of leading Yahweh's people astray, predicated of Samaria's prophets in v. 13 and of Judean ones in v. 32; Yahweh's ongoing investigation, detecting (v. 11), seeing (v. 14), and hearing (v. 25); the destructive violence of true prophecy, symbolized by storm wind (v. 19) and fire and hammer (v. 29); and Yahweh's denial that the prophets under review had ever been sent (vv. 21, 32). In the first composition there are four units, vv. 9–12, 13–15, 16–20, and 21–24. Bookends are provided in that the first unit mentions a filled "country" (v. 10) and the fourth unit a filled "earth" (v. 24), using the same noun, *ʾereṣ*. The verb *rʾh*, "see," with a divine first person subject (vv. 13–14 and 24) also functions as a framing device. All four units contain variations of a basic term, *rāʿâ*, "bad, badness, a bad fate," three times in the first (vv. 10, 11, 12); *mĕrēʿîm*, "people who behave badly," and *rāʿâ*, "bad behavior," in the second (v. 14); *rāʿâ*, "a bad fate," in the third (v. 17); and *rāʿ* and *rōaʿ*, "bad," in the fourth (v. 22). In the third unit the synonymous *rĕšāʿîm*, "the wicked," appears at v. 19. The Hebrew roots *rʿʿ*, "be bad," and *rʾh*, "see," dominate the composition and provide a summary of its meaning, namely, that Yahweh sees what is bad among Judean prophets, and the result for its perpetrators can only be a bad fate. At beginning and end this double truth is confirmed by a parallel pervasiveness, whereby pervasive badness finds its punitive match in the pervasiveness of a foreboding divine presence (vv. 10, 24).

[**23:9–12**] The first unit has remarkably general targets, with prophets featuring only in v. 11, admittedly in a climactic role. The unit plays an introductory part for the rest of the composition whereby degeneration in the community at large, including its prophetic element, is roughly sketched before responsibility for it is later laid at the prophets' door. The unit is basically an oracle of disaster, made up of the reason (vv. 10–11) and the announcement (v. 12).

[9] But before the oracle two other components appear. First, the title of the collection is given. It refers to Jeremiah's prophetic rivals. In Yahweh's name they offered optimism in place of his pessimism and so lacked his need to critique Judean society. Second, Jeremiah provides an emotional introduction to the oracle of vv. 10–12 by recording how personally devastated he was by the perspective and prospect that emerged for the community. The outburst reflects the convention of reaction to bad news and is meant to cue readers to the content of the oracle.[162] In general terms this personal introduction to an oracle repeats a pattern of intense responsiveness encountered earlier in the book, at 4:19–21 and 14:17–18; there the style adopted was a report of a distressing vision in the first case and a dirge-like lamentation in the second. Here Jeremiah's response to receipt of the oracle, before delivering it, is total and bodily disorientation. The term "holy" acts as a corrective foil to the "godless" behavior attributed to prophets in v. 11 (cf. v. 15).

[10] The reasons for coming disaster are presented in vv. 10–11. A shift to divine speech, heralded by "his holy message," will become clear from the two cases of the divine "I," both accentuated by quotation formulas in MT (vv. 11, 12). Adultery could symbolize abandoning Yahweh for other gods, as in 3:8–9; 13:27. However, the juxtaposition of v. 14 in the next unit, in which adultery features in a moral context, suggests that for the compiler sexual unfaithfulness was in view, as in 5:7; 7:9; and 9:2 (1). The indictment is interrupted, in order to show its heinousness, by a claim that environmental consequences were already being suffered. Mourning is a metaphor for infertility and drought, as in 12:4. Here was evidence of an interim divine "curse" already in operation. The concept is one encountered previously at 12:4 (see the commentary there). Yahweh's further intervention to deal with the root of the problem was necessary to restore equilibrium. Further accusations consist of a damning generalization and then the misuse of power.

[11] The climax features religious personnel, priests and evidently prophets on the temple staff. The singling out of these two groups recalls 5:31 and 6:13. Their wrongdoing is left unspecified as godlessness (or defilement) and badness. But to Yahweh it came as "an appalling surprise" (Holladay 1:628). God expected better of them.

[12] Inevitable disaster was to follow for all those indicted earlier, as the linking "Therefore" implies. God's blessing is typically portrayed in the OT and especially in the Psalms as an open road to the future, an unimpeded journey, "the

---

162. See Hillers, "Convention," 86–90; cf. 6:24; Isa 21:3.

path of life" (Ps 16:11). Its opposite, a "way" that is "dark and slippery" (Ps 35:6) and a sudden end to any progress (cf. Jer 6:21), is predicated here. Such a sinister consequence is then traced back to Yahweh's own activity, with an insistence that the *rāʿâ*, "badness," evidenced in vv. 10–11 can only issue in the other kind of *rāʿâ*, "a bad fate," when the announcement of disaster was fulfilled.

[13–15] The second unit is also an oracle of disaster, with a reason (v. 14), an announcement, formally introduced with "Therefore" and the quotation formula (v. 15a*a*), and a clinching reason (v. 15b). "Jerusalem's prophets" frame the body of the oracle. Verse 13 represents an expansion of the first reason, which sets the scene with an unflattering comparison between Jerusalem's prophets and Samaria's.

[13–14] Yahweh's investigation of the prophets (v. 11) continues. In 3:11, which is to be distinguished from the redactional explanation in 3:3–10, Judah was accused of sinking lower than the now defunct northern kingdom in apostasy. Here, with the prophets of the two capitals in view, divine discrimination assesses those of Jerusalem to be, if not worse, at least as bad as Samaria's were, though their respective delinquencies lie in different spheres, religious in the north (cf. Hos 13:1) and ethical in the south (but cf. Jer 2:8 and v. 27 below for religious deviation earlier in Judah's history). The unspoken implication of the comparison is sinister; everybody knew Samaria's fate.[163] The emotion-laden accusation is that the prophets who distanced themselves from Jeremiah's own prophetic stand lived at the same low level as their constituency and felt no need for a moral challenge in their messages. So neither in word nor in deed did they set a good example. The general ethical context suggests that "deceit" refers to a part of their lifestyle shared with their public (cf. 9:3, 5 [2, 4]), rather than the specificity of false prophesying (cf. 5:31; 14:14; 20:6). Similes relating to the prophets and their urban public alike bring closure to the accusatory section, as later in v. 29.[164] Sodom and Gomorrah constitute a paradigm of general immorality, as in Isa 1:10, though the charge of adultery forges a loose link with the sexual violence in Genesis 19.

[15] The thematic expansion "about the prophets" in MT looks ahead to v. 15b. Verse 15a*b* has in view their constituency, Jerusalem's "residents" (v. 14). Their punishment at Yahweh's hands is represented metaphorically as bitter and fatal, using images both of which were reused in 9:15 (14), while the second has a parallel in 8:14. The finger of underlying blame is pointed firmly in the prophets' direction, with a charge of "godlessness" that echoes v. 11 in the first unit and a magnifying of their sphere of influence from the capital to the whole country, which returns to the national note of v. 10.

---

163. Thomas W. Overholt, *The Threat of Falsehood: A Study in the Theology of the Book of Jeremiah* (SBT 2/16; Naperville, Ill.: Allenson, 1970), 53.
164. Watson, *Classical Hebrew Prophecy*, 65.

[16–20] Second plural references frame the unit, with redactional amplifications in the former case. The unit follows the basic pattern of an oracle of disaster, with the reason (vv. 16a*b*–17) introduced by an exhortation (v. 16a*a*) and capped by a pair of rhetorical questions (v. 18), while the announcement (vv. 19–20a) has appended to it an assurance of its fulfillment (v. 20b). However, the series of third person divine references reveals it to be a prophetic counterpart of a divine oracle of disaster. Verse 17b contains the poetic basis for diction redeployed in prose sermons (e.g., 11:8; McKane 1:579–80).

[16–18] Jeremiah gives three serious warnings to the public about his prophetic rivals, arguing that their brand of prophesying lacks authenticity. First, he claims that they are not divinely inspired. Their own psyches, instead of being channels of revelation, have created the messages they bring. Second, he observes the glaring gap between their audience's lifestyle and the reassuring messages they provide. Moral discrimination is given no role in determining who should receive predictions of *šālôm*, "peace," and denials of *rā'â*, "a bad fate." Yahweh's true prophetic "message"—such as Jeremiah gives—is marked by a moral emphasis, and to oppose it should spell only doom. Third, and here the text changes to prose (NJB), there is a restatement of the first point, which depicts visionary access to the heavenly council of Yahweh (cf. 1 Kgs 22:19–23; Ps 89:7 [8]; Isa 6:1–8) as a mark of the true prophet and denies that his rivals, who in the context must be in view, have any such privilege. Verse 22 will return to this concept in a poetic format. The three points belong together. The first and last ones express heartfelt convictions; any of Jeremiah's rivals could have retaliated with similar sincerity. These points are meant to receive their bite, their basic logic, from the central thesis, an accusation of indiscriminate oracles of salvation that were not grounded in moral realities such as one would judge of prime importance in Yahwism. It is a variation of Paul's eschatological argument to the Christian community in 1 Cor 6:9–10 and of John's in 1 John 2:8–11. The composition has already added a divine amen to Jeremiah's argument. The glib promise, "No bad fate will befall you," was preceded in v. 12 by the similarly worded threat, "I will inflict a bad fate on them"—one could render "I will cause a bad fate to befall them."

[19–20] Jeremiah gives a vision report corresponding to the ironically used "visions" of v. 16 (cf. Holladay 1:634). Whereas "visions" referred to prophetic revelations in general, including the vision genre, here an actual vision is in view. It appears in a brief and simple form in the first three cola of v. 19, introduced by a telltale *hinnēh*, "Look." Then, by way of interpretation, the fourth colon and v. 20a make counterassertions about the future, challenging those decried in v. 17. Divine "fury" and "anger" dominate as an inevitable response to community members who have shrugged off the prophetic testimony of Jeremiah and his ilk and continued in their bad lifestyle. In conclusion the prophet gives advice—"Mark my words!"—to the public he began to address in v. 16, about fulfillment as a criterion of truth (cf. Num 24:14). There are two ways to learn, and the second is the hard way.

[21–24] This final unit is an oracle of disaster. It can begin abruptly because it is closely associated in topic with the previous unit. The first person references indicate divine speech clearly enough, while a closing quotation formula occurs in v. 24b and a formula introduces the announcement in v. 23. The prophetic saying in vv. 16–20 has a prefatory role, introducing in v. 18 the divine council of v. 22 and concretely expressing in vv. 19–20a the disaster sketchily nuanced in vv. 23–24. By the same token, the oracle also authenticates Jeremiah's prophetic stand, somewhat like the divine responses to Jeremiah's confessions in 11:21–23 and 15:11–12.

[21–22] There is a further indictment of the so-called prophets who appeared in the second and third units. The blanket disowning of v. 21 is elaborated in v. 22 in terms of the amoral stand they took, along the lines of v. 17b and also of v. 14. Such a premise confirmed their lack of admission to the divine council of v. 18 and the consequent denial that what they prophesied could be identified with "my messages," which essentially had a moral basis (cf. Lam 2:14). The repetition of "bad" in v. 22 accentuates a dominant motif of the composition. Its use within the reason for disaster leads the reader to expect an announcement of that disaster in what follows, indeed, a restatement of the "bad fate" present in vv. 12 and 17.

[23–24] Rhetorical questions by their nature often involve a surprising leap that taxes the hearer. These three are posed in a particularly enigmatic way, and McKane (1:587) speaks for many exegetes in claiming that "these verses have no intrinsic connection with any context in chapter 23." Rudolph (153), following Albert Condamin and followed by several commentators, NRSV, and GNB, attaches them to the next unit, but that is less likely if they are poetry.[165] The second question is the most crucial of the three, around which the first and third space-related questions cluster in reinforcement. The second half of this question is more literally "so that I cannot see him." The nuance of this verb with Yahweh as subject is clarified by comparing passages in which a denial of God's seeing implies that one may sin with impunity: Pss 10:11; 94:7; Isa 29:15; 47:10; Ezek 8:12; 9:9. In a comparable set of passages God's seeing is a prelude to punishment: Gen 6:5, 12; 11:5; Job 11:11; 34:21. Similar results are found in some passages that refer to the divine eyes: Job 34:21 (again); Prov 5:21; Jer 16:17; Amos 9:3 (lit. "from my eyes"). One of the most significant of all these passages is Gen 6:5, "The LORD saw that the wickedness of humankind

---

165. Most commentators and most EVV take vv. 23–24 as poetry; Cloete, *Versification*, 140, does so without question. Rhetorical questions can close a poetic piece (cf. Watson, *Classical Hebrew Poetry*, 342). Already the Aleppo and Leningrad codices of MT, unable to use the prose-poetry criterion, linked vv. 23–24 to vv. 25–28 by their use of minor paragraph markers after vv. 22 and 29 (cf. Lundbom 2:193, 200).

was great," where "wickedness" renders rāʿat, "badness," one of the group of cognate terms that run through the composition of Jer 23:9–24. Another is Isa 47:10, which begins, "You felt secure in your wickedness (rāʿātēk)," and continues in v. 11, "But evil (rāʿâ) will come upon you." Some of the passages include the motif of trying to hide from God, namely, Job 34:21; Isa 29:15; Jer 16:17; Amos 9:3; and also Heb 4:13. So the second question alludes to deserved disaster and is tantamount to an announcement of disaster. It is tied into the preceding context as part of a network of related terms. None of the prophets can hide from the bad fate to which their bad behavior, all too visible to divine eyes, makes them liable. There is a glance back to v. 14, at the horrifying sights Yahweh has seen in the case of Jerusalem's prophets. Then the preceding and following spatial questions fall into place simply as parallel reinforcements for the second. The first means that God is not shortsighted, so localized in any one spot as to miss what is happening elsewhere, but has long-range vision (cf. Ps 139:2), while the third question implies the universal God's total range of visibility.[166]

The composition in 23:9–24 vehemently castigates Jeremiah's prophetic rivals for their morally irresponsible lifestyle and message. It can only predict a bad end for them at the hands of a God whom they have misunderstood and misrepresented.

23:25–40 Popular and Unpopular Types of Prophecy

25 "I have heard what the prophets say, those who prophesy falsehood in my name when they say, 'I have had a dream! I have had a dream!' 26 How long will this go on? Is it in the minds of the prophets who prophesy falsehood and who prophesy[a] delusions generated by their own minds— 27 is it[b] their intention to use the dreams they relate to one another to make my people[c] forget my name, just as their forebears forgot my name for that of Baal? 28 The prophet who has a dream has only a dream to relate, but the one who has my message can speak my message truly. What is chaff compared with grain?" *declared Yahweh.* 29 "Is not[d] a message of mine like fire," *declared Yahweh,* "or like a hammer smashing rock? 30 Therefore, look, I am opposed to those prophets," declared Yahweh, "who steal my messages from one another. 31 Look, I am opposed to those prophets," *declared Yahweh,* "who just move their tongues and recite the oracular formula. 32 Look, I am opposed to those who prophesy false dreams," *declared Yahweh,* "who by relating them use their false and reckless claims to lead my people astray—when I never sent them, never gave them any orders—and fail to be of any use to this people," *declared Yahweh.*

---

166. See Fretheim, *Suffering of God*, 61–62, for the divine presence in the created order.

33 "Whenever you are asked by this people or by a prophet or priest, 'What is Yahweh's burdensome pronouncement?' you are to tell them: 'You are Yahweh's burden,[e] and I will throw you down,'"[f] declared Yahweh. 34 "As for any prophet or priest or any other member of the people who mentions 'Yahweh's burdensome pronouncement,' I will deal with them individually and with their families. 35 This is the expression you are to use to each other, among friends and relatives: 'What answer did Yahweh give?' or 'What message did Yahweh give?' 36 Yahweh's 'burdensome pronouncement' you are never to mention again, because the 'burdensome pronouncement' is what the person with his message has,[g] and so you are distorting the messages of the living God, Yahweh Almighty, our God. 37 This is the way you[h] are to address a prophet: 'What answer did Yahweh give you?'[i] or 'What message did Yahweh give?' 38 *If you do use the expression 'Yahweh's burdensome pronouncement, therefore'*—here is what Yahweh said—'because you have used this expression, "Yahweh's burdensome pronouncement," after I categorically told you not to use it, 39 therefore I am here to pick *you* up[j] and throw you down, along with the city I gave you and your forebears, *right away from my presence.* 40 I will give you instead lasting humiliation, lasting and unforgettable shame.'"

a. See *BHS* and Holladay 1:641 for the repointing of MT, which LXX[L] supports.

b. The *hē* is interrogative (McKane 1:588–89). For the anacoluthon cf. GKC §167b.

c. The omission of "my people" in LXX is probably accidental (Janzen, *Studies*, 21; cf. *BHS*). An antecedent seems to be required for "their."

d. MT is conflated; in the LXX tradition *kōh*, "thus," is incorporated in a prehexaplaric revision (Ziegler, *Beiträge*, 100; Janzen, *Studies*, 201 n. 76; cf. *BHS*).

e. MT provides an echo of the previous question, "As for 'What is the *maśśāʾ* (burdensome pronouncement or burden)?'" LXX "You are the burden" presupposes a redivision of consonants (see *BHS*, though its inclusion of Vg. is dubious since it paraphrases MT [Barthélemy, *Critique textuelle*, 2:648], perhaps with one eye on LXX). This reading is generally preferred as a logical preface to Yahweh's sharp reply. EVV reflect it, except for NIV and NJPS, whose judgment, as Lundbom 2:215 bluntly states, "perpetuates the error." Barthélemy explains MT both here and at Job 7:20 as theological corrections to safeguard the transcendence of Yahweh, to whom nothing can be burdensome.

f. For this sense of the verb here and in v. 39 see Holladay 1:650–51 and cf. *HALOT* 2:695b.

g. The syntax of the causal clause and the antecedent of the suffix have been variously interpreted. McKane 1:600–601 has seen that the polemical use of *maśśāʾ* that underlies the ban points to the sense that the prophet of doom is in fact Yahweh's true representative, and this is the reason given for the ban on ridicule. Two exegetical conclusions follow. First, *hammaśśāʾ*, "the burdensome pronouncement," is the emphatic subject, as the word order suggests. Second, *ʾîš dĕbārô* belong together in a construct phrase, as Tg. construes, but, unlike Tg., in the sense "the man of his word" with the suffix relating to

Yahweh. A major difference between McKane's thorough study, "*mś'* in Jeremiah 23:33–40," in *Prophecy: Essays Presented to Georg Fohrer on His Sixty-Fifth Birthday, 6 September 1980* (ed. J. A. Emerton; BZAW 150; Berlin: de Gruyter, 1980), 35–54, esp. 46–49, and the presentation in his commentary is that in the latter he moves to this interpretation. It is shared by NEB and by Thompson 505; Jones 316; Wanke 1:219.

h. See GKC §144h for the indefinite sense of the second singular in MT. However, the plural in the subsequent Greek tradition accords with vv. 35, 36, 38; MT has probably suffered careless assimilation to the singular address of the prophet in v. 33.

i. LXX omits vv. 36b and 37 thus far, probably by accidental loss of a line (cf. Janzen, *Studies*, 99–100, 223 n. 35).

j. See *BHS* for the repointing that is generally adopted (thus EVV except NIV and NJPS). Barthélemy, *Critique textuelle*, 2:649–51, finds in MT a theological correction, as in v. 33.

This composition consists of two prose units, vv. 25–32 and 33–40. They are both concerned with issues of the nomenclature for prophetic oracles and communal opposition to Jeremiah's messages of coming doom. Their former role was to round off the collection of prophetic sayings that began in v. 9, as a distinct section; now they have been adopted as a composition. The issue of prophetic truth versus falsehood in the first unit is paired with a respect for the divine reality revealed in Jeremiah's oracles in the second.

[25–32] This oracle refers to Jeremiah's prophetic rivals in the third person. It consists of two reasons (vv. 25–29) and a triple announcement of disaster (vv. 30–32) introduced by the conventional "Therefore." Meyer has proposed that 23:9–32 was compiled as a pamphlet, based on Jeremiah's teaching, that circulated in Jerusalem.[167] McKane (1:596–97) has suggested something similar concerning vv. 25–32, noting that exilic concerns are absent. The sheer complexity of the unit, its third person orientation, and the abbreviated usage of the formula of hostile orientation (vv. 30–32) do suggest that the unit constitutes a compressed summary.

[25–29] This section falls into two separate halves, one reason relating to Yahweh's "name" (vv. 25, 27 [twice] and the other reason to Yahweh's "message" (vv. 28 [twice], 29). Both halves conclude with a series of questions, in each case a single one followed by a double one (vv. 26–27, 28b–29). This parallelism suggests that a basic statement incorporating a contrast opens each half, in vv. 25 and 28a, though the latter case is generally taken as an exhortation, following LXX.

[25–27] Yahweh's "name" refers objectively to the prophets' use of the quotation formula that included the divine name, "Here is what Yahweh said" (cf. 28:2), and/or the version "declared Yahweh," to which v. 31 will explicitly refer

---

167. Ivo Meyer, *Jeremia und die falschen Propheten* (OBO 13; Freiburg: Universitätsverlag; Göttingen: Vandenhoeck & Ruprecht, 1977), 140.

Doomed Kings and Discredited Prophets 271

(cf. 28:4). Two charges of misrepresentation are offered, one relating to content and the other to form. The content of the prophets' teaching is branded as "falsehood," as in 14:14, while the form is that of a dream. <u>Falsehood constitutes a perversion of true faith in Yahweh; it did not entail conscious deceit.</u>[168] Dreams were traditionally regarded as an acceptable form of divine revelation (e.g., Gen 28:12; Num 12:6; 1 Sam 28:6, 15; Joel 2:28 [3:1]; Matt 1:20), yet in the book of Jeremiah they are deprecated, not only in this oracle but in 27:9 and 29:8. In these cases they acquire a bad reputation or guilt by association. That they were used to convey prophetic material quite alien to that of Jeremiah's God has here ruled them out as an admissible form (cf. 29:8–9; Deut 13:1–5 [2–6]). It is striking, however, that Jeremiah's receipt of divine truth depended at times on the similar genre of visions, notably in the next chapter, despite the derogatory references to visions in 14:14 and 23:16. The popularity of dream revelations evidently posed a greater threat.

[25] The oracle begins with Yahweh's response to the claims made by Jeremiah's prophetic rivals. The excited double cry would certainly attract a crowd of hearers, but Yahweh for one was not impressed.

[26–27] The series of questions starts with a brief expression of deep exasperation, borrowed from the world of the complaint psalm (NAB; cf. Pss 6:3 [4]; 90:13; Isa 6:11). The next, doubled question explores the prophets' motivation in parading such untruths and wishful thinking. Did they have a sinister purpose that matched the result? Certainly the result was a misrepresentation of Yahweh, ironic in view of their explicit use of Yahweh's name. To forget Yahweh is elsewhere associated with pagan worship (2:32; 3:21; 13:25; 18:15; cf. Hos 2:13 [15]), but not here. "[I]t is just as much idolatry to worship God according to a false mental image as by means of a false metal image."[169] "One another" may reflect a clique that gave mutual moral support before going public with their dreams.[170]

[28–29] The second reason makes the point at issue not "my name" but "my message," which is different from a prophetic dream. "Truly" is a positive counterpart to "falsehood" in the corresponding statement in v. 25. The first, short question uses a metaphor for worthlessness and worth to contrast the value of each type of revelation. The second, double question presents the content of the latter type in terms of violent destruction, the only proper oracle for the times (cf. 5:14 and as NT parallels for God's adversarial word Heb 4:12; Rev 2:12, 16). There is an implicit contrast with bland assurances of *šālôm*, "peace," and blatant denials of disaster characteristic of Jeremiah's rivals (v. 17).

[30–32] The announcement of disaster consists of a series of formulas of hostile orientation; they are in each case expanded with further grounds for

---

168. Martin A. Klopfenstein, "*šqr* to deceive," *TLOT* 3:1399–1405, esp. 1403.
169. William Temple, *Christian Faith and Life* (London: SCM, 1931), 24.
170. Meyer, *Falschen Propheten*, 136.

disaster. Elsewhere in the OT, for instance in 21:13, the formula is followed by specific reprisals Yahweh was to initiate. In this case separate announcements seem to have been condensed. The truncated form focuses on the extra reasons, just broaching Yahweh's opposition in response. There are loose links between the first two statements and what has preceded them. The first statement reverts to the notion of a clique ("one another") and echoes "my message," from vv. 28–29. The fact that any of these prophets had "my messages" may indicate an original separate setting from the foregoing. The second statement echoes the use of Yahweh's name in prophetic oracles (v. 25) and claims unwarranted use of the quotation formula "declared Yahweh." MT retaliates by supplementing the formula in v. 30 with five more significant ones in vv. 28–32.

[32] The third statement is much longer and represents an effort to summarize several elements of vv. 25–28. The vocabulary of prophesying dream-mediated falsehood in vv. 25–26, the construction of v. 27a, and the motif of usefulness expressed in metaphor at v. 28b all reappear. The metaphors of destruction in v. 29 find as their counterpart the ominous hostility of Yahweh.

[33–40] Whereas the dream as a popular means of prophetic revelation was the issue in the former unit, this one deals with the oracular term *maśśāʾ*, here rendered "burdensome pronouncement." The unit has an intricate structure in that it interweaves an oracle of disaster with material belonging to a question-and-answer format. Failing to perceive this amalgamation, commentators have tended to brand vv. 34–40 as a clumsy secondary development and to misunderstand their meaning. The elements of the oracle of disaster appear in the crucial v. 36, in which the prophet gives the reason, and then in vv. 38–40, which present the announcement. The initial question-and-answer format has occasioned an anticipation of the divine announcement of disaster in vv. 33–34 and lingers in a wrapping around of the basic reason in v. 36 with further material belonging to the question part of the format in vv. 35 and 37. The unit falls into three consecutive sections. In vv. 33–34 Yahweh addresses the prophet and gives a message for him to transmit to the community. In vv. 35–37 Jeremiah addresses the community, in view of the third person divine references at the end of v. 36 that include "our God." In vv. 38–40 there is a divine oracle to the community that resumes and develops v. 33b. There seems to be no good reason for not regarding this prose unit as a reminiscence of an experience of Jeremiah.

[33] This question-and-answer format directly addressed to the prophet has appeared earlier in the book, notably at 13:2–14; 15:1–4. The present case has been characterized as "the simplest and probably oldest example from the prophets."[171] The issue involves wordplay. The term *maśśāʾ*, "utterance," a noun derived from the verb *nāśāʾ* (*qôl*), "lift (the voice)," was used in the prophetic sense of oracle; it appears alongside the cognate verb in 2 Kgs 9:25,

---

171. Long, "Question and Answer Schemata," 135.

"the LORD uttered this oracle." By itself the noun is used in prophetic literature as a heading for an oracle against a foreign nation, especially in the book of Isaiah (e.g., Isa 13:1), and for a collection of oracles in Zech 9:1; 12:1; and Mal 1:1. But the noun can also mean "burden" and was used four times with the verb in Jer 17:21–27 with the sense "carry loads." Here the question posed to Jeremiah is a derogatory one that even as it seemed to respectfully solicit an oracle sarcastically dismissed it as another unnecessary burden Jeremiah was to place on the constituency's shoulders. The term became the focus of opposition to his oracles. Yahweh's set retort anticipates by way of summary the formal announcement of disaster in vv. 38–39. It throws the term back in an exasperated way, branding the constituency itself as a burden too heavy for Yahweh to carry any longer (cf. Exod 19:4). That constituency was not simply made up of the community at large, but included temple representatives and Jeremiah's prophetic rivals.

[34] The resumption of the triple definition of the constituency uses inversion, a common stylistic ploy when terms are repeated.[172] Here the focus is not on the punishment of the community at large but on that of specific individuals who with smirks engaged in the wordplay that refused to take seriously Yahweh's oracles through Jeremiah. The pinpointing is reminiscent of Pashhur (20:6), by which he and his family would receive special attention when the general destruction of the community took place (cf. too 11:22–23).

[35–37] The answer format continues in vv. 35 and 37, evidently now addressed to members of the community who are envisioned as first talking among themselves and then inquiring of a prophet. In both these situations the mandate is to avoid the ambiguous term *maśśāʾ* because of its use as an unwarranted term of abuse, as v. 36 states plainly. Verse 36 is spoken by the prophet and paves the way for the announcement of disaster in vv. 38–40 by presenting a sinister reason. Ironically those who rejected an oracle of disaster were confronted with one just for them. The piling up of divine labels highlights the reality of God's power and covenant as conveyed in Jeremiah's oracles.

[38–40] MT smooths the connection. The oracle of disaster continues with a standard "therefore" and then a blunt restatement of the reason before moving to the announcement with a resumptive "therefore." Mention of the city associates the disaster with the overthrow of Jerusalem. Only here is the city, rather than the country, said to be given to forebears. MT adds to the agony by incorporating the notion of exile in its addition, "right away from my presence," an interpretive touch probably inspired by 2 Kgs 23:27 that does not quite fit the imagery of a dropped load but nicely prepares for the topics of exile and restoration in ch. 24.

---

172. Cf. Shemaryahu Talmon, "The Textual Study of the Bible—A New Outlook," in *Qumran and the History of the Biblical Text* (ed. F. M. Cross and S. Talmon; Cambridge: Harvard University Press, 1975), 321–400, esp. 358–62.

The note of permanent humiliation provides solemn closure to the announcement, one calculated to remove any remaining smirks.

The composition in 23:25–40 addresses two obstacles Jeremiah faced, the medium of dream revelations adopted by his optimistic rivals and a heckling, dismissive retort from the public. Both issues broach the nature of true prophecy and especially its destructive content at this juncture of Judah's history.

24:1–10 Restoration and Judgment

24:1 Yahweh directed my attention to two baskets of figs placed[a] in front of Yahweh's temple. (It happened after King Nebuchadnezzar of Babylon had deported from Jerusalem King Jeconiah ben Jehoiakim of Judah, along with the *Judean* officials and the craftsmen and smiths, and taken them home to Babylon.) **2** There was one basket of very good figs, the quality of early ones, and another of very bad figs, so bad they were inedible. **3** Yahweh asked me, "What can you see, Jeremiah?" "Figs," I replied, "the good figs very good and the bad figs very bad, so bad they are inedible." **4** Then I received the following message from Yahweh: **5** Here is what Yahweh, Israel's God, said: "These good figs symbolize the good consideration I will give the group of Judean deportees I sent away from this place to the Chaldeans' country. **6** I will look out for their good, bringing them back to this country and building them up instead of demolishing them, planting them instead of uprooting them. **7** I will give them the will to acknowledge me as Yahweh; then they will be my people and I will be their God, because[b] they will come back to me wholeheartedly. **8** The bad figs, on the other hand, so bad they are inedible, surely"—here is what Yahweh said—"symbolize the way I will treat King Zedekiah of Judah and his officials, along with the other survivors from Jerusalem, left in this country—or living in Egypt. **9** I will turn them into people all the other kingdoms in the world shudder at;[c] they will be ridiculed and regarded as infamous, they will be taunted and cursed—in whatever places I drive them away to. **10** I will let loose among them sword, famine, and pestilence, until they have died off the land that was my gift to them *and their forebears*."

a. See BDB 417a; *DCL* 4:241a. The third emendation listed in *BHS*, adopted by McKane 1:606, needs to be weighed against the negative assessment of John A. Emerton, "A Further Consideration of D. W. Thomas's Theories about *yādaʿ*," *VT* 41 (1991): 145–63, esp. 158.

b. "When" (NJPS) or "if" (Drinkard in Craigie et al. 357, 360) does not suit v. 7aα, unless the clause qualifies v. 7a, which seems unlikely despite MT's punctuation and Deut 4:29; 30:10; Jer 29:12–14. See the discussion of Hermann Stipp, "Jeremia 24: Geschichtsbild und historischer Ort," *JNSL* 25 (1999): 151–83, esp. 160–65.

c. LXX lacks MT's *lĕrāʿâ*, "for bad, as bad." NAB and REB omit, as RSV did. It does not fit the formulaic context and doubtless arose as a marginal comment on v. 8, supplying a counterpart of *lĕṭôbâ*, lit. "for good," in v. 5, which was derived from 21:10. It was attracted into the text at this point by the series of nouns with this preposition prefixed. The supposition that it originally closed v. 8, as a parallel to v. 5 (Volz 247; cf. *BHS*) requires in its support a text-critical explanation of its omission.

This prose piece functions as a short composition that closes the block of chs. 21–24. Its nonprophetic topic differentiates it from the collection and group of compositions that spanned 23:9–40, while it works admirably as the final half of a frame for the whole block, along with the first (prose) unit of the first composition, 21:1–10. The piece is at heart a combination of a proclamation of salvation and an announcement of disaster. It achieves this dual end by means of an oracle-vision report in an autobiographical style, rather like the two reports in 1:11–16. In this case a description of two entities (vv. 1a, 2) and a dialogue of question and answer (v. 3) are followed by an interpretation of each entity (vv. 4–10), in which the opposing statements are made. This form-critical unity is not the last word, inasmuch as at least two literary stages of composition emerge on closer examination. Verses 6, 7, 9, and 10 are pervaded by the standard language of the prose sermon.[173] Accordingly, the original interpretations (vv. 5 and 8) are followed by redactional elaborations that develop their significance for the reading constituency with "a sustained attempt at theological reflection."[174] This factor explains the presence of the two quotation formulas in v. 5 and, rather awkwardly placed, in the course of v. 8. They are unexpected in a simple report of Yahweh's interpretation for Jeremiah and prepare rather for public transmission. The formulas here announce the elaborations that follow a little later and lay claim to their own authority via the redactor-prophet.

[24:1–2] The description of the vision is interrupted by a literary footnote stating the chronological setting as after 597, a good fit for the report. It is a historical interpretation of v. 5 and has made intertextual use of 2 Kgs 24:14–16; the name "Jeconiah" ("Jehoiachin" in 2 Kings) accords with the form used in the prose of Jer 27:20; 28:4; and 29:2, though there it has a shorter Hebrew ending. The note was placed here because of its introductory nature and also just before the description of "good figs," which it elucidates. The topographical setting of the vision indicates that it took place in the temple area. Whether what Jeremiah saw could have been seen by others present or whether it was a trance experience is unclear, but the former may well have been the case, so that the very oddness of the presence of such bad figs initially attracted the prophet's attention and

---

173. Cf. Stulman, *Prose Sermons*, 33–44. Although Stulman does not study this passage individually, these listings of prose sermon vocabulary indicate its presence in ch. 24; see nos. 4, 11, 17, 28, 39, 44, 52, 56, 69, 86.

174. Burke O. Long, "Reports of Visions Among the Prophets," *JBL* 95 (1976): 353–65, esp. 359.

suggested a providential intention. Presumably the figs were gifts of firstfruits "set down before the LORD" (Deut 26:10), awaiting a priestly decision about their acceptability (cf. Lev 22:20–21).[175] Thus the scene is set for the divine verdict in the vision. Early figs were especially prized (Hos 9:10; Mic 7:1).

[3] First, however, comes the question-and-answer dialogue, a feature of a number of visions (Jer 1:11–14; Amos 7:7–8; 8:1–3; Zech 5:1–4). Jeremiah's attention and thereby the reader's are drawn to what he has just described, as a preliminary to the interpretation that will focus on "good" and "bad."

[4–5] After the oracle reception statement and quotation formula in which "Israel's God" anticipates v. 7, the interpretation takes the form of a simile ("Like . . . so . . . ," NRSV), as later in v. 8. In neither case is the adjective given any moral or spiritual meaning—indeed, in v. 7 future reformation is a necessity for those representing the splendidly good figs! Jeremiah's diverse reactions model Yahweh's. Moreover, $rā^côt$, "bad," is interpreted against an implicit background of $rā^câ$, "a bad fate, disaster," ubiquitous in the book thus far, while $tōbôt$, "good," is explained in line with $tôb$ (6:16; 8:15; 14:19; 15:11; 17:6) or $tôbâ$ (14:11; 18:10; 21:10; and here in v. 6) in the sense of a good outcome. Not merits but prospects are in view, so that the interpretations function not as reasons in a statement of disaster or salvation but as announcements of what was to happen. This forward look associates Jehoiachin's truncated reign with hope and Zedekiah's contemporary reign with doom. The former claim is not so much a reversal of 22:24–30 as a positing of a new and positive future for those exiled in 597, whereas earlier the particulars of the personal return of Jehoiachin and royal rank for his heirs had been denied. Now Jehoiachin and company stand in a postjudgment position; Zedekiah and company, however, still occupy a prejudgment place and have yet to face divine judgment. "This place" has a parallel in "this country" at vv. 6 and 8 and so refers to Judah; v. 1b represents a translation from Judah and "the Chaldeans' country" (v. 5) to urban terms, "Jerusalem" and "Babylon."

[6–7] The elaboration of the interpretation, which the quotation formula in v. 5 was meant to herald, provides the reader with a summary of Yahweh's saving plans, first in external and then in relational terms. Return from exile would be the first step of the positive work of divine renewal of the community that was to follow on the heels of radical judgment. These verses depict these past and future events using the book's characteristic vocabulary (cf. esp. 1:10; 31:28; 42:10); implicitly, demolishing and uprooting lay in the past. Verse 7 announces the fulfillment of covenant ideals, giving a central role to the double covenant formula (cf. 7:23 and 11:4 in prose sermons). It would come true only by means of the eschatological inner transformation to be wrought by God. Only that could bring proper appreciation of Yahweh and of Yahweh's purposes

---

175. Zimmerli, "Visionary Experience," 110, but Reventlow, *Liturgie*, 88–89, is doubtful.

for the covenant community (cf. 31:33–34; 32:38–40; Ezek 20:44; 36:26). Only that would enable a spiritual return that spelled complete allegiance (cf. 3:10). Logically the experience in the causal clause falls between the two preceding ones (Bracke 1:195).

[8] The sinister side of the vision is applied to the substitute regime of Zedekiah. The "survivors" are those not included among the deported in 597 (v. 5). The closing qualification "or living in Egypt" strikes a dissonant note, yet a deliberate one in that it is matched by "in whatever places I drive them away to" at the end of v. 9. Verse 10 makes clear that inhabitants of Judah were initially in view. Judah, and Judah alone, was to become their grave. This sentiment was subsequently given a historical update by lumping together with them in the judgment the refugees to Egypt after 587 as part of the same group (cf. "who live[d] in Egypt," 44:1, 13, 15, 26). The addition in v. 9 has the same intention, just as in 23:8 "from any of the other countries I have driven them to" was meant as a literary echo of Jehoahaz's deportation to Egypt.

[9–10] What did the negative statement of v. 8 mean? Again the elaboration uses prose sermonic language to spell out the terribly bad prospects. The "inedible" nature of the figs is interpreted as the shocked reaction of the rest of the world to the Judeans' fate (cf. 15:4; 26:6; 42:18; 44:8)—whether in Judah or in the Egyptian (etc.) Diaspora, where exile would spell only doom (cf. 8:3). The novel elements *lĕmāšāl lišnînâ*, "regarded as infamous, taunted," are quoted from Deut 28:37 (NRSV "a proverb and a byword"). The triple curse of the redacted book is borrowed in v. 10 to explain the basis of the reaction, in terms of devastating military invasion and siege that would bring about a dead end and an annulment of earlier promises. MT "and their forebears" creates a link with 23:39.

This complex message was obviously intended to dash hopes of a successful future associated with Zedekiah's reign, like 21:1–10. It stood under the dire judgment of God. As there, hope is real but ironic. In 21:9 survival was possible only by getting out of Jerusalem, while here it is keyed into a past event. Yet the evenhanded depiction and explanation (both primary and secondary) in roughly equal parts mean that vv. 5 and 6–7 may not be subordinated to vv. 8 and 9–10, but stand in their own right as promises (cf. 23:5–6), opening a restricted channel to Israel's future receipt of divine grace. The two-sided message, "an *ad hoc* message, directed to a particular situation,"[176] presents premonitions of good and bad to come, which tied grace and judgment to different regimes. The redactor eventually updated the bad side (to some extent, but cf. 34:1–5), but did not (know how to?) update the good side in a similar way, yet presumably assumed that the originally unenvisioned Judean exile after 587 somehow nestled under the earlier exilic category (cf. Fretheim 347). MT says

---

176. Peter R. Ackroyd, *Exile and Restoration* (OTL; Philadelphia: Westminster, 1968), 55.

as much in 29:14, 16–18. In the divine purpose the road to restoration lay only via the detour of displacement, whether to Babylonian exile or to the lands of the Diaspora (cf. 32:36–41). It is interesting to speculate that Jeremiah was echoing popular political support for the earlier king against the Babylonian nominee or that the redactor intended to side with later Babylonian exiles in a quarrel over legitimacy with contemporary groups in Judah and Egypt, but the present text is not interested in such speculations; in the second case the argument is not made sufficiently clear for this interpretation.

25:1–38 Doom for Judah and Other Nations

25:1 A message for all the people of Judah that Jeremiah received in the fourth year of King Jehoiakim ben Josiah of Judah *(that is, the first year of King Nebuchadnezzar of Babylon)*, 2 which *the prophet Jeremiah* told all the people of Judah and *all* the residents of Jerusalem: 3 "Since the thirteenth year of King Josiah ben Amon of Judah up to now, actually for twenty-three years, I have been *receiving each message from Yahweh and* telling you over and over again,[a] *but you have not listened.* 4 Moreover, *Yahweh* has been sending to you over and over again *all his* prophetic servants, but you have not listened, you have turned a deaf ear *instead of listening* 5 to what they said, that you should renounce, every single one of you, your bad practices, the bad you have been perpetrating, so you could live[b] on the land *Yahweh* long ago gave you and your forebears forever, 6 and that you should not follow other gods, giving them homage and worshiping them, 'or else you will upset me with objects your own hands have made and I will treat you badly. 7 But you did not listen to me,' declared Yahweh.[c] 8 'Therefore'—here is what Yahweh *Almighty* said—'because you have failed to listen to my messages, 9 look out, I am going to send for and get *all* the northern clans,' declared Yahweh, 'and for my servant King Nebuchadnezzar of Babylon, and bring them here to attack this country and those who live in it and also all the other nations around *here*. I will wreak ruin[d] on them and make people react to them with shock, whistles, and unending insults.[e] 10 I will eliminate from them sounds of joy and gladness, such as the shouts of bride and groom, and the noise made by a hand-mill, and the light of a lamp. 11 For seventy years *this* whole country will be turned into *a ruin*, a shocking scene, and the *local* nations will be in subjection[f] *to Babylon's king.* 12 When the seventy years are over, I will deal with *Babylon's king and* that nation,' declared Yahweh, '*for their wrongdoing, namely, with the country of the Chaldeans,* and turn it into a permanently desolate area. 13 I will make all my messages that I directed against that country come true for it—everything written in this book, in which Jeremiah prophesied against *all* the

Doom for Judah and Other Nations

nations. 14 *That means they in turn will be*[g] *in servitude to many nations and powerful kings, and so I will pay them back as their actions deserve, as their hands have perpetrated.*'"

15 *By way of explanation,* here is what Yahweh, Israel's God, said *to me*: "Take from my hand this cup of wine, which represents wrath,[h] and get all the nations to whom I send you to drink *it.* 16 *On drinking,* they will throw up[i] and go berserk, from the impact of the sword I am to send among them." 17 So I took the cup from Yahweh's hand and got *all* the nations to whom Yahweh had sent me to take a drink: 18 namely, Jerusalem and Judah's towns, with its kings and royal officials, turning them into a ruined area and into a catalyst for shock and whistles *and cursing*[j] *(all of which has happened by now)*; 19 Pharaoh, king of Egypt, with his ministers and officials, all his own people 20 and all the foreign groups;[k] and all the kings of *the region of* the Philistines—Ashkelon, Gaza, Ekron, and what is left of Ashdod; 21 Edom, Moab, and Ammon; 22 *all* the kings of Tyre and *all* the kings of Sidon, and the kings of the Mediterranean *coast*; 23 and Dedan, Tema, and Buz, and all the people with shaven temples; 24 and all the other kings of Arabia[l] who live in the desert and all the kings in the region of Uz; 25 *all the kings of Zimki*[m] and all the kings of Media; 26 all the kings of the north, whether adjacent to one another or distant, and the rest of the kingdoms[n] that are on the face of the earth. *After them the king of Sheshach will take a drink.* 27 "You are to tell them: 'Here is what Yahweh Almighty, *Israel's God*, said: "Drink up, get intoxicated, then vomit and fall down and stay down, from the impact of the sword I am to send among you!"' 28 If they refuse to take the cup from your hand and have a drink, then say *to them*: 'Here is what Yahweh *Almighty* said: "You must take a drink 29 because, *look,* the city that is named after me is starting to experience my bad treatment. So how can you be let off?[o] No, you cannot be let off, because a sword is what I am summoning to attack *all* the earth's inhabitants," *declared Yahweh Almighty.*'

30 "Your task is to prophesy *all* this and then say *to them*:

'Yahweh roars from heaven above,
   howling from his holy residence,
   roaring loudly at his homeland.
A vintage song he chants like grape-treaders
   to *all* the earth's inhabitants.
31   The clamor[p] reaches
   as far as the edge of the earth,
because Yahweh has a dispute with the nations,
   bringing to trial all humanity
and handing them over as guilty to the sword,'"[q]

declared Yahweh. 32 Here is what Yahweh *Almighty* said:

"Look, a bad fate is to break out,
   spreading from nation to nation,
and a vehement storm wind will be aroused
   from the remotest parts of the earth."

33 Those slain by Yahweh will cover the earth on that day from one end to the other, *unmourned, ungathered,* unburied, left lying like dung on the surface of the ground.

34 Wail, you shepherd-kings, and bawl,
       throw yourselves about, you flock masters,
    because your time is up—you are to be slaughtered and shattered (?),[r]
       falling like precious pottery![s]
35 Running away will not be an option for the shepherd-kings
       nor will escape for the flock masters.
36 Hark at the bawling from the shepherd-kings,
       at the wailing from the flock masters!
    It is because of Yahweh's devastation of their pasture
37   and ruination of peaceful meadows
       from the impact of Yahweh's burning anger.
38 He left, like a lion, his lair—
       yes, the country of each of them has become a shocking place
       from the impact of the oppressor's sword[t]
    and from the impact of his burning anger.

   a. For the form *ʾaškêm* see *BHS* and the discussion of McKane 1:618.
   b. For the idiomatic use of the imperative to express consequence see GKC §110f; Joüon §116f.
   c. MT adds to the shorter text of LXX: "so as to upset me with objects your own hands have made, which will result in bad consequences for you," a doublet of v. 6b that has been inappropriately inserted here from the margin. LXX in v. 6b is somewhat closer to the form of MT in v. 7b (Janzen, *Studies*, 13).
   d. See McKane 1:623; cf. BDB 355b.
   e. As NAB and NRSV judge, LXX is preferable to MT (see *BHS*) on formulaic grounds (cf. MT at 29:18). The plural *ḥrbwt*, "ruins," provides a clue that MT was originally intended as a marginal correction or explanation of *lĕḥorbâ* in v. 18, where a plural might have been expected with reference to Judean towns, and was misapplied, displacing a term in a similar context in the preceding column. For this type of text-critical error see the textual notes on 17:3–4. The influence of 49:13, where the construct phrase occurs, was probably also a contributing factor.

Doom for Judah and Other Nations 281

f. The shorter text underlying the mistranslation in LXX achieves a similar sense by finding here the different meaning of the same verb in v. 14 (BDB 713a), "the nations will be in servitude to them," i.e., "the northern clan(s)" of v. 9 (Streane 151; Goldman, *Prophétie et royauté*, 141–42, 209).

g. Haplography is generally assumed; see *BHS* and cf. 27:7.

h. For the appositional usage cf. Ps 60:5 (3).

i. See *HALOT* 1:200a; LXX, REB, and NJPS understand the verb thus, while v. 27 supports this sense.

j. MT has assimilated to 24:9.

k. MT places here "and all the kings in the land of Uz," which does not fit the geographical context of Egypt and Philistia. Uz is not precisely defined in the OT; it is connected with Edom in Lam 4:21. It may refer to a place in Arabia and hence to vv. 23–24. It is feasible to imagine that it had an original position there, possibly after v. 24. LXX (32:6, 10) represents the phrase in neither place, like MT at an earlier stage; both lost it in v. 24, if that is where it belonged, through parablepsis. A later attempt at restoration in MT misfired because in the phrase that precedes in v. 20, "and all the foreign groups (ʿereb)," in an unpointed text there was confusion with ʿārāb, "Arabia" (cf. the note below on v. 24), a confusion that also underlies the sentence division in MT at v. 20 (cf. *BHS*). The mistake in MT over the placement of the Uz phrase supports a supposition that it was meant to belong to v. 24. NJB is aware of the problem.

l. MT adds to "and all the kings of ʿārāb (Arabia)" a doublet, "and all the kings of the ʿereb," the foreign groups mentioned in v. 20. This is another manifestation of the confusion evident in v. 20. A reference to Arabia is needed in the context of vv. 23–24. LXX (32:10) has only the second phrase, attesting an earlier stage of textual development. MT offers a later stage in which a marginal correction has been inserted alongside the erroneous text. NAB and REB omit, while NJB is again alert to the problem.

m. MT has a conflated text, "and all the kings of Zimri and all the kings of Elam," while LXX (32:11) has just the second phrase. "Zimri" occurs only here as an ethnic name. A widely accepted explanation for the mysterious first phrase, proposed by Felix Perles (cf. McKane 1:639) and mentioned in *BHS*, is that the noun was earlier *zimkî*, a code name achieved by reversal of the order of letters in the Hebrew alphabet (called *athbash*), which stood for "Elam" (ʿylm). An encoding of this type does occur at v. 26b, again in the redacted MT, a phenomenon that suggests its likelihood, in this case as part of the MT redaction. The conflated text attests both the encoded replacement, which MT intended, and the plain text by way of explanation, while LXX bears witness to the underlying original. In the present text the strange name has been assimilated to a well-attested personal name. NJB places the first phrase in parentheses in recognition of the textual problem.

n. MT ungrammatically and tautologously adds "of the earth (hāʾāreṣ),"which LXX (32:12) lacks. In the pointed MT a construct state is prefixed with the article. The phrase is omitted by EVV except NRSV and NJPS. The addition probably represents a marginal explanation of the ambiguous phrase "(on the face of) the ground/earth (hāʾădāmâ)," indicating that it referred not to "the ground" as in v. 33 but to "the world" or "earth." The term was improperly incorporated into the text under the influence of 24:9. Barthélemy, *Critique textuelle*, 2:657, intriguingly observes that Isa 23:17, with its reference to seventy years, already seems to reflect MT even if it does represent a gloss.

o. For the implied question see GKC, §150a; Joüon §161a.
p. Thus NRSV; cf. REB "great noise."
q. For the cola divisions and alignments in vv. 30–31 cf. the discussion of Cloete, *Versification*, 198.
r. MT *ûtĕpôṣôtîkem* is an unresolved crux. It looks like a mixed form, partly based on a noun, "and your scatterings," and partly a verb, "and I will scatter you." LXX (32:20) does not represent it, but may have omitted it as unintelligible, as NAB, REB, and GNB do. If it is an integral part of the text—and unless one can explain it as a gloss or other intrusion one is left with this option—the best that can be done is to disregard the accentuation and pointing of MT and, with Barthélemy, *Critique textuelle*, 2:658–59, to point as a noun, *ûtĕpûṣôtêkem*, with some ancient support and take it as a continuation of the preceding verbal noun "for slaughter," rendering "and (for) your shattering(s)." The root *pwṣ* means "scatter," but a better meaning would be "shatter," in line both with the closing simile and with the sense of the related verbs *npṣ* and *pṣṣ*; this is a common suggestion that Barthélemy takes up as a second semantic option.
s. The reading *kĕʾêlê*, "like rams," presupposed in LXX for *kiklî*, "like a pot," and adopted by NAB, REB, and GNB, is interesting but less likely than MT; it was a secondary attempt to achieve metaphorical uniformity.
t. MT *ḥărôn*, "burning," is generally regarded as a mistake for *ḥereb*, "sword," assimilating to the same term in the next colon; EVV except NJPS and NJB so judge. BHS cites MT MSS, LXX (32:24), and Tg. for support and compares 46:16 and 50:16. For the repointing of *hayyônâ*, "the oppressing (?) (sword)," to *hayyôneh*, "the oppressor's (sword)," which is indirectly supported in Syr. by its exegetical translation as the divine name, see McKane 1:647, 654–56. NIV and REB render thus.

This composition explores the role of Babylon as "destroyer of nations" (4:7). It is made up of three units, vv. 1–14, 15–29, and 30–38, the first two in prose and the third in poetry. The inclusion of the fate of other, local nations with that of Judah in the first unit develops in the second and third into two messages of international doom, with Judah (v. 18) and Jerusalem (v. 29a) explicitly included in the second and Yahweh's "homeland" of Judah (v. 30) mentioned in the third. In the second and third units the balance between Judah and the other nations changes, with the latter being given increasingly greater weight. This composition has the role of a block because it begins in v. 1 with an oracle reception heading used to demarcate a new block. The reader has come to expect a prose sermon in the vicinity of a new block, and it duly appears in the course of the first unit.[177] It pervades vv. 3–12, though it is possible to isolate nonsermonic elements in vv. 9–12 as an earlier base on which the sermon has been editorially imposed; the nonconventionality of "the noise made by a hand-mill and the light of a lamp" (v. 10) is particularly striking. The sermon has a strong affinity with the sermons in chs. 7 and 11, and also overlaps with stylized passages in ch. 16. Focus is laid on the sinister rejection of Yahweh's prophetic revelation that accused Judah of moral degen-

177. See Stulman, *Prose Sermons*, 82–86.

Doom for Judah and Other Nations

eration and pagan worship and threatened the loss of the traditional gift of the land and the elimination of normal daily life. In this respect the first unit serves as a literary buttress, reinforcing the lessons of earlier ones in chs. 7 and 11. At closer range the prophets' call for repentance in v. 5 traces an arc back to the optimistic prophets' failure to do so in 23:14, 22, while the accusation of pagan worship in v. 6 echoes that in 22:9. Not surprisingly the message is presented in v. 3 as containing a summary of Jeremiah's prophetic ministry, while the composition's development to destruction on a grand scale has an air of a conclusion. It has often been observed that Jeremiah's role as "prophet to the nations" (1:5, 10) resurfaces here to provide a frame for chs. 1–25. That and the chronological flashback to 1:2 in 25:3 combine to give the composition a pausal function in the ongoing book.

All three units are integrated by the recurring root r^{cc}, "be bad," in various forms, with reference to Judah's bad behavior (v. 5) and Yahweh's bad treatment of it (v. 6), to Jerusalem's bad treatment at Yahweh's hands (v. 29a), and to the bad fate of the nations in general (v. 32). This focal repetition is supported by references to the aggressors' "wrongdoing" in MT at v. 12 and to the nations as "wicked" or "guilty" in the common text at v. 31. The first two units are linked by the shocked reactions to Yahweh's intervention against Judah and adjoining nations in v. 9 and against Jerusalem and Judah in v. 18. As one might expect from the shift of focus, however, closer affinity is evident between the latter two units, due to the "sword" Yahweh was to commission against the nations (vv. 16, 27, 29b and 31, 38). The frame for these latter two units is created by the "wrath" in v. 15 and "burning anger" in v. 37 (cf. v. 38) that were to be inflicted by Yahweh on the nations. An important role is played by vv. 18 and 29a in bonding the first unit to the other two, yet these are initial and final elements whose secondary nature has been suspected. However, if they are secondary, they came in at the compositional level and already predate the complex redactional evidence of LXX, which exhibits both a shorter text in terms of individual components and a much longer text by inserting the originally separate oracles against the nations (chs. 46–51 in MT) after v. 13 (it definitely attests the presence of vv. 18 and 29a). This compositional factor strongly suggests that the large-scale rearrangement in LXX, though widely held to be original, is an intrusion into a text that in this major respect coincided with MT. McKane (2:1110) states that, with the removal of the oracles against the nations, the cup of wrath piece in vv. 15–29 "was left high and dry" in MT, but he can say that only because he characteristically leaves a compositional perspective out of account. By placing vv. 15–38 after the oracles against the nations—at 32:1–24 in LXX—the carefully arranged composition has been bulldozed into separate pieces.[178]

---

178. Cf. Peake 2:4, "The insertion of these oracles at this point tears [ch.] xxv in two, separating sections that are really connected." Peake was arguing for an unattested placing of the oracles after 25:38, a popular expedient for a while and one still taken seriously by Nicholson 1:213.

The final redaction represented in MT has made an ample contribution to the text; Stulman has calculated that the LXX is 29 percent shorter.¹⁷⁹ The redaction took a keen historical interest in the two initial prose units. It brought historical precision by importing clarifying references to Nebuchadnezzar by name or title and to the Chaldeans that were already implicit for the reader by now. "Babylon's king" had been mentioned in 20:4; 21:2, 10, and "the Chaldeans" at 21:4; 22:25; 24:5, while at 24:1 the pre-LXX redaction had referred explicitly to Nebuchadnezzar. This type of amplification reappears in the MT redaction at 25:1 as a synchronism, coordinating Yahweh's word and its historical outworking.¹⁸⁰ Already at 21:1–7 a process of more precise specification was evident at the level of MT; it continued in 22:25 and is more prominent here. Verse 12 underlines and explores Babylon's doom, while extra attention is drawn to it by means of an added sentence in v. 14 and the use of a cryptogram in v. 26b. More generally the fulfillment of Judah's predicted fate is noted in v. 18, with a glance at v. 29.

[25:1–14] After the heading in vv. 1–2, the unit follows the general lines of an oracle of disaster. However, the grounds for Judah's disaster are presented primarily by the prophet himself in vv. 3–7, before the oracular announcement of divinely instigated disaster for Judah and neighboring nations via military agency in vv. 8–10 and its consequences in v. 11. Verse 12 develops in a new direction with an announcement of disaster in which Yahweh intervenes against the agents themselves, while in MT v. 14 adds the consequences and interprets them as a reprisal. For v. 13 see below.

[1–2] An oracle reception heading for the first unit appears along with a date, between March/April 605 and March/April 604. As 46:2 is aware, it was the year when Nebuchadnezzar, then Babylonian crown prince, defeated the Egyptian army at Carchemish in north Syria. This victory, probably in May–June,¹⁸¹ marked a turning point in the history of Syria and Palestine and the dawn of the dominance Nebuchadnezzar subsequently achieved there. It would have been an appropriate time for Jeremiah to reiterate his earlier message about the foe from the north, if material in vv. 9–12 represents the kernel that relates to this dating. Nebuchadnezzar returned home to succeed his dead father in September, and the next eight months were his accession year. This means that the later synchronism is a year off, since his first full regnal year ran from March/April 604 to March/April 603; his accession year is here replaced by his first year.¹⁸² Never-

---

179. *Prose Sermons*, 82. This figure incorporates the text-critical issue of v. 7b.

180. Yohanan Goldman, *Prophétie et royauté au retour de l'exil: Les origines littéraires de la forme massorétique du livre de Jérémie* (OBO 118; Freiburg: Universitätsverlag; Göttingen: Vandenhoeck & Ruprecht, 1992), 205.

181. Donald J. Wiseman, *Chronicles of Chaldaean Kings (625–556 B.C.) in the British Museum* (London: British Museum, 1956), 25.

182. For background discussion of royal chronology see David J. A. Clines, "Regnal Year Reckoning in the Last Years of the Kingdom of Judah," *AJBA* 2, no. 1 (1972): 9–34; idem, "The Evidence

theless, in this, the first of a number of explicit references to Nebuchadnezzar and/or the king of Babylon in the unit, the final redactor is hinting at the vindication of Jeremiah's earlier warnings about the foe from the north (cf. v. 9).

[3–7a] There is a fundamental difference between LXX and MT. The former has first person references throughout (see *BHS*), whereas MT begins with prophetic first person references (v. 3), continues with third person references to Yahweh (vv. 4–5), and switches to first person divine references (vv. 6–7a). At first glance MT looks secondary, especially after the divine "message" announced in vv. 1–2. However, such a heading may refer not to what immediately follows but to a subsequent oracle (see "Genre" in the introduction). In the LXX unawareness of this literary technique prompted the imposition of nearly total consistency, whereas the heading is meant to brood over the unit, awaiting the direct speech of vv. 6b–14. A further factor, at least for the Hebrew text underlying LXX, may have been that the idiom rendered "over and over again" in v. 3 elsewhere occurs only with Yahweh as subject, as in v. 4, but prophetic reuse is not out of the question; indeed, LXX so understood the idiom by taking the prophet as subject in its first clause.[183] MT differentiated between subjects ("receiving each message from Yahweh," v. 3; "declared Yahweh," v. 7) and made third person divine subjects explicit. Another motivation underlies two other additions, "the prophet Jeremiah" and "but you have not listened" in vv. 2–3, namely, a desire to enhance correspondence with the description of the prophets in v. 4; Jeremiah was the last in a long line. In sum, in v. 3 Jeremiah considers his own prophetic ministry, in vv. 4–6a that of like-minded prophets, and in vv. 6b–7 Yahweh's own message through those prophets, in anticipation of v. 8.

[4–7] The ultimate sin in the book of Jeremiah is a failure to heed the prophetic message (cf. esp. 6:17; 7:13, 25–26). Here it is the focus of vv. 4, 7, and 8 and also of v. 3 in MT. Behind the standards of good and bad and of exclusive, aniconic worship of Yahweh implicitly stands the torah, as chs. 7 and 11 made clear. Failure to maintain such standards was serious but forgivable, and the prophetic message permitted a second chance. But rejection of that message was a different matter; it spelled only doom. The rejected summons to repentance in the generalized prophetic teaching at vv. 5–6 (cf. 7:3–7, 25–26) moves

---

for an Autumnal New Year in Pre-exilic Israel Reconsidered," *JBL* 93 (1974): 22–40. See also Henri Cazelles, "587 ou 586?" in *The Word of the Lord Shall Go Forth: Essays in Honor of David Noel Freedman in Celebration of His Sixtieth Birthday* (ed. Carol L. Meyers and M. O'Connor; Winona Lake, Ind.: Eisenbrauns, 1983), 427–35.

183. H. St. John Thackeray, *The Septuagint and Jewish Worship: A Study in Origins* (2d ed.; Schweich Lectures 1920; London: British Academy, 1932), 34, observed that elsewhere in the book—including v. 4—*haškêm*, "rising early," is rendered *orthrou*, "in the morning," to avoid anthropomorphism, but in v. 3 the literal *orthrizōn* is allowed to stand with a human subject. This differentiation has generally been overlooked.

from admonition and accusation to promise and then from admonition to climatic threat.[184] The promise nicely reinforces the first admonition with Hebrew wordplay, *šwb*, "renounce," and *yšb*, "live," which one might reproduce as "leave . . . live," except that in English wordplay is not so effective. The switch to direct speech in vv. 6b–7a dramatizes the threat and the sin of sins that made the threat inevitable. A whole history of betrayal had to be countered. "This history, with its own irresistible and irreversible momentum, . . . requires drastic measures: it must be brought to an end."[185]

[8–9] The formally introduced announcement of disaster repeats the serious charge before moving to a resumption of the topic of the invasion of the enemy from the north that had dominated earlier presentations of Jeremiah's prophesying. Since the sending of the prophets failed, Yahweh would "send another sort of message" (Drinkard in Craigie et al. 366). The added clarification about Nebuchadnezzar betrays its secondary nature by its awkward placement. The epithet "my servant" reappears in 27:6 and 43:10. It was probably added first in 27:6, but the present addition nicely accentuates Yahweh's commissioning of the invaders as divine agents ("send"), underscores the ironic parallelism with the "servants" sent in v. 4, and facilitates the reversal at God's hands in vv. 12–14. As Jesus told Pilate, "You would have no power . . . unless it had been given you from above" (John 19:11). A new element, though one presupposed in the redactional unit at Jer 12:14–17, is the spillage of the invasion into adjacent states—as MT correctly clarifies—a note that is sounded again in v. 11. It frighteningly magnifies the impact of the invasion as catastrophic, while, on the compositional level, it paves the way for the stronger international flavor of the next units. The phrase "the northern clans" in MT (cf. MT in 1:15) replaces the distinctive "the clan from the north" in LXX, which prepares for the eventual references to "that nation" at v. 12 and "that country" at v. 13 in the common text.

[10] The stereotyped "sounds . . . groom" is part of the sermonic expansion of the piece, as in 7:34 and 33:11 (cf. 16:9). In a slightly awkward way it adds rhetorical fullness to the original features of peacetime normality, the mill grinding grain in the morning for daily bread and the lamp giving its welcome light as darkness fell. This verse is reused in Rev 18:22–23 with reference to the fall of Rome, the new "Babylon."

[11] The duration of the desolation of Judah and the political control of the western nations by the "clan" of v. 9 or, as MT clarifies, "the king of Babylon," was to be very long, "seventy years." This number, which also occurs in 29:10, is left unexplained, though it comes remarkably close to the replacement of the Babylonian Empire by the Persian Empire in 539, a period of sixty-six years,

---

184. Raitt, "Prophetic Summons," 35.
185. Dale Patrick, *The Rendering of God in the Old Testament* (OBT; Philadelphia: Fortress, 1981), 87.

beginning at 605. Nevertheless the prediction has an impressionistic quality, an exceptionally long period of Babylonian hegemony and Judean impotence (cf. Isa 23:15–17).[186] Did it originate as a premonitory rejoinder to Hananiah's "two years" (28:3), somewhat like the relation of "seven" and "seventy-seven" in Matt 18:22? Then the summary of Jeremiah's prophesying includes material from Zedekiah's reign (cf. Jer 29:10), despite the dating in Jehoiakim's reign in 25:1.

The number gripped the attention of subsequent generations. In Zech 1:12 (cf. v. 16; 7:5) its fulfillment is associated with the destruction of Jerusalem and the rebuilding of the temple, so that a period from 587 to 515 appears to be in view. In 2 Chr 36:21 the desolation of Judah is linked with that mentioned in Lev 26:34, and a sabbatical rest of seventy years is envisioned, presumably from 587, with the first return of Judean exiles in 538 in mind; though 2 Chr 36:22, a citation of Ezra 1:1, with its reference to the advent of King Cyrus of Persia, appeals to another Jeremianic text (Jer 51:1). In Dan 9:2, 24–27 the issue is transferred to a much broader chronological canvas by interpreting the seventy years in terms of ten jubilee cycles (10 x 49 years) rather than ten sabbatical cycles (10 x 7 years), an interpretation aided by associating the sabbatical years of Lev 25:2–7 with the jubilee years of Lev 25:8–17.[187] The last seven years of nearly half a millennium are then located in the second century B.C.E., in the era of Judean persecution at the hands of Antiochus IV. In turn the book of Revelation updates these seven years to an era of Christian persecution, with the second half of that period being devoted to an intense form, the great tribulation of Dan 12:1 (Rev 7:14 NIV; 11:2–3; 12:6, 14; 13:5), which itself echoes Jer 30:7.

[12] Whereas in v. 11 "seventy years" refers to a long stretch of time that "stresses the fullness of . . . judgment" (Carroll 495), in v. 12 the phrase implies a limited period of time. The oracle veers from announcing Yahweh's punishment of Judah at the hands of the new superpower to announcing Babylon's own dire punishment, which is expressed in the rhetorical terms of permanent desolation (51:26), 62. Babylon is no longer simply an agent of punishment, but becomes a victim in turn. MT takes great pains over the terse statement it inherited. It identifies who the victims were to be and grounds their punishment in "wrongdoing"; cf. 51:6. "Country" provides an antecedent for "it" in the final clause, though its masculine form in the Hebrew refers back to "(that) nation," which is, after all, a people in a land. Verse 12 in LXX appears to mark the end of the basic oracle; it features a reversal like that in Isa 1:21–26, one that implicitly spells good news for Judah. The overall message is akin to that in Isa

---

186. Comparison is often made to Marduk's ruling that Babylon should lie waste for seventy years, in an inscription of the Assyrian king Esarhaddon (*COS* 2.120:306).

187. Pierre Grelot, "Soixante-dix semaines d'années," *Bib* 50 (1969): 169–86, esp. 182–84; Fishbane, *Biblical Interpretation*, 482–83.

10:5–19, where Assyria, "the rod of" Yahweh's "anger," is threatened for going beyond the divine mandate (cf. Jer 50:18).

[13] Although the divine "I" is maintained, as in MT's addition at v. 14, this sentence prepares for the oracles against Babylon (= chs. 50–51 in MT) included in a continuation of the book of Jeremiah that at a secondary stage already had within it the collection of foreign oracles, as in LXX (MT chs. 46–51) (cf. McKane 1:632). LXX takes the relative clause as a heading for the collection, which leaves the previous phrase hanging in the air, as McKane observes; it is "adapted clumsily" in LXX (Jones 329). The MT placement of the oracles represents a tertiary, post-LXX development that leaves v. 13 isolated as a relic. This conclusion is supported by 46:1 in MT, which evidently adapted the relative clause of 25:13b*b* into a heading like LXX, thus giving a double rendering. For the reader of MT the common text at v. 13 awkwardly refers far forward to chs. 50–51. LXX attests the insertion of the foreign oracles here; they were meant to illustrate the fall of Babylon (v. 12) and the fall of the other nations in the following oracle.

[14] The extra sentence in MT "functions as a patch to repair the place where the oracles had been removed."[188] By echoing 50:29, 41 it hints at the destruction of the Jerusalem temple as divine warrant for a Media-led attack on Babylon; it elucidates the mention of punishment in v. 12 and its added "wrongdoing" taken from 51:6. A motif of reversal appears. The subjection of v. 11b would feature again in the divine comeuppance for the Babylonians (cf. 27:7); the verb ʿ*bd*, "serve," occurs in both places, here in the same construction as in the Hebrew text underlying LXX (v. 11), though not in MT.

[15–29] The second unit is an announcement of disaster at the hands of Babylon for the nations of the world known to Judah; it uses the vivid motif of the cup of divine wrath. The unit is meant to be read alongside the first one. The references to Judah in the common text at vv. 18 and 29 mean that the twin topic of Judah and the nations in vv. 1–14 continues here. Verse 18 employs vocabulary used in v. 9, while the "bad treatment" of v. 29 echoes v. 6. The additions in MT at vv. 9 and 11 clarify that only local nations are in view; but, though exegetically correct, they drive a slight wedge between the units by their less general language, which is lacking in both the second unit and the third unit. However, MT does reinforce their interconnectedness. First, it subordinates this unit to the earlier one as an elucidation (NRSV "For," v. 15). Second, it adds a reference to the judgment of Babylon in v. 26, to match that in vv. 12–14. The unit falls into three sections: vv. 15–17, the divine command to Jeremiah to pass the cup to the nations; vv. 18–26, a list of the nations involved; and vv. 27–29, the oracle to be transmitted. The symbol of the cup dominates the first and third sections, as the joint references to drinking indicate.

---

188. Anneli Aejmelaeus, "Jeremiah at the Turning-Point of History: The Function of Jer. xxv 1–14 in the Book of Jeremiah," *VT* 52 (2002): 459–82, esp. 478.

Doom for Judah and Other Nations

[15–17] This account reads at first like the report of a symbolic action, as in 13:1–11. The three elements of such a report are all present: divine command, prophetic execution, and divine interpretation of the cup in terms of "the sword" in v. 16 and also v. 27, first to Jeremiah himself and then to his rhetorical audience. But such language functions as a striking, quasi-visionary—in the absence of a precise spelling out of a visionary experience—metaphor, for two reasons. First, there is no material cup for Jeremiah to handle. Second, the oracular communication (v. 27) that paraphrases the divine statement to the prophet about consequences (v. 16) functions as the real-life equivalent of the prophetic execution (v. 17). "The whole action . . . is performed by Jeremiah when he announces what he is commanded" (Keil 1:380). The sending of Jeremiah with the cup is tantamount to the rhetorical dispatch of the message of destruction to its intended targets. The "sword" in earlier parts of the book has regularly stood for the invasion that in due course was identified as Babylonian (e.g., 6:25; 14:13; 24:10). The metaphor of the devastating cup of divine wrath is used in the Psalms and prophetic literature to express the execution of God's judgment (Pss 60:3 [4]; 75:8 [9]; Obad 16; Hab 2:15–16). The harsh motif recurs in the NT in Rev 14:10; 10:19; and 18:6, and also in the prayer of Jesus at Gethsemane (Mark 14:36; cf. 10:38–39; John 18:11).

[18–26a] The intimate connection between vv. 17 and 27 has been broken by the inserted, originally independent list of nations, but it was the best place to make the insertion since other possible positions—such as after vv. 15, 16, or 27—all have drawbacks. The purpose of the list was to define the outreach of "the sword." The list of states to be subjugated by Babylon loosely accords with the objects of the oracles against the nations in chs. 46–51 in MT or in the version of them placed in LXX immediately before v. 15, with an important difference that Judah appears only here. Damascus, Kedar, and "the encampments" (NRSV "Hazor") (49:23–24; LXX 30:12–13) are not specified here, but the first is presumably included in "all the kings of the north" (v. 26) and the latter two in "all the other kings of Arabia" (v. 24). Media (v. 25) is missing there as object of an oracle, though it does feature as attacker of Babylon in 51:11, 28 (LXX 28:11, 28). Tyre and Sidon reappear only as allies of Philistia (47:4; LXX 29:4). "All the kings of the north" includes the Syrian states of 49:23–24 (LXX 30:12–13) and is a different usage from the imperial contingents of the Babylonian army descending on Judah from the north at 1:15 and in MT at 25:9. The catchall phrase at the end of v. 26a rounds off the subjects of the world power only here and not in either form of the oracles. In order this list goes its own way, within the context of Babylon's imperial ambition; its order agrees with neither version of the oracles. There appear to be two wide sweeps in vv. 19–25: from southwest, to west, to east (vv. 19–21), and from northwest to southeast, to the far east (vv. 22–25), and finally the northern states (v. 26a). Pride of place is given to Judah. The later note in MT at the close of v. 18 about the accomplishment of its subjugation takes further the initial stage to be mentioned in v. 29. Egypt's "foreign groups" relate to its ethnic immigrant communities, while the reference to Ashdod presupposes its siege at Egyptian hands earlier in the seventh century, mentioned by Herodotus (*Hist.* 2.157). The "kings of the Mediterranean coast" refer to Phoenician maritime colonies, such as Cyprus. Dedan and Tema were in North Arabia, while Buz was a place or tribe in East Arabia (cf. Job 32:2, 6).[189] The Arab group "with shaved temples" appeared earlier at 9:26 (25). Herodotus (*Hist.* 3.8) mentions Arabs who wore their hair in a basin cut and shaved their temples as a religious custom. Uz was a region in northwestern Arabia between Dedan and Edom.[190] Elam (see the textual note m on v. 25) and Media, both east of Babylonia, are somewhat unexpected elements in a western list and may suggest an origin among Babylonian exiles (but cf. 49:34 and commentary).

[26b] The addition in MT crowns the list with Babylon itself, relating this verse to vv. 12–14 and also coordinating it with the presence of Babylon among the oracles against the nations in both textual traditions, at the close in MT (chs. 50–51) and after Egypt in LXX (chs. 27–28). The encoding of the name was extended back to Elam in MT, though not in the earlier LXX. It is a mark not of concealment but of literary sophistication that highlights these states; at 51:41 MT adds "Sheshach," parallel with "Babylon." Does it have a contemptuous ring, like "yob" for "boy" in British back-slang? "After them" betrays an awareness that the addition is going beyond the scope of the list and unit, in that the agent of destruction for other states was itself to be destroyed. The future verb gives an independent perspective after the narrative verb of v. 17, but mention of drinking builds a stylistic bridge back to the continuation of vv. 15–17 that begins with v. 27.

[27–29] The continuation consists of the declaration Jeremiah was to make on Yahweh's behalf, announcing the providential downfall of a host of states at Babylon's hands. As in v. 16, the sword represents the historical outworking of what the cup symbolizes. Verses 28–29 bring closure, affirming the inevitability of the conquest due to the refusal to drink from the cup of divine judgment. Its certainty is grounded not only in the nations' guilt, to which v. 29 makes passing reference with an insistently repeated verb of judicial acquittal, "let off." The seriousness of Yahweh's sponsorship of "the sword" must be judged by the fact that even Jerusalem, the city sacred to Yahweh's name (cf. Ps 48:1, 8 [2, 9]; Dan 9:18–19), had felt the first of its strokes. The capture of the capital in 597 here seems to be an accomplished fact. It was a sure omen of worse to come, not only for Judah but for the other nations within reach of Babylon's far-reaching power, as Yahweh was "rousing the Chaldeans . . . who march through the breadth of the earth" (Hab 1:6).

---

189. See Ernst A. Knauf, "Buz," *ABD* 1:794.
190. Cf. Knauf, "Uz," *ABD* 6:770–71.

[30-38] The third unit continues the theme of the divine judgment of Judah and the nations implicitly by means of Babylonian attack. Its essence is the divine announcement of disaster in v. 32, though v. 31 and perhaps v. 33 hint at grounds for it. The initial prose line uses an introductory directive of Yahweh to Jeremiah to graft the unit to the preceding units and specifically to v. 27; MT reinforces the connection with "all" and "to them," the latter referring to Judah and the other nations. This opening cue corresponds to parallels with earlier material in the poetry. The "sword" of vv. 31 and 38 echoes that of vv. 16 and 27 and has the same historical meaning, while "*all* the earth's inhabitants" (vv. 29, 30) is a focal catchphrase that relates the unit to the former one. The poetic unit falls into two six-line sections, vv. 30–32 and 34–38, bisected by a prose sentence in v. 33. The sections each subdivide into two parts, vv. 30–31 and 32, and vv. 34–35 and 36–38. Four of the five components of the unit appropriately make use of *'ereṣ* ("earth," vv. 31, 32, 33), though in v. 38 the Hebrew word has an individualizing force and means "country" (only vv. 34–35 lack the term). An overall frame for the unit is provided by the references to Yahweh as a destructive lion in vv. 30 and 38,[191] while the reference to the "sword" as Yahweh's instrument of destruction at the end of both poetic sections (vv. 31, 38) provides a forceful parallel climax. The combination of the cup metaphor for destructive judgment and the sword for its outworking in the previous unit is matched by that of the sheep-threatening lion metaphor and the sword here.

[30-32] Underlying the first section is the concept of the heavenly court of justice at which Yahweh holds judicial proceedings and issues verdicts against human felons (cf. 1 Kgs 22:19–23 and the development of the motif in Isa 6:1–13). The forensic setting is made clear in v. 31b, while the verdict is heralded in vv. 30–31a, after the directive, and its contents are revealed in v. 32.

[30-31] The prophet introduces the announcement of disaster in v. 32 with an appropriate four-line fanfare. Two bicola about the universal range of the verdict are framed by two tricola that focus on Yahweh. The roaring of the divine lion occurs in a judicial context at Joel 3(4):16a in connection with a trial of neighboring nations (3[4]:12) in "the valley of decision" or "the Valley of the Verdict" (NJB). There the verdict issues from Jerusalem, but here from the heavenly throne room, while the initial object of divine judgment is Judah, Yahweh's "homeland" (cf. 2:7). The object is widened in the next line to "*all* the earth's inhabitants," so that both Judah and other nations are involved. Now a different metaphor is used for the divine communication, the song sung while treading grapes; the grapes represent those ripe for judgment. Similar imagery is included in a complex of divine judgment motifs at Joel 3(4):13, with reference to the carrying out of the verdict by Yahweh's agents; in Jeremiah "the

---

191. Giorgio R. Castellino, "Observations on the Literary Structure of Some Passages in Jeremiah," *VT* 30 (1980): 398–408, esp. 405.

earth's inhabitants" are the intended victims, and the agency factor is "the sword" at the end of v. 31. The divine cry is so loud that it echoes through the earth, so that all victims may learn their fate. Behind the expansive rhetoric stands the fate of the nations who were to be confronted by the Babylonian advance. An allusion, left unexplained, is made to their "guilty" status. The handing over, a perfect verb in Hebrew, refers to the verdict as itself a performative action. The closing quotation formula harks back to the introduction in v. 30, with reference to the scene-setting message Yahweh told Jeremiah to give about the verdict.

[32] The divine verdict itself is presented in two bicola, in the general terms of a "bad fate" and with the metaphor of a "storm wind" to describe the Babylonian invasion. The same metaphor was used in 23:19, also following a reference to the divine council at which pronouncements of judgment were made (23:18).

[33] The prose sentence describing the extent of the disaster has affinities with the one about the invasion of Judah in 12:12. It is also related to the language of the prose sermon used at 8:2 and 16:4. MT, aware of the latter cross-references, has added a verb borrowed from 8:2 and another borrowed from 16:4. The purpose of the sentence, like that in 12:12, is to focus on Yahweh as author of the disaster in v. 32 and commissioner of the sword in v. 31—even wielding it so that the sword's victims are "slain by Yahweh." It may be relevant that 8:2 (and 16:11) finds pagan religion to be the reason for Judah's disaster, so that the knowledgeable reader gains an implicit explanation for the guilt of v. 31 that echoes v. 6 in Judah's case.

[34–38] Each half of this six-line section spoken by the prophet begins with an exclamatory sentence about mourning (vv. 34a, 36a), continues with a reason (vv. 34b, 36b–37), and finishes with an implicit supplementary reason (vv. 35, 38). The section is suffused with shepherd/sheep imagery, which permits in v. 38 fresh usage of the unit's initial lion metaphor.

[34–35] The first half section summons the kings of the various nations to be attacked to communal lamentation and then predicts the inevitability of their downfall. The lamentation functions as an anticipatory dirge rather than a petitionary prayer. The shepherds' fate of slaughter, normally reserved for sheep (11:19), is ironic (Drinkard in Craigie et al. 375; Holladay 1:681). There is evidently a temporary switch of metaphors at the end of v. 34, expressing sudden disintegration and a reversal of values (cf. Ps 2:9; Lam 4:2).

[36–38] A report takes over, resuming the lamentation advocated in v. 34a, but dramatically finding it duly implemented. This time the cause is traced to Yahweh's violent intervention, so that grim reversal once more occurs. The pastoral scene is shattered by the divine beast. In 4:7 and 5:6 the lion image stands for the human invader, but it is clear that the roarer of v. 30 is reappearing here. McKane (1:654), who interprets it as a human subject, does admit how abrupt it is. The verdict given earlier in the heavenly courtroom and communicated throughout the earth is now carried out by a theophany of judgment on earth. Verses 36b–38 are dominated by divine causality and fittingly clothed in tricola that echo those with a divine subject in vv. 30–31. True, acknowledgment is made of human instrumentality, the "sword," in line with both an emphasis of the unit and composition and the overall prophetic task of interpreting historical experience, but divine commissioning of the sword is in view, as the closing parallelism of "anger" and "sword" in vv. 37 and 38 is meant to indicate. "The oppressor" is to be understood as the Babylonian invader (McKane 1:655).To encounter Babylon is to be confronted by Yahweh. MT prefers to finish on a divine note, emphasizing the role of God.

The composition of 25:1–38 puts the Babylonian invasion of Judah in a wider setting, viewing it as a stark ingredient of international upheaval, but one that remains firmly under the just, long-term control of Judah's God.

26:1–29:32 True and False Predictions

26:1–24 Rejection of God's True Message and Messenger

26:1 In the accession year of King Jehoiakim ben Josiah of Judah this message came from Yahweh. *It said:* **2** "Here is what Yahweh said: 'Stand in the court of Yahweh's temple and address all the Judean *towns*folk coming to worship at Yahweh's temple, giving the entire message I order you to give them—do not leave anything out. **3** Perhaps they will listen and renounce their bad ways, one and all, so I can change my mind about the bad fate I intend for them in reaction to their bad behavior. **4** Say *to them*: "Here is what Yahweh said: 'If you fail to listen to me by walking in the track of my torah that I have put in front of you, **5** by paying attention to the messages of my prophetic servants whom I have been sending to you over and over again, though you have never listened, **6** then I will treat this temple like Shiloh, and *this* city I will turn into a curse word used by every other nation in the world.'"'" **7** Now the priests, the prophets, and all the people heard Jeremiah out, as he said this in Yahweh's temple. **8** When Jeremiah finished giving the entire message Yahweh had ordered to be given to all the people, he was seized by the priests and prophets and by all the people. "You have to die!" they said. **9** "Why have you prophesied in Yahweh's name that Shiloh is what this temple will become like and that this city will be desolated and become devoid of residents?" All the people formed themselves into an assembly to deal with Jeremiah[a] in Yahweh's temple. **10** When the Judean officials heard about this, they came up from the palace to Yahweh's temple and took their seats in the porch of Yahweh's New Gate.[b] **11** The priests and prophets told the officials and all the people, "This man must be tried on a charge that carries the death penalty for prophesying threats against this city, as you have heard with your own ears." 12 Jeremiah, however, said to *all* the officials and all the people, "It was Yahweh who sent me to prophesy everything you have heard about the threat to this temple and city. 13 The upshot is that you must let your conduct, the way you live, be good, in obedience to *your God* Yahweh, so Yahweh can change his mind about the bad fate he has threatened you with. 14 As for me, I am obviously in your hands. Treat me in whatever way you consider right and proper. 15 Only be sure you realize that if you put me to death you will be making yourselves, this city, and its residents guilty of killing an innocent person, because it is true that Yahweh sent me to you to say all this in your hearing." 16 Then the officials and all the people told the priest and prophets, "This man should not be tried on a charge that carries the death penalty. Rather, what he has told us has been in the name of our God Yahweh."

17 Some of the country elders had stood up[c] and said to all the assembled people, 18 "Micah from Moresheth used to prophesy in the reign of King Hezekiah of Judah. He told all the people of Judah, 'Here is what Yahweh *Almighty* said:

"Zion will be turned into a plowed field,
 Jerusalem will become rubble,
 and the temple mount scrub-covered slopes."'

19 In point of fact did *King* Hezekiah *of Judah* and all Judah put him to death? No, he became afraid of Yahweh and begged Yahweh for mercy, didn't he? So Yahweh changed his mind about the bad fate he had threatened them with. In our case, we would be making a big mistake that could cost us our lives."

20 There was another man who used to prophesy in Yahweh's name, Uriah ben Shemaiah from Kiriath-jearim. He prophesied[d] on exactly the same lines as Jeremiah about the threat to this *city and*[e] country. 21 When King Jehoiakim, *all his military officers,* and all the officials heard what Uriah had said, *the king*[f] tried to put him to death, but Uriah heard about it *and ran off in fear* and managed to reach Egypt. 22 King *Jehoiakim*, however, sent men to Egypt, Elnathan ben Achbor and others with him, to Egypt.[g] 23 They fetched Uriah from Egypt and brought him to King Jehoiakim, who had him executed by sword and his body thrown into the burial ground of the common people. 24 However, Ahikam ben Shaphan gave Jeremiah a helping hand, siding with him and preventing him from falling into the people's hands and being put to death.

True and False Predictions 295

a. See the commentary.

b. There is some textual evidence for a longer reading, "the New Gate of Yahweh's temple" (see *BHS*), but it probably reflects harmonization with 36:10. Barthélemy, *Critique textuelle*, 2:663–64, judges that the absence is primitive.

c. For the pluperfect sense see the exegesis; cf. Joüon §118j, k.

d. For the alternation of Hebrew conjugations in v. 20 see 14:14 and note g.

e. See Janzen, *Studies*, 21.

f. LXX (33:21) "they tried." MT and LXX probably developed from a basic reading "he tried," with MT supplying the implicit subject and LXX assimilating to the earlier plural subject. There is similar development in v. 19, where the verbs of fearing and entreaty are made plural in LXX.

g. Talmon, "Double Readings in the Massoretic Text," *Text* 1 (1960): 144–84, esp. 180, sees in MT a conflation of variants, with a general statement alongside detailed information; he compares Exod 20:10 over against Deut 5:14. Janzen, *Studies*, 14, concurs, noting that LXX omits the second, while MT has preserved both variants. On the other hand, the first variant has been deleted by Rudolph 174 (thus *BHS*) and McKane 2:659–61. But are these really variants? Perhaps this awkwardly expressed sentence was written that way, in which case parablepsis has occurred in LXX (cf. Janzen, *Studies*, 22).

The four narratives of chs. 26–29 function as a literary block. The three in chs. 27–29 were clearly placed together because of their concern for how long the deportation of 597 would last, an issue that led to conflict between Jeremiah and rival prophets located in Jerusalem (chs. 27–28) and in Babylon (ch. 29). The negative exhortation that runs through ch. 27, "Do not listen to . . . prophets . . . because they are prophesying utter falsehood to you" (vv. 9–10, 14, 16), echoes in ch. 29 at vv. 8–9, while a denial that Jeremiah's rivals had been "sent" by Yahweh (27:15) is repeated with reference to Hananiah in 28:15 (cf. 28:9) and Shemaiah in 29:31 (cf. 29:23). Chapter 26 has been prefixed to the collection.[192] This first narrative shares the description of Jeremiah's audience as priests, prophets, and people (26:7–8) with his readership (29:1), while in 27:16

---

192. It has often been claimed on linguistic grounds that these three units earlier circulated as an independent collection that attacked false prophecy, but the evidence is not so impressive when the shorter text of LXX is taken into account (cf. Holladay 2:114). The Hebrew name for Nebuchadnezzar is spelled with a medial *n* in MT at 27:6, 8, 20; 28:3, 11, 14; 29:1, 3—though with an *r*, a transcriptionally more correct form, in 29:21, as elsewhere in the book—but all these cases except 27:6 represent redactional amplification in MT. An epithet, "the prophet," appears regularly in ch. 28 and also twice in ch. 29 (vv. 1, 29), but this too is secondary. A more impressive argument, but one that cannot be checked against LXX with its hellenized, standard forms, is the short forms of names that have Yahwistic endings, with *-â* instead of *-āhû*. It occurs especially with Jeremiah's name, in 27:1, six times in ch. 28, and 29:1, though the long form appears in 29:27, 29, and 30. In 29:21–32 the names of Kolaiah, Maaseiah, and Zephaniah are found in a short form, and yet Shemaiah appears in both forms. The deviation of 29:21–32 in using long forms for Jeremiah and the standard form for Nebuchadnezzar may suggest an added layer.

Jeremiah addresses priests and people about the rival prophets, and in 28:1, 5 his altercation with Hananiah occurs in the hearing of priests and people. The prose sermon that readers of the book thus far have come to expect at the beginning of a block duly appears in 26:3–6 (cf. vv. 13, 19). Chapter 26 provides a summary of the tradition of true prophecy, spelling out the inevitability of the divine judgment of 587 and tracing it to Judah's failure to listen to Yahweh's "prophetic servants." The warning not to listen to rival prophets in chs. 27 and 29 receives a counterpoint in the lack of right listening featured in the prose sermon. MT reinforces this initial message at the end of the block (29:19) and associates with it the catastrophe in 597. At 26:18 the eighth-century prophet Micah is adduced as an example of the doom-laden tradition of which Jeremiah regards himself as the heir (28:9). The "bad fate" of 26:3, 13 is repeated at 28:8 only in MT. The common text contrasts this "bad fate" with "peace" for the deportees of 597 in 29:11.

The optimism of Jeremiah's prophetic rivals after 597 about a short term return of the plundered temple artifacts is countered in 27:16 (also in 28:3–4, 14). Instead, a long-term deportation is promised (29:10), lasting the seventy years of Babylonian hegemony. Already in 27:22, MT drew attention to this promise symbolized by the return of the temple artifacts. This climax toward which the block has been working is a development of the promise of doom for Babylonia after seventy years (25:11–12, plus v. 14 in MT), which MT pointedly reinforces in 27:7. Accordingly, the block develops material in ch. 25 to a positive corollary for the deportees of 597.[193] Further definition is added to the program of a "good" future for the deportees set out in 24:5–7 by the "good" promised in 29:32 (also 29:10 MT). MT is well aware of this intended link, as its own clear echo of the "bad figs" (24:8–10) in 29:16–18 shows. While the earlier editor probably thought that those exiled in 587 would share the fortune of the deportees of 597, the MT redactor makes this prospect explicit at 29:14, as comparison with 29:18 shows. Yet 587 opens up a terrible chasm that only God's grace can bridge. The block of chs. 26–29 reflects on the deportation of 597 and the disaster of 587 in a setting of true and false prophecy and builds on chs. 24 and 25 by pointing to restoration as an eventual aftermath of tragedy.

The surface message of ch. 26 is that Jeremiah nearly died. It is spelled out not only by the climax in v. 24 but also by means of the pervasive references to death and dying (vv. 8, 11, 15, 16, 19, and 21). What caused this close shave was his prophesying (so the verb "prophesying" in vv. 9, 11, 12, 18, and 20). That Jeremiah's prophesying led to a public discussion of whether Jeremiah should be tried on a capital charge carries the ironic implication that his audience was hammering a further nail into its own coffin. The community's

---

193. This dependence on 25:1–12 that the block displays in the common text provides a further argument for the intrusiveness of the foreign oracles in ch. 25 in LXX.

True and False Predictions

response to Jeremiah was a measure of its response to Yahweh, because prophesying had been done "in Yahweh's name" (vv. 9, 16, 20).

The composition is made up of three basic elements: a commissioning scene in vv. 4–6, a delivery scene in v. 7, in which the emphasis falls on the reception of the message, and an extensive reaction scene in vv. 8–16.[194] The relative space assigned to scenes indicates that the focus of the narrative is on the reaction scene, which narrates the threat to Jeremiah's life. The main body of the narrative is contained in vv. 1–16. Verses 17–19 and 20–24 function as two separate narrative supplements or postscripts to a narrative already completed in v. 16. They are parallel in their indication of support for Jeremiah and in their contrast of his experience with that of other named prophets, but dissimilar in that the former supplement is more closely integrated with the main narrative. Both shed light on its outcome by furnishing further information.

[26:1] The introductory oracle reception statement is supplied with a date that sets it in the months after the deportation to Egypt of King Jehoahaz by Judah's new master, Pharaoh Neco, who had earlier defeated and killed King Josiah (609), but before the official first year of King Jehoiakim in March/April of 608 (cf. 2 Kgs 23:29–34). The relevance of the dating is not spelled out, though it suggests deep concern in Judah over the political situation.

[2–3] Yahweh's commissioning of Jeremiah with the message of vv. 4–6 is prefaced with "a rare statement of Yahweh's intention," which from the start orients the narrative toward the response of Jeremiah's audience.[195] Emphasis falls on Jeremiah's faithful delivery of the divine message and on the need for a radical change of lifestyle in Judah to avoid Yahweh's intended punishment. Both elements will be resumed later, the first in v. 8 and the other in vv. 13 and 19. Readers will be reassured about the first, but not about the second.

[4–6] The public message Jeremiah was to deliver is often understood to be an abridged version of the temple sermon (7:1–15). Apart from the dire precedent of the destruction of Shiloh's sanctuary (v. 6, echoed in v. 9; 7:12, 14), there are some other parallels in diction, such as the reference to Yahweh's prophetic servants in v. 5 (as in 7:25), and Jeremiah's subsequent call for radical improvement in v. 13 (as in 7:3, 5). A more significant phenomenon in this passage is the use of prose sermonic language in vv. 4–6 and also in vv. 3 and 13.[196] This redactional prose sermon, which will be echoed in v. 19, is not only related to

---

194. John Applegate, "Narrative Patterns for the Communication of Commissioned Speech in the Prophets: A Three-Scene Model, " in *Narrativity in Biblical and Related Texts* (ed. G. J. Brooke and J.-D. Kaestli; BETL 149; Leuven: Leuven University Press, 2000), 69–88, esp. 85–87.
195. Ibid., 85–86.
196. Adam C. Welch, *Jeremiah: His Time and His Work* (New York: Macmillan, 1951), 138–40; Winfried Thiel, *Die deuteronomistische Redaktion von Jeremia 26–45* (WMANT 52; Neukirchen-Vluyn: Neukirchener Verlag, 1981), 3–4. Stulman does not categorize material in ch. 26 as a prose sermon, but in his individual listings he includes material from the chapter, no. 12 in v. 3a, no. 63

the diction of ch. 7. It draws parallels not only with ch. 7 but also with ch. 18. The divine change of mind echoes 18:8.[197] The positive exhortation to improvement of lifestyle (v. 13) does coincide with 7:3, 5, but also with 18:11, where it follows the negative exhortation that occurs again in 26:3. The opening *wĕʿattâ* (NRSV "Now therefore") in v. 13 aligns the appeal even more closely to 18:11. Essentially vv. 3–6, 13, and 19 have been composed in prose sermonic language to supply a summary of the divine message in a narrative that focuses not on that message but on the reaction to it. Apart from the use of general prose sermonic terms, there is a particular dependence on the diction of the prose sermons in chs. 7 and 18. This prose sermon lays blame firmly on the covenant people; Yahweh could not do otherwise than bring disaster. This import may be ascertained by comparing the parallels in chs. 7 and 18. The exhortations and conditions of 7:3–7 have a hypothetical and ironic role in view of the offenses of 7:8–11a. They set up positive possibilities that the context recognized were not realized, and broached negative possibilities that must eventually be realized. In ch. 18 the report of a negative popular reaction in v. 12 turned the argument that culminated in a call to repentance in v. 11 into a virtual oracle of disaster. Both cases were set in contexts of failure; in neither case was appeal or positive possibility to be taken at face value. That the same is true in ch. 26 is demonstrated by v. 9, where the hearers sum up the divine oracle of vv. 4–6 as a straightforward announcement of disaster. Verse 9a (cf. v. 6) seems to preserve a basic form of the message, which, while it shares with ch. 7 a reference to Shiloh, is to be distinguished from it in that here the fall of temple and city are related (cf. MT in v. 20). In ch. 7 the fate of temple and land are interlocked. Correspondingly "this place" in 28:6 and 29:10 will refer not to the land but to Jerusalem.

The sins of disregarding both Yahweh's double revelation of the torah traditions and the subsequent warnings of the prophets were featured in ch. 7 (vv. 5–6, 9, 13 and 23, 25–26), echoing Jeremiah's poetry in 6:16–19. The background of the torah is also emphasized in the prose sermon of 11:1–14, while the one in 25:1–14 defines in vv. 4–7 the failure to heed the messages of Yahweh's "prophetic servants" as the ultimate sin that guaranteed communal disaster. This double accusation of earlier prose sermons is summarized here. In an NT setting of religious persecution, Stephen would repeat it (Acts 7:51–53).

[7] The delivery or reception scene introduces the hearers as "priests," "prophets," and "all the people"; they will have important roles in the next

---

in v. 3b, no. 45 in v. 4b, no. 39 in v. 6b, and no. 82 in v. 13a. As to v. 5, he surprisingly omits references in nos. 5 and 70 (*Prose Sermons*, 33–34, 38–39, 41–42). The quotation formula in v. 2 (contrast v. 4) may affirm the redactional authority of the prose sermon, as in 24:5, 8.

197. Stulman does not include this case among his prose sermonic vocabulary, though he takes 18:1–12 as a prose sermon (*Prose Sermons*, 73–76).

True and False Predictions 299

scene. The grouping will appear in tandem in v. 8. "All the people" will appear in vv. 9 and 12, while it and the first pair will be counterpoised in vv. 11 and 16. It is tempting to regard both priests and prophets as temple officials, as in 23:11, with a common concern for the temple. More likely the priests react to the destruction of the temple in v. 6a (cf. v. 9), while the prophets react to the destruction of the city (v. 6b; cf. v. 9), stung by the implicit denial of their regular message of *šālôm*, "peace," for the community. LXX sensitively renders "false prophets" in vv. 7, 8, 11, 16, and 6:13, where prophesying *šālôm* is an explicit issue, but simply "prophet" in 23:11. The people react to both threats in their two roles as worshipers (v. 2) and as Judeans with a vested interest in the capital.

[8–9a] The reaction scene, which runs through v. 16, begins with the arrest of Jeremiah. The narrative initially glances back at the divine command for complete transmission of the oracle in v. 2 and reports its accomplishment. Jeremiah is shown to be Yahweh's faithful representative, whose proclamation has mirrored the divine will. The rejection of Yahweh is at stake in the community's death wish for Jeremiah, which from v. 8 onward becomes the leitmotif of the unit. The absence of Jeremiah's name until v. 7 indicates that the unit does not have a biographical purpose but instead focuses on the fate of Yahweh's message.[198] Some interpreters have suggested that the reference to "all the people" taking part in the arrest is the result of assimilation to the series of auditors in v. 7. Omission of the phrase would fit the opposite sides taken by "all the people" and "the priests and prophets" in vv. 11 (cf. v. 12) and 16. However, at the end of the unit "the people" are regarded as Jeremiah's attackers (v. 24), an apparent reference to v. 8 in its present form as well as to v. 14.

[9b–11] "All the people" constitute themselves into a kind of judicial assembly.[199] The verb in v. 9b is rendered in EVV in terms of crowding around Jeremiah, whether threateningly or not. The entity addressed by the elders in v. 17 is "the assembled people." This formal assembly seems to be reflected already in vv. 12 and 16, where "all the people" appear alongside "the officials." Presumably they do not cease to be hostile but clothe their hostility in a show of legality. It is from the "hands" of this assembly, in which Jeremiah acknowledges himself to be (v. 14), that Jeremiah is said to be delivered (v. 24). Royal officials appear from the palace next door to the temple and assume a presiding role. The location is defined as a temple gate, the "New Gate," which is often equated with the "upper gate" built or rebuilt by Jotham (2 Kgs 15:35; cf. Jer

---

198. Norbert Lohfink, "Die Gattung der 'historischen Kurzgeschichtes' in den letzen Jahren von Juda und in der Zeit des babylonischen Exils," *ZAW* 90 (1978): 319–47, esp. 323. References to divine deliverance (cf. 1:8; 15:20) are conspicuously absent from ch. 26.

199. Rietzschel, *Problem der Urrolle*, 97 n. 10; Pietro Bovati, *Re-Establishing Justice: Legal Terms, Concepts and Procedures in the Hebrew Bible* (trans. M. J. Smith; JSOTSup 105; Sheffield: Sheffield Academic Press, 1994), 229. Cf. the judicial use of the *Hiphil* of *qhl* in Job 11:10.

36:10) and is probably to be identified with the "Upper Benjamin Gate" on the north side of the temple in Jer 20:2. This is not a full-blown trial that culminates in a formal verdict. McKane (2:678–81), developing Duhm (213), has pointed out the difficulties that lie in the way of this standard interpretation of the text and so urged that the ambiguity of *mišpāṭ* in vv. 11 and 16, "judicial verdict" or judicial case," should be resolved in favor of the latter sense. The officials function as "troubleshooters . . . conducting a fact-finding enquiry" (McKane 2:680). The proceedings represent a preliminary hearing to determine whether Jeremiah should be subsequently tried on a capital charge.[200] The priests and prophets now step forward as the overt accusers. They pointedly mention only Jeremiah's threat against the city in addressing the civil body of the people and the officials; they are primarily addressing the former ("with your own ears"), since the officials arrived on the scene after the prophesying.

[12–15] In his own defense Jeremiah makes three points. First, his speech is framed by an insistence on Yahweh's initiative (Holladay 2:107). It sharpens the simple "prophesying" (v. 11) and addresses the basic complaint of using Yahweh's name to back up his prophesying (v. 9). Again his role as the representative of Yahweh (vv. 2, 8) comes to the fore. As in the accusers' speech (v. 11), the assembled people are still the target, as the ones who heard the oracle. Second, v. 13 is a call to come to terms with the "bad fate" threatened by Yahweh. It reverts to the prose sermonic language of v. 3, repeating not the oracle but Yahweh's intention (v. 3b) and reframing in positive terms the ideal human response (v. 3a). Third, Jeremiah develops his first point, using his claim of divine initiative to argue for his personal innocence and so to warn of bloodguilt that would result from his wrongful death (cf. Gen 4:10; 9:5).

[16] The ruling was a refusal of the accusers' request. There was no case to answer, so judicial proceedings on a capital charge could not occur. Jeremiah's life had to be spared; the risk of incurring the bloodguilt of v. 15 was not worth taking (cf. v. 19). The narrative receives logical closure at this point. The judicial authorities did their work, dealing with the issue of the prophet's fate. But a deafening silence is maintained about the deeper issue of the content of Jeremiah's prophesying, now that its divine source was granted. The implicit tabling of this issue, though outside the judicial scope, brings its own condemnation, along with the communal hostility to the prophet, despite the official restraint.

[17–19] This first supplement can hardly be taken as a continuation of the narrative, though it has "the assembled people" of vv. 9b–16 in view and addresses them, as the speakers did in vv. 11 and 12–15. It attempts to explain the surprising failure to proceed with the case in view of the adamant hostility evident earlier. The intervention of vv. 17–19 was what swayed the official deci-

---

200. Cf. Bovati, *Re-Establishing Justice*, 355.

sion. The postscript functions as a flashback to the stage before v. 16 (Volz 96; Rudolph 171).[201] A prophetic precedent is found for Jeremiah's being spared. Jeremiah is compared to another Judean prophet, Micah, who prophesied a century before. The striking announcement of disaster for the city and temple in the tricolon of Mic 3:12 is cited. So is an otherwise unattested tradition of Hezekiah's repentance. Far from Micah's being executed, the result was contrition on the king's part—a golden exception to v. 5. In the reference to escaping a "bad fate," there seems to be an allusion to the sparing of Jerusalem from Assyrian occupation (cf. 2 Kgs 18:13–19:37; Isa 36:1–37:38). A parallel is being drawn between Micah and Jeremiah as prophets who transmitted Yahweh's announcement of disaster. The prose sermonic terminology of vv. 3 and 13 is reiterated to drive the point home. The "big mistake" is putting Jeremiah to death and incurring bloodguilt (Keil 1:394). This postscript has redactional features, namely, the exact citation of prophetic scripture and the echoing of prose sermonic vocabulary, but the use of a nonscriptural tradition suggests that preliterary factors underlie the postscript. Memories of a prophet from a Judean village could be expected to survive among "country elders."

[20–24] Jeremiah had another ally. The narrative starts again from a different angle; the focus of the second postscript is delayed until v. 24. A member of Jerusalem's social elite gave help, presumably in connection with the incident, since "hands" picks up v. 14, though further particulars are not given. A contrast is drawn with the fate of an otherwise unknown prophet who delivered oracles of disaster, evidently a little later in Jehoiakim's reign than the incident of vv. 1–19 but before the transfer of political control of Judah from Egypt to Babylon after the battle of Carchemish in 605. Uriah lacked the protection Jeremiah was fortunate to have.

[20–23] The MT has embellished the comparison by adding a reference to the city. Jeremiah is portrayed as a prophet of disaster, as in v. 9. The period of Egyptian control of Judah, which ended during Jehoiakim's reign (2 Kgs 24:1), made Uriah's extradition feasible. Elnathan ben Achbor reappears in 36:12, 25 as one of Jehoiakim's officials; he is probably to be identified with the king's father-in-law (2 Kgs 24:8). His involvement reflects how seriously the king viewed the issue, as does the denial of an honorable burial in a family grave (cf. 2 Sam 19:37 [38]; 2 Kgs 23:6), while the repetition of "Egypt" in v. 22 underscores the lengths to which the king was prepared to go.

[24] Remarkably Jeremiah was spared such a fate. In his case the enemy was not (yet) the king but the people. Over against the people's "hands" was a protecting "hand" large enough to prevail. Ahikam ben Shaphan, a trusted and spiritual member of Josiah's entourage (2 Kgs 22:12, 14), whose son Gedaliah was

---

201. The row of initial verbs of speaking in the Hebrew of vv. 11, 12, 16 is noticeably disturbed in v. 17, indicating a break in continuity (Lohfink, "Gattung," 323 n. 16).

later to be governor of Judah (Jer 40:5; 2 Kgs 25:22), used his influence on the prophet's behalf.

Jeremiah 26:1–24 turns out to be good news for Jeremiah, but paints a bleak picture of Judah's spiritual state in that Yahweh's faithful representative becomes the butt of the people's animosity. "Jeremiah survived; neither heeded like Micah nor martyred like Uriah, he survived to be ignored" (Davidson 2:52). So Yahweh's "bad fate" for Judah was confirmed; a divine change of mind was out of the question.

27:1–22 Yoke Symbolism, Part One

27:2[a] Here is what Yahweh had said[b] *to me*: "Make *yourself* ties and crossbars, and put them round your neck. 3 Then send them[c] to the kings of Edom, Moab, Ammon, Tyre, and Sidon by envoys who have come[d] to Jerusalem to visit King Zedekiah of Judah, 4 giving them these instructions for their masters: 'Here is what Yahweh *Almighty*, Israel's God, said: "Here is what you are to tell your masters: 5 'It was I who made the earth— *the humans and animals that are on the earth*[e]—using my great power and outstretched arm, and I can give it to anybody I deem appropriate to have it. 6 *And for now it is* I *who* have given *all* the*se* countries[f] *into the hand of* King Nebuchadnezzar of Babylon, *my servant*[g]—even wild animals *I have given to him* to serve him! 7 *And all the nations will serve him, his son, and his grandson, until the time is up for his own country, when he*[h] *will be in servitude to many nations and powerful kings.* 8 But *what will happen is that* any nation, any realm, that will not *serve him—King Nebuchadnezzar of Babylon—or that will not*[i] put its neck into the yoke of Babylon's king, sword, and famine, *and pestilence* are what I will use to deal with *that nation*,'[j] declared Yahweh, 'until I have used his hand to get rid of them.[k] 9 You then, do not listen to your prophets, diviners, dreamers,[l] magicians, or sorcerers who are telling *you expressly* not to serve Babylon's king, 10 because they are prophesying utter falsehood to you and the result will be that[m] you are taken far away from your own soil—*I will drive you away and you will be destroyed*. 11 But any nation that does insert its neck into the yoke of Babylon's king and serve him I will leave on its own soil,' declared Yahweh, 'to till it and stay on it.'"'"

12 I had addressed King Zedekiah of Judah on exactly the same lines: "Insert your necks *into the yoke of Babylon's king* and serve him[n] *and his people, so you may survive.* 13 *Or else you and your people will die from the sword, famine, and pestilence threatened by Yahweh for any nation that will not serve Babylon's king.* 14 And do not listen to the messages of the prophets who tell you expressly not to serve Babylon's king, because they are prophesying utter falsehood to you. 15 'In fact I never sent them,'

True and False Predictions 303

declared Yahweh. 'They are using my name to prophesy in falsehood, and the result will be that I will drive you away and you will be destroyed, along with the prophets who are prophesying to you.'"

16 I had also addressed the priests[o] and all this people: "Here is what Yahweh said: 'Do not listen to the messages of *your* prophets when they prophesy to you, "Look, the artifacts belonging to Yahweh's temple will be brought back from Babylon *very soon,*" because they are prophesying utter falsehood to you.' 17 *Do not listen to them! Serve Babylon's king so you may survive, or else this city will become a ruin.* 18 If they are prophets and if they do have any message from Yahweh, then let them implore Yahweh[p] *Almighty that the artifacts left in Yahweh's temple, in the palace of Judah's king, and in Jerusalem may not be taken*[q] *to Babylon.* 19 In fact here is what Yahweh *Almighty* said about *the pillars, the vat, the trolleys, and* the remaining artifacts *left in this city,* 20 not taken by King Nebuchadnezzar of Babylon when he deported *King* Jeconiah *ben Jehoiakim of Judah* from Jerusalem *to Babylon, along with all the upper class of Judah and Jerusalem—* 21 yes, here is what Yahweh Almighty, Israel's God, said about the artifacts left in Yahweh's temple, the palace of Judah's king, and Jerusalem: 22 'Babylon is where they will be taken, *and there they will stay until the day when I turn my attention to them,*' declared Yahweh, '*and I will bring them up and bring them back to this place.*'"

a. In v. 1 MT adds to the earlier LXX text (ch. 34): "In the accession year of King Jehoiakim ben Josiah of Judah Jeremiah received this message from Yahweh," whereas the rest of the passage has Zedekiah's reign in view (vv. 3, 12; cf. the post-597 setting of vv. 16–22). The scanty textual evidence for "Zedekiah" (see *BHS*) reflects scribal activity in line with the rest of the chapter and with 28:1; so the name is not simply to be changed with five of the EVV. Friebel, *Sign-Acts*, 138, observes that reports of symbolic actions in the book do not necessarily begin with a date formula (cf. 13:1–11; 16:1–9; 19:1–13). In 13:1 and 19:1 the report of a symbolic action starts with a quotation formula. Here the dating was reserved for the start of the main account in ch. 28, after the preparatory ch. 27. MT's date formula was wrongly borrowed from 26:1 in a careless marginal attempt to provide a supplement, which entered the text (Janzen, *Studies*, 14, 45).

b. For the pluperfect sense in vv. 2, 12, and 16, advocated by Ehrlich, *Randglossen*, 4:312, see the commentary. The Hebrew inverted order in vv. 12 and 16 accords with this interpretation.

c. Thus MT and LXX, followed by NJPS and NJB. The other EVV follow LXX[L] in not representing the suffix and taking the message as the implicit object (cf. *BHS*). The sending of a message is a separate issue (v. 4).

d. LXX adds "to meet them," probably a corruption of "to meet him," for which there is some Greek evidence (cf. *BHS*). It was originally a marginal exegetical comment on "to King Zedekiah of Judah" in which the preposition "to" means "to visit," as in the translation.

e. LXX omits by parablepsis ("earth . . . earth") according to *BHS*; Janzen, *Studies*, 118. However, the interruption of a stereotyped formulation (cf. 10:12; 32:17; 51:15) and the antecedent of "the earth" for "(give) it" suggest a redactional addition (Emanuel Tov, "Exegetical Notes on the Hebrew Vorlage of the LXX of Jeremiah 27 [34]," *ZAW* 91 [1979]: 73–93, esp. 82), which the asyndeton supports. It provides a basis for v. 6b (Holladay 2:115).

f. LXX "the earth" assimilates to v. 5; moreover, the same rendering for the Hebrew plural occurs in 23:3; 32(LXX 39):37; 40(LXX 47):11 (Tov, "Exegetical Notes," 83). The plural does not anticipate the secondary v. 7 (Holladay 2:115), but reflects the list in v. 3. For the addition of "these" in MT cf. 25:9, 11; 28:14.

g. In place of ʿabdî, "my servant," LXX has "to serve him," as if for lĕʿobdô, which does occur in v. 6b and is rendered with a different Greek verb. The verbal phrase represents a separate issue from the nonrepresentation of the noun phrase, a development within the Greek tradition that provided a variant translation of the later term (McKane 2:689). The marginal alternative was subsequently placed in the text at a point that was judged feasible. For the secondary nature of the former of the two Greek verbs in this passage see Janzen, *Studies*, 55–56; McKane 2:688–89.

h. "It" would be easier (cf. *BHS*), but the pronoun is probably used loosely for the extant king of Babylon.

i. MT lōʾ . . . wĕʾēt ʾăšer, missing from LXX, can hardly be explained simply in terms of homoeoteleuton (*BHS*) in view of the secondary elements it contains. Tov, "Exegetical Notes," 85–86, takes the royal specification as redactional, comparing 21:7 and 25:9; it needs to be added that the explanation was supplied here because the previous pronoun "he" (bô) in the redactional v. 7 had a different reference. McKane 2:691 explains wĕʾēt ʾăšer as a stitch joining the insertion to what follows. The initial negative verbal clause supplies a stylistic counterpart to v. 7a and so has a bridging function between the redactional v. 7 and v. 8. Thus the plural verb yaʿabdû, "will serve," strange before the singular one, echoes the plural wĕʿābdû, "and . . . will serve," in v. 7. At the earlier stage one expects immediate mention of the yoke symbolized in vv. 2–3 (cf. v. 11).

j. LXX "them," unless it is a translational element, as McKane 2:691 holds.

k. Cf. Ps 64:6 (7) for a possible transitive use of the Qal (cf. BDB 1070b).

l. MT means " your dreams." The noun is to be pointed ḥāl- as a *nomen agentis*; there are parallels for the feminine in Mishnaic Hebrew (Ehrlich, *Randglossen*, 4:312–13). The ancient versions (*BHS*) may have rendered "your dreamers" simply according to context.

m. For the consecutive sense see Joüon §169g.

n. LXX has "(serve) Babylon's king." LXX lacks most of the direct speech of v. 12 and also vv. 13–14a. Verse 14a must have been lost in error since v. 14b does not make sense without it. From its content, the rest is to be regarded as redactional amplification, though whether it derives from the post-LXX stage of redaction can hardly be established by the criterion of content. From a text-critical perspective Tov, "Exegetical Notes," 87, largely following Hitzig 216, makes the reasonable argument against accidental omission over the span of three verses that such instances are rare and explains the loss of v. 14a at first by homoeoteleuton after v. 13 ("Babylon's king"), but later rightly claims that v. 13 itself was not in the Hebrew text of LXX. Thus v. 14a was lost by homoeoteleuton after "Insert your necks and serve Babylon's king" in v. 12, which Tov plausibly claims to have been the original direct speech in that verse, before the noun phrase was replaced by "him" in consequence of the insertion "into the yoke of Babylon's king." Indeed, the repetition in v. 17 supports this reconstruction.

o. The prefacing of "to you" in LXX (see *BHS*) is part of a doublet in v. 15, both components of which represent assimilating additions (Tov, "Exegetical Notes," 88, following Hitzig 216).

p. For "Yahweh" LXX has "me" (see *BHS*), which reflects either a misunderstanding of an abbreviation of the divine name, Hebrew *bî*, for *byhwh* (Godfrey R. Driver, "Once Again Abbreviations," *Text* 4 [1964]: 76–94, esp. 79), or a translational equivalent of "Yahweh." Either divine or prophetic speech features here, though the latter is more likely, and the redactional addition in MT seems to have so taken it.

q. For the grammatical awkwardness cf. 23:14 and see *BHS*, whose first option is preferable because it can be explained in terms of haplography (Ehrlich, *Randglossen*, 4:313).

Chapters 27 and 28 make up a pair of extended passages that share the topics of false prophecy and the prophetic symbolism of wearing a yoke. Chapter 27 functions as an explanatory preface to ch. 28, filling in its gaps and supplying it within a larger context. The passage falls into three sections, vv. 2–11, 12–15, and 16–22. They all contain the same negative exhortation and reason: "Do not listen to ... prophets ... because they are prophesying utter falsehood to you" (vv. 9–10, 14, 16). The first section concerns a symbolic action that Jeremiah was to perform (it is also mentioned in the second section at v. 12). The issue of false prophecy, which has a minor role in the first section (vv. 9–10) is given relatively more space in the second and becomes the dominant theme of the third. Apart from that link, the third section has little in common with the former two. It serves in part as a preparatory amplification and discussion of Hananiah's prophetic utterance in 28:3, just as the first two sections address other concerns in ch. 28.

The extra editorial material supplied in MT more than compensates for the ancillary role of ch. 27. It has been estimated that MT is 42 percent longer than the Hebrew text of LXX.[202] By isolating the later material, Stulman found that, of the fifteen cases of prose sermonic diction, only six were present in the common text and that all these were phrases unattested in Deuteronomy and the Deuteronomistic History.[203] The MT redaction has two main aims: to integrate the three sections and, in the first and final sections, to lift the reader's eyes beyond the prospect of destruction to an eventual vista of hopeful renewal. The second aim invests the chapter with its own special value.

[27:2–11] The first section and also the first half of the second mention a symbolic action, which typically involves a divine command and interpretation

202. Stulman, *Prose Sermons*, 86.
203. Ibid., 88–89.

and performance by the prophet. Here the report of its performance can be omitted because it is already presupposed by 28:10. Much space is devoted to the interpretation of the action, which is not really supplied in ch. 28. The initial command is provided in an abbreviated form. This section of three parts (vv. 2–4a, 4b–7, and 8–11) is a series of quotations embedded inside quotations.

[2–4a] The sending of the crossbars and ties to the delegates in v. 3 and the fact that Jeremiah himself wore a wooden crossbar according to 28:10, 12 suggest that five extra ones were made for the delegates to take home. The crossbar and ties made up a yoke worn around the neck of a farm animal drawing a plow, threshing sledge, or cart. The term "yoke" is used metaphorically in chs. 27–28 for political subjection. Presumably Jeremiah was initially to wear all six sets, before sending five of them to the delegates.[204] The ancient Near Eastern custom of involving religious personnel and ritual in planning for a military campaign would have made his action and speech appropriate.[205] The addition "to me" after the quotation formula brings the first part of the section closer to the other two first person reports (vv. 12, 16) and to 28:1 (symbolic action accounts are usually written in a first person format). Little interest is shown in the details of the Jerusalem conference, to which Transjordanian and Phoenician states sent delegates (evidently in Zedekiah's fourth year, 594/593; cf. 28:1) with the intention of secession from Babylonian hegemony. The only detail given is the names of the five states involved. Zedekiah's visit to Babylon in the same year (51:59) spelled the suppression of the plot.

[4b–6] After the preliminary formulas, vv. 5–6 provide a theological prologue to the message of vv. 8–11. They explain God's involvement (v. 8; cf. 28:2–4, 11), that the message is grounded not in political factors but in the divine will. Israel's God chooses Nebuchadnezzar (cf. Dan 4:17; Rom 13:1–2). The creator is in sovereign control of the nations. Yahweh's role as creator is prominent in Jeremiah's original poetry (5:22) as well as in exilic poetry in the book (10:12). Traditional creation language is embellished with exodus phraseology (cf. the commentary on 21:5). The reference to wild animals pointedly hints that no creature should harbor thoughts of independence. MT has expanded vv. 5–6 at a number of points. The reference to "humans and animals" interprets "the earth" in animate terms, rather like William Kethe's hymnic paraphrase of "all the earth" in Ps 100:1 as "All people that on earth do dwell." The phrase builds a bridge between "the earth" and the people and "wild animals" of v. 6. "For now" will receive its own elucidation in v. 7. "Give into the hand of" accommodates the verbal phrase to one used earlier in contexts of Yahweh's support of Babylon (20:4; 21:7, 10; 22:25). Moreover, it provides a neat antic-

---

204. Theodor Seidl, *Texte und Einheiten in Jeremia 27–29: Literaturwissenschaftliche Studie* (part 1; ATSAT 2; St. Ottilien: EOS, 1977), 32; Friebel, *Sign-Acts*, 142.
205. Friebel, *Sign-Acts*, 144.

True and False Predictions

ipation of Babylonian power displayed in a negative form at v. 8.[206] "My servant" is a clever wordplay on the verb "serve," expressing what is implicit in the text, that the imperial vassalage connoted by the yoke imagery was given to one who was himself a vassal of a divine overlord. Like the centurion who deferred to Jesus in Matt 8:9 and Luke 7:8, he was "a man under authority," though here the role was not a conscious one (cf. Isa 45:1, 5; Rom 13:4–6).

It can hardly be an accident that the two Hebrew verbs in the initial command to Jeremiah in v. 2, *ʿśh*, "make," and *ntn*, "put," are repeated in v. 5, now with the second verb meaning "give." This little noticed repetition makes interpretation of the symbolic action complex.[207] Verse 8 will focus on the second verb in the sense "put," with the slightly different construction "put its neck into the yoke." In that case Jeremiah models what the neighboring nations (vv. 8, 11) and Judah (v. 12) should do. However, the appeal to divine creation and providential control flows naturally from the enactment, but with a different application: Jeremiah is the model for Yahweh in first making and then giving.[208] From this perspective vv. 5–6 do not simply present a theological preamble but plunge into interpretation, while v. 8 begins a second way of construing the symbolic action. Whereas the first interpretation highlights the two verbs of v. 2, the second emphasizes the second verb and the yoke as object. This different perspective may indicate that the first interpretation was subsequently prefixed to the second.

[7] The temporal limitation "for now" (v. 6) was the first hint of a long-term agenda that the MT redaction in this chapter is concerned to promote: the eventual expiration of Babylon's leasehold. It continues an endeavor already evident in the basic text underlying LXX at 25:11–12 and amplified in MT at 25:14. Indeed, v. 7b repeats 25:14b, with its message of the eventual overthrow of Babylonian power, which was inspired by ch. 50. In turn, the period of its imperial rule over three generations appears to be an interpretive reflection on the "seventy years" of 25:11–12. In fact, though Nebuchadnezzar (605–562) was succeeded by his son Evil-merodach (562–560), by his son-in-law Neriglissar (560–556) and then by his grandson Labashi-Marduk (556), they were followed by the usurper Nabonidus (556–539), whose son Belshazzar, representing his father at the royal seat in Babylon, witnessed its downfall. The generational interpretation is best taken as an exilic forecast that interpreted Jeremiah's laconic "seventy years."

---

206. Goldman, *Prophétie et royauté*, 133.
207. Roy Wells, "Dislocations in Time and Ideology in the Reconception of Jeremiah's Words: The Encounter with Hananiah in the LXX *Vorlage* and the MT," in *Uprooting and Planting* (ed. J. Goldingay), 322–50, esp. 327, observes the repetition.
208. Accordingly the rendering of the first verb in v. 2 should be "Make" with most EVV and not "Take" (REB) or "Get" (McKane 2:684).

[8–11] These verses consist of a conditional oracle of disaster (v. 8) and a conditional proclamation of salvation (v. 11), which frame and bolster a negative exhortation and the immediate reason for it (vv. 9–10).

[8] The first of the alternatives is a deterrent for the neighboring states, to encourage them to continue their political submission and not to make a bid for independence. "Sword and famine" are a standard pair in the book for the rigors of invasion and siege at Babylon's hands, while "pestilence" is a frequent supplement in MT. Such reprisals, here managed by Yahweh through Nebuchadnezzar, apply not merely to Judah, as hitherto in the book, but to its western neighbors. Behind the empire stands Yahweh's sovereign will, supporting it.

[9–10] Now the kings are directly addressed. The issue of false prophecy is here atypically put in a non-Judean setting. The text implies that Jeremiah knew of or assumed political support for rebellion among religious advisers in the other states, as in Judah (vv. 14–15). These advisers are called not only "prophets" and "dreamers" but also by a range of terms that elsewhere in the OT are used disparagingly of foreign religious influence (e.g., Isa 2:6; Mic 5:12 [11]); here they empathically reflect a non-Yahwistic religious situation. This massing of terms also suggests the weight of nationalistic fervor aroused by these professionals, who "seduce . . . into imagining a third alternative, namely, resistance to the empire" (Brueggemann 245). The folly of such a stand is shown by the threat of exile, a fatal antidote to nationalism. MT brings the text into conformity with the next section by importing "you expressly" and "I will drive you away and you will perish" from vv. 14–15.

[11] The final argument presents the second alternative, the assurance of continued, though limited, nationhood. The argument is rhetorically clinched by a wordplay that uses the same verb, ʿbd, "work for" and "work at," for "serve" and "till." The added quotation formula matches v. 8, augmenting the parallelism of the two statements.

[12–15] This section is an echo of the former one. Just as the five kings of v. 3 were addressed through their delegates, now the royal host is addressed. There is a double exhortation, to continue to "serve" the Babylonian king in the vassalage that had begun for Judah in 597 and not to take the advice of false prophets. The additions in MT (vv. 12–13) improve the structural correspondence between vv. 8–11 and vv. 12–15 by using the stylistic feature of resumptive inversion in that the last component in v. 11, the injunctions to insert the neck and serve, is put first in v. 12.[209] The parallelism is made more explicit by the expansion "into the yoke of Babylon's king" from v. 11. Thereafter vv. 12b–13 correspond with v. 8, v. 14 with vv. 9–10a, and v. 15 with (the enlarged) v. 10b. This careful correspondence works out in more detail Jeremiah's claim to address Zedekiah "on exactly the same lines." It prevents the notion that

---

209. See n. 172 on 23:34.

True and False Predictions

Judah had any immunity from Babylonian reprisals against rebellious states. "Any nation" (vv. 8, 13) meant what it said. Indeed, a harsher message than vv. 8-11 is presented at v. 15 in the common text. In vv. 12-14 Jeremiah applies the former oracle to Judah's situation, while in v. 15 an oracle confirms the prophet's application.

[12-13] The plural Hebrew verb and pronoun in the exhortation, "Insert your necks," are reminiscent of the plural verbs after the vocative "David's house" in 21:11-12. This might suggest that the redactional "people" in vv. 12-13 refers to royal staff, as in 22:2, 4. However, the point of v. 13 seems to be to explain the plural references in v. 12 as applying to king and country, in line with the mention of "nation" in v. 8. That v. 8 is being repeated in v. 13 is made explicit by the reference to any nation's refusal to serve. The paraphrase in terms of death in v. 13 and the antithetic "survive" in v. 12 are borrowed from 21:9. The threefold means of death is repeated from the amplified text of v. 8. Verse 13 generated the contrasting additional material at the close of v. 12, complete with "and his people" to balance "(you) and your people."

[14-15] In the basic text the reason for not listening to the prophets is enlarged (cf. v. 10) with a denial of the divine authority they claimed and a prediction of their deportation along with their national constituency (cf. 14:14-15). Verse 15 represents an oracle of disaster, but one that is noticeably unqualified by a condition. Although vv. 12b-13 in MT offer the options of vv. 8 and 11, even in that fuller text, in view of v. 15, the option of survival has a hollow, ironical ring. It was a scenario that would never see the light of day, claims v. 15. There was more hope for the other states than for Judah.

[16-22] The last section has a frame of two divine messages, one in v. 16, followed by prophetic speech in vv. 17-18 or at least in v. 18, and the other introduced by Jeremiah in vv. 19-21 and cited in v. 22. It brings to a climax the topic of false prophecy, but focuses on a different issue, one that will take the foreground in 28:3.

[16] The first divine message is a negative exhortation against a proclamation of salvation made by Jeremiah's rivals. The proclamation is cited as a prophetic statement, like vv. 12-14. The corresponding 28:3 makes it an oracular saying and presents it in the more precise form of a two-year gap before temple artifacts looted in 597 would be returned. Here priests are an obvious audience for this oracle, and so are the people as they worship. This oracle is fundamental to the entire chapter and is the logical presupposition of the distinctive message in vv. 2-15. Hitherto in the book Jeremiah's prophetic rivals have been associated with a message of peace and with a denial of Jeremiah's forecast of a bad fate (e.g., 14:13; 23:17; cf. 28:8-9; 37:19). Evidently the Babylonian attack and sacking of Jerusalem in 597 forced a shift in their "peacemongering" position, namely, that within two years the status quo would be restored and Yahweh's honor satisfied by the return of plundered temple artifacts. It was a powerful slogan that had the

potential of capturing the popular imagination, minimizing the prophets' loss of face by positing an early reversal, and allowing a useful leeway before their claim was put to the test (and failed). This new position necessitated a corresponding adjustment in Jeremiah's message. The simple countercall of a bad fate still to come at Babylon's hands was supplemented by a specific insistence that Babylonian hegemony was here to stay, endorsed by the divine will—the very message of vv. 2–15. It was doubtless the two-year limit that was the stimulus for the extravagant figure of seventy years (25:11–12).

MT's qualification (v. 16), "very soon," has the same role as "for now" (v. 6); in fact it is an amplification of the same Hebrew word, ʿattâ, "now" (cf. NAB "soon now," NIV "very soon now"). It corresponds to "in not more than two years" at 28:3. It will be countermanded in v. 22, which will repeat the long-term agenda of v. 7 in terms of the temple artifacts. The prophets were right about their eventual restoration, but wrong about the timing. "The true prophet must be able to distinguish whether the historical hour stands under the wrath or love of God."[210]

[17] MT supplies a digest of vv. 12–14, continuing the harmonizing process evident earlier and repeating the negative and positive exhortations and incentive and threat.[211] The late redactor is insightfully aware of the organic link between the different messages of vv. 12–15 and v. 16. The addition does disturb the pattern of a single exhortation "do not listen" in the earlier sections and breaks the thematic connection between vv. 16 and 18.[212] The threat now focuses on Jerusalem, in line with the fate of secular artifacts in the capital that will be announced in v. 19 and also anticipated in v. 18 and repeated in v. 21, whereas ch. 28, like 27:16, speaks only of sacred artifacts. In view of v. 22a, the options have no basis in future reality, but are a rhetorical means of indicating a lost opportunity.

[18] Jeremiah's exhortation has an ironic ring and operates from his own premise that true prophecy involves doom. Real prophets would not be taking a positive stand on the issue of the temple artifacts, but would understand their loss as an omen of worse things to come. Then they would endeavor to avert such a disaster by intercession (cf. 7:16, which uses the same verb "implore"). The exhortation paves the way for the oracle of disaster that follows. In v. 18b MT basically interprets the meaning correctly but gives a wider definition of the artifacts by adding secular artifacts to the sacred ones. "This city" (v. 17) becomes a redactional focus, recurring in v. 19 and varied as "Jerusalem" in

---

210. James L. Crenshaw, *Prophetic Conflict: Its Effect upon Israel's Religion* (BZAW 124; Berlin: de Gruyter, 1971), 54, translating Eva Osswald, *Falsche Prophetie im Alten Testament* (Tübingen: Mohr [Siebeck], 1962), 22.

211. The same tendency is independently at work in LXX, in the addition "I never sent them" from v. 15 (*BHS*).

212. Seidl, *Texte und Einheiten*, 32.

vv. 18 and 21 and as "this place" in v. 22 in line with 28:6 (cf. 19:12). Verse 20 will explain the new emphasis on the capital and also on the palace, which appears in vv. 18 and 21. In general the secular concern takes its cue from the initial reference to "all this people" in v. 16, while the sacred artifacts were related to "the priests" there. The repetition of "this" with "city" and "place" in vv. 17, 19, and 22 is a clue to this exegetical connection.

[19–22] A second divine message follows, correcting the optimistic message of the false prophets in v. 16. It is an announcement of disaster that matches the pessimism at the close of v. 15. Yet in v. 22 MT will insist that optimism is in order, in a long-term sense rather than the short-term claim of v. 16.

[19] The quotation formula is redactionally expanded by a list of temple artifacts to be lost. The list projects a poignant arc to the end of the book, the documentation of the destruction of Jerusalem in 587 at ch. 52, which includes the plundering of the bronze pillars, vat, and trolleys, taken just for the value of their metal (52:17–23). The other sacred artifacts left behind are reinterpreted as secular ones, in line with the wider emphasis of vv. 18 and 21.

[20] The historical information about Jeconiah's or Jehoiachin's deportation accords with that supplied in 24:1 as an aftermath of the Babylonian invasion of Judah in 597. The confiscation of temple "treasures" along with palace "treasures" is mentioned in 2 Kgs 24:13, and the latter confiscation is presupposed in the secular interpretation at the end of v. 19. The Hebrew term rendered "upper class" occurs with reference to Judah at 39:6, in connection with the 587 invasion, but the deportation of leading citizens was a feature of the earlier deportation (cf. 24:1 and commentary; 28:4). Like v. 16, v. 20 is a key to the redactional expansion of the artifacts in this section, from sacred ones to secular. The added reference to nonroyal deportees is the clue. The king, wealthy citizens, and "Jerusalem" supply a pattern for confiscations in 597 that supplement the loss of temple artifacts with those taken from the palace and city mansions, a pattern that is reasonably carried over to the 587 situation. One may compare 52:13, which mentions the burning of the temple, palace, and "every house belonging to a dignitary" in 587. This augmentation of artifacts emphasizes the material loss that followed the 587 invasion, as a critique of the false prophets—and also to provide a measure of the restoration to be promised in v. 22.

[21–22] To this end the resumption of the quotation formula from v. 19 permits the repetition of the range of artifacts from the expanded version of v. 18. The basic oracle is one of unmitigated disaster, but it is supplemented with a corollary (v. 7 and 25:12, 14). Disaster was not God's last word. The timing of Yahweh's attention to the artifacts corresponds to the divine dealing with Babylon in 25:12; the same Hebrew verb *pqd* is used, and its positive use depends on 29:10, where it is used with the deportees of 597 as object. If the short-term restoration of the temple artifacts was false, their long-term restoration—and those of other confiscated artifacts since the projected reality would be greater than the false hope—would await Yahweh's providential timing. The focus on the eventuality of reversal ("until") reaffirms v. 7 and by implication the "seventy years" of 25:11–12. The expectation appears to be exilic; literary dependence on Ezra 1:7, 11; 6:5 that is sometimes claimed is difficult to substantiate.[213]

Chapter 27 functions at two levels. At one level it lays a foundation for Jeremiah's encounter with Hananiah in ch. 28. At another level it looks beyond imminent disaster to the positive future Yahweh has in store for the covenant people.

28:1–17 Yoke Symbolism, Part Two

28:1 *In that year,*[a] in the fourth year of King Zedekiah of Judah, in the fifth month, Hananiah ben Azzur, a prophet who came from Gibeon, said to me in Yahweh's temple, in front of the priests and all the people: **2** "Here is what Yahweh *Almighty, Israel's God,* said: 'I hereby break the yoke of Babylon's king. **3** In not more than two years I am going to bring back to this place *all* the artifacts belonging to Yahweh's temple *that King Nebuchadnezzar of Babylon removed from this place and took home to Babylon;* **4** also, *King* Jeconiah *ben Jehoiakim of Judah* and *all* the Judean deportees *who went to Babylon I am going to bring back to this place,* declared Yahweh, because I will break the yoke of Babylon's king.'" **5** Then *the prophet* Jeremiah said to *the prophet* Hananiah in front of the priests and all the people[b] standing in Yahweh's temple— **6** *the prophet* Jeremiah said, "Amen! I hope Yahweh will do[c] so. I hope *Yahweh* will make your message happen, your prophecy that the artifacts belonging to Yahweh's temple and all the deportees will be brought back from Babylon to this place. **7** Listen, however, to this statement[d] I am going to make in the hearing of you and all the people. **8** The prophets who preceded you and me over a long period were ones who prophesied to many countries and powerful kingdoms with threats of war, *a bad fate,*[e] *and pestilence.* **9** If a prophet gives a prophecy of peace, the prophet truly sent by Yahweh can only be recognized when the *prophet's* message comes to pass." **10** *The prophet* Hananiah then took the crossbar off the neck of *the prophet* Jeremiah and broke it. **11** Hananiah said in front of all the people: "Here is what Yahweh said: 'This is how I will break the yoke of King *Nebuchadnezzar* of Babylon off the necks of all the nations *in not more than two years.'"* Then *the prophet* Jeremiah went on his way.

12 Jeremiah received the following message from Yahweh after *the prophet* Hananiah broke the crossbar off *the prophet* Jeremiah's neck:

---

213. See Peter R. Ackroyd, "The Temple Vessels: A Continuity Theme," in *Studies in the Religious Tradition of the Old Testament* (London: SCM, 1987), 40–60, esp. 55–56.

13 "Go and tell Hananiah: 'Here is what Yahweh said: "A wooden crossbar[f] is what you broke, but you[g] should make iron crossbars in its place, 14 because"—here is what Yahweh *Almighty, Israel's God,* said—"an iron yoke is what I have put on the necks of all the*se* nations so they serve King *Nebuchadnezzar* of Babylon, *and they will serve him. Even the wild animals I have given him!*"' 15 *The prophet* Jeremiah also said to *the prophet* Hananiah, "Listen, Hananiah! Yahweh never sent you. You are the one responsible for getting this people to trust in falsehood. 16 Therefore here is what Yahweh said: 'Look out, I am going to dispatch you off the face of the earth. This year you will die *because you have spoken lies*[h] *against Yahweh.*'" 17 *The prophet* Hananiah did die *that year*, in the seventh month.

a. MT adds, "in the accession year of King Zedekiah of Judah," and then continues, "in the fourth year." The former dating represents a harmonizing gloss adapted from 27:1 and influenced by 49:34. The gloss evidently displaced the correct reading preserved in LXX (35:1), which was subsequently added in MT so that MT reflects a conflated text (Janzen, *Studies*, 14–15; GNB). REB "first (year)" for "fourth" follows G. R. Driver's suggestion in "Once Again Abbreviations," 86, which Janzen, *Studies*, 194 n. 24, has critiqued.

b. The transposition in LXX (*BHS*) is explicable as the result of a Greek grammatical necessity (Seidl, *Texte und Einheiten*, 66 n. 85), but it also occurs in 27(34):16.

c. For an imperfect used in a jussive sense see GKC §§75t, 107n.

d. LXX "the word of the Lord" (*BHS*) is an easier and so inferior reading, reflecting that the call for attention regularly introduces an oracle, as in v. 15.

e. NRSV and REB "famine" adopt a variant reading, *rāʿāb* (see *BHS*), in place of *rāʿâ*, "a bad fate." The variant is generally regarded as secondary, prompted by the common triad in MT, "sword, famine, and pestilence."

f. After the singular in v. 10, the plural pointing *môṭôt* is unexpected. Friebel, *Sign-Acts*, 142 n. 154, has observed that in MT the singular construct is written *môṭat* and the plural construct or absolute *mōṭôt* throughout chs. 27–28, apart from here, which suggests an erroneous pointing in this case and that a singular was intended. Then one has to read *taḥtêhā*, "in its place," for *taḥtêhen*, "in their place." The plural *mōṭôt* (v. 13b), surprising in view of the antithetical parallelism, appears to echo the plural reference to "nations" in v. 11 and to anticipate that in v. 14, and so to refer to a series of crossbars such as Jeremiah initially made. LXX consistently renders plural in both chapters, even in 28:12, and so is useless for retroversion in this case.

g. LXX's first singular (*BHS*), adopted by RSV and GNB, wrongly anticipates v. 14. Cf. GKC §112aa for the perfect with *wāw* consecutive used to introduce a command or wish (Seidl, *Formen und Formeln in Jeremia 27–29: Literaturwissenschaftliche Studie* [part 2; ATSAT 5; St. Ottilien: EOS, 1978], 213 n. 51).

h. Rather than "rebellion" or the like in EVV. See *HALOT* 2:769a; Jeffrey H. Tigay, *Deuteronomy* (Jewish Publication Society Torah Commentary; Philadelphia: Jewish Publication Society, 1996), 130–31, 367 nn. 19–20. The similarity of meaning to *šeqer*, "falsehood," in v. 15 was probably a factor that encouraged intertextuality (see the commentary).

Chapter 28 functions as a continuation of the previous chapter and presents a particular example of the false prophesying there reported in general terms and here developed in story form. Thus "to me" (v. 1) carries over the first person references in 27:12, 16 (cf. 27:1). Yet this consistency is editorial in nature, since the rest of the chapter, from v. 5 onward, speaks of Jeremiah in the third person. Indeed, ch. 27 was prefixed at an early stage to an originally independent ch. 28. Hananiah plays a key role, indicated by the way his activities frame the passage in dated statements in vv. 1 and 17 and feature centrally in vv. 10 and 12. The MT redaction creates an extra frame, "(In) that year," which not incorrectly ties this unit to the previous one in the first case and reinforces the month reference in the second.

The passage falls into two sections that relate consecutive encounters between Jeremiah and Hananiah, vv. 1–11 and 12–17; the second encounter is only envisioned in vv. 12–14, but vv. 15–17 imply the realization of the earlier part. The sections are united by two factors. First, a disputation spans the unit.[214] In Yahweh's name Hananiah presents a thesis (vv. 2–4), with which Jeremiah engages in dispute (vv. 6–9); later in Yahweh's name he presents a counterthesis (v. 14), in a setting of further dispute (vv. 13, 15–16; cf. 2:23–25 and commentary). MT has admirably highlighted thesis and counterthesis by filling out their quotation formulas in a parallel fashion. Here were two Yahwistic prophets at loggerheads. LXX is less subtle in rendering "prophet" as "false prophet" in v. 1, as in 26:7, here anticipating v. 15. MT also enters exuberantly into the spirit of the disputation by repeatedly counterpointing the names with the same title "the prophet" at adversarial points in the narrative and in the section endings at vv. 11b and 17; in the latter case both name and title are pointedly added. This stylistic feature is based on Jeremiah's mention of "the prophets who preceded you and me" in v. 8, with the aid of the description of Hananiah as a prophet in v. 1.

Second, the passage interweaves the disputation with the report of a symbolic action, Hananiah's response to Jeremiah's own. It is this action that sparks the debate, or rather its provocative interpretation in vv. 2–4 does so. Its execution follows in v. 10, after Jeremiah's interruption in vv. 5–9, and then a summarizing restatement of its interpretation in v. 11, necessitated by the interruption. Significantly there is no initial command from Yahweh to engage in the symbolic action. This absence of a standard element—in contrast to 27:2–3—sounds a warning. It is an initial clue meant to alert readers to take sides against Hananiah. The presence of ch. 27, as a whole, has already primed them to do so. Text and context have much less interest than modern scholarship does in the contemporary community's problem of differentiating between true and false prophecy. They reflect an unashamedly partisan spirit, bolstered

---

214. Seidl, *Formen und Formeln*, 218, refers to a basic thesis in vv. 2–4 and a retort in vv. 6–9. This analysis does not go far enough.

by a post-587 perspective. "If there had been confusion during Jeremiah's lifetime, there need be no longer" for the exilic and later readers of the book.[215] Readers of LXX find Hananiah's name in Greek dress as Ananias and are thereby reminded that the NT has in Acts 5 its own Hananiah who died a sudden punitive death.

[28:1–11] In the first encounter Hananiah takes the initiative. This section is made up of three parts, Hananiah's proclamation of salvation (vv. 1–4), intended as a preliminary interpretation for his symbolic action (v. 10), Jeremiah's interruption (vv. 5–9) and Hananiah's action and renewed interpretation (vv. 10–11).

[1–4] "Yahweh's temple" is the location of the encounter in the first two parts (vv. 1, 5). It corresponds to the issue of the temple artifacts plundered in 597, already mentioned in ch. 27, that will be broached by Hananiah in v. 3 and picked up by Jeremiah in v. 6. Priests and people are an appropriate audience in v. 1 and also v. 5, since both sacred and secular losses will be specified (vv. 3–4, 6). Thus v. 1 introduces not only the section's spokesperson for the rival prophetic ideology already featured in ch. 27, but also the place and constituencies important for the first two sections.

[1] "To me," the product of early editing, does not correspond to any direct address to Jeremiah in vv. 2–4, but at least indicates his crucial role. Hananiah spoke with one eye on Jeremiah, who was wearing the crossbar on his neck (v. 10); Jeremiah's own symbolic action featured in ch. 27 is presupposed. After the preparatory ch. 27, the reader is aware of a complex situation: Hananiah responds to Jeremiah's own response to the multistate conference planning rebellion against Babylon, a stance supported by prophets in each state, including Judah. Hananiah was reaffirming what Jeremiah had decried. The "fifth month" was July/August 594.

[2–4] By expanding the quotation formula, MT recalls 27:4. Speaking with the quotation formula and so with the same sincere conviction of inspiration as Jeremiah was wont to speak, his rival begins with an interpretation of the symbolic action he was about to perform. In a proclamation of salvation he announces at beginning and end a divine intervention to terminate Babylonian control. The initial Hebrew performative perfect, "I hereby break" (NJPS; cf. 1:10 and commentary) declares Yahweh's intention as already fulfilled in principle in the symbolic action. The implications of this intervention for Judah are spelled out in vv. 3–4a. Destruction of the enemy would mean salvation for Judah, on two scores. First, the temple artifacts lost in 597 would be restored "in not more than two years." According to 27:16 Hananiah is reaffirming a party line. Second, along with the artifacts, those deported at that time, both king and citizens, would be repatriated

---

215. Brevard S. Childs, *Old Testament Theology in a Canonical Context* (Philadelphia: Fortress, 1985), 141.

to Jerusalem. God and realm would have their honor satisfied. With an eye for style MT expands the structure into an ABCC′B′A′ format (Scalise in Keown et al. 54);[216] in v. 3b it also adds information from 27:16, 20.[217] Jeremiah's response (v. 6) will make no specific reference to the king's return.

[5–9] Jeremiah adroitly introduces a new and damaging genre into the scenario, a disputation. It downgrades Hananiah's solemn proclamation to the thesis of a contentious disputation, as he proceeds with the element of dispute. In structure it is similar to his defense in 26:14–15.[218]

[5] Our hero—for so the text means to portray Jeremiah—wrests the limelight from his rival, as the repetition of the public setting from v. 1 connotes. Jeremiah seizes the moment between Hananiah's word and deed to deliberately disrupt the proceedings. The reminder of the location, "Yahweh's temple," paves the way for the renewed mention of the temple artifacts in v. 6.

[6] Jeremiah speaks politely out of respect for the invocation of Yahweh's name that would have impressed the hearers. He starts by citing common ground, with magnanimous panache. His diplomatic affirmation rings out like Benaiah's in 1 Kgs 1:36. Yet the ensuing context makes it sound like little more than ardent desirability. The fulfillment of Hananiah's pronouncement (v. 4) would be a dream come true, the top of everybody's wish list, including Jeremiah's.

[7–8] Jeremiah's dispute moves from the chimera of rosy thinking to a solid argument, whose importance he underlines with a call for attention. He appeals to a long, preexilic prophetic tradition that had struck a mainly negative note of military defeat. Implicitly such a negative prognosis depended on the negative diagnosis of society that these prophets, like Jeremiah, had offered. MT eloquently fills out the negativity with Jeremiah's key term for disaster, "a bad fate," and with the redaction's favorite addition, "pestilence" (cf. 27:8). Hananiah was swimming against the tide of this established prophetic paradigm, it is implied, while Jeremiah was its living champion. The general statement of v. 8 is consistent with the prophetic "lookouts" Yahweh "appointed" for Israel in 6:17 and with the echoes of earlier prophecy in Jeremiah's teaching.[219]

---

216. This is better than the ABCB′A′ chiasm posited by Frank-Lothar Hossfeld and Ivo Meyer, *Prophet gegen Prophet: Eine Analyse der alttestamentlichen Texte zum Thema: Wahre und falsche Propheten* (BibB 9; Fribourg: Schweizerisches Katholisches Bibelwerk, 1973), 95. The C′ element is the repatriates, while the B′ element is "I am going to bring back to this place."

217. See Janzen, *Studies*, 48.

218. Axel Graupner, *Auftrag und Geschick des Propheten Jeremia: Literarische Eigenart, Herkunft und Intention vordeuteronomistischer Prosa im Jeremiabuch* (Biblische-theologische Studien 15; Neukirchen-Vluyn: Neukirchener Verlag, 1991), 67.

219. See in general Hetty Lalleman-de Winkel, *Jeremiah in Prophetic Tradition: An Examination of the Book of Jeremiah in the Light of Israel's Prophetic Traditions* (CBET 26; Leuven: Peeters, 2000).

True and False Predictions

[9] The corollary of v. 8 is that the burden of proof rests on the rival prophetic ideology since it breaks the pattern of what is claimed to be the dominant one. The test of authenticity for a prediction of peaceful restitution can only be its eventual fulfillment, before which judgment on its validity must be suspended.[220]

[10–11a] Hananiah resolutely carries on with the prophetic symbolic action, though its momentum has been lost by the interruption and its skeptical content. He tries to seize back the limelight—so the shorter description of the bystanders may indicate—as he snatches the crossbar from Jeremiah's shoulders, breaking it, and interpreting in terms of Yahweh's breaking the yoke (contrast 27:8, 11). In style the interpretation accords with that found in 13:8; 19:11; and 51:64. Hananiah now addresses the international perspective of the symbolism.

[11b] The final statement of the section typically marks the closure of a narrative episode. However, such closure here stands in tension with the ongoing, uncompleted disputation, which lacks a counterthesis. There is unfinished business; the genre demands a sequel. Why the delay? Jeremiah has presented his dispute and now awaits a divine message to clinch the disputation. The reader confidently expects such a message after the oracles of ch. 27.

[12–17] In fact, this second section of the passage contains three messages (vv. 13, 14, and 16). The separate introductions relating to Jeremiah in vv. 12 and 15 divide the section into two parts, vv. 12–14 and 15–17. This section deliberately counters the first one in particulars that will be noted as they occur. A difference between the two is the lack of publicity in this second section.

[12–14] In 42:7 Jeremiah had to wait ten days for a pertinent message to be revealed to him (cf. 18:2, 5). Here the time lapse is not specified—though it must have been less than two months (v. 17)—but a temporal hinge with the former section is provided in v. 12b. The content of this hinge also prepares for the divine command in v. 12b for Jeremiah to transmit a countermanding oracle about replacement of the wooden crossbar with iron ones. The initial oracle reception statement contrasts with its absence in v. 1. Yahweh tauntingly suggests for Hananiah another symbolic action that does not reverse Jeremiah's original one but reinforces it with a set of iron crossbars lacking the breakability of the first set (cf. "iron from the north," 15:12). Its taunting tone puts the proposal on a par with Jeremiah's suggestion in 27:18 that the false prophets should engage in intercession. A supplementary oracle is cited in v. 14, which provides an interpretation for such a proposed symbolic action. This oracle has such weight in the passage that it is not surprising that it has been redactionally expanded at a number of points in MT, which was aware of its significance as the counterthesis to the thesis of vv. 2–4. First, matching epithets for Yahweh

---

220. Commentators often compare Deut 18:22, but Carolyn J. Sharp, *Prophecy and Ideology in Jeremiah: Struggles for Authority in Deutero-Jeremianic Prose* (London: T & T Clark, 2003), 152–53, observes the crucial difference between the two texts.

are added to both quotation formulas. Second, "these nations," in contrast to "the nations" in v. 11, reminds the reader of the coalition of states in 27:3 and Jeremiah's making a set of crossbars, one for each king. This development explains the plural "crossbars" of v. 13. Third, the blatant assertion of 27:6b is repeated, preceded by the emphatic "And . . . will serve him" that opened 27:7. The last two additions relating to ch. 27 are not surprising since v. 14 constitutes a strong affirmation of 27:8. These additions reinforce the message of unremitting political subordination for the western states, thus elucidating the "iron yoke." By divine mandate Babylon was here for the duration.

[15–17] A personal oracle of disaster addressed to Hananiah is the last of the three oracles. Jeremiah himself speaks the reason; the weight of divine authority is reserved for the dramatic announcement in v. 16.

[15] This final confrontation echoes the call for attention issued to Hananiah in v. 7. Like the first, it relates to his prophesying, but now in a terrifyingly specific manner. The issue of a prophet being sent by God, raised in general negative terms in v. 9, is also now applied to Hananiah. Moreover, it individualizes the charge against Jeremiah's rivals in 27:15. The accusation of prophetic falsehood recalls the structural repetitions of ch. 27 (vv. 10, 14, 16), but now it is put in a solemn setting of Hananiah's guilt. He was advocating a perversion of true faith. "In falsehood" and "truly" (lit. "in truth") in v. 9 are loosely polarized. Hananiah was plainly wrong about God's will.

[16] The announcement of imminent disaster for the false prophet gains extra gravity from the use of wordplay. The Hebrew verb *šlḥ*, "send," is used in an intensive form with the sense "dispatch." The one who prophesied without being sent would in reprisal be sent away—to his doom. The imminence is specified as within the span of a year—an ironically quicker fulfillment than the two years of v. 3. The repetition of "I am going to" confirms that v. 3 is being challenged here. Elsewhere in Jeremiah's oracles the punitive death of individuals or particular groups is linked with the disaster that was to befall the community at large (11:23; 14:15; 20:6; 21:15). In this case an example is made of this ringleader of Jeremiah's rivals. MT reflects a need to explain the exception. It does so by citing as a precedent Deut 13:5 (6), where a death sentence was prescribed for a prophet's advocating idolatry in the community of faith. The intertextual connection probably came about via Jer 23:27, where dreaming prophets (cf. Deut 13: 1, 3, 5 [2, 4, 6]) cause Yahweh's name to be forgotten, as in earlier days Baal's name came to be preferred. Again idolatry and a false view of Yahweh's character and purposes are compared. Hananiah's sin was as gross as idolatry;[221] it warranted an exemplary death, as in Deuteronomy 13.

---

221. Cf. the use of *šeqer*, "falsehood," in terms of believing in unreal gods at 3:23; 10:14; 13:25; and 16:19, where it is variously rendered "delusion," "lie(s)," "false gods."

True and False Predictions

[17] A historical comment seals the counterthesis by recording the fulfillment of the fatal prediction. By comparison with v. 1, it specifies that Hananiah's death occurred two months later (September/October 594). MT rounds off the unit by counterpointing the endings of its two sections, vv. 11b and 17. In the conflict between the prophet Jeremiah and the prophet Hananiah, the former won and the latter lost. Jeremiah's definition of prophecy in terms of "war" (v. 8) and Hananiah's in terms of "peace" (v. 9) was thereby judged in favor of Jeremiah. Yahweh's providential verdict verified Jeremiah's prophesying in that Jeremiah lived on ("went his way"), while Hananiah died.

In 28:1–17 Jeremiah's conflict with rival prophets about Babylonian hegemony, set out in ch. 27, is exemplified in the person and proclamation of Hananiah. Hananiah's contrary symbolic action is itself countered with a disputation that ends with a realized prediction of his death. Under God, Babylon's control of Judah would end no time soon.

29:1–32 *No Quick Return for the Deportees*

29:1 This is the text of a letter sent from Jerusalem by *the prophet* Jeremiah to *the rest*[a] *of* the elders of the community of deportees, to the priests and prophets, and to all the people *Nebuchadnezzar had deported from Jerusalem to Babylon*— **2** after the surrender of King Jeconiah in Jerusalem, along with the queen mother and the eunuchs, the officials[b] of Judah and Jerusalem and the craftsmen and smiths— **3** taken by Elasah ben Shaphan and Gemariah ben Hilkiah, who were being sent by King Zedekiah of Judah to Babylon to see King *Nebuchadnezzar* of Babylon. It read: **4** "Here is what Yahweh *Almighty*, Israel's God, said: 'To *all* the deportees, whom I have deported from Jerusalem *to Babylon*: **5** Build houses and live in them, and plant gardens and eat their produce. **6** Get married and have sons and daughters, and marry your sons and daughters off *so that they can have sons and daughters*, and let your numbers grow *there* rather than get fewer. **7** Urge[c] the peace of the city[d] I have deported you to and pray to Yahweh for it because in its peace you will find your own peace.' **8** In fact here is what Yahweh *Almighty, Israel's God*, said: 'Do not be deceived by the prophets and diviners you have in your community. Do not listen to your dreamers[e] whom you get to dream, **9** because they are prophesying to you in my name in utter falsehood. I never sent them,' *declared Yahweh*. **10** In fact here is what Yahweh said: 'Indeed, just as soon as Babylon's seventy years are up, I will turn my attention to you and keep my *good* promise, the one I have made you to bring you back to this place. **11** Indeed, *I know the plans*[f] I have in mind for you,' *declared Yahweh*, 'plans of peace rather than a bad fate, to give you a *hopeful* future.^g 12 So *when you call on me*, when you *come*^h *and* pray to me, I will listen to you.ⁱ 13 When you look for me, you will find [me]. When you urge me wholeheartedly, 14 I will let you find me,'^j *declared Yahweh, 'and I will restore your fortunes, collecting you from all the nations and places I will have driven*^k *you away to,'* declared Yahweh, *'and bringing you back to the place I have deported you from.'* 16 ¹*In fact here is what Yahweh said: 'Concerning the king now seated on the Davidic throne and concerning all the people residing in this city, your kin who did not leave with you at the time of deportation'*— 17 *here is what Yahweh Almighty said*—*'look, I am going to let loose among them sword, famine, and pestilence, and make them like awful*^m *figs, so bad they are inedible.* 18 *I will chase after them with sword, famine, and pestilence and make them people all the other kingdoms in the world will shudder at, people to whom all the nations I will have driven them away to will react with cursing and shock and with whistling and insults.* 19 *The reason is their not listening to my messages,' declared Yahweh, 'when*ⁿ *I sent to them my prophetic servants over and over again*—*nor did you listen either,' declared Yahweh.* 20 *As for you, listen to Yahweh's message: 'All you deportees whom I have sent away from Jerusalem to Babylon,* 15 because you say, "Yahweh has provided prophets for us in Babylon"'— 21 here is what Yahweh Almighty, Israel's God, said—'concerning Ahab *ben Kolaiah* and Zedekiah *ben Maaseiah, who have been prophesying falsehood to you in my name*: Look, I am going to hand them over to King *Nebuchadnezzar* of Babylon, who will execute them right in front of you. 22 They will give rise to a curse used by all the Judean deportees in Babylon, "May Yahweh treat you like Zedekiah and Ahab, roasted to death by Babylon's king!" 23 because they have done what is scandalous in Israelite tradition, committing adultery with their neighbors' wives, and have given in my name *false* messages I never authorized. But I am *someone who knows and* a witness,' declared Yahweh.

24 "Also to Shemaiah from Nehelam you are to say *as follows*: 25 '*Here is what Yahweh Almighty, Israel's God, said:* "Because you have sent *a letter* in your own name^o *to all the people in Jerusalem,* to the priest Zephaniah ben Maaseiah, *and to all the priests,* with the message, 26 'Yahweh himself has appointed you priest in succession to the priest Jehoiada in order that there may be officers^p in Yahweh's temple to deal with any prophesying^q madman so you can put him in the stocks or in irons. 27 The point is, why haven't you reprimanded Jeremiah from Anathoth, who has been prophesying to you [all]? 28 The reason [I write] is that he has sent word to us in Babylon that the situation will last a long time and we are to build houses and live in them and plant gardens and eat their produce.'"'" 29 *The priest* Zephaniah read out *this* letter for *the prophet* Jere-

miah to hear. 30 Jeremiah then received the following message from Yahweh: 31 "Send word to *all* the deportees: 'Here is what Yahweh said: "Concerning Shemaiah from Nehelam: Because Shemaiah has prophesied to you without my sending him and gotten you to trust in falsehood, 32 therefore"—here is what Yahweh said—"look, I am going to deal with Shemaiah *from Nehelam*, along with his progeny. He will have nobody *living* among this people, nobody who will enjoy seeing the good I am going to bring about for my people," declared Yahweh, "because he has spoken lies against Yahweh."'"

a. The meaning of *yeter*, "the rest of," in this context is baffling; see McKane 2:727. The term was used of artifacts in 27:19. Conceivably it is a misplaced gloss on "all the people" (Volz 270; *BHK³*; Bright 204–5; cf. 36:9; 52:15).

b. LXX (cf. *BHS*) refers instead to the upper class, *ḥōrîm*, mentioned in MT at 27:20 (Ziegler, *Beiträge*, 92).

c. The phrase means to "seek a *šālôm* oracle on behalf of the city of Babylon" (Jonathan P. Sisson, "Jeremiah and the Jerusalem Conception of Peace," *JBL* 105 [1986]: 429–42, esp. 440). Calvin 3:420 considered this type of interpretation, but rejected it.

d. LXX "the land" (*BHS*) is an easier and so inferior reading (Holladay 2:132). The conception in vv. 1–14a is of deportation from Jerusalem to the capital city, Babylon.

e. See textual note 1 on 27:9. LXX "dreams" reflects MT in this case.

f. The omission in LXX may be accidental (*BHS*; Janzen, *Studies*, 118). However, it seems to be associated with the quotation formula added in MT, which pauses before the repeated "plans."

g. LXX^{OL} have preserved the original reading, telescoped in LXX (*BHS*, *HUB*), though Ziegler does not adopt it.

h. None of the EVV follows the accentuation of MT, which links with the previous clause: "when you call to me, you will go," presumably out of exile, in anticipation of v. 14. Gillian Greenberg, "Some Secondary Expansions in the Masoretic Text of Jeremiah: Retroversion Is Perilous, But the Risk May Be Worthwhile," in *Biblical Hebrew, Biblical Texts: Essays in Memory of Michael P. Weitzman* (ed. A. Rapaport-Albert and G. Greenberg; JSOTSup 353; London: Sheffield Academic Press, 2001), 222–43, esp. 235, relates the verb to making pilgrimage to Jerusalem, evidently taking v. 14a*b*-b as a means to that end.

i. For the juxtaposition of logically subordinate and main clauses see GKC §112ff, kk.

j. LXX "I will reveal myself to you" (see *BHS*) is striking but may well be a case of theological exegesis (Goldman, *Prophétie et royauté*, 66–68; *HUB*). Jones 366 argues for its originality, especially in a play between the verb *glh*, "reveal," and *gôlâ*, "deportation."

k. For the future perfect here and in v. 18 see Joüon §112i.

l. In MT the irrelevance of v. 15 for vv. 16–20 and connection with vv. 21–23 suggests that v. 15 was dropped by homoeoteleuton (*bābelâ*, "to Babylon," v. 20; *bābelâ*, "in Babylon," v. 15) and wrongly reinserted before the quotation formula of v. 16 rather than that of v. 21 (Janzen, *Studies*, 118). As Janzen observes, the order of topics in

vv. 1–14 and 16–20 accords with that in ch. 24, first the deportees of 597 and then those left in Jerusalem. LXX^L preserves the order vv. 16–20, 15, 21–23, whether by tradition or critical reconstruction we do not know; cf. NAB. LXX has only vv. 15, 21–23, leaving out vv. 16–20 probably because they were not in its Hebrew text.

m. *HALOT* 4:1618b prefers "rotten."

n. Strictly the conjunction means either "to whom" (Holladay 2:134) or "concerning which," loosely linking with what precedes.

o. LXX omits "Because" and renders "I did not send you in my name." This represents an exegetical translation (Ziegler, *Beiträge*, 50–51), which has an oracle in view. It tried to ease somewhat the awkward complexity of MT; see the commentary.

p. LXX and other versions (see *BHS*) have a singular noun referring to Zephaniah (cf. 20:1–2); REB, GNB, and seemingly NIV follow suit. MT has in view security officers reporting to Zephaniah (Barthélemy, *Critique textuelle*, 2:678–79, comparing 2 Kgs 11:18). MT is preferable as a more difficult reading.

q. See textual note g on 14:14 for the verb here and in v. 27.

This passage tells of two letters sent by Jeremiah to the deportees of 597, one in vv. 1–23 and a second in vv. 24–32 replying to a response to the first received by a temple official. Throughout the chapter MT has used at certain points the same expanded quotation formula, "Here is what Yahweh Almighty, Israel's God, said" (vv. 4, 8, 21, and 25). These seem to highlight certain oracular passages (vv. 4–7, 8–9, 21–23, and 25–32). Apart from the first, the other three passages involve false prophecy. The identical beginnings promote vv. 4–7 by contrast as the true message of Yahweh. Jeremiah got it right; the prophets in Babylon did not. Verses 8–9 have an important role in the collection of chs. 27–29, in that they reiterate the triple warning sounded in ch. 27, "Do not listen to . . . prophets . . . because they are prophesying utter falsehood to you." This message is now relayed to the deportees. It is echoed in MT at vv. 21 and 23, but it is already reinforced in the common text at v. 31. MT creates its own link with ch. 28 by ending at v. 32 on the same note as 28:16 in a doom-laden denunciation of false prophets. Shemaiah abroad was as reprobate as Hananiah at home.

[**29:1–23**] The first letter does not possess any epistolary features apart from the address in v. 4b (cf. REB).[222] Only the body of the letter is transmitted; it consists of a series of oracles. After a superscription in vv. 1–3, it falls into two distinct parts, vv. 4–14 and 16–19, and vv. 20 + 15 + 21–23, in which vv. 4 and 20 correspond as introductory components. The first part consists of a main section, vv. 4–7, and three subsidiary sections, vv. 8–9, 10–14, 16–19, each intro-

---

222. Dennis Pardee, "An Overview of Ancient Hebrew Epistolography," *JBL* 97 (1978): 321–46, esp. 331 n. 47, finds here an indirect object with the quotation formula, with most EVV, but the change of person from "Yahweh" to "I" is significant. There is a mixture of prophetic and epistolary styles. The claim that "witness" in v. 23 refers to a countersignatory (Holladay 2:138, 144) is unlikely, since the first person language relates to Yahweh throughout.

True and False Predictions

duced by a quotation formula prefaced by *kî* ("For," NRSV, but left unrendered in v. 16), here translated "In fact." This phenomenon raises the issue of the literary integrity of the letter, since in the poetic compositions earlier in the book this conjunction was often used to introduce originally independent or editorial units. It reflects redactional activity, though not necessarily the addition of secondary material (cf., e.g., 22:6–7). Verse 20 has been inserted as an introduction in MT in order to integrate vv. 15 + 21–23, which provide an example of the false prophets (vv. 8–9) at work in the Babylonian community. Verses 16–19 have been supplied in MT to supplement vv. 10–14. The letter attested in the common text coheres and is part of a larger whole, chs. 27–29, to which it now belongs. As in ch. 27, the stereotyped language of the prose sermon belongs primarily to the expansions of the literary tradition represented in MT, which Stulman has calculated is 37 percent longer than the text shared by LXX (ch. 36) and MT.[223]

[1–3] This superscription to the letter supplies information about its historical context.

[1] The letter was sent to the recognized leaders of the deported Judean community (cf. Ezek 8:1). The letter both explicitly and implicitly protests against the claims of the prophets, who are identified in v. 15. Accordingly MT prolongs the adversarial stance of ch. 28 by qualifying Jeremiah as "the prophet" here and in v. 29, now prophesying by mail, while LXX interprets "prophets" as "false prophets" here and in v. 8. Mention of priests and prophets triggers the reader's memory about the controversy over the temple artifacts plundered in 597 and the claim of Jeremiah's prophetic rivals at home that they would be returned with the deportees (28:3–4) within two years. The reader is meant to recall the claim as the background to the letter. The letter identifies the people at large as the object of both positive and negative exhortations. MT has clarified who this community was by providing the historical sequel to the information of v. 2; it makes use of v. 4, appropriately adapting it to a secular version (cf. too 27:20).

[2] This information is a helpful early amplification, like 24:1b, which interrupts vv. 1 and 3. It too is based on 2 Kgs 24:14–16 and uses "Jeconiah" for the royal name.

[3] The arrangements for delivering the letter are explained. A royal delegation to Babylon, whose purpose readers are not told, furnishes an opportunity to take it "in the diplomatic mail bag" (Thompson 545). Elasah ben Shaphan was presumably the brother of Jeremiah's protector Ahikam in 26:24 and so a sympathizer.

[4–7] The quotation formula characterizes the exhortations as an oracle, which the divine subject in vv. 4 and 7 reflects. "I have deported" provides a frame explaining to the deported community that their situation was part of

---

223. *Prose Sermons*, 89–94.

God's will. The oracle combats a belief in a quick return home espoused in Judah (28:3–4) and evidently shared by the deportees.

[5–6] The unwanted advice of building homes and growing food, marrying and having families echoes ironically traditional formulas concerning ongoing blessing in the God-given homeland.[224] Babylon was now to be regarded as their new home, and such activities were expressions of the divine will for those in exile. They were to settle down, as if in their own land, living life to the fullest possible extent.

[7] The triple use of *šālôm*, "peace," is a barbed denial of earlier expectations. It implicitly recalls the earlier claims of Jeremiah's prophetic rivals that Yahweh would bring about for Judah not a bad fate but peace. These claims had been wrecked by the Babylonian invasion and deportation of 597 and replaced by the assurance of a short deportation (cf. the commentary on 27:16). The claims are here ironically recalled; *šālôm*, yes—but on enemy territory! It is a corollary of the divine warning to Babylon's vassal states, including Judah, in ch. 27 (esp. v. 11) not to rebel against their overlord. The community is told to accept and make the best of the divinely ordained situation, even to pray for Babylon (cf. Ezra 6:10; 1 Tim 2:1–2). Thus they would survive what was to be a prolonged situation, to endure as long as Babylon was the agent of Yahweh's will. Its interim nature will emerge in v. 10, in the reference to seventy years, but MT has already given redactional expression to its length at v. 6, in the reference to a third generation who would live to see a reversal of the situation (Duhm 229; cf. v. 32; 27:7). The third person reference to Yahweh stresses the presence and power of "Israel's God" (v. 4) in the very place where pagan gods were worshiped (Rudolph 184).

[8–9] A second oracle draws out the implication of the foregoing (mainly) positive exhortations by a pair of negative ones that shows their polemical nature; so "it follows naturally" (Jones 363). The oracle is a warning that denies the contrary advice of local prophets who shared the viewpoint of Jeremiah's rivals back home. The blame, however, was shared, in view of the complicity of the deported community. The prophets were responding to "the pressure exerted by public opinion."[225] In light of 27:9, the listing of "prophets, diviners, dreamers" here has a pejorative ring. The coup de grace is the closing denial

---

224. Cf., e.g., Deut 20:5–7; 28:30–32; Isa 65:21–23. Adele Berlin, "Jeremiah 29:5–7: A Deuteronomic Allusion," *HAR* 8 (1984): 3–11, has reviewed this background. Her claim of intertextual dependence on Deut 20:5–7, 10 has been critiqued by Sharp, *Prophecy and Ideology*, 107 n. 12. Daniel L. Smith, "Jeremiah as Prophet of Nonviolent Resistance," *JSOT* 43 (1989): 95–107, esp. 103–4, has also closely linked the passage with Deuteronomy 20, finding a call to nonviolent resistance.

225. J. Alberto Soggin, "Jeremiah 29, 8b," in *Old Testament and Oriental Studies* (BibOr 29; Rome: Biblical Institute Press, 1975), 238–40, esp. 240.

that reapplies the denials delivered to Jeremiah's rivals in Jerusalem (27:15; 28:15).

[**10-14**] The third oracle in the letter is a proclamation of salvation, a bittersweet promise of long-term hope over against short-term optimism. It presents Yahweh's positive purposes for the deported community. Yahweh's response to the issue of return was not "no" but "not yet." "God's own way . . . is with utter freedom and, in the end, with caring fidelity" (Brueggemann 263).

[**10**] The virtual promise of 25:11-12 is resumed. The verb *pqd*, used negatively of Babylon's eventual punishment in 25:12 with the meaning "deal (with)," is repeated here in a positive sense, "turn my attention (to)." MT has built a bridge between 25:12 and 29:10 by applying the verb to the restoration of the temple artifacts (27:22), which was an omen for the return of the Judeans who were deported with them. The period of seventy years until Babylon's downfall is related to Judah's restoration. The relevance of the seventy years is its likely origin as Jeremiah's prophetic retort to the two years claimed by his rivals to be the time lag before restoration. The return of the deportees, denied by Jeremiah in 28:6 on Hananiah's short-term premise, could be affirmed on a long-term basis. LXX interprets the final "you" as "your people."

[**11**] The focus on *šālôm*, "peace," for the deportees in v. 7 is developed, but now with reference not to making the best of their present experience but to their future lot (v. 10). The *šālôm* of v. 7 was relative, but now an absolute *šālôm* is in view. Yahweh's ultimate plans for them involved the manifestation of *šālôm* and a positive "future" beyond Babylon's period of power. MT carefully defines this future as "hopeful," borrowing the term from 31:17; "future" had been used negatively in 5:31 (rendered "final outcome") and 23:20 (rendered "when time has elapsed"). MT also reinforces the divine planning with a reassuring reference to Yahweh's knowledge. A similar reference is added to v. 23, there in rebuke, while here in reassurance (cf. 15:15).

[**12-14a***a*] Triple parallelism is eloquently used to indicate Yahweh's gift of accessibility to the praying community, though v. 13 may be an early editorial flourish if it is a citation of Deut 4:29.[226] "Pray" and "urge" repeat inversely verbs used in v. 7 concerning Babylon's peace in which the deportees could share. This might suggest that the span of a good future includes the time spent in deportation. However, the focus on the aftermath of deportation in MT's addition at v. 14a*b*-b indicates otherwise, doubtless correctly. While v. 7 relates to prayers that embrace the present stage of God's will for the deportees, here prayers that anticipate the next stage are in view. Return was the intended goal of prayer; the praying was to consist of ardent laments along the lines of Psalm 102 and Dan 9:4-19. "Come" in MT apparently refers to communal lamentation (cf. 2 Chr 20:4).

226. Parke-Taylor, *Formation*, 226-27, so argues.

Verses 12–14a*a*, with their assurance of the need for and efficacy of prayer in realizing God's gracious promises, are a spiritual jewel in the book of Jeremiah (cf. Matt 7:7), as 31:31–34 is a theological jewel. The Chronicler set high value on this section. In a quest for scriptural answers to postexilic Judah's problem of a spiritual exile, he chose three texts relating to a literal return from exile, Lev 26:34–45; Jer 29:10–19; and Ezekiel 18.[227] This second text became the basis of the epigrammatic 2 Chr 7:14 and of the spiritual principle, "If you seek (Yahweh), he will be found by you," in 1 Chr 28:9, and 2 Chr 15:2, and it supplied the keyword *drš*, "seek," used throughout the book to refer variously to repentant return to Yahweh and normative worship and way of life.

[14a*b*–b] MT envisions not simply the Babylonian deportees of 597 but a much wider constituency, the Diaspora. So it enlarges "you" and "your" beyond their original scope, just as v. 10 did generationally. Moreover, "all the nations I will have driven you away to" presupposes v. 18 and so includes even those exiled in 587 in its purview.[228] Terrible judgment would not finally exclude its victims from redeeming grace. This addition incorporates two divine promises from elsewhere in the book. The beginning and end anticipate the terminology of restoration in 30:3, 18, while sandwiched between them is the gathering from the Diaspora mentioned in 23:3; use is also made of "places" (24:9) and, as already noted, of "nations" (v. 18).[229]

[16–19] This is an oracle of disaster with the announcement (vv. 17–18) and then the reason (v. 19). An introductory quotation formula, like that in v. 10, is MT's way of integrating it into the context. A frame is provided for the passage by the repetition of the same Hebrew verb, *šlḥ*, in an intensive form ("let loose") in v. 17 and in a simple form ("send") in v. 19. The oracle contrasts with the proclamation of salvation in vv. 10–14. While the deportees had no "bad fate" in store (v. 11), the Judeans back home were like "bad" figs in their prospects (v. 17). This digression in MT reminds the reader of the judgment to befall the Judeans in 587. God's purposes did not proceed in a straight line between the 597 deportation and the distant restoration, but worse punishment was to intervene, though, in line with v. 14a*b*-b, its victims would not be beyond redemption.

[16] The digression moves from King Jeconiah and others deported from Jerusalem in 597 (vv. 1–2) to his successor Zedekiah and those left in Jerusalem in the post-597 period.

[17–18] This material basically derives from 24:8–10, the interpretation of Jeremiah's vision of bad figs, and presupposes the reader's knowledge of it; the

---

227. See Leslie C. Allen, "1 and 2 Chronicles," *NIB* 3:302–3.
228. Cf. Goldman, *Prophétie et royauté*, 73.
229. Ibid., 70–73.

deportees had never had the opportunity of hearing it. The connection was sparked by the similarity of elements in vv. 10–14 to the preceding interpretation of the good figs in 24:5–7, namely, "bringing back to their country" (24:6; cf. 29:10, 14) and "they will come back to me wholeheartedly" (24:7; cf. 29:13). The references to building and planting, though used differently, may also have played a part. Prose sermonic language, a feature of the earlier contexts carries over. The order of the material was slightly changed so that v. 17a echoes 24:10 and vv. 17b–18 echo 24:8–9. The switch made possible the stylistic framing in vv. 17a and 19, whereby the punishment fits the crime since both relate to divine sending.[230]

[19] In order to provide a reason for the disaster, the redactor moves on from ch. 24 to ch. 25, to 25:8 and 25:4, the latter verse employing prose sermonic language.[231] According to ch. 25, Yahweh's reprisal through (Babylonian) invasion (25:9) and then of the imperial power would be wielded for seventy years (25:11–12), to which 29:10 has also referred. The redactor is reminding readers of the judgment that was soon to occur in 587 with Babylonian power as its instrument. Yet the invasion of 597 had been an initial part of that judgment, and he pauses to reflect that the same sin had occasioned it as the Judeans committed under Zedekiah. The reflection provides a neat transition to v. 20, where the 597 deportation is portrayed as a divine judgment. The recurrence of the intensive form of šlḥ, "let loose," from v. 17, now with the meaning "send away," suggests a punitive sense.

[15, 20–23] The warning against prophets in the community (vv. 8–9) develops this oracle of disaster directed against two prophets. The announcement of disaster (vv. 21–22) precedes the reason (v. 23) again.

[20] The call to attention added in MT dovetails vv. 21–23 with v. 19, while the address integrates the passage into the overall structure of the letter by loosely echoing v. 4. The verb "sent away" represents a last glance at the vision report of ch. 24, but now at a feature that relates to the good figs (24:9).[232]

[15] The oracle is set in a communal framework by two public warnings, the deportees' resentment of Jeremiah's interference in v. 15 and the phrase "right in front of you" in v. 21. Claims of Yahweh's patronage of such prophets are countered by Yahweh's oracle to the contrary.

[21] Yahweh's handing over of Judahites to Babylon's king or the like has frequently expressed Judah's fate earlier in the book (see 27:6 and commentary). Here the phrase is dramatically reused about specific individuals. The involvement of the Babylonian authorities suggests that their prophesying

---

230. Ibid., 85, 95.
231. Ibid., 91–92.
232. Ibid., 96, 104.

included a political dimension. No specific description of its content is provided, but MT makes explicit its implicit tenor of a radically different message, cementing the connection with v. 9 by its added relative clause and also by supplying the adjective "false" in v. 23.

[22] The punishment is reinforced obliquely by use of a curse formula. The grim wordplay of *qĕlālâ*, "curse," and *qālām*, "roasted" (cf. Dan 3:6), has been developed in MT by adding the patronymic "ben Kolaiah (*qôlāyâ*)" in v. 21.

[23] They are indicted not only for illicit prophesying but also for a supporting criterion of sexual immorality (cf. 23:14). The strong language of doing *nĕbālâ* (NJPS "vile things") in Israel typically refers to sexual offenses (cf., e.g., Gen 34:7; Judg 20:6). The assurance that Yahweh knows about sins presumed to be secret clinches the certainty of doom (cf. 13:27).

[24–32] The second part of the chapter concerns a reply to a response to the first letter, as v. 28 shows. Verse 24 is a divine directive to Jeremiah, like 21:8. Verses 24–28 should be read as instructions to send a letter, instructions that are redefined in vv. 31–32. Readers expect an individual oracle of disaster when a reason is provided in v. 25. However, vv. 26–28 cite the return letter and vv. 29–30 take a narrative form. The expected announcement of disaster comes only in v. 32, but after a second reason that seems different from the first one. This awkward disjointedness has upset commentators, yet it is not intolerable and has a discernible logic within the recognizable contours of an oracle of disaster.

[24–25] An individual, "Shemaiah from Nehelam," took it upon himself to reply to Jeremiah's letter of vv. 1–23. However, he did so by reporting him to the temple authorities in the person of "Zephaniah ben Maaseiah" (cf. 21:1; 37:3). MT supplies other addressees to accommodate the Hebrew plural "you" that occurs in the letter at the end of v. 27. The added quotation formula introduces an accusation and will be resumed (v. 30) with the message reported and the associated quotation formulas (vv. 31 and 32).

[26–27] Evidently Zephaniah had recently been promoted to the rank of chief security officer, a post once occupied by Pashhur (20:1–6). Shemaiah reminds him of his divinely given responsibility to protect worshipers in the temple courts from the clamor of those claiming to be prophets (cf. 2 Kgs 9:11). He reports a flagrant case that he complains has gone unchecked—Jeremiah! He insists on an official reprimand and suggests appropriate measures, to which Jeremiah was no stranger (cf. 20:2).

[28] Clarification of the complaint reveals that the offense had not been committed orally or on sacred ground but in the form of a letter sent to the deportees. Did Shemaiah assume or have information that Jeremiah was promoting notions already promulgated in the temple area? The reader recalls from 28:1 that Hananiah's initial encounter with Jeremiah had taken place at the temple;

the hearers mentioned there are repeated by MT in v. 25. The letter is summarized, using the technique of quotation inversion.[233] While the second component cites the memorable language of v. 5, the first interprets the reference to "seventy years" (v. 10) as an extended stay.

[29] Readers have been listening with Jeremiah to Yahweh's directive and accusatory message that quotes Shemaiah's own words back at him. Suddenly they find the scene shifting to a narrative mode and the voice becomes that of Zephaniah reading out the letter of vv. 26–28 to Jeremiah. The interview demanded by Shemaiah (v. 27) is now taking place. Readers are not informed of the atmosphere of the interview, whether frosty or friendly. That Zephaniah had not interviewed him before—or so Shemaiah had complained—may push the pendulum toward the latter alternative.

[30–31] Again, the reader is not told how this oracle of disaster relates to the one begun in v. 25. They differ in that the former one is addressed to Shemaiah, but this oracle is to be sent to the deported community announcing Shemaiah's fault and fate (cf. vv. 21–23). Verse 31 has a climactic role. The earlier part of the text took at face value the letter and the individual who wrote it. Now v. 31 reveals the significance of writing "in your own name" (v. 25), which could have meant "without the official authorization of the elders" (Rudolph 187). Shemaiah had failed to declare a conflict of interest, that he was a professional prophet of the same ilk as Jeremiah's rivals at home. The same language is here used of him as of Hananiah in 28:15, and MT will sharpen the analogy in the closing clause of v. 32 (cf. 28:16). The new revelation of v. 31 starkly exposes his manipulative disguise as a concerned member of the public, though Yahweh had already seen through it in v. 25. Now perhaps readers can appreciate that there had been no mention of the false prophets of vv. 8–9, 15, 21–23 in Shemaiah's summary of the first letter.

[32] Shemaiah's fitting punishment was to be his family's extinction and so disqualification from Yahweh's eventual reversal of the deportation—far from its number growing in size (v. 6; cf. Ezek 13:9). MT draws an exegetical arc back to v. 10 by inserting "good" there in accord with this verse. While the community would return in the persons of their posterity (v. 10), Shemaiah never would. MT adds another word, "living." The prophet would have no one "living" or dwelling in the community when the time came. The verb is a ricochet from v. 28 and thence from v. 5, triumphantly echoing Yahweh's earlier message through Jeremiah.

In 29:1–32 homesick deportees are told by letter that repatriation, though sure, will not be soon, and an angry reply from a deported prophet disqualifies his family from the promised repatriation.

---

233. For such resumptive inversion see Talmon, "Textual Study," 375–78.

30:1–31:40 Covenant-Centered Hope

30:1–31:1 Future Reversal of Past Reprisals

30:1 A message received by Jeremiah from Yahweh that said: **2** Here is what Yahweh, Israel's God, said: "Write down all the messages I have told you in a book, **3** because look, the time is coming," declared Yahweh, "when I will restore the fortunes of my people Israel and Judah," said Yahweh, "bringing them back to the country that was my gift to their forebears, so they can occupy it." **4** Now these are the messages Yahweh gave about Israel and Judah.

5 Here *in fact* is what Yahweh said.

    A cry of fright we heard;
        there was terror instead of peace.
6 Ask and find out
        whether a male can bear a child!
    Why then did I see every man
        with his hands on his middle *like a woman giving birth*
        and *every* face turned pale?
7 Oh!^a That day was momentous—
        when has its like occurred?
    It was a time of trouble for Jacob,
        from which, however, he will be saved.

8 "*What will happen* on that day," declared Yahweh *Almighty*, "*is that* I will break 'his yoke off your neck' and your ties I will tear off. No longer will he be in servitude to aliens. **9** Instead they will serve their God Yahweh and their king David, *whom* I will appoint for them.

10 "*As for you, do not be afraid, my servant Jacob*,"
     declared Yahweh,
        "*do not be scared, Israel*,
    because here I am, about to save you out of anywhere distant,
        your progeny out of their countries of exile.
    Jacob will come back^b and live quietly,
        securely with nobody to frighten him.
11 Yes, I am with you,"
     declared Yahweh,
        "ready to save you,
    because, while I will completely do away with all the nations
        among whom I have scattered you,
    I will not do away with you completely,

though I have been chastising you in judgment,
unable to leave you unpunished."

12 Here *in fact* is what Yahweh said:

"Your wound was incurable,[c]
　your injury so severe.
13　Nobody took on your case to deal with the abcess;[d]
　　you had no remedies to promote healing.
14　All your allies forgot you,
　　they did not care *about you*,
　when I inflicted on you an enemy's injury,
　　chastisement from someone cruel,
　because your wrongdoing had been so great,
　　your sins so numerous.[e]
15[f]　Why did you cry out[g] over your wound,
　　that your pain was incurable?
　It was because your wrongdoing had been so great, your sins so numerous,
　　that I took this action regarding you.
16　Therefore all those who devoured you will be devoured.[h]
　　All your foes[i] will go off as prisoners.
　Those who plundered you will get plundered,
　　and all who looted you I will expose to looting.
17　Yes, I will restore you to health,
　　healing you of your injuries,"
　declared Yahweh,
　"because you have been called 'outcast,'
　　'That is Zion[j] who has nobody that cares.'"[k]

18 Here is what Yahweh said:

"Look, I am going to restore the fortunes of Jacob*'s tents*
　and to his homes I will show compassion.
Each town will be rebuilt on its mound,
　each fortified house will stand where it should.
19　From them will emanate thanksgiving
　　and the noise of revelers.
　I will increase their numbers so they do not diminish;
　　I will give them prestige so they are not insignificant.[l]
20　The children he has will be as many as they used to be,
　　and his community will be well established under my attention,
　while I will deal with *all* his oppressors.

21 His leader will be one of his own,
    his ruler will come from among him
    and I will permit him to come near and he will approach me.ᵐ
    Whoⁿ wouldᵒ ever put his courage on the line
    and approach me otherwise?"
    declared Yahweh.
22 "'Then you will be my people and I in turn will be your God.'"
23 "Look, Yahweh's storm wind,
    the onset of fury!
    The wind is sweeping across.ᵖ
    Around *the heads of* the wicked it will whirl.
24 Yahweh's burning anger will not subside till he has worked through it
    and till he has accomplished the purposes he had in mind.
    When time has elapsed,
    you will understand this."

31:1 "At that time," declared Yahweh, "I will be the God of *all* the families of Israel and they will be my people."

a. Hebrew *hôy* is a general exclamation of dismay (*DCH* 2:503).
b. The verb does not have an adverbial sense, "again" (Ehrlich, *Randglossen*, 4:317; Rudolph 190; cf. the majority of EVV), but means "return" (NRSV, NJB, GNB). Nelson Kilpp, *Niederreissen und aufbauen: Das Verhältnis von Heilsverheissung und Unheilsverkündigung bei Jeremia und in Jeremiabuch* (Biblisch-theologische Studien 13; Neukirchen-Vluyn: Neukirchener Verlag, 1990), 114, observes that the word order so implies.
c. Hebrew *ʾānûš* is used either as an impersonal passive verb (cf. Isa 53:5) or as a noun (cf. Jer 17:6).
d. Repointing is necessary with *BHS*.
e. The infinitive construct is continued with a finite verb (Rudolph 192).
f. LXX (ch. 37) omits v. 15a and places v. 15b after v. 16a, but with a third plural verb to fit the new context (McKane 2:769; cf. Ziegler, *Jeremias*, 352–53). If v. 15b is authentic, it does require v. 15a. The probable explanation is that v. 15 was overlooked because of the similarity of vv. 14b and 15b; then only v. 15b was retrieved, but the marginal reading was misplaced.
g. For the unexpected masculine verb cf. GKC §145t.
h. In the Hebrew text underlying LXX an exegetical gloss on this colon probably displaced the next, similar-looking colon (cf. *BHS*). For this type of error see the textual notes on 17:3–4.
i. Though widely attested (see *BHS*), *kullām*, "all of them," is unnecessary for the sense and difficult for the meter. Did it originate as a gloss on the next colon, the only one to lack "all"?
j. LXX's strange "your prey" (cf. McKane 2:769–70 over against *BHS* and Ziegler, *Jeremias*, 353) is perhaps to be explained as originating in a gloss, *ṣydyk* (*ṣayyādêk*,

"your hunters"), as a textual variant of *ṣryk* (*ṣārayik*), "your foes," in v. 16; it was misunderstood as *ṣēdêk*, "your prey," and subsequently taken as a correction of the somewhat similar looking *ṣîyôn*, "Zion," and displaced it. The Greek translation rendered the singular suffix collectively as a plural, just as in v. 21 it made the two third singular references plural in the last colon of the tricolon (cf. *BHS*).

k. For the construction see S. R. Driver, *Revised Translation*, 366, who compares v. 13b and 49:1 for the word order.

l. LXX omits the last colon, probably by oversight because of its similarity to the previous one (Janzen, *Studies*, 119). A 3 + 3 bicolon fits well in v. 19b.

m. The two tricola in vv. 20–21a are shown to be such because they share the features of perfect consecutive verbs with the verb "to be" in the first cola and different first singular ones in the third (Holladay 2:159).

n. For the reinforced interrogative cf. Ps 24:10; Esth 7:5.

o. For this use of the perfect in surprised questions cf. Joüon §112j.

p. Cf. BDB, 176a.

This new literary block is "an anthology of poems and prose pieces that form a tapestry of hope" (Stulman 258); it consists of three compositions, 30:1–31:1; 31:2–26; and 31:27–40. The oracle reception heading in 30:1 indicates that a fresh block consists of 30:1–31:40 since the heading next appears at 32:1. The block introduces ch. 32 by amplifying Jeremiah's prophetic declaration of reoccupation of Judah. Chapter 32 begins a lengthy new prose unit, on the heels of those in chs. 26–29. The short units in 30:1–31:40 represent an editorial collection of originally independent material.[234] The block cites a series of oracles Jeremiah had delivered concerning the return of the exiles of the northern kingdom and crowns them with a number of post-Jeremianic oracles of hope. Thus the block also functions as a development of the sketch in chs. 26–29 of a positive future for God's people that would follow the period of exile. What would happen after the seventy years of 29:10 (cf. 25:12) is now defined.

In the first composition Yahweh's past punishment of the covenant people is matched three times over with the sure consequences of future restoration. The structure of 30:1–31:1 is marked by signposts, the quotation formulas at the head of sections, in vv. 5, 12, and 18 (Duhm 237; he associated them with those in ch. 31). These formulas are differentiated from the formula in v. 2 that introduces the composition and is adorned with the divine epithet "Israel's God," which together with the closing "I will be the God . . . of Israel" in 31:1 forms an overall frame.[235] Six units, with a seventh added in MT at vv. 10–11, have

---

234. Cf. Alexander Rofé, *The Prophetical Stories: The Narratives about the Prophets in the Hebrew Bible, Their Literary Types and History* (trans. D. Levy; Jerusalem: Magnes, 1988), 114, who envisions the insertion of chs. 30–31 and also ch. 33. Chapter 33 is a subsequent development.

235. Marvin A. Sweeney, "Jeremiah 30–31 and King Josiah's Program of National Restoration and Religious Reform," *ZAW* 108 (1996): 569–83, esp. 573, makes a structural distinction between the quotation formulas in vv. 2 and 18 and the formulas in vv. 5 and 12 that have *kî* prefixed ("*In*

been organized into three sections, vv. 5–11, 12–17, and 30:18–31:1. Four of the units—five including vv. 10–11—are in verse and two in prose. The three sections have a pattern of past punishment and future hope.[236] This basic AB pattern is followed simply in the first and second sections of the common text, in vv. 5–7 and 8–9 and vv. 12–15 and 16–17; however, MT has enlarged to an ABB structure by adding vv. 10–11. In the third section the component of hope is enlarged by inserting another one at the beginning (BAB), in vv. 18–21; it amplifies the final positive component of 31:1 that follows the negative one of vv. 23–24. To this end the added v. 22 proceeds to draw a thematic parallel with 31:1. The composition appears to be rooted in the period of Babylonian exile, looking back to earlier woes endured at Yahweh's hands and forward to restoration.

[30:1–4] These verses present a preface to the block and the first composition. The block has three motifs running through it, the restoration of the exiles of Israel and Judah to the land, the reinstatement of Zion, and, most significantly, the validation and upgrading of Yahweh's covenant with the people. This preface introduces the first motif. Formulas that will be structurally important in the block are also introduced to readers, the quotation formula in v. 2 and the temporal formula, "look, the time is coming," in v. 3.

[2] The oracle reception heading also introduces the oracle of v. 2b, which quotes one part of another oracle to Jeremiah (36:2). This reuse signals that not only oracles of disaster, which 36:2 has in view and which predominate in chs. 2–25, should be included in the book, but also other oracles that point to a positive future (Duhm 237–38; McKane 2:750–51). Although chs. 30–31 (or 30–33) are often called "the book of consolation" on the basis of v. 2, in the present context the book of Jeremiah, or at least the book so far, is in view (cf. 25:13). The quotation formula of v. 2a will be considered in relation to v. 3.

[3] If "Israel's God" (v. 2) along with the longer phrase in 31:1 forms a frame for the composition, so does "my people," repeated in 31:1. Restoring fortunes is an apt comprehensive phrase, borrowed from v. 18; it introduces a motif of the composition in a summary fashion. Repetition of the Hebrew verb šûb pro-

---

fact"; NRSV "For" in v. 12, but left untranslated in v. 5). He regards the former cases as indications of two main divisions in vv. 2–17 and 30:18–31:1 and the latter of two subordinate ones in vv. 5–11 and 12–17. However, the absence of the conjunction from LXX is significant for analyzing the basic structure of the text, which MT does not necessarily change.

236. Cf. Kilpp, *Niederreissen*, 106–7, 123, who, though he sets vv. 5–7 in present and future time, does differentiate between the roles of vv. 12–15 as future-oriented in Jeremiah's preaching but as a lament over a past crisis in the literary context. Weiser 2:262, 271 translated with past tenses in vv. 12–13, supposing that Jeremiah was referring to the fall of Samaria. Other advocates of past/future perspectives in vv. 12–17 are Monica Gerlach, "Zur chronologischen Struktur von Jer 30, 12–17: Reflexionen auf die involvierten grammatischen Ebenen," *BN* 33 (1986): 34–52, esp. 45–51; Bob Becking, *Between Fear and Freedom: Essays on the Interpretation of Jeremiah 30–31* (OtSt 51; Leiden: Brill, 2004), 174–75, 186–87.

vides a narrower definition of restoring fortunes envisioned as a return to the promised land. The old political terms "Israel and Judah" have been taken over from 31:27, 31, influenced by the use of oracles originally given for the northern kingdom (31:2–6, 15–17, and 18–20). The phrase functions as a definition of "Jacob" (vv. 7 and 18), who as the father of the twelve tribes was an appropriate model for Israel as a whole, both north and south (McKane 2:756). The closing reference to the ancestral land as Yahweh's gift is a motif frequently encountered in prose sermons and similar redactional material.[237] It is particularly appropriate in this comprehensive context, since the land was a gift to all the tribes. Verse 3, along with vv. 8–9, fills the explanatory role of the prose sermon that regularly follows the structural oracle reception heading and divine command to Jeremiah at the beginning of a block. The editorial nature of vv. 2b–3 accords with the use of the quotation formula in v. 2a. The formula legitimates editorial material as divinely inspired, and this significance applies here, as it did in 24:5, 8; and 26:2.

[4] This introduction to particular units organized into sections flows on from vv. 2–3, utilizing "messages" and "Israel and Judah" from there.

[5–11] The first section falls into three originally separate units, a poetic one (vv. 5–7), a prose one (vv. 8–9), and a supplementary poetic one in MT (vv. 10–11).

[5–7] The trauma undergone by the covenant nation is recalled. Verses 5–6 adapt an original audition and vision report, transposing it to the past, while v. 7 reflects on its severity and builds a bridge to the promise of vv. 8–9.

[5a*a*] This first of three quotation formulas used to demarcate units in the composition is awkward at first sight in that manifestly human speech follows as far as v. 7. This phenomenon has occurred earlier in the book, at 14:1, 17; and 17:5, and here indicates that what precedes v. 8 is a preface to the positive material.

[5a*b*–6] The reader expects parallelism between "we heard" and "did I see" to extend to a pair of singular verbs; the advice in *BHS* to so read in the first case, taken by GNB, is understandable. What was an audition and vision report of future calamity from Jeremiah, like 4:19–21, has been transformed into a reaction to bad news like 6:24 and becomes a mixture of individual and communal lament over a crisis that has already occurred. In this case, however, the crisis is a past experience that has not itself continued except in memory and aftermath. It appears to refer to the experience of the fall of Jerusalem in 587, but both "Jacob" (v. 7) and "Israel and Judah" (vv. 3–4) indicate that the fall of the northern kingdom in 721 is caught up in the purview. The emotional bombardment caused by the generic experience comes to the fore; readers encounter it via the extreme reactions of those who had to undergo it. The paradoxical question of v. 6a is the rhetoric of stress, preparing the way for the male body

---

237. Cf. 7:7, 14; 11:5; 16:15; and 24:10 in Stulman's list in *Prose Sermons*, 33 (no. 4).

language that follows, which MT has carefully explained with the aid of 6:24. In the present literary setting the absence of "peace" vindicates Jeremiah's challenge to Hananiah in 28:9.

[7] This verse is transitional, looking back historically to "That day" and forward to the experience of being "saved."[238] It reflects on that day's awful uniqueness, but finds comfort in the language of rescue.

[8–9] There is to be another "that day," a day of salvation in blatant contrast to the day of judgment in v. 7. This prose proclamation of salvation, legitimated as divine by a quotation formula, presents Yahweh's saving intervention (v. 8a) and its welcome results, negative and positive (vv. 8b–9). The proclamation, beyond its sectional significance, has a wider role, to tie this block to the previous one and to develop it in terms of promise. Chapters 27–28 had narrated in prose the symbolic action of the yoke worn by Jeremiah and his subsequent encounter with Hananiah.

[8] The interpretation of Jeremiah's action in terms of submission to Babylon had featured the terms "yoke" and neck" (27:8, 11–12; 28:14) and "ties" (27:2), while breaking the yoke was also mentioned (28:2, 4, 11). In reaction to Hananiah, Jeremiah had promised long-term deliverance. This deliverance is now described in terms of breaking the yoke, but, unlike Hananiah's optimistic claims, here the divine pledge comes only after the extremes of judgment that Hananiah and his fellow prophets had denied.[239] Serving Babylon's king (27:9, 11, 12, 14; 28:14) was to be a mark of Jacob's past, not of his future; mention of "aliens" glances back to the exilic punishment of 5:19 (a redactional passage). The vocabulary of servitude echoes 25:14 and 27:7. The switch of persons in v. 8, to second and then back to third, and the unheralded reference to "his yoke" indicates the existence of an intertextual appeal to an older prophecy, to the language of Isa 10:27, which corroborates the present promise of liberation from Babylonian servitude.[240]

[9] The happy reversal stays with the notion of service and develops it in two positive directions. First, it connotes the service of worship directed to Yahweh as "their God"—the obverse of "my people" in v. 3. Second, in MT at least, instead of serving the king of Babylon, they would serve their own king, a descendant of David. The assurance looks forward to v. 21 and backward to 23:5.

[10–11] This impressive oracle of salvation recurs in 46:27–28 with some recensional differences. There it is attested in the common text of LXX (ch. 26) and MT but not so here, and it is unlikely that it was present in the Hebrew text

---

238. Levin, *Verheissung*, 179; Kilpp, *Niederreissen*, 110.
239. Georg Fischer, *Das Trostbüchlein: Text, Komposition und Theologie von Jer 30–31* (SBB 26; Stuttgart: Katholisches Bibelwerk, 1993), 248.
240. Barthélemy, *Critique textuelle*, 2:682.

underlying LXX.[241] It reinforces the message of vv. 8–9; by comparison with the second section, vv. 12–17, it is strictly redundant in that a positive message corresponding to vv. 16–17 has already been given. It provides a good redactional fit with the context, echoing "fright" of v. 5 in "frighten," v. 10; "be saved" of v. 7 with "save," v. 10 (and also in v. 11, an addition to the parallel 46[26]:28); and "Jacob," v. 7, also in v. 10; while "my servant" provides a hinge with "serve their God Yahweh" in v. 9. Moreover, the first reference to judgment in v. 11 nicely anticipates vv. 12–15, as MT acknowledges by its addition of "In fact" (NRSV "For") to v. 12; indeed, the root *ysr*, "chastise," occurs in both vv. 11 and 14. The Diaspora is in view, rather than simply the Judean exiles in Babylonia.

The poem largely follows the pattern of an oracle of salvation: a preliminary exhortation not to fear, the assurance of the divine presence,[242] the promise of divine intervention, a description of its consequences, and an explanation (cf. 1:17–19). The genre is prominent in Second Isaiah (e.g., Isa 41:8–13); the characterization of the people as Yahweh's "servant" there—not a natural characteristic of salvation oracles—outside such oracles (Isa 44:21; 45:4; 48:20) suggests a late exilic setting for this oracle.[243] In v. 11 the explanatory promise not to do away completely with the people is consistent with other texts in the book of Jeremiah. It echoes the editorial insistence of 4:27; 5:10, 18; 44:14, 28; and 46:28. Moreover, the second colon of the closing tricolon reuses the language of 10:24, though in a different sense. The definition of past suffering in terms of judgment and punishment adds a moral dimension to the description of vv. 5–7, which will be a firm ingredient of the other negative passages (vv. 14–15, 23–24).

[12–17] The second section of the composition repeats the pattern of past suffering (vv. 12–15) and of future salvation (vv. 16–17). It is a composite unit addressed to a feminine person, who is identified only at the end as a personified "Zion." REB accordingly adds "to Zion" to its translation of the quotation formula in v. 12, providing implicit information not available to the non-Hebraist concerning a switch to second feminine pronouns. Within the block Zion stands not simply as Judah's capital, but also as a Mecca for the northern tribes (31:6, 12; cf. 3:14).

[12–15] This material reflects an oracle of disaster, with the results of Yahweh's intervention (vv. 12–14a) followed first by a statement of the intervention, then by a reason (v. 14b), and finally by a recapitulation of the oracle

---

241. Some argue that LXX omitted these verses as the second occurrence of a doublet in the LXX ordering of chapters (e.g., Bright 279). See, however, the general discussion of Janzen, *Studies*, 91–96, and the specific one of Parke-Taylor, *Formation*, 124–25.

242. This assurance normally follows the exhortation, as it does in 46(26):28, where the exhortation is repeated. So the present version of the oracle is an abbreviated form.

243. Siegmund Böhmer, *Heimkehr und neuer Bund: Studien zu Jeremia 30–31* (GTA 5; Göttingen: Vandenhoeck & Ruprecht, 1976), 61–62; Kilpp, *Niederreissen*, 117.

(v. 15). The oracle has been projected into the past; it probably develops one of Jeremiah's own oracles, like vv. 5–6.

[12] After the section marker announcing the divine message, Zion's plight is depicted as a "wound." Such medical metaphors have been an important feature in Jeremiah's oracles (8:21–22; 10:19; 14:17; and, in a confession, 15:18).

[13–14a] The metaphor is first developed (v. 13) and then interpreted (v. 14a). The judicial language "take on a case" constitutes a unique metaphor within a metaphor; in English "case" can reflect either situation, unlike its Hebrew counterpart. Zion's helplessness is interpreted as a lack of "allies" (cf. 4:30; 13:21; 22:20, 22).

[14b] The intervention continues the note of extremity with its description of the human enemy providentially used by Yahweh as "cruel" (cf. 6:23), and so does the reason with its emphasis on the magnitude of the wrongdoing.

[15] The recapitulation prefaces the reason with an exasperated question, which MT reinforces by adding an elucidating clause that echoes "incurable" (v. 12). The sequence of reason and intervention in v. 15b goes over the ground of the last two bicola of v. 14 in an inverted form, focusing on the extreme degree of liability. Zion deserved its inordinate punishment and had no grounds for protest.

[16–17] "But where sin increased, grace abounded all the more" (Rom 5:20). This exilic proclamation of salvation was designed to cap vv. 12–15 in its present literary setting. The reversal of the reprisal is now worked out. First, the tables would be turned against Yahweh's agents of destruction (v. 14), its victims are reassured. Then the incurable injuries (v. 13) would be wonderfully healed. The closing reason serves to explain "Therefore" at the start of the announcement of reversal, for which one may compare 15:19 and 16:14. It harks back to the suffering of Zion, abandoned by its allies (v. 14). Its citizens' fate is transferred to the city: it is an "outcast," driven away (cf. 27:15). The unspoken link that makes the reason reasonable is divine compassion that comes to Zion's rescue. Yahweh heard and saw Zion's lament over its humiliation and abuse and evidently "took notice" (Exod 2:25). Zion did have someone who cared after all. Yahweh was "moved by the hurt of the covenant partner and the general abuse of the nations."[244]

[30:18–31:1] The third section of reversal falls into three parts (vv. 18–22, 23–24, and 31:1). It breaks the pattern of the first two sections by adding a positive passage at the beginning.

[18–22] The first part is primarily a further proclamation of salvation that mingles divine intervention and its results in three pronouncements (vv. 18–19a, 19b–20, and 21). The results are presented in separate impressionistic

---

244. Brueggemann, "The 'Uncared for' Now Cared for (Jer 30:12–17): A Methodological Consideration," *JBL* 104 (1985): 419–28, esp. 427.

sketches of a happy future for the community. The winsome focus is on the restoration of the status quo ante; there would be a return to the thriving normality that marked life in the land before tragedy struck. Each pronouncement refers to or hints at a deprivation the people had suffered. The poem is probably an exilic prophecy; in subject matter it has affinities with the redactional complex in 23:3–6. It takes up such hopes as prisoners of war would cherish.

[18–19a] At the top of the list is a territorial home to be enjoyed again. Restoring fortunes is a comprehensive heading for a list of specific promises that reverse Yahweh's earlier judgments presented in Jeremiah's messages of disaster.[245] "Tents" in MT may recall Num 24:5 in a context of blessing for Israel. The implied compassion in v. 17 now finds expression. Ruined tells would be reoccupied and flourish with ordered dwellings where happy, hospitable families would live. Towns destroyed by divine judgment (cf. 2:15; 4:7, 26, 29; 9:11) would rise again. The cessation of social celebration had been a recurring note in earlier descriptions of disaster; 16:1–9 offers a striking example.

[19b–20] The ongoing life of the community would be guaranteed by strong population growth and a powerful community undergirded by God's positive blessing and maintenance of national security in keeping would-be oppressors at bay in the future. Especially the loss of children in previous divine judgment (2:30; 5:17; 10:20) would be reversed.

[21] The national monarchy (cf. v. 9), sturdily independent of foreign pressure (cf. v. 8; Deut 17:15) and linked to Yahweh by a special bond of access made possible by divine initiative, would provide the key to communal prosperity. One may compare Ezek 44:3; 45:17, 22–25; and 46:2, passages that presumably reflect preexilic cultic practice (cf. 2 Kgs 23:3). As mediator between Yahweh and the people, the ruler would be the continual agent of blessing for them.

[22] MT adds a concluding statement, which is a quotation from 11:4. Its role as a quotation explains the change from third person to second in referring to the people and suggests its character as prose rather than poetry. The restoration of a community vibrant with life and order is hailed as the outworking of the covenant relationship between Yahweh and the nation. In 11:4–5 the covenant formula was linked with the gift of the land "awash with milk and honey," and its preexilic fulfillment was noted. Now this gift is to be enjoyed once more (cf. v. 3). A concern underlying the insertion was the structural fit of vv. 18–21 in this section. The answer was to tie vv. 18–21 with 31:1 by understanding these verses as an exposition of the communal blessings that flowed from a covenant relationship.

[30:23–31:1] The final two parts cover past reprisal in vv. 23–24 and future reversal in 31:1.

---

245. See John M. Bracke, "*šûb šᵉbût*: A Reappraisal," *ZAW* 97 (1985): 233–44, esp. 237–39.

[**30:23-24**] A quotation of 23:19-20, with a few recensional differences, supplies the reprisal; quotation marks in the translation so indicate. Whereas in the previous two sections adaptation to a past setting was applied to Jeremiah's oracles of future disaster, in this case straightforward citation of a message now known to be fulfilled is employed. The passage originally looked forward to the catastrophe of 587, but it is conveniently expressed in generic language and is explained in terms of punishment for "the wicked," which here refers to the covenant people.[246] The advantage of the quotation is that—somewhat like v. 7—it states that divine anger will end after a limited period of time. Now the exilic community, standing on the far side of such catastrophe, was better able to "understand" and to hear an implicit pointer toward promise.

[**31:1**] The fulfillment of the covenant promise is offered as the element of renewal. The ending of Yahweh's work of judgment triggered a laying aside of anger (v. 24) that boded well for the scattered community of faith. Readers who want further details are urged by MT's addition (v. 22) to look back to vv. 18-21. "The families of Israel" harks back to the comprehensiveness of 30:3; MT's addition of "all" accentuates the link.

In 30:1-31:1 past judgment at Yahweh's hands is presented as a precursor to restoration. The God who punished the covenant people promises to reestablish them.

31:2-26 Promises of Homecoming and Blessing

31:2 Here is what Yahweh said.

Favor was found in the wilderness
   by the people who survived the sword.
Coming to give rest to them, to Israel,[a]
3   Yahweh appeared to them[b] at a distance.
"So with an age-old love I love you,
   which is why I prolong my loyalty to you.[c]
4   Once more I will build you up so you are rebuilt,
   virgin Israel.
Once more you will deck yourself with hand drums
   and go out to join the revelers' dance.
5   Once more you will plant vineyards—
   on Samaria's mountains—
   planters will eat the crops they planted.[d]
6   Yes, the time will come when the guards shout out
   on Ephraim's mountain ridge,

---

246. Barbara A. Bozak, *Life "Anew": A Literary-Theological Study of Jer. 30-31* (AnBib 122; Rome: Pontifical Biblical Institute, 1991), 68.

Covenant-Centered Hope

'Come on, let us go up to Zion,
to our God Yahweh!'"

7 In fact here is what Yahweh said.

Sing joyfully[e] for Jacob,
exclaim about the top nation,
shout out in praise and say,
"Yahweh has saved his people,[f]
Israel's remnant!"
8 "Look, I am going to bring them home from the north *country*
and collect them from the remotest parts of the earth.
Blind and lame among them,
pregnant women along with those in labor,
as a vast crowd they will come back here.
9 In tears they will come,
making supplication[g] as I bring them.
I will lead them by streams of water
on a level path where they will not stumble,
because I am a father to Israel
and Ephraim is my eldest son."

10 Listen to Yahweh's message, you nations,
tell it in the distant coastlands, saying,
"The one who once scattered Israel will collect them,
protecting them as a shepherd does his flock."
11 In fact Yahweh will ransom Jacob,
redeeming him from the clutches of one too strong for him.
12 They will come and sing on Zion's height,
radiant over Yahweh's bounty,
over grain, wine, and oil,
and over the young of flocks and herds.
Their stomachs[h] will be like gardens sated with water;
they will no more be faint with hunger.
13 Then girls will enjoy the dance,
so will men, young and old alike.[i]
"I will turn their grief into gladness
and comfort them, giving them joy after sorrow.
14 I will sate the priests' stomachs with rich fare,
while my people will have their fill of my bounty,"

declared Yahweh.

15 Here is what Yahweh said:

"Hark, in Ramah[j] can be heard wailing,
    bitter crying.
Rachel is crying *for her children*,
    refusing to be comforted
for her children because none of them[k] is there."

16 Here is what Yahweh said:

"Stop your sounds of crying
    and dry your tearful eyes,
because there is to be a reward for your input,"
declared Yahweh,
    "when they come back from the enemy's country,
17 and there is hope for your future,"
declared Yahweh,
    "when the children come back to their own territory."
18 I can clearly hear
    Ephraim grieving,
"You chastised me, and I got chastised
    like an untrained calf.
Have me back so I can come back
    because you, Yahweh, are my God,[l]
19 and because after I turned back, I repented,
    and after I wised up,[m]
    I slapped my thigh.
I felt ashamed—humiliated, I may add—
    to be enduring the consequences of my disgraceful youth."
20 "Is it because Ephraim is a dear son to me,
    because he is a favorite child,
that, every time I denounce him,
    I cannot help remembering him?[n]
Yes, that is why my heart yearns for him,
    so I have to show him compassion,"
declared Yahweh.

21 Set up markers for yourself,
    erect signposts *for yourself*.
Concentrate on the road,
    the path you came by.
Come back, virgin Israel,
    come back to these towns of yours.

Covenant-Centered Hope   343

22 How long will you waver,
       backsliding daughter?
    No need, because Yahweh is creating something new in the world:
    A female courts° a man!

23 Here is what Yahweh *Almighty, Israel's God,* said: "Once more people in the country of Judah and its towns will use this expression when I restore their fortunes,

'May Yahweh bless you,
   righteous home,
   sacred mountain!'

24 The people of Judah will live there, including all its townsfolk and plowmen along with those who journey^p with the flocks, 25 because I will have sated the thirst of the weary and fully met the hunger of all the faint."

26 At this point I woke up and looked around,^q having had a pleasant sleep.

   a. Cf. REB; McKane 2:780–81.

   b. LXX (ch. 38) implies *lô*, "to him/them" (Israel), which most EVV prefer. NJPS and NJB ("to me") and NIV ("to us") retain MT *lî*. A third person reference suits the context. Sweeney, "Jeremiah 30–31," 574–75 n. 11, has plausibly argued that a copyist was influenced by the first person reference in v. 26.

   c. Similarly EVV, apart from NIV. The suffix is datival (GKC §117x); cf. Pss 36:10 (11); 109:12.

   d. The line is an ABA' tricolon with the middle colon having a pivotal role; cf. Watson, *Classical Hebrew Poetry,* 181–82.

   e. LXX does not omit "joyfully" (*BHS*), but has a condensed translation (*HUB*).

   f. Thus LXX and Tg. instead of MT's direct address, "Yahweh, save your people." A celebratory hymnic statement seems to be appropriate here, rather than a petition of lament. Apart from NJPS, NIV, and NRSV, EVV have adopted LXX. 4Q72 has an intermediate text, the verb *hwšy^c* like LXX but the object *^cmk* as in MT.

   g. NRSV ("with consolations"), NAB, and REB follow LXX (see *BHS*). However, NJPS claims the MT reading can mean "with compassion," comparing Zech 12:10. Barthélemy, *Critique textuelle,* 2:685–86, likewise claims that the issue is exegetical rather than text-critical, but prefers the standard sense for MT in view of the parallelism (cf. 3:21), finding marks of conversion here.

   h. KJV has "soul" here and in v. 14 for Hebrew *nepeš,* lit. "throat" as the seat of appetite. See Wolff, *Anthropology,* 11–13.

   i. REB ("will rejoice") and NRSV adopt the pointing of LXX as a verb (see *BHS*). However, Barthélemy, *Critique textuelle,* 2:687, has observed that the syntax of MT has parallels at 6:12; 13:14; 31:8; 48:7; 49:3.

   j. The pointing of MT lacks the article that, apart from Neh 11:33, elsewhere accompanies the place name (*BHS*; cf. 40:1), which LXX and Syr. recognized.

k. The singular has an individualizing force, referring to none of the exiles; cf. GKC §145m.

l. Thus NJPS; cf. 3:22.

m. REB "now that I am submissive" merits the criticism mentioned in textual note a to 24:1.

n. Cf. NJB, REB. For the syntax cf. 48:27 and see Joüon §169e; Adrianus van Selms, "Motivated Interrogative Sentences in Biblical Hebrew," *Semitics* 2 (1971/72): 143–49.

o. NJPS; cf. NJB. The medieval Jewish expositor Rashi understood this disputed verb as going after a man with the intent of marrying him. This sense is plausible and fits well here as a metaphor of marriage for the covenant; cf. the personal use of the verb in Deut 32:10 (NRSV "he shielded him"; REB "He protected him").

p. Probably a participle should be read (*BHS*; NRSV); MT assumes a relative clause. A similar case occurs at the end of v. 25.

q. So NIV.

A fresh composition of six units begins with v. 2 and ends with the statement in v. 26, while the address "virgin Israel" in its initial and final units (vv. 4, 21) provides a frame, along with the rehabilitating expression "once more" in vv. 4–5 and 23. The composition gives assurances of Israelite and Judean return to the land and blessed resettlement in it. The style of demarcating new units by the quotation formula used in the former composition continues here to a limited extent; it is absent from the start of three of the six units (vv. 10, 18, and 21). However, the pattern of past reprisal and future reversal that pervaded 30:1–31:1 is now dropped. A technique of using the quotation formula not to introduce immediately following divine speech but to give advance notice of such speech later in the unit was employed once in the earlier composition, at 30:5, looking ahead to vv. 8–9 or 8–11. This technique becomes a regular feature of the present composition. The formula in 31:2 paves the way for Yahweh's speech in vv. 3b–6, while the one in v. 7 anticipates vv. 8–9, and the one in v. 15 anticipates vv. 16–17. Similarly in the unit of vv. 10–14, where a call to hear "Yahweh's message" (v. 10) stands in place of the quotation formula, the message finally appears in vv. 13b–14. In the unit of vv. 15–17 the quotation formula in v. 15 is resumptively repeated in v. 16 and its preparatory role in v. 15 is thereby revealed. It is significant that the unit in vv. 18–20 also closes with divine speech (v. 20), though in this unit an initial quotation formula is lacking. However, its place is taken by a closing quotation formula in v. 20, the only place in the composition where it occurs in the text shared by LXX and MT. As for vv. 21–25, the widespread phenomenon of final divine statements in the other units of this composition suggests that these verses are meant to make up a composite unit; as in v. 16, the quotation formula directly precedes divine speech. Then all six units move from a preparatory human saying to a divine one.

[2–6] The introductory passage in vv. 2–3a is intended to explain the "age-old love" of Yahweh in v. 3b, which finds fresh illustration in the coming events of vv. 4–6. New life in the land had its roots in a covenant relationship established long before. That relationship provides a frame for the unit in that it is described at some length from a divine standpoint (vv. 2–3a) and then acknowledged on the human side in the brief tribute to "our God" (v. 6).

[2–3a] What guaranteed Israel's homecoming was not simply Yahweh's promise but also the theological continuity to which it bore witness. This continuity depends on the exodus or, more precisely, Yahweh's self-revelation in the wilderness in a covenant-making role (cf. 2:2). It is summed up as "favor," a term that moves in a similar theological orbit to the terms Yahweh will use, "love" and "loyalty." Surviving the sword reflects an exodus tradition (Exod 5:21; 15:9; 18:4).[247] So too does the occurrence of the Sinai theophany "at a distance" (Exod 19:12–13; 21:23–24; 24:1–2).[248] The self-revelation of the holy, majestic God was an act of gracious condescension. It was the first stage in a process that was to bring Israel to a resting place in the land after wandering in the wilderness.

[3b] There is a switch from past to present. The scene has been set for the divine theological statement that grounds future blessing in the motivation of a past relationship. "The mercy of God would not be evanescent, but would follow the people from year to year in all ages" (Calvin 4:56). God had not changed, and so the present generation could cherish an assured hope that trusted in a faithful God. "The gifts and calling of God are irrevocable" (Rom 11:29). The prolonging of divine "loyalty" (ḥesed) has a parallel in the deprecating of Yahweh's prolonging of anger rather than displaying "steadfast love" (ḥesed) in Ps 85:5, 7 (6, 8).

[4–6] The rest of the oracle consists of a proclamation of salvation; it begins with Yahweh's saving work in v. 4a and continues with the results of that work in human experience. "Once more" rings out three times at the outset of the first three statements. God-given life in the land would be resumed; the reference to "rest" in v. 2b has implicitly paved the way. A dual structure operates in vv. 4–6. While the introductions in terms of time differentiate the bicola in v. 6 from the bicola and tricolon in vv. 4–5 (AAA/B), the content functions as action and reaction within v. 4 and in vv. 5–6 (AB/A'B'). The building up of "virgin Israel" refers to the creation of a family of descendants, repopulation as the basis for future generations (cf. 30:19–20).[249] A response was to be a communal, joyful celebration, as in 30:19a after the building of v. 18b. The A and A' elements in vv. 4a and 5 couple building and planting, paired terms in the book for the positive work of God that would follow terrible judgment (cf. 1:10). Jeremiah 24:6 provides a virtual commentary on these elements, "bringing them back to their

---

247. Böhmer, *Heimkehr*, 55.
248. Kilpp, *Niederreissen*, 136 n. 13; cf. also Israel's finding divine favor in Exod 33:16.
249. Cf. BDB 124b.

country and building them up instead of demolishing them, planting them instead of uprooting them." The second element here concerns human planting, though it clearly reflects the divine purpose. Both the A' and B' elements relate to vineyards in that the task of the "guards" was to protect the vineyards (cf. Isa 27:3). They would announce the time to be ripe for pilgrimage to Zion. The celebration of v. 4b now assumes a religious character (cf. Ps 122:1, 4; Luke 2:42). Life was to consist of communal cycles of work and joyful fruition, of work and worship that linked a "people" (v. 2) and "our God" in covenant fellowship.

The references to "Samaria" and "Ephraim" have encouraged a widespread scholarly conviction that this oracle emanated from Jeremiah's early prophesying about the restoration of the former northern kingdom. It has affinities with such oracles preserved in 3:12–13, 14 that have members of the erstwhile northern kingdom in view and envision reunited worship in Zion (cf. 3:6a*a* and commentary). One of Jeremiah's oracles has been reused in the exilic medley of divine promise and hope represented in this composition. In the present literary setting the theocratic term "Israel" relates to the undivided people, while the references to "Samaria" and "Ephraim" cite the northerners by way of example.

[7–9] How could such blessings in the homeland materialize for those now far away from home? The next unit is meant as an answer, as the initial conjunction (NRSV "For") implies. Yahweh was to bring the people home. The introductory statement after the quotation formula in v. 7 consists of a so-called eschatological song of praise that by faith elicits praise even now for God's future work. The oracle (vv. 8–9) is a proclamation of the coming salvation. Yahweh's work of restoration is announced at beginning and end (vv. 8a, 9b), and the human results in the center (vv. 8b, 9a). The reference to Yahweh's "people" (v. 7) and the two-sided covenant metaphor in the closing bicolon (v. 9) are bookends for the unit. The unit is probably exilic, though the last bicolon in v. 9 may derive from Jeremiah's own oracles about the fallen northern kingdom.

[7] "Jacob," as in 30:7, 18, stands for the whole of Israel, the exiled heirs of the northern and southern kingdoms, and so does "Israel." The happy imperatives set an enthusiastic tone for the unit. The addressees of the call to praise are not identified; the focus is on the reason and the divine and human parties to be involved in Yahweh's praiseworthy work. The eschatological song of praise, with its imperative summons and hymnic praise that uses a perfect verb to describe a future event, is a feature of Second Isaiah (e.g., Isa 40:10–13; 52:9–10).[250] Jacob's description as "top nation" refers to its role as divinely elect, like the metaphor in v. 9 (cf. Deut 32:8–9; Ps 18:43 [44]).

[8a] The opening bicolon of the divine proclamation weaves in language from Jeremiah's oracles of disaster (6:22; 25:32), reapplying it to the return. Earlier references in the book to deportees leaving the northern country (3:18;

---

250. See Westermann, *Praise and Lament*, 143–45.

Covenant-Centered Hope

16:15; 23:8) have been redactional; MT provides closer alignment by adding "country."

[8b–9a] Here the focus is on the results that Yahweh's activity would achieve. A full return is predicated. Nobody was to be left behind, not even people with disabilities or pregnant women. The contrition of the returnees, an element upon which vv. 18–19 will enlarge, is a positive spiritual note.

[9b] Yahweh's abundant provision for the journey home matches oracles in Second Isaiah (e.g., Isa 40:3–4; 41:17–18). The theological motivation for such blessing is the covenant relationship expressed in terms of close family kinship (cf. Jer 3:19; Exod 4:22; Hos 11:1). Over against other nations Israel as a whole had a prime role as Yahweh's elect. The prophet affirms that northerners ("Ephraim") shared in this relationship.

[10–14] The oracle duly appears at the close (vv. 13b–14). The initial call to hear "Yahweh's message" here replaces the quotation formula that opens half the units in this composition. The earlier part of the unit is a prophetic preparation for the oracle in excited tones. It discusses first the return from exile (vv. 10b–11) and then Yahweh's blessings in the reoccupied land (vv. 12–13a) and so mulls over the topics of the two earlier units in reverse order. In particular v. 10b functions as a retrospective summary of vv. 7–9, echoing "collect" from v. 8 and interpreting the leading by water of v. 9 in pastoral terms (cf. Ps 23:2; Rev 7:17). Links with Second Isaiah (vv. 10–11) suggest that the unit is late exilic.

[10–11] The rhetorical address to the nations is a fanfare of praise that announces Yahweh's imminent work for Israel as news that must be broadcast. The oracular switch from sorrow to joy in v. 13b is elucidated in the factual terms of Yahweh's rescue operations that contrast with the earlier work of judgment. The shepherd analogy is consistent with 22:3, a redactional text and adds a further covenantal note to the composition. The news is explained in terms of Yahweh's intervening in power, using strong theological verbs that Second Isaiah had exploited (e.g., Isa 43:1; 50:2; 51:10–11).

[12–13a] Now the "joy" and "bounty" to be promised in vv. 13–14 are directly anticipated in the exposition, in a reverse order that permits a smooth transition from the joy of v. 13a to its divine promise in v. 13b. First, as in v. 6b, the bounty in v. 12 is associated with cultic thanksgiving in Zion, which is therefore related to "priests" in v. 14; then it is elaborated in mouth-watering detail. The prospect of such plentifulness is contrasted with what was evidently an exilic experience of comparative deprivation. Yahweh would amply meet Israel's basic needs. In turn "joy" is illustrated in terms of communal dancing, as in v. 4b. "The 'then' that is promised is sharply contrasted with the 'now' which is still deathly and exilic" (Brueggemann 286).

[13b–14] Finally the oracle itself caps the unit with a summary of future transformation, including a covenantal reference, "my people." The lavishness of the priests' share of Israel's cultic offerings is a measure of the covenant people's own abundance of blessing.

[15–17] This unit combines the ending of human grief (v. 13) with the promise of return to the land (v. 8). Its concern with the exilic fate of the northern kingdom suggests that, as in vv. 2–6, one of Jeremiah's early oracles has been woven into the later composition. Its presence affirms that northern exiles would share in the restoration. An auditory vision (v. 15) sets the tone for divine reassurance (v. 16a) that is grounded in a proclamation of salvation (vv. 16b–17).

[15] The prophet (cf. 3:21; Lundbom 2:434–35) reports a dramatic vision of Rachel inconsolably mourning her exiled children. The tone is that of a funeral lament, not an imploring psalm lament. Rachel was the ancestral mother of the Joseph tribes, Ephraim and Manasseh, and also of Benjamin (Gen 30:22–24; 35:16–18, 24). The vision reflects the real-life mourning of those left in the area, still bemoaning the absence of their fellow citizens exiled in 721 B.C.E. The implicit factor linking the vision and the underlying reality is the location of Rachel's tomb in Benjaminite territory. One of two OT traditions places the tomb near Bethlehem (Gen 35:19; 48:7; Matt 2:16–18 conveniently adopts it, or rather conflates the two traditions). The other tradition locates her burial in the tribal region of Benjamin (1 Sam 10:2), and the reference to Ramah here seems to echo it.

[16–17] Funeral-like laments expect no answer, but in a direct address the divine message amazingly announces what the matriarch never imagined to be possible, a solution to the problem that caused her grief. Her efforts in raising her children would not be in vain (Volz 294). The prospect of repatriation is spelled out persuasively and painstakingly in a pair of double statements.[251]

Matthew's Gospel applies v. 15 to King Herod's slaughter of the innocents in Bethlehem (Matt 2:17–18), viewing the text from the perspective of Jesus' own time and context and finding in it a remarkable omen of the consequences of opposition to the divine will.[252] In an enhancement of the funereal tone of the lament, dead victims feature in the fulfillment, rather than exiled ones. This is significant because Herod's action inaugurated the authorities' opposition to Jesus that was to culminate in his own death.[253]

[18–20] The theme of return develops in a spiritual dimension, involving a renewed relationship with Yahweh, which was a precondition of physical return to the land. The structural pattern of the units in this composition suggests that Yahweh is not the speaker in the opening part. Accordingly the element of audi-

---

251. The double *yēš*, "there is," is a positive denial of the negative *ʾên*, lit. "there is not," in v. 15 (Holladay 2:188).

252. Cf. Michael Knowles, *Jeremiah in Matthew's Gospel: The Rejected-Prophet Motif in Matthaean Redaction* (JSNTSup 68; Sheffield: JSOT Press, 1993), 33–52.

253. Christine Ritter, *Rachels Klage im antiken Judentum und frühen Christentum: Eine auslegungsgeschichtliche Studie* (AGTU 52; Leiden: Brill, 2003), 123–26.

Covenant-Centered Hope

tion in a visionary context (v. 15) continues here (cf. 4:19, 31; Lundbom 2:441). In vv. 18–19 a report of Ephraim's prayer of lament is provided, and in v. 20 Yahweh's affirmative reaction in a response to the prophet concerning Ephraim. The name "Ephraim" introduces each half of the unit. Once more one of Jeremiah's oracles concerning the former northern kingdom has been worked into the hope-filled composition. The piece would have originally referred to northern Israelites still living in the land, as in Yahweh's appeal in 3:12–13; indeed, the two passages may have been organically related, with "come back" in 31:18 echoing 3:12 and "my God" picking up "your God" in 3:13. In this context, however, the overheard voice becomes that of the community of northern exiles hoping for return to the land and to favor with God. There is a triple play on the Hebrew verb šûb. It is used in v. 19 of the earlier turning back spiritually from Yahweh and in v. 18 of a spiritual return ("Have me back") as the condition for a physical return.

[18] The note of lamentation continues from v. 15, but now, in contrast, it is associated with prayerful and hopeful repentance and harks back to an earlier part of the composition (v. 9a). There returning exiles, including representatives of Ephraim (v. 9b), were lamenting, but now there is a flashback to the same thing happening before the return journey. The topic of divine reprisal that dominated the former composition briefly resurfaces (cf. especially the "chastisement" of 30:4); it is blended with the theme of returning in the spiritual sense of confession and a yearning for fellowship with God to be restored. The original covenant relationship is owned afresh ("my God") as motivation for the appeal. The admission of guilt is accentuated by the simile of a calf not yet broken in to wear the yoke (cf. 2:20; 5:5).

[19] The seriousness of Ephraim's repentance is conveyed by a report of a conversion experience intended to prompt Yahweh's acceptance in reconciliation. Slapping the thigh is a gesture of grief; GNB paraphrases, "we hung our heads in grief." In Ezek 21:12 (17) it accompanies verbal mourning, and so here it echoes the grieving mentioned initially in v. 18. Similarly the closing confession of sin reinforces the confession of v. 18.

[20] Yahweh responds in warm tones to Ephraim's overtures. Deep commitment to the covenant relationship, which is again expressed in father-son terms, as in v. 9, is poignantly expressed as a factor that stands in tension with the demands of justice, as in Hos 11:8–9. In both cases the fact that judgment had previously been meted out holds out hope that compassionate love would triumph (contrast Jer 13:14). Yahweh's memories were clearly positive ones of a period that antedated Ephraim's misspent "youth" (cf. 2:2). "Compassion" echoes the parade of gracious terms that introduced the composition, "favor," "love," and "loyalty" (vv. 2–3). In a context of guilt, especially of confessed guilt, such terms appropriately shade into "compassion" (cf. Ps 103:13). The unit serves as a magnificent summary of the message of the parable of the Prodigal

Son, as a number of commentators have observed (e.g., Duhm 250). It especially aligns with the stage when the father saw his son in the distance making his way back and "was filled with compassion" (Luke 15:20).

[21–25] This composite unit challenges and coaxes its addressees. It combines the twin themes of the composition, coming back to the land (v. 21) and experiencing blessing in the land (vv. 23–25). It reverts to a feminine address for Israel, "virgin daughter," used at the outset of the composition (v. 4). The first, poetic half of the unit develops the motif of the homeward journey broached in v. 9b, while the end of the second, largely prose half echoes the divine meeting of human needs promised in vv. 12 and 14. "Once more" in v. 23 resumes vv. 4–5. Both parts of the unit appear to derive from an exilic setting. Originally independent, they have been paired as a preparatory prophetic message and a divine one, and are hinged by "towns" in vv. 21 and 23–24.

[21–22] The poem offers a barrage of real and virtual imperatives to prepare for the imminent journey home and especially to make the necessary psychological adjustments. Two examples are given. First, the prophet urges Israel to "fix your mind" (NJB) on the journey that would reverse the one into exile. The divine promise must be taken seriously and implemented. Second, and more importantly, there was a need to shake off doubts that had their roots in the old spiritual alienation. "Daughter" echoes the covenant relationship expressed by "son" (v. 20) and "eldest son" (v. 9). "Backsliding" (*šôbēbâ*) recalls the preexilic turning back (*šûb*) (v. 19). But, wonder of wonders and defying all precedent, even that was no disqualification. It was a barrier Yahweh could and would overcome, by a transforming work of grace (cf. Isa 43:19). Israel would be empowered to show initiative as covenant partner, so that "the woman, instead of holding aloof and waiting to be sought by the man, ... will affectionately cling round her divine husband."[254] So Yahweh would enable Israel to meet the necessary spiritual commitment—"My people encompass Me with love unfeigned" (Berrigan 129). There is a mixture of covenant metaphors in v. 22, as in 3:19–20, whereby the father-daughter imagery changes to a marital one.

[23–25] A solid divine basis is provided for the exhortations. This proclamation of salvation maintains the inclusion of the Judean exiles in the invitation and promise of vv. 21–22 issued to the generic Israel. Earlier in the composition material relating to the people of the northern kingdom had played a large role. Now the balance is restored by finally specifying Judah too as the focus of promise. Moreover, the allusion to Jerusalem (v. 23) appropriately caps the Zion references (vv. 6 and 12). Divine blessing upon Jerusalem was the key to Judah's own blessing.

[23] Yahweh's work of rehabilitation (cf. 30:3, 18) is summed up in a forecast of the renewed use of what was evidently a preexilic formula invoking

---

254. S. R. Driver, *Revised Translation*, 188 n. d.

Covenant-Centered Hope 351

divine blessing on the holy city, Yahweh's own "home" (cf. Exod 15:13). The formula is comparable in spirit to Ps 122:6–9. The reference to "righteous home" reminds the reader of Isa 1:21, 26, which also seems to be using traditional material. The invocation implies restoration of a worship-centered community occupying its former land.

[24] A wistful sketch of this community "there"—"in the country of Judah," v. 23—is supplied. A full range of urban populations and rural workers would be represented in the restoration.

[25] Yahweh would underwrite their continued existence by seeing that their basic needs were met. As in vv. 5 and 12, the coherence of vv. 23–25 lies in a healthy sequence of work, sufficient reward, and worship. The middle element, normally beset by risk from year to year, is placed under God's special blessing.

[26] The human "I" in this observation relates to that in v. 18. Evidently the redactor-prophet reencountered Jeremiah's visionary experiences of vv. 15 and 18 as his own. The observation marks the end of the composition and refers to its content as given in a dream (cf. 1 Kgs 3:5, 15; Job 4:12–21). Then the welcome "sleep" refers by synecdoche to the dream revelation, which is here favorably regarded in contrast to 23:25–32.

In 31:2–26 assurances are given of Israelite and Judean return to the land and to covenant fellowship with Yahweh, which would result in rich blessing.

31:27–40 Divine Guarantees for Israel's Future

27 "Look, the time is coming," declared Yahweh, "when I will seed *the communities of* Israel and Judah with seed that produces people and livestock. 28 As I was watchful over them with the intent of *uprooting and tearing down,* demolishing, *destroying,* and treating badly, I will be just as watchful over them with the intent of building and planting," declared Yahweh. 29 At that time people will say no more,

"Parents have eaten sour grapes,
  but children's teeth feel rough!"

30 Instead people will die for their own wrongdoing. *All* those who eat sour grapes will find their own teeth feeling rough.
31 "Look, the time is coming," declared Yahweh, "when I will make with the communities of Israel and Judah a new covenant, 32 unlike the covenant I made with their forebears when I took them by the hand to bring them out of Egypt, because[a] they have broken my covenant and I in turn have had to show myself their master,"[b] declared Yahweh.
33 "Rather, this is the covenant I will make with the community of Israel after that period," declared Yahweh: "I will internalize[c] my torah, writing

it on their minds, and then I will be their God and they in turn will be my people, **34** and so no more will anybody have to teach other members of the community or family to know Yahweh, but[d] all of them, ranging from lowest to elite, will know me," *declared Yahweh*. "[This will happen] because I will forgive their wrongdoing and remember their sinning no more."**35**[e] Here is what Yahweh said—

> the one who has provided the sun for light by day,
> the moon and stars[f]
> for light by night,
> the one who rouses the sea so its waves toss about,
> Yahweh Almighty is his name—
> **36** "If these regular features are removed
> from my presence,"
> declared Yahweh,
> "then also the line of Israel will stop
> being ever a nation in my presence."

37 *Here is what Yahweh said:*

> "If the skies above could be measured
> or earth's foundations below explored,
> Then also I would reject *all* the line of Israel[g]
> for all they have done,"
> declared Yahweh.

38 "Look, the time is coming,"[h] declared Yahweh, "when the city will be rebuilt as Yahweh's from Hananel Tower to[i] the Corner Gate. **39** *Once more* a measuring line will be stretched straight[j] out over Gareb Hill and then round to Goah. **40** The entire valley, with its corpses and altar ashes,[k] and all the fields as far as Wadi Kidron, up to the corner of the Horse Gate on the east, will be consecrated to Yahweh. No more will it be uprooted or demolished forever."

 a. So NIV; cf. NAB "for"; Rudolph 202. For a causal sense cf. BDB 83b. LXX and Aquila rendered "because" and Symmachus "for." A relative clause is awkward here.

 b. So NAB, following Rudolph 26, 202, and *BHS* with some ancient support; *HALOT* 1:142b.

 c. The Hebrew perfect must be "prophetic" (cf. Joüon §112h). Levin, *Verheissung*, 258 n. 6, regards LXX "giving I will give" as a rendering of such certainty.

 d. As in v. 33, *kî* is adversative after a negative (Rudolph 202, following the traditional German translation; Walter Gross, "Erneuter oder neuer Bund? Wortlaut und Aus-

Covenant-Centered Hope 353

sage in Jer 31, 31–34," in *Bund und Tora: Zur theologischen Begriffsgeschichte in alttestamentlicher, frühjüdischer und urchristlicher Tradition* [ed. F. Avemarie and H. Lichtenberger; WUNT 92; Tübingen: Mohr (Siebeck), 1996], 41–66, esp. 50). Cf. NJB "No" in v. 33 and here.

e. For the transposition in LXX noted in *BHS* see Rudolph 204; Janzen, *Studies*, 220 n. 17; Becking, *Between Fear and Freedom*, 41–42, 67–68.

f. MT prefaces with *ḥuqqōt*, "the regular features of," which is lacking in LXX and unexpected in terms of parallelism. It represents the mistaken incorporation into the text of a marginal comparative gloss that contrasted the masculine *ḥuqqîm* in v. 36 with the feminine form used in 33:25; Job 38:33 (cf. Duhm 258; Janzen, *Studies*, 49). NAB and GNB delete. For the AB/A′/B′ parallelism in the tricolon cf. v. 19a.

g. While MT gives rhetorical reinforcement by adding "all," LXX does the same by adding a negative, "[even so] I would not reject" (cf. REB).

h. See *BHS*.

i. See *BHS*.

j. For the sense with a reflexive suffix see BDB 617a.

k. For the appositional construction see *IBHS* 231. The omission in LXX noted in *BHS* was caused by a copyist's eye jumping to the next *wkl*, "and all" (Barthélemy, *Critique textuelle*, 2:691–92).

This composition, most of which is written in prose, offers a series of assurances about Israel's and Judah's future security. It has an air of conclusion and climax after the two previous compositions and so also reflects an exilic setting. Indeed, the composition's varied units all seem to have originated then, poised between the judgment of 587 and an expectation of restoration. For example, the literary telescoping of 1:10, 12 in v. 28, and the allusion to Ezekiel 18 in vv. 29–30 so suggest. The composition falls into three sections, like the first one (30:5–31:1). In this case, however, each section begins with temporal and quotation formulas, "'Look, the time is coming,' declared Yahweh" (vv. 27, 31, 38). Each section is made up of two sayings. In the central section, which is much longer than the other two, the poetic passage in vv. 35–37 demarcated by initial and closing quotation formulas complements the prose passage in vv. 31–34. MT has split the poetry into two by prefacing a quotation formula in v. 37 to match the one in v. 35. In the first section the use of initial and closing quotation formulas (vv. 27–28) separates the first statement from the saying (vv. 29–30). In the third section two topographical statements concerning the city and the valley to the south are supplied (vv. 38–39 and 40). Each of the three sections features "no more," which strikes a strong note of discontinuity, yet in the interests of a greater continuity, Israel's survival as the covenant people. In the large middle section "no more" occurs twice (v. 34) and provides closure for the divine saying. Elsewhere it does so for the section (vv. 29, 40). The combination of a temporal formula, "Look, the time is coming," and a "no more" statement throughout this composition recalls the usage in redactional material at 7:32; 16:14–15 (= 23:7–8); and 19:6. The quotation formula "Here is what Yahweh said" had important structural roles in the two earlier compositions, but here it appears at v. 35 and likewise at v. 37 in MT as a subsectional marker, a stylistic variant of the initial "declared Yahweh" in the rest of the composition, which LXX has in v. 37. A frame is provided for the composition by repetition of demolishing (and uprooting in MT) in vv. 28 and 40 as divine activity relegated to the past and ruled out for the future.

[27–30] The two sayings in this section both begin temporal formulas, the second in v. 29 resuming the first.

[27–28] This proclamation of salvation has a recapitulating role. The motif of divine blessing in the previous composition is summarized in v. 27, while that of the reversal of divine reprisal, which characterized the composition of 30:5–31:1, is sketched in v. 28.

[27] The reference to "Israel and Judah," which MT expands in line with v. 31, recalls the repeated report of a reunited people (30:3). Yahweh promises an abundance of human population (cf. 3:16; 23:3; 30:19) and supply of livestock. The metaphor of seeding is reminiscent of the positive, postjudgment interpretation of "Jezreel" ("God sows") in Hos 2:22–23 (24–25). There is a hint of reversal since the 587 disaster had, earlier in the book, been presented as taking a toll on humans and animals (Jer 7:20; 9:10 [9]; 21:6; cf. 32:43; 33:10).

[28] The image of sowing seed is not far from those of building and planting, especially as "building" can connote having a family and "seed" can mean progeny, as it does in vv. 36–37 (rendered "line"). The blessing of being built up addressed to virgin Israel (31:4) is now echoed and developed into the theme of reversal after reprisal. To this end the contrasting programmatic language of 1:10 is used to indicate restoration after judgment in a two-part divine purpose. It is combined with Yahweh's alert monitoring in the vision of 1:12. There it was associated with Yahweh's message of judgment; here there is a shift from the fulfillment of messages of woe (and weal) to the people who would figure in them. "Treating badly," which drops the metaphor, has occurred earlier at 25:6, 29; the corresponding noun, "a bad fate," occurs in association with the negative metaphorical verbs in 18:7–8; 42:10; 45:4–5, and here it may echo 1:14. MT amplified the negative verbs with extra ones taken from 1:10, thus underlining the source; another reason for "uprooting" is to supply a structural parallel with v. 40. An exilic setting is implied, midway between past judgment and restoration.

[29–30] The "no more" statement that is a feature of this composition and contributes to the motif of reversal is consistent with the change of speech promised in 3:16 and 16:14–15 (= 23:7–8). It is borrowed from Ezek 18:3; indeed, the perspective present in vv. 29–30 summarizes Ezek 18:1–20, which proclaims a new freedom from the crippling shackles of the past.[255] In the process v. 30a makes use of the related Deut 24:26b.[256] At v. 30b there is a reuse of the metaphor to illustrate the plain speaking of v. 30a; it accentuates the note of reversal. The saying is not expressed in oracular terms, but readers are meant to recognize the original as an oracle given to Ezekiel (Ezek 18:1). In the present context restoration to the land is the setting of the reversal. The punishment that continued in the exilic period, which thereby affected generations not directly involved in the sins that led to the disaster of 587, would be brought to a close by the restoration. There is some tension between this representation of the conditions of the restoration and the exuberantly eschatological ones in vv. 33–34. There is an unfolding, upward movement to the greater blessings set out in the next section.[257] The main point of the saying, in the wake of v. 28, is the ending of past guilt, a crucial issue for the exiles to which v. 34b will return.

[31–37] The second section's greater length demarcates it as the focus of the composition. It falls into two proclamations of salvation (vv. 31–34 and 35–37). Traditional displays of Yahweh's immense power are used to back up both, references to the exodus in the first case and to the divine role as creator in the second.

[31–34] Renewal and blessing continue, but rise to eschatological heights. The oracle amplifies the "something new" Yahweh was to create (v. 22). Prose sermonic terminology features in vv. 32–33, exodus language reflecting 7:22, 25; 11:4, 7; and 16:14–15 (= 23:7–8), and the covenant formula reminiscent of 7:23; 11:4; and 24:7. The new covenant oracle appears to be the product of post-Jeremianic prophecy; it presupposes and caps the prose sermons in chs. 7 and 11 with a triumphant reversal.[258] Moreover, the promise of a new exodus (16:14–15) is now matched by a new covenant. The topic of covenant that ran all through the earlier two compositions is now developed in this long oracle. In vv. 32–34 the contrast drawn between the new covenant and the earlier one is formally parallel in that a statement of covenant making with first person verb and reference to its beneficiaries is followed by a causal clause, in v. 32a and b

255. See Leslie C. Allen, *Ezekiel 1–19* (WBC 28; Dallas: Word, 1994), 270–77, 280–81. For the dependence on Ezekiel see Hendrik Leene, "Ezekiel and Jeremiah: Promises of Inner Renewal in Diachronic Perspective," in *Past, Present, Future: The Deuteronomistic History and the Prophets* (ed. J. C. de Moor and H. F. van Rooy; OtSt 44; Leiden: Brill, 2000), 150–75, esp. 170–72.

256. Joel S. Kaminsky, *Corporate Responsibility in the Hebrew Bible* (JSOTSup 196; Sheffield: Sheffield Academic Press, 1995), 146. The change of noun from ḥāṭāʾ), "sin," and of verb from the Hophal was doubtless due to Ezek 18:20.

257. Rudolph 201 suggests that vv. 29–30 represent a realistic corrective to vv. 31–34, and Holladay 2:163 concurs, but the compositional structuring sets vv. 29–30 firmly with vv. 27–28, not with vv. 31–34.

258. Stulman does not so designate the passage, but he lists parallels in *Prose Sermons*, 33 (no. 2), 38 (no. 44, where 31:33 is intended).

on the one hand and vv. 33a and 34b on the other. The first spells the closing of one door, and the second the opening of another. Verses 33b–34a supply a definition of "this" second covenant; a slight adaptation has to be made in the translation of v. 34b to clarify the structure.

[31] That a reunited people would be prominent in the restoration is spelled out by use of the old political terms "Israel" and "Judah," as in v. 27; it paves the way for the glance back at the history of apostasy in v. 32b. On the other hand, the resumptive reference in v. 33 uses the theocratic term "Israel," which by itself has this wider sense, as frequently earlier in the literary block. The covenant will be presented as new not in substance but in form (Calvin 4:127).

[32] God's gracious care associated with the first covenant (cf. vv. 2–3a) is conveyed by a unique phrase in this context, "taking by the hand" (cf. Isa 42:6; Exod 19:4; Hos 11:3–4). It will bring out the heinousness of Israel's breach of the covenant and the propriety of the consequent punishment. The issue of the radical breaking of the covenant by both communities consciously reiterates 11:10, while the reference to the exodus echoes 11:4. The closing verb is often understood to mean Yahweh's overall role in the covenant relationship, such as "though I was their husband" (NRSV). However, it depicts Yahweh's punitively seizing back control because of the otherwise inexplicable temporal phrase "after that period" (v. 33), which must refer to the time of Yahweh's reprisal of punishment for Israel before the restoration, a time of inescapable disaster (so 11:11).[259] This use of the verbal phrase imparts a new sense to the one employed in 3:14, though LXX so interpreted there. There is here a backward glance at the moral reprisals of the first composition.

[33] Instead of the people's breaking the covenant, Yahweh would give the torah, in the sense of the written revelation of the will of the God of the covenant, an inner power. The writing on the seat of the human will contrasts with an external writing on tablets at Sinai in view of v. 32a (cf. 2 Cor 3:3) or on scrolls.[260] It also contrasts with the writing of sin on Judah's hearts (Jer 17:1). This miraculous transformation is concerned with motivation and expresses theologically the "new" willingness forecast in v. 22. It is consistent with the divine gifts of character to Israel in Hos 2:19–20 (21–22; see REB) and with the new heart of Ezek 36:26. When internal cues replaced external ones, the two-sided covenant formula would find perfect fulfillment in the mutuality of its partners. The prospect of 31:1 and of 30:22 (MT) here receives elucidation. In broader terms the unrealized ideal of 7:23 and 11:4 was to find fulfillment on the lines of 24:7.

[34a] After the divine intervention of v. 33 comes its human result. The first of the two contrasting "no more" statements strikingly describes the wonderful inter-

---

259. Bernard Renaud, *Nouvelle ou éternelle alliance? Le message des prophètes* (LD 189; Paris: Cerf, 2002), 38–40, 54.
260. Levin, *Verheissung*, 261, rightly sees no direct link with Isa 51:7 or Ps 37:31.

nalization as instinctive knowledge of Yahweh (cf. 8:7).[261] This knowledge was revealed in the torah (cf. the parallelism of Hos 4:6); earlier in the book it had been summed up in Jer 9:24 (23) and 22:15–16. It would render obsolete the old traditions of the priestly teaching of torah to the community (cf. Hos 4:6 again) and parental instruction to children (cf. Deut 6:7; Ps 78:5). The lack of such acknowledgment of Yahweh's will and even repudiation of it (9:3, 6 [2, 5]) were intolerable blemishes on the old era of revelation; soon they would cease. The social pervasiveness of sinning, "from lowest to elite" (6:13; 8:10; cf. 5:4–5), would be replaced by one of compliance with the divine will. All levels of society would possess it as God's supernatural gift to the covenant people. In Joel 2:28–29 (3:1–2) the social distinctions are widened beyond class to gender and age.

[34b] But what of the past guilt that hung like a cloud over the present community of exiles? Verses 29–30 had broached the problem and given one answer. Now it is addressed again, in response to the haunting anxiety it caused. The pair of causal clauses about broken covenant and divine reprisal (v. 32b) contrasts with Yahweh as the sole, positive subject. A gracious act of amnesty would be declared, the forgiveness of the covenant community's sins, something declared to be impossible before God's work of judgment (5:1, 7). The way to a fresh relationship would thus be opened up. Here is the precondition of the new covenant, what Calvin (4:138) calls "the foundation of God's kindness" (cf. Ezek 36:25–26).

Recognition of the theological importance of vv. 31–34 comes from the reverberations it produces in the NT.[262] The very title "New Testament" is a rendering of the Greek term via the Vulgate's understanding of it in the light of the exegesis in Heb 9:15–17, which exploits the double meaning of the Greek word *diathēkē*, "covenant" and "will" (cf. 2 Cor 3:5–14; Gal 3:15–18). Paul's account of the Last Supper in 1 Cor 11:25 associates the cup of wine with the "new covenant"; the long text in Luke's Gospel that includes 22:20 does the same. Mark's and Matthew's Gospels refer to Jesus' "blood of the covenant" (Mark 14:24; Matt 26:28), alluding to the sacrifice that ratified the Sinai covenant (Exod 24:1–8). Matthew 26:28 goes on to state the purpose as "for the forgiveness of sins," an equally clear allusion to Jer 31:34b.[263] Matthew's account already associates Exodus 24 and Jeremiah 31, as does the exegesis of Heb 9:15, 18–22. This coupling of texts suggests that the same is true for the description of the cup as "the new covenant in my blood" in 1 Cor 11:25, thus comparing in principle what Jer 31:31–32 contrasts. The NT echoes of the oracle of Jer 31:31–34 retain

---

261. Helga Weippert, "Das Wort vom neuen Bund in Jeremia xxxi 31–34," *VT* 29 (1979): 336–51, esp. 339–40.

262. For echoes at Qumran see the summaries of Lundbom 2:473–74; Knowles, *Jeremiah in Matthew's Gospel*, 261–63.

263. Cf. Knowles, *Jeremiah in Matthew's Gospel*, 208–9.

something of its forward-looking role. The accounts of the Last Supper all closely tie its celebration to the future kingdom of God or to the second coming of Christ. Even the Letter to the Hebrews, which quotes the whole of vv. 31–34 from LXX in 8:8–12, seems to envision its complete fulfillment in the coming age, as is implied by the need for teaching in Heb 5:12, with which one may compare the omission of the lack of teaching in v. 34 from the quotation in 10:16–17. The NT claims an inauguration of the new covenant and looks forward to its consummation.

[35–37] This oracle is a two-part proclamation of salvation that reinforces the promise of the perpetuity of "Israel" with an oath.[264] "Line" in vv. 36–37 is literally "seed" (KJV) in the sense of progeny, and so the promise of v. 27 is developed here. In both parts of the oracle Yahweh's work in the world of nature is used to explore the covenant relationship and to guarantee its validity (cf. 5:22; 8:7; 18:14). The exiles are encouraged to "entrust themselves to a faithful creator" (1 Pet 4:19).

[35–36] There is unusual overlap between the introduction (v. 35) and the oracle (v. 36), in that "these regular features" in the latter presuppose the terms cited in the former. The statement takes the form of a participial hymn, a type of hymn earlier encountered at 10:16. Here, as often, it is associated with creation and oath taking.[265] The second half recurs at Isa 51:15, which probably indicates another instance of reliance on Second Isaiah.[266] Yahweh's control of sky and ocean in the production of light for the world and of storms at sea (cf. Ps 107:24–25) exhibits a divine constancy that may logically be predicated of the same God's covenant relationship with Israel. The common factor is God's "presence." There are natural and spiritual components in the overall economy, like staff serving or standing before the divine householder (cf. Exod 33:18, where "leave" renders the verb here translated "are removed"; Ps 103:21).[267] Should one render "Yahweh Almighty" in v. 35 literally as "Yahweh of hosts," as an element of the imagery? "If" is, of course, the "if" of argument, not of doubt. "Nothing, not even 587, can separate Israel from God's relentless love" (Brueggemann 297). The term "nation" recalls the description of Jacob as "top nation" (v. 7). Since a nation is a people in a land, and the context has in view restoration to the land, Rudolph (204) correctly sees a political future for Israel posited here.

---

264. Claus Westermann, *Prophetic Oracles of Salvation in the Old Testament* (trans. Keith Crim; Louisville: Westminster/John Knox, 1991), 146–47.

265. Crenshaw, "Form-Critical Analysis," 164–65.

266. In this case, however, the incongruence of "I" and "his" at Isa 51:15 may be a sign of secondary usage (Levin, *Verheissung*, 199).

267. Konrad Schmid, *Buchgestalten des Jeremiabuches: Untersuchungen zur Redaktions- und Rezeptionsgeschichte von Jer 30–33 in Kontext des Buches* (WMANT 72; Neukirchen-Vluyn: Neukirchener Verlag, 1996), 175 n. 597, aptly compares the close syntactical parallel to v. 36b in 2 Sam 19:14 (13) (KJV "be before me"), though here he sees a reference to cultic presence.

[37] The same logic is applied as in vv. 35–36, now using an unrealizable condition. Sky and earth replace the phenomena of sky and sea; now their overwhelming vastness is in view and implicitly taken as windows to Yahweh's power. These vast entities that extend as if forever are pictures of enduring stability divinely caused and maintained. Israel, sinful though it had been and so troubled in heart about Yahweh's negative reaction (cf. 14:19), could rest assured: "God is greater than our hearts" (1 John 3:20; cf. Eph 3:18–19). The rejection represented by Yahweh's earlier work of judgment (Jer 6:30; 7:29; cf. 14:19) was over.

[38–40] The final proclamation of salvation has Jerusalem as its subject. Its prosaic subject matter exemplifies the grounding of spirituality in the material and mundane. This passage provides climax to a topic that has kept on surfacing in this compositional block, the importance of Zion in Yahweh's purposes and in Israel's future (30:17; 31:6, 12, 23). The epithet "sacred mountain" (v. 23) is developed here, and the motif of building (vv. 4, 28; cf. 30:18) is applied to a capital languishing in ruins. Even the disreputable area to the south of the city would be redeemed and incorporated as a consecrated zone. The city itself would regain its old status as God's own city (Ps 48:1–2, 8 [2–3, 9]). The verses include a nostalgic knowledge of urban topography. Though the details are not clear, the intent seems to be to sketch the city limits apart from the temple area in the northeast sector that was already consecrated. The places mentioned in v. 38 cover the western extent of the north wall from east to west. The two places in v. 39 are unknown, but presumably represent the western side of the city. In v. 40 the broad "valley" is the Valley of (Ben) Hinnom on the southwest, which stretches around to Wadi Kidron on the southeast. In turn the latter extends north and marks the eastern boundary of the city. The Horse Gate was probably in the middle of the eastern wall of the city.[268] The Valley of Hinnom (7:31–32) is the site of a pagan sanctuary; the "corpses" assume a fulfillment of the prediction in 7:33. The "altar ashes" are presumably associated with the non-Yahwistic cult; the "fields" of Wadi Kidron were used as a rubbish dump according to 2 Kgs 23:4, 6. The defiled area would no more exist as an affront to Yahweh; the sanctity of the temple was to extend even there. This southern area, and with it doubtless the whole city, would share in the blessing of building (cf. v. 38) and planting promised in v. 28, and nevermore lose it. "Once more" (MT) echoes a framing feature of the previous composition (vv. 4–5, 23).

The Letter to the Hebrews has in view a "heavenly Jerusalem" (12:22), rather than the earthly one of this oracle, but at least vv. 31–34 are applied in the letter to a Jewish-Christian group. Elsewhere in the NT their beneficiaries are a mostly Gentile church, presupposing the eschatological admission of the

---

268. For vv. 38–40 see the discussion in Jan J. Simons, *Jerusalem in the Old Testament* (Leiden: Brill, 1952), 231–33; cf. *Macmillan Bible Atlas*, maps 114 and 169.

nations into God's elect community (cf. Jer 4:2; 12:14–17; 16:19–21), whereby each part of the two-sided covenant formula might be applied to them (Isa 25:9; Zech 2:11 [15]). There are hints, however, of a cherished expectation of a more literal fulfillment in the NT. In Acts 1:6 the disciples' question to the risen Jesus, "Is this the time when you will restore the kingdom to Israel?" is not dismissed out of hand but regarded as irrelevant for their immediate ministry. According to Luke 21:24 the trampling of Jerusalem by Gentiles had a time limit that echoes the reconstructive program of Dan 8:13–14 (cf. Rev 11:2).[269] And Paul concludes a discussion of Israel's spiritual future in Romans 9–11 with a passage that, though primarily dependent on other OT texts, reads remarkably like a digest of Jer 31:31–40, even finding room for Zion: "All Israel will be saved . . . 'Out of Zion will come the Deliverer. . . . And this is my covenant with them, when I take away their sins'" (Rom 11:26–27).

Jeremiah 31:27–40 predicts the permanent restoration and blessing of Israel and Judah and their former capital and a transcendent realization of the covenant relationship. Subsequent history proved very different. The postexilic return to the land failed to live up to its promise. Yet it marks the inauguration of the biblical eschatological program.[270] More serious is the nonreturn of the northerners. Hosea too had looked forward to the eventual homecoming of the northern exiles in renewed fellowship with God (Hos 2:14–23 [16–25]), while Ezekiel predicted a reunited kingdom by means of the symbolic action of two sticks held end to end to represent a scepter (Ezek 37:15–24a).[271] This expectation evidently fired the Chronicler's postexilic conviction that northern Yahwists should be accepted by Judah, for example, his portraying an Israel made up of twelve tribes (1 Chronicles 1–8) and adapting Neh 11:4 by slipping "Ephraim and Manasseh" into 1 Chr 9:3. And it doubtless underlay the early Christian mission to Samaria (Acts 1:8; 8:5–23; cf. John 4:1–42).

32:1–33:26 Covenant-Centered Joy

32:1–44 Hope against Hope

32:1 A message received by Jeremiah from Yahweh in the tenth year of the reign of King Zedekiah *of Judah*, which was Nebuchadnezzar's eighteenth year. 2 *At the time* the king of Babylon's army was besieging

---

269. See in general Richard Bauckham, "The Restoration of Israel in Luke-Acts," in *Restoration: Old Testament, Jewish, and Christian Perspectives* (ed. James M. Scott; Journal for the Study of Judaism Supplements 72; Leiden: Brill, 2001), 435–87.

270. See Willem VanGemeren, *Interpreting the Prophetic Word* (Grand Rapids: Zondervan, 1990), 186–87, 208–9.

271. See Allen, *Ezekiel 20–48*, 192–93, 195–96. Cf. in general David C. Greenwood, "On the Jewish Hope for a Restored Northern Kingdom," *ZAW* 88 (1976): 376–85.

Covenant-Centered Joy

Jerusalem and *the prophet* Jeremiah was being detained in a guarded courtyard at the king *of Judah*'s palace, 3 where King Zedekiah *of Judah* had detained him after questioning why he had been prophesying as follows: "Here is what Yahweh said: 'Look out, I am going to hand over this city to the king of Babylon, who will capture it, 4 while *King* Zedekiah *of Judah* will not manage to escape the Chaldeans' hands. Instead, he will be handed right over to the king of Babylon, who[a] will interview him in person and confront him directly, 5 and Babylon is where he will take Zedekiah and there he will stay[b] until I turn my attention to him,' declared Yahweh. 'Though you [all] fight the Chaldeans, you will not succeed!'"[c]

6 Jeremiah reported, "I received[d] the following message from Yahweh: 7 'Look, Hanamel, your uncle Shallum's son, is going to visit you with a request that you buy his field in Anathoth since you have the right to purchase as redeemer.' 8 My cousin Hanamel did visit me, *in line with Yahweh's message,* in the guarded courtyard. He duly asked me, 'Buy my field in Anathoth, in the Benjamin region. Because you have the right of ownership in your role as redeemer, buy it yourself.'[e] This was what Yahweh's message was referring to, I realized.[f] 9 So I bought the field from my cousin Hanamel, *the one in Anathoth,* weighing out[g] for him seventeen silver shekels. 10 I also signed[h] a deed, sealed it, and got it witnessed before weighing out the silver in scales. 11 Then I took the purchase deed, in the form of a sealed one *containing the terms and conditions* and an open one, 12 and gave the purchase deed[i] to Baruch ben Neriah ben Mahseiah in front of my cousin[j] Hanamel, the witnesses[k] who had signed[l] the purchase deed, and *all* the Judeans who were present in the guarded courtyard. 13 I gave Baruch instructions in front of them, 14 'Here is what Yahweh Almighty, *Israel's God,* said. Take *these deeds,* this purchase deed, both the sealed one[m] and the[n] open document, and put them in an earthenware jar so they last a long time.[o] 15 The reason is that here is what Yahweh *Almighty, Israel's God,* said: "Once more will houses, fields, and vineyards[p] be bought in this country."'

16 "I prayed to Yahweh after giving the purchase deed to Baruch ben Neriah, 17 'Oh no, Lord Yahweh, *look,* you it was who made sky and earth by your great power and with your outstretched arm, so nothing is impossible for you, 18 who show loyal love to thousands and pay into children's pockets recompense for parents' earlier wrongdoing, great and powerful God—Yahweh *Almighty is his name*—[q] 19 great planner and expert performer, you whose eyes are so *open*[r] to what*ever* humans do that you can allot to individuals what their behavior warrants, *what their conduct deserves,* 20 you who provided signs and portents in Egypt [and have continued to do so] down to the present both in Israel and among people generally, winning for yourself the renown you still have right now,[s] 21 and

you brought your people Israel out of Egypt with signs and portents, with strong hand and outstretched arm, and with fearsome exploits, 22 and then you gave them this country, the one you had promised their forebears on oath *to give them*, a country awash with milk and honey, 23 and they came in and took it over, but they failed to obey you or base their life journeys on your torah requirements—everything you had ordered them *to do* they have failed to do—and so you have made all this bad fate happen to them. 24 Look, mounds have been brought to the city for its capture, and the city is virtually handed over to the Chaldeans who are fighting it and it suffers the impact of sword, and famine, *and pestilence*. What you threatened has come true, *as you see*. 25 Yet you it was, *Lord Yahweh*, who told me to buy the field myself, paying silver, and to get it witnessed—when the city is handed over to the Chaldeans!'"

26 Then Jeremiah received the following message from Yahweh: 27 "*Look*, I am Yahweh, God of all living. Is anything impossible for me? 28 Therefore"—here is what Yahweh said—"look out, I am handing this city over to *the Chaldeans and to* King *Nebuchadnezzar* of Babylon, and he will capture it, 29 whereupon the Chaldeans who are fighting this city will come in and set this city on fire, burning *it* down *together with* the houses where sacrifices have been made on the roof to Baal and libations poured to their gods, making me upset. 30 In fact the people of Israel and Judah since their earliest years have continually done nothing but what I regard as bad—*yes, the people of Israel too made me terribly upset at the objects their hands had made*," declared Yahweh. 31 "Indeed, my anger and fury has been so roused *for me* by this city,[t] ever since it was built and right up to now, that I have to remove it from my presence 32 because of all the bad behavior of the people of Israel and Judah, making me upset at them—their kings, their administrators, their priests and prophets, and people in Judah and residents of Jerusalem. 33 They have turned their backs on me instead of their faces toward me, and, though I repeatedly tried to teach them, they would not listen and accept correction. 34 Instead they have put their detestable images in the temple that goes by my name, defiling it. 35 They have built the Baal shrines that are in Ben Hinnom Valley, burning their sons and daughters in honor of Molech—something I never sanctioned for them, something that never crossed my mind, that they should do such an abominable thing and so cause Judah to sin. 36 The main point *therefore* is"[u]—here is what Yahweh, Israel's God, said about *this* city you [all] describe as handed over to the king of Babylon by means of sword, famine, and pestilence— 37 "Look, I am going to collect them from all the countries I will have driven them away to in my anger and fury and in extreme rage and, bringing them back to this place, I will settle them securely 38 and they will be my people and I in turn will be

Covenant-Centered Joy

their God. 39 I will give them one mind and one way of life so they always revere me, so it goes well with them and their children after them,ᵛ 40 and thus I will make an everlasting covenant with them, in that I will not give up on them *in doing them good* and I will instill reverence for me in their minds so they will not stop relying on me. 41 I will enjoy doing them good, and I will plant them in this country out of faithfulness, doing it with all my heart and soul. 42 In fact"—here is what Yahweh said—"just as I have brought on this people all this overwhelming bad fate, so I am going to bring about for them all the good I am promising them. 43 Landᵂ will be bought in *this* country that you [all] describe as desolate, devoid of humans and animals, and handed over to the Chaldeans. 44 Fields will be bought for silver, and people will write deeds, seal them, and get them witnessed in the Benjamin region, in the vicinity of Jerusalem and in the towns of Judah, towns in the hill country, in the Shephelah, and in the Negeb, because I will restore their fortunes," *declared Yahweh.*

a. For the subject see Andrew G. Shead, *The Open Book and the Sealed Book: Jeremiah 32 in Its Hebrew and Greek Recensions* (JSOTSup 347; London: Sheffield Academic Press, 2002), 92–93.

b. For this sense of the verb, which LXX (39:5) supports, see BDB 226b.

c. LXX lacks v. 5a*b*-b (*BHS*), but it is essential to the context (see the commentary). There is, however, no obvious reason for its loss. Herbert Migsch, *Gottes Wort über das Ende Jerusalems: Eine literar-, stil- und gattungskritische Untersuchung des Berichtes Jeremia 34, 1–7; 32, 2–5; 37, 3–38, 28* (ÖBS 2; Klosterneuburg: Österreichisches Bibelwerk, 1981), 16, suggests eye slippage from *yhyh* to *(tṣl)yhw*, but the skipping of a line may have been the main cause (cf. Shead, *Open Book*, 102).

d. LXX "Jeremiah received" aligns with v. 1, while in v. 26 LXX has a first person reference, assimilating to v. 25. MT suits the wider context; see the commentary.

e. The brief rendering in LXX (see *BHS*), which may presuppose an indistinct text, interprets *qnh*, "buy," in terms of *zqn*, "be old" (Kilpp, *Niederreissen*, 73 n. 17).

f. Cf. 2 Kgs 9:36; Zech 11:11, cited by Schmid, *Buchgestalten*, 87 n. 158. By its addition of "in line with Yahweh's message" (cf. 13:2) MT reinforces the link with the fulfillment.

g. MT adds to the text represented by LXX *ʾet-hakkesep*, "the silver," with a prefixed object marker, which doubtless originated as a marginal correction or variant of the markerless noun in v. 10 and was wrongly incorporated here. In the new context the addition gained the meaning "price" (REB; cf. Gen 23:16).

h. So NRSV, NIV, REB, GNB. NJPS (cf. NAB, NJB) has "wrote." Cf. v. 12.

i. LXX paraphrases as "it." In MT the first article is ungrammatical. Probably a marginal reading *ʾet-hassēper* was intended as a correction of *ʾet-sēper* in v. 14, and a copyist carelessly corrected the wrong instance.

j. See *BHS* for the corrective restoration to MT.

k. As *BHS* notes, LXX attests *hāʿōmĕdîm*, "who were standing," for *hāʿēdîm*, "the witnesses." The reading was originally a marginal equivalent of *hayyōšĕbîm*, "who were present," later in the verse, but lacking in LXX; however, it was taken as a correction of the similar looking group of consonants and displaced it.

l. NJPS ("were named in") and REB follow another textual tradition of vocalization (see *BHS*).

m. The omission in LXX (see *BHS*) is a case of parablepsis (Janzen, *Studies*, 15); the *wāw* may be retained with the sense "both," as in v. 20 (Rudolph 208; most EVV).

n. LXX rightly lacks "this" of MT, wrongly repeated from earlier in the sentence.

o. The plural pronouns are used loosely for the copies of the deed on a single document and are probably original (cf. Migsch, *Jeremias Ackerkauf: Eine Untersuchung von Jeremia 32* [ÖBS 15; Frankfurt am Main: Peter Lang, 1996], 72), while the added "these deeds" in MT has taken the process further (cf. Kilpp, *Niederreissen*, 76 n. 30), perhaps exploiting the singular sense of the plural noun (cf. GKC §124b n. 1).

p. The different order in LXX that puts "fields" first is probably a secondary accommodation to the singling out in v. 44, over against the reconstruction of Holladay 2:204; MT is the more difficult reading.

q. The omitted material does appear in LXX in a conflated text by way of correction (*HUB*; Shead, *Open Book*, 157–64).

r. The shorter text in LXX construes as "eyes are on"; cf. Pss 33:18; 34:15 (16). MT is similar to Zech 12:4 and Job 14:3.

s. For the *kap veritatis* see John Goldingay, "*kayyôm hazzeh*, 'on this very day'; *kayyôm*, 'on the very day'; *kā'ēt*, 'at the very time,'" *VT* 43 (1993): 112–15.

t. Cf. the different formulation in 52:3, borrowed from 2 Kgs 24:20, which accordingly has a different meaning. Joo, *Provocation and Punishment*, 207–8, citing BDB 757b, takes *'al* as "directed toward" a particular goal.

u. See the commentary on 18:11.

v. S. R. Driver, *Revised Translation*, 201; NJPS, taking *ṭôb* as a verb, as in the underlying Deut 5:29.

w. Cf. GKC §126m; Rudolph 212.

Chapters 32–33 form a literary block, as the sequence of oracle reception headings in 32:1 and 34:1 indicate. At an earlier stage of the book, its first chapter capped the series in chs. 26–29, developing the theme of hope beyond exile. Supplementing first with the inserted chs. 30–31 and then with the subsequent stages of 33:1–13 and 14–26 has created a larger body of literature (chs. 30–33), united by the theme of renewed covenant, which is expressed in general terms of hope in chs. 30–31 and in specific expectations of joy in chs. 32–33, namely, the crescendo of divine joy in 32:41 and the central affirmation of human joy in 33:9–11.

The symbolic action of ch. 32 anchors the proclamations of salvation (chs. 30–31) in Jeremiah's own experience of hope for Judah. This unit falls into four sections, an introductory passage that provides background information (vv. 1–5), Jeremiah's report of a symbolic action (vv. 6–15), his perplexed prayer (vv. 16–25), and Yahweh's response (vv. 26–44). The length of the final section and its climactic position indicate that the unit's focus lies there. The perplex-

Covenant-Centered Joy

ity of the third section is mirrored more broadly in the tension between two contrasting motifs that run through the unit, the handing over of Jerusalem to the enemy (vv. 3, 24–25, 28, 36, and 43) and the renewed purchase of land in Judah (vv. 15, 25, and 43–44); the two motifs are also juxtaposed at the end of the third and fourth sections (vv. 25 and 43–44). The latter motif functions as a climax in section two, while the former one is present in sections one, three, and four. The first two sections introduce the motifs separately, suggesting that these sections operate together as preparatory material for the latter two. From another perspective vv. 1–5 prepare for the two following sections by using in vv. 2–5 language that anticipates vv. 8, 12, and 24. So vv. 1–25 as a whole are distinct, paving the way for vv. 26–44. Both perspectives lead to the conclusion that the "message" of v. 1 points forward to v. 26, rather than to v. 6. A further clue to this interpretation is a difference of person; the third person style of v. 26 is related to v. 1, while the first person version in v. 6 ties the oracle reception statement closely to the adjacent first person report of vv. 8–15. Moreover, the "second message" of 33:1 corresponds in its content to a counterpart in 32:26–44, while the third person style of its oracle reception statement corresponds to 32:26.

[32:1–5] A first person account (vv. 6–25), supplied with an introductory passage that picks up the account's factual clues, sets them against a more explicit background. The "guarded courtyard" of vv. 8 and 12 is the focus of v. 2b and the reason for Jeremiah's detention there is given in vv. 3–5. Likewise, the siege conditions imposed by "the Chaldeans" upon Jerusalem in v. 24 are elaborated a little in v. 2a and given grim heightening in vv. 3–5. Verse 1 offers a regnal date formula, but the stage of the siege is left unclarified. Such generality about Jeremiah's prophetic activity also marks v. 3. However, the content of the prophecy offers details about the outcome of the siege, depicting a dark prospect that enhances the overall contrast of darkness and light represented in vv. 6–25.

[1] The year in question is March/April 588–March/April 587. Like the synchronism in MT at 25:1, this one is a year off; Nebuchadnezzar's eighteenth year ran from 587 to 586 according to Babylonian chronology.

[2] The "guarded courtyard" in the palace grounds functioned as an open prison (McKane 2:837). The location will be prominent in chs. 37–39 (37:21; 38:6, 13, 28; 39:15), but the historical relation of this episode to them is left unclarified. MT adds "the prophet," reinforcing Jeremiah's role in v. 3.

[3–5] The text focuses on the king's protest to Jeremiah's prophesying rather than its commissioning or delivery.[272] The prophecy is duly cited; it is an announcement of disaster delivered to the people, according to the Hebrew plural "you" (v. 5). It relates Yahweh's intervention and a series of grim consequences, first for the city and then at length for the king, with the final

---

272. Applegate, "Narrative Patterns," 79–80.

consequence reverting to the city in the form of its citizens ("you"). Its structure is a double sequence of "the king of Babylon," "Zedekiah," and "the Chaldeans,"[273] which leaves Zedekiah a victim trapped between victors, while the doubling stamps the fate of king and city as beyond all doubt. The details of Zedekiah's fate echo 34:2–5, which is set within an oracle addressed to the king, and retain its positive conclusion. That the abbreviated reference is a positive one is indicated both by the content of 34:4–5 and by the usage of the verb in 29:10 and in MT's addition at 27:22.[274]

[6–15] A report of a symbolic action follows, the only positive one in the book. It is presented as a first person account, which is typical of this genre (see 13:1–18; 16:1; 27:2, 12, 16; 35:3–5; cf. 18:3–5). The initial third person reference smooths the transition from vv. 1–5. The report will be continued with a prayer of response introduced in the first person at v. 16. The three constituent elements of a symbolic action, divine command, prophetic performance, and divine interpretation, are scattered through vv. 6–25.

[7] The divine message predicts an imminent event, the visit of Jeremiah's cousin with a request. Report of a command is delayed until v. 25 and of an explanation until v. 15. The delay creates drama, providing punch lines for the symbolic action (v. 15) and for the prayer (v. 25). The narrative continues as if the missing elements were present in v. 7.[275] The cousin's request concerns land belonging to the extended family in Anathoth (cf. 1:1; 11:21–23). Jeremiah is approached as "redeemer," the next of kin responsible for buying back land sold outside the family as a result of personal financial stringency (cf. Lev 25:25–28, 48–49). In this case a preemptive intervention is requested to avoid such a sale.[276] Hanamel's access to the city during the siege is plausible, as McKane (2:838) argues.

[8–10] The predicted visit duly takes place, and so Jeremiah carries out the presupposed instructions that will be revealed to readers at v. 25. The report creates an impression of scrupulous commitment to legal formalities so that there could be no question of denying the transfer of property. "Jeremiah appears as a true 'contrarian,' like an investor who buys shares of stock when prices appear to have hit bottom."[277]

---

273. Migsch, *Gottes Wort*, 119.

274. Cf. Christopher Begg, "Yahweh's 'Visitation' of Zedekiah," *ETL* 63 (1987): 113–17.

275. Cf. the examples of initial telescoping and subsequent supplementing, which are found in 2 Samuel 14 and 24:11–13 by Meir Sternberg, *The Poetics of Biblical Narrative: Ideological Literature and the Drama of Reading* (Bloomington: Indiana University Press, 1985), 384, and the deferring of information traced in Judges 6–8 by Jan P. Fokkelman, *Reading Biblical Narrative: An Introductory Guide* (trans. I. Smit; Louisville: Westminster John Knox, 2001), 126–30.

276. Friebel, *Sign-Acts*, 326 n. 554.

277. Martin Kessler, "The Judgment-Promise Dialectic in Jeremiah 26–36," *ACEBT* 16 (1977): 60–72, esp. 68.

[11–12] The preservation of the purchase deed is now arranged. Evidently the contract was written out twice on a single document. Half of the document was then rolled up and sealed, while the other half contained an open copy that could be unrolled to inspect the wording of the contract.[278] In MT the sealed form is represented as a fuller version and the open one as a summary, but since such a practice is unknown elsewhere the added phrase may have originated in a marginal qualification relating to the first mention of the deed in v. 10 (Volz 306). Baruch is co-opted as the prisoner's agent in preserving the document. This is the first appearance of someone who will appear again later in the book, notably in ch. 36.

[13–15] Apart from the witnesses to the purchase, a wider audience witnesses a symbolic action, a feature that now comes to the fore and requires as public a performance as possible (cf. Isa 8:1–4). The quotation formula in v. 14 has an anticipatory role, preparing for the actual quotation in v. 15. This usage has been observed a number of times earlier in the book. A precise parallel, with repetition of the formula, occurred in 31:15–16. The instructions of v. 14 are more naturally understood as Jeremiah's own, perhaps presupposing an otherwise unspecified divine command. Preservation in clay jars is attested at Elephantine[279] and Qumran. Here it is undertaken as an expression of confidence in the truth asserted by the symbolic action, which is duly disclosed in v. 15; it is a proclamation of salvation, one that contains blessing rather than deliverance.[280] Jeremiah was acting as harbinger of radically changed times, anticipating an outbreak of peace that would again permit normal property transactions. MT's addition "Israel's God" in vv. 14–15, like the common text at v. 36, hints at covenant blessing as the spiritual setting of the economic promise. Verses 14–15 are a good fit in their broader literary context. "Once more" triumphantly echoes a literary frame for ch. 31 (31:4, 23), while "a long time," though different in Hebrew wording, reminds the attentive reader of the length of the exile in 29:28 and so of the seventy years of 29:10. However, the more snugly these verses fit that context, the harder it is to understand the perplexity of the following prayer. Readers are meant to view the text against two horizons, a wider one that spans generations and an immediate focus on the siege and its aftermath. In the latter case the preservation of the purchase deed was presumably meant to survive the risks posed by a long siege culminating in conflagration.

[16–25] It is against that immediate perspective that Jeremiah's prayer springs from the symbolic action as a personal response, unfinished business between the prophet and his God, though vv. 36 and 43 in the divine reply suggest a

---

278. For such practices at Elephantine at the end of the fourth century and the beginning of the third century B.C.E. and elsewhere, see Friebel, *Sign-Acts*, 329 n. 543.

279. Bezalel Porten, *Archives from Elephantine: The Life of an Ancient Jewish Military Colony* (Berkeley: University of California Press, 1968), 191.

280. Westermann, *Prophetic Oracles*, 157.

subsequent public announcement that clarifies the significance of the action. In the prayer basic material comes at beginning and end, in vv. 17 and 24–25. Prose sermonic language, including literary quotations, is manifest in vv. 18–23.[281] A description of divine attributes appears (vv. 18–20) and then a historical version of an oracle of disaster—reason and reprisal—(v. 23a*b*-b), preceded (vv. 21–23a*a*) by an account of divine grace that made the reason so heinous and the reprisal so necessary. Along with vv. 29b–35, vv. 18–23 offer answers to Zedekiah's question "Why?" in v. 3 (cf. Fretheim 453–54). This redactional material takes its cue from the editorial question-and-answer formulations (5:19; 9:12–14 [11–13]; 16:10–12; 22:8–9). It reaffirms the interpretation of the tragedy of 587 B.C.E. as a valid expression of the divine will.

[17] After the introduction and a reference to the crucial vv. 11–15, the prayer begins (v. 16) with the cry "Oh no, Lord Yahweh," a standard expression of protest in the book (1:6; 4:10; 14:13). In the last two cases the protest has related to Jeremiah's besetting problem, the rival ministry of *šālôm* prophets. Does such a context underlie this complaint? If that were the case, an extra reason appears for adding chs. 32–33 to material in chs. 27–29—the issue of true and false prophecy. Was Jeremiah afraid that he had just been constrained to deliver a Hananiah-type message, to be followed by a relatively quick return to normality (cf. 28:2–4)?[282] If so, the basic prayer of v. 17 politely leaves that option open to an all-powerful God, but proceeds to doubt it as fundamentally inconsistent; it is somewhat like Abraham's challenge to God in Gen 18:25–26. The editorial enlargement of the prayer will focus on divine power, but push it in a negative direction, in accord with the negativity in the introduction to the unit (vv. 3b–5). Both passages pave the way for a partial answer (vv. 28–35) in the divine response. Thereby Jeremiah's former messages of disaster (v. 24b) receive solid affirmation. The appeal to Yahweh's role as Creator, here as evidence of divine power, recalls 27:5, especially in its amalgamation of creation and exodus language.

[18–20] Three sketches of divine attributes minister to a destructive power, implicitly or explicitly. The first (v. 18) links divine power to a collective moral framework that leans toward a punitive element. It largely consists of two quotations, from the hymnic Exod 34:7 and from Deut 10:17. MT's addition, basically from Jer 33:2, contributes to the hymnic flavor, but at the expense of an awkward switch to the third person. The second sketch (v. 19) continues a moral emphasis, but now in individual terms and with negative language, which MT supplements from 17:10. The third (v. 20) refers to Yahweh's acts of judgment, a consistent feature in human history, from the Egyptian plagues onward.

---

281. See Stulman, *Prose Sermons*, 94–99.
282. Cf. Terence E. Fretheim, "Is Anything Too Hard for God? (Jeremiah 32:27)," *CBQ* 66 (2004): 231–36, esp. 233.

[21-23] "Signs and portents" are a bridging element between divine attributes and Yahweh's historical relations with Israel. The allusion to the exodus derives from Deut 4:34, while the description of the promised land comes from Deut 26:15. Divine grace is mentioned to enhance Israel's history of ingratitude, gross enough to warrant the calamity of 587.

[24-25] These verses attest to the anomaly of the positive message of the symbolic action in the context of a catastrophic siege, a fulfillment of earlier prophecy. Verses 18-23 argued the validity of such prophecy. Mounds of earth piled against the walls meant the city was doomed. MT has fittingly framed the prayer by repeating from v. 17 the phrase "Lord Yahweh" with its undertones of protest.

[26-44] The divine reply that resolves Jeremiah's consternation is the focus of the unit. After v. 27 it falls into three parts (vv. 28-35, 36-41, and 42-44), each introduced by the quotation formula. The reply exhibits prose sermonic terminology, just like the prayer, from v. 29b through at least v. 41.[283] Accordingly the initial announcement of disaster (vv. 28-29a) and the closing proclamation of salvation (vv. 42-44) have been amplified by vv. 29b-35 and 36-41. Earlier in the commentary I suggested that at times the quotation formula is used to introduce the material of a redactor prophet, and this may be its role at v. 36. Verse 42 represents a structural climax, as a dual summary for the negative and positive poles set out earlier.

[27] The opening precisely matches v. 17. A self-introduction formula introduces Yahweh as the Creator and counters Jeremiah's politely confrontational statement with a provocative question.

[28-30] "Therefore" glides into an unfolding of God's power at work in the future; MT will resume it at v. 36. The announcement of disaster is similar to vv. 3 and 24, echoing the key negative motif of the unit, Yahweh's handing over of the city to the enemy. Divine intervention was to trigger a host of tragic consequences. Two reasons for the disaster are given in vv. 29b-30, affirming and amplifying v. 23. The first repeats charges of pagan worship in Jerusalem made in earlier prose sermons at 7:9; 11:12-13; and 19:4 (a sinister reference to houses). The second reason (v. 30a) is projected on a much larger screen, specifying culprits and their activity. Pagan worship is still in view, as comparison with 7:30 confirms. MT's addition (v. 30b) satisfies a need to explain the sudden introduction of the northern kingdom into the argument; the addition has used 25:6-7, but redirected it from Judah to Israel. The closing quotation formula in MT marks the end of vv. 28-30.

[31-35] The formal pattern of vv. 28-30 is repeated, an oracle of disaster, with an announcement of disaster (v. 31) and reasons for it (vv. 32-35). Israel again appears, but now fleetingly in v. 32, while most of its accusations are related to Jerusalem and Judah. The joint accusation concerning Israel and

---

283. See again Stulman, *Prose Sermons*, 94-99.

Judah's past (vv. 30 and 32) may be compared with their occurrence in chs. 30–31 as future joint beneficiaries of Yahweh's restoring work. The denunciations (vv. 33–35) repeat a series encountered earlier (7:25, 28, 30, and 31) and so function as a summary.

[36–41] What precedes is only half of the story of the divine purpose; the second, positive half is now disclosed. The total message matches the theme of future reversals of past reprisals that pervaded 30:1–31:1. In the introductory v. 36 the key negative motif of the unit is echoed and put in a context of communal lament that now receives an answer. What follows in vv. 37–41 has little to do with the city; it concerns the country and people. The city has a representative role; a similar progression from city to country was a feature of the previous part of the divine answer.

[37–41] The proclamation of salvation is carefully constructed, with a frame (vv. 37 and 41) and a covenant-dominated central passage (vv. 38–40).[284]

[37] Yahweh's "anger and fury" is resumed from v. 31, but amplified with "extreme rage" to accommodate Yahweh's ultimate reprisal of deportation for the people at large (cf. 21:5). Indeed, not simply Babylonian exile but a diaspora is envisioned, only to be reversed. The redactional promise, which looks far beyond a siege situation, is familiar to readers of the book; notably this one reads like a fusion of 16:15 and its parallel 23:8. "This place" refers to the country, in contrast to "the countries" and in view of "this country" in the framing counterpart at v. 41.

[38–40] "My people" picks up "your people" in v. 21. The covenant formula announces the topic of vv. 38–40. The formula has appeared in the book with this order at 11:4, and 24:7, and also in MT at 30:22, and in a reverse order at 7:23; 31:1, 32. Its future significance is enthusiastically defined in vv. 39–40, in terms of divine intervention and its human consequences (v. 39) and a statement of its implications (v. 40). The definition is generally parallel to 31:33–34 in eschatological content, but different terminology is used here, including reverence (cf. 5:22, 24) and a monotheistic mind-set that reverses the polytheism of vv. 29b–30, 32–35. The divine yearning of Deut 5:29 was to come true. This definition again stresses God's role and so provides a similar answer to the problem of a spiritual bridge that kept breaking down at the human end (11:10; 31:32). The emphasis on divine blessing as "good" (vv. 39 ["well"], 41, 42; accentuated in MT at v. 40) counters the "bad" punishment of v. 23, as v. 42 will make clear. The cardinal point is that Yahweh's spiritual engineering would bring its own guarantee of permanence.

[41] Yahweh's commitment to partnership is poignantly brought to the fore. The first clause is a quotation from Deut 30:9 (NRSV "The LORD will again take

---

284. Cf. Schmid, *Buchgestalten*, 101 n. 230; and Migsch, *Jeremias Ackerkauf*, 232–35, who both find a chiastic structure.

delight in prospering you"), while the unique phrase "with all my heart and soul" spoken by God was triggered by its proximity at Deut 30:10. A counterpart to v. 37 is provided, matching its settling with planting and "this place" with "this country" and offsetting strong negative emotion with equally strong positive passion. Covenant and land-related blessing are two sides of the same coin.

[42–44] The reply is rounded off in this third part by a summary of the teaching (vv. 27–41) and a reverting to the significance of the symbolic action that sparked the discussion. Some prose sermonic elements appear in vv. 42 and 43 and in v. 44b.[285]

[42] The comparison matches 31:28, but whereas that one appealed for support to 1:10, 12, this one simply repeats the "good" and "bad" contrasts of vv. 23 and 39–41 (cf. Zech 8:14–15). It exploits the massive tradition of divine judgment presented earlier in the book and correlates it with the divine promises of reversal and restoration as equally weighty and certain of fulfillment.[286] The threatened "bad experience" had come true (vv. 23–24), and so the promised "good" was sure to happen. It was with such confidence that Rabbi Akiba took encouragement from the ruins of the Second Temple, reasoning that now it only remained for God's promises to come true.[287]

[43] A further allusion is made to a communal lament. This time the land rather than the city is in view, and it is defined as "devoid of humans and animals." This conception of an empty land during the exile serves the purposes of the Babylonian exiles in the book and suggests that the exiled redactor prophet was now responding directly to the concerns of his contemporaries.[288]

[44] The divine settling and planting are now expressed in the mundane form of real estate transactions. Jeremiah's example (vv. 9–10) points to Judah's future, and the promise of v. 15 is graphically restated. His deal "in the Benjamin region" (v. 8) provides a prototype for what would happen throughout Judah (cf. 17:26; 33:13). The divine backing for such consequences is reaffirmed in the closing formulation, encountered earlier at 30:3 and 31:23, and also in MT at 29:14, which defines Yahweh as the dynamic agent of renewal.

Chapter 32 justifies Jeremiah's seemingly bizarre symbolic action at such a historical moment. It was not a contradiction of his earlier messages of disaster,

---

285. See Stulman, *Prose Sermons*, 34 (no. 10), 39 (no. 51), 42 (no. 73).
286. Levin, *Verheissung*, 175.
287. *B. Mak.* 24b.
288. See Nicholson, *Preaching*, 131–33. For the relation of the motif of the empty land to history, see on the one hand Hans M. Barstad, "After the 'Myth of the Empty Land': Major Challenges in the Study of Neo-Babylonian Judah," 3–20, and on the other Bustenay Oded, "Where Is the 'Myth of the Empty Land' to Be Found? History versus Myth," 55–74, in *Judah and the Judeans in the Neo-Babylonian Period* (ed. O. Lipschits and J. Blenkinsopp; Winona Lake, Ind.: Eisenbrauns, 2003).

but a confirmation paradoxically based on them. God's power to destroy was also available for renewal and restoration, which were guaranteed by Yahweh's deep commitment to the covenant between God and people.

33:1–26 Jerusalem's Role in the Reversal

33:1 Jeremiah received the following as a second message from Yahweh during his confinement in the guarded courtyard: 2 "Here is what was said by Yahweh who gets things[a] done, *Yahweh* who plans them[a] to make sure they happen—Yahweh is his name: 3 'Give me a call and in reply I will tell you important, secret[b] matters that are unknown to you. 4 For example'—here is what Yahweh, *Israel's God,* said about this city's houses and those of the Judean kings that have been demolished to resist the mounds and sword— 5 'people are coming forward[c] in order to fight with the Chaldeans—and to fill them with the corpses of men whom I will have killed in my furious anger, all their bad behavior having made me hide my face from *this city*.[d] 6 Look, I am going to cure its wounds and bring healing. I will heal them and bring to light for them peace and stability aplenty.[e] 7 I will restore the fortunes of Judah and Israel and rebuild them to their former condition. 8 I will also cleanse them from all their wrongdoing they did in sinning against me, forgiving *all* their wrongdoings they did in sinning against me and rebelling against me. 9 It will become *for me* a focus of joy*ful renown,* of praise and glory expressed by all the nations in the world, as they hear about all the good I am doing *for them* and react with awe and trembling to all the good and all the peace I am providing for it." 10 Here is what Yahweh said: "Once more there will be heard in this place that you describe as ruined and devoid of humans and animals, in Judah's towns and in Jerusalem's streets that lie desolated and devoid of humans[f] and animals, 11 sounds of joy and gladness, shouts of bridegroom and bride, and the cries of people singing,

'Give thanks to Yahweh Almighty
  because Yahweh is good,
  because his loyal love lasts forever,'

as they bring thank offerings to Yahweh's temple. The reason is that I will restore the fortunes of the country to its former condition," said Yahweh. 12 Here is what Yahweh *Almighty* said: "Once more there will be in this place, which is now ruined *and devoid of humans and even animals,*[g] and in all its towns pastures for shepherds to settle their flocks in. 13 In the towns of the hill country, of the Shephelah, and of the Negeb, and in the Benjamin region, in the vicinity of Jerusalem, and in Judah's towns, once more flocks will pass under the hands of those who are counting them," said Yahweh.

14 "Look, a time is coming," declared Yahweh, "when I will bring to realization the promise of good I have made about the communities of Israel and Judah. 15 At that time, at that juncture, I will cultivate a right-dealing scion of David, who will do what is just and right countrywide. 16 At that time Judah will enjoy salvation, while Jerusalem will live securely, and here is what it will be called: 'Yahweh-Is-Our-Righteousness.' 17 The explanation is that"—here is what Yahweh said—"the line of David will not lack a male representative who occupies the throne of Israel's community 18 nor will the priests of Levi lack the continuity of a male representative in my presence who offers whole offerings, burns grain offerings, and performs sacrifices."

19 Jeremiah received the following message from Yahweh: 20 Here is what Yahweh said: "If you [all] can break my covenant with the day and my covenant with the night,[h] so[i] daytime[j] and night do not come when they should, 21 then also my covenant may be broken with my servant David, so he no more has a son reigning on his throne, and also with the men of Levi, the priests who minister to me.[k] 22 Just as the mass [of stars] in the sky cannot be counted and the sand by the sea cannot be measured, such is the degree to which I will multiply the numbers of the line of my servant David and of the men of Levi who minister to me."

23 Jeremiah received the following message from Yahweh: 24 "Are you unaware of what this people has been saying, 'The two clans chosen by Yahweh have been rejected by him'? They are writing off my people, considering[l] it a nation no more." 25 Here is what Yahweh said: "If my covenant with daytime and night does not exist[m] [and if] the regular features of sky and earth were not placed there by me, 26 then also the lines of Jacob and of my servant David will be rejected by me so his line is not a source for rulers over the line of Abraham, Isaac, and Jacob. Indeed,[n] I will restore their fortunes and show them compassionate love."

a. The suffixes refer neither to the earth (LXX 40:2) nor to Jerusalem (Calvin 4:228–30), but are neuter (Ehrlich, *Randglossen*, 4:327; NJPS); cf. Isa 22:11; 46:11. The secondary text of LXX, which assimilates to Isa 45:18, encouraged by Jer 32:17, is followed by the other six EVV.

b. Literally "inaccessible," here to knowledge (Rudolph 214).

c. Cf. NAB, NJPS. LXX hardly omits (*BHS*), but somehow combines with v. 4 (*HUB*).

d. LXX "them." MT provides a nearer antecedent for "its" in v. 6 than v. 4.

e. See *HALOT* 2:906b.

f. LXX lacks MT's intrusion "and without inhabitant" into this fixed formulation. It doubtless originated as a marginal comment comparing 26:9 concerning Jerusalem and/or 34:22 concerning Judah's towns.

g. This material absent from LXX may have originated as a variant of the last six words of v. 10, adapted from 51:62, which has entered the text at a similar point (cf. Janzen, *Studies*, 50). It is not unfitting here.

h. Cf. Lev 26:42 and Joüon §129a n. 4.

i. See *BHS* and now 4Q72 (DJD 15:200).

j. See *DCH* 4:186a for the form of noun here and in v. 25.

k. For the unusual Hebrew see Joüon §§121k n. 1, 129m.

l. Literally "before them," with the sense "in their estimation"; it is an ironic replacement for *lĕpānay*, "before me, in my presence," in 31:36 (cf. Goldman, *Prophétie et royauté*, 33–34; Schmid, *Buchgestalten*, 65). It was taken in the sense "in my estimation"; it has influenced the textual tradition here (see *BHS*).

m. The awkward Hebrew is resolved by the emendation in *BHS*, which is followed by NJB ("I have not created"; cf. NEB). Yet a cosmic covenant does fit the context (Pierluigi Piovanelli, "JrB 33, 14–26 ou la continuité des institutions à l'époque maccabéenne," in *The Book of Jeremiah and Its Reception: Le livre de Jérémie et sa réception* [ed. A. H. W. Curtis and T. Römer; BETL 128; Leuven: Leuven University Press, 1997], 255–76, esp. 266); cf. GKC §159v for a noun clause in a protasis.

n. So NJPS.

This chapter celebrates Jerusalem as the key to Yahweh's purposes for Israel. It consists of six proclamations of salvation, divided into two sets of three (vv. 1–13 and 14–26). The division is more radical than the flow of MT and EVV suggests inasmuch as vv. 14–26 are lacking in LXX and belong to the later redaction attested in MT; it is the longest such addition in the book, made "after the divergence of the two text traditions."[289] The unit is a supplement to ch. 32, tightly linked to it by v. 1. It is presented as a sequel to the revelation of 32:26–44, or more precisely to its positive second half in vv. 36–44, and continues a pattern of moving from Jerusalem (v. 36) to the people at large (vv. 37–44). Jeremiah 33:14–26 reflects on 30:1–33:13 and develops certain aspects of it.

[33:1–13] After the general introduction (vv. 1–3), in which the personal oracle to Jeremiah begins with a quotation formula (v. 2), the passage is made up of three specific proclamations of salvation also introduced by a quotation formula in each case (vv. 4–9, 10–11, 12–13). The symbolic action of 32:6–16, 24a is no longer in clear view. Instead, the wider setting of the siege of Jerusalem that was an ongoing concern in ch. 32 (vv. 2–3, 24, 25b, 28–29, 36, 43) comes to the fore in 33:4–5 (cf. vv. 10, 12) as the focus of reversal; it is a motif by no means unrelated to the symbolic action. The second and third of the three proclamations loudly echo the note of renewed continuity, "once more" (vv. 10, 12, 13), sounded in the interpretation of the symbolic action at 32:15. The return to a "former condition" in the first and second proclamations (vv. 7, 11) is comparable. Other material from ch. 32 is resumed and developed

289. Janzen, *Studies*, 123.

in the passage, so that it is an "elaboration" of ch. 32, "generated by it" (McKane 2:854). There is comparatively little prose sermonic language,[290] and what there is functions as literary quotation, which is a feature of most of the material in vv. 7-13. Verses 3-6 are a core oracle concerning the rebuilding of houses demolished during the siege. It is loosely related to the renewed buying of houses in the interpretation of the symbolic action (32:15).

[1] The editorial introduction harks back to 32:1-2 and so connects with the oracle announced in 32:26.

[2-3] The quotation formula is expanded with a description of Yahweh that closes with a refrain, "Yahweh is his name." The refrain is sometimes associated with Zion as an eschatological symbol, and this connection seems to have caused its presence here.[291] The theological description gives an assurance of the eventual fulfillment of Yahweh's purposes for Jerusalem. The coaxing invitation to Jeremiah alludes to the prayer of 32:16-25, especially the uncertain note of v. 25. He is promised a revelation that, unlike the oracles of disaster the prophet was used to delivering, would take a new and positive turn.

[4-6] A fresh quotation formula explains the occasion and topic of the oracle. The demolition of houses near the city wall was evidently a defensive measure, whether to provide stones and other debris to hurl down on the attackers or to clear sufficient space for defenders to engage them. Such measures are dismissed as doomed, leading only to casualties stored there in the face of deserved divine abandonment, but healing is promised for the city and its houses. For the metaphor one may compare 2 Chr 24:13 and Neh 4:7 (1), where "repairing" reflects the same Hebrew phrase and literally refers to the healing of wounds. The phrase was used of Zion in 30:17 and is now applied to reconstruction.

[7-9] The redactor-prophet amplifies the oracle with five promises that represent the reversal of negative traditions in the book and envision Jerusalem as the key to the people's renewal (cf. 32:29-30, 31-32, 36-37). First, the general language of 32:44b is used and applied to both of the old kingdoms in v. 7a, doubtless via "all the bad behavior" mentioned in 33:5 and linked in 32:32 with Israel and Judah. Second, the literal demolishing in v. 4 triggers a contrasting and metaphorical building in v. 7b, as an echo of the word pair in 24:6; 31:28; 42:10; and 45:4. Third, spiritual renewal is promised in v. 8, reversing the wrongdoing, sinning, and rebelling of 5:6 and 30:14-15 with the cleansing mentioned in exasperation in 13:27 and with the forgiveness of 31:34. Fourth, a frame is provided with v. 6 in v. 9a by reverting to Jerusalem and applying to it the fulfillment of the covenant ideal of 13:11; it is here set in an international context to express the exceptional blessing. MT supplements the allusion by

---

290. See Stulman, *Prose Sermons*, 99-102.
291. Cf. Crenshaw, "Form-Critical Analysis," 171, who cites Isa 48:2 and 51:15-16 and regards this usage as exilic.

adding "renown" from 13:11. The added note of joy (cf. 30:13; 32:41) will be repeated in v. 11. Finally, in v. 9b the "bad behavior" of v. 5 is reversed in the "good" Yahweh was to bestow (cf. 32:42), while the "peace" of v. 6 is echoed in closing.

[10–13] These proclamations of salvation are a pair in view of their common beginning and motif, the reversal of the land's being "devoid of humans and animals," first with respect to humans (vv. 10–11) and then to animals (vv. 12–13). "This place" refers to the land of Judah, as in 32:37, and the phraseology of 32:43 is largely reused.[292]

[10–11] The termination of shouts of happiness in Judah's towns and Jerusalem's streets was foretold in 7:34, while they were banished from "this place" in 16:9. Now the reversal of such eerie silence is celebrated. A new example is added, the singing of the thanksgiving hymn as individuals gathered at the Jerusalem temple for a service in which they thanked Yahweh for deliverance from personal crisis (cf. Pss 100:4–5 and 107:21–22). "Good" reinforces the double use of the noun in v. 9, while "loyal love" recalls 32:18, but now in a more positive context. The closing echo of v. 7 (= 32:44) emphasizes that these happy shouts would occur only as a consequence of Yahweh's own dynamic intervention.

[12–13] Animals too would flourish again, and sheep are chosen as the example of such welcome normality, grazing in pastures and counted to ensure none had strayed. Verse 13 elaborates "in all its towns" in v. 12, referring to the districts listed in 32:44. Such a panorama suitably concludes this litany of future blessings that is a celebratory medley of material from ch. 32 and reversals of divine judgments that appear earlier in the book.

[14–26] This passage is a later supplement to the promises of 30:1–33:13; it reaffirms them and makes them more specific. Verses 14 and 26b provide a general frame. First, Yahweh's good promises in 32:42 are echoed,[293] and their scope is widened to heirs of both of the old political kingdoms, who were mentioned in 30:3; 31:27, 31 (cf. 32:30). In v. 26b there is a closing echo of the announcement of Yahweh's positive intervention that was the leitmotif of these chapters (30:3, 18; 31:23; 32:44; 33:7, 11). The supplement is made up of three proclamations of salvation, vv. 14–18, 19–22, and 23–26. The second

---

292. The influence of Ezek 36:33–38 in the use of *ḥārēb*, "ruined," in vv. 10 and 12 and the Niphal participle, "desolated," in v. 10, over against *šěmāmâ*, lit. "desolation," in 32:43 has been suggested by Alfred Marx, "À propos des doublets du livre de Jérémie: Réflexions sur la formation d'un livre prophétique," in *Prophecy: Essays Presented to Georg Fohrer on His Sixty-Fifth Birthday, 6 September 1980* (ed. J. A. Emerton; BZAW 150; Berlin: de Gruyter, 1980), 106–20, esp. 111.

293. Bernard Gosse, "La nouvelle alliance et les promesses d'avenir, se référant à David dans les livres de Jérémie, Ezéchiel et Isaïe," *VT* 41 (1991): 419–28, esp. 422. Most scholars attempt to relate to 29:10.

and third are closely related, as was the case in vv. 10–11 and 12–13 in the previous passage.

[14–18] Kings and priests, condemned in preexilic contexts, will now have key roles. The oracle reworks 23:5–6, with adaptations both woven into the citation in vv. 14–16 and added separately in the interpretation of vv. 17–18. Monarchy and priesthood are to be vital factors in Israel's future; both are centered on Jerusalem, the first implicitly and the second explicitly.[294] Monarchy was a real but minor concern in 30:1–33:13, appearing in 30:9, 21; the latter text, with its mention of "ruler," will be echoed in the "rulers" of v. 26. Here the sentiments of 23:5–6 become important. It was also an obvious choice in that "their king David whom I will appoint (*ʾāqîm*) for them" in 30:9 is similar to "and I will put in charge (*wahăqīmōtî*) a . . . scion for David" in 23:5.

[14–15] The quotation from 23:5 has been integrated into the introductory general statement of v. 14b; then in v. 15 the text works its way back to 23:5 with a new preface and verb.[295] The old verb is put to fresh use with the sense "I will bring to realization." The continuation of 23:5, apart from abbreviation, makes a small change in that *ṣaddîq*, "righteous" in the sense of "legitimate," is replaced with *ṣĕdāqâ*, "of righteousness" and so "right-dealing," in anticipation of the same noun a little later, rendered "what is right." The double focus on the social justice of the monarchy will be differentiated from a separate meaning given to *ṣedeq*, "righteousness," in v. 16.

[16] The new text removes the original link with monarchy by two changes. First, "in his days" (NRSV) or "in his reign" in 23:6 with reference to David's scion is replaced by "in those days" (NRSV) or "at that time." This is done in order to present a different perspective than v. 14b in reverting to "the days are coming" (NRSV) or "the time is coming" in v. 14a. Second, the royal title is turned into a title for Jerusalem as a consequence of changing "Israel" to "Jerusalem." Why are the royal references replaced? Evidently to make room for the second of the two explanations in vv. 17–18, which is related to priesthood. Verse 15 will be explained in terms of royalty in v. 17, while v. 16 will be given a priestly interpretation in v. 18, in an ABA'B' structuring of text and meaning. A religious role for Jerusalem builds on the promises of 30:1–33:13: the use of its namesake "Zion" in 31:6, 12; Jerusalem's title "righteous home, sacred mountain" in 31:23; and the expanded sanctity of the rebuilt city in 31:38–40. Moreover, "priests" are mentioned in 31:14 and temple worship in

---

294. Johan Lust, "The Diverse Text Forms of Jeremiah and History Writing with Jer 33 as a Test Case," *JNSL* 20 (1994): 31–48, esp. 45, has compared the royal and sacerdotal focus of this passage with the extra references to the temple, palace, and Jerusalem in MT at 27:18, 21, and suggested that in both places the editor "wished to focus attention to the priestly and royal houses as the representatives of Jerusalem."

295. See the layout in Fishbane, *Biblical Interpretation*, 471–72.

33:11. The title "Yahweh-Is-Our-Righteousness" recalls "righteous home" in 31:23. A priestly significance for "salvation" and "righteousness" may be gleaned from Ps 132:9, 16, where the clothing of Yahweh's and Zion's priests with these metaphorical vestments appears to refer to their role in providing oracles of salvation (cf. Pss 24:5, where "vindication" is lit. "righteousness"; 85:9–13 [10–14]).

[17] The interpretations are graced with a quotation formula, here evidently an authentication from a redactor-prophet, as in earlier texts common to LXX and MT. The first interpretation relates to v. 15 and reaffirms the old promise of succession of the Davidic kings in 1 Kgs 2:4; 8:25; and 9:5, now strikingly presented in absolute terms rather than in its earlier conditional setting. Perhaps 1 Kgs 2:4 is especially important, with its particular terminology of promise that forges a link with Jer 33:14.

[18] The interpretation in v. 16 that focuses on priesthood is developed. Here and in vv. 21 and 22 it is consistently given a tribal definition, "Levi," rather than a narrower one of "Aaron" or "Zadok." The royal formula employed in v. 17 is put to new use. The distinctive duty of the priesthood is now defined in sacrificial terms. Burning grain offerings probably refers to part of the morning and evening rituals in the temple (cf. Num 28:1–8; Sir 45:14).[296]

[19–26] If vv. 14–18 were an interpretation of 23:5–6 as a convenient surrogate for 30:9, 21, these two oracles stay within the ensemble of 30:1–33:13 by taking as their point of departure an oracle found in 31:35–37. The protasis and apodosis in vv. 20–21 reflect 31:35–36, and v. 22 has fainter links with 31:37, while vv. 24–25 again use 31:35–36, and v. 26 has a counterpart in 31:37.[297] The basic claim that nature guarantees the covenant—though the term was not used in the earlier text—is left unchanged, but the covenant partners of Yahweh are multiplied in new ways. The ascription of the oracles to Jeremiah (vv. 19 and 23) is unexpected. It presumably springs from the redactor's crediting him with the basic oracles (cf. Ps 72:20; Acts 4:25). The quotation formulas in vv. 20 and 25 reflect those in 31:35, 37 (MT), but they become the voice of the redactor-prophet reworking the primary oracles in Yahweh's name. There is some engagement with a public constituency, directly in the public address in v. 20 and indirectly in the lamenting quotation of v. 24.

[20–21] The motif of covenant was dominant in 30:1–31:40; it was then reinforced in 32:38–40 and in 33:11. Now it is developed further in an application to royal and priestly institutions as jointly participating in a covenant relationship with Yahweh, while the notion of covenant is also related to Yahweh's cosmic rule. The arcing between cosmic time on the one hand and crown and cult

---

296. Cf. Norman Snaith, "Jeremiah xxxiii 18," *VT* 21 (1971): 620–22.
297. See Goldman, *Prophétie et royauté*, 16–21.

on the other in terms of covenant supplies an argument for the permanence of the latter two. The divine covenant with time is one that Israel cannot break! It lacks the fragility of the old national covenant (11:10; 31:32). The tradition of a Davidic covenant is revived, with particular dependence on Psalm 89.[298] A priestly covenant is also mentioned (cf. Num 25:12–13; Deut 33:9; Mal 2:4–9). Monarchy and priesthood are permanent parts of God's plans for Israel.

[22] The transfer of the covenant concept from Israel to nature, royalty, and priesthood prompts a different development on similar lines, now in a comparison. "Stars," "sea" (31:35), and "sky" (31:37) also traditionally appeared in similes for Israel's growth into a great nation (Gen 15:5; 22:17; 32:12 [13]; Hos 1:10 [2:1]). These images too are lavishly reapplied from the covenant with Israel to the covenants with David and Levi's progeny.

[24–26] Verse 24 represents a rhetorical portrayal of complaint within the community as background to the divine answer (vv. 25–26). The genre of a proclamation of salvation overlaps with that of a disputation.[299] The negative thesis of v. 24a is disputed in vv. 25–26a and replaced with a positive counterthesis in v. 26b. It is tempting to interpret the "two clans" in terms of David and Levi, but the sequel in terms of "my people" and the progeny of Jacob and David conspicuously lacks any priestly reference (Rudolph 219). Instead, there is a return to "the communities of Israel and Judah" (v. 14). Although a royal concern persists, a communal need for assurance of Israel's permanence works in tandem with the pull of the original text toward this meaning. Consequently the basic oracle of 31:35–37 is now given a more straightforward interpretation. *Ḥuqqôt*, "statutes, regular features" (cf. *ḥuqqîm*, "regular features," 31:36), parallels "covenant," as in 1 Kgs 11:11. The royal factor persists from v. 21 as an extra confirmation of national survival. The passage fittingly ends with an avowal of Yahweh's coming intervention that reflects a dominant feature of 30:1–33:13. It harks back to 30:18, with its reminder of Yahweh's compassionate love for "Jacob." The allusion generated the use of the name earlier in the verse; that and the patriarchal tradition echoed in v. 22 prompted the list of patriarchs, apt images of survival (cf. Isa 51:2). The issue of Israel's rejection was one that Paul would later wrestle with and need to deny (Rom 11:1).

Can the addition in MT be assigned a date? It may plausibly be regarded as at least early postexilic with a setting in Judah. The pairing of royal and priestly traditions may presuppose the joint leadership of Zerubbabel, the governor of royal lineage, and Joshua, the high priest (Ezra 3:2; 5:2; Hag 1:2; cf. Zechariah

---

298. Lust, "Messianism and the Greek Version of Jeremiah," in *VII Congress of the IOSCS Leuven 1989* (ed. C. E. Cox; SBLSCS 31; Atlanta: Scholars Press, 1991), 87–122, esp. 106–7, citing Timo Veijola. "Covenant" occurs in Ps 89:3, 28, 34, 39 (4, 29, 35, 40) and "servant" in vv. 3, 20, 39 (4, 21, 40); parallels with the natural order occur in vv. 29, 36, 37 (30, 37, 38).

299. Cf. Graffy, *Prophet Confronts His People*, 38–41.

4) or an ideal of government derived from it. The association of the priesthood with Levi is matched in Mal 2:4–9. While the supplement in the common text, vv. 1–13, celebrates the promises of ch. 32 in terms of reversal, the second supplement unique to MT meditates more broadly on the hope expressed in 30:1–33:13 and yet sets a narrower focus on monarchy and priesthood as indispensable elements in a new and permanent Israel.

34:1–51:64 Destruction and Eventual Reconstruction, Part Three

34:1–36:32 The Dangers of Rejecting the Divine Word

34:1–22 Capture of King and Capital: A Reason Why

34:1 A message received by Jeremiah from Yahweh when King Nebuchadnezzar of Babylon and all his army, augmented by all *the kingdoms in* his empire *and all the peoples*, were campaigning against Jerusalem and all its towns, which said: **2** "Here is what Yahweh, *Israel's God,* said: 'Go[a] to King Zedekiah of Judah and tell him, "Here is what Yahweh said: 'Look out, I am going to hand this city over to Babylon's king, who will burn it down. **3** Nor will you escape from his hand; rather, you will be captured—yes, captured—and handed over to him. You will have a direct confrontation with Babylon's king and he will interview you in person,[b] and Babylon is where you will be brought.' **4** However, hear Yahweh's message, King Zedekiah of Judah. Here is what Yahweh said *about you*: '*You will not have death inflicted by the sword,* **5** you will die a peaceful death and, just as your forebears, the previous kings who came before you, had burning ceremonies, the same will be done in your honor, together with public mourning for you with the cry, "So sorry about the sovereign!" Indeed, I *myself* have made a promise,' declared Yahweh."'" **6** So *the prophet* Jeremiah told King Zedekiah *of Judah* all this in Jerusalem, **7** while the army of Babylon's king was campaigning against Jerusalem and *all* Judah's towns *that were left,* namely, Lachish and Azekah, the only fortified towns that remained of Judah's towns.

8 A message received by Jeremiah from Yahweh after King Zedekiah had made a covenant with *all* the people *who were in Jerusalem* that they should make *for themselves*[c] a proclamation of liberty, **9** each promising to let his Hebrew slaves, male and female, go free so that nobody kept[d] a brother [or sister] Judean enslaved. **10** All the officials and all the people *duly listened,* who had entered into the covenant to let the male and female slaves they each had go *free so they were kept enslaved no more. They listened and let them go.* **11** *Later, however,* they turned around *and took back the male and female slaves they had let go free,* forcing them, male and female, to be slaves again. **12** Jeremiah then received Yahweh's message,[e] as follows: 13 "Here is what Yahweh, *Israel's God,* said: 'I made my own covenant with your forebears when I brought them out of Egypt, that slave compound, with the stipulation, 14 "At the end represented by a seventh year"[f] each of you must let go his "Hebrew brother," who "sold himself to you and has served you six years," when "you must let him go free *from your service."* Your *forebears* failed to listen to what I said, turning a deaf ear. 15 You *yourselves* in the present generation have done differently, doing what is right by my standards, by each making a proclamation of liberty to his fellow and covenanting to this effect in my presence, in the temple that goes by my name. 16 Then, however, you turned around and profaned my name by each taking back your male and female slaves you had let go free to live their own lives *and forcing them,* male and female, *to be* your slaves again.' 17 Therefore here is what Yahweh said: 'You for your part would not listen to what I said about making a proclamation of liberty in each case to *your brothers,* your fellow Judeans. Look out, I am going to make a proclamation of liberty where you are concerned,' *declared Yahweh,* 'to sword, pestilence, and famine! I will turn you into people the rest of the kingdoms in the world shudder at. 18 I will hand over the men who have passed up my covenant by failing to implement *the terms of* the covenant they had made in my presence [in the rite of] the calf[g] that they had cut in half and passed between its pieces— 19 the officials from Judah *and those from Jerusalem,* the eunuchs, the priests and *all* the people *of the country,* those who passed between the pieces of the calf, 20 whom I will hand over to their enemies, *to people with designs on their lives,* and their corpses will become forage for birds in the sky and for animals on the ground. 21 King Zedekiah of Judah and his officials will also be handed by me over to their enemies, *to people with designs on their lives,* to the army of Babylon's king that has withdrawn from besieging you. 22 Look out, I am going to give orders,' declared Yahweh, 'and bring them back to this city. Campaigning against it, they will capture it and burn it down, while the towns in Judah I will turn into uninhabited ruins.'"

a. MT adds *wĕʾāmartā,* "and say/tell," to the earlier text represented by LXX (41:2) and it is then repeated. This alternative reflects the usual order (cf., e.g., 28:13; contrast 35:2) by way of correction.

b. The omission of the clause in LXX is due to Greek parablepsis (cf. Janzen, *Studies,* 50; Holladay 2:232). The parallelism is impressive, and in 32:4 there appears to be inverted repetition of the two clauses (see the commentary on 23:34).

c. The suffix is reflexive, a dative of disadvantage (Rudolph 220; cf. Joüon §133d); cf. v. 17b and contrast vv. 15 and 17a.

d. LXX does not represent *bām,* "them," an anticipation of the object that mechanically assimilates to v. 10 (Volz 320). G. R. Driver's suggestion that it means "among them" ("Textual Problems," 121) yields an odd sense alongside the use in v. 10.

e. MT adds "from Yahweh" to the text attested in LXX and Syr., assimilating the oracle reception statement to the oracle reception heading in v. 8 (Janzen, *Studies*, 51).

f. The sequel shows that here the genitive has an appositional role. LXX paraphrases as "when six years are fulfilled."

g. "The calf" stands in loose apposition to "the covenant" (Barthélemy, *Critique textuelle*, 2:711; cf. McKane 2:873). Its distance from the initial verb militates against taking it as its second object, "(I will make . . .) into the calf," which LXX evidently supports and for which Holladay 2:237, 242 opts. Keil 2:86, though he adopts this view, observes that an article is unusual with a second object and that the sense "treat as" expects a comparative particle. Accordingly NRSV adopts Ehrlich's conjecture *kāʿēgel*, "like the calf" (*Randglossen*, 4:331), the same rendering as the other EVV evidently justify as a paraphrase of a second object. See the commentary.

The next literary block (chs. 34–36) has failure to listen to Yahweh's manifold revelation as its motif. Chapter by chapter, it moves methodically along the broad sweep of the revelatory tradition from the torah to the prophetic movement and to Jeremiah's own prophesying, though by so doing the text has to move back in time, from Zedekiah's reign (ch. 34) to Jehoiakim's (chs. 35–36). The initial oracle reception heading suggests a fresh start, though such headings also appear at 34:8 and 35:1. Chapter 36 provides a climactic conclusion to the block. The chapters of this block "return to the motif stated at the beginning of chap. 26."[1] The recollection presupposes a literary setting in which ch. 32 was appended to chs. 26–29 before the addition of its elaboration in ch. 33 or the insertion of chs. 30–31. The core, chs. 27–29, was concerned with how long the 597 deportation would last and countered the short-term expectation of optimistic rival prophets with a long-term one. Its exhortations not to listen to such prophets were matched in the prose sermon of 26:4–6 with an insistence that failure to listen to the divine revelation given in torah traditions and in true prophecy would lead to further disaster. Chapters 34–36 elaborate this warning. In closing, 36:3, 7 revert to the "perhaps" of 26:3, a loophole that sets a premium on a positive human response—which failed to materialize. That failure has already come to the surface in chs. 34–35. Jeremiah 34 narrates disobedience with respect to a torah tradition found in Deuteronomy 15. Chapter 35 exposes Judah's rejection of the long-standing, legitimate prophetic movement by contrasting it with sectarian scrupulousness. By way of climax ch. 36 narrates a drama of royal repudiation of Jeremiah's collected oracles of disaster. Accusations of not listening resound through the block—not listening to Yahweh's torah revelation in 34:14, 17 (reinforced twice in MT at v. 10), to the prophetic revelation in 35:13–16 (reinforced in MT at v. 17), and finally to Jeremiah's own oracles of disaster in 36:31 (cf. MT at v. 25). The motif of not listening to Yahweh appeared in a number of Jeremiah's poetic oracles (6:10, 17,

1. Martin Kessler, "Jeremiah Chapters 26–45 Reconsidered," *JNES* 27 (1968): 81–88, esp. 84.

19; 13:15, 17; 22:21; 23:16) and was used vis-à-vis the torah and prophetic traditions in 6:17, 19, and 22:21. The people "have ears and do not listen" (5:21). The motif was taken up abundantly in prose sermonic material (chs. 7, 11, 13, 17, 19, 25, and 26), and was related to the traditions of torah and prophecy, especially in 7:23–26.

Chapters 26–29 gradually traced a trajectory of long-term hope, which was developed in turn in chs. 30–33. The present block has returned to the trajectory of short-term disaster set out clearly in ch. 26. MT kept this other track in readers' minds by recalling it in 29:19 (cf. 28:8). Chapter 36 is climactic since it refers to Jehoiakim's fourth year (605 B.C.E.), when Nebuchadnezzar's victory at Carchemish over Egyptian forces established his control of Syria-Palestine. This watershed in Judean history, which vindicated Jeremiah's earlier "foe from the north" oracles, was celebrated in 25:1–14 and comes to the fore again in ch. 36 (vv. 1, 29). So not only does this block revert to ch. 26, but ch. 36 reverts to ch. 25, which itself provides a powerful climax for chs. 1–25. The book has returned to this stage as it reaches ch. 36, before the next block of chs. 37–39 moves inexorably to the final months of Zedekiah as king, when dire prophecy would turn into indisputable history.

This chapter proclaims the imminent capture of Zedekiah and Jerusalem for which it finds a torah-based explanation. It is composed of two prophetic messages of disaster (vv. 1–7 and 8–22), each introduced by an oracle reception heading. A frame is provided for the unit by the submission of "this city" (vv. 2, 22) and of Zedekiah (vv. 3, 21) to Nebuchadnezzar in an ABB'A' pattern. The first part of the frame refers to the capture of the king and the second to the capture of Jerusalem.[2] Verses 1 and 22 provided a corroborating frame by mention of campaigning and the inclusion of Judah's other urban centers in both the campaign and the conquest.

[**34:1–7**] The first message announces disaster for Jerusalem and Zedekiah (vv. 2–3), followed by a mitigating proclamation of salvation for the king (vv. 4–5). The message follows a divine directive to Jeremiah (v. 2a) and is introduced by a heading that puts the message in a historical setting (v. 1). Verses 6–7 provide a brief report of Jeremiah's carrying out the directive, together with a restatement of the setting. The focus of the unit lies on the second and longer message.

[**1**] The oracle reception heading is expanded with information about the historical context. The terrible crisis long predicted by Jeremiah earlier in the book had now materialized, in the form of a final Babylonian invasion of Judah. The invasion is overwhelming; it is no longer just Chaldean (e.g., 32:4), but made up of international contingents from the vassal states of the empire (cf. 25:9).

---

2. LXX adds the city's capture to v. 2 (see *BHS*), assimilating to v. 22 (Janzen, *Studies*, 63) and/or to 32:3.

MT enters into the spirit of the text by expanding the engulfment. Evidently Nebuchadnezzar was not involved, but directed operations from his Syrian headquarters at Riblah, leaving the fieldwork to his officers (cf. 38:17–18; 39:5). The campaign is described in general terms (cf. 52:4, 9, 12), though the royal reference, formally presented, is meant to add to a feeling of intolerable pressure (cf. Ezek 26:7). In view of the parallel in v. 7, Jerusalem's "towns" refer to Judah's other urban centers subject to the royal city (cf. 19:15).

[2–3] The initial quotation formula implies a subsequent public announcement (cf. 32:3–5) or else further introduces its penning. There was to be a double handing over of the royal capital and its king, and for the vassal king a formidable calling to account before his overlord and eventual deportation.

[4–5] The fate is surprisingly mitigated. Zedekiah is reassured of a natural death, as MT expounds in v. 3, and even of the honor of a royal funeral, complete with the ritual of burning aromatic spices (cf. 2 Chr 16:14; 21:19) and public mourning (cf. Jer 22:18). At first sight the promise seems to envision the king's reinstatement, but the funeral may simply mark the consolation of respect for the exiled king, such as Jehoiachin enjoyed a different manner (52:31–34).[3] More perplexing is the way the promise cuts across other forecasts made during the same period of Babylonian invasion, a categorical one that Zedekiah was shortly to die (21:7) and a conditional one that he would survive only if he surrendered (38:17–20). The present passage promising survival presupposes his failure to surrender, along the lines of 38:21–23. An attempt at harmonization has been made by regarding the call to attention in v. 4a as an implicit conditional clause signifying, "But if you obey the word of the LORD" (NAB; for the syntax cf. Ps 139:18), and then deleting the following quotation formula as a subsequent misunderstanding of the clause (Rudolph 220–21; BHS; Holladay 2:232–34; cf. Bright 216; Brueggemann 324–25), though NAB retains the formula. This expedient imports a novel element to the text; it is better to take each passage as it stands and think of various prophetic encounters with the king. Nevertheless, the question arises why a concession is made to Zedekiah here. The answer may come from two perspectives. First, the passage is reminiscent of the reward of survival for meritorious service in the cases of Ebed-melech and Baruch (39:15–18; 45:1–5). Indeed, MT's addition in v. 4b intensifies the similarity, when compared with 39:18. Zedekiah is presented in the book as an ambivalent character, and perhaps this message once belonged in a setting of his protection of Jeremiah (cf. 37:20–21; 38:10). It does so no longer, neither here nor in its echo in 32:3–5, where its dignified end for Zedekiah is retained but toned down. Second and more pertinently, the two passages (vv. 1–7 and 8–22) are now meant to be read together, as their parallel

---

3. This interpretation underlies Josephus's claim that Nebuchadnezzar buried Zedekiah "royally" (*Ant.* 10.154 [Thackeray, LCL]).

elements attest. Verses 3–5 correspond with the lesser sentence for Zedekiah at v. 21, in comparison with that to be meted out in v. 20. Verse 21 functions as the implicit reason for the announcement of vv. 4–5, which serves to amplify the understated contrast in v. 21 with the fate of lack of burial in v. 20 and so to enhance the horror of the latter.

[6–7] MT brings out the different social roles of prophet and king in the actual encounter and maintains the longer royal title found in the parallel divine directive and prophetic call to attention (vv. 2, 4). Whereas the background information (v. 1) presented the army itself as an overwhelming element, a complementary focus now lies on Judah's grim losses. Again MT magnifies the effect. A military report from the Judean side is provided in one of the Lachish ostraca: "We are watching the (fire-) signals of Lachish . . . for we cannot see Azeqah."[4]

[8–22] A further announcement of disaster follows, but now one set in an oracle of disaster with a prefixed reason for it in vv. 13–16, which is linked to the announcement with the standard "Therefore." Quotation formulas introduce the two sections of the oracle (vv. 13 and 17). An expansive heading is provided for the oracle (vv. 8–11). Prose sermonic language predominates, occurring extensively in vv. 13–15, 17, and 20, and in a literary quotation from Deut 15:1, 12 in v. 14a, which may be regarded as the text of the sermon.[5] In this case general prose sermonic language of indictment, especially that used in ch. 7,[6] has been given a scriptural grounding by referring to the manumission of debtors after six years of a limited form of slavery, indenture service to repay debt (Deut 15:12–18). This interpretation has been grafted upon an earlier accusation that uses a technical phrase, "make a proclamation of liberty" (vv. 8, 15, 17), not employed in Deuteronomy 15, and is based on the breaking of a religious pledge. At the outset the release of Judean slaves is equated in v. 9 with that of Hebrew males and females specified in Deut 15:12, 17, though the term for female slave is *šiphâ* in Jer 34:9, 11, 16, not *ʾāmâ* as in Deut 15:17.[7] The phrase for release first used in v. 8 occurs in Lev 25:10, in the setting of a jubilee year (cf. Ezek 46:17), and also in Isa 61:1.

[8–11] The heading gives the background to the oracle, but fails to divulge two vital pieces of information that will emerge in the oracle: the temple ceremony involved in the proclamation of release for the slaves (v. 15) and the time of the army's withdrawal (v. 21). The reticence is intentional—so as to present these facts climactically at the end of the reason and announcement; similar literary delay occurred in ch. 32. To help readers, MT has carefully supplemented

---

4. *COS* 3:80. For the progress of the campaign see *Macmillan Bible Atlas*, 124, map 162. Cf. Ze'eb B. Begin, "Does Lachish Letter 4 Contradict Jeremiah xxxiv 7?" *VT* 52 (2002): 166–74.
5. See Stulman, *Prose Sermons*, 102–7.
6. There are significant links with 7:22, 24–26, 30, 33.
7. Cf. Thiel, *Redaktion von Jeremia 26–45*, 40.

a short introduction in the heading with certain details gleaned from the oracle. In LXX " turned around" begins v. 10, as *BHS* records, but the expansion has logically required its move to v. 11. MT restricts the extent of the release to Jerusalem (v. 8; cf. the first addition in v. 19), but the earlier text by featuring Judean officials in v. 19 and including Judah's towns in the punishment in v. 22 suggests a much wider area for the emancipation. The MT addition, "(the people) of the country," (v. 19), also lends belated support, unless it represents independent assimilation to the listing in 1:18. The subsequent easing of the military crisis evidently caused second thoughts, though the historical motivation for the original release is not given.

[13–16] The social covenant organized by Zedekiah is compared with the Sinai covenant as a lead-in to the quotation from Deuteronomy 15. The reference to the exodus is fittingly embellished by a phrase common in Deuteronomy (cf. Exod 20:2; Mic 6:4), "the slave compound," as an allusion to Egyptian captivity. The implicit lesson derives from Deut 15:15, "Remember that you were a slave in the land of Egypt, and the LORD your God redeemed you" (Keil 2:85). The quotation in v. 14 jumps from the introductory Deut 15:1 to 15:12, and Hebrew second singular references distinguish the next citation, which MT rounds off by supplying "from your service" (Deut 15:12 NAB). The jump implies that the release of debt slaves in Deut 15:12 has been reinterpreted in terms of the communal debt remission every seven years in Deut 15:1, although there the timing of the release of particular slaves would have differed according to when each was enslaved. The basic reason for the oracle appears in vv. 15–16, the profaning of the divine name by contravening a covenant made before Yahweh in the temple (cf. 2 Kgs 23:3); a reinforcing reference to Jer 7:10 is appended, "that goes by my name."

[17] The announcement of disaster begins with a prose sermonic reprisal that is an ironic adaptation of the proclamation of liberty (vv. 8 and 15), so that the punishment fits the crime. First comes a recapitulation of the reason, a negative reframing of vv. 8 and 15. The reprisal was generated by an earlier sermon in 24:9–10, in which Yahweh was to "let loose ... sword, famine, and pestilence," and make the offenders "people all the other kingdoms in the world will shudder at." The same Hebrew verb for letting loose (*šillaḥ*) was used in 34:9 and later verses (and in Deut 15:12) for letting the slaves go.

[18] A separate reprisal, which continues vv. 15–16, will be unfolded in v. 19 by identifying the culprits and in v. 20 by elaborating the verb "hand over."[8] It presents a wordplay in the charge of breaking the covenant, ratified though it was by a rite at the temple (vv. 15–16; cf. Gen 15:9–10, 17).[9] The ceremony of

---

8. Barthélemy, *Critique textuelle*, 2:711.

9. Cf. Gerhard F. Hasel, "The Meaning of the Animal Rite in Genesis 15," *JSOT* 19 (1981): 61–78.

"passing" (ᶜbr) between the severed halves of a calf had been forgotten, since the participants had in due course "passed up" (ᶜbr) or transgressed the covenant by reclaiming their slaves.[10] By undergoing the ratifying rite with Yahweh as witness, they had made the covenant Yahweh's as well as their own and dangerously laid themselves open to divine punishment.[11] "My covenant" is shorthand for the covenant made "in my presence."[12]

[19–20] The slave owners are identified as both officials of various kinds and members of the people. Then the divine abandonment is spelled out. Treatment at the hands of "their enemies" is described in terms of a shocking lack of burial taken from prose sermons in 7:33 and 19:7. MT's further qualification, "people with designs on their lives," which it repeats in v. 21, has picked up the second cue by borrowing from 19:7, 9 (in the latter case MT only).

[21–22] There is a supplementary announcement for Zedekiah; the Jerusalem officials have been mentioned in the other camp at v. 19 in MT as partially involved. The differentiation with its lesser punishment suggests that, although the king had arranged the covenant (v. 8), he did not infringe it—and yet he bore a measure of blame for permitting the infringement. Readers are only now informed of the historical circumstances of the manumission, the Babylonian army's temporary lifting of the siege of Jerusalem, to deal with an Egyptian attack according to 37:5. The metropolis and its daughter towns were doomed after all. The import of this finale is that, just as the slave owners had first raised, then dashed, the hopes of their slaves, the urban centers that harbored the opportunistic slave owners would undergo similar reversal at Yahweh's bidding. Peake (2:144) and Lundbom (2:557, 567) note the deliberate echo of "take back" (v. 16) in "bring back," the same Hebrew verb now used for reprisal.

In 34:1–22 the focus lies on flouting the divine torah as paving the way for certain doom.

35:1–19 An Object Lesson in Listening

35:1 A message received by Jeremiah from Yahweh during the reign of King Jehoiakim *ben Josiah* of Judah. It said: 2 "Go to the community[a] of the Rechabites *and talk with them*. Get them to come to Yahweh's temple, to one of the rooms, and offer them wine to drink." 3 So I got hold of Jaaza-

---

10. Cf. Patrick D. Miller, "Sin and Judgment in Jeremiah 34:17–19," *JBL* 103 (1984): 611–13.

11. The common interpretation in terms of a self-imposed curse, despite its appeal to eighth- and seventh-century treaty formulations, is not only syntactically difficult to discern in the text, but produces exegetical difficulties. The wordplay (v. 18) concerning intention and performance and the switch to "my covenant" already make adequate points. Comparison with Ezek 17:19 is not compelling, since that context lays explicit stress on an oath that if broken turns into a curse (vv. 13, 16, 18, and 19).

12. Cf. "my covenant" in Ezek 17:19, for which see Allen, *Ezekiel 1–19*, 259.

niah ben Jeremiah ben Habazziniah, his brothers, *all* his sons, and the rest[b] of the Rechabite community, 4 and escorted them to Yahweh's temple, to the room of the group associated with the man of God, Hanan ben Yigdaliah, which was next to the officials' room and above the room of the guardian of the threshold, Maaseiah ben Shallum. 5 Then I put wine-filled pitchers[c] and cups in front of the members of the Rechabite community, and urged them to drink some wine. 6 "We do not drink wine," they said, "because our founder, Jonadab ben Rechab, gave us instructions, 'You and your descendants must never drink wine; 7 nor should you build houses, sow crops, or plant vineyards. Instead of having such possessions[d] you must spend all your lives in tents; that way you will live long on the land you occupy as transients.' 8 We have obeyed our founder Jehonadab *ben Rechab with regard to all he instructed us*, in respect of drinking no wine—a lifelong commitment, and the same goes for our wives, sons, and daughters— 9 and building no houses to live in, and that we should have neither vineyards, fields, nor crops. 10 We have also lived in tents, thus listening to and practicing all that our founder Jonadab instructed us; 11 but, when *King* Nebuchadnezzar *of Babylon* invaded the country, we decided to move and come into Jerusalem to get away from the Chaldean and Aramaean armies, and so we got to live in Jerusalem."

12 Jeremiah[e] then received Yahweh's message, as follows: 13 "Here is what Yahweh *Almighty, Israel's God,* said: 'Go and tell the Judeans and the residents of Jerusalem: "Will you never learn your lesson and comply with what I say?" *declared Yahweh.* 14 "There has been implementation of what Jehonadab ben Rechab said, when he instructed his descendants to drink no wine. They have not done so *ever since, listening to their founder's instruction.* I, on the other hand, have spoken to you over and over again, but you would not listen *to me.* 15 I have sent you *all* my prophetic servants *over and over again,* telling you one and all to renounce your bad ways in favor of good behavior and to stop following other gods for worship. That way you could continue to live on the land I have given you and your forebears. But you have turned a deaf ear, refusing to listen *to me.* 16 Since[f] Jehonadab ben Rechab's community has implemented the instruction of their founder *which he gave them,* whereas this people has not listened to me,'" 17 therefore "—here is what Yahweh, *God Almighty, Israel's God,* said—"look out, I am going to inflict upon Judah and *all* the residents of Jerusalem all the bad fate I have threatened them with, *because they would not listen when I spoke to them and would not respond when I called them.*"'" 18 *The Rechabite community was told by Jeremiah:* "Here is what *Yahweh Almighty, Israel's God, said:* 'Because *you* have listened to the instruction of *your* founder Jonadab and have kept all his instructions, duly conforming to all that he

instructed you, 19 therefore'—here is what Yahweh *Almighty, Israel's God,* said—'Jonadab ben Rechab will never lack a male representative in my service.'"

a. In the light of vv. 3, 5, and 18, NRSV "house" is not intended literally, but NJPS evidently does so intend, translating with "household" in v. 3 and "family" in v. 18, though retaining "house" in v. 5.
b. For the idiom cf. 34:17 and 36:12, and see H. Migsch, "Zur Interpretation von *wĕʿet kol-bêt hārekābîm* in Jeremia xxxv 3," *VT* 51 (2001): 385–88.
c. So NRSV, NJB; see Friebel, *Sign-Acts*, 129 n. 129.
d. The singular Hebrew verb is either distributive, referring to each of the preceding nouns, or applies collectively to a farmstead containing such elements; cf. v. 9. Contrast NAB, NJB, NRSV, and GNB, which relate only to the vineyards.
e. LXX (42:12) uses the first person (*BHS*) here and in 36:1 (LXX 43:1), standardizing with v. 3 as continuous narrative; see textual note d on 32:6.
f. Unlike modern EVV but like KJV, Ehrlich, *Randglossen*, 4:333, takes *kî* as causal, noting the counterpart "therefore" in v. 17 and the parallelism of the two topics of the Rechabites and the Judeans in reverse order (vv. 16 and 17–19). The third person references to the Judeans common to vv. 16 and 17 suggest taking the verses together.

This chapter accuses Israel of not complying with God's long-term prophetic revelation, a default driven home by a contrasting lesson that exemplifies compliance. The unit's coherence lies in its genre, a report of a symbolic action, complete with its three standard elements of divine commission (vv. 1–2), prophetic execution (vv. 3–11), and divine interpretation (vv. 12–19). A characteristic first person account (cf. 32:6 and commentary) appears in vv. 3–5, whereas the editorial heading (v. 1) is in the third person, and so is the interpretation (v. 12; cf. v. 18). The interpretation has been heavily overlaid with prose sermonic language that reinforces the message, at the close of v. 13, toward the end of v. 14, in most of v. 15, and in v. 17.[13] The text bears similarities with 7:24–26, 28; 18:8, 11; 25:3–6. In turn, MT has expanded the unit with its own reinforcements of the message of noncompliance, including (v. 17b) the addition of material from 7:27 that complements the earlier borrowing from ch. 7. There is elaborate symmetry between the report in 35:1–19 and the denunciation of the reenslavement scandal in 34:8–22.[14] The passages move in tandem. First, an oracle reception heading (34:8a; 35:1) opens a setting of the scene (34:8b–11; 35:2–11). Then an oracle reception statement and quotation formula (34:12–13a; 35:13b–16) preface a reason for disaster (34:13b–16; 35:13b–16) and particular and contrasting announcements of disaster in one case (34:21–22)

13. See Stulman, *Prose Sermons*, 107–11.
14. Elmer A. Martens, "Narrative Parallelism and Message in Jeremiah 34–38," in *Early Jewish and Christian Exegesis: Studies in Memory of William Hugh Brownlee* (ed. Craig A. Evans and William F. Stinespring; Atlanta: Scholars Press, 1987), 33–49, esp. 39–43.

The Dangers of Rejecting the Divine Word

and of salvation in the other (35:18–19). Both incidents are temple-related (34:15; 35:4). The interlocking of the two units by such parallelism reinforces their common motif of not listening to Yahweh's revelation, torah-based in the first case and prophetic in the other.

[35:1–2] An oracle reception heading introduces the commission (v. 2). Its dating in Jehoiakim's reign (608–598 B.C.E.) fits the historical setting given in v. 11, relating to the end of the reign. The unfolding of the story will disclose information about the Rechabites, a religious sect best known to the public for its strange abstinence from wine. The provocative episode staged by Jeremiah demonstrates their tenacity in maintaining this basic tenet.

[3–11] The presentation of this symbolic action follows a three-scene pattern of commissioning, already provided in v. 2, delivery in vv. 3–5, and reaction in vv. 6–11.[15]

[3–5] Jaazaniah, the contemporary leader of the sect, and his male followers are invited to a large room in the temple complex, normally occupied by a group of temple prophets. Its proximity to the rooms of important persons indicates its accessibility to the public, since such personages would normally be provided with convenient locations. Next door the royal officials had a room at their disposal, and close by was the office of a prominent temple officer (cf. 52:24). The room was probably open on one side so that worshipers in the area could observe what transpired (cf. 36:10). Jeremiah sets the scene with full pitchers and individual cups and then issues his invitation.

[6–11] It is predictably declined. As any sect members would, his guests gladly take the opportunity to explain their distinctive stance at length, first stating the historical basis for their convictions (vv. 6–7) and then methodically itemizing their compliance (vv. 8–11). The founder of the group, Jonadab (or Jehonadab) ben Rechab, evidently lived in Elisha's time; he appears in 2 Kgs 10:15–16 as a supporter of Jehu's reformation and purge in the northern kingdom some two and a half centuries before. Jehu evidently picked him for his usefulness as a promoter of certain conservative values in the face of Canaanite inroads into Israelite religion. By comparison, Jeremiah, while making use of the group, holds them at arm's length. In response to Jeremiah's challenge, which selected the most notorious hallmark of the sect in the public's eyes, the wine issue is set first, but carefully combined with a list of the founder's other mandates of nonconformity to social norms. No rationale is provided, nor is it necessary in this context, but their essentially itinerant lifestyle is brought to the fore. Then the group's adherence to the founder's principles is proudly rehearsed. A compromise for survival's sake is uneasily admitted in v. 11 with respect to v. 7b ("tents," "transients"). The Chaldean and Aramaean incursions correspond to the preliminary attacks of 2 Kgs 24:2, which were to lead to a full-scale attack

---

15. Applegate, "Narrative Patterns," esp. 79, 83.

on Jerusalem in 598–597 shortly after Jehoiakim's death. The community recently had to adopt a sedentary lifestyle as refugees in the capital. Living in Jerusalem is contrasted with living in tents.[16] All this information might seem of no direct relevance to the refusal of wine, but even the rueful self-justification backs up the group's stance as sticklers in spirit for their sectarian convictions. Their presence in Jerusalem must have aroused public curiosity, providing a telling opportunity for Jeremiah to exploit their distinctiveness.

[12–19] The interpretation relies on a feature that has appeared earlier in the book, the use of contrast as a means of indictment (cf. 2:11, 32; 8:7; 18:14–15).[17] Here the Rechabites' scrupulous compliance with the founder's mandate not to drink wine sets in relief the people's noncompliance with the divine will. "Listen" is the key word. There is an argument from the lesser to the greater (Calvin 4:308). The interpretation takes the form of a complex oracle of disaster. After an exasperated, accusatory question in v. 13, well captured in REB and NJB, a direct reason appears in vv. 14–16, and an announcement of disaster in the course of vv. 17–19. The basic charge of noncompliance has been greatly expanded with prose sermonic language that elaborates the people's rejection of Yahweh's long provision of prophetic revelation and its admonitions and their preference for moral and religious compromise. The disaster announced in v. 17 in its edited form entirely takes on a prose sermonic shape, further reinforced in MT. Verses 16–19 present various form-critical features, which MT has complicated even more in v. 18. A proclamation of salvation is combined with an oracle of disaster in an ABB'A' order. The Rechabite community was to be rewarded, while Judah and Jerusalem were to be punished. The combination of genres is easier to track in the earlier form of LXX, which has "therefore . . . said," which now opens v. 19 in MT, at the beginning of v. 18 and has third person references to the Rechabites in v. 18. The logic is: Since the Rechabites have complied and since this people has not complied, therefore this people will be punished and therefore the Rechabites will be rewarded. The contrast in destinies nicely caps the contrast in the accusation and accentuates Judah's fate. MT has taken the trouble to highlight the Rechabites' reward even more, presumably to enhance the contrast, by creating a separate oracle addressed to the Rechabites ("you," "your") in v. 18. It has its own narrative introduction that corresponds to the directive "tell" of v. 13, but turns it into a delivery statement. This expansion necessitated pushing the material attested in LXX at the start of v. 18 down to v. 19[18] (a similar displacement occurred in MT at 34:10–11). The generous accolade of v. 19, with its phrase "stand before me" (NRSV), may imply a prophetic role for this

---

16. Ehrlich, *Randglossen*, 4:332; Herbert Migsch, "Wohnten die Rechabiter in Jerusalem in Häusen oder in Zelten? Die Verbformationen in Jer 35, 8–11," *Bib* 79 (1997): 242–57, esp. 254. NAB, NJPS, and GNB envision continued tent living, with Thompson 616.
17. Friebel, *Sign-Acts*, 131 n. 132; cf. Smith 194.
18. Cf. Janzen, *Studies*, 85, 105–6.

group since elsewhere in the book the phrase has prophetic associations (15:1, 19; 18:20).[19] However, the phrase need not be so technical and may simply refer to survival under God's special care (Calvin 4:324; cf. 30:20). Whereas earlier the unit carefully contrasted the sect's adherence to their human founder's wishes with the people's nonadherence to Yahweh's will, admiring the principle of constancy rather than its content, the divine accolade guaranteeing the Rechabites' survival is a climactic tour de force that condemns Judah by setting a higher premium on sectarianism than on nominalism. There was infinitely more hope for this fringe group than for mainstream Judah.

[17] The prose sermonic language that marks this general announcement of disaster suggests it should be revisited. While it may have replaced an earlier, perhaps more specific version, it is more economical to conclude that v. 17a was added to the form-critical mix. In that case the divine interpretation was earlier an ironic proclamation of salvation for the Rechabites, which contrasted its reason with the Judean community's noncompliance with Yahweh. The prose sermon redactor not only expanded the reason in vv. 14–15, but also supplied an announcement of disaster that spelled out a tacit message earlier left to the imagination.

In 35:1–19 the Rechabites are used as a reverse model to shamefully expose Judah's spiritual inconstancy in rejecting Yahweh's prophetic revelation.

36:1–32 Reaffirmation of the Rejected Word

36:1 *It was* in the fourth year of the reign of King Jehoiakim ben Josiah of Judah *that* Jeremiah received this message from Yahweh. It said: **2** "Get yourself a book-sized scroll and write on it all the messages directed against Jerusalem[a] and Judah and all the other nations, which I have given you since the time I spoke to you in Josiah's reign and right up to the present. **3** Perhaps the community of Judah, hearing all the bad fate I am planning to bring about for them, will consequently renounce *one and all* their bad behavior, and then I can forgive their sinful wrongdoing." **4** So Jeremiah summoned Baruch ben Neriah, and *Baruch* wrote down at Jeremiah's dictation all the messages Yahweh had given him, on a book-sized scroll. **5** Then Jeremiah gave Baruch instructions, "I am under restriction and cannot enter Yahweh's temple. **6** So *you go and* read out from the scroll *on which you have written Yahweh's messages at my dictation*, in the hearing of the people present in Yahweh's temple on a fast day. Moreover, all the Judeans who have come in from their towns will hear as you read them[b] out. **7** Perhaps, as entreaties are humbly submitted in Yahweh's

---

19. See Chris H. Knights, "'Standing before Me for Ever,' Jeremiah 35:19," *ExpTim* 108 (1996/97): 40–42.

presence, they will *one and all* renounce their bad behavior, prompted by the intensity of the furious anger expressed to this people by Yahweh." 8 Baruch *ben Neriah* duly carried out all *the prophet* Jeremiah's instructions about reading Yahweh's messages from the book in Yahweh's temple.

9 It was in the ninth month of the fifth[c] year of the reign of King Jehoiakim *ben Josiah of Judah* that a fast in Yahweh's presence was proclaimed for all the people in Jerusalem, *including all the people who could get[d] from the towns of Judah to be in Jerusalem.*[e] 10 So Baruch read Jeremiah's messages from the book in Yahweh's temple, in the room of Gemariah, son of Secretary Shaphan, which was in the upper court by the porch of the New Gate of Yahweh's temple, in the hearing of *all* the people. 11 Micaiah ben Gemariah ben Shaphan, having heard all Yahweh's messages from the book, 12 went down to the royal palace, into the Secretary's office, where a session was being held of all the officials—Secretary Elishama, Delaiah ben Shemaiah, Elnathan ben Achbor, Gemariah ben Shaphan, Zedekiah ben Hananiah, and the rest of the officials. 13 Micaiah reported to them all that he had heard Baruch read *from the book* in the hearing of the people. 14 Then the officials collectively sent Yehudi ben Nethaniah ben Shelemiah ben Cushi to Baruch with the message, "That scroll you have been reading from in the people's hearing you are to bring with you and come here." Baruch *ben Neriah* duly came, bringing the scroll *with him*. 15 "Sit down," they told him, "and read it out for us to hear." So Baruch read *in their hearing*. 16 Then, as they heard these messages, they turned to each other in alarm[f] and said,[g] "We must report all this to the king," 17 while to Baruch they put the question, "*Tell us* how you came to write down all these messages."[h] 18 "He gradually dictated all of them to me," Baruch said *to them*, "and I in turn would write them *in ink* in the book." 19 "Go, hide, along with Jeremiah," *the officials* told Baruch, "*and* do not let anybody know where you both are." 20 Then they went to the king by way of the courtyard, after depositing the scroll in the office of *Secretary* Elishama. They reported everything in the king's hearing. 21 The king sent Yehudi to get the scroll, and he duly fetched it from *Secretary* Elishama's office. Yehudi read it out in the hearing of the king and all the officials standing around[i] the king— 22 the king was sitting in his winter apartment *in that ninth month*, with a brazier in front of him supplied with a fire.[j] 23 Then, as Yehudi read out three or four columns, he would rip off that part with a writer's knife and throw it into the fire in the brazier until the entire scroll ended up in the brazier fire; 24 no alarm was shown, no clothing was ripped by the king or *any of* his courtiers on hearing all these messages, 25 though[k] Elnathan, Delaiah, and Gemariah begged the king not[l] to burn the scroll—*but he would not listen to them*. 26 Then the king ordered Prince Jerahmeel, Seraiah ben

The Dangers of Rejecting the Divine Word

Azriel, and Shelemiah ben Abdiel to arrest *the scribe* Baruch and *the prophet* Jeremiah. However, Yahweh kept them hidden.ᵐ

²⁷ Jeremiah received a message from Yahweh after the king had burned the scroll containing the messages Baruch had written down at Jeremiah's dictation. It said: ²⁸ "Do it again. Get *yourself* another scroll and write *on it* all the *first* group of messages that were on the *first* scroll burned by King Jehoiakim *of Judah*. ²⁹ Then *concerning King Jehoiakim of Judah* you are to say: 'Here is what Yahweh said: "You are the one who burned this scroll, querying 'Why did you write on it that Babylon's king is sure to come and destroy this country, exterminating from it both humans and animals?' ³⁰ Therefore"—here is what Yahweh had to say concerning King Jehoiakim of Judah—"he will have no heir to sit on David's throne, while his corpse will be thrown out to lie exposed to parching heat by day and to frost by night. ³¹ I will deal with him, his children, and his courtiers *for their wrongdoing*, inflicting on them, the residents of Jerusalem, and the Judeans all the bad fate I threatened them with and which they would not listen to."'" ³² So *Jeremiah* got another scroll *and gave it to the scribe* Baruch *ben Neriah*, who wrote on it at Jeremiah's dictation all the messages that had been in the book *King* Jehoiakim *of Judah* burned *in the fire*. Many other messages of a similar nature were added.

a. Thus BHS and REB with LXX (43:2). A frame for the unit appears to be intended here and in v. 31, where Jerusalem and Judah recur in the same unusual order. Israel, in the sense of the northern kingdom, was never the object of Jeremiah's oracles of disaster. See the commentary for a further reason. MT has 30:1–3 wrongly in view.

b. The antecedent has to be supplied from as far away as v. 4. MT has eased the strain by adding it to the earlier text in the form of the relative clause in v. 6a.

c. The relation of LXX "eighth" to MT, whether text-critical or redactional, is not known.

d. So NJB. The participle has a future sense because their coming is a consequence of the proclamation (Rudolph 230).

e. Instead LXX has "and the community of Judah," which represents an independent expansion derived from v. 3, whereas MT has v. 6 in mind (Janzen, *Studies*, 107).

f. For the pregnant construction see *HALOT* 3:922a and cf. Joüon §133b. LXX "took counsel together" is coping with *yḥdw*, "together," for *pḥdw*, in a damaged text.

g. NAB and REB omit MT's addition "to Baruch" to LXX's shorter text; Baruch is not addressed until v. 17, as the word order there indicates. MT carelessly assimilates to vv. 15 and 19 (Janzen, *Studies*, 52).

h. NAB, NJB, and REB omit MT's addition "from his mouth/at his dictation" (cf. vv. 4, 6), which is not represented in LXX and anticipates the answer in v. 18. NRSV, NIV, and GNB take it as a staccato, separate question affirmed in v. 18. In that case it might be better to assume loss of an interrogative particle by haplography (Ehrlich, *Randglossen*, 4:334).

i. Strictly "over" the seated figure of v. 22.

j. For the construction see Joüon §128b.

k. See GKC §160b and Ehrlich, *Randglossen*, 4:336, for this sense of *wĕgam*.

l. For the secondary omission of the negative within the Greek tradition, mentioned by *BHS*, cf. Emanuel Tov, *The Septuagint Translation of Jeremiah and Baruch: A Discussion of an Early Revision of Jeremiah 29–32 and Baruch 1:1–3:8* (HSM 8; Missoula, Mont.: Scholars Press, 1976), 49–50, 116–17, 165–66.

m. The omission of the divine name in LXX and subsequent adaptation to a passive verb may spring from pseudohaplography before *wyhy*; see the commentary.

At first sight the chapter is made up of two sections, vv. 1–26 and 27–32, each introduced by an oracle reception statement. However, closer examination indicates that a sectional break also occurs after v. 8, so that vv. 1–8, 9–26, and 27–32 make up "three links in a chain."[20] There is overall movement from Yahweh's word through Jeremiah being recorded to its being heard and rejected, and then to its reproduction.[21] At the outset vv. 9 and 27 separately echo elements of v. 1, v. 9 its regnal dating and v. 27 its prophetic formula. MT supplements the parallelism by prefixing *wayĕhî*, literally "And it was/happened," to v. 1, matching v. 9 and also v. 27, where it means "And it came." A strong feature of the unit is its use of suspense. This factor was observed at work in chs. 32 and 34, but here it plays a much more prominent role. Readers are continually left wondering over a lean text only to have their queries satisfied at a later point. The device may irritate, but it fixes issues more firmly in a reader's mind than if they had been presented in logical order. The pervasive interest of the unit lies in a book or scroll, which has been called the unit's main protagonist.[22] "The scroll is so much more difficult to resist because it cannot, like a person, be intimidated, banished, or destroyed. It keeps reappearing" (Brueggemann 346).

[36:1–8] This section sets the scene for the other two. It falls into two parts, vv. 1–4 and 5–8, each moving from a commission backed by a reason to execution, with Yahweh's address to Jeremiah being translated into the latter's address to Baruch.[23]

[1] Readers sense that Jehoiakim's fourth year (March/April 605–March/April 604 B.C.E.) was a historical trigger for the oracle, but its significance does not surface until much later in the unit.

[2] The gist of this verse was quoted and reused in 30:2, but its span for Jeremiah's ministry in turn reflects 25:3. Jeremiah 25:3–6 was echoed in the prose sermonic language in parts of ch. 35, and its influence extends here and later to

---

20. Eduard Nielsen, *Oral Tradition: A Modern Problem in Old Testament Introduction* (SBT 11; Chicago: Allenson, 1954), 65.

21. Cf. Martin Kessler, "Form-Critical Suggestions on Jer 36," *CBQ* 28 (1966): 389–401, esp. 391, 393, 397.

22. Yair Hoffman, "Aetiology, Redaction and Historicity in Jeremiah xxxvi," *VT* 46 (1996): 179–89, esp. 182.

23. Wanke, *Untersuchungen*, 63; Wanke 2:331.

v. 29. Moreover, mention of "Jerusalem and Judah and all the other nations" recalls 25:17–26, where "Jerusalem and Judah's towns" head a list of nations, which were all to drink Yahweh's cup of wrath. Jeremiah's foretelling of disaster in ch. 25 is reaffirmed.

[3] Prose sermonic language is used in the reason for the commission, and it is repeated in the parallel v. 7.[24] More precisely, the initial "Perhaps" is cited from 26:3, which is related to 25:5. As there, its uncertain hope is a redactional way of putting a focus on the eventual response to Jeremiah's discharge of the commission, and its repetition in v. 7 only increases a suspense that pushes the reader toward the sequel. MT "one and all" assimilates further to 26:3.

[4] Baruch ben Neriah, encountered earlier at 32:12, was invited to do the actual pen work. MT calls him a "scribe" in vv. 26 and 32, a profession that has been verified by a contemporary seal impression, "Belonging to Berechiah ben Neriah, the scribe," which is generally taken as referring to this Baruch.[25]

[5–8] The details shed light on the divine commission; the precise interpretation of that general commission may remind readers of Josh 1:10–11 after 1:1–6. Baruch was to reprise the sort of role he played earlier in the book (but later in time) when he acted as Jeremiah's representative concerning a written document (32:12–15). At this juncture, however, Jeremiah was not imprisoned, but free enough to hide, as v. 19 will reveal. The nature of the restrictions placed on him is not specified, but in light of 29:26–27 he might have been formally banned from the temple area as a maverick prophet. Baruch was to be a stand-in; his eyes and voice, as well as hand, passed on a summary of Jeremiah's prophesying. Its contents are not disclosed apart from v. 29. Now readers know why writing it down was necessary. Fasting was associated with a time of emergency prayer, when the people's hearts would be open to gather at the temple to confess sin and implore divine help, and so it would be conducive to a maximal and positive hearing for Jeremiah's incriminating messages. The second half-section closes with Baruch's cooperation, corresponding to the prophet's in v. 4.

[9–26] Three consecutive scenes follow in this heart of the unit (vv. 9–10, 11–19, and 20–26). They feature not only Baruch's reading of the scroll in the temple area, but two more readings.

[9–10] The first scene gives details of Baruch's reading at the temple, unpacking Baruch's cooperation in v. 8. Yahweh's messages (vv. 2, 4, 8; cf. v. 6) are now called "Jeremiah's messages" inasmuch as Jeremiah received them (vv. 2, 4). MT's addition "the prophet" (v. 8) paves the way for the change in perspective, which also reflects Baruch's role as Jeremiah's representative

---

24. Thiel, *Redaktion von Jeremia 26–45*, 49; cf. Stulman, *Prose Sermons*, 34 (no. 10).
25. Nahman Avigad, *Hebrew Bullae from the Time of Jeremiah: Remnants of a Burnt Archive* (trans. R. Grafman; Jerusalem: Israel Exploration Society, 1986), 28–29, 130.

(vv. 5, 6). A fast day was not proclaimed until December 604, nine months or more later;[26] MT ties the audience more closely to v. 6. No interest is shown in the reason for the fast, whether nonarrival of the early rains (Rudolph 233; cf. 14:1–10) or, more likely, the Babylonian sacking of Ashkelon in that very month (e.g., Holladay 2:256).[27] The text attests the eventual arrival of an opportunity for the planned intervention. The venue was a room allocated to a royal official (cf. v. 12), evidently open on one side. Gemariah is specified as son of the former secretary of state in Josiah's reign (cf. 2 Sam 8:17; 2 Kgs 22:3), who was involved in multiple readings of the book of the law (2 Kings 22). It is often assumed that the present account is meant to be read against the background of 2 Kings 22, but this fantasy finds little support in the text (contrast Jer 22:13–17).[28] Nevertheless, the next generation of the Shaphan family is presented as supporting Jeremiah here, in v. 25, and in 26:24 (cf. 29:3). One can imagine Gemariah as the royal liaison officer for the temple.[29] The siting of an ad hoc inquiry conducted by royal officials at the New Gate (26:10) would be appropriate outside the liaison office. Tantalizingly, nothing is said about the people's response to the reading; it will be given eventually.

[11–19] The second scene is a development of the first, featuring a fresh reading (vv. 10, 15) and juxtaposing reference to Baruch and Jeremiah (vv. 10, 19). But now the palace is the setting, with Gemariah's son evidently reporting to his father in his liaison role and judging it urgent enough to interrupt a meeting of officials chaired by the present secretary of state. An aide was sent to find the scroll and its reader. The aide's surprisingly long series of patronymics identified him as a naturalized foreigner, as the names "Yehudi" ("Judean") and "Cushi" ("Nubian") suggest (Holladay 2:258). Readers are gratifyingly informed of fitting responses of alarm and a sense of national doom that warranted the king's attention. The bona fide nature of the book was ascertained—Baruch was simply the amanuensis, not the composer[30]—and the interview ended on a staccato note (even more so in LXX), which warned of danger. Readers aware of the king's assassination of another prophet (26:23) can only agree and feel uneasy about the outcome.[31]

---

26. For the time lag see Clines, "Evidence," 24–25, 33–34.
27. See *ABC*, 100; Lawrence E. Stager, "Ashkelon and the Archaeology of Destruction: Kislev 604 B.C.E.," *ErIsr* 25 (1996): 61*–74*.
28. Cf. Graupner, *Auftrag und Geschick*, 105. In v. 24 it would inflict exegetical overload on the text, which has adequate freight to carry.
29. Cf. William McKane, *Prophets and Wise Men* (SBT 1/44; Naperville, Ill.: Allenson, 1965), 122.
30. This insistence and implicitly 43:3 are at odds with the common notion that Baruch edited the book of Jeremiah.
31. Cf. Nielsen, *Oral Tradition*, 68.

[20–26] The final scene closely matches the second.[32] There was another walk (vv. 12, 20a) and another report (vv. 13, 20b), now to the king. Yehudi was sent again for the scroll (vv. 14, 21a), which was read once more (vv. 15, 21b). "Then, as . . ." (vv. 16, 23) prefaces the responses. Readers' sense of déjà vu is meant to maximize the shock of the king's flagrantly discordant response (v. 16). The setting of his winter quarters, complete with brazier—MT reminds readers it was December (v. 9)—paves the way for the dramatic, piecemeal destruction of the scroll in v. 23. Yehudi is possibly the subject of the verb of ripping, but the attribution of the burning to the king from v. 25 onward and especially in v. 29 implies his direct responsibility, another case of delayed clarification. Verse 24 gives a double commentary, contrasting the officials' alarm in v. 16 and what the proper response should have been—ripping one's clothes in grief (cf. 41:5) rather than ripping up the scroll! The play on different uses of the same verb (qr^c) is the narrator's scathing protest. The vocal pleas of three of the officials were in vain; the group pressure of the other courtiers meant they dared not do more. But they had already done more, by urging Baruch to hide with Jeremiah (v. 19), in order to foil the king, for whom silencing the messengers was on a par with destroying the message. The destruction was a symbolic action, like Hananiah's breaking Jeremiah's yoke in 28:10. It signified a disbelieving contempt for the messages of disaster it contained. It is difficult to decide whether the lack of the divine name in LXX at the end of v. 26 is a text-critical issue, on either side, or a redactional one in MT. The claim of divine providence does make for a fitting climax (cf. 15:21; 20:13) and one that is consonant with God's having the last word in the next section.

[27–32] The final section addresses Jehoiakim's ghastly deed, both as a sin to be punished and as a wrong to be put right. The correcting of the wrong (vv. 27–28, 32) is wrapped around an oracle of disaster (vv. 29–31). The vocabulary links of the section to the two preceding ones reveal its two roles. The king's burning of the scroll in vv. 27–29, 32 picks up vv. 23 and 25, and the mention of courtiers in v. 31 picks up v. 24, while the fresh commission to write and its execution by Baruch in vv. 28 and 32 confirm vv. 2 and 4. The royal punishment also overlaps with that of Jerusalem and Judah, namely, their "bad fate" in vv. 2–3; MT reinforces this link by adding "wrongdoing" from v. 3. The echoing of v. 3 means that prose sermonic language appears once more, in v. 31, with the finality of 587 ultimately in view.[33] There is a further trace of such language at the end of v. 29.[34]

[27] One expects a reference to the burning of the scroll to appear in v. 29 as a reason for punishment, but it also spills over into vv. 27, 28, and 32 as a

---

32. Cf. Wanke, *Untersuchungen*, 65–67; Wanke 2:332.
33. Thiel, *Redaktion von Jeremia 26–45*, 50.
34. Cf. Stulman, *Prose Sermons*, 42 (no. 73).

shocking deed that dominates the entire section. Indeed it should, because it corresponds to the crowning, unforgivable sin of rejecting the prophetic word in both Jeremiah's poetry (6:16–19) and the prose sermons (e.g., 7:23–26). The narrator cannot help reverting to it again and again.

[28] If Jehoiakim's act was a kind of symbolic action, Yahweh commissions another one that trumps the king's, the writing of another scroll like the first. "The word of our God will stand forever" (Isa 40:8; 1 Pet 1:25), in this case permitting no escape from its oracles of disaster.

[29] In providing this reason for coming disaster, MT clarifies the addressee with the aid of v. 30. The reason sheds light on the second section of the unit by supplying the king's verbal protest that properly belongs there, and on the first section by referring obliquely to the historical event that triggered the writing of the former scroll. In 46:2 Jehoiakim's fourth year is identified as the year (605 B.C.E.) when Nebuchadnezzar defeated Pharaoh Neco at the battle of Carchemish, which spelled the collapse of Egyptian hegemony in Syria-Palestine and the beginning of Babylonian rule there. The same date was assigned to ch. 25, in which Jeremiah's hitherto unidentified foe from the north mentioned in a series of earlier messages could now be equated with Nebuchadnezzar and his forces (25:9). The climactic identification found in ch. 25 reappears here. Nebuchadnezzar is branded as the agent of Jeremiah's messages of total destruction; the beginning of the end had arrived. Carchemish was the catalyst that turned yesteryear's premonitions into tomorrow's news.

[30–31] The announcement of disaster leans on the royal oracles of 22:19, 30—Jehoiachin's short-lived succession hardly counted (cf. LXX in 37:1)—but in this new context the verb "thrown" acquires fresh poignancy as a counter to the king's throwing the scroll piece by piece on the fire (v. 23). Association of others in a collective punishment accords with 14:15; 17:18; and 20:6. Here not only are the royal family and court (cf. v. 24) involved, but the opportunity is also taken to revert to the people of Jerusalem and Judah (vv. 2–6; cf. v. 9), thereby reaffirming 35:17. At last the response lacking in v. 10 is supplied. Not only the king but also his people had rejected the divine word. The wistful "perhaps" of vv. 3 and 7 went ominously unsatisfied.

[32] Baruch is the subject in the earlier LXX, but MT carefully clarifies the relation between the commission of v. 28 and its execution here. The notice of subsequent addition to the second scroll is distinguished from the scroll's contents by a switch to a passive verb, perhaps indicating another editorial hand. It presumably covers Jeremiah's post-604 oracles of disaster. The notice proclaims the dead certainty of coming destruction; it paves the way for chs. 37–38, which narrate Jeremiah's interaction with Zedekiah.

The unit of 36:1–32 brings the literary block of chs. 34–36 to a close with a melodramatic attempt to deny the truth of Jeremiah's prophesying, which helps to seal Judah's fate.

37:1–39:18 Retribution for Rejecting Message and Messenger

37:1–21 Message and Messenger in Wartime

37:1 Zedekiah ben Josiah came to the *royal* throne in succession to *Coniah ben* Jehoiakim, having been appointed by *King* Nebuchadnezzar *of Babylon* as king over Judah. **2** Neither he nor his courtiers nor the people at large would listen to the messages Yahweh gave via *the prophet* Jeremiah. **3** King Zedekiah, however, did send Jehucal ben Shelemiah and the priest Zephaniah ben Maaseiah to *the prophet* Jeremiah with the request, "*Please* pray to *our God* Yahweh on our behalf." **4** Now Jeremiah was able to move about freely in public, not having been put in jail. **5** Meanwhile Pharaoh's army had set out from Egypt, and when the Chaldeans *besieging Jerusalem* heard news of them, they withdrew from Jerusalem. **6** Then *the prophet* Jeremiah received the following message from Yahweh: **7** "Here is what Yahweh, *Israel's God,* said: 'Here is what you both[a] are to tell Judah's king who has sent you[a] to me to consult me: "Look out, Pharaoh's army that has set out to help you [all] will go back home to Egypt, **8** while the Chaldeans will come back here and attack this city and then capture it and burn it down." **9** Here is what Yahweh said: "Do not deceive yourselves with the belief that the Chaldeans will go away from you once and for all, because they will not. **10** Rather,[b] if you manage to defeat the whole Chaldean army that is attacking you so only wounded men in tent after tent[c] are left to represent it,[d] they will just get up and burn this city down!"'"

11 Now when the Chaldean army had withdrawn from Jerusalem at the approach of Pharaoh's army, **12** Jeremiah proceeded to leave[e] Jerusalem to visit the Benjamin region to participate in [land] division there in a public ceremony.[f] **13** But when he was at the Benjamin Gate, he encountered a checkpoint officer named Irijah ben Shelemiah ben Hananiah, who held *the prophet* Jeremiah back, claiming he was going to the Chaldeans as a deserter. **14** "That is false!" said *Jeremiah*. "I am not deserting to the Chaldeans"—but he would not listen to him. Irijah arrested Jeremiah and took him to the officials, **15** and the officials, furious with Jeremiah, gave him a beating. Then they put him[g] in the scribe[h] Jonathan's house, which was being used as a jail. **16** Actually Jeremiah was put in a dungeon, a cellblock.[i] *Jeremiah* remained there a long time. **17** Then *King* Zedekiah sent and fetched him. *In his palace* the king questioned him secretly as to whether there was any message from Yahweh. "Yes," said *Jeremiah,* adding, "you will be handed over to Babylon's king." **18** Jeremiah also said to King *Zedekiah,* "What wrong have I done you, your courtiers, or this people to warrant my being put in jail by you [all]? **19** And where are your prophets who prophesied to you [all] that Babylon's king would not invade *you and* this country? 20 The point is, *please listen,* my lord, Your Majesty, *please* let me present my humble entreaty to you: Do not[j] put me back in the scribe Jonathan's house or else I will die there." 21 On King Zedekiah's orders Jeremiah was assigned to a guarded courtyard and given a loaf of bread a day from the bakery district until *all* the bread in the city was used up. Jeremiah remained in the guarded courtyard.

    a. LXX (44:7) renders with singular pronouns, as *BHS* observes, as if Jeremiah is addressed; it makes similar changes in v. 18b and earlier in 32(39):32, 43.

    b. LXX[L] rightly takes *kî* as introducing an adversative clause after a negative, as in 7:5, not as "For" (BDB 474b, where "20" is a misprint for "10"). EVV take as emphatic. LXX *kai,* "and," is the same loose rendering as in v. 16; its extra *hoti,* "For," that now begins v. 9 probably originated as a marginal replacement that became misplaced (*pace* Holladay 2:265).

    c. LXX "place" (see *BHS*) has in view wounded men left where they fell on the battlefield (Streane 228).

    d. Ehrlich, *Randglossen,* 4:337, comparing 2 Kgs 9:35, observes that *bām* is partitive; LXX leaves it untranslated. The punctuation in MT is erroneous and unsupported by LXX (McKane 2:925).

    e. For the ingressive sense see Migsch, *Gottes Wort,* 134; cf. *IBHS* 554–55.

    f. A literal meaning "from there" for *miššām* does not seem to fit unless the verb is related to *ḥlq,* "be smooth, slippery," and taken in a developed sense "slip away," with some support from the Greek tradition (see *BHS*) and medieval Jewish exegesis (McKane 2:926–28). The same conclusion has been reached by finding an Akkadian cognate meaning "run away" (Matitiahu Tsevat, "*ḥālaq* II," *TDOT* 4:447–51, esp. 450). However, the order suggests that the purpose of the journey to Benjamin, rather than of leaving Jerusalem, is being qualified. LXX "to buy from there" keeps the literal meaning by means of an exegetical rendering that uses 32:6–15 (cf. *HUB*). Rudolph 238 takes *miššām* loosely as "there," appealing to Isa 65:20. Hermann-Josef Stipp, *Jeremia im Parteienstreit: Studien zur Textentwicklung von Jer 26,32–43 und 45 als Beitrag zur Geschichte Jeremias, seines Buches und judäischer Parteien in 6. Jahrhundert* (BBB 82; Frankfurt am Main: Hain, 1992), 162, suggests a partitive, quasi-pronominal sense, as in 1 Kgs 17:13, "(divide) from it." In either case the verb may be taken as a denominative Hiphil (cf. *IBHS* 443–44), "participate in a division" (BDB, 324a tentatively; *HALOT* 1:323a; cf. *DCL* 3:242a). "Among the people" (NRSV) seems to mean "in a public ceremony" (cf. v. 4).

    g. MT adds to LXX "(in) the prison," which overloads the sentence. It probably originated as a marginal alternative for or explanation of "the/a jail" later (cf. McKane 928–29).

    h. Or "Secretary" (Bright 225, 229; McKane 2:939; NRSV, NIV, GNB), successor to Elishama in 36:12.

    i. Later Hebrew and Aramaic meanings for *ḥānût,* "tent, stall, shop" (Jastrow 482) suggest a specialized sense in a prison context, "cubicle, cell." Then the common explanation as a vaulted room is wrong.

j. LXX *kai ti*, "and why," hardly fits. It probably originated in an exegetical gloss *wĕlāmmâ* on *wĕlōʾ*, "or else," later in the sentence (cf. 2 Kgs 14:10, where NJPS renders *wĕlāmmâ* "rather than"), which by error displaced *wĕʾal*.

A new literary block begins with ch. 37 and extends to the end of ch. 39; it is made up of three chapter-length units. No oracle reception heading graces the beginning of the block, but its fresh and comprehensive start in 37:1–2[35] and return to the historical context of ch. 34, which began the previous block, suggest that it is a new block. The block's main relation to the previous one is that opposition to Yahweh's prophetic revelation through Jeremiah, broached in ch. 36, is developed. A virtual summary of what the block wants to say is provided at beginning and end (37:1–2 and 39:1–2, 4–10), featuring the general rejection of Yahweh's messages through Jeremiah and the catastrophe that befell king, city, and people; it operates as cause and effect. Both passages are editorial summaries with connections to prose sermons. The style of royal accession used in the books of Kings is echoed in 37:1, while v. 2 reuses the prose sermonic language of 36:31.[36] In turn the historical insertion in ch. 39 derives from a version of 2 Kings 25. What these summarizing passages do not mention is the suffering of Jeremiah that occupies so much of chs. 37–38. For all the space it takes up, that theme plays a supporting role to the overall focus. The bad treatment of Yahweh's messenger mirrors the rejection of the message; the so-called confessions of Jeremiah had a similar function earlier in the book. Jeremiah's persecution is the symptom of a refusal to take to heart his prophetic message.[37] Verse 2, understood as a nuanced echo of v. 18, says as much. His persecution takes two forms, not only life-threatening experiences but also a loss of personal freedom. The latter form sets the pace of the block. It is used as "a code": "The prophet, the word of God, was put away and not heard."[38] It is broached

---

35. Sean McEvenue, "The Composition of Jeremiah 37:1 to 44:30," in *Studies in Wisdom Literature* (ed. W. C. van Wyk; OTWSA 15/16; 1976): 59–67, esp. 60.

36. Thiel, *Redaktion von Jeremia 26–45*, 52–53.

37. The interpretation of Heinz Kremers, "Leidensgemeinschaft mit Gott im Alten Testament: Eine Untersuchung der 'biographischen' Berichte im Jeremiabuch," *EvT* 13 (1953): 122–40, in terms of a biographical passion narrative, depends on a treatment of hypothetically selected passages rather than one that relates the material to the present context (McEvenue, "Composition," 61). Kessler, "Chapters 26–45 Reconsidered," 84–85; and Nicholson, *Preaching*, 106–8, are nearer the mark in finding here part of a history of Yahweh's word proclaimed by Jeremiah. Wanke, *Untersuchungen*, 92, developing Kremer, coordinates all the cases of *yšb*, "remain, stay," with Jeremiah as subject (37:16, 21; 38:13, 28; 39:14; 40:6) within a narrative block, 37:11–43:7. However, the last case is quite distinct, with its own nuance of remaining in the land that introduces the topic of chs. 40–43.

38. Else K. Holt, "The Potent Word of God: Remarks on the Composition of Jeremiah 37–44," in *Troubling Jeremiah* (ed. A. R. P. Diamond et al.), 161–70, esp. 164.

in 37:4, which in structural terms envisions not only vv. 15–16 but also further misadventures, and is assigned a structural role at the conclusion of two units (37:21; 38:28a) and of two unit sections (38:13; 39:14; cf. too 37:16). Jeremiah's remaining in the guarded courtyard becomes an interim series of conclusions that impatiently anticipate his eventual release in 39:14. The shabby treatment of the messenger follows on the heels of his proclamation of messages of disaster, in 37:11–21 after vv. 3–10, in 38:4–13 after vv. 1–3, and in 38:24–28 after vv. 14–23. Correspondingly the release of the messenger (39:11–14) comes after the fulfillment of the message (38:28b–39:10). The negative message is tempered with strictly limited positive alternatives (38:2, 17–20), but in advance 37:3–10 has a blunting effect on such hopes.[39] Indeed, the summary of a general refusal to take Jeremiah's messages seriously in 37:2 implies the inevitability of disaster. The announcements of disaster in chs. 37–38 have a truncated form in that they feature not direct divine intervention but only its human results (37:7–10; 38:3 [contrast 21:10]; cf. 38:17–18, 20–23). This imbalance is finally redressed at 39:16, where Yahweh's intervention comes to the fore. Its message of a bad fate repeats 36:31 (cf. 35:17) at the close of the previous block and so has a structural importance beyond its immediate context. The announcement of salvation for Ebed-melech (39:17–18) has the same function as the one for the Rechabites in 35:18–19, as a yardstick against which to measure the shortcomings of others.

The overall structure of the initial chapter is indicated by its double core that occurs twice, Zedekiah's sending to or for the prophet and Jeremiah's consequent "message" for him (vv. 3, 6, and 17). These clues establish two sections for the unit (vv. 1–10 and 11–21), which both present reports of an oracular inquiry. In each case primarily narrative material introduces the message (vv. 1–5 and 11–17a), while Jeremiah's speeches for or to the king occupy the rest of the sections. So each section falls into two subsections (vv. 1–5 and 6–10, and vv. 11–17a and 17b–21). A pervasive concern in both introductory subsections is the "Chaldean" invasion. Not unnaturally, Jeremiah's speeches in the second subsections reflect this concern, though in the second case the equivalent "Babylon's king" is used (vv. 17b, 19), as a direct counterpart to the royal figure of Zedekiah. The new phrase provides an envelope for the unit, as an echo of "Nebuchadnezzar" in v. 1, while MT "King Nebuchadnezzar of Babylon" makes the echo explicit. A second common concern is the capital, referred to as "Jerusalem" in the first subsections (vv. 5, 11–12) and as "this city" or "the city" in the second (vv. 8, 10, 21). The issue of Babylonian pressure on the capital overshadows the unit, and Jeremiah's involvement in it is traced in two respects. MT adds a third concern, that Jeremiah's role is that of a "prophet" (vv. 2, 3, 6, 13). The repeated term is a foil to "your prophets" (v. 19) and usefully

---

39. Seitz, *Theology in Conflict*, 237, 255.

reminds readers of Jeremiah's representative function as a true messenger of God. Of less exegetical importance is the addition "Jeremiah" in MT (vv. 14, 16, 17, and 21), which merely makes the subject of verbs explicit.[40]

[37:1–10] The announcement of disaster in vv. 7–10 lacks a reason, but it is supplied in narrative form by the statement of v. 2.

[1–5] These verses provide a historical background for this first subsection, referring to the king, the prophet, and the phase of the war.

[1–2] These verses create a bridge between the Jehoiakim-related story of ch. 36 and this one. Indeed, the charge of not listening momentarily carries over the key phrase of the previous block, chs. 34–36. The lack of "Coniah" (= Jehoiachin) in the earlier text reflects not only the brevity of his three-month reign in 598 B.C.E. (cf. 2 Kgs 24:8–12, 17 and the similar bypassing of Jehoahaz in 2 Kgs 23:34) but also a literary transition from the king of ch. 36 to that of ch. 37 (Peake 2:161). More precisely, v. 2 presupposes 36:31. There Jehoiakim, his courtiers, and the people in Jerusalem and Judah did not listen to Yahweh's message of disaster. Here the new broom did not sweep clean, and so that scenario of wholesale and ultimate accusation, which summed up not only ch. 36 but also the block of chs. 34–36, is transferred to the reign of the last king of Judah, when utter disaster would strike. The account in ch. 37 starts very near the end of his reign. Already the Babylonian invasion that would spell the downfall of preexilic Judah and its monarchy was in full swing, as v. 5 will disclose. The Chronicler made use of v. 2 at 2 Chr 36:12 in his characterization of Zedekiah's reign. It afforded some grounds for his own distinctive view that Zedekiah, rather than Manasseh as in the Deuteronomistic version (cf. Jer 15:4), was responsible for the disaster of 587, a view that proceeded from his premise that each generation controlled its own destiny under God and was capable of repenting or resisting divine grace ("did not humble himself"). In the present context the tragic summary is a warning to readers not to hold their breath when they reach the prophet's positive offer to the king in 38:17–20.

[3] As in 21:1–2, Jeremiah was regarded with sufficient prophetic authority to receive a delegation from Zedekiah, perversely requesting intercession to avert disaster. He wanted Jeremiah's and Yahweh's "aid," while repudiating Yahweh's "command" (Brueggemann 355). The appeal for prophetic intercession (cf. 7:16 and commentary) in light of v. 5 expresses hope for a Babylonian defeat, please God. The added "our God" sensitively expresses an affirmation of faith that bolsters the request with a tradition of deliverance (cf. 42:20 MT).[41]

[4] This aspect of the introduction ties the first section to the next by implicitly contrasting the prophet's freedom with its loss in v. 15. The reader is alerted to an impending change; Jeremiah should enjoy his freedom while he could.

---

40. LXX did the same in 43(MT 36):18.
41. Cf. Broyles, *Conflict of Faith*, 222–23.

[5] The historical situation underlying Zedekiah's request and Jeremiah's subsequent answer is now explained. It was probably the early summer of 588 B.C.E., and the focus of the Babylonian offensive, though still on Judean soil, had switched from the capital to the advancing Egyptian army responding to Judah's appeals for help after rebelling against its overlord (cf. 2 Kgs 24:20b, though the interruption is not mentioned in 2 Kings). MT adds minimal historical clarification based on 21:4, 9.

[6–10] Jeremiah had naught to say for the king's comfort in his reply to the delegation. The situation was too bad for judgment to be canceled by the intervention of an interceding prophet.

[7–8] Jeremiah downgraded the king's upbeat request for intercession to an ambivalent consultation of Yahweh (cf. 21:2), which paves the way for an announcement of disaster (vv. 7b–8).[42] The announcement develops the information given to readers (v. 5) by specifying its temporary nature. This meant, on the one hand, the Egyptians' eventual abandonment of their military venture and, on the other, the Babylonians' terminal reengagement with Jerusalem, in a double turn around ("go back," "come back"). For readers the latter message is a reiteration of the one to Zedekiah in 34:2, 22. The capital's fate was sealed under this last king of Judah.

[9–10] A fresh quotation formula introduces a demoralizing reinforcement of this double message, which ends on the same unremitting note of the conflagration of Jerusalem. This reinforcement rounds off the first section with a final put-down of the royal expectation (v. 3). It takes the form of a brief disputation.[43] Two standard elements of thesis and dispute are combined in v. 9, while the third, the counterthesis, occurs in v. 10 (see 2:23–25 and commentary). Verse 9 relates to the Egyptian intervention (v. 7b) and issues a warning against an erroneous assumption. Verse 10 takes the form of a supplementary announcement of disaster. It refers to the Babylonian reengagement (v. 8) and scathingly dismisses the bravest and best efforts of the defenders in reprisal as doomed to ultimate failure. The concept of the victory of a feeble minority is an ironic reversal of a tradition of divine power at work through Israel's weakness (cf. Judg 7:2–8; 1 Sam 17:38–50; 1 Cor 1:26–29; for reversal cf. 2 Chr 24:24). The reversal of another ancient tradition in Jer 21:5 is comparable.

[11–21] The second section of the unit takes a disconcerting turn for Jeremiah in its introductory story line, and the turn duly features in his subsequent

---

42. Lalleman-de Winkel, *Jeremiah in Prophetic Tradition*, 220. Similarly Diamond, "Portraying Prophecy: Of Doublets, Variants and Analogies in the Narrative Representation of Jeremiah's Oracles—Reconstructing the Hermeneutics of Prophecy," *JSOT* 57 (1993): 102 n. 9, refers to the consultation as "bias-neutral." However, Rannfrid I. Thelle, "*drš ʾt-yhwh*: The Prophetic Act of Consulting YHWH in Jeremiah 21,2 and 37,7," *SJOT* 12 (1998): 249–56, has argued that consultation should not be differentiated from intercession.

43. Diamond, "Portraying Prophecy," 102, recognizes "a disputational element" in v. 9b.

verbal encounter with the king. The end of the narrative (v. 21), which supplies the king's amelioratory response, presents a new factor. Both this climactic innovation and the section's departure from solely oracular material by its preoccupation with Jeremiah's personal experience raise the question of intention. King and prophet now change roles as petitioners; it is now the prophet who comes cap in hand. The two halves of the section are demarcated by trackings of Jeremiah's location near or at their close, which report improvement in his lot and yet continued imprisonment.

[11–17a] The lead-up to prophetic speech describes a change in Jeremiah's circumstances, when compared with v. 4. Ironically it was the exercise of his freedom, a newfound one permitted by Babylonian redeployment, which caused him to lose it. He apparently wanted to take part in a clan ceremony of land distribution at his home village of Anathoth (cf. 1:1; Mic 2:5); despite LXX there is no necessary connection with the land issue in 32:6–15, which took place later. Jeremiah was stopped at the northern gate of the city as a deserter (cf. 38:19; 39:9; 52:15). Evidently the Benjamin region had already come to terms with the invading forces.[44] His pro-Babylonian pronouncements after 605 made him an obvious suspect. The narrative has already made the falsity of the charge clear; the officer's not listening echoes v. 2. Jeremiah's treatment went from bad to worse, as he was first beaten and then interned and left to starve, as vv. 20b–21 will imply (Rudolph 237). He had had some royal officials taking his side in ch. 36 during the previous reign, but they were doubtless deported in 597 or had recently defected (cf. 38:19), and now he encountered only hostility. The reminder in MT (v. 13) that his prophetic role was involved is an insightful clue that Jeremiah's ill treatment was a measure of the community's rejection of Yahweh. In other words, v. 2 has vv. 13–16 as its counterpart and illustration. The sending in v. 17a that parallels v. 3 now has a summons and interview as its sequel. Zedekiah's secrecy relates to the inexpediency of public knowledge of association with so politically incorrect a figure as Jeremiah, just as in 38:24–26 the officials would be kept in the dark.

[17b] The oracular message is a terse, intransigent reiteration of inevitable disaster, now involving the king. Like vv. 7b–8, it echoes ch. 34, in this case vv. 3a, 21.

[18–20] Imprisonment was not a legal punishment, but a form of detention pending a trial.[45] Accordingly Jeremiah took the royal audience as an opportunity for a judicial appeal, protesting his jailing as unwarranted, like the original

---

44. Seitz, *Theology in Conflict*, 256.
45. Karel van der Toorn, "Prison," *ABD* 5:468–69; Pietro Bovati, *Re-Establishing Justice: Legal Terms, Concepts, and Procedures in the Hebrew Bible* (JSOTSup 105; Sheffield: JSOT Press, 1994, 227.

charge (v. 14); a royal hearing and verdict (v. 21) duly followed.[46] He conducted a spirited defense with a twofold argument. First—and the terms of v. 2 are significantly repeated, "king," "courtiers," and "people"—he claimed the community to be the guilty party rather than himself. "Courtiers" and "officials" clearly overlap, as in 36:21, 24, and the phrase "your courtiers" may reflect court style.[47] The king's active involvement or at least passive complicity in his officials' action now comes to the fore as a challenging factor (cf. 32:2–3). Jeremiah's prophetic role is still implicitly in view, because, second, he contrasts his record and fate with those of his prophetic rivals, whose word Zedekiah and the rest of the community had embraced ("your prophets"). Evidently they had not lost their freedom, though their denials about Babylonian invasion had proved embarrassingly mistaken (cf. 28:2–4, 11); the form of question is like that in 2:28. Jeremiah's announcements of disaster relating implicitly and explicitly to Nebuchadnezzar had turned out to be true—his army was still on Judean soil—and so his accusations of communal guilt had been shown to be correct. Verses 18–19 mirror the pattern of an oracle of disaster. The community had been at fault rather than Jeremiah, while Jeremiah's rivals had been proved wrong over the punishment, and Jeremiah right. He closed with a passionate plea for release from jail, enhanced in MT by extra touches.

[21] The royal decision is ambivalent. It is almost an admission of Jeremiah's prophetic validity—almost, because his freedom was not restored. He was transferred to more congenial quarters, evidently the open prison (32:2) in the palace grounds, and supplied with bread for as long as possible. The narrative presentation is complex. Jeremiah's continued imprisonment was tantamount to an indictment of a community that rejected the messenger along with his divine message. Yet the king's response is at the same time meant to be read as an acknowledgment of sorts that the prophet was in the right, that in another's words, "we indeed have been condemned justly, for we are getting what we deserve for our deeds, but this man has done nothing wrong" (Luke 23:41).

38:1–28a Message and Messenger in Wartime Again

38:1 Shephatiah ben Mattan, Gedaliah ben Pashhur, Jucal ben Shelemiah, and Pashhur ben Malchiah[a] heard the following types of message being given by Jeremiah to *all* the people: 2 "Here is what Yahweh said: 'Any who stay in this city will die from sword or famine *or pestilence*, but any who surrender to the Chaldeans will survive. They will get away with just

---

46. Cf. Migsch, *Gottes Wort*, 42–43, 259–60; Bovati, *Re-Establishing Justice*, 110–11; Mark Roncace, *Jeremiah, Zedekiah, and the Fall of Jerusalem* (Library of Hebrew Bible/Old Testament Studies 423; New York: T & T Clark, 2005), 56–58.

47. Stipp, *Jeremia im Parteienstreit*, 170 n. 72, who notes that "your officials" never occurs.

Retribution for Rejecting Message and Messenger

their lives, and they will survive.' 3 Here is what Yahweh said: 'This city will be handed over—yes, handed over—to the army of Babylon's king, and he will capture it.'" 4 Then *the officials* told the king, "That man should be put to death, *we urge,* inasmuch as he is demoralizing the troops left in this city and also all the people by talking to them like this. In fact that man's aim is not the welfare of this people but their harm." 5 King *Zedekiah* said, "Look, he is in your hands. In fact the king cannot[b] gainsay you!"[c] 6 They *took Jeremiah off and* threw him into a cistern, one that belonged to Prince Malchiah,[d] located inside the guarded courtyard, lowering *Jeremiah with ropes.* The cistern contained no water, only mud, and *Jeremiah* sank into the mud. 7 Now Ebed-melech, a Nubian *eunuch,* heard while in the palace that they had put Jeremiah into the cistern. The king was holding a judicial session[e] at the Benjamin Gate, 8 and *Ebed-melech* left *the palace* and spoke with the king. 9 "*My lord, Your Majesty,*" he said, "it is *all* wrong what those men[f] have done to *the prophet Jeremiah,*[g] *throwing him into the cistern.* He will die[h] of famine where he is because[i] there is no more bread left in the city." 10 The king ordered *the Nubian* Ebed-melech, "Take thirty[j] men from here with you and lift *the prophet Jeremiah* out of the cistern before he dies." 11 So Ebed-melech took the men *with him* and went into the palace grounds to the basement[k] of a storehouse. He took from there some old rags and tatters, and lowered them into the cistern to Jeremiah *with ropes.* 12 *The Nubian Ebed-melech* told *Jeremiah* to put the old rags and tatters[l] *under his armpits,* beneath the ropes. Jeremiah did so. 13 Drawing *Jeremiah* up by the ropes, they lifted him out of the cistern. But Jeremiah remained in the guarded courtyard.

14 King *Zedekiah* sent and had *the prophet Jeremiah* brought to him, at the third entrance to Yahweh's temple. "I want to ask you for a message,"[m] the king told *Jeremiah.* "Do not hold anything back from me." 15 Jeremiah said to Zedekiah, "If I tell you, you are going to put me to death, aren't you? And if I counsel you, you won't listen to me!" 16 King Zedekiah swore an oath to *Jeremiah secretly,* "By the life of Yahweh who has given us these lives of ours I swear I will not put you to death or hand you over to those men *who have designs on your life.*" 17 Then Jeremiah said to *Zedekiah,* "Here is what Yahweh, *God Almighty, Israel's God,* said: 'If you surrender to the officers of Babylon's king, you will survive. Then this city will not be burned down, and both you and your family will survive. 18 But if you do not surrender *to the officers of Babylon's king,* this city will be handed over to the Chaldeans, who will burn it down, while you yourself will not escape *from their hands.*'" 19 King *Zedekiah* said to Jeremiah, "I am worried about the Judeans who have deserted to the Chaldeans. I may be handed over to them and get abused by them." 20 "You will not be handed over," said Jeremiah. "*Just* obey Yahweh

in the way I am informing you so things may go well for you and you survive. 21 If, however, you refuse to surrender, this is the message Yahweh revealed to me in a vision: 22 I saw all the womenfolk left in the Judean royal palace being led out to the officers of Babylon's king, and noticed them intoning,

> 'You have been set up and outmaneuvered
> by men who were your friends!
> Your feet are sunk into the mire,
> so they have turned tail.'

23 All your wives and sons will be led out to the Chaldeans, and you yourself will not escape *from their hands*, but will be captured and in the hands of Babylon's king,[n] while this city will be burned[o] *down*."

24 Zedekiah said to *Jeremiah*, "Do not let anybody know about this interview or else you will die. 25 If the officials hear I have been talking with you and come and ask you to report to them what you have told the king—warning you not to hide anything from them or they will put you to death—and what the king told you,[p] 26 tell them you were presenting your humble petition to the king not to get sent back to Jonathan's house, to die there." 27 The officials did all come to Jeremiah with their inquiry, and he gave them a report along the same lines as the king had ordered. They stopped the interview and left, having heard nothing about the earlier one. 28a Jeremiah remained in the guarded courtyard up to the time Jerusalem was captured.

a. LXX (45:1) omits the fourth person, probably by parablepsis (Janzen, *Studies*, 119). This would have more naturally occurred at the Greek level of transmission, involving —*iou* endings.

b. See *BHS* and Joüon §75i. However, BDB 407b finds a relative clause here.

c. The construction is uncertain. For a direct object after *ykl* see Ps 13:4 (5). Then *dābār* is a loose accusative, "in respect of a word"; the judicial context suggests "word" in the sense of accusation or decision rather than "anything."

d. See GKC §127f. But the grammatical anomaly may indicate that the name and title are an early and correct gloss (cf. McKane 2:946, 950–51, following Ehrlich, *Randglossen* 4:339; REB).

e. So GNB; Bright 231; cf. Volz 342.

f. In LXX the king alone is directly addressed (see *BHS*), continuing a secondary trend in evidence at 37:18 (Stipp, *Sondergut*, 160).

g. LXX "that man," as in v. 4.

h. Cf. GKC §111l; *IBHS* 557–58.

i. Or possibly, relating to the future, "when" (NIV) or, as a narrative comment outside the direct speech, "For (there was)" (NJPS). LXX and other EVV accord with the translation above.

Retribution for Rejecting Message and Messenger 411

j. "Three" (*BHS*, NAB, NRSV, REB, and GNB) follows one late Hebrew MS, Kennicott 96. Over against the grammatical difficulty in the present text mentioned by McKane 2:946, 954, and Holladay 2:267, Rudolph 240, following Keil 2:112, cites cases in 2 Sam 3:20; 2 Kgs 2:16–17.

k. For the emendation adopted by EVV except NIV and NJPS and misprinted in *BHS*, see McKane 2:954–95.

l. LXX "them" is probably translational (McKane 2:955).

m. Cf. NJB; Weiser 2:339. Lundbom 3:80 helpfully compares 50:2. For *higgîd*, "tell," in v. 15 in the sense of transmitting a divine revelation, see 9:12 (11); 42:4, 20–21.

n. Rudolph 242 notes the pregnant construction, comparing v. 3; cf. REB.

o. MT "you will burn" is implicitly repointed to the passive of LXX, Syr., and Tg. by modern EVV (cf. *BHS*); so Barthélemy, *Critique textuelle*, 2:720–22. KJV "thou shalt cause to be burned" is hardly a valid rendering, though apparently MT so intended.

p. As *BHS* notes, LXX has the second object clause also where MT has the first one. The interruption of the warning may suggest that LXX has a composite text that combines different positions for its object clause and that MT represents a differentiating development (cf. McKane 2:961–62). However, the clumsiness of MT may be original.

This narrative unit, which largely coincides with the chapter division, continues to make Jeremiah's suffering the measure of the community's rejection of the God whose message he brought. The unit falls into two similar sections (vv. 1–13 and 14–28a). Their similarity is fourfold. First, they both close with a refrain about Jeremiah's prison location (vv. 13b and 28a). Second, they are structured around reports of two pairs of interviews (vv. 4–5 and 8–10, and vv. 14–26 and 27). The first two are interviews with the king about Jeremiah, initiated by royal officials and a palace worker, while the second two are interviews with Jeremiah inaugurated by the king and the officials. Third, the general prophetic messages in vv. 2–3 are applied to Zedekiah and expanded in vv. 17–23. Fourth, threats to Jeremiah's life brood heavily over both sections, finding expression in vv. 4 and 9–10 on the one hand and in vv. 15–16 and 24–26 on the other. This multiple evidence of parallelism within and between the sections suggests that they each divide into two subsections, vv. 1–6 and 7–13a and vv. 14–23 and 24–27, to which the sectional refrains of vv. 13b and 28a are added. There is an ABBA ordering in that the officials dominate the first and fourth subsections and Zedekiah plays key roles in the second and third, though the development of vv. 2–3 in vv. 17–23 means that the first and third subsections are closely aligned.

The structuring of this unit in two sections, each with two subsections, echoes the previous one. The units are an obvious pair; they also exhibit close contacts in content. The royal request for intercession (37:3) is comparable to the one for a prophetic message (38:14). J(eh)ucal ben Shelemiah, mentioned in 37:3, reappears in 38:1. The king's rescue of Jeremiah from potentially fatal imprisonment occurs in both units. However, the radical message of 37:1–10 does not match the general and specific offers of a safe surrender and the sparing of the city from destruction (38:2–3, 17–23), though a failure to accept such offers explicitly leads to the same fate as in ch. 37. The relationship between the two units is tantalizingly complex; similarities jostle with pronounced differences. "The narratives in Jer 37–38 exhibit all the problems of a cycle of scenic narratives redacted into a continuous story."[48] Some scholars have found a common source in the accounts. There are strange links between them. The Benjamin Gate of 37:13 returns in 38:7, though in quite a different role. There is a reference, odd at first sight, in 38:26 to Jonathan's house, the former death trap in 37:15, 20, rather than to the cistern of 38:6–13. Jeremiah's preaching to "*all* the people" (38:1) might suggest that, as in 37:4, the prophet was not yet imprisoned, but MT has simply copied an impassioned "all" from 38:4. What cannot be denied is that ch. 38 continues the story of ch. 37 and so further illustrates the fatal rejection of the divine message due to maltreatment of the messenger. MT's perceptive addition of "the prophet Jeremiah" in both sections, in vv. 9–10 in a context of his likely death and in v. 14 at the outset of the second section, reinforces this agenda.

[**38:1–13**] Death is the grim leitmotif of this first section. Whereas in the previous unit it raised its head only once (37:20), now it rampages through the text and on into the next section. Projections of death are polarized, the predicted death of those in Jerusalem who refuse to surrender (v. 2) and a retaliatory bid to put the predictor to death (v. 4), which was duly instigated but foiled by a rescue permitted by the king (vv. 9–10). The punishment of death by famine (v. 9) exquisitely fits Jeremiah's prediction of such a death (v. 2). By way of reprisal the messenger almost became the victim of his own message. There could be no greater rejection of the divine message than a death sentence for the prophet of death.

[**1–6**] The first interview that lies at the heart of the first subsection is prefaced by a report of its occasion (vv. 1–3) and concluded with the implementation of its outcome (v. 6). From another perspective the subsection has the narrative pattern of two scenes relating to the delivery of prophecy (vv. 1–3) and the reaction to it (vv. 4–6).[49]

[**1–3**] MT's identification of the individuals of v. 1 as royal "officials" (v. 4) gives implicit information, as mention of officials in the final subsection (vv. 25 and 27) suggests. The ongoing narrative assumes that Jeremiah was still in the open prison of the guarded courtyard and had access to the public (cf. 32:8, 12). The first summary of Jeremiah's prophesying is strikingly different than that in ch. 37, but is closely related to 21:8–9 (cf. "Pashhur ben Malchiah" in

---

48. Mary C. Callaway, "Telling the Truth and Telling Stories: An Analysis of Jeremiah 37–38," *USQR* 44 (1990/91): 253–65, esp. 262.

49. Applegate, "Narrative Patterns," 81–82.

21:1; 38:1). However, 21:10 went on to predict the categorical burning down of the city, in line with 37:8, 10, while the second summary (38:3) mentions only its capture, and 38:17–18 will accordingly make the destruction conditional. The text takes such inconsistencies in its stride. The alternatives of v. 2 will be prominent in the second section. Babylon's capture of Jerusalem was nonnegotiable, and so dreams of regained national sovereignty were doomed to disappointment (cf. 27:12–15).[50] Hope at a lesser level lay only in complying with Babylon.

[4–6] The officials' accusatory report to the king includes its own suggested verdict. Jeremiah is portrayed as a deliberate agitator, and his bad influence is described—perhaps exaggerated to bolster the accusation—as percolating through the city, affecting the military stationed in Jerusalem and civilians alike, and damaging the war effort. Not even the king could deny the accusation or verdict, and he assigned the officials to carry out the verdict (cf. 26:14). Publicly committed to the war effort, he had no option but to accede to their demand, which led to Jeremiah's being moved to wretched conditions of imprisonment. The addition "with ropes" in MT will be repeated in v. 11 and depends on their mention in vv. 12–13.

[7–13a] How wretched his new conditions were is explained in the course of the second interview (vv. 9–10). He was left to die a lingering death. As in the first subsection, the background to the interview occurs first (vv. 7–8) and then the execution of the royal command (vv. 11–13a). Both subsections (vv. 1–6 and 7–13) begin with the same verb, "heard," and engage in accusation and decision, but to quite different ends. The kindly intervention of Ebed-melech stands as a disparaging foil to the officials' cold-blooded cruelty. Just as foreign sailors in the first chapter of Jonah show up the prophet's spiritual deficiency, so this foreigner's compassion shines out against the dark scheming of native Judeans. MT sensitively underlines his foreign status (vv. 10 and 12). His description as a "eunuch" in MT recalls 29:2 (cf. 34:19) and suits a palace setting.[51] His name, which means simply "king's servant," enriches the story. He had his master's true interests at heart, helping him to reach relative levels of justice and spiritual perception he would otherwise not have attained. The judicial setting implicit in 37:18–20 is explicit here; the location of a city gate for court hearings is not unusual (cf., e.g., Isa 29:21; Amos 5:12, 15). Ebed-melech reopened Jeremiah's case before the court. The charge of severe injustice apparently touched personal qualms and political misgivings that lurked behind the

---

50. Applegate, "The Fate of Zedekiah: Redactional Debate in the Book of Jeremiah: Part I," *VT* 48 (1998): 138–60, esp. 156, has observed that 27:12–15, set early in Zedekiah's reign, provides a theological background for 38:17–23, where 38:2–3 are developed with respect to the king.

51. For a discussion of his eunuch status see Tom Parker, "Ebed-Melech as Exemplar," in *Uprooting and Planting* (ed. J. Goldingay), 253–59, esp. 255–57.

king's public facade. The logic of the reason (v. 9b) is hard to fathom except in terms of hyperbole, as 52:6–7 suggests, but it functions as a powerful rhetorical ploy and reinforces the main clause, which is a deliberate counterpart to v. 2. The dispatch of so large a rescue party presumably reflects the newfound vigor of Zedekiah's determination to rescue the prophet. Ebed-melech deftly turned the royal permission into pragmatic realism, rummaging for likely resources and getting the job done in a considerate manner. In v. 12 MT plausibly fleshes out the leanness of the earlier text.

[13b] As in 37:21, the royal response reverses Jeremiah's prospect of death, but does not extend to setting him free. Jeremiah returns to the limbo between a death trap and exoneration. This sop to his prophetic veracity only underlines the inevitability of coming disaster.

[14–28] The second pair of interviews focuses on the first one; its greater length and detail so indicate. Death was still a real option for Jeremiah. Reassuringly dismissed in the king's case (vv. 15–16), it disconcertingly resurfaces in his closing threat (v. 24) and in his warning about the officials (v. 25; cf. too v. 26). As in the first section, the prospect is finally commuted to continued incarceration.

[14–23] Jeremiah was summoned for a personal interview with the king, as in 37:17–20. The request for a prophetic message channels the interview into a specific reissue of the two messages of vv. 2–3. The two quotation formulas that opened vv. 2 and 3 are paralleled by the one in v. 17 and the comparable introductory language in v. 21. Accordingly the subsection falls into three parts, the initial narrative and interchange (vv. 14–16), then the discussion of two options (vv. 17–20), and the reinforcement of one of the options (vv. 21–23). All three parts bring to the fore the factor of a divine message (vv. 14, 17, and 21).

[14–16] We can no longer understand the precise location; it presumably gave private access to the temple area from the palace (cf. 2 Kgs 16:18 and perhaps Ezek 44:1–3). The king's demand for full disclosure will find a structural contrast in v. 24 at the head of the next subsection. Jeremiah's personal concerns here initiate his speech to the king, whereas they had a concluding and also larger role in 37:18–20. His concerns of fatal reprisal and of lack of trust in the prophetic mission express in a nutshell the polar opposites of the whole narrative. Jeremiah knew all too well the nexus between message and messenger, especially between rejection of the message and the killing of the messenger. Readers are meant to catch an echo of 37:2 in the charge that the king would not listen. The king professed in an oath his religious respect for life and his resolve to protect Jeremiah from the officials, to whose murderous intent MT gives dramatic vent. The addition of "secretly" in MT, perhaps originally intended to qualify v. 14, alerts the reader to a parallel with 37:17. Zedekiah significantly left unanswered Jeremiah's second concern. Again, the royal sanction and silence epitomize the unit.

[17–20] The king's silence did not bode well for reception of the message, which adapts the limited alternatives of vv. 2–3 to the royal situation and begins and ends with an opportunity for survival. Abandoning the siege would spell survival for the (captured) king and royal family and for the (occupied) city. Only thus could the destruction of the city and an ominous personal fate be avoided. The king raised a smokescreen of objection—party politics could be vicious—but Jeremiah waved it away. The whole question is reduced to a religious issue between the king and his God. "Obey" (*šmʿ bqwl*) is a stronger form of listening (*šmʿ*). Verse 20b is probably a redactional prose sermonic elaboration (cf. 42:6 and commentary).

[21–23] In v. 22 Jeremiah communicates a vision with auditory content, which sums up the second alternative and aims to induce Zedekiah to take the other option. It counters the king's imagined humiliation of v. 19 with another one. The women of the royal harem, who survived the capture of Jerusalem in 597 only to appear in its coming capture, were chanting a taunt song (Volz 345; Lundbom 3:76). It is expressed in two poetic bicola with a dirge meter and mockingly describes the treacherous desertion of royal supporters, who would prove fair-weather friends. More specifically there is a reference to the officials, as the Hebrew wordplay shows.[52] Then comes an interpretation of the vision (v. 23), which repeats v. 18 and adds the factor of the royal family mentioned in v. 17. The metaphor of mire (v. 22) echoes psalm imagery for a crisis (Pss 40:2 [3]; 69:2, 14 [3, 15]). Closer at hand, a parallel is drawn between Jeremiah's recent sinking into the mud (v. 6) and the prospect of Zedekiah's feet sinking into metaphorical mire. The two crises are linked as cause and effect. The rejection of the prophetic message that resulted in Jeremiah's dire predicament, despite the partial amelioration granted by the king, was to land Zedekiah himself in a comparable predicament.[53]

The offer of positive and negative alternatives in v. 2 (here and in 21:8–10) underscores the fate of the city and, in the present case, also the fate of the Jerusalem-based monarchy. The close of v. 17 so hinted. Verses 21–23 develop this hint and expose the reason for the prediction of disaster in the negative alternative, namely, the failure to comply with the condition of the positive alternative. This failure has the role of the accusation in an oracle of disaster.[54] Readers have already been warned of the failure by 37:2.

[24–27] The officials are prominent at the close of the unit, as they were at its outset. Again, what they heard is at stake (vv. 1, 25, 27). The king's

---

52. The verb *ykl* ("outmaneuvered") has occurred in v. 5 ("cannot gainsay"); cf. the significantly abbreviated name "Jucal" in v. 1 (Christof Hardmeier, *Prophetie im Streit vor dem Untergang Judas: Erzählkommunakative Studien zur Entstehungssituation der Jesaja- und Jeremiaerzählungen in II Reg 18–20 und Jer 37–40* [BZAW 187; Berlin: de Gruyter, 1990], 243).

53. Polk, *Prophetic Persona*, 162.

54. Diamond, "Portraying Prophecy," 103 n. 10.

paramount desire to present a united front with his ministers meant that he should not be exposed as discussing affairs of state with this persona non grata nor as appearing to take his prophetic options seriously. A death threat from the king—to make him keep quiet—discouraging a security breach counters the likelihood of a death threat from the officials—to make him not keep quiet. It functions as constraint for a cover story that reuses 37:20, a plausible appeal not to be put in the officials' deadly clutches again. Return to Jonathan's house, rather than to the slimy cistern in the palace grounds, would have brought him under their direct control (cf. 37:15). Jeremiah duly played the game assigned to him. His lie invites comparison with Bonhoeffer's ethical principle that there are people who have no right to be told the truth because confidentiality that respects a real-life relationship trumps disclosure in the specious name of absolute honesty.[55]

[28a] The concluding note of v. 13b is repeated, harping on Jeremiah's continuing loss of freedom (cf. 37:4). Ironically freedom would come only with the fall of Jerusalem, as ch. 39 will narrate. The implicit link between his imprisonment and the city's capture is the divine judgment shown to be justified by the rejection of both message and messenger.[56] The foregone conclusion of v. 3 had to come; when, not if, was now the issue.

38:28b–39:18 Vindication of Message and Messenger

38:28b When Jerusalem was captured— **39:1** in the tenth month of the ninth year of the reign of King Zedekiah of Judah, King Nebuchadnezzar of Babylon had advanced on Jerusalem with his whole army, and they laid siege to it; **2** on the ninth day of the fourth month of Zedekiah's eleventh year an opening was made into the city— **3** the officials of Babylon's king all came and sat in council in the Middle Gate, namely, Nergalsarezer Samgar; Nebusarsechim,[a] chief eunuch; Nergalsarezer, chief Mag; and all the rest of the officials of Babylon's king— **4**[b] when he saw them, King Zedekiah of Judah and all the soldiers made their getaway. They left the city at night through the royal garden and the gate between the two walls. He left to get to the Arabah, **5** but the Chaldean army chased after them and caught up with Zedekiah at Jericho Plains. He was apprehended and taken up to King Nebuchadnezzar[c] of Babylon at Riblah in Hamath territory, where he pronounced sentence on him. **6** Babylon's king had Zedekiah's sons executed at Riblah before his eyes; all the

---

55. Dietrich Bonhoeffer, *Ethics* (ed. E. Bethge; trans. N. H. Smith; New York: Macmillan, 1955), 213–14, 326–34.

56. The exegetical translation in LXX at the close of v. 27, "the word of the Lord was not heard" (see *BHS*), though inappropriate as a narrative detail, shows remarkable insight into the purpose of the unit.

Judean nobles were also executed by Babylon's king. 7 Then he had Zedekiah's eyes put out and shackled him in bronze chains, ready to take him home to Babylon. 8 The palace and the people's housing were burned down by the Chaldeans, and the walls of Jerusalem were demolished. 9 The rest of the people left in the city, along with the deserters who had gone over to him and any others of the people who were left, were deported to Babylon by Nebuzaradan, chief of the guards. 10 Members of the people left in Judah by Nebuzaradan, chief of the guards, were the poor who had no property. He assigned them vineyards and fields[d] at that time. 11 King Nebuchadnezzar of Babylon had issued the following orders relating to Jeremiah, to be carried out by Nebuzaradan, chief of the guards: 12 "Take responsibility for him and keep a kindly eye on him. Do not do him any harm—let him dictate the way you treat him." 13 So a delegation was sent by Nebuzaradan, chief of the guards, and by Nebushazban, chief eunuch, Nergalsarezer, chief Mag, and all the other chiefs of Babylon's king. 14 They sent and had Jeremiah brought from the guarded courtyard. They entrusted him to Gedaliah ben Ahikam ben Shaphan, releasing him *to the official residence*;[e] and he lived at liberty.

15 Jeremiah had received[f] Yahweh's message *during his detention* in the guarded courtyard. It said: 16 "Go and tell the Nubian Ebed-melech *as follows*: 'Here is what Yahweh *Almighty*, Israel's God, said: "Look, I am about to fulfill the messages I directed against this city in terms of a bad fate rather than good fortune, *and you will witness them materializing at that time*. 17 But I will rescue you at that time," *declared Yahweh*, "and you will not be handed over to the men you are scared of. 18 Rather, I promise your escape. You will not be struck down by a sword, but will get away with your life because you have put your trust in me," declared Yahweh.'"

a. MT links "Nebu" with the preceding word, but LXX (46:3) rightly separates them (thus NIV, REB).

b. The absence of vv. 4–13 from LXX will be considered later. Verses 1–2 are present in LXX, but marked with an asterisk in LXX^{OL}, which usually signifies material absent from the old LXX; they are absent from OL (Ziegler, *Jeremias*, 411). These data are better explained in terms of a scholarly rationalization that queried obviously secondary material than as evidence for an early stage of LXX claimed by Bogaert, "La libération de Jérémie et le meutre de Godolias: Le texte courte (LXX) et la rédaction longue (TM)," in *Studien zur Septuaginta—Robert Hanhart zu Ehren: Aus Anlass seines 65. Geburtstages* (ed. D. Fraenkel et al.; MSU 20; Göttingen: Vandenhoeck & Ruprecht, 1990), 312–22, esp. 313–15. A subsequent restoration of only vv. 1–2 to the general LXX MS tradition is unlikely.

c. Holladay 2:269 claims that the name is expansionist in MT. The shorter text of 52:9 suggests its redactional nature, but it probably antedates the redaction in MT as a

structural feature (see the commentary). Likewise in v. 11, where Holladay makes the same judgment, it functions as a structural correspondent to the full title in v. 1.
 d. See *HALOT* 2:385a.
 e. Literally "to the house"; cf. NEB "to the Residence," following Keil 2:123.
 f. The inverted Hebrew order indicates a pluperfect sense (cf. Joüon §§118d, 166j).

The basic material in 38:28b–39:18 provides closure for the previous unit in two different respects. First, the unit's final clause about Jeremiah's imprisonment (38:28a), with its hint of reversal, raises the question of whether and how he was released; the answer is supplied in 38:28b; 39:3, 11–14. Second, Ebed-melech, the compassionate rescuer of Jeremiah (38:7–13), is the subject of a reassuring oracle by way of divine commendation in the flashback of 39:15–18. These two positive supplements are strikingly different from each other in content and form, the first being a secular narrative and the other the report of a divine oracle. What unites them, apart from their upbeat tone, is their evident intent to present a contrast to the attitudes of Zedekiah and his officials in the first case and to Zedekiah's fate in the second. Their treatment of God's spokesperson is thereby shown up as justifiably inviting the tragedy duly experienced by the king, the city, and the people whom the king and his officials represented. What that tragedy was is briefly explained in an editorial insertion in vv. 1–2, 4–10, taken either from material in ch. 52 or from the literary source of ch. 52 in 2 Kings 25.[57] This insertion of selected material has been integrated into the first supplement, demonstrating how Jeremiah's message of disaster came terribly true. In so doing it sheds light on the capture of Jerusalem broached in 38:28a and laconically picked up in 38:28b and on the dire consequences for city, king, and people. The expanded passage (38:28b–39:18), consisting of two short, separate positive pieces enlarged by a negative insertion, now functions as a composite unit in its own right. It is a continuation of the previous unit and coheres with it by employing motifs of reversal, contrast, and fulfillment. By such means it spells vindication for Yahweh's message and messenger.[58]

[38:28b–39:14] The insertion of vv. 1–2 and 4–10 has created a composite narrative, the first of two sections for the unit. It falls into two subsections (38:28b–39:10 and vv. 11–14). Both subsections introduce the imposing figure of "King Nebuchadnezzar of Babylon" (vv. 1, 11), first in relation to "King Zedekiah of Judah" and then in relation to "Jeremiah," and so each subsection stakes out its own concern at the outset. Two further divisions emerge for the

---

57. The closer relation of the insertion to ch. 52 is indicated notably in v. 5, where "Zedekiah" reflects 52:8 rather than "him" of 2 Kgs 25:5; in v. 6a, where the singular verb "slaughtered" with "Babylon's king" as subject aligns with 52:10 instead of the plural verb of 2 Kgs 25:7; and in v. 6b, which is essentially present in 52:10 but absent from 2 Kgs 25:7. However, the lack of reference to the king in 52:7 sets that text over against 39:4 and 2 Kgs 25:4.
 58. Nicholson, *Preaching*, 108.

first subsection. "King Zedekiah of Judah" fittingly signals their respective openings in vv. 1 and 4.

[**38:28b–39:3**] The historical details of the siege are sketched, based on 52:5–7a. King confronts king as military enemies, though evidently the Babylonian king is only represented by his troops (cf. v. 5). Verse 1 gives the gist of 52:4, while v. 2 abbreviates material from 52:5–7a. The fate of the city comes to the fore in vv. 1–2 and will be resumed in vv. 8–9; the sequence "Jerusalem . . . city" will be repeated there. Verse 3 interrupts the quotation and stands between vv. 1–2 and 4–10, the basic text that broaches Jeremiah's release from punishment, which v. 11 will resume. The "officials of Babylon's king" were mentioned in 38:17, 22 hypothetically and in a visionary context; here they rule in Jerusalem as an occupying government. Zedekiah's own officials, who were intent on Jeremiah's imprisonment and death, uneasily shared ch. 38 with the Babylonian officials, but now the latter have taken over and releasing Jeremiah would be part of their agenda. If the Nubian eunuch was a foil to the cruel Judean officials in ch. 38, here the Babylonian officials are poised to play that role. For all their foreign names, they exposed their Judean counterparts as barbaric in their treatment of the prophet.[59] The "Middle Gate" was evidently in the middle of the northern wall of the city (see Holladay 2:291). If Zedekiah, sitting in an adjacent gate at 38:7, released Jeremiah from a deadly incarceration but withheld his liberty, now justice was to be fully done.

[**4–10**] This passage has been demarcated from the earlier literary context (vv. 3 and 11) by its own chronological frame, "when he saw them" and "at that time," both of which have been set around the quoted text.[60] The absence of vv. 4–13 from LXX is most probably to be explained as a textual oversight due to the similarity of vv. 3 and 11 and especially their closing words (e.g., Rudolph 243).[61] Alternatively it has been widely explained as a redactional addition that first materialized in MT; McKane (2:977–78) has argued that this is the economical conclusion to be drawn since the material seems to be redactional. However, the issue is not the presence of redactional material but at what stage it entered the text. The appearance of vv. 1–2 in the general LXX tradition, verses that belong to the same redactional process as vv. 4–10 and presuppose their

---

59. "Samgar" appears to refer to an administrative office (see *HALOT* 2:759a), here qualifying the personal name in an uncoordinated way. The second personal name has a corrupted Hebrew form beyond restoration. Underlying *sārîs*, rendered "eunuch," is a transliteration of Akkadian *ša rēši*, "the one at the head (of the king)," but it would have been understood as "eunuch" by Hebrew readers. For Akkadian *rab mugi* with reference to a high military official, which underlies "Mag," see *CAD* 10/2:171. For a discussion of the names and titles in MT and LXX see Barthélemy, *Critique textuelle*, 2:725–28; McKane 2:973–76; and in LXX Ziegler, *Beiträge*, 80–81.

60. Hardmeier, *Prophetie im Streit*, 193, 197–98.

61. Janzen, *Studies*, 118, prefers this explanation. Rofé, *Prophetical Stories*, 209 n. 36, envisions the loss of a Hebrew column by a copyist's eye skipping across.

presence, indicates the complexity of the matter. Separate redactional and textual factors appear to have been at work in different stages, and the latter factor cannot be sidestepped.

[4–7] The terrible fate of the king is described by means of 52:7b–11, 13–14. The added initial clause "when he saw them" loosely integrates the resumed citation with the basic v. 3, while the added phrase "King Zedekiah of Judah" repeats v. 1 as a counterpart to the other royal title in v. 5. King confronts king again, now in person, after an abortive flight. Zedekiah found himself "captured and in the hands of Babylon's king" (38:23; cf. 37:17). Having rejected the possibility of survival for his family (38:17), his last sight was a demonstration of the ghastly alternative. Ironically he himself survived, though death would have been preferable (cf. 8:3).

[8–10] The burning down of city buildings, taken from 52:15, records the fulfillment of 38:17–18, 23, and also of 37:8. The focus soon turns to the fate of the people. Systematically "the people" has displaced or amplified earlier references in ch. 52 at three points and so augmented the original reference in v. 9a. First, "(every) house belonging to a dignitary" in 52:13 becomes "the people's housing"; second, "the craftsmen" in 52:15 becomes "the people who were left"; third, "some of the poor" in 52:16 is expanded with "members of the people."[62] The people who had not listened to Yahweh's messages via Jeremiah (37:2; cf. v. 18) paid the price in social upheaval, including forced labor in a Babylonian agricultural enterprise.[63]

[11–14] The insertion from ch. 52 introduces readers to Nebuzaradan (vv. 9–10), who, otherwise unannounced, plays a key role in the account of Jeremiah's liberation. He acted at the behest of the great Nebuchadnezzar, who, in the enlarged narrative, turns from being Zedekiah's foe (vv. 1, 5) to Jeremiah's friend.[64] Scholars often surmise that at an earlier stage of the text vv. 11–12 belonged with 40:1–6, where Nebuzaradan also appears and his "kindly eye" and deferential accommodation to Jeremiah's wishes (40:4) look like an outworking of his master's sentiments in 39:11–12. Then v. 13, which resumes v. 3, was integrated into the inserted vv. 11–12 by the incorporation of Nebuzaradan. If such a literary reconstruction is correct, a structural desire to balance Nebuchadnezzar's dual role (vv. 1 and 11) was the reason for deliberately altering the shape of the text into its present form.

Zedekiah had saved Jeremiah from death at Ebed-melech's prompting, but his benevolence only went so far. Jeremiah's continued confinement (37:21;

---

62. Barthélemy, *Critique textuelle*, 2:730–32.
63. See J. Nigel Graham, "'Vinedressers and Plowmen': 2 Kings 25:12 and Jeremiah 52:16," *BA* 47 (1984): 55–58.
64. Roncace, *Fall of Jerusalem*, 126–27, has observed the reversal in vv. 5–7 and 12 by repeating three Hebrew terms, *lqḥ*, "was apprehended/take responsibility for," *ʿyn*, "eye(s)," and *dbr*, "pronounced/dictate."

38:13, 28) was a far cry from the freedom he had enjoyed in 37:4. Nebuchadnezzar's considerate behavior trumped Zedekiah's and put the Judean king to shame. It was a reward for services rendered, a concession accorded not even to Judean deserters to his cause (v. 9). The text says nothing about any embarrassment this implication of political collaboration caused Jeremiah; in view of 27:6, 11 it infers an outworking of divine providence. Verse 3 is resumed in the bridging v. 13, where Nebuzaradan cooperates with the occupying council, though surprisingly a new name is given to the chief eunuch. Jeremiah was freed at last. Mention of giving custody to Gedaliah introduces readers to the postwar governor who will feature in 40:1–6 and so gives a full family background (cf. 32:12). Reference to him accords with the account of Jeremiah's liberation (40:1–6). The addition of the inexplicit phrase "to the house" in MT at v. 14 is best taken as a reference to the governor's residence that fills out the text based on 40:6.

[15–18] This passage should not be moved back to ch. 38, as for example Holladay (2:269) does. Its position should be respected, though enlargement earlier in the chapter has distorted its role as a companion piece to vv. 3, 11–14, or perhaps at an earlier stage to vv. 3, 14. The "guarded courtyard" (vv. 14 and 15) functions as a hinge for the two diverse pieces. MT has facilitated the amalgamation of a communal announcement of disaster in v. 16 and an individual, fear-allaying proclamation of salvation in vv. 17–18 by the clause that concludes v. 16, which integrates Ebed-melech's involvement and repeats from v. 17 the earlier text's link "at that time." Setting Ebed-melech's survival against the background of Jeremiah's oracles of disaster reassures readers of the expanded text of ch. 39 that Jerusalem's fate described earlier with the aid of ch. 52 functioned as a fulfillment. The definition of its "bad fate" in 21:10 as being handed over to Babylon's king and burned down confirms the intended connection between v. 16 and the earlier borrowed material. The proclamation of salvation (vv. 17–18a) has a powerful ABABA framework of positive and negative elements, in which the latter reinforce the former. The inferred significance of the proclamation can be gauged from the central element, a divine promise of "escape." It contrasts with Yahweh's refusing escape for Zedekiah in 38:18, 23 (cf. 32:4; 34:3).[65] The foreigner ("Nubian," v. 16) was to achieve what Judah's royal representative would not—and did not (39:4–5). In view of 22:25 the invaders were evidently the ones Ebed-melech feared. The reason for the proclamation is put prominently at the end (v. 18b). Ebed-melech's "trust" is a spiritual interpretation of his intercession for and rescue of the prophet in 38:7–13. His treatment of the messenger was evidence of his trust in the message sender. Such trust stands over against the king's refusal to listen to Yahweh's messages of disaster through Jeremiah at 37:2 and taking refuge in a false

---

65. Kilpp, *Niederreissen*, 89; cf. Rudolph 249; Wanke, *Untersuchungen*, 111–12.

security (37:9; cf. Rudolph 249). Ebed-melech's promised good fortune underscores the propriety of Zedekiah's fate.

Jeremiah 38:28b-39:18 triumphantly rounds off the narrative of Jeremiah's prophetic ministry in Zedekiah's reign with two positive passages that corroborate that ministry and with a third, negative one inserted in the first that corroborates his messages of disaster.

40:1-45:5 Self-Imposed Exile

40:1-43:13 A God-Given Opportunity Squandered

40:1 A message that Jeremiah received from Yahweh after Nebuzaradan, chief of the guards, had let him go from Ramah, where he had him removed *while he was manacled* in chains among *all* the deportees from *Jerusalem and* Judah, who were being deported to Babylon. 2 The chief of the guards had *Jeremiah* removed and said to him, "It was Yahweh your God who threatened this place with such a bad fate. 3 Yahweh *has inflicted it* and brought it about *as he had threatened*, because you had [all] sinned against *Yahweh* and did not obey him, *and so this threat has materialized for you [all].* 4 *What I want to say is,* look, *today* I am releasing[a] you from the manacles on your hands.[b] If you consider it right to come with me to Babylon, then do so, and I will keep a kindly eye on you. If, however, you consider it wrong[c] *to come with me to Babylon,* then do not. *See, the whole country is available to you*"[d]— 5 *he was still not turning to go—*"so go back to Gedaliah ben Ahikam ben Shaphan, whom Babylon's king has put in charge of the towns[e] of Judah, and stay with him among the people. *Or* go wherever else you consider it suitable to go." The chief of the guards supplied him with *rations and* gifts, and let him go. 6 *Jeremiah* came to Gedaliah *ben Ahikam* at Mizpah and stayed *with him* among the people left in the country.

7 Now when all the army commanders and their troops in the rural areas heard that Babylon's king had put Gedaliah *ben Ahikam* in charge of the country, committing into his care men and women *and children belonging to the poorest in the country,* consisting of those who had not been deported to Babylon, 8 they came to Gedaliah at Mizpah—namely,[f] Ishmael ben Nethaniah, Johanan[g] ben Kareah, Seraiah ben Tanhumeth, the sons of Ephai from Netophah, and Jezaniah whose father was from Maacah, all accompanied by their troops. 9 Gedaliah *ben Ahikam ben Shaphan* assured them and their troops on oath, "Do not be afraid of being subject to[h] the Chaldeans. Stay in the country as subjects of Babylon's king and things will go well for you. 10 I, for my part, am staying here at Mizpah as representative[i] to the Chaldeans when they visit us. As for you,

commandeer^j wine, fruit, and olive oil, storing it in your own containers, and stay in your towns, the ones that will have come^k under your control." 11 Similarly all the Judeans in Moab, Ammon, Edom, and any other countries heard that Babylon's king had set a remnant in Judah and that he had put Gedaliah ben Ahikam *ben Shaphan* in charge of them. 12 So *those Judeans all returned from all the places they had been driven to*. They came to Judah, to Gedaliah at Mizpah, and commandeered plentiful supplies of wine and fruit. 13 Now Johanan ben Kareah and all the other army commanders in the rural areas came to Gedaliah at Mizpah 14 and asked him, "Do you have any inkling that King Baalis^l of Ammon has commissioned Ishmael *ben Nethaniah* to kill you?" Gedaliah *ben Ahikam* did not believe them. 15 Johanan *ben Kareah* then said privately to Gedaliah at Mizpah, "Just let me go and kill Ishmael *ben Nethaniah*, unbeknownst to anybody. Otherwise he will kill you and then all the Judeans who have gathered around you will be scattered and the Judean remnant destroyed." 16 Gedaliah *ben Ahikam* told Johanan *ben Kareah as follows*, "Do not do any such thing! What you are saying about Ishmael is false." 41:1 But in the seventh month Ishmael ben Nethaniah ben Elishama, a member of the royal family, came to Gedaliah *ben Ahikam* at Mizpah, accompanied by the king's chiefs^m and ten men, and they shared a meal there *at Mizpah*, 2 when suddenly Ishmael *ben Nethaniah* and the ten men accompanying him killed Gedaliah *ben Ahikam ben Shaphan with their swords. He put him to death*, the one Babylon's king had put in charge of the country, 3 and all the Judeans who were with him, *with Gedaliah,* at Mizpah and the Chaldeans who were present. *The soldiers were killed by Ishmael.* 4 What happened two days^n after he had put Gedaliah to death, before anybody was in the know, was that some men arrived from Shechem, Shiloh, and Samaria, 5 eighty in number, with their beards shaved off, their clothes torn, and their bodies mutilated. They were carrying grain offerings and frankincense to present at Yahweh's temple. 6 Ishmael *ben Nethaniah* walked out *of Mizpah* to meet them, shedding tears as he walked. *On reaching them,* he said *to them,* "Come and meet Gedaliah *ben Ahikam*." 7 But when they got inside the town, *Ishmael ben Nethaniah* slaughtered them [and threw them]^o into a cistern, *with the assistance of the men who accompanied him.* 8 However, ten members of the group had said to Ishmael, "Do not put us to death! We have supplies hidden in the open country, wheat, barley, olive oil, and honey." So he refrained from putting them to death along with their companions. 9 The cistern into which Ishmael had thrown all *the corpses of the men* he had killed was a large cistern,^p one constructed by King Asa in case of attack from King Baasha of Israel. Ishmael *ben Nethaniah* filled it with the casualties. 10 Then Ishmael ben Nethaniah took prisoner all the people left behind at Mizpah, including the princesses[q] whom *Nebuzaradan*, the chief of the guards, had committed to the care of Gedaliah ben Ahikam. *Bringing them as prisoners, Ishmael ben Nethaniah set off to cross over to Ammon.* 11 But when Johanan ben Kareah and all his fellow army commanders heard all about the crimes Ishmael *ben Nethaniah* had committed, 12 they took all their troops and set off to fight *Ishmael ben Nethaniah*. They encountered him by the large reservoir at Gibeon. 13 The people with Ishmael all *cheered* on seeing Johanan *ben Kareah* and *all* his fellow army commanders. 14 *Then the people whom Ishmael had brought as prisoners from Mizpah all turned around and* went back to *and joined* Johanan *ben Kareah*. 15 But Ishmael *ben Nethaniah* escaped *from Johanan* with eight men and set off for Ammon. 16 Johanan *ben Kareah* and all his fellow army commanders took control of all the remnant of the people, whom he had taken back from Ishmael *ben Nethaniah*,[r] men,[s] women, and children, and also eunuchs, all of whom he brought back from Gibeon. 17 They set off and then halted at Chimham's holding[t] near Bethlehem, intending to travel on to *go into* Egypt 18 to get away from the Chaldeans, of whom they were afraid because Ishmael *ben Nethaniah* had killed Gedaliah *ben Ahikam* whom Babylon's king had put in charge of the country.

42:1 Then all the army commanders, including[u] Johanan *ben Kareah* and Jezaniah ben Hoshaiah,[v] and the entire people ranging from the lowest to the elite approached 2 the prophet Jeremiah and said, "Please consent to our humble request! Pray to Yahweh your God *on our behalf*, on behalf of this *whole* remnant here, now that we, once so many, have been left so few, as you can see *we are* with your own eyes. 3 We want Yahweh your God to tell us the direction we should go and the action we should take." 4 "I hear you," *the prophet* Jeremiah told them. "Look, I am going to bring your request to Yahweh your God in prayer, and what*ever* reply Yahweh gives *for you* I will tell you without keeping anything back from you." 5 They for their part told Jeremiah, "May Yahweh be a true and faithful witness against us if we do not act in complete accord with the decision Yahweh *your God* commissions you to give us. 6 Whether it is welcome or not, we will obey Yahweh our God to whom we are sending you, so things may go well for us for obeying Yahweh our God." 7 Ten days later Yahweh's message was received by Jeremiah. 8 He called a meeting of Johanan *ben Kareah, all his fellow* army commanders, and the entire people from the lowest to the elite 9 and told them, "Here is the message of Yahweh, *Israel's God, to whom you sent me to present your humble petition.* 10 'If you are prepared to stay[w] in this country, I will build you up instead of demolishing you and plant you instead of uprooting you, because I will have changed[x] my mind about such a bad fate as

Self-Imposed Exile

I brought about for you. 11 Do not be afraid of Babylon's king, of whom you are now so afraid. Do not be afraid of him,' declared Yahweh, 'because I will be here with you, ready to save you and rescue you from his clutches. 12 I will generate compassion for you so he treats you compassionately and allows you to stay^y on your own soil.' 13 If, however, you keep saying 'We will not stay in this country'—disobeying Yahweh *your God*— 14 *and say instead, 'No!* Rather, Egypt is where we will go, where we will see no warfare and hear no trumpet blast, nor starve for food. That is where we will stay,' 15 in that case *the point is,* hear Yahweh's message, *you Judean remnant.* Here is what Yahweh *Almighty, Israel's God,* said: 'If you *do* set your sights on *going into* Egypt and go and live there as aliens, 16 then^z the sword you fear will catch up with you *there* in Egypt, and the famine you dread will hound you *there* into Egypt, and that is where you will die. 17 All the men who set their sights on *going to* Egypt to live there as aliens will die from sword or famine *or pestilence.* None of them will have any family members who *survive and* escape the bad fate I am going to inflict on them.' 18 'In fact'—here is what Yahweh *Almighty, Israel's God,* said—'just as the residents of Jerusalem felt the deluge of *my anger and* my fury, you too will feel the deluge of my fury when you go into Egypt. You will face reactions of cursing and shock and of oaths and insults, and you will never see this place again.' 19 Yahweh has told you, 'Do not go into Egypt,' you Judean remnant. You must realize that I am giving you a warning^{aa} today. 20 The reason is that you were fatally deceptive^{bb} when you yourselves sent me *to Yahweh your God* with the promise, 'Pray to Yahweh *our God* on our behalf, and whatever Yahweh *our God* says *just tell us and* we will do it!' 21 *And I have told you today,* but you fail to obey Yahweh *your God or any part of* the message he commissioned me to give you. 22 So the point is, *you must realize that* sword and famine *and pestilence* will be what you die from in the place where you want to go and live as aliens."

43:1 When Jeremiah had finished telling *all* the people the entire message from Yahweh *their God,* which Yahweh *their God* had commissioned him to give them—the entire message quoted above— 2 Azariah ben Hoshaiah, Johanan ben Kareah, and all the troops, *who were insolent,*^{cc} said to Jeremiah, "It is false, *what you are stating*! Yahweh our God^{dd} never commissioned you to say, 'You must not go into Egypt and live there as aliens.' 3 Rather, Baruch ben Neriah has been inciting you against us, wanting us to be handed over to the Chaldeans so they can put us to death or deport us to Babylon." 4 Neither Johanan *ben Kareah*^{ee} nor the other army commanders nor the entire people would obey Yahweh by staying in Judah. 5 Instead, Johanan *ben Kareah* and the other army commanders took control of the whole Judean remnant—those who had come back *from the various nations to which they had been driven away*[ff] in order to settle for a while in the country *of Judah*,[gg] 6 men, women, and children, and the princesses, and *all* the other persons Nebuzaradan, *chief of the guards,* had left with Gedaliah ben Ahikam *ben Shaphan,* including the prophet Jeremiah and Baruch ben Neriah— 7 and they went into Egypt, disobeying Yahweh, and arrived at Tahpanhes.

8 Jeremiah received Yahweh's message in Tahpanhes, as follows: 9 "Get hold of some large stones and cover them up *with mortar on the brick pavement that is*[hh] by the entrance to Pharaoh's building in Tahpanhes. [Do so] in the presence of some Judean men 10 and say *to them*: 'Here is what Yahweh *Almighty, Israel's God,* said: "Look out, I am going to send for *my servant,* King Nebuchadnezzar of Babylon, and bring him here. He will put[ii] his throne on top of these stones I have covered up, and spread out his canopy[jj] above them. 11 He will come and attack Egypt. Those designated for plague [will go] to plague, those for captivity to captivity, and those for the sword to the sword. 12 I will set fire[kk] to the temples of the Egyptian gods, and he will burn them and carry them off as captives. He will pick Egypt clean of lice[ll] just as a shepherd picks his cloak clean of lice, and then he will leave *there* unscathed. 13 He will smash the obelisks of the Egyptian Beth-shemesh, while the temples of the Egyptian gods he will burn with fire."'"

a. For the perfect see GKC §106m; Joüon §112g.

b. Cf. *BHS*.

c. LXX (47:5) has "But if not," a paraphrase of MT or vice versa. Then LXX *apotreche*, "run away," appears to render *ḥădal*, "cease" (here translated "then do not").

d. LXX lacks "to wherever is right and to wherever you consider it suitable to go there, go" added in MT and representing two marginal variants of v. 5*ab*. LXX implies *ṭôb*, "right," for MT *yāšār*, "suitable," and so the first variant is an old one.

e. LXX "country" (see *BHS*) assimilates to v. 7.

f. Thus Duhm 315; cf. *BHS*.

g. LXX and the parallel 2 Kgs 25:23 lack MT's "and Jonathan," which probably conflated two variant names that are confused elsewhere, and then made *ben*, "son," plural (Janzen, *Studies*, 17; NAB, NRSV). "Jonathan" does not appear in the subsequent narrative.

h. LXX and 2 Kgs 25:24 have "(afraid) of the servants/ministers (of the Chaldeans)," which NEB adopted here. A marginal reading *mēʿabdê* was probably intended as an (incorrect) exegetical comment on *rabbê*, "chiefs," in 41:1, with the sense "one of the ministers (of the king)"—a syntactical interpretation most EVV side with—and was wrongly taken as a correction of the similar-looking *mēʿăbôd* in the previous column (cf. 17:3–4 and pertinent notes and a similar mistake in 41:9–10).

i. Ehrlich, *Randglossen*, 4:344, compares Deut 5:5 for this sense, and Rudolph 248 compares Jer 15:1.

j. Not "gather" in the sense of harvesting, but "take away, expropriate," already harvested and processed produce (McKane 2:1004).

Self-Imposed Exile   427

k. The verb has a future perfect sense (Duhm 315).

l. A Judean version of Ammonite *Baʿal-yîšaʿ*; see Bob Becking, "Baalis, the King of the Ammonites: An Epigraphical Note on Jeremiah 40:14," *JSS* 38 (1993): 15–24, esp. 20–22.

m. LXX (48:1) omits this former group by homoeoarcton, while the omission in 2 Kgs 25:25 accords with the nature of that passage as a digest (Barthélemy, *Critique textuelle*, 2:741–43). For the syntax NJB is a better guide than other EVV; see note h on 40:9.

n. EVV, except NAB and NJPS, find an inclusive reckoning here, referring to the next day.

o. For the pregnant construction see GKC §119gg.

p. EVV, except NIV and NJPS, adopt the reading underlying LXX, *bôr gādôl*, "a large cistern," in place of MT *bĕyad gĕdalyāhû*, "by the hand of Gedaliah," which NIV takes as "along with Gedaliah" and NJPS "in the affair of Gedaliah." The phrase in MT doubtless originated as a marginal comment on v. 10 that clarified the role of *ʾet-gĕdalyāhû* as using a preposition meaning "with, in the care of," and took "the people" and "the princesses" as the antecedent objects of the verb, the very construction that appears in 40:7b and one that NAB, NRSV, and NJB rightly find here. The different subject, Nebuzaradan rather than Babylon's king, indicates that this is not the authorization formula (cf. 43:6). Cf. *hipqîd bĕyād*, "entrust into someone's hand," in Ps 31:5 (6) and *hipqîd ʿal-yād* with the same meaning in 1 Kgs 14:27 and 2 Chr 12:10. The gloss was misunderstood as a correction of the similar-looking phrase in v. 9 and displaced it despite its scant significance here.

q. MT adds "and all the people who had been left behind at Mizpah," whereas earlier in the sentence it has "all the remnant of the people who had been at Mizpah." In LXX only the first phrase occurs, but in the earlier position. MT in the first case reflects assimilation to v. 16 and in the second case the incorporation of a marginal correction into the text (cf. Janzen, *Studies*, 17; McKane 2:1015).

r. MT adds "from Mizpah after he had struck down Gedaliah ben Ahikam," lacking in LXX and ill-fitting here. It probably represents a wrongly incorporated marginal annotation relating to v. 14. "From Mizpah" functions as a cue element referring to v. 14, while the temporal clause recapitulates v. 2. The presence of "all . . . the people whom . . . Ishmael" earlier in both vv. 14 and 16 encouraged the mistake. NRSV, NAB, NJB, and GNB cope by emending *hēšîb mēʾēt*, "he had taken back from," to *šābâ ʾōtām*, "he had carried them away captive," with *BHS*, following Hitzig 333.

s. Both MT and LXX add "soldiers," which interrupts the standard listing found in 40:7 and 43:6. The preceding *gĕbārîm*, "men," was misunderstood as *gibbôrîm*, "warriors," here and in 43(50):6 (Ziegler, *Beiträge*, 101), and the military addition was made by way of explanation in an unpointed text that was so understood (Hitzig 334). EVV stay with the traditional text, ignoring a scholarly consensus.

t. Thus REB and McKane 2:1022, following Alt. See the commentary.

u. For the use of the copula for singling out, Rudolph 254 refers to GKC 484 n. 1(b).

v. The patronymic is new, compared with 40:8, while "Azariah ben Hoshaiah" in 43:2 is a fresh surprise. The textual tradition underlying LXX[OL] here (49:1), "Jezaniah ben Hananiah and Azariah ben Hoshaiah," may be an authentic reading, telescoped in MT, as Barthélemy, *Critique textuelle*, 2:746–48, tentatively argues.

w. See *BHS*. EVV so understand.

x. The verb has a future perfect sense, as Holladay 2:274 renders.

y. MT has wĕhēšîb, "and he will let you return (to)"; LXX agrees, but with a first person verb. The group's presence in Judah (41:17) and the protest in v. 13 favor a pointing wĕhōšîb, "and he will let you stay (on)" (cf. BHS); a first person variant of this is attested by Aquila, Syr., and Vg. Thus, e.g., S. R. Driver, *Revised Translation*, 253 n. b; Streane 250. RSV and REB change thus; NJPS notes the variant as significant. The roots were confused in MT at v. 10. See the commentary.

z. For the rare grammatical attraction noted in BHS here and in v. 17, see GKC §112y.

aa. The perfect is performative according to Delbert R. Hillers, "Some Performative Utterances in the Bible," in *Pomegranates and Golden Bells: Studies in Biblical, Jewish, and Near Eastern Ritual, Law, and Literature in Honor of Jacob Milgrom* (ed. D. P. Wright et al.; Winona Lake, Ind.: Eisenbrauns, 1995), 757–66, esp. 763. He compares Deut 4:26 and 30:19. NJPS, REB, and GNB translate thus. The omission in LXX (see BHS) was an oversight from kî, "that," to kî, "The reason is that" (Janzen, *Studies*, 118).

bb. See BHS; McKane 2:1030, 1038, who follows Ehrlich, *Randglossen*, 4:348; NAB, NJB; cf. NJPS. LXX substitutes "you did wrong," assimilating to 7:26 and 16:12 (cf. 38:9).

cc. This exegetical amplification reappears in LXX at 42:17 (47:17) in a corrupted form, evidently attached to the previous column in a Hebrew MS (Janzen, *Studies*, 65). The addition of ʾōmĕrîm, "(who were) saying/speaking," in both MT and LXX (50:2) is syntactically problematic.

dd. For the LXX variant ʾēlēnû, "(to say) to us," for ʾĕlōhênû, "our God" (see BHS), cf. 2Q13 ʾlwhymh, "their God," for ʾlyhm, "to them," at 42:9 (DJD 3:63; *HUB*).

ee. The absence of the patronymic in LXX is supported by 4Q72a here and also in vv. 5 and 6, and so is that of Nebuzaradan's title in v. 6 (DJD 15:204; *HUB*).

ff. The brevity of LXX is misrepresented in BHS; it extends to šām, "there." 4Q72a probably agreed with LXX (Janzen, *Studies*, 183; Stipp, *Sondergut*, 79 n. 5, against Tov, DJD 15: 203).

gg. "Of Judah" is a correct exegetical expansion in MT, necessitated by the verb gûr, rendered "settle for a while" (see the commentary). 4Q72a may have read "Egypt" (Janzen, *Studies*, 183), an easier reading.

hh. The absence of these words from LXX was probably a feature of 2Q13 in view of the spacing (DJD 3:63–64). However, 4Q72a has a lacuna that indicates an even longer text than MT (DJD 15:203, 205).

ii. The first person in MT has probably been assimilated to the next verb and to the preceding suffix. The third person of LXX and Syr. is generally preferred (cf. BHS). Of the EVV only NIV and NJPS retain MT.

jj. Or "carpet"; the meaning is uncertain. See *HALOT* 4:1636.

kk. The third person of LXX, Syr., and Vg. fits the context more obviously than the first of MT (see BHS), which only NJPS and GNB keep. However, elsewhere in the book this verbal phrase is used with a divine first person subject (17:27; 21:14; 49:27; 50:32), except for 11:16, where Yahweh is the third person subject. This factor may have led to assimilation, but MT deserves to be kept as a more difficult reading. After 15:2, which underlies 43:11b, a first person verb of divine intervention occurs.

ll. NIV, NJB, and NJPS opt for the meaning "wrap around himself" for the repeated verb, but the other four EVV follow LXX "pick clean of lice, decontaminate," which *HALOT* 2:814a advocates here. See the discussion of John A. Emerton, "Lice or a Veil in Song of Songs 1. 6?" in *Understanding Poets and Prophets: Essays in Honour of George Wishart Anderson* (ed. A. G. Auld; JSOTSup 152; Sheffield: JSOT Press, 1993), 127–40, esp. 134–38.

The literary block of 40:1–45:5, begun as is customary with an oracle reception heading, consists of three units. The coherence of the first two lies in a willful human choice to journey to Egypt and settle there. Jeremiah and Baruch were forced to go with the group of Judean refugees who made that choice, and faced their displeasure. The third unit records a consoling divine promise of survival for Baruch. The first unit, an unusually long one, is found in 40:1–43:13, the second in 44:1–30, and the third, a short one, in 45:1–5. The oracle reception heading at 40:1 introduces the entire composition and the first unit, while another one and a variation of it at 44:1 and 45:1 introduce the second and third units. Redactional material is incorporated, the book's final prose sermon (ch. 44) that condemns the pagan worship that was a cause of Judah's collapse in 587 and would doom the Egyptian Diaspora; short ones appear within 40:2–3, by way of introduction, and in 42:10–12, and there are touches elsewhere.

The first unit describes Judeans left in the land according to the glowing terms of a positive theological scenario set out in ch. 27, only to continue with how and why the potential beneficiaries chose to abandon the scenario and migrate to Egypt. Despite its length, the unit possesses an inner coherence; it is presented as a consecutive account, though the first section in 40:1–6 functions as a loose preface and the placing of the final one in 43:8–13 is editorial. Within the unit the coherence of 40:1–42:22 is evident from the function of 40:2–3 as a theological prologue to the negative side of Jeremiah's complex message of 42:9–22, namely, 42:13–22. The initial short passage, 40:2–3, and the final long one, 42:13–22, share three motifs. First, the "bad fate" of 587 is matched with a future "bad fate" to be brought about in Egypt (40:2; 42:17). Second, "this place" (40:2) reappears in 42:18, as a synonym of "this country" (42:13; cf. v. 10) and an antonym of the other "place," Egypt (42:22). Third, the cause of the disaster is traced back to a failure to obey Yahweh (40:3; 42:13, 21; cf. v. 6). MT sensitively augments this evidence of a parallel frame by adding the verb "inflict" in 40:3, to match 42:17 (cf. 44:2). An inner correspondence emerges between 40:5 and 40:7–41:18. In 40:5 there occurs for the first time the authorization formula, "Babylon's king had put Gedaliah in charge" of Judah or the like; it recurs four times in pivotal positions (40:7, 11; 41:2, 18).

This strategic vocabulary helps to establish 40:1–42:22 as a coherent whole that falls into three sections. First, 40:1–6 by way of a preface supplies three headlines for the rest of the passage in vv. 1, 2–3, and 5, including the introduction of a coming message. Second, 40:7–41:18 narrates the shocking story of the assassination of Babylon's Judean representative. Third, in 42:1–22 the previously announced message that presupposes the story is duly solicited (vv. 1–7) and given (vv. 8–22). Jeremiah 40:1 is meant to be an advance announcement of the oracle that appears in ch. 42. Calvin (4:441) so understood it, quaintly remarking that Jeremiah "seems throughout the chapter to have forgotten the introduction." Apart from Schreiner (2:219), however, scholars have looked askance at the isolation of 40:1 and been loath to link its oracle reception heading with so distant an oracle. What has been overlooked is a practice of delaying oracles after their formal introduction (see the introduction under "Genre"). The suspenseful distance between 40:1 and 42:7, though much greater, constitutes another case. Readers are expected to wait for the next but one section of the unit; the inordinate size of the preparatory next section makes the wait a long one. The other evidence for the interlocking structure of 40:1–42:22 adds weight to this conclusion. Both 40:1–6 and 40:7–41:18 pave the way for ch. 42 from different perspectives.

The three sections in 40:1–42:22 are rounded off by a fourth section, 43:1–7, so that 42:1–43:7 shows a typical narrative pattern of three scenes. The second scene (42:8–22) presents the delivery of the oracle, and the third (43:1–7) the public reaction to it, while the first scene (42:1–7) unusually highlights an initial request for the oracle.[66] Jeremiah 43:8–13 must have the role of a fifth and final section since it interprets the "sword" of 42:16–17, 22 in terms of Nebuchadnezzar's reprisal in 43:10–11 and in so doing expresses the shadow side of a major theme of 40:1–42:22.

[40:1–6] The triple preparatory roles of this first section have been outlined above. Since v. 6 explains in advance how it was that the prophet was available to be consulted in 42:1–6,[67] it anticipates his message in 42:7–22. How did he come to belong to the Mizpah community associated with Gedaliah that ended up heading for Egypt under Johanan's leadership? Jeremiah 40:6 and the verses that lead up to it provide the answer.

[1] Attempts to discern the oracle reception heading of v. 1 in vv. 2–3 founder on the explicit setting of the oracle in a post-Ramah context. This section provides another version of Jeremiah's release at Babylonian hands after the fall of Judah, parallel to the one in ch. 39. However, this version has its own distinct literary function. In comparative terms it fundamentally differs from the previous one in locating the release in Ramah, rather than at an earlier time in Jerusalem. It is possible to harmonize the versions by focusing on "go back" in v. 5 and envisioning Jeremiah as subsequently caught up in a military sweep. However, the text is not interested in harmonization; it just selected this version from narrative tradition for its own ends. Ramah, five miles north of Jerusalem, was evidently the location of a holding camp for the deportees before their trek north to Riblah and then far beyond. The addition of "Jerusalem" in MT, which amplifies a standard phrase used in 24:5; 28:4; and 29:22, creates a contextual

---

66. Applegate, "Narrative Patterns," 83.
67. Graupner, *Auftrag und Geschick*, 119.

link to 39:9. The heading in v. 1 anticipates Jeremiah's removal from the crowd in v. 2 and being let go in v. 5, while presumably other details were editorially moved from their places in the story told in vv. 2–6.[68]

[2–3] Nebuzaradan's offer (vv. 4–5) has been prefaced with a redactional prose sermon.[69] It recapitulates the catastrophe of 587 in theological terms as a preface to the same interpretation of a looming catastrophe that will appear in the oracle of ch. 42. One way Hebrew narrative has of expressing theology is via direct speech (cf. 2 Chr 35:21). The reference to Yahweh as Jeremiah's God identifies him as the source of this interpretation in his prophesying before the fall of Jerusalem. In v. 3 MT focuses on fulfillment.

[4–6] The generous options offered to Jeremiah are reduced to a single decision. At the beginning of v. 4 MT integrates the options with the sermon. At the end it adds a statement modeled on Abraham's offer to Lot in Gen 13:9 and Abimelech's to Abraham in Gen 20:15. It is developing a motif that will emerge in the basic text in the next section, that nondeported Judeans would be faced with a great opportunity to settle in the land, which, however, they ultimately failed to take. Here Jeremiah is regarded as an anticipatory role model for this potential. The addition at the beginning of v. 5 is best understood as a parenthetical narrative reference to Jeremiah's indecision, which vividly breaks up and justifies the lengthy presentation of options (cf. Keil 2:127–28; NJPS). As in 39:14, Gedaliah's family background is mentioned, here doubtless to remind the reader of the help given Jeremiah by his father Ahikam ben Shaphan in 26:14. His role as postwar governor of a Babylonian province of Judah provides a headline for the next section. Mizpah, the provincial capital, is generally identified with Tell en-Naṣbeh, three miles north of Ramah, an identification that fits the itinerary of northern pilgrims in 41:4–7, though hardly the mention of Gibeon at 41:12, which is in the wrong direction for a journey to Ammon (see Holladay 2:294–95), unless, as Bright (255) suggests, a circuitous route was taken, perhaps to evade capture. In the light of 40:11–12 Jeremiah is presented as throwing in his lot with a new community of hope—hope that later would be tragically dashed. But his choice represents a validation of that community.[70] A theological reason will gradually materialize.

[40:7–41:18] There are two surprises in this section of the unit.[71] First, it does not mention Jeremiah at all, but briefs the reader about the community who

---

68. Ibid., 125.
69. Thiel, *Redaktion von Jeremia 26–45*, 58–59. Stulman does not designate the passage as such, but his list includes the cases of "obey" (*Prose Sermons*, 33, no. 1) and "threatening a bad fate" (44, no. 91; cf. esp. 35:17; 36:31) and in MT "inflicting a bad fate" (34, no. 10), though it appears in Jeremiah's poetry at 23:12 (cf. 17:18).
70. Hardmeier, *Prophetie im Streit*, 214–17.
71. A digest of this section appears in 2 Kgs 25:22–26. The span of text used there features the corruption in 40:9 (2 Kgs 25:24) found in LXX and based on a portion of the text in 41:1 not utilized in the 2 Kings summary.

will ask Jeremiah for an oracle in 42:1–6. Second, it reads like a human, nontheological account. However, the section is dominated by the authorization formula first used in v. 5; its recurring presence not only tracks the narrative progress of this section but also hammers out an implicit theological agenda. The narrative falls into three subsections (40:7–12; 40:13–41:9; and 41:10–18), each divided into two parts. The second and third are each marked by its own key word, the verbs *hikkâ*, "kill," and *hālak*, "go," here rendered "set off."[72] The verbs sum up the dissolution of the section's positive opportunity. The dissolution is also marked by an overarching motif of fear. An assurance not to be afraid occurs in the first subsection (40:9), and a motivation of fear grips the community by the end of the third subsection (41:18). This contrast will reappear in Jeremiah's oracle at 42:11, 16. The explicit link between doing the divine will and the absence of fear in the oracle is implicit in the preceding narrative.

[40:7–12] If the third subsection will focus on going, the first focuses on coming, coming "to Gedaliah at Mizpah," in both parts, in vv. 7–10 at v. 8, picking up v. 6, and in vv. 11–12 at v. 12. This centripetal movement, which will be reversed in the eventual centrifugal one, is in both cases a response to hearing (vv. 7, 11). Hearing builds a bridge back to the authorization formula of v. 5, whose significance is unfolded in vv. 9–10.

[7–10] A sensitive meeting takes place between remnants of the Judean army—led by regional officers, each one a potential warlord—and the new governor. MT refers back to 39:10, though it uses the terminology of 2 Kgs 25:12, to pinpoint the dire economic state of the population, for whom, however, a new era of peace and plenty could be dawning. Gedaliah's speech is conciliatory and reassuring. His role as "representative" or liaison to the imperial authorities made him "an advocate for his people" (Brueggemann 378). The note of things going well is a prose sermonic element that will be picked up in the community's request for an oracle at 42:6.[73] It will be associated with divine blessing, a meaning not far from the surface here. The reader is expected to hear in v. 9 an echo of Jeremiah's 594/593 oracle during the conference of western states at Jerusalem in ch. 27. Any nation that served or was subject to Babylon's king was promised that Yahweh would "leave it on its own soil to till it and stay on it" (27:11). The situation of postwar Judah is here interpreted in the light of this scenario, and the interpretation will be developed in the oracle at 42:10–12. Although Jeremiah does not appear in 40:7–41:18, one of his earlier messages emerges as the interpretive backdrop to the intervening drama. Submission to Babylon is presented as the path to security and prosperity. The book of Joshua is virtually revisited in v. 10, as settlers are invited to requisition the fruits of

---

72. Martin Kessler, "New Directions in Biblical Exegesis," *SJT* 24 (1971): 317–25, esp. 322–24.

73. See Stulman, *Prose Sermons*, 35, no. 21.

harvest abandoned by deportees, reaping where they had not sown, as a bonus to tide them over while they tilled and sowed for a coming year.

[11–12] There is a rerun of vv. 7–10, now featuring Judean fugitives. Mention of "Moab, Ammon, Edom" creates another link with ch. 27 (27:3), so that in a tenuous sense these Judeans have an extra qualification for that chapter's promise. MT enters into the spirit of temporary optimism by reusing a formula of return from exile (cf., e.g., 24:9 and in MT 29:14) and envisioning a minireturn here and also later in 43:5.[74] MT is inspired by the verb "gathered" in v. 15 and the term "remnant," which itself opens up vistas of hope.

[40:13–41:9] This second subsection is dominated by the key word "kill," which is varied by "slaughtered" (41:7), "put to death" (41:8; in MT also 41:2), and "casualties" (41:9). Its combination with the authorization formula in 41:2 spells a reversal of the hopeful scenario in the first subsection. The two parts of the subsection are 40:13–41:3 and 41:4–9.

[40:13–41:3] Repetition of "came to Gedaliah at Mizpah" in 40:13 and 41:1 represents a grim parody of its former usage since it is now set in a context of assassination, first as a rumor and then as a reality. The rumor brought by the regional militia leaders about one of their number and Gedaliah's response of naive disbelief are storm clouds that gather over the sunny hope of the first subsection. The purveyor of realism (v. 15) receives short shrift; his offer of a preemptive strike is turned down. Careful readers find the language of Johanan's warning particularly worrying, because his description of the consequences sounds remarkably like those of refusing to serve Babylon's king in 27:15, that Yahweh would drive such people away so they would be destroyed.[75] In 41:1 readers are reintroduced to Ishmael in his own right. They are told for the first time that Ishmael was an (evidently minor) member of the royal family, and so a motive of resentment at a commoner's elevation to power presents itself, one that fits his seizing the princesses in 41:10. With hindsight one may discern that in 40:14 the Ammonite king was behind a royalist plot, perhaps honor-bound by a former alliance with Zedekiah. The "king's chiefs," in view of the use of "chiefs" in 39:13, were high-ranking Babylonian officials, to be referred to as "Chaldeans" in 41:3.[76] So Ishmael's crime is compounded. In vv. 2–3 MT not only raises the emotional temperature in shock but also identifies "all the Judeans" who were killed as Gedaliah's guards, to leave room for the mass of survivors in v. 10.[77] In v. 1 "the seventh month" (September/October) anticipates the cold-blooded massacre of 41:4–9; its seemingly premature position reflects the subsequent commemoration of the massacre on an annual fast day

---

74. Cf. Lust, "Gathering and Returning," 130–31.
75. Cf. the correspondence of *hăpīṣôtîkā*, "I scattered you," and *hiddaḥtîkā*, "I drove you away," in the parallel texts 30:11 and 46:28.
76. Bogaert, "Libération de Jérémie," 321.
77. McKane 2:1017–18; cf. Barthélemy, *Critique textuelle*, 2:743–44.

(Zech 7:5; 8:19), the third of the seventh month. The year is left unspecified, and so the duration of Gedaliah's governorship is not known.[78]

[41:4–9] If Ishmael's earlier death orgy had a modicum of reason, this one does not. His killing spree—no wonder MT involves his companions—marks the utter breakdown of law and order and a senseless abuse of power, and so underscores the ruination of the earlier positive scenario. The visit of northern pilgrims from the neighboring province of Samaria reflects Josiah's earlier annexation of the area and his destruction of local sanctuaries in favor of the Jerusalem temple (2 Kgs 23:15–20). The visit attests the long-lasting success of his religious policy. The pilgrims were in mourning (cf. Jer 16:6) for the recent destruction of the temple (2 Kgs 25:9, 13; Jer 52:13, 17); they expected to worship at its site, celebrating the Feast of Tabernacles as best they could. Readers are meant to detect a wistful semblance for the hope of northerners' worship at Zion expressed in 3:14 and 31:6. It emerges only to be smothered at birth. Ishmael's invitation to the pilgrims to interrupt their journey by paying their respects to the governor (v. 6) turns out to be an act of cunning deception, facilitated by pretending to share their grief over the temple's destruction. In v. 8 he adds to his vices openness to bribery. The historical reference (v. 9) to the events of 1 Kgs 15:16–22 ironically underlines Ishmael's perversity in using what was intended for the sustenance and protection of life as a place to dump his victims' corpses.

[10–18] This third subsection falls into two parts (vv. 10–14 and 15–18). Both are marked by a double use of a new key word, *hālak*, literally "go," rendered "set off." In v. 10 Ishmael sets off for Ammon, while in v. 12 Johanan and his troops set off to intercept him. In v. 15 Ishmael and his depleted group set off for Ammon once more, and in v. 17 the other, augmented company set off for Egypt. In principle the key word marks the final collapse of the high hopes expressed at the beginning of the section. The comings and the fine talk of staying now give way to frantic goings. The subsection ends with a recapitulation of 41:2 and the contravention of the authorization formula that implies submission to the will of Nebuchadnezzar's divine patron. No wonder the assurance not to fear (40:9), which was itself grounded implicitly in Yahweh's positive purpose, is replaced by a report of fear!

[10–14] Readers' hopes are initially raised again as they read of the rescue of Ishmael's prisoners.[79] MT makes much of the volte-face in vv. 13–14, adding a vivid emotional touch, cheering.

---

78. Pohlmann, *Studien*, 115 n. 311.
79. For a photograph of the reservoir see *ABD*, 2:1011. It was thirty-seven feet in diameter at the top.

Self-Imposed Exile

[15–18] Such hopes fade as the militia leaders plan a self-chosen exile to escape the punitive solidarity the Babylonians might exact against the community. In such a context "remnant" (v. 16) can be used only in irony, recalling 40:15. The role of the "eunuchs" mentioned in v. 16 was to attend the princesses of v. 10 (cf. Esth 2:3; 4:5). "Chimham's holding" (v. 17) seems to refer to tenure of land assigned centuries before by royal grant to a son of David's benefactor Barzillai (cf. 2 Sam 19:37–38, 40; 1 Kgs 2:7).[80] It makes the observation that such a token of strong and beneficent monarchy was now only a fragment of memory. Bethlehem—another place with royal associations—was evidently not far from the southern border of the province of Judah (cf. 13:19 and commentary).

[42:1–22] In this third section of the unit the scene for a divine oracle is set by its public solicitation and its receipt by the prophet in vv. 1–7, before its communication and a prophetic commentary on it in vv. 8–22. Each of the two subsections begins with an explicit identification of the assembled group with the whole of the nondeported Judean community. In v. 1 they are equated with the remnant of 40:11, 15; and 41:16, which, apart from the army units, was regarded as clustered at Mizpah (40:15). The listing of the constituent parts of the remnant in 43:5–6 will confirm that this whole group migrated to Egypt. The significance of this mass exodus in reverse is that the scenario of 40:9–10 based on ch. 27 is finally ruled out as a possibility, in line with Johanan's foreboding in 40:15.

[1–7] The community's request (vv. 1–3) leads to Jeremiah's reply (v. 4), which is countered by a response (vv. 5–6) before the prophet receives an oracle (v. 7). The focus of the interchange is on what the community says and on its self-representation as desiring to discover the divine will. The oracle reception statement at last resumes the oracle reception heading of 40:1 (cf. 32:1, 26).

[1–3] Readers have not been told earlier of Jeremiah's presence among the civilians, though they were meant to assume it from 40:6. Reference to his prophetic role in the narrative (cf. MT in v. 4) continues in the request ("your God"). They solicit his intervention as intercessor, pleading the remnant status of the community as a motive for divine help and claiming openness to Yahweh's will for them.

[4] In a guarded reply the prophet pointedly reminds them of their commitment to Yahweh ("your God") and promises openness in communicating a divine response. In view of his later negativity in vv. 20–21, he seems to be expressing skepticism about their openness in affirming his own.[81] Certainly the preceding narrative gave the impression their minds were made up

---

80. Albrecht Alt, "Der Anteil des Königtums an der sozialen Entwicklung in den Reichen Israel und Judah," in *Kleine Schriften zur Geschichte des Volkes Israel* (ed. M. Noth; Munich: Beck, 1959), 3:348–72, esp. 358–59; cf. Duhm 319–20.

81. Graupner, *Auftrag und Geschick*, 136; cf. Streane 248–49.

(41:17–18), so that what they now want is confirmation of their own calculated decision. Verse 20 will so judge in retrospect.

[5–6] The community hurriedly reassures the prophet, protesting suspiciously overmuch their sincere desire to accept the divine will. Verse 6 appears to be an editorial reinforcement of their response.[82] Its prose sermonic language develops 40:3, 9, and sums up the issue as one of obedience, starting a trend that will be continued in vv. 13b and 21. The challenging "your God" of v. 4 is capped with an affirming double "our God." If—but only if—their words are a measure of their hearts, they are eminently trustworthy.

[7] The delay is surprising (cf. 28:5, 12) and embarrassing. The garrulous community, straining at the spiritual leash, is confronted by a doubting and then silent prophet. At least the quiet waiting is a pointer to eventual inspiration. Insincerity and sincerity are set side by side.

[8–22] Jeremiah responds with an oracle (vv. 10–18) and then reinforces it with his own comments (vv. 19–22). MT eases the movement from vv. 1–7 to the oracle by adding in v. 9b a combination of phrases from vv. 2 and 6, though the addressee of the request of v. 2 is changed from the prophet to his God. The prophet's role falls short of the intercessory one he was asked for; "it is not so much Jeremiah, the intercessor, who appears as Jeremiah, the proclaimer of the word of Yahweh" (McKane 2:1041).

[10–18] Alternative scenarios are presented, with a conditional proclamation of salvation and an oracle of salvation (vv. 10–12) and a conditional oracle of disaster (vv. 13–18). The weight of the message is given to the latter option. "There is a strong sense of the inevitability of disobedience and doom."[83] The message has been framed at beginning and end with prose sermonic affirmations to bring out its significance.

[10–12] The basic conditional offer was evidently, "If you are prepared to stay in the country, do not be afraid of Babylon's king, of whom you are so afraid; he will allow you to stay on your own soil." Prose sermonic language and confirmatory literary allusions enhance the offer and clarify the length and breadth of the divine grace on which the community was turning its back. Underlying the offer is the scenario of 40:9–10 that is now openly expounded, while the fear of 41:18 that denied 40:9 is countered. The scenario is once more an application of the thematic ch. 27, and 27:11 ("on its own soil . . . and stay on it") is in mind at v. 12b. A redactional overlay amplifies the message in vv. 10a*b*-b, 11b, and 12a. The programmatic promise of building and planting instead of the opposite and the chance of a divine change of attitude reflect the alternatives of 18:7–10, while the particular choice of "demolishing" echoes the

---

82. Thiel, *Redaktion von Jeremia 26–45*, 64; cf. Stulman, *Prose Sermons*, 30, no. 1; 35, no. 21; Pohlmann, *Studien*, 126–27.

83. Peter R. Ackroyd, "Historians and Prophets," *SEÅ* 33 (1968): 18–54, esp. 49.

alternatives of 24:6.[84] In v. 11b the oracle of salvation given to Jeremiah in 15:20b–21a (cf. 1:19), with its promise of rescue and divine basis of assurance, is collectively reapplied, while v. 12a borrows from 1 Kgs 8:50. The sense of v. 10b is that the community's compliance would prevent the disaster that their present propensity was about to reap at Yahweh's hands, a disaster that would repeat their ordeal of 587 in another form (cf. v. 18; 40:2–3).

[13–18] The negative alternative of vv. 13–14 is used as a reason for the announcement of disaster in vv. 16–17, which is reaffirmed in the climax of v. 18. Verses 13–18 also comprise a disputation, made up of a thesis (vv. 13–14), a dispute (vv. 15–17), and a counterthesis (v. 18). This form largely accounts for its lengthy, repetitive nature. Allowance must still be made for prose sermonic additions to drive the lesson home, one at the close of v. 17 (cf. MT in 40:3) and the catastrophe formula near the end of v. 18.[85] Furthermore, a characteristic definition regarding lack of obedience breaks in at the end of v. 13, with a telling third person divine reference. The community's attitude put into words (v. 14) is an unfolding of the fear (v. 11; and 41:18) concerning Babylonian military reprisals and the famine that would again accompany them if they stayed in Judah, as the rebuttal in v. 16 makes clear. The focus on "sword and famine" (plus "pestilence" at times in MT) in vv. 16–22 corresponds to the fate of the nation that does not serve Nebuchadnezzar in 27:8, which is reinforced in MT at 27:13. This factor underlies the correction that such would still be their fate if they left Judah, which was within his sphere of influence. The fresh emphasis on living as aliens ($g\hat{u}r$, vv. 15, 17) disputes the verb "stay" in v. 14 and insists that the verb can be properly applied only to settling in the homeland (vv. 10, 12; cf. v. 13). The switch to the third person in v. 17 reflects the conditional use of a relative clause, with the sense "If any of the men (among you). . . ."[86] The literal "men" (NAB, NJPS) is to be retained in translation since heads of families are in view (cf. 2 Kgs 10:11). The vertical solidarity of punishment is consistent with 11:22–23 and 20:6 (cf. Exod 20:5). A bleak picture of expatriation, warfare, starvation, and extinction, and consequently no possibility of a homecoming, replaces the fantasy of peace and plenty in Egypt. It is all summed up (v. 18) as a terrible divine intervention that in intensity would match the disaster that overwhelmed Jerusalem in 587. The door is slammed on a potential scenario based on ch. 27 of continuing life in the land and also on an Egyptian diaspora. So "the future of Israel lay with the Babylonian diaspora."[87] The other scenario of ch. 24 was the only door to good prospects. The prose sermonic redactor has endorsed this conclusion at v. 10 by echoing 24:6

---

84. Cf. Stulman, *Prose Sermons*, 44, no. 86.
85. See ibid., 38, no. 39.
86. Cf. Davidson, *Hebrew Syntax*, §132, remark 2.
87. Nicholson, *Preaching*, 111.

and may also have 24:9 in specific view at v. 18. The promise of building and planting lay elsewhere, not with the Egypt-bound refugees.

[19–22] The divine disputation is reinforced with the prophet's closing reprimand. The oracle is curtly summarized and put in a human setting of deceit that exposes the pretensions of the oracle-seeking community in vv. 1–6. In v. 21 the prose sermon's catchword "obey" in v. 6 is flatly denied in an echo of v. 13. MT continues the prophet's challenge over pronouns from v. 4, doubly echoing "your God" in vv. 20–21 and distastefully quoting the community's double "our God" from v. 6. Finally the facade of alternatives, which took the community's words at face value, is stripped away and the outcome of the prechosen option is addressed in all its starkness by reaffirming the dispute of v. 16. "Now that they have chosen the road to Egypt, there is virtually no way out."[88]

[43:1–7] Following the oracle is the communal response (vv. 1–4), and then a narrative that acts upon that response (vv. 5–7). Both subsections conclude with a prose sermonic definition in terms of disobedience, in v. 4 and in the middle of v. 7; it reinforces the redactional message throughout ch. 42.[89]

[1–4] Jeremiah's faithful compliance with 42:4 is recorded as a foil to the people's response—or at least that of the military component (cf. 40:7a, 9; 41:12), with Azariah now taking the lead (cf. 42:1 and note v)—which belies their pledge in 42:5. MT embellishes this contrast by continuing the double divine apposition it adopted in 42:20–21 in dependence on 40:6; the apposition now takes the narrative form "their God." MT also shakes its fist at the responders, calling them "insolent," in shock at their categorical rejection of the oracle (cf. Deut 1:43). Judging attack the best form of defense, they finger Baruch as the "*eminence grise*" responsible for Jeremiah's negative message (Jones 477). The community projects the content of its own underlying fear in 41:18 and 42:10 onto Baruch in self-justification and derogatory blame. Baruch, whom readers meet for the first time in a postwar setting, was earlier encountered as Jeremiah's copyist and agent in his enforced absence (32:13, 16; 36:19, 32). Here he is branded as the human source of the message, a role he virtually denied in 36:17–18. Thereby Jeremiah is dismissed as a false prophet (Weiser 2:363; McKane 2:1052). "False" (*šeqer*) in v. 2 is ironic at two levels. At one level it is an echo of Gedaliah's inauspicious answer to Johanan in 40:16, while at another it redirects the "falsehood" often predicated of Jeremiah's rivals earlier in the book (e.g., 5:31; 14:14; 23:25; 27:10; 29:9).

[5–7] In vv. 5a and 7 the journey of 41:16–17 is willfully resumed, as if 42:1–43:4 could be erased. Unfortunately "the prophet Jeremiah" stubbornly remains in v. 6, recalling 42:2. Verses 5b–6 provide a portmanteau listing of the various elements of the heterogeneous remnant community listed hitherto

---

88. Ackroyd, "Historians and Prophets," 49.
89. Pohlmann, *Studien*, 158; cf. Thiel, *Redaktion von Jeremia, 26–45*, 67–68.

(40:6, 12, 15; 41:10, 16), "including Jeremiah and Baruch," in order to convey a sense of migration en masse, as in 42:1, 8. The old prophet was taken where he did not wish to go, like Peter (John 21:18; Berrigan 172). In v. 5 MT recollects with a sigh the minireturn from exile it had celebrated in 40:12. The verb *gûr*, rendered "settle for a while" and earlier as "live as aliens" (42:15, 22), is unexpected here; one expects "stay," as in 40:9 and 42:10. Its use, unless it reflects careless writing, has the ironic force that indeed Judah did not turn out to be their homeland. Tahpanhes (v. 7) was a fortress town in northern Egypt in the eastern Nile Delta; it was mentioned in 2:16.

[8–13] The final section in this extended unit functions as a climactic conclusion. It trumps the dream of Egyptian peace and plenty in 42:14 with a picture of doom that clarifies the oracular forecast of war (42:16–18) by specifying the "sword" (42:16–17; 43:11). The coherence of the section within the unit emerges at three points. First, apart from the overall topic of Egypt, "Tahpanhes" (vv. 7, 8) is a hinge fastening this section to the previous one. Second, there is the "sword" link with ch. 42. Third, "King Nebuchadnezzar of Babylon" traces an arc back to "Babylon's king" in the authorization formula at 40:5, 11; 41:2, 18, and also in the scenario of 40:10 and 42:11. The section presents divine commands to Jeremiah to engage in a symbolic action in the presence of some of the refugees (v. 9) and to proclaim what it meant in an announcement of disaster (vv. 10–13). The normal report of the prophet performing the symbolic action is omitted to keep the focus on the interpretive oracle.

[9] The action took place outside the royal administrative building in the frontier town. Similarly the southern frontier town of Elephantine had in it "the king's house" with the same sense.[90] What Jeremiah was to do with the stones is not clear. The sense of the verb here rendered "cover up" is ambiguous. Was he to bury them to "mark the spot" where Nebuchadnezzar's throne was eventually to be set (cf. NRSV, NIV, GNB)?[91] Or was he to build a dais for the throne, with a mortar overlay providing a level surface for the stones (cf. REB, NJPS)? The problem is compounded by the terms of uncertain meaning that are missing from LXX, possibly by oversight,[92] unless they are an explanatory elaboration in MT. As to their meaning, they may refer to an open area outside the government building and to the application of clay mortar to the stones to hide them or cover them.

[10–13] This announcement of disaster spells out in two phases Yahweh's intervention and the human consequences (vv. 10–11, 12–13). In both cases the consequences highlight the demonstration of Nebuchadnezzar's control of

---

90. See Arthur E. Cowley, *Aramaic Papyri of the Fifth Century B.C.* (Oxford: Clarendon, 1923), 3–7, no. 2, lines 12, 14, 16.
91. Friebel, *Sign-Acts*, 357, 359.
92. Janzen, *Studies*, 183.

Egypt. The oracle appears to be a premonition of his incursion in 568/567 B.C.E., when he probably invaded and plundered the Delta (cf. Ezek 29:17–20).[93]

[10–11] If the details of the symbolic action are blurred, its significance is clear. The focus on Nebuchadnezzar throughout the oracle is meant to remind the reader of the foundational use of ch. 27 in chs. 40 and 42. In line with that divinely willed dominion over the Palestinian states, he was now to extend his punitive power into Egypt. MT, aware of the connection to ch. 27, spells it out by adding "my servant" to the formal designation, as in 27:6 (cf. 25:9). The carefully laid stones pledged a divine end for an ornate display that triumphantly flaunted Babylon's presence and power outside the building symbolizing Egyptian control. The oracle falls into the category of oracles against the nations, like those in chs. 46–51, and does not mention the Judean refugees, some of whom were bystanders during the symbolic action (v. 9). Such oracles, even those that address foreign nations, are really aimed at a Judean constituency. The implication here is that those who wanted to evade Babylonian military action (42:14) had walked into a situation ripe for its resurgence. Verse 11b is an abridged quotation of 15:2. Its crucial element is "sword," which has been moved to a climactic place. It looks like the compiler's endeavor to clinch the section's connection with an earlier section of the unit, the "sword" in 42:16–17. The editorial contrivance clarifies this section as an elaboration of the fate that was to befall the Judean migrants. They would be tragically caught up, it is implied, in Nebuchadnezzar's raid on this Egyptian border town. The literary allusion to 15:2 matches those in 42:11–12 and suggests the work of the prose sermonic redactor.

[12–13] The second divine intervention and its human results feature irresistible power. "Fire" and the overpowering of Egypt's protective deities provide a frame. In the middle the colorful simile of hunting for lice develops the plundering of divine images into systematic looting, carried out as casually as a shepherd with time to spare can work over his lice-infested cloak. Then Egypt's inability to check or harm the invader continues the note of masterful ease. However, the redactor who added v. 11b found a human reference in the simile, the selection of victims in a gruesome triage for plague, captivity, or sword. This reinterpretation, along with the addition in v. 11, increases the coherence with the oracle in 42:16–17 and with the refugees' retort in 43:3. Verse 13 develops v. 12a, claiming the sacred precincts and architectural symbols ("obelisks") of the great Egyptian sun god Re to be at risk, nearly a hundred miles to the south of Tahpanhes. His sanctuary at On (Hellenistic Heliopolis, "Sun City"; cf. Gen

---

93. *ANET*, 308b. The text is fragmentary and unclear. See Donald J. Wiseman, "Babylonia 605–539 B.C.," in *Cambridge Ancient History*, vol. 3, part 2: *The Assyrian and Babylonian Empires and Other States of the Ancient Near East, from the Eighth to the Sixth Centuries B.C.* (ed. J. Broadman et al.; 2d ed.; Cambridge: Cambridge University Press, 1991), 229–51, esp. 236.

Self-Imposed Exile

41:45) is identified as an Egyptian counterpart of the Palestinian Beth-shemesh, "house/temple of the sun (god)."

In 40:1–43:13 an opportunity to stay in the land under divine blessing is abandoned. Instead, the nonexiled Judeans move to Egypt, a sphere fraught with disaster.

44:1–30 *Fatal Consequences of a Besetting Sin*

44:1 A message received by Jeremiah, which was intended for all the Judeans who lived in Egypt, that is, in Migdol, Tahpanhes, *Noph*, and the Pathros area, as follows. 2 "Here is what Yahweh *Almighty*, Israel's God, said: 'You have seen for yourselves the utterly bad fate I inflicted upon Jerusalem and *all* the towns in Judah. Look, they are uninhabited ruins *today* 3 as a result of their bad behavior that made me so upset—going off and sacrificing[a] to other gods never known *to them or* to you *or to your forebears*. 4 I sent *all* my prophetic servants to you over and over again, with a *strong* warning not to engage in that abominable conduct, which is so hateful to me, 5 but they would not listen, they turned a deaf ear to the warning to renounce their bad behavior by refraining from sacrificing to other gods. 6 So my fury and anger fell in a deluge, burning up Judah's towns and Jerusalem's streets and making them the ruined and desolate areas they are today.[b] 7 The point is'—here is what Yahweh, *God* Almighty, *Israel's God*, said—'why are you ensuring for yourselves an extremely bad fate, namely, the extinction of men and women, of children and infants from your Judean families, so you will have no remnant left for you, 8 by upsetting me with images your hands have made, by sacrificing to other gods in Egypt, where you have come to live as aliens, with the result that you face the extinction of your families and universal reactions of cursing and insults? 9 Have you forgotten those bad things done by your forebears and by Judah's kings and its officials,[c] and the bad things done *by yourselves and* by your wives, committed in Judah and on Jerusalem's streets? 10 They have shown no contrition to this day or fear, nor have they walked in the track of my *torah and* rulings that I put in front of *you and your* forebears.[d] 11 Therefore'—here is what Yahweh *Almighty, Israel's God*, said—'look out, I am setting my sights on *a bad fate for you,* the extinction of all *Judeans.* 12 *I will seize*[e] the *Judean* remnant *who set their sights on coming to Egypt to live there as aliens, and they will all perish* in Egypt. They will be struck down by a sword or perish from famine. From the lowest to the elite *they will die by sword or famine,* and they will face reactions of *cursing,* shock, and oaths and insults. 13 I will deal with those who live in Egypt in the same way I dealt with Jerusalem, using sword and famine *and pestilence.* 14 There will be no survivor, *nobody who escapes* among the Judean remnant, those who *have come to* live as aliens[f] in Egypt and then to go back to Judah, where they are longing to go back *and stay*. But they will not go back, except for individual survivors."

15 Jeremiah received the following response from all the men, who were aware their wives were sacrificing to other gods, and from all the women *who were present*, a large group, and from all the people who lived [elsewhere] in Egypt, in Pathros: 16 "That message you have given us in Yahweh's name—we do not intend to listen to you. 17 Instead, we mean to carry out all the commitments our mouths have made to offer sacrifices and pour libations to the Queen[g] of Heaven, just as was previously done by us and our forebears and by our kings and officials, in Judah's towns and on Jerusalem's streets. We had plenty of food as a result and enjoyed good fortune, and we never laid eyes on a bad fate. 18 But ever since we gave up offering sacrifices *and pouring libations* to the Queen of Heaven, we have lacked for everything and have been perishing from sword or famine. 19 When we used to offer sacrifices[h] and pour libations to the Queen of Heaven, was it without the support of our husbands that we made for her cakes *bearing her image*[i] and poured libations to her?"

20 Then Jeremiah said to all the people, men and women, all the people who had given him this response, as follows, 21 "The sacrificing done in Judah's towns and on Jerusalem's streets by you and your forebears, by your kings and officials as well as by the people at large—did not Yahweh remember *such acts* and call this to mind? 22 Yahweh could stand it no longer, reacting to your bad conduct, to the abominable things you were doing. So your country has become the ruined and shocking area, curse-worthy *and devoid of inhabitants*, it is today. 23 It was in reaction to your sacrificing, your sinning against Yahweh, disobeying Yahweh, and refusing to walk in the track of his torah, rulings, and terms. That is why you have experienced this bad fate *that lasts to this day*."

24 Jeremiah went on to tell *all* the people, and particularly *all* the women, "Hear Yahweh's message, *all you Judeans in Egypt*. 25 Here is what Yahweh *Almighty*, Israel's God, said: 'You *and your* wives have used both[j] your mouths to speak and your hands to implement that promise of yours, "We mean to keep our vows, the ones we made to offer sacrifices and pour libations to the Queen of Heaven." Go ahead and carry out[k] your vows! Go ahead and keep your vows! 26 Therefore'—hear Yahweh's message, all you Judeans who live in Egypt—'look out, I swear by my powerful name,' said Yahweh, 'that my name will never again be used[l] anywhere in Egypt on the lips of any Judean man for the oath "By the life of *the Lord* Yahweh." 27 Look out, I am going to watch over them with a

bad fate in view, not good fortune, so every Judean man in Egypt will perish from sword or famine until they are all gone, 28 though a few survivors of the sword will come back *from Egypt* to Judah. *All* the Judean remnant, those who have come to Egypt to live there as aliens, will find out whose promise comes true, *theirs or mine.* 29 Here is a sign for you,' declared Yahweh, 'to show I am going to deal with you in this place, so you will be able to recognize that my message of a bad fate for you[m] will indeed come true.' 30 Here is what Yahweh said: 'Look, I am going to hand over *Pharaoh*, King Hophra of Egypt, to his enemies, to people who have designs on his life, just as I handed over King Zedekiah of Judah to King Nebuchadnezzar of Babylon, his enemy who had designs on his life.'"

a. The grammatically intrusive *la‘ăbōd*, "to serve, worship," in MT, which LXX (51:3) lacks (*BHS*), probably represents the incorporation of a gloss that had the contextually similar 35:15 in view. NEB omits it.

b. See textual notes on 32:20 for the phrase here and in v. 22 and also in MT at v. 23.

c. "Their wives" in most EVV conceals a textual problem. MT *nāšāyw*, "his wives," must be intended in a distributive sense, "the wives of each of them," as Symmachus renders (see Barthélemy, *Critique textuelle*, 2:753), but can hardly be correct. Aquila's rendering, "his/its officials," implies an original *śārāyw* (cf. LXX "your officials" [*BHS*], followed by NJB, with contextual assimilation of the pronoun); the suffix refers to Judah, as in 8:1 (Ehrlich, *Randglossen*, 4:350, following Houbigant). This is surely the source from which other readings developed. Cf. vv. 17 and 21 for the combination of kings and officials. MT suffered assimilation to "wives" later in the sentence.

d. LXX "their forebears" is doubtless the earlier reading, in line with the third plural references earlier in the sentence. MT has rhetorically widened the scope to direct involvement in both vv. 9*ab* ("*by yourselves*") and 10b, in the latter case with 26:4 in mind; cf. too v. 21 below.

e. Or "do away with," as in 15:15 (Rudolph 260).

f. MT adds *šām*, "there," which is rightly missing from LXX (*BHS*). It assimilates to vv. 12 and 28 and a number of earlier passages (see Janzen, *Studies*, 58), but is inappropriate here.

g. See *BHS* and textual note g on 7:18 for this case and for vv. 18, 19, 25.

h. For the anomaly of a masculine form see GKC §145n; Joüon §149c.

i. See GKC §58g.

j. Rudolph 262.

k. See *BHS* and GKC §72k for the form. For the use of an imperfect in an imperatival sense cf. Joüon §113m.

l. The omission in LXX may be translational (McKane 2:1080).

m. The omission from LXX is probably accidental (Janzen, *Studies*, 108, 118; cf. *BHS* and *HUB*).

The complex unit in ch. 44 is a disputation that forecasts the virtual extinction of the Judean community in Egypt for illicit worship and insists on a

Yahwistic interpretation of Judah's downfall. It begins with two narrative scenes, a commissioning scene (vv. 1–14) and an audience reaction scene (vv. 15–19).[94] It continues with two more, a counterreaction scene (vv. 20–23) and a fresh commissioning scene (vv. 24–30). Accordingly the unit falls into an ABB'A' structure, with a divine voice at beginning and end, and human voices, those of Jeremiah's audience and of Jeremiah, in between. The divine contributions are oracles of disaster, with reasons (vv. 2–10 and 25) and announcements (vv. 11–14 and 26–30). The dynamic of the unit is supplied by a disputation.[95] Instead of the usual three-part scheme that finds truth in the counterthesis, this one has a four-part scheme that promotes the thesis. There is a divine thesis (vv. 1–14), the audience's counterthesis (vv. 15–19), Jeremiah's dispute of the counterthesis (vv. 20–23), and a divine reaffirmation and confirmation of the thesis (vv. 24–30).[96] There is continuity with the preceding unit in that "the prophet Jeremiah" who was taken to Egypt and delivered an oracle there (43:7–13) now delivers two further oracles. Moreover, the present unit adduces an extra reason for condemning the Egyptian community. The focus on the Judean remnant's coming to live as aliens in Egypt in the thesis (vv. 8, 14; also v. 12 in MT) and in its reaffirmation (v. 28) takes up a climactic phrase used previously (42:15, 17, 22; 43:2), thus carrying forward earlier accusations. Also, "in this place" (44:29) recalls 42:22.

Scholars have tended to identify much redactional material in the unit due to its repetitiousness, even though the genre of disputation is open to repetition because of its argumentative nature. Nevertheless, regard must be paid to MT's amplifications to a text already augmented with prose sermonic language. The prose sermonic elements appear primarily in two clusters (vv. 2–10 and 20–23). They contribute a final prose sermon to the book, in order to drive home the meaning of Judah's destruction. This was done by adapting and expanding an earlier form of disputation, a thesis (vv. 11–14), a counterthesis (vv. 16–19), a dispute (v. 25), and reinforcement of the thesis (vv. 26–30). This earlier form, which represents Jeremiah's last known message, was closely associated with ch. 42 and made the remnant's migration to Egypt (44:14; anticipated at v. 12 in MT) the basic accusation that was to incur divine reprisal of mass destruction (cf. McKane 2:1089–90). The counterthesis affirmed that, on the contrary, resumed worship of the Queen of Heaven would guarantee good fortune, as was the case in preexilic times. The dispute challenges this claim, focusing on v. 17, while the reinforcement of the thesis repeats the accusation (v. 28) and its coming recompense. The prose sermonic pieces grafted onto the earlier text alter

---

94. Cf. Applegate, "Narrative Patterns," 79, 81.

95. Cf. Long, "Stylistic Components," 388.

96. Cf. the disputation in Isa 10:5–15, which comprises thesis (vv. 5–6), counterthesis (v. 7), dispute (vv. 8–14), and reestablishment of thesis (v. 15), according to Murray, "Rhetoric of Disputation," 106–10.

the balance and focus of the unit. The migration to Egypt plays a lesser role, while the comparison with the 587 disaster (v. 13) and the specific aberrant worship already practiced in the preexilic period (v. 17) are now far more prominent. Pride of place is given to the tragedy of 587 and to its interpretation as Yahweh's reprisal for pagan worship in general.

[**44:1**] The oracle reception headings found here and in 45:1 introduce not literary blocks of material but divisions within the block, as in 34:8, and 35:1 after 34:1. As in 25:1, the present heading lacks the usual "from Yahweh." The addressees in the first oracle (vv. 7, 12, 14) and also in v. 28 are the Judean remnant whose misadventures that took them to Tahpanhes were recounted in chs. 40–43. Here, however, they are editorially widened to existing communities of Judean colonists. Mention is made of Migdol, located somewhere in the eastern Delta, and also of Pathros, a term for Upper (southern) Egypt. MT completes the general picture by adding Noph (Greek Memphis), an important city in northern Egypt, mentioned in 2:16; it creates a connecting link with that toponym in 46:14, 19, in material placed after ch. 45 in MT. The text apparently reflects a meeting of representatives as v. 15 suggests. The intention was to virtually exclude the Egyptian Diaspora from the reversal of fortunes to be enjoyed by other displaced Judeans (cf. 24:8).

[**2–14**] The thesis of the disputation, which will come under fire and then be defended later in the unit, is presented as an oracle of disaster. Its reason (vv. 7–10) is embellished in vv. 2–6 with an illustration of the dire consequences from the recent war, while the announcement follows in vv. 11–14. The three parts are each prefaced by a quotation formula.

[**2–10**] This is the first of two prose sermonic supplements to the unit.[97] It reinforces a lesson taught in earlier prose sermons and given priority in Jeremiah's poetry (2:4–19, 20–37), that pagan worship had made Judah's destruction inevitable.

[**2–6**] The reminiscence is given greater punch by its chiastic arrangement (cf. Brueggemann 405). It builds on a characteristic interplay of "bad fate" and "bad behavior." Yahweh's tragic intervention in Judah's affairs in 587, bringing ruin (vv. 2, 6), was retaliation for its "bad behavior" in "sacrificing to other gods" (vv. 3, 5b). Its fate was sealed by refusal to listen to prophetic revelation, Yahweh's second chance (vv. 4a, 5a). At the heart of the chiasm stands the double description of its sin in passionate terms as "abominable conduct, which is so hateful to me" (v. 4b). Torah allusions refer to the rejection of the first chance

---

97. Cf. Thiel, *Redaktion von Jeremia 26–45*, 69–72; Stulman, *Prose Sermons*, 112–17. The inflicting of a bad fate (v. 2) merits inclusion in the latter's analysis (cf. Stulman, *Prose Sermons*, 34, no. 10). So do the last phrase (v. 9; cf. v. 6) and the torah allusion (v.10b), which MT clarifies in line with v. 23 (see Stulman, *Prose Sermons*, 39, no. 45). Both Thiel and Stulman, however, follow older scholarship in including vv. 11–14 in the sermon's scope; for the attribution of vv. 11–14 to the core oracle cf. Pohlmann, *Studien*, 171, 182.

Yahweh had given, in v. 3 the novelty of pagan worship and in v. 4b a citation of Deut 12:31, which was set in a context of warning against pagan worship.

[7–10] The reason for coming disaster makes lively use of rhetorical questions. It reapplies some of the sinister language of vv. 2–6 to the current situation, the "bad fate" of v. 2 and "bad behavior" of vv. 3 and 5, now "bad things" in v. 9, and the "sacrificing to other gods" in v. 8, also from vv. 3 and 5. In addition, the prevalence of aberrant religion (v. 9) matches that of the disaster (v. 6), while the torah allusions (vv. 3–4) are clarified (v. 10b, as later in v. 23), with exclusive worship of Yahweh in mind. In v. 8 a further reason for disaster, the migration to Egypt, anticipates vv. 14 and 28, but essentially the passage describes the worship of the Queen of Heaven (vv. 17–19, 25) in the general terms of vv. 3 and 5 as "sacrificing to other gods" and so meriting condemnation. The explicit reference to "wives" in v. 9, which will be capped in v. 15 and which anticipates their worship in v. 19, clinches the application. MT reinforces the break with tradition by adding in v. 7 "Israel's God" from v. 2. The combination of preexilic generations and groupings with "by your wives" at v. 9 in the common text anticipates v. 17, while MT amplifies it with "by yourselves," with the husbands of v. 19 in view. In the common text the particular fate of "extinction" in vv. 7–8 is borrowed from v. 11 and embellished with the aid of 9:21 (20) ("infants"). A "bad fate" (v. 7) not only anticipates v. 17 but looks back to v. 2 by way of comparison, and so exemplifies the bridging role between past and present that vv. 7–10 play.

[11–14] This announcement of disaster makes a double move from divine intervention to human consequences (vv. 11–12, 13–14). It has been integrated with the preceding prose sermon by the paraphrase of the catastrophe formula of v. 8 in v. 12, while MT does the same by adding "a bad fate" (v. 11). The basic message condemning migration, which repeated the one in 42:15–22, was thus made part of a larger message of reprisal for the pagan worship condemned in vv. 2–10. MT enhances the similarity to 42:15–22, insisting on a sealed fate, doubly merited—for leaving Judah as well as for illicit worship. It does so in v. 12, which has been crammed with echoes of 42:15 and 17, and in v. 14. Its added relative clause in v. 12 neatly balances Yahweh's purpose in v. 11 with that of the remnant. The futile nostalgia for a squandered opportunity in v. 14 not only sums up the message of chs. 40–43, but recalls for the reader the frustration predicted for two other exiles, King Jehoiachin and the queen mother in 22:27. The significant modification at the end of v. 14 will be repeated in v. 28a.

[15] The narrative introduction looks back both to the setting of the oracle reception heading in v. 1 and to the prose sermonic phrase "sacrificing to other gods" used earlier (vv. 3 and 8). The latter echo has a transitional role. The mention of "women" paves the way for v. 19, where the wives are clearly speaking in their own right, but the introduction invites readers to hear voices of the men or of both the men and the women in vv. 16–18.

Self-Imposed Exile

[16–19] The counterthesis was meant to deny the announcement of disaster in vv. 11–14. The sinister consequences of vv. 12 and 14 are denied by setting alongside them not personal experience but "a historical memory" (McKane 2:1087), the happy consequences of cultic worship of the Queen of Heaven in preexilic times before Josiah's reform (see 7:18 and commentary). The assumption is that those good old days would be enjoyed once more if only they maintained such worship, as they intended. Good fortune, not a bad fate, was their destiny, they claimed. The perspective changes somewhat in the larger redactional setting and focuses on the religious aspect. The refusal to listen now is related to the nonlistening of v. 5. The traditional and socially acceptable nature of their worship, which only exacerbated the problem in v. 9, is a matter of pride, which acquires for the reader a negative, defiant perspective from v. 9, and to this end the added prose sermonic element "in Judah's towns and on Jerusalem's streets," which implicitly stands in contrast with temple worship, underscores the cross-reference. The cult was evidently swept away among Josiah's religious reforms in 621 B.C.E., though private worship persisted (cf. 7:18). Its latter-day devotees, applying a contrary interpretation of *post hoc* as *propter hoc*, credit subsequent disasters to its cessation and state their determination to reestablish it as a means of blessing. Verse 17 refers to the discharging of vows, using a technical phrase (cf. Num 30:2, 12; Judg 11:36). The women add their husbands' approbation of and cooperation in their religious practices as further justification. MT elucidates the form of the ritual cake offerings as stamped before baking with a representation of the goddess.[98]

[20–23] The dispute continues the prose sermonic thesis of vv. 2–10. It rejects the counterthesis by maintaining the cogency of the Yahwistic interpretation of Judah's downfall. So it recalls the language of vv. 2–10, echoing vv. 2, 6, 8, 9, and 10b. Fresh prose sermonic language is used in vv. 22–23.[99] The divine remembering in v. 21 ironically counters the imputed human forgetting in v. 9.

[24–30] The thesis of vv. 11–14 is first reaffirmed in vv. 25–28 and then confirmed in vv. 29–30. The reestablishment of the thesis is almost completely free of prose sermonic elements—"people who have/had designs on his life" in v. 30 are the only instances[100]—nor does it echo vv. 2–10 or 20–23. This component of the disputation is another oracle of disaster. It is divided into three parts, a reason for disaster (v. 25), an announcement (vv. 26–28), and a confirming sign

---

98. See Martin Rose, *Der Ausschliesslichkeitsanspruch Jahwehs: Deuteronomische Schultheologie und die Volksfrömmigkeit in der späten Königszeit* (BWANT 106; Stuttgart: Kohlhammer, 1975), 254 n. 1.

99. For "bad conduct" and "disobeying" see Stulman, *Prose Sermons*, 41, no. 63; and 33, no. 1. Stulman does not count vv. 20–23 as a prose sermonic composition, but it is widely taken as such; see esp. Thiel, *Redaktion von Jeremia 26–45*, 74–76.

100. Stulman, *Prose Sermons*, 43, no. 77.

(vv. 29–30). The parts are signaled by calls for attention (vv. 24 and 26) and by parallel quotation formulas (vv. 25 and 30). The first part functioned earlier as the dispute, but the redactional incorporation of vv. 20–23 as the prose sermonic dispute with its own narrative introduction and the separate narrative introduction in v. 24a mean that v. 25 has been associated with what follows.

[25] The wives were in view in the Vorlage of MT, as the mostly feminine Hebrew verbs throughout indicate, whereas MT has roughly widened the address in line with the narrative introduction that involves both husbands and wives. Verse 29 implies a more general address, and the vocative in v. 26, which MT has copied in v. 24, concurs. The dispute challenges v. 17, which raises the question whether v. 17 and indeed vv. 16–18 were originally spoken by the wives along with v. 19. The present form of the text, introduced by the narrative of v. 15, says no, and despite scholars' suspicions the text may be permitted a careless lack of consistency. The call to honor vows prefaces its aftermath that will be stated in the announcement of disaster; it sarcastically challenges the counterthesis at the point of v. 17a.

[26] "Yahweh's name," disdained in the counterthesis at v. 16, turns into a "powerful" boomerang. Over against the oath formula used by syncretistic Yahwists invoking Yahweh's name is pronounced a countermanding divine oath that strikingly implies the end of Yahwism among Egypt-based Judeans, which vv. 27–28a will explain in terms of death or departure. If they want to reject an exclusive Yahweh and so forfeit the right to use the oath, on their own heads be it! The sentence gains rhetorical effect from its frame of a divine oath ratified by Yahweh's own name and a human oath in the same name, with the former oath outranking the latter. The singling out of each "(Judean) man" in vv. 26–27, overlooked in LXX and removed in most EVV, appears to be as intentional as "men" was in 42:17. "Husbands" (v. 19) and "men" represent the same Hebrew word, just as "wives" and "women" did in v. 15. This women-centered cult that met with the approval and participation of husbands would spell doom for these husbands and heads of families, not simply for the wives who sponsored it (cf. v. 7).

[27–28] In v. 27a the counterthesis of vv. 16–19 that ruled on the issue of good fortune or a bad fate (v. 17b) is denied, while v. 27b reaffirms the thesis with reference to v. 12. Verse 28a repeats the modification found at the end of v. 14, denying totality. Both corrections are due to later editing (cf. 4:27; 5:10, 18), but not merely in reflection of knowledge that some Judeans did manage to return. Rather, it incorporates a subsequent awareness of divine grace that would include some of the Egyptian Diaspora in the restoration to the land, eventual grace that the book could celebrate in its later form (see 23:3 and commentary, the initial comment on chs. 21–24 with reference to 23:8 and 24:9, and "Purpose" in the introduction). Verse 28b returns to the promise of v. 25 (and

Self-Imposed Exile 449

v. 17). Yahweh's announcement of disaster would trump the community's vows to the Queen of Heaven that were meant to guarantee good fortune.

[29–30] A confirming sign buttresses the preceding "promise" with its assurance of "a bad fate." Hophra (589–570 B.C.E.; Greek Apries), the pharaoh who had earlier tried to help Zedekiah (37:5), would be overthrown by Yahweh's intervention. The precedent of Zedekiah's demise at Yahweh's hands is cited to bolster the confirmation of the thesis. The sign is a premonition of Hophra's loss of his throne to his general Amasis in a coup and his later being put to death.[101] In terms of fulfillment the sign fared better than what it betokened. The Judean Diaspora in Egypt seems to have continued, despite setbacks;[102] in due course the LXX, produced by later immigrants from Judah, became a tribute to its importance and influence. The value of the thesis is its oblique and rhetorical affirmation that the real destiny of the Judeans lay with the Babylonian Diaspora, whose return was to trigger the ongoing development of mainstream Judaism under the providence of God for centuries to come.

Chapter 44 adds a further reason for the coming doom of Judeans in Egypt, such aberrant worship as that of the Queen of Heaven, which had earlier set Judah on the road to ruin.

45:1–5 Promise of Survival to Baruch

45:1 A message spoken by the prophet Jeremiah to Baruch ben Neriah, when he was writing down these messages on a scroll at Jeremiah's dictation, in the fourth year of King Jehoiakim ben Josiah of Judah, *which said:* 2 "Here is what Yahweh, *Israel's God,* said about you, Baruch. 3 You[a] are saying, 'Wretched me! Yahweh has added sorrow to the pain I have. I am worn out from my groaning and cannot find any rest.' 4 '*This is what you are to* say to him:" "Here is what Yahweh said: 'Look, what I have built up I am going to demolish, and what I have planted I am going to uproot, *and that applies to the whole earth.*[b] 5 You, on the other hand,[c] have your expectations of great things.[d] Do not expect them! Instead,[e] although, look, I am going to inflict a bad fate on everyone[f] else,' declared Yahweh, 'I will let you get away with your life in all the places you go to.'"'"

a. LXX (51:33) facilitates the connection with v. 4 by prefacing "Because" (cf. *BHS,* NAB).

101. Herodotus, *Hist.* 2.161–163, 169; see Donald B. Redford, "Hophra," *ABD,* 3:286–87.
102. Cf. Bezalel Porten, *Archives from Elephantine: The Life of an Ancient Jewish Military Colony* (Berkeley: University of California Press, 1968), 278–98. Josephus, *Ant.* 10.182, preserves a tradition that Nebuchadnezzar deported Judean immigrants from Egypt.

b. MT has incorporated an interpretive gloss absent from LXX. It awkwardly repeats the earlier object sign, which was unnecessary with the addition of *hî*, "that is." An object sign can be the clue to a gloss, whether grammatically suitable or not, as in Isa 7:17; Hag 2:5 (cf. Godfrey R. Driver, "Glosses in the Hebrew Text of the Old Testament," in *L'Ancien Testament et l'orient* [Orientalia et Biblica Lovaniensia 1; Louvain: Publications Universitaires, 1957], 123–61, esp. 127). See the commentary.

c. The pronoun expresses antithesis to "I" in v. 4 (cf. *IBHS*, 295–96).

d. GKC §150a and Joüon §161a take it as a question, like EVV except REB and NJB. Cf. the discussion of Holladay 2:310. The force of *lĕkâ* is not reflexive (most EVV "for yourself") but centripetal, indicating what is of special interest to the subject (cf. Takamitsu Muraoka, "On the So-Called *Dativus Ethicus* in Hebrew," *JTS* 29 [1978]: 495–98; Joüon §133d; *IBHS* 208–9), as Pieter A. H. de Boer, "Jeremiah 45, Verse 5," in *Symbolae biblicae et mesopotamicae Francisco Mario Theodoro de Liagre Böhl dedicatae* (ed. M. A. Beek et al.; Leiden: Brill, 1973), 31–37, esp. 35, realized.

e. The focus of the two-clause sentence is on the second, while the first has a concessive force (cf. Joüon §171f; *IBHS* 677, with reference to 2 Kgs 7:19); *kî* has an adversative sense after a negative clause.

f. Literally "all flesh." See the commentary.

This divine commendation of Baruch is strikingly similar to that of Ebed-melech in 39:15–18. Both function as deliberate flashbacks and positive supplements to their literary blocks. Whereas 39:15–18 looks back to Ebed-melech's role in 38:7–13, this postscript similarly has in view the mention of Baruch at 43:3, 6. In this case, however, material belonging to the historical context of ch. 36 and evidently available in a fund of oracles has been reused. It recalls an old promise of survival then made to Baruch over against doom promised for the heedless King Jehoiakim and his people. In its new context the promise is relevant to the later context of looming crisis; it implicitly draws a sinister parallel between the great tragedy of 587 and the threat to befall the Judeans in Egypt (cf. 44:13). The block in chs. 40–45 was originally more compact in design, with the slighted theme of staying in the land with God's blessing turning into a reason for total disaster, while the postscript threw that disaster into greater relief with a foil of coming deliverance for Jeremiah's faithful companion. The structure of the block became more complex with the addition of prose sermonic material to the unit in ch. 44. The material related the refugees' worship of the Queen of Heaven to the pagan worship that had been a cause of Judah's downfall at Yahweh's hands, and so permitted that crucial tragedy to be explained and justified once more. Moreover, the message of total extinction in ch. 44 was qualified with promises of partial return from Egypt. The latter change to that unit shed different light on ch. 45 and gave extra editorial significance to its presence. Now it functions not only as a footnote to 43:3, 6, and as a foil to the punishment of those who shook the dust of the holy land off their feet, but also as an illustration of redeeming grace, just as Jere-

Self-Imposed Exile 451

miah had been a potential model for staying in the land at the beginning of the block (40:6). The much later tradition of allocating a separate chapter to this piece, unlike that in 39:15–18, fittingly reflects its enhanced status; it has become a final unit for the block, one that pushes open a small window to a positive future. This was the note on which the book at an earlier stage ended, as it does in LXX, apart from the appendix in the last chapter.

Perhaps the most striking feature of this piece is that it cites an older oracle and leaves readers to coordinate it with the present context. One could put quotation marks around the entire piece. There is a parallel in 30:23–24, where, in a paired series of past negative oracles and future positive ones, 23:19–20 is quoted with its future tenses left unchanged, though the new context indicates that by now it has been fulfilled and relates to the past. This parallel might indicate that the promise to Baruch has been honored by his subsequent survival of many vicissitudes up to his safe arrival in Egypt (cf. Rudolph 265). However, the closer precedent of 39:15–18 suggests that its promise is held to have continuing validity for the future. As to genre, the climactic focus of the piece lies in the individual proclamation of salvation to Baruch (v. 5b*b*). As in 39:15–18, it is preceded by a communal announcement of disaster in order to express Baruch's role as a foil. In this case the divine oracle begins by citing a lament of Baruch and proceeds to answer it. There are still elements that lie outside such an analysis, and they are best explained by positing the presence of a disputation in vv. 3–5a, in which Baruch's dispute is answered by affirming a hitherto implicit thesis, then Baruch's counterthesis is met with a divine dispute.[103] There is rich evidence of redaction at work in this passage. A series of literary processes makes it a redactional showcase. The editorial placement of a prewar oracle in a postwar setting offers initial evidence. Another is the heading of v. 1 that supplies a setting for the oracle. Within the oracle a prose sermonic statement occurs in v. 5b*a*, while the later edition of MT makes a telling comment in v. 4b besides minor pluses earlier.

[45:1] The oracle reception heading one expects in line with 44:1 is replaced by what one might call an oracle delivery heading. It focuses on the prophet's communication of the oracle; there is a parallel in 29:1, which expresses the human phenomenon of sending a letter to convey a divine oracle.[104] The oracle belongs to the long-past situation of ch. 36 in 605/604 B.C.E. (cf. 36:1, 4). "These messages" stands baldly in tension with the new context; it matches the wording in 36:16–18, 24 (cf. "this scroll" in 36:29). It cannot refer to the oracles against the nations in chs. 46–51, because LXX attests the absence of this material from the stage of redaction represented in MT. The heading is meant to shed light on the oracle.

---

103. Cf. the two stages of dispute that Murray, "Rhetoric of Disputation," 112–14, detected in Mal 1:6–9.
104. Graupner, *Auftrag und Geschick*, 171–72.

[2] The expanded quotation formula makes clear that "message" in v. 1 refers to a divinely given oracle (cf. "Jeremiah's messages" in 36:10) and indicates the addressee. This introduction looks ahead to the oracle of vv. 4–5, while v. 3 continues Jeremiah's initial speech of v. 2, supplying the context of the ensuing oracle.

[3] Baruch's lament is cited as a prelude to Yahweh's answer (vv. 4–5). The lament has three elements: an exclamation of distress (cf. 15:10 and comment), a description of Baruch's trouble that traces its cause to Yahweh, and a description of personal distress. The second and third elements are common in individual laments, though the second usually has a divine reference in the second person. The second element is an expression of complaint laid against Yahweh.[105] The sentiment of the latter part of the third element occurs in Ps 22:2 (3) with different wording; it refers to the lack of a satisfying answer to the implicit prayer of v. 5, a failure to find what was sought. The heading in v. 1 helps readers to gauge that Baruch was failing to come to terms with the contents of the scroll, which reflected the crucial event of the battle of Carchemish in 605 B.C.E., when Nebuchadnezzar wrested power in the west from the Egyptian pharaoh, so that the "foe from the north" that featured in Jeremiah's early oracles as spelling doom for Judah could now be identified (36:29). The earlier oracles had evidently distressed Baruch, and now their confirmation in history was too much and he vehemently protests. Baruch's language of distress is employed elsewhere with reference to the Babylonian attacks on Jerusalem in 597 and 587, and they have this foreboding significance here.[106] The lament is consistent with the officials' alarm on hearing the scroll in 36:16 and even more with the narrator's missing a reaction of lamenting in 36:24.

[4a] Baruch's lament also functions as a dispute over Yahweh's purposes of disaster for Judah. The initial directive, in shorter and longer forms in LXX and MT, respectively, has been viewed with scholarly suspicion (see, e.g., *BHS*). However, the switch from "you say" with which Jeremiah refers to Baruch in v. 3 to "*you are to* say" whereby Yahweh refers to Jeremiah in v. 4 fits the to-and-fro aspect of a disputation admirably (cf. Ezek 33:34–35). Along with Jeremiah's statement to Baruch in vv. 2–3 it accords with the focus on communication between Jeremiah and Baruch in v. 1. The pair of double images that is a programmatic element in the book and that often reflects redactional work is here

---

105. Cf. Broyles, *Conflict of Faith*, 37–40, 76–78.
106. Graupner, *Auftrag und Geschick*, 173–76, compares for *yāgôn*, "sorrow," 8:18; 31:13; Ezek 23:33 (but in Jer 20:18 it is used differently), and the cognate verb in Lam 1:5, 12; 3:32–33; for *makʾāb*, "pain," 30:15; Lam 1:12, 18; and for *ʾănāḥâ*, "groaning," Lam 1:22, and the verb in Ezek 21:11–12; Lam 1:4, 8, 11, 21.

Self-Imposed Exile 453

used in a unique way that suggests authenticity; the building and planting refer to past rather than future divine activity.[107]

[4b] The explanatory addition in MT is at first sight ambiguous, since *ʾereṣ* can refer either to land (most EVV) or the earth (REB, GNB). However, as part of a redactional stage that places the oracles against the nations immediately after ch. 45 in chs. 46–51, the latter meaning is certain. In MT, 45:1–5 builds a bridge to the next oracles, indicating that Yahweh's work of destruction that began with Jerusalem and Judah was to be succeeded by worldwide destruction (cf. 25:17–26, 29, 30; 36:2).

[5a] Baruch's counterthesis is spelled out and then attacked in Yahweh's own dispute. The passage explains the counterthesis in terms of Yahweh's desire to miraculously deliver Judah.[108] It represents a petition accompanying the lament (v. 3). An objection that one would hardly expect a national concern in an individual lament is easily met by reference to Psalms 77 and 102, individual laments over which communal concerns loom heavily. "Great things" (*gĕdōlôt*) in the OT refer primarily to the great acts of Yahweh (e.g., Deut 10:21; Ps 106:21). Baruch hoped that Yahweh would act in accord with "all his wonders (*niplāʾôt*)" (21:2); the two Hebrew terms are parallel in Job 9:10. Such a hope is here categorically denied.

[5b] Nevertheless, divine appreciation of Baruch's efforts in writing the scroll (v. 1) prompts an accolade of personal deliverance for him. A primary goal for placing the material of 45:1–5 here is to reclaim that deliverance after the mention of the two men (43:3, 6). Presumably the prophet himself, now aged, was soon to die a natural death in Egypt, but in his stead his younger ally was promised life and independence. Although he now found himself among the accursed refugees in Egypt, he was to be one of the survivors (44:14, 28); the promise there finds illustration here. "In all the places" seems to have a Diaspora flavor (cf. 8:3; 24:9; 29:14; MT 40:12), warning that Judah's redemption awaited a later time. Baruch "was a type of the one on whom promise rests."[109] Baruch was somewhat like the OT heroes in Heb 11:13, who "died in faith without having received the promises, but from a distance they saw and greeted them." At the head of v. 5b a prose sermonic statement has been inserted.[110] It

---

107. Robert Bach, "Bauen und Pflanzen," in *Studien zur Theologie der alttestamentlichen Überlieferungen* (ed. Rolf Rendtorff and Klaus Koch; Neukirchen: Neukirchener Verlag, 1961), 7–32, esp. 29, regarded this passage, on form-critical grounds, as the oldest in the book, with reference to the termination of salvation history, whereas the other texts refer to its resumption. Graupner, *Auftrag und Geschick*, 177–79, rightly dismisses as eisegetical attempts to see in v. 4 a reference to Yahweh's sorrow, made by Kremers, "Leidensgemeinschaft," 138–39, and many others.

108. See de Boer, "Jeremiah 45, Verse 5," 31–37.

109. Ackroyd, "Historians and Prophets," 53. The singular is collective.

110. Thiel, *Redaktion von Jeremia 26–45*, 86; Stulman, *Prose Sermons*, 117–18.

reinforces v. 4 with an echo of 44:2 that refers to the destruction of Jerusalem in 587, and so further links this passage with the foregoing. The combination with "everyone," literally "all flesh," occurs only here. The phrase has different meanings according to context. It primarily refers to wholesale destruction in Judah (cf. 12:12 NJPS). However, other levels of meaning are present. The reader is meant also to apply it to the extinction of the Judean Diaspora in Egypt announced in ch. 44, in line with the use of the prose sermonic statement in 42:17. And the reader of MT, after its addition in v. 4b, cannot help thinking ahead to the doom announced for the nations in chs. 46–51 (cf. 25:31).

Chapter 45 caps earlier negativity with a positive note, a promise of survival for Baruch, who had shared Jeremiah's harassment because of commitment to God's cause.

46:1–51:64 Oracles against the Nations

46:1–47:7 Egypt and Philistia

46:1–28 Egypt's Comeuppance and Israel's Security

46:1 What the prophet Jeremiah received as Yahweh's message about the nations. **2** Concerning Egypt: About the army of Pharaoh, King Neco of Egypt, situated by the River Euphrates at Carchemish and defeated by King Nebuchadnezzar of Babylon in the fourth year of the reign of King Jehoiakim *ben Josiah* of Judah:

3 "Get your shields ready, both round and body-length,
    and approach for battle!
4 Harness the horses
    and get mounted, riders!ᵃ
And take up your positions, with helmets on.
    Polish your lances!
    Put on your armor!
5 Why do I foreseeᵇ
    them scared,
    turning back?
Their warriors are beaten and run headlong,
    and do not look back, with terror everywhere,"
declared Yahweh.
6 "The swiftᶜ cannot run away,
    the warriors cannot escape.
In the north, beside the *River* Euphrates,
    they trip and fall.
7 Who is it that rises like the Nile,

>   like the streams with *its* surging waters?
> 8 It is Egypt that rises like the Nile,
>   *like the streams with surging waters,*[d]
>   that says, 'Let me rise[e] and cover the earth.
>   Let me destroy *each town and*[f] its populace.'"
> 9 Advance, horses,
>   make a frenzied dash, chariots!
>   *And let* the warriors march out,[g]
>   Nubia and Put carrying round shields,
>   and Lud stringing[h] their bows!
> 10 But that day belongs to *Lord* Yahweh Almighty,
>   a day of vengeance, so he may be avenged on his foes.
>   The sword will devour all it can
>   and drink its fill of their blood,
>   because *Lord* Yahweh *Almighty* is holding a sacrifice
>   in the north country, by the River Euphrates.
> 11 Climb Gilead and get balm,
>   virgin Lady Egypt.
>   In vain you have applied many remedies
>   without getting healing.
> 12 The nations hear of your disgrace,[i]
>   and your cries resound through the earth,
>   now that warrior has tripped over warrior,
>   both of them falling together.

13 *A message* spoken[j] by Yahweh to *the prophet* Jeremiah about the coming of King *Nebuchadnezzar* of Babylon to attack Egypt:

> 14 Tell it *in Egypt and announce it* in Migdol,
>   announce it in Noph *and Tahpanhes*!
>   Say, "Take up your position and get ready
>   because the sword has devoured what is around you."
> 15 Why does Apis run away?[k]
>   [Why] does your bull[l] not stand firm?
>   Because Yahweh has struck it down.
> 16 He makes many trip,[m]
>   and they fall over one another,
>   and say, "Get up, let us go back to our own people
>   *and* to our native country
>   to get away from the oppressor's sword."[n]
> 17 Nickname[o] King Pharaoh of Egypt
>   "Boaster[p]-who-missed-his-chance."

18 "By my life I swear,"
    declared *the King, whose name is* Yahweh Almighty,
    "one like Tabor among other mountains,
        one like Carmel by the sea, will come."
19 Pack your bags to take into deportation,
        population of Lady Egypt!
    Noph will become a shocking place, that is why,
        ruined and uninhabited.
20 Egypt is a very beautiful[q] heifer—
        a gadfly from the north comes to land on her.[r]
21 Also its mercenaries inside her
        are like fatted calves.
    Yes, they too turn,
        they run away en masse, unable to stand firm,
    because their day of calamity comes upon them,
        the time when they are dealt with.
22 The sound she makes is like a snake as it moves,[s]
        because in force they march.
    With axes they come to attack her
        like men chopping down trees.
23 "They cut down her forest,"
    declared Yahweh,
        "impenetrable as it is.[t]
    They are more in number than locusts, that's why;
        they are past counting."
24 Lady Egypt is humiliated,
        handed over to a people from the north.

25 Yahweh Almighty, Israel's God, said: "Look, I am going to deal with Amon of No[u] and Pharaoh and those who put their trust in him.[v] 26 *I will hand them over to men with designs on their lives, to King Nebuchadnezzar of Babylon and his officers. But afterward it will be inhabited, as in times past,"* declared Yahweh.

27 "But, as for you, do not be afraid, my servant Jacob,
        do not be scared, Israel,
    because, look, I am going to save you out of anywhere distant,
        your progeny out of their countries of exile.
    Jacob will come back and live quietly,
        secure with nobody to frighten him.
28 You must not be afraid, my servant Jacob,"
    declared Yahweh,

Oracles against the Nations 457

"because I am with you,
because, while I will completely do away with all the nations
I have driven you away to,
I will not do away with you completely,
though I have been chastising you in judgment,
unable to leave you unpunished."

a. Or "mount the steeds" (NRSV, NIV). See *HALOT* 3:978a; McKane 2:1113.

b. The omission in LXX (26:5), noted in *BHS*, may be due to inner-Greek homoeoteleuton from *ti hoti* to *dioti* (*HUB*; cf. Janzen, *Studies*, 108–9). For the lack of *kî*, "that," introducing an object clause after *rāʾâ*, "see," see Judg 9:48 (cf. GKC §157a).

c. For the force of the negative see GKC §§107p, 109e; Joüon §114k.

d. This colon, lacking in LXX here, appears in this form in v. 7b in LXX. Probably in MT a marginal correction of v. 7b has been incorporated here and retained by the redacted text. At an earlier stage v. 8 was a tricolon.

e. MT points as if the sense is "bring up." Repointing to *qal ʾeʿĕleh* is necessary in the context (S. R. Driver, *Revised Translation*, 272; Holladay 2:315).

f. Janzen, *Studies*, 59, explains MT in terms of assimilation to 8:16 and 47:2. The latter passage was especially influential.

g. LXX simply has an imperative.

h. The ungrammatical *tōpĕśê*, "carrying," is generally taken as an accidental repetition of the earlier word. LXX already seems to represent it; see the discussion of Barthélemy, *Critique textuelle*, 2:761–62, and the critique of McKane 2:1116. NJPS retains it. For the rendering "stringing" cf. REB and note a on 9:3 (2).

i. LXX implies *qôlēk*, "your voice," as *BHS* notes; REB adopts it in place of MT *qĕlônēk*. It appears to be an easier and so inferior reading (Holladay 2:322), though BDB 885b and McKane 2:1120 prefer it. Cf. Ps 83:17 for the use of MT's noun in a context of national defeat. Carolyn J. Sharp, "'Take Another Scroll and Write': A Study of the LXX and MT of Jeremiah's Oracles against Egypt and Babylon," *VT* 47 (1997): 487–516, esp. 493, observes a semantic fit, that of the six cases of the noun in the prophetic literature three, including this one, have an adjacent form of *kšl*, "trip."

j. LXX "That which was spoken."

k. As Barthélemy, *Critique textuelle*, 2:763–64, acknowledges, MT's running together as *nshp* must be rejected in favor of LXX's attestation of *nās ḥap* (cf. *BHS*), "Apis ran away" (thus EVV except NIV and NJPS). MT failed to recognize the name of a god (Egyptian *ḥp*; Egyptian Aramaic *ḥpy*; Greek *Apis*). The resulting verbal parallelism between vv. 15 and 21 is appropriate. See the commentary.

l. Both the poetic division into cola and the singular suffix ("it") in the next colon require a singular noun with many MT MSS (*BHS*) and LXX; the contextual meaning is then "bull" rather than "warrior."

m. Cf. NJB and NJPS.

n. See textual note t on 25:38.

o. The MT vocalization *qārĕû šām*, "They call there," is often corrected—and Barthélemy, *Critique textuelle*, 2:765–66, agrees—to *qirʾû šēm*, "Call the name of," with

LXX, Vg., and probably Syr. NIV and NJPS retain MT fully, while NJB keeps its pointing of the verb.

p. Cf. běnê šā'ôn, "boasters," in 48:45.

q. See BHS.

r. See BHS. NJPS retains MT.

s. Syr. and Tg. render thus (BHS); so do NAB, NRSV, and NJPS. The other EVV follow LXX, for which, however, see Barthélemy, *Critique textuelle*, 2:768–69.

t. Anneli Aejmelaeus, "Function and Interpretation of kî in Biblical Hebrew," *JBL* 105 (1986): 193–209, esp. 206 n. 40, denies that after a main clause kî can be concessive, as most EVV take it here, and finds an indirect causal clause that is loosely explanatory.

u. MT adds to the shorter text of LXX: "and Pharaoh and Egypt and its gods and kings," which apparently incorporates a marginal note that interpreted the next words, with "and Pharaoh" functioning as a cue. "Egypt" corresponds to "those who put their trust in him," while "gods and kings" are generic plurals that paraphrase the first two nouns. NAB and REB duly omit.

v. The repeated preposition 'al, "with," after 'el earlier indicates that Pharaoh is meant.

A collection of oracles against foreign nations appears in many prophetic books. Although this one reminds readers of Jeremiah's direct dealings with foreign ambassadors (ch. 27), in terms of genre such oracles are another mode of communicating to God's own people, even though they address the other nations at times. This collection celebrates Yahweh as the Lord of the nations who uses the imperial power of Babylon, which is unwittingly subservient to Israel's God; later redaction in the common text and in MT sometimes makes the means explicit. These foreign oracles constitute a series of proclamations of disaster. A reason is occasionally supplied, but more to reinforce the proclamation than to explain the disaster.[111] Two factors make this collection unusual: the different order of the nations in LXX and MT and their different placement, within ch. 25 in the case of LXX and at the end of the book in MT. The latter difference is best explained as the result of separate redactional choices. An independent collection of foreign oracles belonging to the Jeremianic tradition was inserted secondarily into the book by LXX and MT at different points.[112] It was inserted first into ch. 25 in the LXX tradition (25:14–32:24 in LXX). It was subsequently moved to its present place in MT, as the renewed rendering of the close of 25:13 in 46:1 suggests (see the commentary on 46:1).

As for the order of nations, the radical difference between LXX and MT is puzzling and defies complete explanation. The order in MT is: Egypt, Philistines, Moab, Ammon, Edom, Aramaeans, Arab tribes, Elam, and Babylon: whereas

---

111. Beat Huwyler, *Jeremia und die Völker: Untersuchungen zu den Völkersprüche in Jeremia 46–49* (FAT 20; Tübingen: Mohr Siebeck, 1997), 273.

112. So Henry B. Swete, *Introduction to the Old Testament in Greek* (Cambridge: Cambridge University Press, 1902), 241–42; cf. Janzen, *Studies*, 115.

Oracles against the Nations   459

in LXX it is: Elam, Egypt, Babylon, Philistines, Edom, Ammon, Arab tribes, Aramaeans, and Moab.[113] Compared with MT, in the LXX order Babylon now sits next to its fellow world power, Egypt; Elam has first place, leaving a group of five small nations a quartet in which an ABCD order has become BADC; and Moab appears last.

On various grounds the MT ordering has its own redactional coherence. First, it falls into four blocks, (1) three compositions about Egypt supplemented by the Philistines poem, (2) the two Moab compositions, (3) a composition relating to five nations,[114] and (4) the two Babylon compositions plus its supplementary narrative. These four blocks that make up a large block of foreign oracles exhibit three common patterns, either wholly or in part. First, concern for Israel appears prominently in all four blocks. (1) An oracle of salvation for Israel is appended to the compositions about Egypt (46[LXX 26]:27–28). (2) At the end of the first Moab composition its fate is due to having mocked Israel (48[LXX 31]:27). (3) In the multiple composition Ammon is evidently set first because of its relation to Israel. It seized Israelite territory, which Israel would regain (49[LXX 30]:1–2). (4) In the first Babylon composition its disaster is set alongside homecoming for Israel and Judah (50[LXX 27]:4–5, 19, 28; cf. vv. 33–34) and in the second composition alongside the vindication of God's people (51:24, 35–36, 50–51). As a result all the oracles against the nations function as implicit pronouncements of salvation for Yahweh's own people, inasmuch as they involved disaster for Israel's foreign enemies. Jeremiah 30:16–17a provides a miniature counterpart of the phenomenon; a closer parallel involving a particular foreign nation occurs in Isa 13:1–14:2. In 45:4–5 MT understood the foreign oracles only in terms of destruction, but the collection itself traces a wider agenda. The same pattern appears in the LXX order, except in the third case, which can work only by placing Ammon before Edom.

Second, only some of the foreign oracles engage in polemic against national gods, namely, those of Egypt (46[LXX 26]:15, 25), Moab (48[LXX 31]:7, 13, 35; also v. 46, lacking in LXX), Ammon (49[LXX 30]:1, 3), and Babylon (50[LXX 27]:2, 38; 51[LXX 28]:17–18). That feature is highlighted in MT, comprising or heading literary blocks in order to focus on Yahweh's supremacy. Again, the different positioning of Ammon achieves this comprehensive pattern.

Third, in the cases of Egypt, Moab, and Ammon there is mention of deportation (*gôlâ*; 46[LXX 26]:19; 48[LXX 31]:7, 11; 49[LXX 30]:3). This is important for MT because MT, but not LXX, concludes each of these oracles with a promise of restoration (see the commentary on 46:25–26). These paradigmatic promises

---

113. It may be significant that in the LXX order the headings to the first four oracles (counting the Egypt oracle as two) are long and those to the remaining six are short, apart from the one to the Arab tribes (Henry St. John Thackeray, *The Septuagint and Jewish Worship: A Study in Origins* [2d ed.; Schweich Lectures 1920; London: Oxford University Press, 1923], 35–36).

114. For the coherence of these five oracles see the commentary on ch. 49.

of a positive postjudgment future for important nations supplement the sole promise to Elam, the first nation in LXX (25:19; MT 49:39). Once more Ammon's position in MT is crucial.

A fourth factor that governs the MT order is word patterning. The five national oracles in ch. 49 will be shown to be literarily integrated. Moreover, the Philistines oracle has a number of lexical links with the two preceding Egypt poems (see the commentary on 47:2–7), and the Moab oracle starts in 48:1–2 with a strong vocabulary overlap with ch. 47, while the Ammon oracle begins in 49:3–4 with language that echoes the preceding Moab material. This stylistic factor explains the MT order of Egypt, Philistines, Moab, and Ammon; it also fixes the position of Moab, something the earlier three patterns did not do. All this evidence, in which Egypt, Moab, and Ammon keep coming to the fore, attests a sophisticated arrangement marked by a high degree of reflection and stylistic concern.

As for the LXX order, the propinquity of Egypt and Babylon accords with the political status they share as great powers. Was the mass of Babylonian material, which is almost as large as chs. 46–49, originally a separate document from the material in those chapters (cf. 51:60), and was it inserted in separate places in the two editions? The priority of Elam could be a redactional phenomenon of LXX, reflecting an internal distinction that in LXX out of all the foreign nations only Elam is privileged with a positive future it shares with Israel.[115] As the sole representative of the book's recurring hope of the nations' moving beyond destruction to renewal, it deserved priority. However, the restoration formula may have been attached to it simply because it was the first oracle and represented the rest. Whether or not Egypt headed the original list, MT's beginning with Egypt dovetails with the focus on Egypt in chs. 42–44, together with the common dating in 45:1 and 46:2. MT's concluding with Babylon accords with MT's addition at 25:26b that developed 25:12, whereby Babylon's king was to be the last to drink from the fateful cup, after Babylon had made the other nations drunk.[116] Chapter 25, with an emphasis on disaster for foreign nations and explicit mention of the oracles against the nations in v. 13, had a strong but

---

115. Bernard Gosse, "Les évolutions du livre de Jérémie et la rédaction massorétique," in *Structuration des grands ensembles bibliques et intertextualité à l'époque perse: De la rédaction sacerdotale du livre d'Isaïe à la contestation de la Sagesse* (BZAW 246; Berlin: de Gruyter, 1997), 47–67, esp. 51. On the other hand, Pierre-Maurice Bogaert, "Les deux rédactions du livre de Jérémie," *RB* 101 (1994): 363–406, esp. 379–80, regards the oracle reception heading to the Elam oracle in MT at 49:34 as another development of 25:13 and so echoing the earlier priority of that oracle. The lack of reference to the nations and the presence of the same type of heading in MT at 47:1, independently of LXX, render this conclusion uncertain.

116. In other respects neither of the lists in LXX and MT appears to be significantly closer to the order in the list of nations at 25:19–26 (LXX 32:5–12). Each diverges at different points. If "the kings of the north" (25:26) refer to or are meant to include the Aramaeans, the LXX order differs with respect to Moab and Elam, and the MT order with respect to Edom and the Aramaeans.

Oracles against the Nations

separate influence on both the LXX and MT redactions of the foreign oracles. In the LXX tradition the collection was inserted into the middle of ch. 25, after the preparatory v. 13, as a thematically congenial home for it, thereby disturbing the prior compositional arrangement. The MT tradition took a cue from 25:12 and especially its own addition in 25:26b by placing Babylon at the end of the list, alongside the earlier ones. Indeed, the size of the Babylon compositions sets them apart from the rest, while their content reveals a climactic role in their literary echoes of the earlier foreign oracles. Moreover, the distinctive role of Babylon as ultimate victim after its series of earlier victories detaches them from the other oracles. Overall, both LXX and MT show signs of following their own agendas, and the latter's agenda is clearer.

Modern scholarship has tended to deny the attribution of the oracles of the nations to Jeremiah. However, leaving out for now chs. 50–51, there is little reason for such a judgment in the case of most of the poetry of the foreign oracles in chs. 46–49, with the notable exclusion of the derivative material in the Moabite anthology of 48:28–47.[117] They probably belonged to the prophet's later ministry.

The first composition in the collection, introduced by an oracle reception heading as usual at the start of a major literary division, is made up of four units, three relating to Egypt (46:2–12, 13–24, and 25–26), and a fourth to Israel (vv. 27–28).

[46:1] The italics in this case do not mean absolutely new material in MT. MT has made use of the general heading to the collection of foreign oracles that LXX renders in 25:14 (Ziegler's text) and that in MT already appeared as a relative clause at the end of 25:13. The doubling reflects the complex redactional history of these chapters, which had been inserted into ch. 25 in the text represented by LXX and were moved in MT to a position after ch. 45. However, MT has adapted the heading to a type of oracle reception formula that at times introduces blocks of material (1:2; 14:1) and has added "the prophet" (cf. v. 13). MT makes a repeat use of the clause in 25:13 under the influence of the redaction attested in LXX.

[2] The first of the two headings introduces the first composition in the literary block. The second heading supplies historical background for the first unit within the period of Jeremiah's prophetic ministry. The dating repeats that of the introductions to chs. 25 and 36 and—here only—defines the radical significance of 605 B.C.E. as the year of the battle of Carchemish, from which Nebuchadnezzar, who was crown prince at the time, emerged victorious as heir to the Assyrian Empire. He went on to wrest Syria-Palestine from Egyptian control that had prevailed since 609 (2 Kgs 24:7). For Jeremiah it meant vindication for his "foe from the north" oracles, replacing anonymity with a name to

---

117. Cf. the similar conclusion of Huwyler, *Jeremia und die Völker*, 387–88, who, however, excludes the Elam oracle. He makes a positive comparison between the foreign oracles and the oracles against the foe from the north in chs. 4–6.

conjure with and marking the beginning of the end. In the heading, mention of the Euphrates sets the stage for vv. 6 and 10, and "the north" in those verses is here pinpointed as Carchemish in north Syria, while "the sword" in v. 10 is identified with Nebuchadnezzar (cf. 25:9 [MT], 16).

[3–12] The first poem contains the elements of a basic oracle of disaster that has been fleshed out with passionate poetry. The reason appears in vv. 7–8, Egypt's proud ambition of aggressive conquest. This reason is anticipated in the "Why" of v. 5. A divine intervention in the announcement of disaster occurs in v. 10, while its human consequences are given a broader scope, appearing in vv. 5–6, in the center of v. 10, and in vv. 11–12. What of the introductory battle orders in vv. 3–4 and 9? They accentuate the coming disaster by using the motif of contrast. The historical setting of the poem is difficult to judge. Holladay (2:317) thinks the poem looks back at Egypt's defeat and accordingly takes it as a taunt song, a designation that does account for its mocking elements. However, most of the poem seems to anticipate the battle and forecast its outcome (Rudolph 269), and the backward glance (vv. 11–12) may simply dramatize its certainty.

The poem falls into two stanzas (vv. 3–8 and 9–12) (Holladay 2:316). The first and third person divine references (vv. 5 and 10, respectively) indicate that the first stanza as a whole is spoken by Yahweh, and the second, while integral to the poem, is a reflection of the prophet that continues and reviews the first, bringing out its significance. Each stanza has three parts, vv. 3–4 (three lines), 5–6 (four lines), and 7–8 (three lines) in the first and vv. 9 (two lines), 10 (three lines), and 11–12 (four lines) in the second. The stanzas are marked by consecutive parallelism. Initial battle orders occur in both vv. 3–4 and 9. The second parts (vv. 5–6 and 10, respectively) give a central role to Yahweh's overriding purposes for the battle. The third parts go their own ways, in vv. 7–8 glancing back to the reason and in vv. 11–12 looking forward to the sequel, but both are concerned directly or indirectly with the certainty of Egypt's defeat. A pattern of consecutive parallelism is also apparent in the repetition of specific words throughout the poem. The battle orders in vv. 3–4 and 9 have three terms in common, "round shields," "horses," and the imperative ʿălû, rendered "get mounted" in v. 4 and "Advance" in v. 9. The progression continues with "the north" and "the Euphrates" in vv. 6 and 10 and reference to "Egypt" (vv. 8a and 11a) and of "the earth" (vv. 8b and 11b). At the close this sequencing has been deliberately skewed by delaying the second mention of "warriors" and of tripping and falling—first in vv. 5–6—until v. 12 in order to provide a climax. The poem as a whole has a unifying key word, the root ʿlh, evidenced in the imperative ʿălû three times (translated "get mounted," v. 4; "Advance," v. 9; and "Climb," v. 11a), the imperfect and cohortative forms yaʿăleh and ʾeʿĕleh, "rise" (vv. 7–8), and the noun tĕʿālâ, "healing" (v. 11b).[118] Thereby the impulse

---

118. Watson, *Classical Hebrew Poetry*, 383.

Oracles against the Nations 463

of the initial imperatives in vv. 4 and 9 is explained by the ambition of the verbs in vv. 7-8, only to be succeeded by the mocking imperative in v. 11a and the flat denial of healing for Egypt's military wounds in v. 11b.

[3–8] Not until the end of the first stanza is the identity of the losing army disclosed, but the reader has been prepared by the phrase "the army of Pharaoh" in the heading. The stanza is dominated by two questions, "Why" (v. 5) and "Who" (v. 7), the second of which goes on to answer the first.

[3–4] The battle orders are rhetorically addressed to the Egyptian army, as the explicit parallel in v. 9 indicates. They imitate those barked out by Egyptian officers and switch hectically from infantry to chariotry (or cavalry) and back to infantry. The polishing of the lances is a nervous "last-minute burnishing" (McKane 2:1113).

[5–6] The poem abruptly and disconcertingly flashes forward to the army's defeat, which was summarized in the heading. The transition is facilitated by the verb "see," which, the closing quotation formula suggests, refers here to divine foresight, a development from a prophetic visionary experience of remote viewing (cf. 1 Kgs 22:17; Jer 30:6; John 1:48). A motif of panic frames the description in v. 5; it encloses broken formations and ragged flight. But escape proves impossible, as the Egyptian troops are chased and struck down. Their enemies remain unnamed in the poem itself, apart from Yahweh in the next stanza (v. 10).

[7–8] The question that began v. 5 receives the answer that pride goes before a fall. It was Egypt's aggressive ambition that was to be struck down. Judah was still licking the wounds Egypt had inflicted in King Josiah's defeat and death at Neco's hands in 609 B.C.E., but the accusation stays at a general level. The annual inundation of the Nile that beneficially supplied water to adjacent crops is here given a megalomaniac twist (cf. Amos 8:8; 9:5).

[9–12] The second stanza continues the vein of defeat by employing negative wordplay on Egypt (*miṣrayim*, vv. 8, 11), namely, *miṣṣārāyw*, "on his foes," in v. 10 and needed *ṣŏrî*, "balm," in v. 11.[119] The prophet continues the poem, developing earlier elements.

[9] The brisk military orders revert to vv. 3–4; they indicate Egypt's dependence on mercenary troops for its infantry division (cf. Ezek 27:10; 30:5). Here they appear to be African. LXX identifies "Put" as Libya, while "Lud" apparently refers not to the Lydians of west Asia Minor, but to a North African group.[120]

[10] A sudden switch of perspective occurs, as in v. 5. The implicit providence of the first stanza is now clarified as Yahweh's timely and punitive intervention. Egypt was not only Babylon's foe, but Yahweh's; the inferred agency

---

119. Ibid., 382–83.
120. See David W. Baker, "Lud," *ABD* 4:397; idem, "Put," *ABD* 5:560a. For "Nubia" see Donald B. Redford, "Kush," *ABD* 4:109–11.

of Babylon echoes 25:8–11; 27:1–15; and 43:8–13. The complex of motifs—the day of vengeance, the vampire-like sword, and the divine sacrifice—is very similar to that in Isa 34:5–6, 8, but here is crisper, a rat-a-tat succession.[121] Yahweh, Lord of the nations, was using Babylon to punish Egypt's lust for power.[122] MT amplifies framing expressions of divine power that convey the inevitability of Egyptian defeat.

[11–12] A jeering tone enters the prophetic elaboration. Egypt's war wounds, unhealed, would fester. Perhaps the famed balm from the mountainous region of Gilead in Transjordan (cf. 8:22) should be procured as a last resort, since nothing else would work.[123] "Lady [lit. "daughter"] Egypt" has been explained as a reference to national culture, since daughters are "associated with stability, with the building up of society, with nurturing the community at its very heart and center."[124] The epithet "virgin" refers tauntingly to the unexpected, violent defeat of Egypt. The "disgrace" linked with the army's collapse reverses the vainglory pictured as a rising flood in vv. 7–8. Judah is warned that, as the heading in v. 2 implies, the international significance of Egypt's defeat was that it opened up the west to the foe from the north.[125]

[13] The prose oracle reception heading introduces a fresh unit. The heading supplies a feasible setting for the next poem; it especially echoes the verb "come" that pervades the poem in vv. 18, 20–22 and interprets it in terms of Nebuchadnezzar's invasion. As in 43:10–13, there seems to be a premonition of his punitive raid in 568/567 B.C.E., though Jeremiah may have expected it and prophesied about it earlier. At the close of 601 the Babylonians achieved no victory in an encounter with Egypt near its border.[126] The occupation and conquest of Egypt had to await the Persians' attack in 525.

[14–24] The second poem moves to a later stage of events, a Babylonian invasion of Egypt itself. This poem is modeled on the first and is meant to be its inexorable sequel, as the lavish overlap of vocabulary shows. In v. 14 "Take up your position" and "the sword has devoured" echo vv. 4 and 10, respectively, while "Why" in v. 15 echoes v. 5. Running away in vv. 15 and 21 recalls vv. 5–6, and tripping and falling in v. 16 hark back to vv. 6 and 12. The "sword" of v. 10 reappears in v. 16, and the fateful "day" of v. 10 in v. 21. "Lady Egypt"

---

121. Hans Wildberger, *Isaiah 28–35* (trans. T. H. Trapp; CC; Minneapolis: Fortress, 2002), 329, 331, agreed with Eissfeldt in attributing Isaiah 34 at the earliest to the end of the sixth century and envisioned possible dependence on Jeremiah 46.
122. Peels, *Vengeance of God*, 179–81.
123. John G. Snaith, "Literary Criticism and Historical Investigation in Jeremiah Chapter xlvi," *JSS* 16 (1971): 15–32, esp. 17, suggests a taunting reference to Egypt's temporary control of Gilead until 605 B.C.E.
124. Elaine R. Follis, "The Holy City as Daughter," in *Directions in Biblical Hebrew Poetry* (ed. E. R. Follis; JSOTSup 40; Sheffield: JSOT Press, 1987), 173–84, esp. 177.
125. Huwyler, *Jeremia und die Völker*, 315–17.
126. *ABC*, 20, 101.

appears in v. 11 and also in vv. 19 and 24. The humiliation of v. 24 corresponds to the "disgrace" in v. 12. Also "north" in vv. 20 and 24, and "turned" (*hipnû*) in v. 21 resemble the cases in vv. 5 (rendered "look back"), 6, and 10, respectively, but function differently.

Like the earlier poem, this one falls into two stanzas, vv. 14–19 and 20–24 (Rudolph 271). They are here indicated by framing, using for this purpose "Noph" in vv. 14 and 19 and "from the north" in vv. 20 and 24. "Lady Egypt" concludes both stanzas in vv. 19 and 24. However, the dense consecutive parallelism of the former poem is lacking here, though the running away and not standing firm in v. 15 is repeated in v. 21. A hallmark of this poem is its vivid use of imagery in vv. 18, 20–23. In genre the poem is substantially an announcement of disaster for Egypt, though a reference to a reason (v. 17) makes it an oracle of disaster. However, the insistent third person references to Yahweh (vv. 15–16) suggest divine speech near the ends of the stanzas (vv. 18 and 23) so that the heading anticipates the later citations, as often elsewhere (see "Genre" in the introduction). The quotation formulas (vv. 18 and 23) point to a divine speaker, as the heading indicates. Yahweh's intervention is mentioned in v. 15 and implicitly at the end of v. 21, but the poem focuses on the human consequences of the defeat. The chronology is again not clearly expressed, but prediction rather than historical commentary appears to be in view.

[14–19] The focus on Noph at beginning and end highlights a city near Egypt's northern border and so a likely victim of foreign attack. The imperatives (vv. 14, 17, and 19) provide a structure for the stanza that yields three divisions of five, two, and two lines each (vv. 14–16, 17–18, and 19).

[14–16] A rhetorical announcement of military emergency, warning of adjacent enemy activity, specifies the frontier towns of Migdol and Noph. MT has widened the scope to Egypt as a whole, echoing v. 13 and also providing a general antecedent for the Hebrew second masculine singular references (vv. 14b and 15). Its mention of "Tahpanhes" creates a redactional hinge with earlier references in 43:7, 8; and 44:1, while the preexisting "Migdol" now connects it with 44:1. Noph is given religious relevance in v. 15 since the cult of the bull god Apis, who was closely associated with another Egyptian god, Ptah, was located at the latter's sanctuary in Noph.[127] Verses 15–16 flash forward to coming defeat, which in v. 15 is portrayed in terms of a religious contest won by Yahweh. Yahweh's backing of the Babylonians is implicitly at work. Verse 16 continues to describe Yahweh's activity, but shifts the focus from a religious perspective to a military one, attributing to the mercenaries who here represent the Egyptian army an intention to desert and go home. Both the religious and military power bases in Egypt were to be struck palpable blows.

---

127. See Donald B. Redford, "Apis," *ABD* 1:278–79.

[17–18] This second part of the stanza polarizes the pharaoh as the loser vis-à-vis the one whom v. 13 ("coming") has interpreted as the powerful winner, the Babylonian king. MT, reusing 51:57, takes an opportunity to underscore divine involvement in the fray, repeating "name" and calling Yahweh "King" in opposition to "King Pharaoh of Egypt," and thus amplifying involvement already implied in the vehement oath that expresses the divine will. A powerful statement counters the Egyptian's pretentious claims that failed to materialize, an echo of the vainglory in vv. 7–8. MT adds a hymnic note by its expansion with a doxology, which a divine oath sometimes triggers in a judgment context (cf. 48:15).[128] Neither Mount Tabor nor Mount Carmel is very high, but they give an impression of lofty grandeur, rising as they do from the adjacent plain, the Valley of Jezreel, in the first case, and sheer from the sea in the second. So Tabor is contrasted with other mountains, which though higher do not impress the viewer as much. "Among" and "by" have the force of "in comparison with." The prepositions introduce a standard of comparison, as in the similes of Song 2:2–3, "As a lily among brambles, so is my love among maidens. As an apple tree among the trees of the wood, so is my beloved among young men." In this case other mountains and the sea implicitly correspond to the Egyptian king.

[19] The third imperative continues in the military vein of the first one in v. 14, but urges the country's civilian population to prepare for the deportation that typically follows conquest. The call is justified by claiming the coming desolation of Noph.

[20–24] Derogatory statements about Egypt, now referred to with feminine forms that take their cue from "Lady Egypt" in v. 19,[129] punctuate the second stanza (vv. 20, 22a, and 24). They divide it into three parts, vv. 20–21 (four lines), 22–23 (four lines), and 24 (one line). The framing phrase "from the north" evokes the dire early oracles Jeremiah delivered about the foe from the north that was to menace Judah; such anonymity is by now simply a rhetorical and confirmatory feature.

[20–21] The sinister verb "comes" frames this first part, continuing the topic of Babylonian attack. The powerful one (v. 18) is now metaphorically described as a "gadfly" that can sting and stampede the Egyptian "heifer," for all its magnificence (cf. Isa 7:18). Stampeding is the implicit fate for the heifer, as it is explicitly for the calves or mercenaries.[130] The mercenaries of v. 16 reappear, once more in a context of defeat and flight. Pampered and for too long preoc-

---

128. See Crenshaw, "Form-Critical Analysis," 156–61.
129. Holladay's inclusion of v. 19 in the stanza for this reason (2:326) does not fit on other grounds.
130. Bourguet, *Métaphores de Jérémie*, 392.

cupied with the perquisites of peace, they would be no match for the enemy.[131] Divine involvement is implied in "the time when they are dealt with," echoing vv. 15–16.

[22–23] Further figurative language is used, now in rich profusion. First, Egypt is compared to a snake slithering away from the approach of its massed enemies. Its sound, almost inaudible, provides an ironic contrast to the noisy boasting of v. 17. Second, the soldiers' axes, carried to clear brushwood (Judg 9:48) and for demolition work (Ps 74:5), suggest woodcutters ruthlessly hacking away. The "forest," a metaphorical element suggested by the simile, is left undefined. With the military dispersed and the civilian population packing its bags, what remained? In the light of 22:7, 23, where cedars stand for royal buildings, it apparently refers to Egyptian palaces and temples, though they would have been constructed of stone in Egypt, and so to the massive complex of institutions that gave Egypt its cultural identity.[132] Third, the certainty of the Babylonians' success in combating Egypt's acknowledged power is grounded in their military superiority ("locusts").

[24] The final statement functions as a triumphant summary of Egyptian defeat at Babylonian hands.

[25–26] The third unit of the composition is a prose supplement to the second, echoing "deal with" from v. 21 and "Pharaoh" from v. 17. Its core is the brief announcement of disaster due to divine intervention (v. 25). In MT it has been lavishly augmented with a quotation formula that echoes the epithet "Almighty" of v. 18 (also twice in v. 10), an expansion of the announcement of disaster that comments on the handing over of v. 24b, and an unexpected proclamation of salvation. The basic text resumes the religious concern of v. 15 and extends the defeat of Apis of Noph at Yahweh's hands to that of "Amon of No." Amon was the state god whose chief sanctuary was at the temple of Karnak in No (Hellenistic Thebes) in Upper Egypt.[133] So Yahweh's religious supremacy over Egypt would be demonstrated, brooking no rivals. But political defeat is also envisioned, for "Pharaoh and those who put their trust in him." In terms of the previous poem, the latter are the mercenaries (v. 21) and the general population (v. 19). Is the king's divinity in view or political allegiance? In either case the major Egyptian entities in the poem, divine, military, and civilian, are addressed comprehensively. In MT v. 26a expands v. 24b, explaining "the people from the north" as Babylonians and thus resuming the heading in v. 13 and providing the latter half of a frame for vv. 13–26. The prose sermonic phrase

---

131. Herodotus, *Hist.* 2.152, 154, refers to Ionian and Carian mercenaries a few years earlier as being well paid and assigned prime land on either side of the Nile.
132. Bourguet, *Métaphores de Jérémie*, 402–3.
133. See Theodore J. Lewis, "Amon," *ABD* 1:197–98.

regarding fatal intent reuses 44:30, where it already had an Egyptian setting. The reversal (v. 26) looks back to "Lady Egypt" (v. 24) as its subject and to its prospect of deportation (v. 19) and also to Noph's lack of habitation there. The reversal does not simply reflect the temporary nature of Nebuchadnezzar's attack, but makes a theological connection with other late OT promises regarding Egypt (cf. Isa 19:18–25; Ezek 29:13–16). Closer to home, it is connected to a group of promises concerning reversal of fortunes for Moab (48:47), for Ammon (49:6), and for Elam (49:39), all of which are absent from LXX except for 49:39 (LXX 25:19; see the commentary at 49:39).[134] In the Jeremianic tradition they take their cue from 12:14–17. The promise of Israel's return in v. 27 has triggered the application of the overspill of grace to Egypt in MT here. "Come back" implicitly recalled "bring back" in 12:15 with reference to Israel's neighbors, and so the way was paved for a statement of God's final word. A further factor in the MT additions seems to have been that the Egyptian, Moabite, and Ammonite oracles are the only ones that mention *gôlâ*, "deportation" (46:19; 48:7, 11 [cf. v. 46 in MT]; 49:3; cf. v. 36 with reference to Elam), which in 28:6 is associated with bringing back Judean deportees.[135] For Judah the judgment of deportation was the necessary condition of restoration, and so it would be for the nations. Another factor relating to the reversal was the calls in the Babylon compositions for ethnic groups deported there to escape and return home (50:8, 16; 51:9);[136] Babylon's fall was to trigger the release not only of Judeans (50:34). From a broader perspective the double program for the nations in 1:10 is developed. Within the oracles against the nations, the promise takes its place alongside promises of return or reoccupation for Israel in the common text at 46:27; 49:2; 50:4–5, 19, 28, 34 (cf. 51:10).

[27–28] The last unit is a two-part oracle of salvation, which with some recensional differences was used at 30:10–11 in MT. A key factor behind the oracle's incorporation was the distinguishing of Israel's destiny from the fate of other nations. By the same token, the positive v. 26b in Egypt's case is shown to be the latest in a series of editorial revisions, which modify earlier statements. The commentary on 30:10–11 has given an account of the text, including its probably late exilic dating. It remains to be said that the link in this occurrence is the verb "be scared" in v. 27, which is connected with "scared" in v. 5 (*ḥtt* in both cases). Also the formula of divine intervention, "look, I am going to . . ." in

---

134. For the verbal variation between Egypt and the other nations cf. *yšb*, rendered "reside," in 23:8 and *hšyb*, "bring back," in the parallel 16:15. Here *škn*, a synonym of *yšb*, is used.

135. Cf. Bernard Gosse, "Le rôle de Jérémie 30, 24 dans la rédaction du livre de Jérémie," *BZ* 39 (1995): 92–96, esp. 95. Gosse sees the influence of *bēʾaḥărît hayyāmîm* (rendered "When time has elapsed") at 30:24 on 49:39 and (in MT) 48:47 (rendered "eventually"). However, despite the detail of Yahweh's "burning anger" in 30:24 and 49:37, the difference of context does not favor this as an intertextual link.

136. Gosse, ibid.

v. 27 provocatively cuts across the one in v. 25. So vv. 27–28, beginning with a contrasting "But, as for you," represent a coda to the preceding Egyptian oracles as a group, reassuring Israel that Egypt's fate would not be Israel's, despite the temporary period of punishment it was still undergoing at Yahweh's hands in the Diaspora. Moreover, the text implies that Egypt was itself Israel's enemy, and so Egypt's destruction and Israel's salvation reflect two sides of the same theological coin. From a historical perspective the reader would more naturally have understood the oracles against Egypt as warnings to Judah not to ally itself with Egypt against Babylon and so as virtual oracles of disaster for Judah, but the coda implies an interpretation of Egypt as the enemy not only of Yahweh (v. 10) but also of the covenant people. One can now appreciate the passion behind the MT additions throughout the chapter, "the Lord," "Almighty," "King," "Israel's God," and a doxology of praise. On a larger scale the reprieve of v. 28b corresponds to the redactional insertions of 4:27b; 5:10, 18, and to MT at 30:11.

Chapter 46 presents three oracles of disaster forecasting doom for Egypt and caps them with an oracle of salvation for Israel and a promise of ultimate renewal for Egypt.

47:1–7 The Flooding of Philistia

> 47:1 What the prophet Jeremiah received as Yahweh's message about the Philistines, *before Pharaoh defeated Gaza.*
>
> 2 Here is what Yahweh said:
> "Look, waters are going to rise from the north
>   and will turn into a wadi in flood.
> They will flood the country and everything in it,
>   each town and its populace.
> People will cry out
>   and all the country's population will wail
> 3[a] at the sound of the pounding hooves of his steeds,
>   at the rattling of his chariots, the rumbling of their[b] wheels.
> Parents will not turn back for their children,
>   being so demoralized
> 4 by the day that is coming for ravaging
>   all the Philistines,
> for wiping out from Tyre and Sidon
>   every ally that is left."
> Yahweh is about to ravage *the Philistines*, that is why,
>   descendants[c] of those from the coast *of Caphtor*.[d]
> 5 Shaved heads have appeared in Gaza,
>   Ashkelon has fallen silent.[e]

You descendants of the Anakim,[f]
how long must you mutilate yourselves?
6 *Oh*,[g] sword of Yahweh,
how soon before you take a rest?
Put yourself[h] in your scabbard,
relax and keep still!
7 How can it take a rest,[i]
when Yahweh has commissioned it?
Ashkelon and the seaboard
are where he has assigned it to attack.

a. See *BHS* for the sentence alignment in vv. 2–4, misjudged in MT, as NJB recognizes.

b. "His" (so LXX, KJV, NJB) misinterprets. The suffix refers to the collective *rikbô*, "his chariotry," in a tightly structured colon.

c. For this sense of *šaʾărît* here and in v. 5, unrecognized in EVV, cf. BDB 984b; *HALOT* 4:1380b. Volz 404 so interprets; so does Ernst Kutsch, "'. . . denn Jahwe vernichtet die Philister': Erwägungen zu Jer 47, 1–7," in *Die Botschaft und die Boten: Festschrift für Hans Walter Wolff zum 70. Geburtstag* (ed. Jörg Jeremias and Lothar Perlitt; Neukirchen-Vluyn: Neukirchener Verlag, 1981), 253–67, esp. 254.

d. LXX has a generic plural, "coastlands." MT has in view a specific stretch of coast, which was subsequently identified. In 2Q13 *ʾyy kptwr*, "coasts of Caphtor" (DJD 3:65), also attested by Syr. and Tg., is an intermediate reading.

e. Cf. *HALOT* 1:226b; thus EVV except REB and NJPS. For the sentence alignment, adopted by most commentators and by EVV except REB, which preserves that of MT, see McKane 2:1149–50.

f. Even Barthélemy, *Critique textuelle*, 2:771–72, adopts LXX (see *BHS*), judging MT a simple writing error (*n/m*). Although RSV had "Anakim," EVV surprisingly retain MT, rendering either "valley/plain" (NIV, NJB, NJPS), or "power/strength" (NAB, NRSV [with a confused note], REB; cf. *HALOT* 2:848b–49a).

g. A Greek exclamation *ē* possibly underlies LXX *hē*, "the" (*HUB*).

h. For the copying error in the Leningrad Codex see *BHS*.

i. The third person references in the rest of v. 7 suggest that the second person here is a careless assimilation to v. 6 (cf. *BHS*). EVV so judge.

[47:1] The Philistines occupied the southwest coast of Canaan in a series of city-states, two of which are mentioned in v. 5. The terse heading in LXX, which was inspired by v. 4, has been amplified in MT. The quotation formula that begins v. 2 has been expanded into an oracle reception heading, which does not indicate a major division here, in 46:13, or in 49:34, unlike 46:1. In MT a historical setting has also been supplied for the future invasion mentioned in the poem. It is hardly "merely a chronological notation," as Bright (311) suggests (cf. Keil 2:199), but specifies the military content of the oracle, as the use of the same verb "defeated" in 46:2 and 49:28 implies. The reasoning behind the identification is transparent. The rising waters of v. 2 were interpreted of the Nile

Oracles against the Nations

and related to an Egyptian attack because of similar language in 46:7, which comes just before in the MT order of international oracles. The reference was narrowed to "Pharaoh" as an explanation of the unidentified "his" with reference to the invader in v. 3. "Gaza" came from the first Philistine town mentioned in the poem, at v. 5; that a particular city was in view was understood from the reference to "the city" (NRSV) in v. 2, taken not generically but as a true singular. However, the poem features a Babylonian invasion (see below), and the heading in MT represents a historical reapplication, evidently using a tradition of an Egyptian attack on Gaza known to the redactor, perhaps in 609 by Neco as part of his conquest of Palestine (cf. 2 Kgs 23:29), or in 601 when he defeated the Babylonian army near the frontier, or in 588 when Hophra challenged Babylon's grip on Judah (cf. Jer 37:5).[137]

[2a*a*] The quotation formula seems to apply to the poem as far as v. 4a.[138] Thereafter the poem employs the divine name in the third person (vv. 4b, 6–7); the prophet speaks in explanatory amplification (*kî*, NRSV "For").

[2a*b*–7] This poem is an announcement of disaster that twice prefaces divine intervention (vv. 4b, 6–7) with its human outworking and/or consequences (vv. 2–4a, 5). No reason is given, in contrast to Ezek 25:15 and Joel 3(4):4–6; the focus of the poem is on the destructive work of Yahweh that is its double climax. There is affinity between the vocabulary of the poem and that of the two preceding ones against Egypt in 46:3–12, 14–24, which was evidently a factor in the placement of the Philistine poem next to them. Parallels with the first poem in 46:3–12 are the rising waters (46:7 [and 8 in MT]; 47:1), "its populace" (46:8; 47:2), and not turning back (46:5; 47:3). There are two parallels with the second poem in 46:14–24, "from the north" (46:20, 24; 47:1) and the coming day (46:21; 47:4). The "sword" of 47:6 aligns with both Egyptian poems (46:10, 16). The three poems constitute a tightly knit group. The patterns of speech suggest two stanzas, seven lines in vv. 2a*b*–4a and seven in vv. 4b–7. The poem exhibits suspense in not identifying the victims of attack until the start of the second stanza; the attackers need not be identified by name.

[2a*b*–4a] Crisis is the keynote of the first stanza, and it is described in three different ways. So the stanza falls into three parts (vv. 2a*b*, 2b–3a, and 3b–4a). The first part paints the looming crisis in terms of a vehement metaphor; the second presents a reaction of lamentation to the crisis, which is interpreted as a military invasion; and the third gives a reaction of flight and describes the crisis from the standpoint of the invaded nation.

[2a*b*] The usual formula of imminent divine intervention in an announcement of disaster, "Look, I am going to . . . ," is replaced by a metaphor of natural

---

137. For the first case cf. Herodotus, *Hist.* 2.159, and see the discussion of McKane 2:1141–44.
138. Cf. the first person verb at v. 4a*b* in both 2Q13 and LXX. Did an elucidating comparative gloss from another Philistine oracle, Ezek 25:16 or Amos 1:8, displace the form in MT?

catastrophe, and the intervention is delayed until the second stanza. The metaphor will be explained as an army in the second part. The source of the crisis, "from the north," and its national and urban reach (cf. 8:16b) already hint at that military reality.[139] "From the north" framed 46:20–24 with obvious reference to Babylonian attack. Moreover, its earlier role in "foe from the north" oracles (4:6; 6:1, 22; 10:22; 13:20; cf. 1:3) leads the reader to expect such a meaning here.[140] The metaphor appropriately springs from a Palestinian setting, while the comparable one in 46:7–8 had the Nile in view. In earlier prophecy Isaiah applied a flood metaphor to the Assyrians by referring to the Euphrates (Isa 8:7–8). Here a wadi is envisioned, filled to overflowing with excessive winter rains and sweeping everything away in its headlong course, as it floods the coastal plain.

[2b–3a] Mourning cries are mentioned as a reaction to military invasion (cf. 8:16a), which interprets the metaphor. "His" is left unidentified, but the reticence is a rhetorical one, stimulating readers to identify it in their minds.

[3b–4a] Another reaction follows, an attempt to escape so desperate that a panic-stricken instinct for self-preservation triumphs over parental care that would cause delay and death for all (cf. 14:5; 49:11). For the first time the victims of the onslaught are identified; a wider scenario is disclosed, envisioning a strategy against the Phoenicians and a subsidiary attack on their Philistine allies. There is no separate oracle against Tyre or Sidon, though they appear in the list of nations at 25:22. The Babylonians engaged in a thirteen-year siege against the island of Tyre, generally set in 586–573 B.C.E.

[4b–7] The frame of the three-part second stanza presents a wider scenario still, that behind the human assailants stood Yahweh as the ultimate attacker (vv. 4b, 6–7). The executive role of Babylon in the outworking of divine providence, which pervades the book of Jeremiah, is plainly perceptible here. "Ashkelon" looms large in the stanza, which may suggest that the poem originally envisioned Nebuchadnezzar's attack on it in 604 (cf. the commentary on 36:9).[141]

[4b] MT expands the reference to v. 4a from the verb of ravaging to its ethnic object. It also identifies the traditional maritime home of the Philistines before they migrated to Palestine as "Caphtor" (cf. Deut 2:23; Amos 9:7), which probably refers to Crete.[142]

[5] Mourning rites and numb shock echo the lamentation of v. 2b. For head shaving compare Isa 22:12 and Amos 8:10; for self-mutilation see the commentary on 16:6. The rhetorical question with its direct address gives a lively twist to the narrative catalog. "How long" functions not as a sympathetic expression of lament, as in Isa 6:11, but as an unaffected comment, as in 1 Sam

---

139. Kutsch, "Erwägungen," 258.
140. For the unlikelihood that an attack on Gaza by Neco after his return from Carchemish in the north was intended, see already Keil 2:197–99.
141. Cf. *ABC*, 20, 100.
142. See Richard S. Hess, "Caphtor," *ABD* 1:869–70; *HALOT* 2:495b–96a.

16:1, here in anticipatory rhetoric. The Anakim were an aboriginal group that once occupied Philistine territory (cf. Num 13:28; Josh 11:22).

[6–7] The previous question triggers two more in which Yahweh's Babylonian "sword" is the subject. These and a rhetorical appeal function as a vivid means of affirming Yahweh's inexorable role as destroyer, using military means to effect the divine will. There was to be no letup in this grisly work against Philistia (contrast Zech 9:7).

48:1–47 Moab under Threat

48:1–27 Moab's Coming Conquest and Destruction

48:1 Concerning Moab.

Here is what Yahweh *Almighty, Israel's God,* said.

> Alas for Nebo that it is ravaged,
>   that Kiriathaim is captured,[a]
>   Misgab humiliated and defeated![b]
> 2 Moab's renown is no more.
>   In Heshbon a bad fate for it is devised,
>   "*Come on,* let us wipe it out as a nation!"
> You also, Madmen, will fall silent,
>   chased by the sword.
> 3 Hark, a cry comes from Horonaim,
>   "Havoc and sheer brokenness!
> 4 Moab is broken!"
>   *The cry* can be heard as far as Zoar.[c]
> 5 Yes, the road up to Luhith—
>   in tears people go up by it.[d]
> Yes, on the road down to Horonaim
>   the cry[e] about brokenness is heard.[f]
> 6 Run away, escape with your lives!
>   Let them[g] exist like junipers[h] in the desert.
> 7 Or else, because your trust has been put in what you have made,[i]
>   you too will be captured.
> Chemosh will leave and be deported
>   together with his priests and officials.
> 8 The ravager will attack every town
>   so not one town escapes.
> The plain will perish
>   and the plateau be devastated,
>   as Yahweh said:

9   "Give wings to Moab
       because it must fly away. (?)ʲ
    Its towns will become desolate
       and uninhabited."

10 A curse on anyone who is slack in doing Yahweh's work! *A curse on anyone who holds his sword back from bloodshed!*

11 Moab has been tranquil since its young days,
       resting on its lees
       and never poured from jar to jar—
    it never went into deportation—ᵏ
    That is why it has retained its flavor,
       and its bouquet has never altered.

12 "Therefore, look, the time is coming," declared Yahweh, "when I will send to it decanters to decant it, emptying its jars and then smashing theirˡ vessels." 13 Then Moab will be disappointed in Chemosh, just as Israel's community was disappointed in Bethel after putting its trust in it.

14 How can you say,
       "We are heroes,
       warriors ready for the fight"?
15 The ravagerᵐ of Moab and its towns moves up,
       while its finest young men are taken down in slaughter.ⁿ
16 Moab's calamity is coming close
       and its bad fate is approaching very fast.
17 Mourn for it, all you who are its neighbors
       and all you who knew its former fame.
    Say, "How terribly broken is the powerful scepter,
       the splendid mace!"
18 Step down from your glory and sit on the hardᵒ ground,
       population of Lady Dibon.ᵖ
    Moab's ravager has moved up against you, that is why,
       demolishing your fortifications.
19 Stand by the road and keep looking,
       population of Aroer.
    Interrogate any male runaway or any female escapeeᑫ
       and ask what has happened.
20 Moab is humiliated; yes, it is defeated.ʳ
       Wail and cry out,
    report along the Arnon
       that Moab is ravaged.

21 Judgment reaches the plateau region—Holon, Jahzah, Mephaath,
22 Dibon, Nebo, Beth-diblathaim, 23 Kiriathaim, Beth-gamul, Beth-meon,
24 Kerioth, Bozrah, and any other Moabite town, however far or near.

25 "Moab has had its horn cut off,
its arm broken,"
declared Yahweh.

26 Get it intoxicated, because Yahweh is the one it has challenged. Let Moab empty its stomach^s with its vomit^t and become a laughingstock in its turn. 27 Israel was a laughingstock to you, wasn't it? Was it because it was ever caught in the company of thieves that, *whenever you spoke*^{u} *of it,* you shook your head in scorn?

a. For the verb added in MT see *BHS*, with which Janzen, *Studies*, 59, agrees.

b. McKane 2:1156–57 argues against the changes advocated in *BHS*.

c. See *BHS*, but the form should be *šĕ'ôrâ* (Ehrlich, *Randglossen*, 4:356; Barthélemy, *Critique textuelle*, 2:774–75), which appears in a few Hebrew MSS. It developed into K and then, as in 14:3, to Q. NAB and REB reflect the emendation. The place name appears in the underlying Isa 15:5.

d. LXX (31:5) already reflects the repetitious "with weeping . . . weeping," though it lacks the following *kî*. I adopt the solution of *BHS*, with the backing of Isa 15:5. Perhaps the second occurrence originated as a marginal correction of the first, which assumed that the verb was Hiphil, "one causes weeping to ascend" (cf. the Qal in 14:2), but it displaced *bô*, "by it." NAB and NJB make the change.

e. MT prefaces with a contextually awkward *ṣārê*, "distresses of" or "foes of," which LXX lacks, as does the parallel Isa 15:5. McKane 2:1159–60 disputes Barthélemy's interpretation as "disasters" that gave rise to the cry (*Critique textuelle*, 2:778). Was it originally meant as a marginal comment on the second colon of v. 2, explaining that the subject of the plural verb was not the citizens of Heshbon but its enemies or perhaps besiegers? If so, the term slipped and was related to another plural verb, "they heard." NAB and NJB omit.

f. For the ABB'A' pattern in vv. 3–4 and the ABA'B' one in v. 5, cf. Watson, *Classical Hebrew Poetry*, 185–86.

g. The feminine plural verb relates *ad sensum* to the collective *nepeš*, "lives, selves" (S. R. Driver, *Revised Translation*, 368).

h. The expected form is *'ar'ār*, "juniper," as in 17:6 and as Aquila attested with his rendering "tamarisk," followed by Vg. (cf. KJV "heath," NIV "bush"). Barthélemy, *Critique textuelle*, 2:778–80, rightly finds assimilation to the place name "Aroer" in v. 19 and considers the underlying form a recensional variant of the verb *yĕ'ō'ērû* in Isa 15:5 (cf. *BHS* there).

i. MT "in your deeds/things made and in your treasur(i)es" is suspicious because of its length and mismatched pairing; it looks like a doublet (Janzen, *Studies*, 19). The second term could be an incorporated comparative gloss with 49:4 in view (cf. Barthélemy,

Critique textuelle, 2:781). LXX "in your fortifications" (31:7; cf. *BHS*) represents a displacing of the first term with the second one and a rendering that related to the root *bṣr*; the Greek term was used to translate *mbṣr*, "fortification," in v. 18. REB "arsenals" for the second term interprets as stores of weapons, as in 50:25. In light of v. 7b the first term has a religious sense, as in Isa 41:29. In v. 7 "you" and "your" are feminine singular, evidently referring to Moab in general (cf. vv. 2, 9, 20a K).

j. This bicolon is an enigma. To make sense of it requires finding coherence between the noun in the first colon and the verbs in the second. EVV divide into three interpretive groups, none of which has a ring of certainty. In MT, as pointed, two different verbs appear: "in ruins she shall go out" (Holladay 2:341–42). This unusual construction is generally abandoned to produce two forms of a single verb. NJB and NJPS make that verb *yṣʾ*, "go out, leave," which appears in v. 7, and assign to *ṣîṣ* a sense "wings," as in Targumic Aramaic: "Give wings to Moab, for she must go hence" (NJPS); similarly Barthélemy, *Critique textuelle*, 2:782–85. A refinement of this position is to relate the verbs to *nṣh*, "fly," with the support of LXX as to the consonantal text (S. R. Driver, *Revised Translation*, 369; RSV), as in the translation above. BDB 663a questions the existence of this root, while *HALOT* does not recognize it, but *DCH* 5:737, in a lexicon that prizes homonyms, accepts it in principle and as a possibility here. The figure in v. 28 lends some support to this interpretation and either view of the verb (cf. "Abandon," v. 28a). NRSV and NIV find here a curse-like call for infertility, relating the noun to Ugaritic *ṣṣ*, "saltfield " (thus Holladay 2:341; McKane 2:1155, 1163–65, but his rendering, "Make Moab a salt waste," is difficult to derive from the Hebrew), but give it the meaning "salt" (see the caution of *HALOT* 3:1023b), and then relate the verbs to *nṣh*, "be destroyed," a meaning that does accord with the next colon: "Put salt on Moab, for she will be laid waste" (NIV). The same verbal basis is also presupposed in NAB, REB, and GNB (and also *BHS*), but with a reading *ṣîyûn*, "marker," for the noun on the evidence of LXX, where, however, it appears to be an exegetical rendering born of despair: "Give a warning signal to Moab, for she will be laid in ruins" (REB), "Set up a memorial for Moab, for it is an utter wasteland" (NAB).

k. Rudolph 280 claims that this clause is necessary as a poetic colon, but what is left is a tricolon.

l. The switch to a plural is strange. Cf. *BHS*.

m. A pointing as a participle (*BHS*) is necessary to provide a subject for the next verb (cf. v. 8; thus NAB, NRSV, REB, and even Lundbom 3:271); for the double genitive see Joüon §129b; *IBHS* 139. MT has assimilated to v. 20. The feminine suffix (cf. v. 9) is tolerably discordant here.

n. Under the influence of 46:18 and 51:57 (cf. the contextual similarity of 51:56a), MT adds a structurally unfitting expanded quotation formula, "declared the King, whose name is Yahweh Almighty," which LXX lacks (*BHS*; cf. Janzen, *Studies*, 79). The doxology does reflect the context of judgment and idolatry (Crenshaw, "Form-Critical Analysis," 160).

o. Literally "thirsty, dry," G. R. Driver, "Textual Problems," 124, found here a noun with the sense "dry land" (cf. Keil 2:220).

p. Cf. 46:19. For LXX see Janzen, *Studies*, 29, over against Ziegler, *Jeremias*, 318.

q. The accent in MT construes it as a finite verb in an asyndetic relative clause; see McKane 2:1175–76. S. R. Driver, *Revised Translation*, 369, refers to GKC, §112n.

r. See *BHS*, but for the gender disparity cf. v. 15 and also v. 38 after v. 36. Moab tends to be treated as feminine in the first unit and masculine thereafter.

s. See Godfrey R. Driver, "Difficult Words in the Hebrew Prophets," in *Studies in Old Testament Prophecy: Presented to Theodore H. Robinson on His Sixty-fifth Birthday* (ed. H. H. Rowley; Edinburgh: T & T Clark, 1950), 52–72, esp. 61–62; NJPS.

t. For the exegetical translation "with its hand" in LXX (*BHS*), see McKane 2:1180.

u. See *BHS*. For the syntax of the second question see textual note n on 31:20.

It is Moab's turn to be threatened, in a chapter that is a medley of material with its own heading in v. 1 and two conclusions in v. 47. It is a large collection of different units that reminds the reader of blocks of earlier compositions in which originally separate poetic and occasionally prose units were strung together with editorial intent, and even more of the topic-specific collections of oracles, royal in 21:1–23:8 and relating to Jeremiah's prophetic rivals in 23:9–40. This collection seems to fall into two roughly symmetrical compositions, vv. 1a*b*–27 and 28–44, to which MT had added vv. 45–47.[143] A loose overall frame is provided by two factors, the lamenting exclamations "Alas" in v. 1 and "How terrible" in v. 39, at the beginning of the first and final units, and the extinction of Moab as a national entity in vv. 2 ("nation") and 42 ("people"; cf. v. 46). The compositions close with the same pair of motifs: Moab's being made a laughingstock (vv. 26 and 39), and the challenging of Yahweh (vv. 26 and 42). A striking clue to division into units is a novel technique of closing with a divine citation, evident in vv. 9 (introduced in v. 8), 12, 35, 38, and 44 and so explained by MT in vv. 25 and 30 (cf. v. 47a); Keil (2:210) tried his hand at this clue, but overlooked vv. 12 and 30. This technique was developed from Isa 15:9, its sole instance in Isaiah 15–16, a major literary source for this chapter, though that particular text was not quoted here; a similar technique was used earlier in the composition of Jer 31:2–26. Another clue is a climactic prose statement frequently added to a poetic piece (vv. 10, 13, 21–24, and 34); vv. 26–27 function as a similar conclusion to the composition (cf. v. 47b in MT, closing the pair of compositions). Most of these statements offer theological interpretation.[144] These structural criteria establish an overall shape of three complex units in the first composition (vv. 1a*b*–10, 11–13, and 14–27) and four in the common text of the second (vv. 28–30, 31–35, 36–38, and 39–44), to which MT has added a fifth (vv. 45–46).

---

143. Cf. Duane L. Christensen, *Transformations of the War Oracle in Old Testament Prophecy: Studies in the Oracles against the Nations* (HDR 3; Missoula, Mont.: Scholars Press, 1975), 244, who, implicitly followed by Carroll 792, saw two major divisions, vv. 1–28 and 29–44, because of the latter verses' dependence on earlier foreign oracles.

144. Georg Fohrer, "Vollmacht über Völker und Königreiche: Beobachtungen zu den prophetischen Fremdvölkersprüchen anhand von Jer 46–51," in *Wort, Lied und Gottesspruch: Festschrift für Joseph Ziegler*, vol. 2: *Beiträge zu Psalmen und Propheten* (ed. J. Schreiner; Würzburg: Echter Verlag, 1972), 145–53, esp. 149. Fohrer did not find any structural value in the statements.

The difference between the two compositions is that the latter one consists almost entirely of quotations from other texts, whereas the former has just one (vv. 5–6). This literary practice was one of the telltale signs of the prose sermon in earlier chapters, and the quotations are perhaps to be attributed to the same hands. The reader has to respect the anonymity of these poems; they have no oracle reception heading mentioning Jeremiah, but it is not unreasonable to envision some of the poetic material in the first composition going back to him, since implicitly, at a macrostructural level, the Babylonian invasion of the west continues to be in view.[145] Although Moab sent delegates to the anti-Babylon conference in Jerusalem in 594/593 B.C.E. (27:3), it had earlier taken Babylon's side by attacking Judah (2 Kgs 24:2). It survived Nebuchadnezzar's western campaign that brought about Judah's downfall (cf. Jer 40:11), but Josephus (*Ant.* 10.181–82) reflects a tradition that Nebuchadnezzar attacked and subdued Moab and Ammon in 582. A prophetic premonition of such an attack seems to underlie the collection, which has incorporated a variety of material. Moab later collapsed under the infiltration of Nabateans from the eastern desert, a process that was complete by the fourth century B.C.E.

Apart from the divinely spoken conclusions, the pieces formally consist of human reflections on the dire situation confronting Moab. They often take the form of funeral lamentation that expects no happy ending, a rhetorical way of expressing an announcement of disaster in terms of human consequences, since reasons and divine threats of intervention are intermittently added. The whole is an unusual multiple oracle of disaster. The timing in the pieces is erratic, oscillating between past and future, but the overall impression is that the past references function here as "prophetic perfects" that seal the inevitability of Moabite defeat.

The overlap of vocabulary with ch. 47 was the obvious reason for the placement of ch. 48 here: "cry out and wail," 47:3, which occurs in reverse at 48:20; "ravage," 47:4a, b; 48:1, 8, 15, 18, 20; "wipe out," 47:4; 48:2; "head shaving" (*qorḥâ*), 47:15; 48:37; "fall silent," 47:5; 48:2; "sword," 47:6; 48:2. The conglomeration of cases in 48:1–2 was probably the main stimulus for the linkage.

[**48:1a***a*] Moab lay along the eastern side of the Dead Sea, with its maximal northern and southern boundaries stretching beyond it at either end. The quotation formula is relevant for the divine statements placed at the end of units. "Israel's God," added in MT, here points up a contrast with the Moabite god Chemosh, to whom several references are made (vv. 7, 13, 35, and in MT 46).

[**1a***b***–10**] This composite unit falls into two stanzas (vv. 1a*b*–5 and 6–9); the second concludes with divine speech (v. 9) and a prose general statement is

---

145. Cf. the endeavors of Holladay 2:347–52 to find an authentic core via links with Jeremiah's poetry. Huwyler, *Jeremia und die Völker*, 154–55, ascribes twenty-six verses or parts of verses to Jeremiah.

Oracles against the Nations 479

added (v. 10)—the first instances of a pattern for units in this collection. Woven into the end of the first stanza and the start of the second (vv. 5–6) is a citation of Isa 15:5. It is so well integrated into the poem that it is difficult to decide whether it is woven in or the poem has been woven around it. The collection of anti-Moabite messages in Isaiah 15–16 will be extensively reused in the second composition. Overall the compositions echo two long passages (Isa 15:2–9 and 16:6–11). The individual cases, which include obvious reordering and reinterpretation, make clear that the borrowing lies on the side of Jeremiah 48.[146] When Isa 15:5 is revisited in v. 34, what has already been quoted in this unit is carefully passed over, apart from mention of Zoar.

[1a*b*–5] This stanza celebrates the military destruction of the northern half of Moab, north of the River Arnon (vv. 1–2), and reports the reaction to the news in the southern half (vv. 3–5).[147] An enemy from the north is envisioned. The ominous listing of cities is a traditional prophetic technique in both foreign and domestic oracles of disaster.

[1a*b*–2] The first stanza begins with a mock funeral lamentation (*hôy*, "Alas"; cf. 22:18) that typically bemoans the loss of a glorious past ("renown").[148] It engages in ominous wordplay that seals the fate of the cities, "Heshbon" and *ḥšb*, "devise," and "Madmen" and *dmh*, "be silent." Heshbon is represented as already taken and now serves as headquarters for a campaign of national destruction.

[3–5] The key word of the report in the second part is "broken(ness)." The shocked reaction to the bad news resounds through southern Moab. Zoar was its southernmost city. In Isa 15:5a, which underlies v. 5 here, fugitives from the north are in view, but the novel use of the verbs of hearing (vv. 4–5) indicates an interpretation in terms of southerners spreading the grim news about the north up hill and down dale.

[6–10] A divine thread runs through this second stanza and the prose supplement. Yahweh's word and work come to the fore in vv. 8–10, over against Moabite religion in v. 7. Gone is the cataloging of cities. The bustling of v. 5 slides into the excitement of strategic imperatives and exclamations (vv. 6, 9–10) that frame static statements of general destruction.

[6] In a summons to flee, the refugee motif is now allowed a place, but with reference to southerners ("you too," v. 7). The strange verb *yĕʿôʿĕrû* that closes

---

146. Cf. Hans Wildberger, *Isaiah 13–27* (trans. T. H. Trapp; CC; Minneapolis: Fortress, 1997), 124–25.

147. For most of the place names see *Macmillan Bible Atlas*, maps 128 (p. 97) and 130 (p. 98), and especially Wildberger's map of sites (*Isaiah 13–27*, 130) and subsequent discussion. Madmen, which occurs only here, is often tentatively located in central Moab, e.g., by Yohman Aharoni, *The Land of the Bible: A Historical Geography* (trans. and ed. A. F. Rainey; rev. ed.; Philadelphia: Westminster, 1979), 56, 338, 439, but the context suggests otherwise.

148. The exclamation does not introduce a woe oracle here; cf. Ernst Jenni, "*hôy*, woe," *TLOT* 1:357–58, esp. 357.

Isa 15:5, probably read as *yĕʿarʿērû*, "rouse" (*BHS* there), is given a midrashic sort of interpretation as *ʿarʿār*, "juniper," as one must read in the Jeremiah text, a desert shrub (cf. 17:6). The townspeople can survive in a wilderness existence east of Moab.

[7] A reason for the flight is supplied. In the light of v. 7b and v. 13, "what you have made" must be a reference to divine images. Moabite pagan worship was to receive its comeuppance. The capture and deportation of the religious establishment, carrying the image of Chemosh, are envisioned; "officials" seems to refer to ancillary temple staff here and in 49:3.

[8] The northern half of Moab, reflected in vv. 1b–2, is now revisited. The northern "plateau" stretches from the Arnon, while the "plain" is the low-lying area farther north, east of the Jordan and the counterpart of "Jericho Plains" (39:5) on the west side.

[9] An older oracle about the towns of v. 8a is evidently cited. The interpretation of the enigmatic v. 9a in the translation is the least objectionable one because it honors the contextual emphasis on displacement, whether as refugees or as deportees.

[10] The curse in the prose supplement energetically applies the foregoing appeal to Yahweh's word and sees a fulfillment of its providential purpose in the "sword" of v. 2.

[11–13] This short unit, demarcated at its close by its divine speech and prose statement, has a satellite role. It is meant to develop three motifs from the preceding one, the reversal of a desirable past, deportation, and the disillusionment of trust in Chemosh. Moab's wine industry surfaces a number of times in the chapter, here, in v. 26, and in vv. 32–33. This first reference, like the third one, is initially positive in tone and continues the dirge motif of that which is good being brought to a bad and shocking end. Here long-lasting security is compared to aged wine that was deliberately left on its sediment until strained just before use (cf. Isa 25:6).[149] An interpretive note is added midway, contrasting its stability with deportation, the fate of v. 7. The divine announcement of intervention continues the wine metaphor, taking the decanting as a disruptive process, which the smashing of the empty storage jars vehemently underscores. The oracular formula beginning with "Therefore" would have been more appropriate after a preceding accusation; the juxtaposition of two genres has caused some awkwardness. The closing comment reverts to the religious theme of v. 7. Yahweh's intervention would prove the inability of Moab's god to sustain his people's blessing. The final comparison refers to the fall of the northern kingdom. Whether "Bethel" refers to a deity, as the parallelism suggests, or more loosely to the Israelite sanctuary, viewed as non-Yahwistic (cf.

---

149. Cf. David J. Clark, "Wine on the Lees (Zeph 1.12 and Jer 48.11)," *BT* 32 (1981): 241–43, who, however, finds a negative meaning here.

Hos 10:5–6), is not certain.[150] The latter is preferable since the deity is not associated with the northern kingdom elsewhere.

[14–27] This composite unit is made up of poetry in vv. 14–20, 25, and prose supplements in vv. 21–24 and 26–27. The key words of the poetry are "ravager/ravaged" (vv. 15, 18, 20) and "broken" (vv. 17, 25), perpetuating vv. 1 and 8 and vv. 3–5, respectively. Moreover, an up-and-down contrast features in both vv. 15 and 18 (cf. v. 5). This evidence demarcates two poetic stanzas, vv. 14–17 and 18–20, 25.

[14–17] The first stanza takes the lively form of a disputation.[151] It has a standard format; a dispute in vv. 14–17a challenges the thesis expressed within v. 14 and replaces it with a counterthesis in v. 17b (cf. 2:23–25; 8:8–9). "Say" (vv. 14, 17), introducing rival propositions, is a fitting frame; so are the contrasting cases of "How," used in doubting inquiry at v. 14 (*ʾêk*) and in lamenting exclamation at v. 17 (*ʾêkâ*; cf. Lam 1:1). The stanza continues the previous dirge-like note of reversal, now with the prospect of the overthrow of previous sureties—a resolute army, "fame," and power. The call to territorial neighbors to "mourn" is nicely matched by the dirge meter used in the closing exclamation (Rudolph 280). The metaphors for national power complement the initial reference to military might.

[18–20] The second stanza, whose last line has been deferred to v. 25, returns to the topographical specificity of the stanza in vv. 1a*b*–5. Just as in vv. 1a*b*–2 the northern part of Moab was under attack and in vv. 3–5 reactions in the southern part were described, here enemy action focuses on Dibon, still north of the Arnon, while Aroer on the river's north bank reacts to the bad news by seeking information and the settlements in the deep valley along the river were soon to hear the news, as refugees poured in. Hordes of refugees are envisioned in the inclusive alternation of gender. The motif of reversal persists in this stanza, in that Dibon's lost throne of "glory" spells humiliation for Moab (vv. 18, 20).

[21–24] The prose statement is a somber catalog of towns in the northern plateau (cf. v. 8). It defines the towns of Moab ravaged at the start of the unit in v. 15. "Jahzah" is another form of "Jahaz" in v. 34. What was earlier defined in terms of military attack is now characterized as "judgment," another way of expressing "Yahweh's work" (v. 10).

[25] The last line of the poem, after the prose interruption, has been taken as divine speech in MT. MT has taken its cue from the distinctive format of units in ch. 48. It may also envision divine agency for this destructive activity on the lines of v. 38; 49:35; Ezek 30:20, 24, where breaking is expressed within divine

---

150. Cf. Edward R. Dalglish, "Bethel (Deity)," *ABD* 1:706–10.

151. David L. Petersen, "The Oracles against the Nations: A Form-Critical Analysis," in *SBLSP 1975* (ed. G. W. MacRae; 2 vols.; Missoula, Mont.: Scholars Press, 1975), 1:39–61, esp. 49. Huwyler, *Jeremia und die Völker*, 169, finds a thesis and antithesis in vv. 14–15.

speech. The horns of the wild ox, tossed in a successful fight, were a metaphor for triumphant power (cf. Deut 33:17; Ps 75:10 [11]).

[26–27] This prose passage concludes the first composition. It anticipates the motifs of challenging Yahweh and becoming a laughingstock that will draw the second to a close in vv. 39 and 42. Significantly the motifs relate respectively to a reason for disaster and for the consequent disaster itself, and so the passage embraces in its own way the elements of a two-part oracle of disaster, thereby unfolding the "judgment" of v. 21. Verse 27 finds in the disaster a tit-for-tat response for Moab's undeserved mockery of Israel, which here stands for Judah (cf. Zeph 2:8, 10). This second reason is related to the first, challenging Yahweh, and seems to function as a definition of it. To deride Yahweh's people was to defy Yahweh. The portrayal of Israel as innocent does not comport well with its representation earlier in the book, most recently in 46:28, but perhaps the author thought that it had done Moab no harm, as LXX "your thefts" suggests. The motif of drunkenness (v. 26) puts to negative use Moab's wine industry. It echoes the theme of the cup of divine wrath to be drunk by the nations in 25:15–29 (especially 25:27). Moab did appear in the list of nations at 25:21. Deriding a drunk as a metaphor for the humiliation that follows disaster also occurs in Ezek 23:32.

48:28–47 A Moabite Anthology

28 Abandon the towns and make the rocks your home,
    you who live in Moab,
and take after the doves that make their nests
    around the top of a canyon.
29 We have heard of Moab's pride—
    it is extremely proud—
its *insolence,* pride, arrogance,
    and high-and-mighty attitude.
30 "I myself know,
declared Yahweh,
"its hubris,
    and its boasting is wrong, bringing about[a] what is wrong."
31 Here is why I bewail Moab,
    cry out for the whole *of Moab,*
    and groan[b] for the men of Kir-heres.
32 More than Jazer weeps I weep for you,
    vine[c] of Sibmah.
Your tendrils used to spread to the sea,
    and reach as far as[d] Jazer.
On your summer fruit *and* on your vintage
    the ravager has fallen.

Oracles against the Nations 483

33 Joy and gladness have disappeared
from *the fertile fields and* country of Moab—
"I have eliminated[e] the flow of wine from the vats."
There is no treading with a vintage shout—
the shouting is no vintage shout.

34 From the cries of Heshbon as far as Elealeh[f]—as far as Jahaz their voices reach, from Zoar as far as Horonaim or Third Eglath, because even the watercourse of Nimrim has become a desolate scene. 35 "So I will eliminate," declared Yahweh, "any Moabites who present burnt offerings at a shrine[g] or make sacrifices to their god."
36 Here is why my heart sighs for Moab with the pathos of flutes; my heart sighs for the men of Kir-heres with the pathos of flutes. Here is why the abundance it gained has been lost.[h] 37 It is because every head has been shaved bare and every beard clipped off; every hand bears slash marks, while waists wear sackcloth; 38 on all the roofs of Moab and in its squares there is general mourning.[i] It is because "I have broken Moab like an unwanted jar," declared Yahweh.
39 How terrible that it is defeated![j] How terrible that Moab has turned its back in humiliation! Moab has become a laughingstock and a cause of dismay to all its neighbors. 40 By way of explanation here is what Yahweh said.
Look, eagle-like someone will dart, spreading his wings over Moab.

41 The cities will be captured
and the fortresses seized,[k]

while the morale of Moab's warriors on that day will be on a par with that of a woman in painful labor.

42 Moab is to be devastated, a people no more,
because it challenged Yahweh.
43 A scaring device, a pit, and a snare
threaten you who live in Moab.[l]
44 Anybody who runs away to avoid the scaring device
will fall into the pit,
while anybody who climbs out of the pit
will be caught by the snare,
"Yes, I will inflict this[m] on Moab
in the year when they are dealt with,"
declared Yahweh.

45 *In Heshbon's shadow stand
powerless runaways,
because fire has leaped out of Heshbon,
flames from Sihon's domain,*[n]
*consuming foreheads in Moab
and the scalps of boasters.*
46 *What a pity for you, Moab—
Chemosh's people has perished—
now that your sons have been taken off as captives
and your daughters as prisoners!*

47 *"Yet I will eventually restore Moab's fortunes," declared Yahweh.
Here ends the material about Moab's judgment.*

a. The preceding plural noun is the subject. For the punctuation in the former clause see *BHS*.

b. See *BHS*; EVV so render, including implicitly GNB. The third person verb may be linked with the two such verbs earlier in the parallel Isa 16:7.

c. Cf. *BHS*.

d. See *BHS*. LXX already presupposes the consonants of *yām*, "sea," reading ʿ*rym*, "cities," for ʿ*d ym* (Ziegler, *Beiträge*, 104; *HUB*), and so the erroneous repetition occurred at an early stage. EVV except NIV and NJPS delete.

e. It is tempting to read *hošbat*, "has been eliminated," with LXX of Isa 16:10, adopted by NRSV there (cf. *BHS* here), but over against this easier reading, MT respects the first person verb in its source, going on to echo it in v. 35.

f. LXX reflects this not very coherent text, which implies an anacoluthon. NIV and NJPS struggle with its retention, while other EVV change in line with the parallel Isa 15:4: "Heshbon and Elealeh cry out" (NRSV).

g. An accusative of place (BDB 749b).

h. For the plural verb see Rudolph 282 and GKC §145b.

i. McKane 2:1191 judges LXX defective in its omission (cf. *BHS*), which includes "Moab." The latter term may have been lost when the quotation formula was brought forward next to the verb, where it now is in LXX.

j. See textual note r on v. 20. The next verb, *hêlîlû*, "wail," looks suspiciously like a marginal correction of the form in v. 20, which was wrongly attached to the next column. REB omits. LXX already attests it, if the plausible Greek emendation in Ziegler, *Jeremias*, 323 (see his *Beiträge*, 30) is correct. The first part of the note in *BHS* is erroneous; see Barthélemy, *Critique textuelle*, 2:792.

k. For the collective feminine singular forms see GKC §145k; Joüon §150g.

l. MT adds "declared Yahweh," which LXX lacks. The addition is fitting at the close of v. 44, but not here. MT was trying to reduce the delay between the quotation formula in v. 40a and the quotation in v. 44b (see the commentary).

m. See *BHS*. EVV concur except NIV and NJPS.

n. See *BHS*. NAB, NRSV, and NJB emend thus.

Oracles against the Nations 485

[48:28-30] The first unit of the second composition is delimited at its close by the divine speech of v. 30. A summons to flight typically opens a unit.[152] It usually precedes an announcement of disaster, but here simply warns of such a disaster; its motifs of urban threat and a refugee status echo the first composition. Verses 29-30 are taken from Isa 16:6, with minor variations, except that the close has been detached and applied to a new but not unexpected divine quotation.[153] The accusation of pride has a major role in the Moab collection, providing justification for its predicted downfall (cf. 46:8 in the Egyptian oracles). Yahweh corroborates human testimony concerning Moab's pride.

[31-35] A prose supplement to the poetry in vv. 34-35 and divine speech in v. 35 mark the end of the unit. Verses 31-33 are borrowed from Isa 16:7-10 with a few variants, in continuation of the previous quotation, while v. 34 is abstracted from Isa 15:4-6a and v. 35 is inspired by Isa 16:12.

[31-33] A human voice appears in the first person lamentation of vv. 31-32a*a*, as in the Isaiah texts,[154] where a divine voice concludes the unit (the clearly divine first person voice that breaks in at v. 33 complicates the issue). The initial "Here is why" seems to look forward to the ensuing description of disaster, and so *lākēn*, "therefore," in Isa 16:7 has been changed to a more flexible *ʿal-kēn* that can point ahead.[155] Kir-heres or Kir-hareseth (cf. Isa 16:7, 11) was the capital city of Moab (cf. 2 Kgs 3:25). Jazer was the northernmost city, while Sibmah was evidently near Heshbon (cf. Isa 16:8). As Moabite beneficiaries of Sibmah's wine, the people of Jazer would naturally be distressed, but the Judean observer claims to be even more distressed by the destruction. The metaphor of a vine symbolizing Moabite prosperity reminds readers of Ps 80:8-16 (9-17) in Israel's case. The huge vine, here personified and addressed, stretched from Jazer in the northeast to the Dead Sea in the southwest. At the end of v. 32 "ravager," a regular element in earlier Moabite units, has replaced *hêdād*, "vintage cry" or "war cry," in Isa 16:9, showing an awareness of the sinister meaning that appears here in v. 33b and later in 51:14. In v. 33 MT has added "the fertile fields" from the source, Isa 16:10. The divine voice appears in v. 33, making plain the source of the disaster.

[34] The lamentation of the human commentator is augmented by a chorus of Moabite cries from north and south. Wherever the Nimrim wadi was on a

---

152. Huwyler, *Jeremia und die Völker*, 163 n. 366, citing Bach, *Aufforderungen*, 15 n. 2.
153. There are also distant echoes of Isa 16:1-2 in v. 28 (Brian C. Jones, *Howling over Moab: Irony and Rhetoric in Isaiah 15-16* [SBLDS 157; Atlanta: Scholars Press, 1996], 100, following Eduard König).
154. See Wildberger, *Isaiah 13-27*, 118-21, 138, 149, 151.
155. BDB 487a cites Esth 9:26. Rintje Frankena, "Einige Bemerkungen zum Gebrauch des Adverbs *ʿal-kēn* im Hebräischen," in *Studia biblica et semitica: Theodoro Christiano Vriezen dedicata* (ed. W. C. van Unnik and A. S. van der Woude; Wageningen: Veenman, 1966), 94-99, esp. 97-98, found five cases of a prospective use, including Gen 32:32 (33) but not Jer 48:31, 36.

north-south axis, like other Moabite rivers and wadis that brought rainwater down from the almost impervious sandstone beneath limestone, it was perennial.[156] The absence of flow was due to enemy attack (cf. 2 Kgs 3:25). Third Eglath, evidently near Horonaim, may have been so called because two other places bore the same name.

[35] The "proper" divine saying enlarges on the earlier one, picking up its first person verb "eliminate." Now a religious polemic appears; although not a quotation from Isaiah 16, it leans on Isa 16:12, where "shrine" (*bāmâ*; NRSV "high place") appears. Two terms, "eliminate" from Isa 16:10 and "shrine" from 16:12, are made the basis of a new interpretation, rather as in v. 6 above. The Isaiah reference is to a prayer of lament (cf. Isa 15:2a), but "he wearies himself" may already refer to the effort of bringing animal sacrifices as well[157] or at least have suggested it, and so provided a source for the sacrificial application here.

[36–38] The only new material in this prose unit is the divine saying in v. 38b that develops v. 12; it may represent a sophisticated fusion of Jer 19:11 and 22:28. What precedes has been directly mined from three separate places, Isa 16:11 in v. 36a, Isa 15:7a in v. 36b, and Isa 15:2b*b* and 3b in vv. 37–38a. The quotation from Isa 16:7–10 continues with 16:11, then there is a flashback to 15:7, attracted by its initial "Here is why"; "abundance" refers to the harvest (cf. Jer 48:31–33; Isa 15:6), partially retrieved in Isa 15:7, but here lost. Finally, as in the previous unit, there is a movement away from individual lamentation to a general manifestation of grief, and material from 15:2–3 is used to express this emotion. There seems to have been a desire to create a unit parallel to the previous one. As before, "Here is why" is prospective. The repeated conjunctions are balanced by repeated cases of "because" later. There is an ABA′B′ structure of effects and causes in which the first and third elements and the second and fourth correspond. The intensity of sympathy, enhanced by new repetition in v. 36a*b*, is striking. In the present context this reference to the heart "is employed as a way to announce, in other terms, the reality of destruction" (Smothers in Keown et al. 318). Wanke (2:412) finds a mocking lament here.[158] In either case, it is an emotional pointer to doom. The simile of the harp or lyre (NAB, NJPS) in Isa 16:11 is here changed to a flute, Dryden's "soft complaining flute" (cf. Matt 9:23). The use of flutes at a funeral in the latter case is fitting for a dirge here.

[39–44] The last unit in the common text involves a quotation from another Isaianic passage (Isa 24:17–18 in vv. 43–44a) to illustrate the intensive scope

---

156. Cf. Aharoni, *Land of the Bible*, 36.
157. Wildberger, *Isaiah 13–27*, 151.
158. Cf. the irony found in vv. 31–32 and the mock sympathy and sarcasm found in Isa 16:9a that underlies v. 32a*a* by Jones, *Howling over Moab*, 130, 267–68.

of the disaster; it recontextualizes by changing "the earth" to "Moab," doubtless understanding it as "the land" and interpreting Moab in the light of Isa 25:10–12.[159] Before that, vv. 39–42 tread for the last time a course from lamentation to definitions of the disaster and to a trigger of the disaster. By way of wrap-up, motifs from the close of the first composition (v. 26) reappear, and so do some terms from the very beginning (v. 1a*b*-b).

[**40a**] The quotation formula is an advance notice of the divine saying that will appear in v. 44b, which is a theological interpretation that will clarify the human phenomenon of v. 39 (see "Genre" in the introduction).

[**40b, 41b**] MT has embellished v. 41a with Edomite material from 49:22 adapted to Moab, to add military motifs of first attack and then defeat. Whereas Yahweh was in view in the original form of v. 40b, here the context makes clear that the human enemy is described (cf. Ezek 13:3, 12).

[**43–44a**] Quite a different part of the book of Isaiah has been visited to express the all-inclusive extent of the disaster. Isaiah 24:17–18 belongs within Isaiah 24–27, which has been assigned a date very soon after Second Isaiah.[160] There is powerful alliteration in the Hebrew, *paḥad*, "scaring device," *paḥat*, "pit," and *paḥ*, "snare," to consolidate the catchall process of hunting. The first term is rendered "the hunter's scare" in REB; it used noise according to the Isaiah text.

[**44b**] The requisite divine saying borrows an announcement of disaster from Jer 23:12b, which follows a reference to falling.

[**45–46**] MT supplements the series of literary quotations in the second composition with poetic material about Moab drawn from a new source. In vv. 45b–46 extracts from an ancient victory song, Num 21:28a and 29a–b*a*, are wrapped around part of Balaam's fourth oracle that predicts Moab's defeat, Num 24:17b*b*. The supplement by no means lacks rapport with its fresh setting; it functions as a context-sensitive conclusion. A conquered Hebron that is headquarters for a national defeat traces an extra arc back to v. 2; it remakes the meaning of the Numbers text in its own image. Boasting resonates with vv. 29–30; the exclamation of mocking lamentation with those in vv. 1, 17, and 39; the mention of Chemosh with vv. 7, 13, and 35; and deportation with vv. 7 and 11. Closer to hand, the whole citation exemplifies the metaphor of hopelessness in vv. 43–44a (Rudolph 283). The first bicolon (v. 45a) does not come from Numbers. It is related to the metaphor; "runaways" echoes v. 44, as well as vv. 6 and 19. Fugitives seeking shelter in Heshbon find it already occupied and so are doomed.

---

159. Cf. Richard L. Schultz, *The Search for Quotation: Verbal Parallels in the Prophets* (JSOTSup 180; Sheffield: Sheffield Academic Press, 1999), 311.

160. Wildberger, *Isaiah 13–27*, 462, though he considered that in this case material from Jeremiah 48 is quoted (*Isaiah 13–27*, 479). The contextual propensity to quote in this half of Jeremiah 48 reduces the likelihood of the suggestion.

[47a] As in 46:26b, God's last word is one of grace, which surprisingly tempers the message of Moab's destruction. A note of positive reversal ironically caps the Moabite collection, which has made so much negative use of reversal in its dirges. The irony is expressed in Hebrew by an alliterative shift from *šĕbî . . . šibyâ*, "as captives . . . as prisoners," in the last bicolon of v. 46 to *wĕšabtî šĕbût*, "and I will restore the fortunes" in v. 47a (cf. Brueggemann 451). For the phrase see the commentary on 49:39.

[47b] The close of the extensive collection is announced by this colophon. "Judgment," borrowed from v. 21, fittingly sums up the collection in 48:1–47 as a virtual oracle of disaster for Moab. The colophon seems to have nothing to do with the fact that in LXX the Moab material is the last of the oracles against the nations.

49:1–39 A Quintet of Foreign Oracles

49:1 Concerning the Ammonites.

> Here is what Yahweh said:
> "Does Israel have no sons,
>   no heir of his own?
> Why then has Milcom[a] disinherited Gad
>   and his people taken up residence in its towns?
> 2   Therefore, look, the time is coming,"
>   declared Yahweh,
> "when I will get raised against Rabbah *of the Ammonites*
>   the cry of battle.
> Then it will turn into a ruined mound,
>   and its satellite villages will burn down,
>   while Israel will disinherit those who disinherited it,"
> *said Yahweh.*
> 3   "Wail, Heshbon, because Ai is ravaged.
>   Cry out, Rabbah's satellite villages,
> put sackcloth around your waists, mourn,
>   and run to and fro gashing yourselves,[b]
> because Milcom will depart and be deported,
>   his priests and officials as well.
> 4   Why do you boast of the valleys—
>   *[claiming] your valley is so fertile—*[c]
>   rebellious lady,
> you who trust in your[d] resources,
>   [asserting] 'Who can attack me?'
> 5   Look out, I am going to inflict dread on you,"

declared the Lord Yahweh *Almighty*,
     "from everywhere around you,
and you [all]ᵉ will be driven away in different directionsᶠ
     with no possibility of *the fugitives* being regrouped.
6 *Afterward, however, I will restore the fortunes of the Ammonites,*" declared Yahweh.

7 Concerning Edom.

Here is what Yahweh *Almighty* said:
"Is there no longer wisdom in Teman?
     Have the discerning lost their acumen?
     Has their wisdom rotted away?ᵍ
8   Run away, get turned around, find deep caves to live in,
          you who live in Dedan,
     because Esau's calamity I will inflict on him
          at the time I deal with him.
9   If grape pickers come *to you*,
          they will leave no gleanings.
     If thieves do so at night,
          they will destroy as much as they want.
10   What this means is that I myself will strip Esau bare.
     I will expose his hiding places
          so he cannot stay concealed.ʰ
     His children and relatives will be ravaged.
     So will his neighbors, and he will cease to exist.
11   Leave your orphans behind for me to keep alive
          and let your widows rely on me!"ⁱ

12 Here, by way of explanation, is what Yahweh said: "*Look*, those who are not the typeʲ to drink the cup will have to drink it *anyway*. So should you be let off?ᵏ No, you cannot be let off, *but must drink up*. 13 In fact I have sworn an oath by my very self," declared Yahweh, "that a place people react to with shock, insults,ˡ and oaths is what Bozrah will become and all its towns will be turned into permanent ruins."

14   I have heard news from Yahweh,
          while an envoy has been dispatched through the nations:
     "Mobilize and invade it,
          and prepare for battle!"
15   *Here it is:* "Look out, I will reduce you to the smallest of nations,
          one despised by the rest of humanity.

16 What horror you will evoke! (?)[m]
You have been led astray
by your presumptuous attitude,
you community populating rocky retreats,
occupying hilltops.
Though you have a nest as high as an eagle's,
even from there I will get you down," *declared Yahweh.*

17 "Edom will become a shocking place. Every passerby will be *shocked and* react with whistling *to all the damage it has suffered.* 18 As in the case of the overthrow of Sodom and Gomorrah and neighboring towns," said Yahweh, "no one will live there, nobody will settle in it.

19 "Look, like a lion coming up
from Jordan's jungle to year-round pasture,
surely I will suddenly chase it away from it
and appoint over it whoever may be chosen.
Who, after all, is there like me? Who can challenge me?
And what shepherd-king can stand up to me?"
20 Therefore listen to the plans Yahweh
has made for Edom,
to the purposes he has in store
for the residents of Teman.
He guarantees shepherd boys[n] will drag them away.
He guarantees their pasture will be shocked[o] at their fate.
21 At the noise of their downfall the earth will quake.
The shouting will be heard at the Red Sea.[p]

22 Look! Eagle-like he will *soar and* dart, spreading his wings over Bozrah, and the morale of Edom's warriors on that day will be on a par with that of a woman in painful labor.

23 Concerning Damascus.

"Hamath and Arpad are humiliated,
having heard bad news.
They are tossed with anxiety,[q] like the sea[r]
that cannot rest.
24 Damascus, demoralized, has turned around to run away,
gripped[s] by panic.
Distress and pain have seized it, such as a woman in labor feels.
25 How was it the famous[t] city was not[u] abandoned,
the town that brought me such delight?[v]

Oracles against the Nations

26 That is why its young men will fall in its squares and all the soldiers will lie silent *on that day,*" declared Yahweh *Almighty.*

27 "Then I will set fire to the wall of Damascus,
   while Ben-hadad's fortified houses will be consumed by it."

28 Concerning Kedar and the realms of encampments,[w] which were defeated by King Nebuchadnezzar of Babylon.
  Here is what Yahweh said:

"Up! Attack Kedar
   and ravage the easterners.
29 Men will seize their tents and flocks,
   their canvas sheets and other gear.
They will appropriate their camels
   and shout at them 'Terror everywhere!'
30 Run away, beat a retreat in urgency,
   find deep caves to live in, you who now live in encampments,"
declared Yahweh,
"because King *Nebuchadnezzar* of Babylon has a plan for you,
   a purpose he intends for you.[x]

31 "Up! Attack a complacent nation,
   which lives carefree,"
declared Yahweh,
"with no double doors or bars,
   so isolated is the region they inhabit.
32 Their camels will get plundered
   and their plentiful cattle looted.
I will disperse them on every wind,
   those whose temples are shaved,
   and from every side[y]
I will bring their calamity,"
declared Yahweh.
33 "Then the encampments will each be turned into a haunt for jackals,
   a perpetual waste,
where no one will live,
   in which nobody will settle."

34 What was received *by the prophet Jeremiah* as Yahweh's message about Elam, in the accession year of King Zedekiah *of Judah.*

35 Here is what Yahweh Almighty said:

"*Look, I am going to break*^{z} Elam's bow,
their chief instrument of power.
36 Then I will bring four winds to Elam
from the four corners of the sky

"and I will disperse them on all those winds so there will be no nation
unvisited by Elam's outcasts.

37 "And so I will shatter^{aa} Elam as they face their enemies,
as they face people with designs on their lives,
and I will inflict on them a bad fate,
my burning anger,"
declared Yahweh,
"and I will commission the sword to chase them
until I get them finished off.
38 Then I will set up my tribunal in Elam
and get rid of^{bb} its king and government,"
declared Yahweh.

39 "But eventually I will restore Elam's fortunes," declared Yahweh.

a. See *BHS* for the pointing here and in v. 3; cf. 1 Kgs 11:5. Thus EVV except NIV "Molech." MT *malkām*, "their king," lacks an antecedent; secondary influence from Amos 1:15 is likely.

b. The omission of this colon in LXX (30:3) probably reflects difficulty of comprehension; such unusual vocabulary is unlikely in a redactional addition. For the conjectural emendation of the noun, adopted by Duhm 353, see *BHS* (thence NAB, NRSV, and REB) and the discussion of McKane 2:1206–8.

c. MT may have originated in an explanatory marginal comment (McKane 2:1209–10), but it remained as a redactional incorporation. For the rendering "strength" in EVV except NIV and NJB see textual note f on 47:5.

d. For the idiomatic third person suffix see GKC §144p.

e. The pronoun changes here from singular to plural.

f. For the idiom see *HALOT* 3:942a; and Godfrey R. Driver, "Linguistic and Textual Problems: Isaiah i–xxxix," *JTS* 38 (1937): 36–50, esp. 48. Holladay 2:369 compares Amos 4:3.

g. The initial interrogative carries over to the next two cola; cf. GKC §150h. EVV so construe.

h. The participle seems to have the force of an infinitive, which is expected here, as in v. 23; cf. Barthélemy, *Critique textuelle*, 2:613–17.

i. Symmachus and LXX^L (see *BHS*) lost the unexpectedly positive tone by subordinating the bicolon to the close of v. 10 as a quotation and supplying "one who says": "and there is no one who says. . . ." Rudolph 288 and Bright 328 (cf. Thompson 718; Holladay 2:370–71, 376) advocate this dubious expedient. REB and McKane 2:1220,

Oracles against the Nations 493

building on G. R. Driver, "Textual Problems," 125, achieve the same negative end by reading ʿōzēb in v. 11, deriving it from a second root meaning "help," attaching it to v. 10, and then taking the *hē* of MT ʿ*zbh* with the next word as an interrogative: "there is no one to deliver him. Am I to keep alive your fatherless children? Are your widows to depend on me?" Barthélemy, *Critique textuelle*, 2:803–4, followed by Huwyler, *Jeremia und die Völker*, 212, adopts Calvin's recourse to irony. Barthélemy notes the uncertainty of a homonym with such a sense; *HALOT* does not recognize it. See the commentary.

j. For this nonforensic and amoral sense cf. BDB 1049a. S. R. Driver, *Revised Translation*, 294, rendered "they to whom it pertained not to drink of the cup."

k. The absence of the question in LXX, as in the similar 25:29 (LXX 32:15), may simply reflect the translator's failure to recognize it (Sven Soderlund, *The Greek Text of Jeremiah: A Revised Hypothesis* [JSOTSup 47; Sheffield: JSOT Press, 1985], 226–27).

l. MT adds to LXX (29:14) *lĕḥōreb*, "with desolation," which does not fit the stereotypical series of nouns, inserting an external factor into emotional reactions (Rudolph 288; McKane 2:1221). It may be explained as a marginal variant for *lĕḥorbôt*, "into ruins," in v. 13b, which was mistakenly associated with the earlier list of nouns with *lāmed* (cf. Bright 329; cf. the singular form in Isa 61:4).

m. GKC §147c takes the strange noun as an exclamation, as the disjunctive accent in MT suggests, and it is certainly difficult to integrate syntactically. The parallel Obad 3 lacks it. "There is no satisfactory solution" (McKane 2:1224).

n. NJPS, as also in Zech 13:7; Holladay 2:371, 377; and McKane 2:1214, 1227, following Rashi and Luther via Duhm 356 and Volz 417. Cf. *ṣĕʿîrêhem*, "their minions," in 14:3 (Q) and *ʾaddîrê haṣṣōʾn*, "flock masters," in 25:34–36.

o. An internal Hiphil (cf. BDB 1031a; McKane 2:1227).

p. MT adds *qôlāh*, "its sound," lacking in LXX and the parallel 50:46 (= LXX 27:46), to comply with the masculine verb *nišmaʿ*, "will be heard." MT strictly means "As for the shouting, its sound will be heard at the Reed Sea" (Barthélemy, *Critique textuelle*, 2:809).

q. G. R. Driver, "Textual Problems," 126, explained the noun as an accusative of cause.

r. The meter belies the masoretic punctuation; Symmachus and Vg. divide accordingly. For MT *bayyām*, "in the sea," EVV, including NJPS, follow a minor masoretic reading *kayyām*, "like the sea" (cf. Isa 57:20). Did MT suffer careless assimilation to the form in v. 21? Perhaps LXX (30:12), which does not represent it, omitted it as incomprehensible.

s. See *BHS* and cf. 6:24; 8:21.

t. Q implies a double-duty first singular suffix on the parallel noun (GKC §80g, comparing Exod 15:2), "the city that is the object of my praise." A reverse order of nominal phrases would have made this interpretation more plausible.

u. *BHS* and EVV except NIV, REB, and NJPS omit the negative with Vg. and take the clause as an exclamation of regret. For REB see de Waard, *Handbook*, 203. See the commentary.

v. *BHS* and EVV except NIV and NJPS delete the suffix, already attested in LXX (see Ziegler, *Jeremias*, 314). The other ancient translations reflect an easier reading.

w. For this collective term cf. Gen 25:13–16; Lev 25:31; Isa 42:11 (cf. Barthélemy, *Critique textuelle*, 2:813; *HALOT* 1:343b, 345a).

x. For K, which aligns with v. 31, see note k on 3:13.

y. Literally "all its sides," with "nation" in v. 31 as the evident antecedent. The ancient versions rendered with a plural pronoun.

z. LXX (25:15) "Let . . . be broken." More naturally its underlying Hebrew verb would be taken as an imperfect, indicating a future human event in the announcement of disaster.

aa. NIV; cf. NAB, REB, and NJPS "break." See McKane 2:1247, who cites Tg. and Syr. in support.

bb. For LXX, queried in *BHS*, see Ziegler, *Beiträge*, 46–47.

These five oracles have been grouped together into a single chapter, though without an introductory headline. The oracle against Ammon has been given pride of place in the group because of its reference to Israel (v. 2), which recalls the oracle of salvation for Israel appended to the oracles against Egypt at 46:27–28 and thus indicates a new stage within the overall collection. The structural principle of word echoes that linked the Philistine oracle to the Egyptian pair of oracles and the Moabite series to the Philistine oracle reappears here, in that 49:3–4 echo earlier phraseology, "Heshbon" in 48:2 (and 48:45 in MT), "trust" in 48:7, and the deportation of the national god in 48:7 again. In the MT collection of foreign oracles, the oracle against Elam seems to pave the way for the Babylonian oracles in chs. 51–52. However, within the group in ch. 49 the oracles against Ammon and Elam constitute a frame, mentioning wide dispersal for their inhabitants (vv. 5, 36). MT has capped this framing in allocating for Ammon (v. 6) the restoration of fortunes predicted for Elam (v. 39). The three inner oracles share three verbal expressions for defeat. "Run away, get turned around, find deep caves to live in" in the oracle against Edom (v. 8) resounds in different double echoes in the following oracles against Damascus and the desert tribes (vv. 24, 30). The curse of an empty land in both v. 18 for Edom and v. 33 for the desert tribes creates a frame for this inner group. The third of these inner oracles prepares for the one against Elam by the dispersal on the wind(s) in vv. 32 and 36. The group of five oracles in ch. 49 has been welded together by a series of word patterns.

[49:1–6] The oracle against the Ammonites consists of two interconnected oracles of disaster, with an introductory heading and in MT an appended promise of restoration. The connections between the oracles of vv. 1a*b*–2 and 3–5 consist of the Ammonite god Milcom and the capital city of Rabbah with its satellite villages.

[1a*a*] Ammon's territory lay north of Moab as far as the River Jabbok and east of Gilead in the Transjordan. Ammon was a close neighbor of Judah; it participated along with Moab and Edom in both the anti-Babylon conference (27:3) and appears in the cup of wrath listing (25:21).

[1a*b*–2] This oracle of disaster moves from a reason for disaster to an announcement, with prose introductions to the poetry. These two elements are tightly bonded by references to Israel and to disinheriting. The Ammonites'

Oracles against the Nations

grabbing of land that traditionally belonged to Israel would be reversed. The stakes are raised to a religious level by attributing the seizure to the Ammonite god as well as to his people, which provokes Yahweh's retaliatory intervention on behalf of Israel. The significance of "Israel" slides from the patriarch Israel or Jacob in v. 1 to the people in v. 2.

[**1a*b***] Three rhetorical questions echo the style of Jeremiah's poetry earlier in the book (e.g., 2:14; 8:22). They add argumentative vigor to the justification for coming disaster by challenging the legality of the westward annexation, which was doubtless an aftermath of the fall of the northern kingdom. There were plenty of other members of Israel's family who had a prior claim. "Gad," for which LXX gives an exegetical equivalent "Gilead," Gad's territory, stands both for one of Jacob's sons and for the tribe descended from him (EVV mostly "its," but NJPS mg. "his").

[**2**] Yahweh's intervention, instigating military attack, was to issue in two human consequences, negative for Ammon and positive for Israel. Earlier I mentioned Nebuchadnezzar's invasion of Moab and Ammon in 582 according to Josephus, and it is plausible to see here a premonition of the latter attack. Assigning the oracle to the post-587 period of Gedaliah's governorship of Judah would explain its affinity to the language of Jeremiah's poetry and give a plausible setting for a positive prospect for Israel. It would also connect with Ammonite involvement in Gedaliah's murder (40:14; 41:15).

[**3–5**] The second oracle of disaster presents its reason in v. 4 and announcement in v. 5; it addresses Ammon. It has a somber introduction in v. 3, a call to collective lamentation in anticipation of the disaster, particularly the loss of the religious mainstay of the state (cf. 48:7b and commentary).

[**3**] Heshbon, normally Moabite (cf. 48:2), is here regarded as under Ammonite control, as the parallelism with Rabbah's villages suggests; national frontiers fluctuated at different periods. A Transjordanian Ai was presumably nearby (cf. Lundbom 3:320).

[**4–5**] Rabbah is now addressed until the individualizing second plural takes over in v. 5b. There are accusations of presumptuous pride and false security in the economy, namely, the agricultural fertility of the upper Jabbok valley, as the added explanation in MT clarifies. External parallelism suggests the same sense for Rabbah's "resources" (NJB) or "storehouses." The epithet "rebellious" is best taken as a political term, with Babylonian sovereignty in implicit view (Smothers in Keown et al. 324–25; Lundbom 3:322). Ammon was a compliant subject during Judah's rebellion that led up to the invasion in 587 (cf. 2 Kgs 24:2), but its own later rebellion is evident from the plot to assassinate Babylon's governor Gedaliah.

[**6**] In a striking reversal MT aligns Ammon's future with that of Egypt (46:26b; see the commentary there) and of Moab (48:47), taking its cue from Elam's positive future in 49:39, already attested in LXX (25:19).

[7–22] After the heading there is a medley of three Edomite pieces (vv. 7ab–13, 14–18, and 19–22). In each case a poem is supplemented by a prose conclusion (vv. 12–13, 17–18, 22). The first two supplements resemble the prose sermons earlier in the book, in both their language and their literary allusions. In vv. 7 and 20 the medley has a double frame, wisdom and Teman, the southern region of Edom; in v. 20 wisdom terminology is used ironically, pitting Yahweh's wisdom against that of Edom. The three pieces are bonded by the motif of shock at or near their close (vv. 13, 17, and 20). The motif occurs in the supplements in the first two cases; MT enhances the second case. The first and third units end with a reference to the Edomite capital, Bozrah, in their prose conclusions (vv. 13, 22).

[7a*a*] Edom, Moab's southern neighbor, south of the Dead Sea and east of the Arabah, now has its turn. Its presence in the overall collection of chs. 46–52 is expected after its inclusion in the account of the conference of western states (27:3) and in the listing of foreign nations (25:21). Nothing is known of an attack by Nebuchadnezzar on Edom, though a later emperor, Nabonidus, probably mounted one in 552.[161] Edom seems to have abruptly left Judah's side when the Babylonians attacked Jerusalem in 588, and thus incurred the angry denunciations of Ps 137:7; Lam 4:21–22; Ezek 35:5, 15; and especially the postexilic Obad 10–16. It is likely that the same motivation underlies the present material, especially in view of the overlap with Obad 5–6 and 1–4 in vv. 9–10a and 14–16, but it is not made explicit. The priority of this overlapping material has not been satisfactorily resolved; both may depend on an earlier version.[162] Eventually the Edomites settled in the Negeb and southern Judah under pressure from the Nabateans infiltrating from the east.

[7a*b*–13] The first unit, after the introductory quotation formula, is a poem supplemented by a prose conclusion. It is basically an announcement of disaster that includes both Yahweh's intervention (vv. 8b, 10a; cf. v. 11) and human consequences, namely, invasion (v. 9) and death and destruction (vv. 10b, 12–13).

[7a*b*–8] The announcement is prefaced with a taunt about Edom's traditional wisdom (cf. Obad 8), soon to be conspicuous by its absence, and with a warning to flee for which the announcement includes the reason. Dedan is in north-

---

161. See John Lindsay, "The Babylonian Kings and Edom, 605–550 B.C.," *PEQ* 108 (1976): 23–39, esp. 33–36; *ABC*, 105, 281.

162. Bert Dicou, *Edom, Israel's Brother and Antagonist: The Role of Edom in Biblical Prophecy and Story* (JSOTSup 169; Sheffield: JSOT Press, 1994), 58–70; and Paul R. Raabe, *Obadiah: A New Translation with Introduction and Commentary* (AB 24D; New York: Doubleday, 1996), 22–31, opt for Obadiah's dependence on material from Jeremiah. Ehud Ben Zvi, *A Historical-Critical Study of the Book of Obadiah* (BZAW 242; Berlin: de Gruyter, 1996), 99–109, envisions the borrowing of material in both books from a common source. The source was orally proclaimed according to Hans W. Wolff, *Obadiah and Jonah: A Commentary* (trans. M. Kohl; CC; Minneapolis: Augsburg, 1986), 40.

west Arabia, and the reference seems to be to visiting traders (cf. Isa 21:13); Edom's economy was based on trade. "Esau" was Edom's ancestral name.

[9] This pair of bicola is a counterpart to Obad 5; MT has added "to you" by assimilation, disturbing the flow of third person references to Edom in vv. 8 and 10. Whereas in Obad 5 the references are hypothetical and interrogative for purposes of comparison, here metaphors for the enemy illustrate the certainty of not only invasion but also wanton destruction (see NAB, GNB mg.).[163]

[10] The certainty is reinforced by the explanatory disclosure that behind the invaders would stand the person of Yahweh, who was to give them access to property and human life, resulting in the loss of both. Verse 10a is related to Obad 6.

[11] The exhortation, taken at face value, can hardly be squared with Yahweh's siding with the enemy and the wholesale loss of Edomite lives. It is best regarded as a sardonic offer that climactically seals Edom's fate by reinforcing v. 10b.[164] "God taunts the Idumeans . . . , 'What! Dost thou expect that I should be a father or protector to their orphans? . . . This thou expectest in vain from me'" (Calvin 5:72).

[12–13] The prose supplement adds its own reinforcement by twice drawing on ch. 25. First, the language of 25:29 is paraphrased (cf. too Obad 16). Edom could in no way avoid drinking from the cup of Yahweh's wrath along with other nations, even with Judah, utterly unexpected as that was at first sight, given Yahweh's relationship with Judah. Second, just as Jerusalem and other Judean towns suffered shocking ruin at Yahweh's hands in 25:18, so would Edom's capital and towns.

[14–18] Before the prose conclusion in vv. 17–18 there is a poem that also appears in Obad 1–4 with recensional variants. Its substance is an announcement of disaster (vv. 15–16), which incorporates in it elements of a reason for disaster.

[14] A prophetic report of a divine audition introduces the oracle. "I have heard" seems to be an earlier version of the generalizing "we have heard" in Obad 1. Yahweh's voice had been heard both sending a messenger to the nations with a summons to attack Edom and giving to the prophet "news" that is reproduced in the oracle.

[15–16] MT clarifies the link with the "news" of v. 14 with "Here it is" (NRSV "For"). MT also assimilates to the Obadiah text by adding "Look out" and the closing quotation formula. The oracle predicts doom for Edom. Yahweh's

---

163. For Obad 5 see Leslie C. Allen, *The Books of Joel, Obadiah, Jonah, and Micah* (NICOT; Grand Rapids: Eerdmans, 1976), 148–49.

164. Linda Haney, "YHWH, the God of Israel . . . and of Edom? The Relationships in the Oracle to Edom in Jeremiah 49:7–22," in *Uprooting and Planting* (ed. J. Goldingay), 78–115, argues that Yahweh is envisioned as the God of Edom here, showing covenant care.

intervention would decisively challenge the self-sufficient sense of impregnability derived from Edom's high mountains with their natural strongholds.

[17–18] Edom's overwhelming defeat and its reflection in outsiders' reactions, broached in v. 15, are echoed here with the help of 19:8, to which MT assimilates further. They are expanded with the tradition of the overthrow of Sodom and Gomorrah, taken from Deut 29:23 (22), which specifies the adjacent towns as Admah and Zeboiim. The supplement also connects with the poem at v. 16b, linking Edom's downfall with overthrow (McKane 2:1225). Verse 18b borrows from v. 33.

[19–22] This complex unit, which lacks an introduction, combines a divine oracle (v. 19) with prophetic elaboration (vv. 20–22); they share images involving sheep. Thus the eagle in the prose of v. 22 is presumably a vulture preying on the flock; Hebrew *nešer* can mean either. A rendering "eagle" does echo v. 16 toward the end of the previous piece; the Edomite eagle would meet its match. MT has framed the piece by adding *ʿlh*, "soar," literally "go up," the same Hebrew verb used in v. 19 of Yahweh as a lion. The addition, which is lacking in MT's use of this material in 48:40, presupposes a divine subject.

[19] "It" is the object of the verb, referring to a flock representing the people of Edom.[165] A lion emerging from the cover of the thick plant growth around the river Jordan into well-watered pastureland nearby (see 12:5 and commentary) becomes a figure for Yahweh's attacking Edom. The dense shrub forests covering the western slopes of Edom's mountains presumably suggested the comparison. Now Edom's grim future is portrayed in terms of a social revolution that brought new government, displacing the present "shepherd" at Yahweh's formidable behest.

[20–22] An ironic put-down of Edomite wisdom (cf. v. 7) reinforces Yahweh's superior power. The dragging away of sheep implies dead bodies (cf. 15:3; 22:19). Earthquake and distant reverberations[166] hyperbolically reflect the immensity of Edom's ruin and reinforce a reaction of emotional shock. Edom's two centers of power, the administrative capital and the army, would bear the brunt of Yahweh's attack. The looming wingspan and panic-stricken screams provide a gruesome climax both to the unit and to the poetry about Edom (vv. 7–22).

[23–27] For all its brevity, this oracle against Damascus, a province of Assyria and then of Babylonia, poses interpretive problems. At first sight the provinces of Hamath and Arpad, in northern Syria, far to the north of Damascus, react in v. 23 to the bad news of a military threat to Damascus, while they themselves are not directly involved. However, the convention of reacting to

---

165. "Them" in the parallel 50:44, to which LXX, Syr., and Tg. assimilate, has the same sense. Bourguet, *Métaphores de Jérémie*, 169, 172–73, taking as "him," finds an anticipatory reference to the replaced shepherd; so do Lundbom 3:344 and REB.

166. The Gulf of Aqabah may be in view. See John R. Huddlestun, "Red Sea," *ABD* 5:633–42, esp. 634.

bad news extends into v. 24a, and the addition in MT in v. 24b still reflects the convention and presupposes its presence in v. 24a.[167] Then a plausible background for the oracle is the Babylonian campaign against Egypt's army in northern Syria, which culminated in the battle of Carchemish in 605, though no attack on Syrian communities is recorded. The uneven style of vv. 25–27 suggests a later testimony to the importance of that period, when Babylon gained control of Syria. The oracle falls into two parts, with vv. 23–24 reporting a preliminary response to the Babylonian threat and vv. 25–27 flashing forward and focusing on the fall of the city of Damascus. The heading highlights the double mention of Damascus (vv. 24 and 27; cf. "Gaza" in 47:1, 5); the oracle's content is directed more generally against the Aramaeans (Duhm 357). The grouping of Hamath, Arpad, and Damascus loosely corresponds to "all the kings of the north" included as victims of the cup of divine wrath (25:26).

[24b] MT escalates the emotional level with material most similar to 6:24 and Isa 13:8. In both cases the Hebrew verb *rph* precedes, as here (rendered "demoralized"), and has acted as an intertextual trigger.

[25–26] The complex bicolon in v. 25 is best understood as a reproving question closely linked to v. 26 (NIV; cf. 2 Sam 1:14, especially in REB and NJB).[168] It functions as a preface to the announcement of judgment presented in the prose of v. 26 and the poetry of v. 27. If the city had been formally evacuated and surrendered, the demise of its defending forces would have been averted. Their dogged resistance meant the destruction of a preeminent city (cf. 38:17–18 in Jerusalem's case). For v. 25b one may compare expressions in the book of Jonah, the description of Nineveh as literally "great to God" (Jon 3:3) and the horticultural metaphor of divine solicitousness for its population (Jon 4:10–11). In the present context the divine hostility of v. 27 reverses former appreciation in a tragic turnaround.

[27] The climactic announcement of divine intervention and its consequences appears to have been written with Amos 1:14a and 4b in view. Benhadad was a dynastic name for the earlier kings of Damascus.

[28–33] This oracle against the tribes in the eastern desert falls into two largely parallel poetic units. Each is made up of three elements: first, a summons to battle addressed to their attackers (vv. 28b, 31; cf. v. 14); second, an announcement of the disastrous outcome to be caused by the attackers resulting in loss of property and livestock (vv. 29, 32a*a*). For the third element the units go their own ways. The first unit closes with a summons to the objects of

---

167. Cf. 6:24; 50:43; Isa 13:7–8 and see Delbert R. Hillers, "A Convention in Hebrew Literature: The Reaction to Bad News," *ZAW* 77 (1965): 86–90, esp. 87–88.

168. Barthélemy, *Critique textuelle*, 2:811–12; cf. McKane 2:1234–35, who, however, considers Jerusalem to be in view in v. 25. The initial *lākēn*, usually rendered "therefore," does not function here as a form-critical bridge from a reason of disaster to its announcement, but, as in 1 Sam 27:6, has the general sense of ʿ*al-kēn*, "that is why," developing the nonabandonment.

attack to flee and also with a prose reason that discloses the identity of the prospective attacker (v. 30). The second ends with divine interventions of disaster and their consequences (vv. 32a*b*–33). The motif of flight in v. 30a is developed in v. 32a*b*.

[**28a***a*] The tribe of "Kedar" in the heading is obtained from v. 28b (cf. 2:10), "encampments" from vv. 30 and 33, and the Babylonian identity of the enemy also from v. 30. The royal government of the encampments is consistent with "all the kings of Arabia" (25:24). The heading notes the fulfillment of Nebuchadnezzar's campaign, which accords with his expedition to Syria in December 599, when his army, dispatched to the desert, "took much booty from the land of the Arabs, (also) their herds and divine images in great number."[169] So it is not unreasonable to credit Jeremiah with the oracle; its language is similar to his poetry earlier in the book (Holladay 2:385).

[**29**] The desert dwellers' homes and animals that were part of their distinctive lifestyle would be lost. The phrase "Terror everywhere," used in a military context in 6:25, evidently functions here as a battle cry (Bright 336).

[**31–32**] Now their characteristic independence and sense of security are threatened. The unusual hairstyle sported among the desert tribes was mentioned as an identifying factor earlier in the book (9:26 [25]; 25:33).

[**33**] The encampments themselves would be destroyed. The oracle has focused throughout on the idiosyncrasies of the tribes' seminomadic lifestyle. The divine judgment carried out by the campaign takes the form of a catastrophic loss of cultural identity.

[**34–39**] The closing oracle against Elam is an announcement of judgment consisting of a phalanx of divine interventions that confronts the power of this state. A vivid survey of salient factors, military defeat and deportation, in vv. 35–36 is revisited in slow motion in vv. 37–38. The poetic oracle is capped with a later prose proclamation of salvation (v. 39). Throughout there is an awesome focus on Yahweh's personal involvement in one-on-one encounters with Elam, whose name is repeated over and over again. In MT the oracle forms a fitting climax to chs. 46–49 inasmuch as Yahweh directly executes the judgment, while the extending of the punishment of the nations to distant Elam accentuates it "as an exclamation point after the fullness of the seven nations."[170]

[**34**] As if countering the unfeasibility of Jeremiah's prophesying against distant Elam, the editorial heading insists on attributing the oracle to Jeremiah and his time; only here among the foreign oracles is a Judean chronology mentioned. The addition in MT merely makes latent information explicit; for the shorter text

---

169. See *ABC*, 101.

170. H. G. L. Eric Peels, "God's Throne in Elam," in *Past, Present, Future: The Deuteronomistic History and the Prophets* (ed. J. C. de Moor and H. F. van Rooy; OtSt 44; Leiden: Brill, 2000), 216–29, esp. 223.

in the oracle reception heading one may compare the oracle reception statement in 26:1 (LXX 33:1). LXX (26:1) places this material as a statement at the end of the oracle, introducing the oracle with a reference simply to Elam (LXX 25:14).[171] Elam was east of Babylonia and north of the Persian Gulf, with its capital at Susa. It was a rebellious part of the Assyrian Empire until the latter's fall. Mention of a king in v. 38 suggests it may have been independent for a while (Rudolph 296). Nebuchadnezzar's campaign along the Tigris in 596/595 may well have included an attack on Elam; the text of the Babylonian Chronicle is damaged here, but the restoration is plausible.[172] Such a setting would suit the general tenor of the foreign oracles as a testimony to Babylon's supremacy by divine providence. If there was editorial knowledge of this campaign, the extra MT dating at 28:1, which refers to Zedekiah's accession year early in 597 and so links with the present dating, associated the Elam oracle with the conference of western states planning rebellion in ch. 27—which actually occurred in 594—and here the oracle was appropriately placed in 597, before Nebuchadnezzar's campaign. One may then perhaps compare Hezekiah's negotiations with Babylon as part of a rebellion against Assyria (2 Kgs 20:12–19; Isa 39:1–8), though there is no historical evidence for any political connection between Judah and Elam. Elam does feature in the cup of wrath listing at 25:25 (see textual note m there), but nowhere else in the OT heads a foreign oracle. The vagueness of the oracle reveals a lack of acquaintance with this remote state, apart from its military expertise in archery, known from its vassal contingent's contribution to the Assyrian army (Isa 22:6). The presence of the oracle is an implicit testimony to Babylon's power and the universality of its empire under God (Holladay 2:389). Holladay (2:388) has enumerated links with Jeremiah's poetry earlier in the book.

[37] As in 19:7 and 21:7 (cf. MT), Babylon is presumably in view. The pursuing sword is associated with deportation in 9:15 (16) and 29:18 (cf. 42:16).

[38] A change of government recalls v. 19 in the Edom oracle, though here the reference is more developed, including a tribunal to set up a new regime (cf. 1:15; 43:10). In broader terms a connection is made with Elam's "kings" in 25:25 (Jones 520).

[39] The reversal is especially striking in this case since Elam falls far outside the range of western states whose submission to Nebuchadnezzar would spell peace in 27:11 and which after their deportation had the potential to return according to 12:14–17. Nevertheless, Elam belonged like them to the Babylonian Empire and so an extension to Elam is not unreasonable, though it seems strange that in the earlier Vorlage of MT only Elam was to be so blessed. It presumably had a typifying role in LXX, at the head of the foreign oracles, so that

---

171. There *ta Ailam* appears to be a separate heading, "The Elam material."

172. See *ABC*, 20, 102; cf. Donald J. Wiseman, "Babylonia 605–539 B.C.," in *Cambridge Ancient History* 3/2: 229–51, esp. 233.

what was predicated of the first was meant to be applied to the rest. MT has retained this feature here despite its change in order, but perceptively added it to other nations that came to play key structural roles in chs. 46–49, though not to Babylon in chs. 50–51. This evidence is an indication that MT adapted the earlier LXX-type text. The stark transition from an announcement of disaster to a proclamation of salvation is reminiscent of the pattern of the composition in 30:1–31:1 in which Yahweh's past punishment of Israel was matched with a future reversal three times. That reversal was expressed in terms of restoring fortunes in an introduction at 30:3, 18. The Israelite model has been strikingly applied to Elam, and the positive phrase found in ch. 30 has been borrowed here. MT also used it in the oracles against Moab and the Ammonites (48:37; 49:6), applying it to two other nations as if recollecting the threefold alternating pattern of 30:1–31:1. MT used different language for a further reversal, at 46:26b in Egypt's case.

The group of oracles in ch. 49 has brought five more nations under Yahweh's sway. While only the fourth explicitly mentions Babylon's king (vv. 28, 30), his providential agency is in implicit view, as in chs. 46–47.

50:1–51:64 Oracles against Babylon and Their Recitation

50:1–46 Babylon's Fate and Israel's Fortune

50:1 A message spoken by Yahweh about Babylon, *about Chaldea, via the prophet Jeremiah.*

2 "Report it among the nations and get it heard,
   and raise a signal, get it heard,
      do not hide it, state it:ᵃ
   'Babylon is captured,
   Bel humiliated,
   Merodach discredited—
   its idols are humiliated, its images discredited.'
3 Here is why. It is attacked by a nation from the north
      that will turn its country into a shocking scene
   in which will live
      neither human being nor animal.
   They will have run off, they will have gone.

4 In those days, at that time," *declared Yahweh,* "Israelites will come and Judeans will accompany them.

   They will be in tears as they go
      and search for their God Yahweh.

5 They will ask the way to Zion
    with their faces toward it^b
    and will come^c and join themselves to Yahweh
    in a permanent covenant never to be forgotten.
6 A lost flock is what my people have been,
    whose shepherds led them astray,
    turning them away^d to the mountains.
  From mountain to hill they went,
    forgetting where they used to lie down.
7 All who found them fed on them
    and their adversaries said, 'We are not guilty,'
  because they had sinned against Yahweh,
    the rightful pasture
    and their forebears' hope, *Yahweh*.

8 "Run off out of Babylon,
    leave Chaldea,
  and be like the male goats
    leading the flock.
9 Here is why. Look, I am going to arouse against *and get to
    attack* Babylon
  a coalition of *powerful* nations
  from the north country, and they will be deployed against it.
    From there it will be captured.
  Their arrows will be like a trained^e warrior's,
    who never returns empty-handed.
10 Chaldea will get plundered.
    All its plunderers will get as much as they want,"
  declared Yahweh.
11 "Though you are glad, though you are elated,
    you looters of my property,
  though you are as frisky as any heifer after threshing^f
    and neigh like stallions,
12 your mother city will be severely humiliated,
    the one who gave you birth disgraced."
  Look, the last of the nations, a wilderness,
  a dry land, and a desert,
13 Yahweh's rage will cause to be uninhabited,
    all turned into a desolate scene.
  Every passerby will react to Babylon with shock,
    whistling at all the damage it has suffered.

14 Deploy yourselves around Babylon,
        all you stringers of the bow.
    Shoot at it,
        sparing no arrow,
    because it has sinned against Yahweh.
15 Raise a battle cry against it *all around.*
    It has surrendered, its towers have fallen,
        its walls are demolished.
    Because this is Yahweh's vengeance, take vengeance on it,
        treat it as it has treated others.
16 Deprive Babylon of sower
        and of sickle wielder at harvesttime.
    To escape the oppressor's sword^g
        let them one by one turn back to their own peoples,
        one by one run away to their own countries.
17 A scattered sheep is what Israel became,
        driven away by lions.

The first to feed on it was Assyria's king and now the next to gnaw its bones has been King *Nebuchadnezzar* of Babylon.

18 Therefore here is what Yahweh *Almighty, Israel's God*, said: "Look, I am going to deal with Babylon's king and his country, just as I dealt with Assyria's king.

19 Then I will bring Israel back to its own pasture,
        and it will graze in Carmel *and Bashan,*
    while in Ephraim's mountain and Gilead,
        it will get as much as it wants.

20 In those days, at that time," declared Yahweh,^h "there will be a search for Israel's wrongdoing, but it will not be there, and for Judah's sins, but they will be nowhere to be found, because I will forgive those I leave as a remnant."

21 "Attackⁱ the country of Merathaim,
        mount an attack on it
        and on those who live in Pekod.
    Put to the sword and wreak ruin,"^j
    declared Yahweh,
        "thus fully carrying out my orders to you."
22 Hark, there is fighting in the country
        and immense calamity!

Oracles against the Nations

23 How badly splintered and cracked
    is that hammer of the whole earth!
   How shocked a reaction
    to Babylon the nations have!
24 You set a snare[k] for yourself and actually got captured, Babylon,
    though you had no inkling.
   You were tracked down and actually got taken;
    you had challenged Yahweh, that was why.
25 Yahweh has opened his arsenal
    and brought out the weapons that express his fury,
   because *the Lord* Yahweh Almighty has work to do
    in the Chaldeans' country.
26 "Converge on it from all sides,[l]
    open its granaries,
   pile up its property like heaps of grain and wreak ruin on it,
    letting nothing that belongs to it be left.
27 Put to the sword all its bullocks,
    taking them down for slaughter."
   Alas for them, because their day is now here,
    their time for being dealt with!
28 Hark! Fugitives and escapees
    from Babylon's country
   are about to declare in Zion
    the vengeance of our God Yahweh,
   vengeance for his temple!
29 "Summon against Babylon archers,
    all stringers of the bow.
   Encamp around it,
    let nobody belonging to it escape.
   Pay it back as its actions deserve,
    treat it just as it has treated others,
   It has acted presumptuously against Yahweh, that is why,
    against Israel's Holy One.

30 "Therefore its young men will fall in its squares and all its soldiers will lie silent *on that day*," declared Yahweh. 31 "Look out, I am your opponent, you personification of presumption," declared *the Lord* Yahweh *Almighty*,
   "because your day is now here,
    the time for me to deal with you.
32 Presumption personified will trip and fall,
    with no possibility of being helped up.

>   I will set fire to its towns
>   and everything around it will be consumed by it."
>
> 33 Here is what Yahweh *Almighty* said:
>   "The Israelites suffered oppression
>   and so have the Judeans.
>   Their captors have all kept a strong grip on them,
>   refusing to let them go.
> 34 But[m] they have a strong champion—
>   Yahweh Almighty is his name.
>   He will certainly take up their cause,
>   intending to give rest to the earth
>   but stress to those who live in Babylon."
> 35 "A sword threatens the Chaldeans,"
>   *declared Yahweh*,
>   "those who live in Babylon,
>   including its officials and experts.
> 36 A sword threatens the oracle givers, who will be proved fools.
>   A sword threatens its warriors, who will be shattered.
> 37 A sword threatens its horses and its chariots,[n]
>   and all the foreign groups that are in it,
>   who will turn into women.
>   A sword threatens its treasuries, which will be ransacked.
> 38 A sword[o] threatens its water, which will dry up.
>   The reason why? It is a country of idols,
>   where dreaded images drive them mad.
> 39 Therefore wildcats will live there along with jackals,
>   and ostriches will live in it.
>   It will never be lived in again,
>   *never occupied for generations to come.*

40 "As in the case of the divine overthrow of Sodom, Gomorrah, and its neighboring towns," declared Yahweh, "no one will live there, nobody will settle there.[p]

> 41 "Look, a people is coming from the north,
>   a powerful nation,
>   and many kings are being aroused
>   from the remotest parts of the earth.
> 42 Bows and javelins they grip;
>   a cruel entity, they are merciless.

> The noise they make is like the roar of the sea,
>   as they ride upon horses.
> Each of them is deployed for battle[q]
>   against you, Lady Babylon.
> 43 Babylon's king has heard news of them
>   and lost his nerve.
> He is gripped with anguish,
>   with pain such as a woman in labor feels.
> 44 Look, like a lion coming up
>   from Jordan's *jungle* to year-round pasture,
> surely I will suddenly chase them away from it
>   and appoint over it whoever may be chosen.
> Who, after all, is there like me? Who can challenge me?
>   And what shepherd king can stand up to me?"
> 45 Therefore listen to Yahweh's plans
>   he has made for Babylon,
> to the purposes he has in store
>   for the Chaldeans' country.
> He guarantees shepherd boys will drag them away.
> He guarantees the pasture will be shocked at their fate.
> 46 At the cry "Babylon is taken"
>   the earth will quake
>   and the shout will be heard among the nations.

a. The MT punctuation does not suit the meter (see *BHS*).

b. EVV except NJPS follow the 3 + 2 line of LXX (27:5), Syr., and Vg. (McKane 2:1254; cf. Volz 423).

c. Ehrlich, *Randglossen*, 4:363, rightly follows LXX (cf. *BHS*), over against the imperative in MT. NRSV adopts LXX; cf. NIV, NJPS, and GNB. Cf. the discussions of Barthélemy, *Critique textuelle*, 2:817–19; and McKane 2:1254–55.

d. See *BHS*.

e. See *BHS*, which EVV follow; NJPS mg. "who bereaves" explains the other option in the masoretic tradition. Barthélemy, *Critique textuelle*, 2:819–21, keeps the latter reading, claiming it to be older.

f. *BHS* prefers LXX, along with KJV, NRSV ("on the grass"), NAB, and NJB.

g. See textual note t on 25:38; cf. 46:16.

h. LXX locates the quotation formula at the end of the verse; *BHS* is misleading.

i. See *BHS* for the redivision of consonants, which EVV except NJPS adopt, thus avoiding a grammatical anomaly. The noun phrase is an accusative of place (cf. BDB, 748a). The military orders in v. 21 are unusually in the singular, addressing the anonymous collective enemy, perhaps "the oppressor" of v. 16.

j. LXX and Syr. lack ʾaḥărêhem, "after them," which probably originated as a dittograph (S. R. Driver, *Revised Translation*, 308). NAB and GNB omit.

k. *BHS* rightly repoints as feminine second person; so do NRSV, NAB, and REB. The divine name in the next bicolon so suggests.

l. *miqqēṣ* is evidently used with the sense of *miqqāṣeh* at 51:31; Gen 19:4 (Barthélemy, *Critique textuelle*, 2:829–31).

m. See *BHS*.

n. The two suffixes in this colon are unexpectedly masculine singular, which LXX renders as plural, relating to "warriors"; cf. *BHS*.

o. MT *ḥōreb*, "drought," breaks the symmetry of tricolon/colon/colon/tricolon/colon/colon, each containing one instance of *ḥereb*, "sword," in vv. 35–38a (cf. Barthélemy, *Critique textuelle*, 2:833–35). The latter is attested here in LXX^OL and probably Syr.; NAB and REB adopt it. MT adapted the pointing to accommodate "water" as the object of attack, but already in v. 37b "treasuries" occurred as inanimate object of the sword, which has the sense of instrument of destruction (McKane 2:1290).

p. The sentence is better taken as prose, as in 49:18, with NJPS.

q. See note b on 6:23.

The block of prophetic material directed against Babylon in 50:1–51:64 consists of a heading in 50:1, two compositions primarily in poetry (50:2–46 and 51:1–58), and a prose narrative that was subsequently added (51:59–64). Although the block belongs to the overall collection of oracles against the nations, it differs from the earlier ones (chs. 46–49) in three respects. First, the Babylon compositions are nearly as large as the rest of the international oracles put together, in MT amounting to 110 verses over against 121 in the prior chapters. Second, apart from MT in 47:1, the earlier oracles presupposed and sometimes expressed attack from Babylon as the means of divine punishment, but now it is Babylon's turn to face retribution. A third surprise for the reader of the second composition is that its daringly precise content concerning Babylon's conquest failed to be fulfilled literally. When Babylon did fall, it was not to the Medes from the north (51:11, 27–28), but to King Cyrus of Persia from the east. Further, the destruction and desolation featured here did not take place during Cyrus's takeover of Babylon.[173] In hindsight they function as rhetorical expressions of Babylon's total loss of imperial power, which had become necessary on theological grounds. Ezra 1:1 had no hesitation in finding Jer 51:1 fulfilled in Cyrus's achievement.

The length of the twin compositions and the vehemence of their language both express deep passion. "The piling up of words and motifs serves an obvious rhetorical purpose: the writer wished to make his point with extraordinary emphasis and passion."[174] The passion wells up from a situation of communal lament. At one point this situation is explicit: in 51:34–37 a description of dis-

---

173. See the Nabonidus Chronicle, 7. iii.15–19 (*ABC*, 109–10); Cyrus Cylinder, lines 22b–28 (*COS* 2:315); Herodotus, *Hist.* 1.191; 3.159.

174. Martin Kessler, *Battle of the Gods: The God of Israel versus Marduk of Babylon: A Literary/Theological Interpretation of Jeremiah 50–51* (SSN 42; Assen: Van Gorcum, 2003), 177.

tress and prayerful wishes for Babylon to suffer for its wrongdoing are answered by a divine assurance of vengeance and destruction (cf. 50:33–34). But, even when it is implicit, both compositions are a series of impassioned responses to equally impassioned grievances. The whole is a testimony that "God heard their groaning ... and God took notice of them" (Exod 2:24–25). It was to be heard by those who pleaded for the punishment of their oppressors, as in Ps 83:9–17 (10–18). The promises of homecoming in ch. 50 correspond to the petitions, "Do good to Zion in your good pleasure; rebuild the walls of Jerusalem," in Ps 51:18 (20). The promises of the people's vindication in ch. 51 correspond to the wish in Ps 79:10, "Let the avenging of the outpoured blood of your servants be known among the nations before our eyes" (cf. Ps 58:10 [11] and esp. Ps 137:8 concerning Babylon). And the promises of Yahweh's own vindication, also in ch. 51, implicitly answer laments that Judah's God too had suffered loss amid Judah's suffering, as Pss 74:4–8 and 79:1 protest. As Carroll (834) says, "a good liturgy of the events of the sixth century would read 50–51 after the reading of the book of Lamentations." A host of grief-stricken prayers find their divine amen in chs. 50–51. In a lectionary their passionate spirit on behalf of the oppressed could be matched by Luke 18:1–8 and 2 Thess 1:6–10.

The present form of the compositions in the common text of LXX and MT reflects a perspective on Babylon later than the time of Jeremiah's prophetic ministry. On the basis of 51:46, they have been dated between 560 and 555.[175] A similar estimate assigns them to the decade before 550, the year Cyrus broke the power of the Medes (Jones 545). The compositions derive from earlier prophetic literature. They reuse material from other foreign oracles, from the Damascus oracle (49:26; LXX 50:15) in 50:30 and from the Edom oracle (49:18–21; LXX 29:19–22) in 50:40, 44–46. They also pick up material from old oracles of Jeremiah to Judah, especially concerning the foe from the north, who turned out to be Babylon; the wholesale insertion of 6:22–24 in 50:41–43 is a long example. Now Babylon was to be confronted by its own foe from the north (50:3, 9, 41; 51:48)! Habakkuk 2:13 is finely exploited in the climactic Jer 51:58. Moreover, echoes of Isaiah 13 and Second Isaiah will emerge, while Jer 10:12–16, itself exilic, is recycled in 51:15–19. Such allusions attest to a late composition. However, this evidence stands in tension with the added postscript, 51:59–64, especially its redactional claim in v. 60b that the compositions go back to 594/593 B.C.E. By painstakingly tracing parallels between the language of the compositions and that of Jeremiah in earlier oracles, Holladay (2:401–11) attributes as many as 82 out of 104 verses to the prophet, but this judgment underestimates the extent to which earlier literature has been reappropriated. Nonetheless, at

175. Klaas A. D. Smelik, "The Function of Jeremiah 50 and 51 in the Book of Jeremiah," in *Reading the Book of Jeremiah: A Search for Coherence* (ed. M. Kessler; Winona Lake, Ind.: Eisenbrauns, 2004), 87–98, esp. 96.

least one poem (51:20–23), with a pro-Babylonian stance, seems to be a genuinely old piece used for the first time here to form a contrast with Babylon's new, negative role in the divine plan.[176] Jeremiah may well have had a prophetic inkling that, while Babylon's empire would last a long time, it would ultimately pass away, just as the forces of Babylon and Media had overthrown Assyria in his lifetime. If the limitation of Babylonian power to seventy years (25:12; 29:10–14) goes back to Jeremiah's premonition, as I urged earlier in the commentary, a solid foundation was thereby laid for chs. 50–51. So a nucleus of older material may well underlie the two compositions, but its extent remains a matter of speculation. As now constituted, the twin compositions speak with a later message that claims the reader's attention.

In the book of Revelation, Jeremiah 50–51 plays a major role among other OT texts in its eschatological claim that imperial Rome was a new Babylon likewise doomed to fall. The preliminary warning in Rev 14:8–11, the description of the fall in 16:1–21, and the delineation of the character and judgment of Babylon in 17:1–19:4 bear clear and extensive signs of a reuse of these chapters.[177]

Babylon was to fall, but Israel was to have a new lease on life, declares 50:2–46. At first sight the composition is a hodgepodge of random, repetitive material, but closer examination reveals some landmarks. There is a frame, the nutshell statements "Babylon is captured/taken" in vv. 2 and 46. It is enhanced at v. 2 by a report to be "heard among the nations" and at v. 46 by a cry, also to be "heard among the nations," both of which celebrate the conquest.[178] Babylon's conquest appears elsewhere in the composition in such synonymous terms; the capture is predicted in v. 9 and both capture and taking are rhetorically regarded as accomplished in v. 24, which will be echoed in 51:41. The fourfold reference appears to be significant for internal structuring because the motif of a positive future for Israel, sometimes coupled with its tragic past, also appears four times (vv. 4–7/8, 17–20, 28, and 33–34). Moreover, "nations" are mentioned four times (vv. 9 and 23 as well as vv. 2 [cf. v. 3] and 46). If one regards this quadrupling of motifs as structurally relevant, the composition falls into four sections, a short one (vv. 2–7) and three long ones (vv. 8–20, 21–32, and 33–46). The rough divisions of Rudolph (299, 301) coincide with the first two of these sections, and those of McKane (2:1271, 1284) with the last two.[179]

---

176. Alice O. Bellis, *The Structure and Composition of Jeremiah 50:2 51:58* (Lewiston, N.Y.: Edwin Mellen, 1995), 148–49.

177. See Jan Fekkes, *Isaiah and the Prophetic Traditions in the Book of Revelation: Visionary Antecedents and Their Development* (JSNTSup 93; Sheffield: JSOT Press, 1994), 86–91.

178. Kenneth T. Aitken, "The Oracles against Babylon in Jeremiah 50–51: Structure and Perspectives," *TynBul* 35 (1984): 25–63, esp. 30.

179. Here McKane implicitly follows Aitken, "Oracles against Babylon," 36–44. Bellis, *Structure and Composition*, 54–76, isolates vv. 21–32 and also its three subsections. Kessler, *Battle of the Gods*, 62, 95, regards vv. 33–46 as a section.

Oracles against the Nations 511

In the first section, negative and positive oracular claims, about Babylon and Israel, respectively, are simply set side by side in a pair of subsections (vv. 2–3 and 4–7). The second section also closes with positive material (vv. 17–20), following an abundance of negative material (vv. 9–16), though v. 8 does provide a positive transition from vv. 4–7. The third section is made up largely of negative material about Babylon, with Israel's hope figuring briefly just past the middle, at v. 28. The fourth section of two units opens with a positive treatment of Israel (vv. 33–34), while the rest deals negatively with Babylon. Babylon's downfall is the major focus of the composition, but the persistent echoing of Israel's prospects reveals a strong secondary theme of reassurance that this political upheaval was to be the means for the rehabilitation of Yahweh's own people. "Judgment on the oppressor must be the beginning of salvation" (Pixley 149).

[50:1] An oracle reception heading introduces the pair of prophetic compositions (50:2–46 and 51:1–58). MT adds two items. The first, "Chaldea," often recurs in parallelism with "Babylon" in the following compositions and so reflects the content more broadly. The attribution to Jeremiah—in the style of 37:2—is a deduction drawn from his writing down "all the messages against Babylon written here" according to 51:60 (cf. 36:2).

[2–7] This short section has an introductory and summarizing role.[180] It announces Babylon's coming defeat and ties it to Israel's spiritual and spatial restoration.

[2–3] There is a flash forward to the prospect of Babylon's capture at enemy hands and the devastation of its country.

[2] A virtual announcement of disaster, with an implicit reason, is wrapped in the rhetorical dress of a command to report its capture. The command, given to unspecified messengers, is evidently delivered by Yahweh, as in 4:5 and 46:13 (cf. v. 21b below). The nations subject to the Babylonian Empire were to hear the glad news. The discrediting of Marduk, Babylon's chief god, whose title was Bel, removes a challenge to Yahweh's own supremacy. (This religious note was struck in previous foreign oracles, in the cases of Egypt [46:15, 25], Moab [48:7,13, 35, 46], and Ammon [49:1, 3].) MT makes two additions, dramatically highlighting both the report and the religious resolution. The former addition was originally a marginal comparison of Isa 13:2, the opening of another oracle against Babylon, with a cue element attached; there the invaders were summoned. The latter one is explanatory, anticipating v. 38b in different language.

[3] The bare report is amplified, referring to the attacker and the catastrophic consequences of the assault. The attacker is ironically defined in terms of the foe from the north, which appeared in Jeremiah's early oracles (see, e.g., 4:6;

---

180. Cf. Kessler, "Rhetoric in Jeremiah 50 and 51," *Semitics* 3 (1973): 18–35, esp. 33.

6:4, 22) and was eventually identified with Babylon, from 20:4 onward (cf. 36:1, 29 and commentary). Verses 9 and 41 will expand this introductory reference, but leave the enemy unspecified; the next composition will be more forthright. Babylon was to experience a fate it had, as God's agent, meted out to others, as vv. 15 and 29 will explicitly declare. The shocking nature of its devastation paves the way for vv. 13 and 23, while its emptiness looks ahead to vv. 39–40. MT harmonizes the general destruction with the sparing of Israel's exiles by glancing ahead to their running off (v. 8) and their going (v. 4).

[4–7] A proclamation of salvation for Israel follows (vv. 4–5). Verses 6–7 set it against the background of an account of the disaster that had earlier befallen them, a retrospective oracle of disaster including both announcement and reason. The prodigal would return to the father's home and favor. The "covenant" (v. 5) bridges the twin phrases "their God" (v. 4) and "my people" (v. 6). Yahweh again appears to be the speaker throughout, as the quotation formula added in MT indicates.

[4a] After a transitional formula, the initial prose statement applies the restoration to exiles from both the northern and southern kingdoms, in the manner of later prophecies in the book (3:18; 23:6; 30:3; 31:27, 31; 33:7, 14). Verses 20 (also in prose) and 33 will express a similar inclusiveness.

[4b–5] The contrition of the returnees echoes 31:9; it provides a frame for the poem of vv. 4b–7, along with the explanatory sinning of v. 7b. As again in v. 28, "Zion" has a religious connotation, here in the context of a willing return to worship in Yahweh's presence and self-commitment to a permanent bonding (cf. 32:40). They would eagerly embrace the divine will. This focus suggests that they, rather than Yahweh, would not forget the covenant, unlike v. 6b (Keil 2:270).

[6–7] The metaphor of a flock imaginatively pervades the account of disaster, alluding to 23:1–2, where Judah's shepherd-kings were indicted. They are here blamed for religious sin (cf. 2 Kgs 21:9, 11). "Mountain" and "hill" refer to illicit sanctuaries, as in 3:23; "went," like "go" in v. 4, connotes worship. The devouring by wild animals that represent national enemies evokes 2:3, but here by contrast they were no longer guilty. The difference is explained in v. 7b. EVV extend the quotation to the close of v. 7, but commentators tend to judge otherwise. Holladay (2:416) observes that the Hebrew causal conjunction *taḥat ʾăšer*, "because," in 29:19 relates to Yahweh's own explanation. "Rightful pasture" interprets in a new and beautiful way the Hebrew phrase in 31:23, there rendered "righteous home" but here in contrast with the wrong worship of v. 6. MT's addition of the divine name is motivated by a stylistic concern, to round off a chiastic series of nouns.

[8–20] This first long section appropriately devotes more space than the former one to Babylon's future overthrow, but again closes with good news for Israel (vv. 17–20). Verses 9–13 consist of an extended announcement of disas-

Oracles against the Nations

ter, in which a reason is incorporated at v. 11a. The temporary tangent to direct address to Babylon (vv. 11–12a) will be matched in the next section (v. 24). Verses 14–16 are a series of battle calls to the attacking nations. Yahweh is the speaker in vv. 8–12a and 18–20.

[8] First, by way of transition Judean exiles in Babylonia are urged to leave the doomed area—like Lot and his family in Genesis 19—in a summons to flight. They, of all the foreign deportees, were to take the lead. The flock imagery (vv. 6–7) is applied to the new development of v. 4 or at least to its Judean element; flocks could be a mixture of sheep and goats.

[9–13] Divine intervention opens the announcement; the rest is devoted to a series of human consequences. The announcement falls into three phases (vv. 9–10 [duly delimited in MT at the close], 11–12a, and 12b–13 [delimited in MT at its opening by repeating "Look" from v. 9]).

[9–10] Babylon's capture by the foe from the north, reported in vv. 2–3, is announced in v. 9a. MT enhances the link by adding "get to attack" (cf. Joel 3[4]:12); "powerful" glances ahead to v. 41. In vv. 9b–10 the military references to archery and looting seem to be connected by the implicit imagery of a hunter shooting and retrieving its quarry. The initial reference to a skilled warrior is borrowed from 2 Sam 1:22.

[11–12a] The present national pride of Babylonia is ominously contrasted with its future degradation. The second colon of v. 11 justifies the coming doom. The poet imaginatively portrays Babylonian hubris by means of animal similes, an unmuzzled ox freely allowed to eat grain as it threshed (cf. Deut 25:4) and a sexually rapacious stallion (cf. Jer 5:8).

[12b–13] The description of doom ends conventionally with the consequences of desolation and shock, but divine "rage" incorporates the personal intervention (v. 9) and the personal affront (v. 11), relating all three parts of this subsection. "Last of the nations" reverses Babylon's supremacy (cf. Amos 6:1), while "wilderness" strips away its misappropriations. MT elaborates the disaster with a phrase from 51:43.

[14–15] The barrage of battle calls begins with the deployment and "arrows" of v. 9, rhetorically translating future facts into barked orders. MT, glancing ahead to v. 29, adds a reason that matches Israel's own in v. 7 and paves the way for v. 15b; Babylon was liable for divine retribution. The note of reprisal in vv. 10–11 is sounded again in v. 15b and now formulated more clearly. Yahweh had a personal stake in accomplishing justice on the covenant nation's behalf. At times prophetic literature combines the notions of Israel's enemies as Yahweh's moral agents (v. 7) who then incur their own guilt, requiring that Yahweh punish them in turn. Isaiah 10:5–15 provides a rationale for such tension, and v. 18 here may allude to that passage.

[16] Disruption of the agricultural routine is a feature of invasion (cf. Isa 37:30). The link between v. 16a and b seems to be the use of deportees as forced

labor (Streane 295). That topic permits a return to the departure motif of v. 8, here echoing Isa 13:14b, and so provides a transition to vv. 17–20.

[17–20] As in vv. 4–7, a comprehensive survey describes Israel's past fate and future prospects. The polarity of northern and southern kingdoms is here represented by a prose historical review that gives a reason for the announcement of disaster that follows (v. 18). The announcement expresses an assuring argument that, one eastern superpower having fallen, providential history would simply repeat itself. A corresponding proclamation of salvation (vv. 19–20) focuses on divine intervention, unlike vv. 4–7 (Holladay 2:409). The flock imagery of vv. 6–7 is reused but also applied to the territorial restoration. The poem's material blessing is supplemented with reference to God's forgiveness (v. 20). The former sins that hung over Israel's survivors like a cloud, causing its punishment and preventing their covenantal fellowship with God, would be forgiven (cf. 31:33–34; 33:8). Five terms employed in vv. 4–7 are reused in a new way: turning away and bringing back (both šôbēb), shepherding ("shepherds" and "graze" from the same root, r^ch), "mountain(s)," sinning, searching, and finding.[181] Predominantly negative terms are shaken up in a literary kaleidoscope, producing a hopeful pattern of renewal.

[21–32] Three sets of battle orders punctuate this section, inaugurating its three subsections (vv. 21–25, 26–28, and 29–32).[182] Each subsection develops Babylon's punishment in its own way and ends with a strong negative term of divine judgment, "fury," "vengeance," and "fire." Another such term, the root pqd, "deal with," occurs in all three subsections (v. 21 [as a punning name, "Pekod"], 27, and 31). These divine terms are a retort to Babylon's pervasive provocation, expressed by "Merathaim" or "Double Rebellion" (v. 21), challenging Yahweh (v. 24), and acting presumptuously against Yahweh (vv. 29, 30, and 31). Yahweh's voice is heard clearly at vv. 21 and 30–32 and probably also in the orders of vv. 26–27a and 29.

[21–25] The "country" of Babylonia frames the whole subsection and also its second part, vv. 22–25.

[21] Two places in southern Babylonia are specified in the commands: "Merathaim," an adaptation of the marshy region called marratum;[183] and the area of "Pekod," an Aramaean tribe (cf. Ezek 23:23). They mean, respectively, "Double Rebellion" and "Just Dealing," shorthand for disaster's reason and announcement.

[22–25] The sequel of the battle orders is first described (v. 22) and then interpreted.

---

181. Aitken, "Oracles against Babylon," 34. Aitken regards vv. 4–20 as a section marked by chiasm, a feature he endeavors to find throughout chs. 50–51.
182. Aitken, "Oracles against Babylon," 36; Bellis, *Structure and Composition*, 60–62.
183. Bill T. Arnold, "Merathaim," *ABD* 4:699.

[23] The mock funeral lamentation contains the typical "How!" and contrasting transformation of circumstances. The lamentation flows from the descriptive comment of v. 22 by means of the root *šbr*, "break," which underlies both "calamity" (*šeber*, "breaking") and "cracked" (the related verb). Babylon, the embodiment of imperial violence, finds itself at the receiving end of sledgehammer blows (cf. 23:29) and broken beyond repair. The shocked reaction of its earlier victims forms an interim conclusion (cf. v. 13).

[24] A vehemently direct address that recalls vv. 11–12a celebrates and justifies Babylon's capture. Within a larger sphere of divine theodicy, Babylon had unwittingly dug a trap for itself and fallen in it; it was the cause of its own destruction (cf. Ps 9:15 [16]; Prov 28:10). It could not get away with provoking Yahweh, implicitly by its treatment of Israel.

[25] Just as Yahweh's orders were carried out by the invading army (v. 21), it and its weapons represented divine "fury" at work. The phrase is taken from Isa 13:15, where it occurs in an oracle against Babylon.

[26–28] The general pattern of vv. 21–25 is followed here.

[26–27a] The second series of battle orders, developing the first, envisions the capture of Babylon and the complete destruction of all its property and leading citizens. "Granaries" is a metaphor for its wealth, which then veers to a simile (McKane 2:1279); "bullocks" is another metaphor, representing leading citizens.

[27b–28] Another mock lamentation announces judgment day for the "bullocks." As in v. 22, it is continued by "Hark," but attention is switched to Israel's refugees, who return to Zion to celebrate in grateful worship the vindicating feat of "our God," Babylon's fall (cf. 51:10; Ps 145:4).[184] MT adds from 51:11 a prime component of Jerusalem's destruction at Babylonian hands, which had impugned Yahweh's honor (cf. Ps 79:1).

[29–32] The third subsection proceeds on the lines of the previous two.

[29–30] For Babylon's citizens there was to be no "escape," unlike the Judean "escapees" of v. 28. The military commands reapply the material destruction of v. 26b to humans and then turn into formulations of reprisal like the last colon of v. 15. The accusation of presumption (cf. 49:16) is developed in vv. 31–32, but first v. 30 is borrowed from 49:26 (LXX 30:15) in the Damascus oracle, attracted by the common sequel of Yahweh's setting of fire in v. 32b and 49:27, as well as by the motif of falling. These verses elaborate the lack of escape.

[31–32] The closing announcement of disaster begins with a formula of hostile orientation, like 21:13; the similarity of v. 32b to 21:14b seems to indicate literary dependence. The reason, Babylon's presumption, is incorporated in the announcement. Verse 27b is amplified to refer to utter defeat.

---

184. Calvin 5:169 interpreted thus. For *higgîd*, "tell," in the sense of cultic praise see Claus Westermann, "*ngd* hi. to communicate," *TLOT* 2:714–18, esp. 717. Psalm 92:13–15 (14–16) in REB is particularly relevant.

[33–46] A quotation formula gives a formal introduction to the section. As in 48:40, it anticipates Yahweh's speaking later in the section. The section falls into four subsections (vv. 33–34, 35–40, 41–43, and 44–46). MT not unreasonably indicates divine speech beginning in v. 35, which may well extend beyond v. 40, as far as v. 44.

[33–34] An account of the disaster that befell the northern and southern kingdoms provides the background for a report of a reassuring proclamation of salvation; the repeated term "strong" (ḥzq) points to a struggle that Yahweh would win.[185] The divine role as "champion" (gōʾēl, NRSV "Redeemer") is redolent of Second Isaiah (cf. 31:10–11 and commentary). Its combination with a hymnic refrain recurs in Isa 47:4 in a context of judgment upon Babylon.[186] That is probably the source of v. 34, in which case "Israel's Holy One" (v. 29) may also echo the divine phrase in Isa 47:4. "Give rest . . . but stress" is an attempt to reproduce the assonance of hirgîaʿ and wĕhirgîz. The latter term provides a transition to the next subsection.

[35–40] The "sword" poem (vv. 35–38a) picks up the denominative verb "put to the sword" used in vv. 21 and 27 and provides a series of reversals that war would impose on bastions of power, including defeat of its army, manned by mercenaries and vassal contingents, and interference with the irrigation canals on which Babylon's agricultural economy depended. The poem announces disaster that is justified by a religious reason (v. 38b; cf. v. 2). Verse 39 presents a consequence of further disaster, complete desolation, which reverts to a motif used earlier in vv. 3 and 12b–13a (cf. v. 32); in this case its inspiration was Isa 13:20–22a, which already had Babylon in view. The prose supplement in v. 40, borrowed from 49:18 (LXX 29:19), underscores it, and so does MT at the end of v. 39. The supplement was prompted by its similarity to Isa 13:19b, while the masoretic addition is a direct citation of Isa 13:20ab.

[41–43] This is the first of two lengthier borrowings that give even greater weight to Babylon's downfall. They are both introduced by "Look." The common imagery of anxiety in 6:24 (= 50:43) and 49:24, sandwiched between the source of the second quotation, 49:19–21, and that of 50:30 (= 49:26), was one factor that suggested the pairing. Another, more potent underlying factor was the juxtaposition of the divine lion attacking the sheep and the arousal of disaster "from the remotest parts of the earth" in 25:32–38; already in 50:16 "the oppressor's sword" evoked 25:38. The former borrowing cites 6:22–24 with a few necessary adaptations. It accomplishes with broader strokes what was done earlier at vv. 3 and 9—create a ricochet effect by reuse of Jeremiah's "foe from the north" motif.

---

185. Aitken, "Oracles against Babylon," 42.
186. Cf. Crenshaw, "Form-Critical Analysis," 156–57, 160–61.

[44–46] The Edom oracle, already sampled in v. 40, is now milked more extensively. The quotation of 49:19–21 (LXX 29:20–22) with a few variations beside essential ones continues that of 49:18 in v. 40. It provides in closing the basic claim that the foe from the north was backed by divine providence. As before, the change of setting necessitates fresh labeling in vv. 45–46.

Chapter 50 broaches the coming downfall of Babylon and envisions it as the catalyst for Israel's territorial and spiritual restoration.

51:1–58 Babylon's Downfall and Israel's and Yahweh's Vindication

51:1 Here is what Yahweh said:

"Look, I am going to arouse against Babylon
    and against Leb-qamai's[a] population
        a destructive wind.[b]
2 Then I will send winnowers[c] to Babylon,
    who will winnow it and leave its country bare,
as they attack it from every side
    on the day of a bad fate.
3 Let[d] the archer string his bow
    and put on[e] his armor.
Do not spare its young men,
    wreak ruin on its entire army
4 and let them lie as casualties in Chaldea,
    mortally wounded in its streets."
5 The reason is that neither Israel nor Judah is left widowed
    by his God, by Yahweh Almighty,
while their country is accounted full of guilt
    by[f] Israel's Holy One.
6 Run away out of Babylon
    and save yourselves each and every one.
Do not be wiped out in its punishment,[g]
    now that it is Yahweh's time for vengeance,
        as he pays it back with retribution.
7 Babylon has been a gold cup in Yahweh's hand,
    one that made the whole earth drunk.
The nations tasted its wine;
    that is why *the nations*[h] have gone berserk.
8 Suddenly Babylon has fallen and gotten injured.
    Cry out in concern for it,
bring balm to relieve its pain
    in hope of a possible cure.

9   "We have tried to cure Babylon,
        but it proved incurable.ⁱ
    Leave it and we will go to our several countries."
    The explanation is that its judgment reaches as high as the sky,
        piled right up to the clouds.
10 Yahweh has brought to light the justice of our claims.
        Come on, let us testify in Zion
        what our God Yahweh has done.
11 "Polish the arrows,
        fill the quivers"ʲ—

Yahweh has aroused the impulse of the kingsᵏ of Media because Babylon is the object of his plan of destruction.

The explanation is that this is Yahweh's vengeance,
    vengeance for his temple.
12 "Give the signal to attack Babylon's walls.
        Set a strong blockade,
    post sentries.
        Prepare ambushes."
    The explanation is that Yahweh has both planned and is now executing
        his threats against those who live in Babylon.
13 You city situated by a lot of water,
        possessing a lot of treasure,
    your end has come,
        when you must be cut off from life's loom.ˡ
14 Yahweh *Almighty* has sworn an oath by himself:ᵐ
    "I promise to fill you with people as many as a locust swarm,
        who will sing over you a victory song."
15 He is the one who made the earth by his might,
        fixed the world in place by his wisdom,
        and by his insight spread out the sky.
16 At the sound of his shouting there is a massing of water in the sky,
        as he brings clouds up from the ends of the earth.
    Lightning flashes he makes for the rain
        and he brings wind out from his warehouses.
17 Everybody is shown to be stupid, devoid of knowledge.
        Every metalsmith is discredited by the idols
    because those metal figures of his are a lie,
        lacking any breath.
18 They are nonentities, ludicrous, made objects.
        At the time when they are dealt with they will perish.

Oracles against the Nations

19 Not like them is Jacob's portion;
   rather, his possession is the one who shaped the universe—ⁿ
   Yahweh *Almighty* is his name.
20 "You are my club
      and weaponº for war.
   I use you to club nations,
      I use you to destroy kingdoms,
21 I use you to club the horse and its rider,
      I use you to club the chariot and its driver.
22 I use you to club the man and the woman,
      I use you to club the old person and the young one,
      I use you to club the youth and the girl.
23 I use you to club the shepherd and his flock,
      I use you to club the plowman and his pair of oxen.
   I use you to club governors and prefects.ᵖ

24 "But I will pay back Babylon and all Chaldea's population for all their bad behavior, what they did in Zion—for you [all]ᑫ to see," declared Yahweh.

25 "Look out, I am your opponent,
      you destructive mountain,"
   declared Yahweh,
      "you destroyer of the whole earth.
   I will slap you with my hand
      and roll you down from the rocks,
      turning you into a burned-out mountain,
26 so none of your stones can be used as a cornerstone
      or any for foundations.
   Instead, you will be permanently desolate,"
   declared Yahweh.

27 "Raise banners worldwide,
      blow trumpets among the nations.
   Draft nations to fight it,
      summon against it kingdoms,ʳ
      Ararat, Minni, and Ashkenaz.
   Appoint a strategistˢ to fight it,
      move up as many horses as bristly locusts.

28 "Draft to fight it nations, Media's kings, its governors and all its prefects, and all the territory each controls."

29 The country shakes in anguish,
   because Yahweh's purposes for Babylon are being realized,ᵗ
   to make Babylon's country
   a shocking place devoid of inhabitants.
30 Babylon's soldiers have stopped fighting
   and are staying in the fortresses.
   Their soldierly valor sapped, they are as weak as women.
   Its homes have been set on fire,
   its gate bars broken.
31 Courier runs to meet courier,
   messenger to meet messenger,
   reporting to Babylon's king
   that all the edges of his city have been captured,
32 the river crossings have been taken,
   and the fortsᵘ burned down,
   leaving the troops in confusion.

33 In explanation here is what Yahweh *Almighty, Israel's God*, said:

"Lady Babylon has been like a threshing floor when itᵛ is trodden down—
very soon the harvest*time* will arrive for her."

34 "I have been devoured, drainedʷ by King Nebuchadnezzar of Babylon,
and put down, an empty jar.

He has swallowed me up like a dragon,
   filling his belly with my tasty parts, then throwing me up.ˣ
35 May Babylon suffer for the violence done to me and my kin!"ʸ
   let Zion's population say.
"And may Chaldea's population be held responsible for my bloodshed!"
   let Jerusalem say.

36 Therefore here is what Yahweh said:

"Look, I am going to take up your cause
   and get you avenged
   by drying up its river
   and parching its source,
37 so Babylon becomes
heaps of rubble, a haunt for jackals,
   a place people react to with shock *and whistling*,ᶻ
   devoid of inhabitants.

38 One and all like lions *they roar*,^{aa} they growl
        like lion cubs.
39 While they are excited,^{bb} I will prepare them drinks
        and make them so drunk they get the shakes ^{cc}
    and fall into a permanent sleep
        from which they never wake up,"
    declared Yahweh.
40 "I will take them down like lambs for slaughter,
        like rams or goats."
41 How terrible *Sheshach*^{dd} has been captured and taken,
        what once was praised worldwide!
    How shocked a reaction
        to Babylon the nations have!
42 A veritable sea has swept over Babylon,
        covering it with its roaring waves.
43 Its towns have become *shocking places*, dry areas and deserts,
        where^{ee} nobody lives,
        where people never travel.
44 "So I will deal with Bel in^{ff} Babylon
        by making him disgorge what he has swallowed
    so nations never come flooding to him again.

    "Yes, Babylon's wall has fallen.^{gg}
45   Get out of it, my people,
    saving yourselves each and every one
        from Yahweh's burning anger.

46 "So no need^{hh} for your hearts to be timid! Don't be afraid of rumors heard in the country, one rumor coming one year and anotherⁱⁱ the next, of violence in the country and of ruler fighting ruler.

47 "Therefore, look, a time is coming
        when I will deal with Babylon's idols
    so all its country is humiliated
        and its casualties all lie fallen in it.
48 Then singing over Babylon
        will issue from heaven and earth
        and from all in them.
    From the north the ravagers are coming to attack it, that is why,"
    declared Yahweh.
49 Babylon has responsibility for the falling^{jj}
        of Israel's casualties,

just as for Babylon's sake have fallen
casualties worldwide.
50 You survivors of the sword,[kk]
go, do not delay!
Remember Yahweh long ago[ll]
and call Jerusalem to mind,
51 [how] humiliated we felt when we heard the disgraceful truth—
shame spread over our faces—
that aliens had attacked
the sacred areas in Yahweh's temple.
52 "Therefore, look, a time is coming,"
declared Yahweh,
"when I will deal with its idols
so that throughout its country
casualties will groan.
53 Though Babylon rises to the sky,
though it fortifies its defenses to the heights,[mm]
ravagers sent by me will come to attack it,"
declared Yahweh.
54 Hark, shouting from Babylon
and immense calamity from Chaldea!
55 Here is why: Yahweh is ravaging Babylon
and making its noisy clamor cease.
Their[nn] waves roar like those of a great ocean,
their noisy din resounds.
56 Here is why: there is coming to attack it,[oo]
to attack Babylon, a ravager.
Its soldiers will be captured,
their bows broken.[pp]
Here is why: Yahweh is a God of retribution,
who is sure to repay.
57 "So I will make drunk its officials and experts,
its governors and prefects, and its soldiers,

and they will fall into a permanent sleep from which they will never wake up," declared the King, whose name is Yahweh Almighty.
58 Here is what Yahweh *Almighty* said:

"Babylon's broad wall[qq]
will be completely leveled
and its tall gates
burned with fire,

Oracles against the Nations 523

so the peoples will have toiled in vain
and only for fire the nations, wearing themselves out."

a. For the literary encoding that alphabetically writes *kśdym*, "Chaldea," backward as *lbqmy*, pointed as "the heart of my opponents," cf. textual note m on 25:25 and commentary on 25:25–26, and v. 41 below. LXX "Chaldeans" (28:1) is an exegetical rendering (Barthélemy, *Critique textuelle*, 2:837; *HUB*).

b. Or "the wind of a destroyer." See the commentary.

c. See *BHS* for the repointing, adopted by NRSV, NAB, NJB, and REB, in line with the following verb. This would be the natural pointing of a consonantal text. MT is interpretive.

d. MT implies two asyndetic relative clauses (cf. 2:8 and Joüon §158a, d) to wrest meaning out of what were originally two inappropriate negations, which were added in careless anticipation of *wĕʾal*, "and not," in v. 3b; LXX rightly lacks both cases. Then, in order to have a main verb, MT was forced to repeat the first verb, omitted in Q, with the tortuous sense, "At him who bends (the bow) let the one who bends the bow bend (it) and at the one who. . . ." Direct and positive exhortations for the attackers are expected in a summons to battle, especially since the attackers are addressed in v. 3b. NAB and NJPS, uncommon companions, follow LXX. The other EVV assume negatives, following the main textual tradition (cf. *BHS*).

e. Literally "put himself into" and so "put on," with most EVV. Cf. 46:4, with a different Hebrew verb, and the sense "be worn" for the Qal of this verb (Lev 19:19; Ezek 44:17). Avoiding the *hysteron proteron*, NAB (cf. NJB) prefers "flaunt" and NJPS "stand ready in."

f. BDB 579b. "Against" in NJB and GNB follows Ehrlich, *Randglossen*, 4:368, who claims Lev 4:2 in support.

g. See Rudolph 306–7; Holladay 2:421–22. EVV have "for their iniquity" and the like.

h. The unnecessary repetition, absent from LXX, Syr., and Vg., may reuse an annotation that specified the addressees of the imperatives in v. 8b and the speakers in v. 9a.

i. See Holladay 2:422.

j. See *HALOT* 4:1:522a–23b. LXX and most EVV render thus.

k. LXX "king," here and in v. 28, is followed by REB (and by NAB only in v. 28). The plural accords with 25:25 (LXX 32:11). See the commentary.

l. Literally "the measured part for your cutting," in apposition to "your end"; see *HALOT* 1:62a, 148a.

m. LXX "arm" (*BHS*) probably originated in a marginal note *zĕrôaʿ*, "arm," relating to *ʾmt* in v. 13, which LXX took not as *ʾammâ*, "arm, cubit, measure," but as *ʾĕmet*, "truth." The note was improperly related to v. 14, as a correction of *nepeš*, "self," with Isa 62:8 in view and displaced it. Cf. 17:3 and textual note g for this type of textual error.

n. See textual note j on 10:16 and Janzen, *Studies*, 61.

o. The repointing (see *BHS*) is followed by EVV except NJPS. The tradition of MT is old, found in all the ancient versions; it assumes the noun was the object of *mappēṣ*, taken as a Hiphil participle.

p. A monocolon closes the poem (cf. Watson, *Classical Hebrew Poetry*, 171–72). In v. 26 a closing monocolon (Rudolph 309) ends the section, while in v. 48 one ends a subsection.

q. The suffix is second plural.
r. For the repointing cf. *BHS*.
s. For the Akkadian loanword see *HALOT* 2:379a; McKane 2:1317–18.
t. Cf. Joüon §150g.
u. See *HALOT* 1:11a and the discussion of McKane 2:1320–21; cf. NAB, NJB, and REB.
v. *gōren*, "threshing floor," is feminine according to *HALOT* 1:203a; *DCH* 2:376a.
w. See *HALOT* 1:251a.
x. See *DCH* 2:425a.
y. Similarly RSV, NJPS, and NIV mg.
z. What preceded originally constituted a single colon.
aa. The verb is missing from LXX and doubtless originated as a comparative note (cf. Isa 5:29) on the following rare one, which LXX itself misunderstood. The meter was 3 + 2.
bb. NRSV "inflamed," NIV "aroused"; lit. "are hot." Cf. Luke 24:32.
cc. Cf. REB "writhe and toss." See McKane 1329–31 and cf. Barthélemy, *Critique textuelle*, 2:849–50.
dd. See 25:26 and commentary. Possibly LXX omitted as incomprehensible (Barthélemy, *Critique textuelle*, 2:837), but the external parallelism suggests otherwise (cf. 50:23).
ee. See *BHS*. The earlier noun has been accidentally repeated in MT.
ff. "Bel in," absent from LXX by a textual accident (Janzen, *Studies*, 119), is presupposed by the following masculine suffixes.
gg. LXX does not represent vv. 44b–49a, most probably because of oversight due to the repetition of *gam . . . bābel* in vv. 44b and 49b (*BHS*; Janzen, *Studies*, 119). The lost passage and vv. 49b–53 are not sufficiently similar to regard them as doublets.
hh. See Joüon §168g n.3.
ii. The masculine suffix of *ʾaḥărāyw*, "after it," has a neuter sense (Rudolph 312).
jj. Cf. RV "Babylon hath caused the slain of Israel to fall" and GNB, implicitly following Vg.; Keil 2:312; Harrison 189. The parallelism so suggests. The construction seems to be a loose, poetic variant of *ʿal bābel* or *lĕbābel*, "it was Babylon's responsibility," before *lāmed* and an infinitive (cf. 2 Sam 18:11; 2 Chr 26:18). A gerund with the sense "Babylon must fall" is present here.
kk. LXX "country" (cf. *BHS*) has suffered assimilation to 50 (LXX 27):28 (Ziegler, *Beiträge*, 27).
ll. Cf. McKane 2:1340–41; Holladay 2:430. Cf. Isa 22:11.
mm. The parallelism and Vg. suggest an absolute *mārôm*, as in Isa 22:16 (cf. Ehrlich, *Randglossen*, 4:371; McKane 2:1343).
nn. Evidently the antecedent is the human ravagers of v. 53; the metaphor in v. 42 so suggests (Holladay 2:431). Aquila, Symmachus, and LXX[O] imply *galleyhā*, "its waves," with reference to Babylon (cf. *BHS*). The absence of *gallêhem*, "their waves," from LXX is probably not significant.
oo. LXX and Syr. lack *ʾāleyhā*, rendered "to attack it." MT may represent an expanded text, but both elements seem metrically necessary, in which case the shorter text is due to oversight or abridgment.
pp. See GKC §52k. The query in *BHS* suggests a normal form.
qq. Cf. *BHS*. Thus NRSV, NIV, and NJPS.

Oracles against the Nations

The composition in 51:1–58, like the former one, contains a dual message of Babylon's doom that also spells Israel's gain, but it has four notable differences from the former one. First, in this composition Babylon's attackers are explicitly identified (vv. 11, 27–28). Second, while Israel's restoration was envisioned earlier, the focus shifts to Israel's being vindicated by Babylon's downfall. Third, a crusade launched by Yahweh against Babylon's religion, adumbrated in 50:2, 38, now has a major role, in order that Yahweh in turn might be vindicated. Fourth, Israel and Judah are mentioned only once (v. 5a) as a transitional echo of the first composition. Thereafter the single covenant community of Israel or Jacob, which implicitly means Judah, is the subject. As before, the key to sorting out an overwhelming mass of units is to look for persistent repetition of words and motifs that reflects sectional patterns. There seem to be five cases: (1) the drunkenness caused by Babylon as Yahweh's instrument (v. 7) and that experienced by Babylon itself in reversal (vv. 39 and 57); (2) the designation of the attackers as Medes (vv. 11 and 27–28) but also simply as northerners, like ch. 50 (v. 48); (3) Yahweh's punitive dealing with Babylon's idols (vv. 18, 44a) and then in twin references (vv. 47 and 52); (4) the Hebrew root *šbr*, "break," with reference to the capture of Babylon (vv. 8) ["gotten injured"], 30 ["broken"], and 54 ["calamity"]; and (5) the grievance of Jerusalem's heinous experiences (vv. 24, 35, and 50–51). The distribution of these key components, which are related to the distinctives of the composition, points to three sections (vv. 1–26, 27–44a, and 44b–58). The first is bounded by a double frame (vv. 1–2 and 24–25), *mašḥît*, "destructive," and *rāʿâ*, "a bad fate" and "bad behavior," in an ABBA order (cf. Volz 433). Moreover, "Lebqamai's population" in parallelism with "Babylon" in v. 1 corresponds to v. 24, where "Chaldea's population" appears. The third section also has a frame, the collapse of "Babylon's wall" (vv. 44b and 58). The two sets of battle orders to attack Babylon (vv. 3, 11–12) and the single call to Israel to leave Babylon (v. 6) in the first section are roughly matched by one set of battle orders in the second section (vv. 27–28) and two parallel calls to Israel to leave in the third (vv. 45, 50). In this case the first and longest section has the cardinal role, while two subsidiary sections provide echoes. Another such case relates to the word field composed of the terms "vengeance," "pay back," and "retribution," which are clustered in the first section (vv. 6, 11, 24) and appear individually in the second (v. 36) and third (v. 56). A third case seems to be the repeated reference to Zion in the first section (vv. 10 and 24) and the single citations of Zion paired with Jerusalem in the second (v. 35) and of Jerusalem in the third (v. 50). However, only the first instance anticipates worship at Zion, a lingering echo of ch. 50; the rest look back to the destruction suffered by Jerusalem and its citizens, so that vv. 24, 35, and 50 are of primary importance. All the sections basically contain combinations of a summons, whether to fight or to flee, and an announcement of disaster.

[51:1–26] This section uses a variety of genres to convey a dual message in three subsections, that Babylon's coming destruction would bring about Israel's vindication (vv. 1–10 and 20–26) and also Yahweh's own vindication (vv. 11–19).

[1a*a*] The opening quotation formula recurs in v. 58. The pair provides a frame for the composition, extending an aura of divine authority over the whole and so endorsing the interpretive focus on Yahweh's planning and purpose (vv. 11–12, 29).

[1a*b*–10] A divine announcement of disaster for Babylon (vv. 1a*b*–2) and summons to battle (vv. 3–4) are followed by prophetic interpretation (vv. 5–10) that incorporates summonses to flee (vv. 6a, 9b) and a mock lamentation (vv. 7–8a).

[1a*b*–2] The agricultural procedure of winnowing, whereby the wind scattered the chaff, while the heavier grain normally fell to the ground, is the basis of a metaphor for Babylon's destruction at the hands of enemies. In this case the wind was to be so strong that everything would be swept away, as in 4:11–12, which may echo here. The divine arousal is meant to recall 50:9, 41 and will be amplified in v. 11 at the beginning of the next subsection. Fulfillment of the announcement is hailed in Ezra 1:1 (NRSV "stirred up the spirit") as found in the Persian king Cyrus's capture of Babylon in 539 B.C.E.[187] The text was presumably understood as "the spirit of the destroyer," as Rudolph (306) and NIV render here.

[3–4] The summons to battle unpacks the earlier metaphor as utter military defeat.

[5] The prophetic explanation is a two-way bridge that uncovers Babylon's guilt (v. 5b) as the reason for the foregoing and also Yahweh's concern for the covenant communities (v. 5a), a corollary that will be developed in vv. 6 and 10. The motivations are connected in that Babylon's guilt implicitly consists of ill treatment of Yahweh's own people, as v. 10 and later vv. 24 and 34–35 will reveal. Verse 5 is related to other texts. First, 15:7–8 used winnowing and widowhood together concerning the Babylonian campaign in Judah (and also "suddenly," as in v. 8 below), so that vv. 1–2 and 5a offer implicit reversals for both Babylon and Judah. The inclusion of the northern kingdom provides a link with ch. 50. Furthermore, Isa 54:4–6 shares a cluster of vocabulary with v. 5, "widowhood," "the LORD Almighty" (NIV), and "the Holy One of Israel" (cf. too "your God"), and its promise of vindication—since Yahweh had "created the destroyer" (Isa 54:16 NIV)—carries over here. Closer to hand, the divine titles echo Jer 50:29, 34.

[6] The summons to flight in order to avoid the punishment (cf. 50:16) will enable the faith community's vindication, secured by divine "vengeance," as in 50:15.

---

187. Hugh G. M. Williamson, *Ezra, Nehemiah* (WBC 16; Waco: Word, 1985), 9–10.

[7–10] Mock lamentation is evident both in the contrast between Babylon's divine role hitherto and its imminent fate, and in the call for mourning. Babylon's imperial role correlates with 25:15–17, 27, where it was the implicit wielder of the sword that carried out the purpose of the cup of wrath in Yahweh's hand. Only here is Babylon identified as the cup, with its economic power ("gold") contributing to its fatal attraction. A second phase consisting of overwhelming divine "judgment" (v. 9b) that pits vertical extent over the horizontal extent of v. 7 ("the whole earth") is not expressed in terms of drinking from the cup, as it was in MT of 25:26b; the metaphor is abandoned in favor of a fatal wound from an unmentioned sword. The urgent call for medical care issued to resident aliens and the countercries of hopelessness and abandonment convey Babylon's dire fate. Its "judgment" or "punishment" (NJPS) is set in external parallelism with Judah's own need for vindication as effect and cause. "Our God" picks up "his God" (v. 5). The prophet speaks for his fellow exiles in looking forward to the reestablishment of worship in Jerusalem as an opportunity to celebrate the success of Yahweh's second phase carried out for Israel's sake (cf. 50:28).

[11–19] A divine summons to fight Babylon (vv. 11a*a*, 12a) is accompanied by two explanations, the first in terms of Yahweh's own vindication. The violation of Yahweh's temple (cf. v. 51; 28:3; 52:13, 17–23) would find retributive justice in the perishing of "idols" (vv. 17–18), Babylon's idols. Verse 14 adds a divine assurance of victory; reference to "fill" reinforces that of v. 11, providing a border for vv. 11–14.[188]

[11a*b*] A separate prose explanation identifies the addressees as "the kings of Media." The explanation not only marks a development of the general statement at the head of the previous subsection, where the phrase $hē^cîr\ rûaḥ$, here rendered "has aroused the impulse," was translated "arouse a wind," but also looks ahead to vv. 27–28, which suggest that Media's "kings" were its own king and those of subject kingdoms. Yet the verse also seems to allude to Isa 13:17, "I am stirring up [or "arousing," $mē^cîr$] the Medes against" the Babylonians. Isaiah 13 did influence ch. 50, in the common text at the poetry of 50:25 and the prose of 50:40 and in MT at 50:2, 39. The powerful empire of Media was Babylon's northern rival until 550 B.C.E., when Media passed into the control of Cyrus, Babylon's eastern ally and eventual conqueror (cf. Isa 41:2).

[12b–14] The summons of v. 12a expresses the divine will. In the renewed form of a mock lamentation, the text draws a contrast between Babylon's natural/economic resources (cf. 50:37b–38a)[189] and its inevitable demise, which is eloquently described in terms of a weaver's cutting off threads after weaving a batch of cloth (cf. Isa 38:12). The demise is endorsed by an announcement of

---

188. Lundbom, *Hebrew Rhetoric*, 69–70.
189. For water in and around Babylon see Thorkild Jacobsen, "Babylon (OT)," *IDB* 1:334–38, esp. 335–36.

disaster, expressed in the solemn tones of a divine oath, which ominously counters Babylon's massive resources with a massive army.

[15–19] The prophetic speaker reverts in closing to the grateful worship of v. 10 at the end of the previous subsection. He anticipates it by citing 10:12–16, a participial hymn of exilic origin. Its contextual relevance is Yahweh's dealing with idols (v. 18b), which are understood as Babylon's idols, as a reprisal for sacrilege (v. 11b). By such reprisal Yahweh would be vindicated as the true God, who acts as powerfully in history as in the creation and maintenance of the world of nature. Belief in such natural power encourages Israel's trust in its God's control of history yet to happen. Babylonian folly, illustrated by image worship, contrasts with Yahweh's wisdom both in creation and in planning Babylon's fall (v. 12). MT finds here an unfolding of "Yahweh Almighty" in v. 14.

[20–26] The third subsection falls into place by means of the prose statement (v. 24), which envisions Israel's vindication for the fall of Jerusalem. Here is the window through which the rest of the subsection is meant to be viewed.

[20–23] The poem about a "club" recalls the equally repetitive one concerning a sword (50:35–38a).[190] There Babylon was to be the future victim. Here, however, that can hardly be the case. The oracular poems (vv. 20–23 and 25–26) fall into the contrasting pattern encountered in the earlier subsections, where Babylon's divine role and/or grand status up to now was to give way to a future terrible reversal. Among EVV, NJB, NJPS, and GNB reflect this interpretation. The destroyer (vv. 20, 25) was eventually to be destroyed. The "hammer [a different Hebrew term] of the whole earth" (50:23) would be irreparably damaged. Then the addressee is either Babylon's king (cf. vv. 31, 34) or possibly Babylon itself, with its normal Hebrew feminine gender attracted to the masculine of the predicate, the metaphorical "club."[191] The destruction of "nations" and "kingdoms" is never the mandate of Babylon's attacker in chs. 50–51, only the destruction of Babylon and the liberation of subject nations (50:16; 51:9).[192] In order to convey comprehensive destruction the poem falls into a fine chiastic arrangement whereby the objects of the ominously repeated verb are plural pairs at the edges, a double series of a singular noun with a suffixed singular accompaniment just inside the frame, and a triad of singular pairs in the middle.[193]

[24] The prose bridges the two poems and prepares for the second. The "I-you" pattern of both poems does not convey the whole truth. There was a third entity, momentarily addressed, the aggrieved exiles on whose behalf the reprisal was to take place (cf. vv. 10, 35).

---

190. For the club or mace see Yigael Yadin, *The Art of Warfare in Biblical Lands in the Light of Archaeological Study* (trans. M. Pearlman; 2 vols.; New York: McGraw-Hill, 1963), 1:124–25, 142.
191. Cf. GKC §145u and n. 3; Joüon §149c.
192. Bourguet, *Métaphores de Jérémie*, 318.
193. Lundbom, *Hebrew Rhetoric*, 120–22.

[25–26] The announcement of disaster opens with a formula of hostile orientation, like 50:31. The divine club wielder, Babylon's patron, was to change sides. The metaphor of a mountain broaches powerful Babylon's seeming permanence only to dismiss it. God can move mountains (Mark 11:22–23; 1 Cor 13:2)! Here, however, the mountain is not just moved but disintegrates, losing in the process even the value of a quarry. The rolling from the rocks seems to be a lapse from the overall imagery, unless perchance adjacent mountains are in view (cf. NRSV, NJB, NJPS "crags"). The "burned-out mountain" reflects the searing fire of divine anger (cf. v. 45; Lam 4:11). The motif of permanent desolation provides grim closure for the section.

[27–44a] This second section of the composition falls into three subsections: vv. 27–33, where the theme of Yahweh's new, negative policy dominates; vv. 34–40, which interpret Babylon's coming fall from power in terms of Jerusalem's vindication, and vv. 41–44a, which celebrate Babylon's loss of its empire and religious prestige.

[27–33] The subsection moves from divine speech (vv. 27–28), to prophetic (vv. 29–32), and back to divine (v. 33).

[27–28] The renewed summons to fight takes up the vocabulary of the poem about a club and empowers its victims one by one to fight back against Babylon, "nations," "kingdoms," "horses," and "governors and prefects." In both poetry and prose the identity of the assailants as Medes is reaffirmed at the head of this fresh section. Urartu ("Ararat"), Mannea ("Minni"), and Scythia ("Ashkenaz") were nations to the northwest of Media that were under Media's control until 550.[194]

[29–33] The implicit link between the prospect of the country's fate (v. 29) and the vivid description of the city's fall (vv. 30–32) is the motif of bad news, to which the country (NRSV, NIV) responds with anxiety and which is reported to the king in a series of agitated communiqués. The significance of the battle orders as inaugurating Yahweh's new policy for Babylon is affirmed in v. 29, while the attribution of the future capture of the city to Yahweh's providential influence is implied in the oracle of v. 33. The oracle is best taken in terms of a fresh contrast (cf. Peake 2:273). Babylon's imperial assets were like grain spread richly over a threshing floor after the harvested sheaves had been trodden down—but the agricultural simile for wealth switches dramatically to a metaphor of harvest as warfare (cf. Joel 3[4]:13).

[34–40] The aggrieved exiles, once "Zion's population," are now given a collective voice in an individual lament (vv. 34–35), which receives a reassuring answer in the form of an announcement of disaster for Babylon (vv. 36–37). Another announcement that emphasizes contrast is added (vv. 38–40).

---

194. See Yamauchi, *Foes from the Northern Frontier*, 29–47, 63–66.

[34–35] The exiles are encouraged to engage in a psalm lament, which brings injustice to God's ears by giving vent to a description of an enemy's oppression and the consequent emotional distress, and to prayerful wishes for relief. Nebuchadnezzar's plundering and deportation are depicted in the grisly terms of a monster's savagery. Israel's loss ("empty") had been his gain ("filling"). The wishes complain of human suffering and loss of life.

[36–37] The promised relief takes the form of Babylon's destruction at the point of its major resource, the Euphrates. This would spell moral vindication for Israel. The motif of devastation brings satisfying closure, on which MT lingers by expansions from 9:10 and 19:8.

[38–40] As in v. 33, a note of contrast ends the subsection. Babylonian lions, ever growling for prey to kill (cf. 50:17), would end up as slaughtered lambs! The means reverts to the cup of wrath imagery of v. 7, now with Babylon as its victim (v. 39). Delirium tremens would be followed by death, not just a drunken stupor.

[41–44a] The prophet's mock lamentation and a divine announcement of disaster for the major Babylonian god Marduk (cf. 50:2) are attached by the frame of Babylon's magnetism, first secular and then religious. The frame poses a contrast of prior international praise and subsequent loss of pride (cf. Isa 2:2).

[41–43] Verse 41b echoes 50:23b and here reverses former praise. The sea stands for massive invasion, as in 47:2 and 50:42, which causes devastation in reiteration of v. 37.

[44a] At the heart of Babylon's empire stood its religion. So, in a new response to the lament of v. 34, repeating the motif of swallowing, Bel, not the king, is the focus. But because Yahweh is the subject, the vindication of Yahweh is at stake, a motif that will be developed in the closing section.

[44b–58] The first two subsections (vv. 44b-48 and 49–53) are twin passages that end with closing quotation formulas. Each consists of an initial statement about Babylon, then a summons to flee, a separate exhortation that mentions hearing, and an announcement of disaster; in the last case much vocabulary is shared. The third subsection (vv. 54–58) starts with a triple description of Babylon's conquest, in each case followed by references to its divine or human source of attack, and caps it with two announcements of disaster.

[44b–48] There is a time change between vv. 44b–45 and what follows. The first passage anticipates Babylon's conquest in triumphant imagination, while the continuation realistically faces up to human factors of uncertainty over a national struggle for power after Nebuchadnezzar's death in 562 and until Nabonidus's accession in 555, and answers them with divine reassurances. The call to flee echoes v. 6 and "my people" correlates with "his God" in v. 5, but Babylon's "punishment" is now traced back to divine anger. "Casualties" in

v. 47 echoes v. 4. The prose exhortation not to fear recalls Yahweh's answer to the lament in v. 36, in that it is a regular ingredient of an oracle of salvation used for this purpose (cf. 46:27). "Therefore" (v. 47) blames Babylon for the unrest. The universal chorale of v. 48a (cf. Isa 14:7; 44:23; 49:13) is the enhanced counterpart of the praise and singing in the first section at vv. 10, 14, and 15–19. Verse 48b is a reminder of the human means behind v. 47, but reverts to the northern provenance of ch. 50 with implicit reference to Babylon's reverse role as victim.

[49–53] The second subsection goes through the same motions but with significant differences. "Casualties," to be repeated in the sense of v. 47 at v. 52, provides a reason for the later announcement of disaster so that it becomes a retaliatory feature. Babylon would face its trial for war crimes against the world and not least against Israel, whose "survivors" would thus find vindication. But Yahweh was also to be vindicated. Bad memories of the desecration of the temple in 587 (cf. v. 11), handed down in the exilic community, made Babylon's downfall inevitable in order to satisfy divine honor. So Babylon's own religious matériel, its "idols," would feature in the reprisal. The closing reference to "ravagers" echoes the end of the previous subsection, but now Yahweh's superintendence invests them with invincibility.

[54–56] The report of Babylon's downfall reflects the turmoil of battle by oscillating between the noisy victims and their defeated troops on the one hand and the noisy human victors on the other (cf. v. 42), with constant glances behind the scenes at the divine victor who is vindicated.

[57] The cup of wrath was to take its toll on the Babylonian government; terms from the poem about the sword (50:35) and, in a reversal, from the poem about the club (51:23) are gathered up by way of finale. MT reinforces the reminiscences by echoing the finality of the earlier reference to a cup (v. 39) and also ties the oracle into its immediate context by repeating "its soldiers" from v. 56. A hymnic refrain, anticipating the future praise of v. 48, accompanies the quotation formula; MT had copied it earlier in 46:18 and 48:15. Yahweh's kingship superseded that in Babylon, for all its imperial bureaucracy.

[58] God's last word opens with a description of the destruction of the city's defenses, formidable as they were; it adds consequences to the divine intervention in v. 57. What makes it special is the reflection borrowed from Hab 2:13, itself set in a cup of wrath context (2:15–16), which by means of intertextuality ("fire") creates a damning epitaph for a regime built on exploiting its human infrastructure by tribute and forced labor. In God's world such a regime could not last.

The composition in 51:1–58 reiterates the certain demise of Babylon and finds in it vindication for both Israel and Yahweh.

51:59–64 Babylon's Fate Announced and Enacted

59 A message from the prophet Jeremiah, giving instructions[a] to Seraiah ben Neriah ben Mahseiah, when he visited Babylon with King Zedekiah of Judah in the fourth year of his reign, Seraiah being in charge of travel accommodations.[b] **60** Jeremiah had written all about the bad fate that was to befall Babylon on a scroll—that is, all the messages against[c] Babylon written here. **61** Jeremiah told Seraiah, "When you get to Babylon, see that you read aloud all these messages **62** and then pray, 'Yahweh, you yourself have stated about this place that you will destroy it so neither humans nor animals can live in it but it is[d] permanently desolate.' **63** When you have finished reading out this scroll, you are to fasten a stone to it and throw it into the Euphrates, **64** declaring, 'This is how Babylon will sink, never to come up again, victim of "the bad fate I am going to inflict on" it.'"

"Wearing themselves out" marks the conclusion of Jeremiah's messages.

a. LXX (28:59) turns it into a divine oracle (cf. *BHS*), influenced by the divine "I" in v. 64. It did not interpret thus in the similar case of 45:1 (LXX 51:31).

b. "Officer of tribute" (Holladay 2:432, 434) follows LXX, which vocalized a basic *mnḥh* not as *měnûḥâ* (MT), "resting place," but as *minḥâ*, "tribute." This interpretation envisions Seraiah as delivering tribute money and is consistent with the modification in LXX that he did not accompany Zedekiah but was sent by him.

c. Or "concerning" (NRSV, NIV, NJPS; cf. GNB), but v. 62, as well as v. 60a, suggests messages of disaster.

d. *tihyeh*, "you will be," from v. 26 is retained, evidently now as an ungrammatical third feminine.

This narrative unit is the report of a commissioning with two assignments, to read out a scroll (vv. 61–62) and to engage in a symbolic action (vv. 63–64). Elsewhere in the book commissioning reports relate divine commissions to Jeremiah, but here the prophet commissions somebody else. The assignments are presumably to be understood as going back to Yahweh's command, as the divine "I" in v. 64 may intimate, but the text is reporting a stage in human transmission. The report of a symbolic action typically consists of three elements, a divine instruction, a report of the prophet's executing it, and a divine interpretation. The prophet here functions in the divine role, and the nature of the passage as only a commissioning report leaves no space for the execution; the interpretation occurs in v. 64a*a*. Each of the two assignments closes with corroboration of the divine intent to destroy Babylon (vv. 62, 64a*b*).

[59] The heading is like that in 45:1, though there a divine oracle was in view, introduced in v. 2. The focus was on Jeremiah's passing on the divine message, as in 29:1 via the medium of a letter, and the same situation seems to apply here.

Readers are meant to understand that Seraiah was Baruch's brother (32:12) and so someone sympathetic to Jeremiah's cause, like Elasah and Gemariah in 29:3. Seraiah was a minor official involved in a royal visit to the imperial capital. The date of 594/593 recalls the conference of dissident western nations in Jerusalem mentioned in ch. 27, which occurred in that year according to 28:1. Zedekiah's summons to Babylon evidently marked the end of the proposed rebellion.

[60] The relation of this passage to the preceding context is now disclosed to the reader. Verse 60a supplies a parenthetical background to the assignments. The prophet's commitment of oracles to writing, as in 36:2, 28, doubtless involved another person's scribal activity, perhaps Baruch's, as in 36:4, 32. Verse 60b has the air of a redactional afterthought; by way of integration it identifies the contents of the scroll with chs. 50 and 51 as far as v. 58. Echoes of chs. 50 and 51 in vv. 62 and 64 lend warrant to such a conclusion. Nevertheless, the compositions concerning Babylon leave a different impression on the reader. REB follows scholars who delete v. 60b, but it is a redactional part of the common text attested by LXX and MT.

[61] Seraiah was to read out the contents of the scroll to an audience, evidently the Judean deportees of 597, to whom Jeremiah's two letters in ch. 29 were sent.[195] Like Baruch in ch. 36, this reader was to represent the prophet to others. The objection that the scroll's anti-Babylonian sentiments would fan the hotheadedness the first letter was meant to cool is not cogent if the letter already balanced its denial of short-term optimism with a long-term hope of Judean restoration and Babylon's downfall (29:10–14a; cf. 25:12).

[62] Seraiah's concluding prayer functions as an amen. It cites material from 50:3 and 51:26 that refers to desolation, which often indicated closure in those compositions, and it has a similar function here.

[63–64a*a*] The symbolic action portrays Babylon's destruction, somewhat like that of the sash in 13:1–11. Did Seraiah drop the scroll over the bridge? To make the papyrus—not leather—scroll sink, it was weighed down with a stone (Holladay 2:434). Now the scroll is given a quite different function; it represents Babylon. The verbal interpretation is the indispensable guide to the meaning of the symbolism; it is not the divine word that was to be sunk, but its target (cf. 25:27). "This is how" (*kākâ*) also appears in interpretations at 13:9; 19:11; and 28:11. The symbolic action provocatively carried out in Babylon parallels Jeremiah's own symbolic action before Judean migrants in a public place in Egypt at 43:8–13. The action and interpretation are repeated on a grander scale in Rev 18:21.

[64a*b*] The pattern of corroboration (v. 62) by citing an anti-Babylonian oracle is repeated. The "bad fate" echoes not only v. 60 but also v. 2. There it occurred in a passage spoken by Yahweh; correspondingly here it is expanded

---

195. See Friebel, *Sign-Acts*, 162–64.

with a prose sermonic expression to indicate its nature as a divine citation, in which Yahweh's intervention clinches the human consequences of v. 64a*a*. The citation assumes the divine origin of the "message" of v. 59.

[**64b**] MT adds a colophon that differentiates the foregoing from the appendix subsequently added from 2 Kings in ch. 52. The phrase "Jeremiah's messages" harks back to 1:1 and so gives the dimensions of the prophetic book.[196] The "cue" expression actually occurs in v. 58, and its presence indicates that the unit of vv. 59–63a was a subsequent insertion, though the unit appears in LXX;[197] the rubric was retained just before ch. 52 despite the awkwardness. Bright (212; cf. Duhm 375) supposes the unit earlier followed ch. 29. Verse 64b naturally does not appear in LXX, which inserted all the oracles against the nations into ch. 25.

52:1–34
Epilogue: A Tale of Two Kings

52:1 Zedekiah was twenty-one years old when he came to the throne. He reigned in Jerusalem eleven years. His mother's name was Hamutal bat Jeremiah of Libnah. **2** *He behaved badly by Yahweh's standards, just as much as Jehoiakim had.* **3** *In fact Yahweh's anger was the cause of what transpired in Jerusalem and Judah, to the point that he threw them out of his presence. Zedekiah rebelled against Babylon's king.* **4** Now it happened in the ninth year of his reign, in the tenth month, on the tenth of the month, that King Nebuchadnezzar of Babylon advanced on Jerusalem with his whole army. They encamped by it, building siege structures all round it. **5** The city underwent the siege until King Zedekiah's eleventh year. **6** *In the fourth month*, on the ninth of the month, when the city was in the grip of famine so the common people had no food, **7** an opening was made into the city. The troops all *tried to make a getaway*[a] *and* left *the city* at night through the gate between the two walls, which was near the royal garden, even as the Chaldeans were surrounding the city. They made for the Arabah, **8** but the Chaldean army chased after the king and caught up with *Zedekiah*[b] at Jericho Plains after his army had all left him, going in different directions. **9** They captured the king and took him up to Babylon's king at Riblah *in the region of Hamath*, where he pronounced sentence on him. **10** Babylon's king had Zedekiah's sons executed before his eyes; all

---

196. Lundbom, *Hebrew Rhetoric*, 39.

197. This might suggest that chs. 46–51 were moved to ch. 25 and the annotation dropped, but on other grounds that is unlikely.

the Judean officials were also executed by him at Riblah. 11 Then he had Zedekiah's eyes put out and shackled him in bronze chains. Babylon's king took him home to Babylon and kept him in a guarded building until the day of his death. 12 On the tenth day of the fifth month—*that is, in the nineteenth year of the reign of King Nebuchadnezzar of Babylon*—Nebuzaradan, chief of the guard, came and served as the representative of Babylon's king in Jerusalem. 13 He set fire to Yahweh's temple, the royal palace, and all the buildings in Jerusalem; every house belonging to a dignitary he burned down. 14 The walls around Jerusalem were all demolished by *all* the Chaldean army accompanying the chief of the guard. 15 The rest[c] of the people left in the city, the deserters who had gone over to Babylon's king, and the rest of the craftsmen, were deported by Nebuzaradan, chief of the guard. 16 However, some of the poor in the country[d] were left behind by *Nebuzaradan*, chief of the guard, as vinedressers and farmers. 17 The bronze pillars of Yahweh's temple and the trolleys and bronze vat in Yahweh's temple were broken up by the Chaldeans, who carried off to Babylon all the bronze of which they were made. 18 The ash tubs,[e] *shovels*, wick trimmers,[f] tossing bowls, *ladles*—in fact all the bronze artifacts used for worship—were taken away.[g] 19 Also the basins, *fire pans*, tossing bowls,[h] ash tubs, lampstands, ladles, and libation bowls that were in some cases made of gold and in other cases made of silver[i] were taken away by the chief of the guard. 20 As for the two pillars, single vat, twelve bronze oxen underneath the vat, and [j] trolleys, made by King Solomon for Yahweh's temple, the weight of their bronze was incalculable [in the case of] *all these artifacts*. 21 As for the pillars, the first was eighteen cubits high and a tape twelve cubits long would go around it; it was hollow and [the metal] was four fingers thick. 22 It was surmounted by a capital made of bronze. The height of the first capital was five cubits; it had a network and pomegranates all around the capital, also made of bronze. The second pillar was the same. As for pomegranates, 23 there were ninety-six pomegranates open to view (?)[k] and a total of a hundred pomegranates around the network. 24 The chief of the guard arrested the head priest *Seraiah*, the deputy priest *Zephaniah*, and the three threshold guardians, 25 and *from the city he arrested* a eunuch who had supervised the troops, seven men belonging to the king's inner circle, who were present in the city, the clerk of the army *commander*, responsible for mobilizing the common people, and sixty of the people at large, who were also present in the city. 26 They were arrested by Nebuzaradan, chief of the guard, who brought them to Babylon's king at Riblah. 27 Babylon's king had them flogged[l] *and put to death* at Riblah in the region of Hamath. *Moreover, Judah was deported from its own soil.* 28 *Here is the number of the people deported by Nebuchadnezzar: in his seventh year 3,023 Judeans;* 29 *in Nebuchadnezzar's eighteenth year 832 individuals from Jerusalem;* **30** *in Nebuchadnezzar's twenty-third year Nebuzaradan, chief of the guard, deported 745 Judeans. The total number of individuals involved was 4,600.*

31 Now it happened in the thirty-seventh year of the period of deportation for King Jehoiachin of Judah, in the tenth month and on the twenty-fifth day of the month, that King Evil-Merodach of Babylon showed favor to King Jehoiachin of Judah in the year he came to the throne. He freed him from prison, **32** had a good talk with him, and gave him a seat above those of his fellow kings in Babylon. **33** He changed out of his prison clothes and ate at the royal table regularly for as long as he lived. **34** *As for his food allowance*, a regular daily allowance was given to him by Babylon's king until the day of his death, *for as long as he lived.*

a. A clause that made reference to the king (v. 8) must have been present at an earlier stage, though now lacking in 2 Kgs 25:4; cf. 39:4 and BHS. The imperfect in the partial assimilation to 39:4 MT has a conative sense (cf. Ehrlich, *Randglossen*, 4:372).

b. LXX and 2 Kgs 25:5 have "him."

c. MT, but not LXX, has clumsily inserted at the beginning a marginal annotation explaining or providing a variant of the similar phrase that begins v. 16 (Barthélemy, *Critique textuelle*, 2:856–57). Cf. *ûmin hāʿām haddallîm*, "And some of the people were the poor," in 39:10 and *dallat ʿam hāʾāreṣ*, "the poor of the people of the country," in 2 Kgs 24:14. NAB, REB, and GNB omit (cf. NJPS and NJB).

d. LXX omitted v. 15 and the first part of v. 16 by jumping from *hnšʾrym*, "who were left," to *hšʾyr*, "he left" (Janzen, *Studies*, 119; Jannes Smith, "Jeremiah 52: Thackeray and Beyond," *BIOSCS* 35 [2002]: 55–96, esp. 75).

e. Cf. Exod 27:3.

f. LXX reflects instead *mizgālôt*, "meat forks," in line with the lists in Exod 27:3; 38:3. MT accords with the list in 1 Kgs 7:50.

g. LXX placed this verb in v. 17 (*HUB*).

h. Instead LXX places here the wick trimmers that MT, like 2 Kgs 25:14, put in v. 18; cf. 1 Kgs 7:50, where they are gold, and 2 Kgs 12:13 (14), where they are silver.

i. The Hebrew repetition has a distributive sense (Rudolph 320); cf. GKC §123d (rather than §123e).

j. See Janzen, *Studies*, 111; cf. BHS. Barthélemy, *Critique textuelle*, 2:858, gives *taḥat*, "underneath," an adverbial sense (cf. Gen 49:25; Deut 33:13).

k. Literally "to (the) wind" and so perhaps "(open) to the air and light" and visible to the viewer (cf. REB, NJPS, GNB); see McKane 2:1375–76.

l. In the shorter text underlying LXX, the verb had a fatal sense. LXX's rendering "struck" can refer to a fatal blow, as in 48(MT 41):4; cf. OL *interfecit*, "killed," perhaps influenced by the next verb in Vg., but, if so, a good secondary decision. For the indirect connotation in MT cf. Deut 25:2, where the added "in his presence" is significant.

The final chapter is a later appendix to the book, as MT has acknowledged in 51:64b. The prophet does not appear in it, and Calvin provided no commentary in his lectures on Jeremiah. Still, it is part of the redacted book, already available in LXX. Its initial topics of the ending of Zedekiah's reign and the deportation of Jerusalem's citizens trace a framing arc back to 1:3. In more general terms readers can discern a fulfillment of 1:14–15[1] and even a hint of rebuilding after demolishing (1:10). It is taken largely from 2 Kgs 24:18–25:21, 27–30 and in essence presents two contrasting cameos of vindication, the destinies of Zedekiah and Jehoiachin as a testimony of disaster and an omen of restoration in vv. 1–30 and 31–34.[2] At the earlier redactional stage of the text attested in LXX, when ch. 45 (LXX 51) immediately preceded it, the appendix functioned as an echo of the doom presented in 45:4–5. However, in MT, after the foreign oracles of chs. 46–51, ch. 52 fits remarkably well; it reflects the structural parallelism of the present book (see "Macrostructure" in the introduction). The incorporation presupposes 2 Kings and certainly a time after 561 B.C.E. The two historical reports in the appendix, one long and the other short, summarize the double message of the book of Jeremiah, mainly negative but to some extent positive, and report the fulfillment of the prophetic message, in token at least in the second case. The relationship of the two reports is indicated by the parallelism of "Now it happened . . . that" and of "King Nebuchadnezzar of Babylon" and "King Evil-Merodach of Babylon," in vv. 4 and 31, and of "until the day of his death" in vv. 11 and 34.[3] In two places (vv. 2–3 and 27b), MT has added material from 2 Kings 24–25 in order to heighten the contrast and to improve the structural coherence of the first report. The "bad" behavior of Zedekiah in Yahweh's eyes (v. 2) is countered by the "good" or friendly talk the Babylonian king had with Jehoiachin (v. 32). This pair of adjectives takes on nuanced significance. Readers are meant to recall the polarity of a "bad behavior/fate" and "good fortune" throughout the book and especially as it appears in the report of the vision of the two baskets of figs in ch. 24, where "good" and "bad" referred to the respective destinies of those deported in 597 B.C.E., who included Jehoiachin, and of Zedekiah and his administration.

There is further material of different kinds added in MT.[4] First, the list of deportations in vv. 28–30 does not occur in 2 Kings. Second, a host of details

---

1. Georg Fischer, "Jeremia 52—ein Schlüssel zum Jeremiabuch," *Bib* 79 (1998): 332–59, esp. 356, compares the same Hebrew phrase in 1:16 (rendered "present my case") and 52:9 (rendered "pronounced sentence").

2. The Gedaliah section in 2 Kgs 25:22–26 may have been omitted not merely because it was covered in Jeremiah 40–41 but mainly because it obscures the intended polarization. However, more probably it had not yet have entered the underlying text of 2 Kings, dependent as it is on the Jeremiah text (see. n. 71 on ch. 40).

3. Cf. too *wayĕdabbēr ʾittô mišpāṭîm*, "and he pronounced sentence on him," in v. 9 and *wayĕdabbēr ʾittô ṭōbôt*, "and he had a good talk with him," in v. 32.

4. For the relation between the Greek and Hebrew texts of Jeremiah 52 and the 2 Kings parallel, cf. Raymond F. Person, *The Kings-Isaiah and Kings-Jeremiah Recensions* (BZAW 252; Berlin: de Gruyter, 1997), 80–113; Smith, "Jeremiah 52."

have been borrowed from the 2 Kings passage for consistency's sake: "the city" (v. 7), the synchronism (v. 12), "shovels" and "ladles" (v. 18), "fire pans" (v. 19), "and trolleys" and "all these artifacts" (v. 20), the two names (v. 24), "from the city he arrested" and "commander" (v. 25), "and put to death" (v. 27), and "As for his food allowance" and "for as long as he lived," resulting in a doublet (v. 34). This itemizing process of assimilation to 2 Kings seems to be separate from the major recasting in vv. 3a and 27b, as the conflation at the close of v. 34 suggests. Third, there are at least two cases of assimilation to the overlapping passage in ch. 39, "In the fourth month" in v. 6 from 39:2 and making a getaway in v. 7 from 39:4. Fourth, "in the region of Hamath" in v. 9 is copied internally from v. 27[5] and "Nebuzaradan" in v. 16 from v. 15, unless 39:10 is the source.

The text common to LXX and MT already diverges from 2 Kings in a number of other respects. It adds the execution of Judean officials (v. 10b with 39:6), Zedekiah's lifetime detention (at the close of v. 11), some artifacts (vv. 18–19), the distributive element (v. 19), the oxen reference (v. 20), the pillar's circumference and ensuing details (v. 21), and the data about pomegranates (at the end of v. 22 and in v. 23). The common text has some significant differences, the "tenth" day instead of the "seventh" (v. 12), "craftsmen" (*?mwn*) in place of "population" (*hmwn*) (v. 15—perhaps as a counterpart to Jer 24:1 and 29:2, though a different Hebrew term appears there), "five" cubits, as in 1 Kgs 7:16, instead of "three" (v. 22) for the height of the capital, and "seven" men for "five" (v. 25).[6] Moreover, the cultic artifacts in vv. 18–19 are strikingly different. The 2 Kings text may be secondary in some of these divergences, but the Jeremiah text stands out as having a fascination with temple equipment and its tragic loss.

[52:1–30] At the LXX stage of the text, the portrayal of contrasts was important. Its clearest objective indication was the addition to the 2 Kings text of a tradition of the lifelong detention of Zedekiah in v. 11b*b*, as a contrast to Jehoiachin's lifelong sustenance in v. 34. While the second account in vv. 31–34 has only a royal concern, the first one expatiates on its terrible consequences for Jerusalem and Judah. In structure this first section already falls into two subsections at the LXX stage, vv. 1–11 and 12–30; the chronological element in v. 12 echoes the longer one in v. 4. The addition of v. 3b in MT from 2 Kgs 24:20 distinguishes between the fate of Jerusalem and Judah and envisions the expulsion of their population, and also mentions Zedekiah. In so doing it provides a menu of topics for the first section. In the first subsection Jerusalem was besieged and fell, and Zedekiah was permanently removed. In the second Zedekiah's subsequent fate (vv. 12–14) and the deportation of Jerusalem's cit-

---

5. Janzen, *Studies*, 63.

6. Separate mention should be made of the "twenty-fifth" day in MT at v. 31, for which LXX has "twenty-fourth" and 2 Kgs 25:27 "twenty-seventh."

izens (v. 15) are recorded first, with a qualification about some Judeans (v. 16). Then the fate of the temple broached in v. 13 is expanded in terms of the loss of metal artifacts and the arrest of high-ranking priestly staff (cf. 35:4) from Jerusalem is reported (vv. 17–24); the arrest of laypeople and the removal of them all are added (vv. 25–27a). Finally the deportation of Judeans is covered, first in v. 27b, added from 2 Kgs 25:21b, and then in the course of vv. 28–30, which were generated by v. 27b. The addition of vv. 3b and 27b has clarified the coherence of a mass of comparatively heterogeneous information by highlighting four topics.

[1–11] Nebuchadnezzar dominates the first subsection, as the agent of divine punishment. This role, implicit in the shorter text of LXX, is given clearer expression by MT's addition from 2 Kings in vv. 2–3. Yahweh is mentioned twice in vv. 2–3a, first as offended and then as engaging in reprisal. The pattern is repeated on an earthly plane in vv. 3b–4 and continued in vv. 9–11, and the force of the correlation is that Nebuchadnezzar was the vehicle of divine reprisal (cf. 32:28–31). The focus on the Babylonian king resorts to literary license in v. 4, since he was there only in spirit according to v. 9.

[12–30] These verses sketch the fate of Jerusalem and Judah in July/August 587; now Nebuchadnezzar's henchman, Nebuzaradan, replaces him as archenemy (apart from vv. 27–29). The deportation of Judeans who lived outside the capital is assumed (v. 16). Those left were forced to work in an imperial enterprise (see the commentary on 39:10).

[17–23] The destruction of the temple mentioned in v. 13 is developed here in terms of its metal artifacts. The interest of the 2 Kings text is sparked by the focus on the construction of the glorious temple in 1 Kings 6–7, including its metal artifacts in 1 Kgs 7:13–51; now a tragic work of deconstruction was carried out. The reader of Jeremiah, however, is meant to recall the draining of such artifacts to Babylon mentioned in 27:16, 18–22; 28:3, 6. MT was responsible for the emphasis on artifacts in 27:18–22, and this passage adds a historical affirmation to the grim prediction made there, whose precise mention of pillars, vat, and trolleys already paved the way for the same itemizing in 52:17.[7] Jeremiah was vindicated, over against the false hopes of Hananiah and his ilk. The text common to LXX and MT enthusiastically adds to the artifacts of vv. 18–19 "tossing bowls" (v. 18), "basins" (v. 19), and the last four items.[8] With

---

7. Yohanan Goldman, "Juda et son roi au milieu des nations: la dernière rédaction du livre de Jérémie," in *The Book of Jeremiah and Its Reception* (ed. A. H. W. Curtis and T. Römer; Leuven: Leuven University Press, 1997), 151–82, esp. 166–67, finds an echo of 27:10 "from your own soil" intended in MT's incorporation of 52:27b from 2 Kings.

8. The item in v. 18 is derived from 1 Kgs 7:45, the first, fifth, and sixth items (in MT numbering) in v. 19 from 1 Kgs 7:49–50, and the seventh from Exod 25:29 and 37:16. The strange inclusion of the fourth item in v. 19 is unparalleled.

an excess of enthusiasm it adds a reference to the bronze oxen that supported the vat; King Ahaz probably had sent them as tribute to Assyria (2 Kgs 16:17–18). The common text displays a special interest in the pillars, adding the information of vv. 21b–32. The further addition about the pomegranates gives the impression of having originated as a marginal annotation that began with the cue word "pomegranates," referring to the term earlier in v. 22 (cf. 1 Kgs 7:42).[9]

[24–30] The rest of the section develops the reference to deportations from Jerusalem (v. 15), while MT in line with v. 3a fills out the scant allusion to Judah (v. 16) by loosely referring to deportations from there (vv. 27b, 28, 30a) as well as from Jerusalem (v. 29).

[28–30] The addition in v. 27b from 2 Kgs 25:21b concerning deportation generated the incorporation of an independent omnibus list of deportees to Babylon in separate chronological stages, the first in 597, the second in 587, and the third in 582, presumably as a reprisal for Gedaliah's assassination (see the commentary on 40:13–41:3). In the second case the list refers to an earlier deportation from Jerusalem prior to that of "the rest" mentioned twice in v. 15 (cf. McKane 2:1368–69, 1385). This list has two features of interest. First, it uniquely numbers Nebuchadnezzar's regnal years in accord with the Babylonian Chronicle; the "eighteenth year" equals the "nineteenth" in v. 12 (see the commentary on 25:1; 32:1). Second, the numbers seem surprisingly small when compared to descriptions of a relatively emptied land given earlier in the book. Much larger figures for the deportation of 597 appear in 2 Kgs 24:14, 16. The present context limits the purport of v. 29 as preliminary to the deportation in 587 mentioned in v. 15. However, the list itself has a precise and comprehensive ring, though its original purpose and scope are no longer verifiable.

[31–34] After v. 30 the text jumps more than twenty years, to an act of amnesty performed by Nebuchadnezzar's successor in 561. Perhaps other deported kings, those mentioned in v. 32, had their situation eased at the same time, but the focus is on Jehoiachin as a foil to Zedekiah. The 2 Kings text may be regarded as obliquely referring to the compassion hopefully to be shown to deportees by divine providence (1 Kgs 8:50; cf. 2 Chr 30:9; Ps 106:46).[10] In a similar vein, the focus here is on "good," certainly in MT in light of v. 2 and probably already at the earlier level. The intention here is to pick up a key term in the book that has connoted the positive, future work of God on Israel's behalf. It invests Evil-Merodach's action with providential value, if only in token; in particular it reminds the careful reader of 24:5–6. The tide was starting to turn. The first readers were given a hint that "salvation is nearer to us now . . . the

---

9. Cf. LXX's own addition at the end of v. 22, explaining the number 96 in terms of eight pomegranates in each of the twelve cubits.

10. See Jon D. Levenson, "The Last Four Verses in Kings," *JBL* 103 (1984): 353–61, esp. 360.

night is far gone; the day is near" (Rom 13:11–12). In the regnal year of v. 31 there sounds "a signal . . . that the exiled community has served just over half its requisite seventy-year term."[11]

The polarized pair of reports in ch. 52 vindicates the messages of doom that pervade the book and points to the realization of its messages of hope.

---

11. Christopher R. Seitz, "The Prophet Moses and the Canonical Shape of Jeremiah," *ZAW* 101 (1989): 3–27, esp. 27.

INDEX OF MODERN AUTHORS

Ackerman, S., 98n63, 190n71
Ackroyd, P. R., 277n176, 312n213, 436n83, 438n88, 453n109
Aejmelaeus, A., 64, 288n188, 458
Aharoni, Y., 163n44, 288n188, 458
Aitken, K. T., 510nn178–79; 514nn181–82; 516n156
Albertz, R., 50n17
Albrektson, B., 4n8
Allen, L. C., 5n11, 56n26, 197, 214n99, 326n227, 355n255, 360n271, 388n12, 497n163
Alt, A., 427, 435n80
Anbar, M., 55n24
Anderson, F. I., 248
Andreason, N.-E. A., 163n43
Applegate, J., 297nn194–95; 365n272, 391n15, 412n49, 413n50, 430n66, 444n95
Arnold, B. T., 514n183
Avigad, N., 397n25
Avi-Yonah, M., 163n44

Bach, R., 453n107
Bailey, K., 48n15
Bak, D. H., 146, 219n114
Baker, D. W., 463n120
Barr, J., 148n22, 230n119,
Barstad, H. M., 190n71, 371n288
Barth, C., 34n27
Barthélemy, D. 4, 46, 50n16, 53, 60, 64, 68, 72, 107–8, 114, 130, 134–35, 143, 151, 162, 178–79, 188, 197, 204, 211–12, 248, 269–70, 281–82, 295, 308, 322, 336n240, 343, 353, 383, 387n8, 411, 419n59, 420n62, 427, 433n77, 443, 457–58, 470, 475–76, 484, 492–93, 499n168, 507–8, 523–24, 536
Baukham, R., 360n269
Baumgartner, W., 144n13, 169n47, 174n55, 182nn59, 61; 205n87, 206n89, 220, 220n108, 230n120
Becking, B., 334n236, 353, 427
Begg, C., 366n274
Begin, Z. B., 386n4

Bellis, A. O., 510nn176, 179; 514n182
Ben Zvi, E., 496n162
Berlin, A., 324n274
Berridge, J. M., 31n22, 65n33, 86n49, 148n22
Berrigan, D., 350, 439
Beuken, W. A. M., 168n46
Biddle, M. E., 34n26
Blank, S. H., 149n25, 184n67
Boer, P. A. H. de, 450, 453n108
Bogaert, P.-M., 196, 417, 433n76, 460n115
Bohmer, S., 337n243
Bonhoeffer, D., 416
Böttcher, F., 130
Bourguet, D., 158nn37–38; 160n42, 223, 466n130, 467n132, 498n165, 528n192
Bovati, P., 299n199, 300n200, 407n45, 408n46
Bozak, B., 340n246
Bracke, J. M., 2, 277, 339n245
Brekelmans, C., 214n99
Bright, J., 9, 12, 40, 80, 124, 130, 143, 321, 385, 402, 410, 431, 470, 492–93, 500, 534
Brockington, L. H., 143
Broyles, C. C., 6n14, 32n23, 112n.8, 132n95, 148nn21–23; 182n60, 230n18, 405n41, 452n105
Brueggemann, W., 18n46, 41, 43n17, 55n23, 66, 95n57, 157n35, 216n102, 308, 325, 338n244, 347, 358, 385, 396, 405n3, 432, 445, 488

Callaway, M. C., 412n48
Calvin, J., 139, 155–56, 158, 321, 345, 356–57, 373, 392–93, 430, 493, 497, 515n184, 536
Carasik, M., 232n123
Carroll, R. P., 201n84, 250, 287, 477n143, 509
Castellino, G., 291n191
Cazelles, H., 285n182
Childs, B. S., 12–13n41, 34n28, 103n69, 315n215
Christensen, D. L., 477n143
Clark, D. J., 480n149
Clark, G. R., 35n29

Index of Modern Authors 543

Clements, R. E., 12n38, 95nn59–60; 145n15, 234n130
Clines, D. J., 22n113, 230nn119, 121; 232n125, 284n182, 398n26
Cloete, W. T. W., 2n2, 46, 53, 68, 75, 83, 123, 130, 144, 152, 157, 162, 173, 179, 196, 212, 224, 248–49, 262–63, 267, 282
Condamin, A., 84, 267
Cowley, A. E., 127n89, 439n90
Crenshaw, J. L., 128n91, 192n78, 310n210, 358n45, 375n291, 466n128, 476, 516n186
Crüsemann, F., 128n90
Culley, R. C., 144n13
Cunliffe-Jones, H., 175

Dalglish, E. R., 481n150
Daniels, D. R., 41n4
Davidson, A. B., 437n86
Davidson, R., 191, 302
Day, J., 98n62, 120n81
De Roche, M., 35n29, 41n4
De Vries, S. J., 37n28
Diamond, A. R., 50n16, 136n1, 144, 150n29, 152n32, 184n65, 233n128, 406nn41–42; 415n54
Dicou, B., 496n162
Drinkard, J. F., Jr., 224, 232, 274, 286, 292
Driver, G. R., 60, 72, 135, 243n140, 305, 313, 382, 450, 475–76, 492–93
Driver, S. R., 2n1, 75, 333, 350n254, 364, 428, 457, 475–76, 493, 507
Duhm, B., 46, 93, 124, 183n62, 197, 262, 300, 324, 333–34, 350, 353, 426–27, 435n80, 492–93, 499, 534

Ehrlich, A. B., 48n14, 53, 87, 93, 211–12, 224, 236, 303–5, 332, 373, 392n16, 390, 396, 402, 410, 426, 443, 475, 507, 523–24, 536
Eissfeldt, O., 464n121
Ellison, H. L., 7
Emerton, J. A., 80, 90, 114, 151, 162, 274, 428
Eynde, S. van den, 48n13

Fekkes, J., 510n177
Finkelstein, I., 97n61
Fischer, G., 12, 336n239, 477n144, 537
Fishbane, M., 69n36, 192n77, 204, 207nn90, 94; 287n187, 377n295
Fohrer, G., 12, 336n239, 477n144
Fokkelman, J. P., 366n275
Follis, E. R., 464n124
Forbes, R. J., 92n53
Frankena, R., 485n155
Freedman, D. N., 4n7, 248
Fretheim, T. E., 15, 206, 213n95, 215n100, 233, 268n166, 277, 368, 368n.282

Friebel, K. G., 156, 157nn35–36; 189n69, 190n72, 303, 306nn204–5; 313, 366n276, 367, 390, 392n17, 439n91, 533n195

Gerlach, M., 324n236
Glazov, G. Y., 29n15
Goldingay, J., 364
Goldman, Y. A. P., 46, 255, 281, 284, 307n206, 326nn228–29; 327nn230–32; 374, 378n297
Gosse, B., 196, 376n293, 460n115, 539n7
Graffy, A., 109n72, 379n299
Graham, J. N., 420n63
Graupner, A., 316n218, 398n28, 430n67, 431n68, 435n81, 451n104, 452n106, 453n107
Greenberg, G., 321
Greenberg, M., 60
Greenwood, D. C., 360n271
Grelot, P., 287n187
Grol, H. W. M. van, 168n46
Gross, W., 352
Grossberg, D., 38
Gunn, D. M., 229n113, 230nn119, 121; 232n125

Hadley, J. M., 48n13
Haney, L., 497n164
Hardmeier, C., 415n52, 419n60, 431n70
Har-El, M., 150n31
Harrison, R. K., 524
Hasel, G. F., 387n9
Hayes, K. M., 68, 144
Henderson, J., 111n75
Hermisson, H.-J., 65n32, 219n07
Herrmann, S., 21, 24, 207
Hess, R. S., 472n142
Hillers, D. R., 91n51, 248, 264n162, 428, 499n167
Hitzig, F., 208, 304–5, 427
Hoffman, Y., 259n158, 396n22
Holladay, W. L., 6n15, 22n3, 29n14, 35n30, 36n32, 38, 43n9, 48n5, 53, 54n20, 60, 64, 68, 72, 75, 76n39, 86n49, 88, 90, 92n53, 97, 103n69, 113n77, 115, 118, 119, 121n82, 123, 125, 131n93, 138n6, 147n20, 152, 157, 159n11, 161–63, 167, 170, 173n53, 179 181, 183n62, 187–88, 189n69, 193, 197, 198n80, 201n84, 211, 224, 231, 248–49, 252, 254, 263–64, 266, 269, 295, 295n12, 300, 304, 321–22, 322n222, 333, 355n257, 364, 382–83, 385, 398, 402, 411, 417, 419, 421, 428, 431, 450, 457, 462, 466n129, 476, 478n145, 492–93, 500–501, 509, 512, 514, 523–24, 532–33
Holt, E. K., 27n12, 403n38

Hopper, S. R., 234
Hossfeld, F.-L., 316n216, 501, 509, 512, 514, 523–24, 532–33
Houbigant, C. F., 443
Houseman, A. E., 4n8
Hubmann, F. D., 136n1, 138n7, 139n10, 140n11, 143, 147n24, 149nn26–28; 150n30, 152n32, 179, 183n62, 184n67, 197
Huddlestun, J. R., 498n166
Hunter, A. V., 17n45
Huwyler, B., 458n111, 461n117, 464n125, 478n145, 481n151, 485n152, 493
Hyatt, J. P., 88n50

Isbell, C. D., 99n65
Ittmann, N., 229n116

Jackson, M., 99n65
Jacobsen, T., 527n189
Janzen, J. G., 4, 28n13, 32n24, 33, 46, 53, 78n44, 93, 95n56, 100, 102n68, 110, 114–15, 118, 124, 134, 170nn49, 51; 173, 181n57, 191nn75–76; 196–97, 211, 223 236, 249, 251n146, 255, 262, 269–70, 280, 295, 303–4, 313, 316n217, 321, 333, 337n241, 353, 364, 374, 374n289, 382–83, 384n2, 392n18, 395, 410, 419n61, 426–28, 439n92, 443, 457, 458n112, 475–76, 523–24, 536, 538n5
Janzen, W., 248, 251n146, 257n153
Jenni, E., 479n148
Job, J. B., 7n17
Johnson, A. D., 80
Jones, B., 485n153, 486n158
Jones, D. R., 10n31, 27n10, 132, 181n57, 208, 233, 251, 270, 288, 321, 324, 438, 501, 509
Joo, S., 99n64, 364
Jost, R., 98n62
Jünglung, H.-W., 29n14

Kaminsky, J. S., 355n256
Keel, O., 40n2
Keil, C. F., 91, 140, 289, 301, 383, 387, 411, 418, 431, 470, 472n140
Kelley, P. H., 132
Kessler, M., 174n54, 366n277, 383n1, 396n21, 403n37, 432n72, 508n174, 510n179, 511n180
Kethe, W., 306
Kidner, D., 121, 152
Kilpp, N., 332, 334n236, 336n238, 337n243, 345n248, 363–64, 421n65
King, P. J., 214n97
Kiss, J., 214n99, 219n107
Klein, R. W., 258n156

Klopfenstein, M. A., 271n168
Knauf, E. A., 290nn189–90
Knights, C. H., 393n19
Knowles, M., 348n252, 357nn262–63
Köcker, M., 27n10
König, E., 485n153
Kremers, H., 403n37, 453n107
Kruse, H., 102n67
Kuhl, C., 137n4
Kutsch, E., 470, 472n139

Labuschagne, C. T., 123
Lalleman-de Winkel, H., 316n219, 406n42
Le Déaut, R., 62n30
Leene, H., 355n255
Levenson, J. D., 540n10
Levin, C., 139n8, 336n238, 352, 355n255, 356n260, 371n286
Lewis, T. J., 467n133
Lipschits, O., 251n148
Lohfink, N., 299n198, 301n201
Long, B. O., 54nn19, 21; 78n43, 160n40, 175n56, 191n74, 245nn143–44; 272n171, 275n174, 444n95
Lundberg, M. J., 126n87
Lundbom, J. R., 4, 4n7, 6n15, 10n30, 25, 29n14, 40n1, 72, 80, 85n46, 119n79, 131n93, 185n68, 193, 197, 211–12, 236, 244n142, 248, 250, 263, 267n165, 269, 348–49, 357n262, 388, 411, 415, 476, 495, 527n188, 528n193, 534n196
Lust, J., 255, 377n294, 379n298, 433n74

Margaliot, M., 127n88
Martens, E., 390n14
Martin, J. D., 54n22
Marx, A., 376n292
McAlpine, T. H., 251n148
McConville, G., 7n17
McEvenue, S., 403nn35, 37
McKane, W., 3nn3–4; 10n31, 27n10, 33, 46, 53, 66, 80, 93, 102n67, 107–8, 108n74, 119, 123, 125, 134–35, 143–44, 147n18, 158, 160nn41–42; 163, 167n45, 170n51, 176, 191, 193, 197, 201n64, 204, 207, 211, 219, 224, 233, 237, 243, 248–49, 257, 259, 260n161, 262–63, 266–67, 269, 270, 274, 280–83, 288, 292–93, 295, 300, 304, 307, 321, 332, 334–35, 343, 366, 375, 383, 398n29, 402, 410–11, 415, 419, 419n59, 426–28, 433n77, 436, 438, 443, 444, 447, 457, 463, 470, 471n137, 475–77, 484, 492–94, 498, 499n168, 507–8, 510, 515, 524, 536
Meier, S. A., 5nn11, 13
Mendenhall, G. E., 74n38

Index of Modern Authors

Metzger, M., 201n85
Meyer, I., 167, 270, 271n70, 316n216
Michaelis, J. D., 130
Migsch, H., 363–64, 366n273, 370n284, 390, 402, 408n46
Milgrom, J., 41n3, 43nn8, 10; 102n66, 242n139
Miller, P. D., Jr., 2, 30n17, 96, 171n52, 257, 388 n10
Mosis, R., 224
Muilenburg, J., 183n63
Muraoka, T., 450
Murray, D. F., 5n10, 47n11, 95n58, 444n96, 451n103, 540

Neumann, P. K. D., 10n29, 21n1, 25n7, 94n.55
Nicholson, E. W., 17nn42, 44; 31n20, 183n62, 250, 283n178, 371n288, 403n37, 418n58, 437n87
Nielsen, E., 396n20, 398n31
Norris, K., 184n64

O'Connor, K. M., 50n16, 218n104, 230n119, 233n127, 234n131
Oded, B., 371n288
Olmo Lete, G. del, 27n11, 170n50, 192n79
Olyan, J. M., 120 n80
Osswald, E., 310n210
Overholt, T., W., 22n3, 47n12, 265n163

Pardee, D., 322n222
Parker, T., 413n51
Parke-Taylor, G., 147n18, 325n226, 337n241
Parunak, H. V. D., 5n12
Patrick, D., 286n185
Peake, A. S., 88, 194, 220, 283n178, 388, 405, 529
Peels, H. G. L., 74n38, 464n122, 500n170
Perles, F., 281
Perlitt, L., 138n7
Person, R., 9n28, 537n4
Petersen, D., 481n151
Piovanelli, P., 374
Pitard, W. T., 74n38
Pohlmann, K.-F., 91n52, 112n76, 241n138, 434n78, 436n82, 438n89, 445n97
Polk, T., 201n83, 206n89, 229n117, 415n.53
Porten, B., 367n279, 449n102
Preuss, H., 125n85
Prijs, L., 224, 233n129

Raabe, P. R., 496n162
Rad, G. von, 125n86

Raitt, T. M., 56n27, 184n66, 216n101, 246n145, 286n184
Redford, D. B., 162, 449n101, 463n120, 465n127
Renaud, B., 25n5, 356n259
Rendtorff, R., 5n13
Reventlow, H. Graf, 29n16, 276n175
Rietschel, C., 29n14, 299n199
Ritter, C., 348n253
Rofé, A., 12, 333n234, 419n61
Römer, T., 137n5
Roncace, M., 408n46, 420n64
Rose, M., 447
Rosenberg, J., 9n25
Rosenthal, F., 124
Rowley, H. H., 102n67
Rudolph, W., 4, 7n16, 23–24, 27n10, 43, 64, 84, 86n49, 93, 118–19, 121, 124, 135, 138, 162, 176, 180, 189n70, 208, 219, 244, 262, 267, 295, 301, 324, 329, 332, 352–53, 355n257, 364, 373, 382, 385, 395, 398, 402, 411, 419, 419n59, 426–27, 443, 451, 462, 465, 476, 481, 484, 487, 492–93, 501, 510, 523, 526, 536

Sasson, J. M., 121n82
Sawyer, J. F. A., 201n84
Scalise, P. J., 316
Schick, C., 158
Schmid, K., 358n267, 363, 370n284, 374
Schmidt, W. H., 47n11
Schmuttermayr, G., 76n40, 77nn41–42
Schreiner, J., 60, 66, 430
Schultz, R. L., 487n159
Schulz-Rauch, M., 36n32
Seidl, T., 10n29, 306n204, 310n212, 313, 314n214
Seitz, C. R., 404n39, 407n44, 541n11
Selms, A. van, 344
Sharp, C. J., 317n220, 324n224
Shead, A. G., 4n6, 363, 364
Shields, M. E., 54n18, 60n29
Simons, J. J., 35n268
Sissons, J. P., 321
Skinner, J., 26n8
Smelik, K. A. D., 509n175
Smith, G. A., 7n17, 392n17
Smith, D. L., 324n224
Smith, J., 536, 537n4
Smith, M. S., 144, 145n14
Snaith, J. G., 464n123
Snaith, N., 378n296
Soderlund, S., 493
Soggin, J. A., 324n225
Stager, L. E., 39n27
Steiner, R. C., 75, 121n83

Sternberg, M., 366n275
Stipp, H.-J., 11n32, 21, 274, 402, 408n47, 410, 428
Strawn, B. A., 26n9
Streane, A. W., 118, 124, 192, 206, 281, 402, 428, 435n81, 514
Streete, G., 10n31
Stulman, L., 8nn21, 23; 9, 9n26, 11nn33–34; 13n41, 30n18, 56, 104n71, 136n2, 137n3, 167n45, 189n70, 190n72, 207, 213n96, 225n110, 240n134, 243n141, 275n173, 282n177, 284, 297n196, 298n197, 305nn202–3; 323, 333, 335n237, 355n258, 371n285, 368n281, 369n283, 375n290, 386n5, 390n13, 397n24, 399n34, 431n69, 432n73, 436n82, 437nn84–85; 445n97, 447nn99–100; 453n110
Sweeney, M. A., 214n99, 258n157, 333n235, 343
Swete, H. B., 458n112

Talmon, S., 31n21, 55n24, 178, 273n172, 295, 329n233
Tate, M. E., 132n94
Temple, W., 271n169
Thackeray, H. St. J., 285n183, 385n3, 459n113
Thelle, R. I., 406n42
Thiel, W., 17n43, 27n10, 135, 137n4, 154n33, 167n45, 204n86, 237n132, 240n135, 249, 297n196, 397n24, 399n33, 403n36, 431n69, 436n82, 438n89, 445n97, 447n99, 453n110
Thompson, J. A., 188, 270, 323, 392n16, 492
Tigay, J. H., 313
Toorn, K. van der, 407n45
Tov, E., 7n19, 8, 10n30, 124n84, 304, 305, 396, 428
Tromp, N. J., 251n148
Tsevat, M., 402
Tucker, G. W., 21n2

Unterman, J., 257
Urbrock, W. J., 197n82

Vaggione, R. P., 65n32
VanGemeren, W., 360n270
Veijola, T., 379n298
Volz, P., 275, 301, 321, 348, 367, 382, 410, 415, 470, 493, 507, 525

Waard, J. de, 4n8, 7n18, 493
Wal, A. J. O van der, 12n35
Walton, J. H., 217n103
Wanke, G., 25n6, 214n98, 226n111, 396n23, 399n32, 403n37, 421n65, 486
Watson, W. G. E., 2n2, 38, 81n45, 119, 144, 166, 188, 248, 251n147, 253n149, 265n164, 267n165, 270
Watts, J. W., 4n6
Weinfeld, M., 244n142
Weippert, H., 9, 241n136, 357n261
Weiser, A., 208, 242, 334n236, 411, 438
Welch, A. C., 2n1, 297n196
Wells, R., 307n207
Wessels, W. J., 253n150
Westermann, C., 33n25, 41n5, 47n11, 54n19, 65n31, 85n48, 109n72, 112n76, 143, 206n88, 229nn114–15; 257, 346n250, 358n264, 367n279
Whybray, R. N., 109n73
Wijngaards, J., 139n9
Wildberger, H., 464n121, 179nn146–47; 485n154, 486n157, 487n160
Williams, M. J., 9n24
Williamson, H. G. M., 526n187
Willis, J. T., 12n40
Wilson, R. R., 104n70, 167
Wiseman, D. J., 284n181, 440n93, 501n172
Wolff, H. W., 12n39, 54n20, 147n19, 343, 496n162

Yadin, Y., 588n190
Yamauchi, E. M., 65n32, 529n194

Zachary, M., 197
Zenger, E., 232n124
Ziegler, J., 3n3, 80, 269, 321–22, 332, 417, 419n59, 427, 461, 476, 484, 493–94, 524
Zimmerli, W., 69n35, 276n176

www.ingramcontent.com/pod-product-compliance
Lightning Source LLC
Chambersburg PA
CBHW060527080526
44586CB00012B/648